KNOWLEDGE
ENCYCLOPEDIA

DK SMITHSONIAN

KNOWLEDGE
ENCYCLOPEDIA

**LONDON, NEW YORK, MELBOURNE,
MUNICH, AND DELHI**

US Senior Editor Rebecca Warren

US Editor Kate Johnsen

Senior Editors Shaila Brown, Daniel Mills, Ben Morgan

Senior Art Editors Vicky Short, Smiljka Surla

Editors Lizzie Munsey, Sam Priddy, Alison Sturgeon

Designers Daniela Boraschi, Tannishtha Chakraborty, Richard Horsford,
Hedi Hunter, Fiona Macdonald

Visualizer Peter Laws

Illustrators Peter Bull, Rob Cook, FOREAL™, Mike Garland, Mark Garlick,
Gary Hanna, Jason Harding, Arran Lewis, Maltings Partnership, Medi-Mation,
Peter Minister, Gerson Mora and Anna Luiza Aragão/Maná e.d.i., Moonrunner
Design, Ian Naylor, Alex Pang, Dean Wright and Agatha Gomes

DK Picture Library Emma Shepherd, Rob Nunn

Jacket Design Development Manager Sophia MTT

Jacket Designer Laura Brim

Jacket Editor Manisha Majithia

Producer, pre-production Francesca Wardell

Producer Alice Sykes

Managing Editors Julie Ferris, Paula Regan

Managing Art Editor Owen Peyton Jones

Publisher Sarah Larter

Art Director Phil Ormerod

Associate Publishing Director Liz Wheeler

Publishing Director Jonathan Metcalf

Contributors Kim Bryan, Robert Dinwiddie, Jolyon Goddard, Ian Graham,
Reg G. Grant, Jacqueline Mitton, Darren Naish, Douglas Palmer,
Philip Parker, Penny Preston, Sally Regan, David Rothery,
Carole Stott, Paul Sutherland, Chris Woodford, John Woodward

First American Edition, 2013
Published in the United States by DK Publishing, 345 Hudson Street
New York, New York 10014

14 15 16 17 10 9 8 7 6 5

006–187527–Oct/13

ISBN: 978-1-4654-1417-5

DK books are available at special discounts when purchased in bulk for sales
promotions, premiums, fund-raising, or educational use. For details, contact:
DK Publishing Special Markets, 345 Hudson Street, New York, New York
10014 or SpecialSales@dk.com.

Printed and bound in Hong Kong

Discover more at **www.dk.com**

Smithsonian
Institution

THE SMITHSONIAN

Established in 1846, the Smithsonian—the world's largest museum and
research complex—includes 19 museums and galleries and the National
Zoological Park. The total number of artifacts, works of art, and specimens
in the Smithsonian's collection is estimated at 137 million. The Smithsonian
is a renowned research center, dedicated to public education, national
service, and scholarship in the arts, sciences, and history.

CONTENTS

SPACE

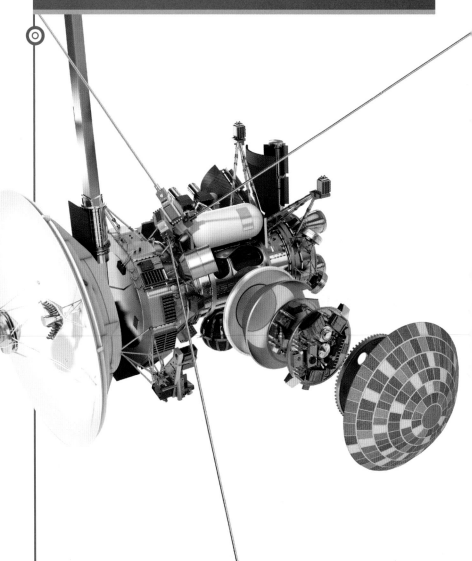

EARTH

NATURE

HUMAN BODY

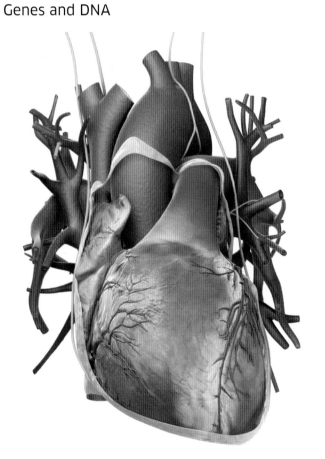

SCIENCE

HISTORY

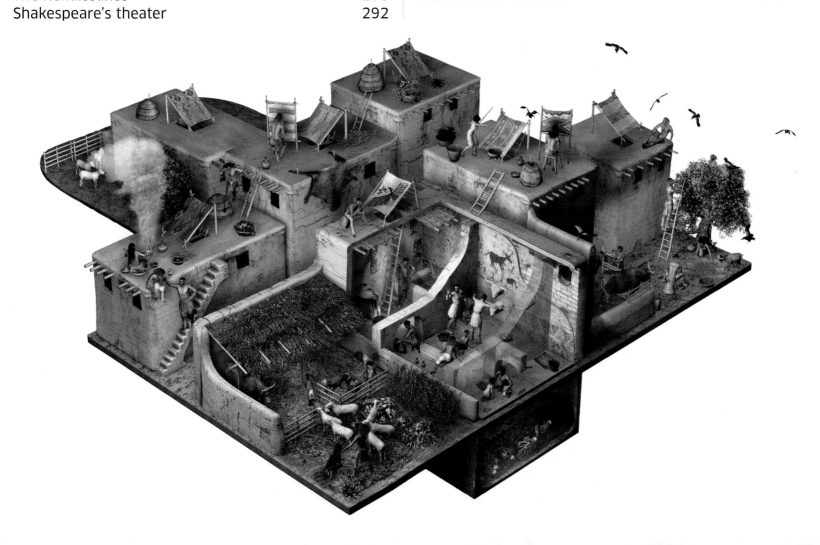

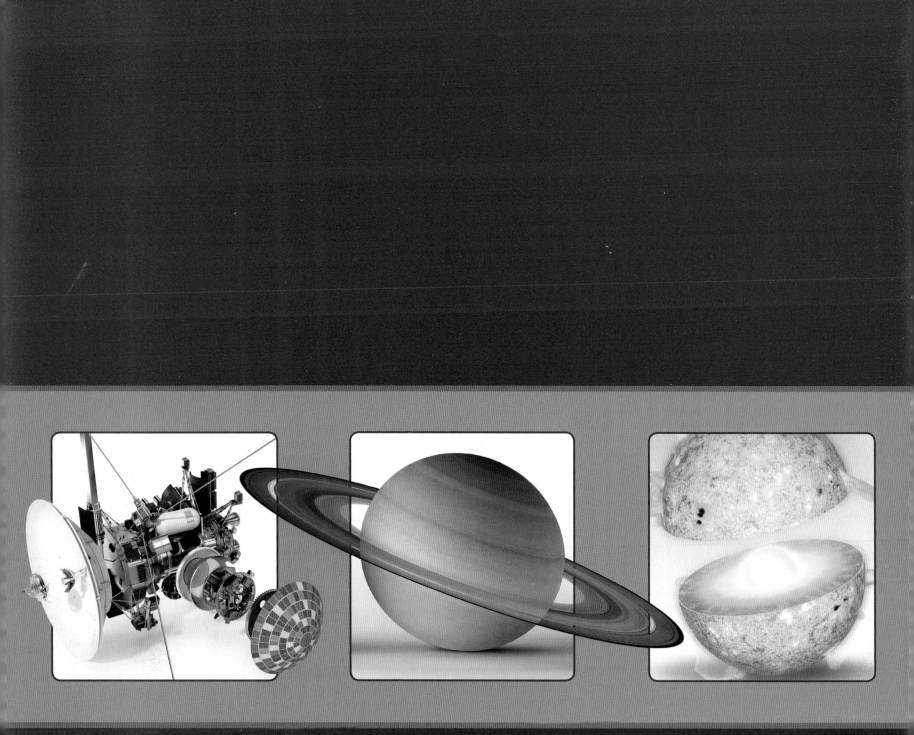

SPACE

When you look into the blackness of the night sky, you are peering into the fathomless depths of the Universe. Stars, planets, and galaxies stretch into space, not just farther than you can see, but farther than you can imagine.

THE UNIVERSE

The Universe is the whole of existence—all of space, matter, energy, and time. The Universe is so vast that it seems unimaginable, but we do know that it has been steadily expanding following its beginning 13.8 billion years ago in an explosive event called the Big Bang.

CELESTIAL BODIES

The Universe is at least 99.999999999999 percent empty space. Floating in this vast, dark void are all sorts of different objects, which astronomers call celestial bodies. They range from grains of dust to planets, stars, and galaxies. Our Solar System includes a star (the Sun) and a large family of planets and moons that formed from the same cloud of gas that gave birth to the Sun. In recent years, planets have been seen around hundreds of other stars, showing that our Solar System may be one of billions in our galaxy.

Asteroid
Rocky lumps left over from the formation of the Solar System are called asteroids. They range in size from boulders to bodies close to the size of a dwarf planet.

UNDERSTANDING THE UNIVERSE

People used to think of the Universe as a giant sphere, but we now know that things are not so simple. The Universe probably has no center or outer edge. Only a fraction of it—the observable Universe—is visible to us. The whole Universe may be vastly bigger than this, perhaps infinitely so.

The shape of space

The three dimensions of space are bent by the force of gravity from matter in the Universe into a fourth dimension that we can't see. This is hard to visualize, so scientists use the metaphor of a two-dimensional rubber sheet to explain the idea. The mass of the Universe could bend this rubber sheet in one of three ways, depending on how densely packed with matter the Universe is. Most scientists now think the shape of the Universe is flat

Closed
A dense Universe would bend itself into a closed shape. Traveling in a straight line would bring you back to your starting point.

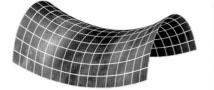

Open
If the Universe isn't dense enough, it might stretch into an open shape, making it infinite in size with no outer edge.

Flat
Just the right amount of matter would give the Universe a flat shape. This would also be infinite in size with no outer edge.

Looking back in time

Because light takes time to travel, when we look into space we are looking back in time. The most distant objects visible are galaxies photographed by the Hubble Telescope. We see them as they were 13 billion years ago. The Universe extends far beyond these, but it's impossible to see objects much further because their light hasn't had time to reach us.

Furthest objects
The light from the faintest galaxies in this photo from the Hubble Space Telescope took 13 billion years to reach Earth.

What's the matter?

The elements hydrogen and helium make up 98 percent of the matter we can see in the Universe. But there doesn't seem to be enough matter to account for the way stars and galaxies are pulled by gravity. As a result, astronomers think galaxies contain dark matter, which we cannot see. There is also an unknown force making the Universe expand, known as dark energy.

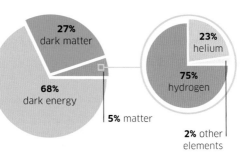

27% dark matter
68% dark energy
5% matter
23% helium
75% hydrogen
2% other elements

MAKEUP OF THE UNIVERSE

THE SCALE OF SPACE

The Universe is so vast that we cannot appreciate its size without making leaps of scale. In this series of pictures, each stage represents a microscopic speck of the image to its right. When dealing with the vast distances in space, miles aren't big enough. Instead, astronomers use the speed of light as a yardstick. Light is so fast it can travel around the Earth 7.5 times in a second. One light year is the distance light travels in a year: nearly 6 trillion miles (10 trillion km).

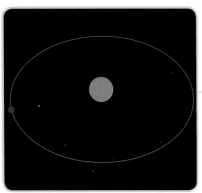

Earth and Moon
Earth is 7,926 miles (12,756 km) wide. Our nearest neighbor in space—the Moon—orbits Earth at a distance of 238,855 miles (384,400 km). If Earth were the size of a soccer ball, the Moon would be the size of a cantaloupe about 69 ft (21 meters) away.

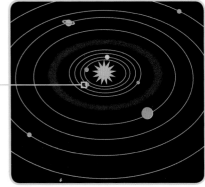

Solar System
The Sun's family of eight planets occupy a region of space 5.6 billion miles (9 billion km) wide. If Earth were a soccer ball, it would take five days to walk across this part of the Solar System. The nearest star would be a 58-year walk away.

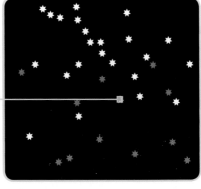

Stellar neighborhood
The nearest star to the Sun is Proxima Centauri, which is just over four light years away. There are around 2,000 stars within 50 light years of the Sun. These make up our stellar neighborhood, which is a tiny fraction of the Milky Way galaxy.

Comet
Comets are chunks of ice from the outer reaches of the Solar System. Some grow long tails of gas and dust as they approach the Sun and are warmed by it.

Moon
Also called a natural satellite, a moon is a body that orbits a planet. Earth has only one moon but the planet Jupiter has 67, including Io (above).

Dwarf planet
Dwarf planets are larger than asteroids but smaller than planets. Like planets, they are round in shape. Pluto (above) is the best known dwarf planet.

Planet
A planet is a large and nearly spherical object that orbits a star and has swept its orbital path clear of debris. The Solar System has eight planets.

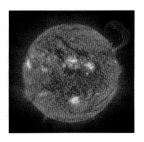

Stars
These luminous balls of gas, such as the Sun, shine by generating their own nuclear power. Stars come in a wide range of types, temperatures, and sizes.

Nebula
A glowing cloud of gas and dust in space is known as a nebula. Some nebulae are clouds of wreckage created by dying stars. Others give birth to new stars.

IS THERE ANYBODY OUT THERE?

One of the biggest questions in science is whether life is unique to Earth or has arisen on other worlds. And if life has appeared elsewhere, could intelligent beings have evolved? Scientists have set up projects to watch and listen for signals from extraterrestrials, and messages have been sent to the stars to inform any aliens out there of our existence.

SETI

Astronomers involved in the SETI (search for extraterrestrial intelligence) project use powerful radio telescopes to scan the skies in search of artificial radio signals broadcast by alien civilizations. The SETI project has been running since 1960, but it has so far found no conclusive evidence of alien signals, despite some false alarms.

RADIO TELESCOPE

Arecibo message

In 1974, scientists used the giant Arecibo radio telescope in Puerto Rico to broadcast a radio message toward the star cluster M13. The message contains symbols (right) that represent human beings, our base-10 counting system, the DNA molecule, and the Solar System. More a publicity stunt than a serious attempt to contact aliens, the broadcast will take 25,000 years to reach M13, and a reply will take 25,000 years to return.

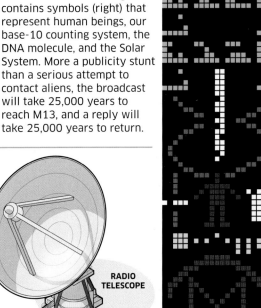

Numbers 1 to 10 in binary, reading left to right

Chemical formula of DNA (the molecule that carries the blueprint of life)

Shape of DNA molecule

Human figure and population of Earth in 1974

Earth's position in Solar System

Arecibo Telescope, which sent message

Pioneer plaque

The robotic spacecraft *Pioneer 10* and *Pioneer 11* visited the planets Jupiter and Saturn in 1973–74 and then flew off into deep space. If aliens ever discover either craft drifting through interstellar space, they will find a gold-plated plaque engraved with a message from Earth.

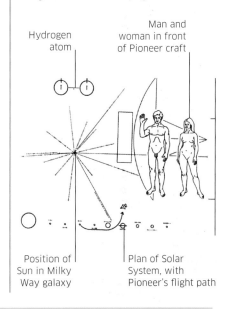

Hydrogen atom

Man and woman in front of Pioneer craft

Position of Sun in Milky Way galaxy

Plan of Solar System, with Pioneer's flight path

Milky Way galaxy
The Milky Way is a vast cloud of 200 billion stars. Its shape resembles a pair of fried eggs held back to back, with a central bulge surrounded by a flat disk. It measures 100,000 light years across the disk and 2,000 light years deep through the bulge.

Local Group of galaxies
The Milky Way is just one of perhaps seven trillion galaxies in the observable Universe. Galaxies exist in groups called clusters, held together by gravity. The Milky Way is part of a cluster known as the Local Group, which is about 10 million light years wide.

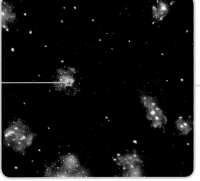

Supercluster
Clusters of galaxies exist in even larger groupings called superclusters. We live in the Virgo Supercluster, which is one of millions of superclusters in the known Universe. Between these are immense empty areas called cosmic voids.

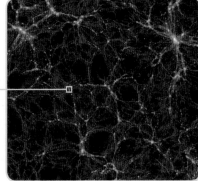

Universe
Superclusters are thought to form a vast web of filaments riddled with enormous voids containing no galaxies. The true size of the Universe is a mystery, and only a fraction of it is visible to us. The Universe may even be infinite in size.

The Big Bang

About 14 billion years ago, the Universe materialized out of nothing for unknown reasons. Infinitely smaller than an atom to begin with, the Universe expanded to billions of miles across in under a second—an event called the Big Bang.

Time came into existence when the Universe began, so the question "What happened before?" has no meaning. Space also came into existence. The Big Bang was not an explosion of matter through space—it was an expansion of space itself.

At first the Universe consisted of pure energy, but within a trillionth of a second some of this energy turned into matter, forming a vast soup of subatomic particles (particles smaller than atoms). It took nearly 400,000 years for the particles to cool down enough to form atoms, and then another 300 million years before the atoms formed planets, stars, and galaxies. The expansion that began in the Big Bang continues to this day, and most scientists think it will carry on forever.

The Universe began
as something called a singularity: a point of zero size but infinite density.

The expanding Universe

The illustration below does not show the shape of the Universe, which is unknown. Instead, it is a timeline that shows how the Universe has expanded and changed since the Big Bang. We know the Universe is expanding because the most distant galaxies are rushing apart at rapid speeds. By running the clock backward, astronomers figured out that the expansion began 13.8 billion years ago at a single point: the Big Bang.

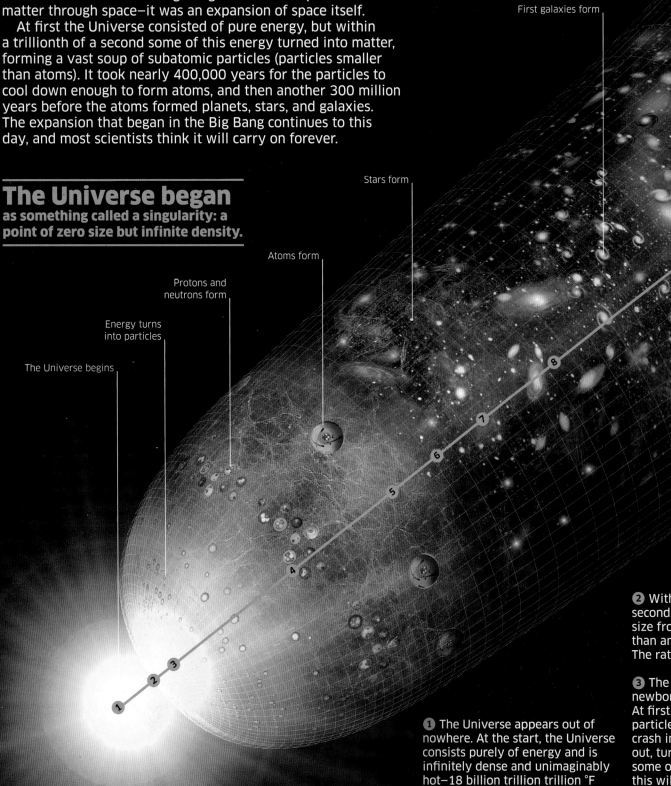

Rate of expansion increases

First galaxies form

Stars form

Atoms form

Protons and neutrons form

Energy turns into particles

The Universe begins

❷ Within a tiny fraction of a second, the Universe balloons in size from trillions of times smaller than an atom to the size of a city. The rate of expansion then slows.

❸ The intense energy of the newborn Universe creates matter. At first, the matter is a soup of particles and antiparticles. These crash into and cancel each other out, turning back into energy. But some of the matter is left over—this will eventually turn into atoms and later stars and galaxies.

❶ The Universe appears out of nowhere. At the start, the Universe consists purely of energy and is infinitely dense and unimaginably hot—18 billion trillion trillion °F (10 billion trillion trillion °C).

Solar System forms

Discovery of the Big Bang

The first scientific evidence for the Big Bang was found in 1929, when astronomers discovered that light from distant galaxies is reddened. This color change happens when objects are moving away from us, making lightwaves stretch out and change color. The more distant the galaxies are, the faster they are rushing away. This shows that the whole Universe is expanding.

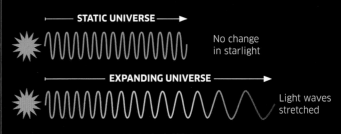

———— STATIC UNIVERSE ————▶   No change in starlight

———— EXPANDING UNIVERSE ————▶   Light waves stretched

Big Bang afterglow

More evidence of the Big Bang came in the 1960s, when astronomers detected faint microwave radiation coming from every point in the sky. This mysterious energy is the faded remains of the intense burst of energy released in the Big Bang.

MICROWAVE MAP OF WHOLE SKY

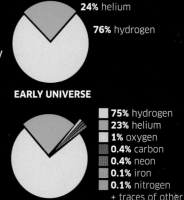

Changing elements

For hundreds of millions of years, the Universe consisted almost entirely of hydrogen and helium —the very simplest chemical elements. After stars appeared, new elements began to be made in the cores of dying stars. All the complex elements in our bodies were forged in dying stars this way.

24% helium
76% hydrogen

EARLY UNIVERSE

■ **75%** hydrogen
■ **23%** helium
■ **1%** oxygen
▥ **0.4%** carbon
▥ **0.4%** neon
■ **0.1%** iron
■ **0.1%** nitrogen
+ traces of other

UNIVERSE TODAY

④ The Universe is now about 1 microsecond old and 60 billion miles (100 billion km) wide. The leftover particles begin to form protons and neutrons—the particles that today make up the nuclei of atoms. But the Universe is too hot for atoms to form yet. Light cannot pass through the sea of particles, so the young Universe resembles a dense fog.

⑤ After 379,000 years, the Universe cools enough for atoms to form. The Universe is now an enormous cloud of hydrogen and helium. Light can pass through space more easily, and the Universe becomes transparent.

⑥ Half a million years after the Big Bang, matter is spread out almost evenly in the Universe, but tiny ripples exist. Working on these denser patches, gravity begins pulling the matter into clumps.

⑦ At 300 million years, stars appear. Stars form when great clouds of gas are pulled into tight knots by gravity. The pressure and heat become so intense in the dense pockets of gas that nuclear reactions begin, igniting the star.

⑧ At 500 million years, the first galaxies are forming. Galaxies are enormous clouds of stars, held together by gravity.

⑨ Now 5 billion years old, the Universe consists of vast clusters of galaxies arranged in threads, with gigantic voids between them. The voids get ever bigger as space continues to expand. At 8 billion years, the expansion of the Universe begins to accelerate.

⑩ Our Solar System forms at 9 billion years. When the Universe is 20 billion years old, the Sun will expand in size and destroy Earth.

⑪ The Universe will carry on expanding forever, becoming cold and dark everywhere.

Big Bounce theory

What caused the Big Bang? We may never know for sure, but some scientists have suggested that there may have been lots of big bangs, with the Universe expanding after each one and then shrinking again. This theory is called the Big Bounce because the process repeats itself.

Universe expands   Big Bang   Universe shrinks

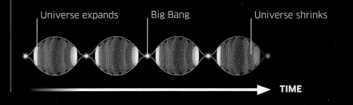

TIME

14   space ○ THE UNIVERSE

200 billion—the approximate number of stars in the Milky Way galaxy.

23—the number of times our Solar System has orbited the Milky Way.

Galaxies

Our Sun belongs to a giant whirlpool of stars called the Milky Way. Huge collections of stars are called galaxies, and like all galaxies the Milky Way is unimaginably vast.

Galaxies come in many shapes and sizes. Some are spirals like our own galaxy, but others are fuzzy balls or shapeless clouds. The smallest have just a few million stars. The largest contain trillions.

Although they look packed with stars, galaxies are mostly empty space. If you made a scale model of the Milky Way with a grain of sand for each star, the nearest star to the Sun would be 4 miles (6 km) away. The furthest would be 80,000 miles (130,000 km) away. The stars in a galaxy are held together by gravity and travel slowly around the galactic heart. In many galaxies, including ours, a supermassive black hole lies hidden in the center. Stars and other material are sucked into this cosmic plughole by gravity and disappear forever.

The Milky Way

If you could look down on the Milky Way galaxy from above, the view would be like flying over a glittering city at night. Most of the galaxy's 200 billion stars are in the central bulge. Curving around this are two vast spiral arms and several smaller arms. The Milky Way is thought to be a barred spiral (see panel), but we can't see its shape clearly from Earth since we view it from the inside. In the night sky, the Milky Way appears only as a milky band of light.

MILKY WAY OVERHEAD VIEW

Orion Arm
Our Solar System lies in this small arm. Many of the stars we see in the night sky are in the Orion Arm.

SCUTUM-CENTAURUS ARM

10,000 light-years

20,000 light-years

NORMA ARM

30,000 light years

40,000 light years

MILKY WAY SIDE VIEW

Main disc containing arms

❶ Galactic center
This photo from an infrared (heat-sensitive) telescope shows stars and gas clouds packing the center of the Milky Way. A supermassive black hole lies hidden somewhere in this area.

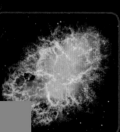

❷ Solar System
Our Solar System is in a minor spiral arm called the Orion Arm. We orbit the center of the galaxy once every 200 million years, traveling at about 120 miles (200 km) a second.

❸ Crab Nebula
Clouds of gas and dust occur throughout the Milky Way, especially in the spiral arms. The Crab Nebula is a cloud of wreckage left behind by a dying star that exploded.

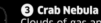

❹ Globular cluster
Not all the Milky Way's stars are in the main disc of the galaxy. Many are in globular clusters—tightly packed balls of ancient stars floating above and below the galaxy in a spherical region called the halo.

7 trillion–the approximate **number of galaxies** in the observable **Universe**.

6,000 years–the **length of time** it would take **to count** the **Milky Way's stars** at a rate of **one a second**.

15

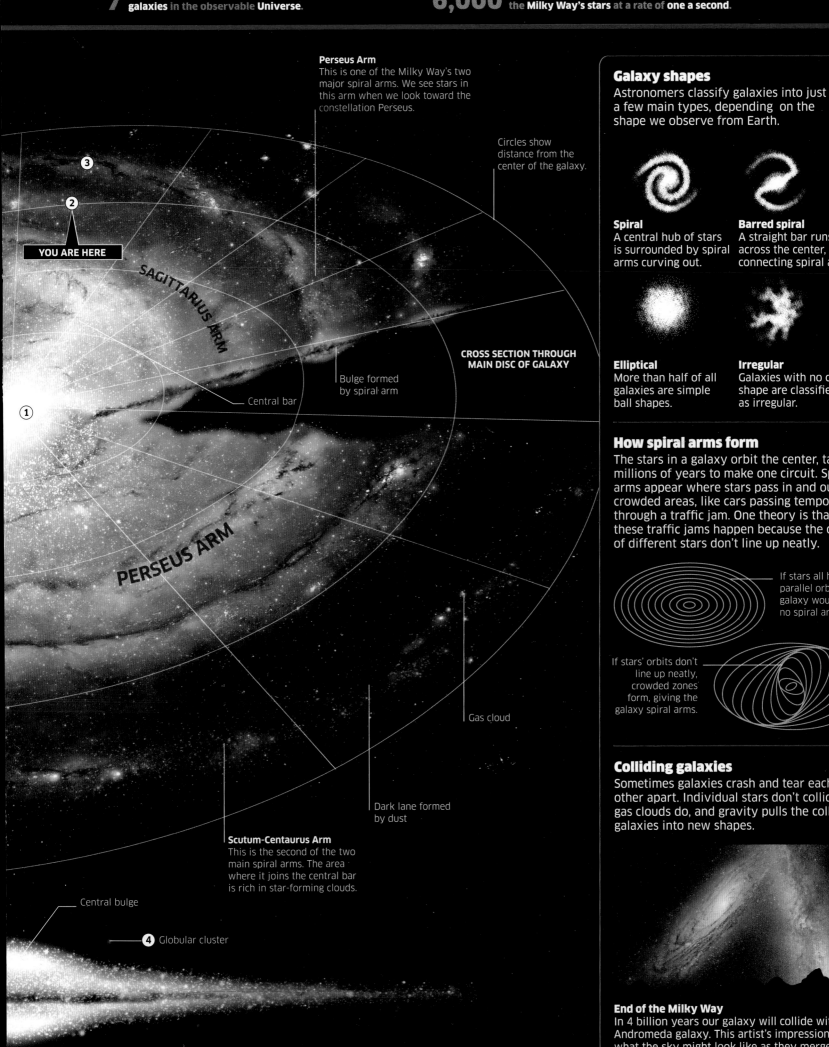

Perseus Arm
This is one of the Milky Way's two major spiral arms. We see stars in this arm when we look toward the constellation Perseus.

Circles show distance from the center of the galaxy.

SAGITTARIUS ARM

YOU ARE HERE

CROSS SECTION THROUGH MAIN DISC OF GALAXY

Bulge formed by spiral arm

Central bar

PERSEUS ARM

Gas cloud

Dark lane formed by dust

Scutum-Centaurus Arm
This is the second of the two main spiral arms. The area where it joins the central bar is rich in star-forming clouds.

Central bulge

④ Globular cluster

Galaxy shapes
Astronomers classify galaxies into just a few main types, depending on the shape we observe from Earth.

Spiral
A central hub of stars is surrounded by spiral arms curving out.

Barred spiral
A straight bar runs across the center, connecting spiral arms.

Elliptical
More than half of all galaxies are simple ball shapes.

Irregular
Galaxies with no clear shape are classified as irregular.

How spiral arms form
The stars in a galaxy orbit the center, taking millions of years to make one circuit. Spiral arms appear where stars pass in and out of crowded areas, like cars passing temporarily through a traffic jam. One theory is that these traffic jams happen because the orbits of different stars don't line up neatly.

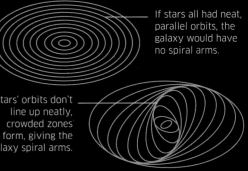

If stars all had neat, parallel orbits, the galaxy would have no spiral arms.

If stars' orbits don't line up neatly, crowded zones form, giving the galaxy spiral arms.

Colliding galaxies
Sometimes galaxies crash and tear each other apart. Individual stars don't collide, but gas clouds do, and gravity pulls the colliding galaxies into new shapes.

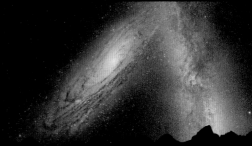

End of the Milky Way
In 4 billion years our galaxy will collide with the Andromeda galaxy. This artist's impression shows what the sky might look like as they merge.

The brightest stars emit 6 million times more light than the Sun.

13 billion years—the age of the oldest known star.

Star birth

Stars have been forming throughout the Universe for most of its life. They take shape in vast clouds where thousands of stars are born at a time.

The clouds that give birth to the stars are cold and dense and consist mainly of hydrogen gas. The newly formed stars are huge spinning globes of hot, glowing gas—mainly hydrogen, with helium and small amounts of other elements. Much of this material is packed tightly into the stars' cores, and it is here that nuclear reactions release energy in the form of heat and light.

The largest stars
in the night sky are big enough to swallow our Sun a billion times.

How new stars form

The star-forming process begins when the cloud becomes unstable and breaks up into fragments. Gravity pulls the material in a fragment into an ever-tighter clump, and the clump slowly forms a sphere as it shrinks. Now a protostar, this star-to-be keeps on shrinking, its core getting denser and hotter. Eventually the pressure and temperature are so high that nuclear reactions begin, and the star starts to shine.

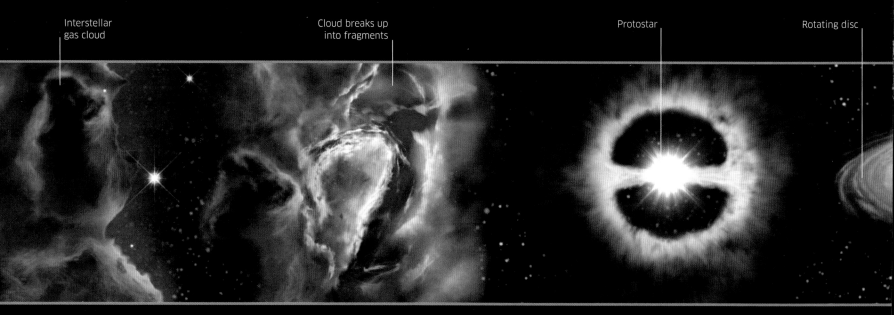

Interstellar gas cloud | Cloud breaks up into fragments | Protostar | Rotating disc

1 Interstellar cloud
Stars are born within enormous, cold, dense clouds of gas and dust. The process of star formation may be triggered if something disturbs the cloud, such as a collision with another cloud or a shockwave from a supernova explosion.

2 Fragments form
Now unstable, the cloud breaks up into fragments of different size and mass. The most massive and dense of these fragments are gradually pulled by their own gravity into tighter clumps. These shrinking fragments will eventually turn into protostars.

3 Protostar
A protostar forms. Gravity pulls material into its core, where the density, pressure, and temperature build up. The more matter the original cloud fragment contained, the greater the temperature and pressure rise as the protostar develops.

Starbirth nebulas

Clouds of gas and dust in space are called nebulas. Much of the gas and dust in a nebula is debris from old stars that exploded when they ran out of fuel. Over millions of years, this material is recycled to make new stars. Starbirth nebulas are among the most beautiful objects in space, their colorful clouds illuminated from within by the blue light of newborn stars.

Orion Nebula
The Orion Nebula is one of the closest star-forming regions to Earth. In the night sky it looks like a fuzzy star in the sword of Orion. In reality, it is a vast cloud of gas and dust thousands of times bigger than the Solar System.

Types of star

A star begins to shine when nuclear reactions in its core convert hydrogen into helium and release energy. It is then called a main sequence star. Not all main sequence stars are the same—they differ in size, temperature, color, brightness, and the amount of matter they contain. When stars begin to run out of fuel and near the end of their lives, they stop being main sequence stars and may swell up and turn into red giants or shrink to become white dwarfs.

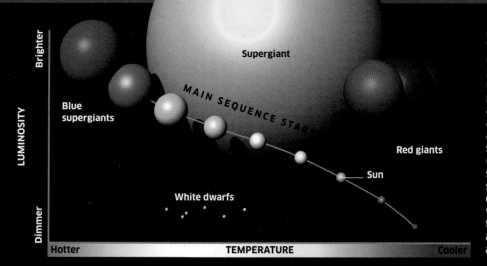

Classifying stars

The Hertzsprung-Russell diagram is a famous graph that astronomers use to classify stars. The graph plots brightness against temperature and reveals that there are distinct groupings of stars, such as red giants (dying stars) and main sequence stars (ordinary stars). Astronomers also classify stars by color, which is linked to their temperature: hot stars are blue; cooler stars are orange or red.

Jets of gas

Star begins to shine

Leftover material may form planets

4 Spinning disc

The growing mass at the center creates a gravitational pull, drawing ever more gas and dust inward. A little like water going down a drain, the material being pulled in starts to spin around. Powerful winds develop, blowing jets of gas out from the center.

5 A star is born

Squeezed by the force of gravity, the protostar's core becomes so hot and dense that nuclear reactions occur, and the star begins to shine. The glowing core produces an outward pressure that balances the inward pull of gravity, making the star stable. It is now a main sequence star.

6 Planets form

Not all the material from the gas cloud has been used to make the star. The leftovers form a spinning disc of gas and dust around the star. This debris may be lost into space, or it may clump together to form planets, moons, comets, and asteroids.

Star clusters

Stars are not formed singly—they are born in clusters from the same cloud of material at roughly the same time. Eventually, the stars of a cluster will drift apart and exist alone in space, or with a close companion or two. Our Sun, like about half of the stars nearest to us, is alone. About a third of the stars in the night sky are in pairs, bound together by gravity.

Pleiades cluster

A handful of the 5,000 or so stars that make up the Pleiades cluster can be seen with the naked eye. In about 250 million years time, the stars will have dispersed and the cluster will no longer exist.

Supergiant stars can grow to **1 billion times** the volume of **our Sun**.

Four ways to die

Stars can die in four different ways, all of which are shown on these pages. Our Sun, a typical star, will follow the central path, but not yet–it has enough fuel to keep shining for 5 billion years. When larger stars die, they turn hydrogen into heavier chemical elements such as carbon and oxygen, which are later recycled to form new stars and planets. All the atoms in your body were created this way.

5 billion tons–the weight of one teaspoonful of material from the core of a neutron star.

Stable star
Every young star goes through a stable phase in which it shines steadily.

Small stars
Stars with less than half the mass of the Sun fade away very slowly. Once the hydrogen in the core is used up, the star begins to feed off hydrogen in its atmosphere. But it doesn't generate enough gravity to use other elements as fuel, so it slowly shrinks to become a black dwarf. This will take far longer than the age of the Universe–up to a trillion years.

Star begins to shrink

Star death

All stars eventually run out of fuel and die. Most fade away quietly, but the most massive stars self-destruct in a huge explosion that can outshine an entire galaxy.

Like Earth, stars generate the force of gravity, which squeezes their hot cores. The more matter a star has, the greater the force of gravity and the hotter and denser the core becomes. The way a star dies depends on how much matter it contains (its mass) and how powerfully its core is squeezed by gravity.

Stars make heat and light by the process of nuclear fusion: hydrogen atoms in the core crash together to form helium, releasing energy. In small stars, when hydrogen in the core runs out, the star's light slowly fades. But in more massive stars, the core is so hot and dense that fusion can spread beyond it, changing the star's appearance. The most massive stars are eventually overwhelmed by their own gravity, which crushes them so violently that they collapse into a pinprick to create a black hole.

Medium stars
When a Sunlike star has used up the hydrogen in its core, nuclear fusion spreads outside the core, making the star expand into a red giant. The core collapses until it is hot and dense enough to fuse helium, but eventually it runs out of helium too. Finally, it becomes a white dwarf, and its outer layers spread into space as a cloud of debris.

Star expands

Massive stars
Stars over eight times more massive than our Sun end their lives in strange and violent ways. The heat and pressure inside the core become so great that nuclear fusion can not only fuse hydrogen atoms together to form helium but can fuse helium and larger atoms to create elements such as carbon or oxygen. As this takes place, the star swells into the largest star of all: a supergiant.

Star expands

1 teaspoonful of material from a red giant weighs less than a grain of salt.

1,600 light years—the distance from Earth to the nearest black hole.

19

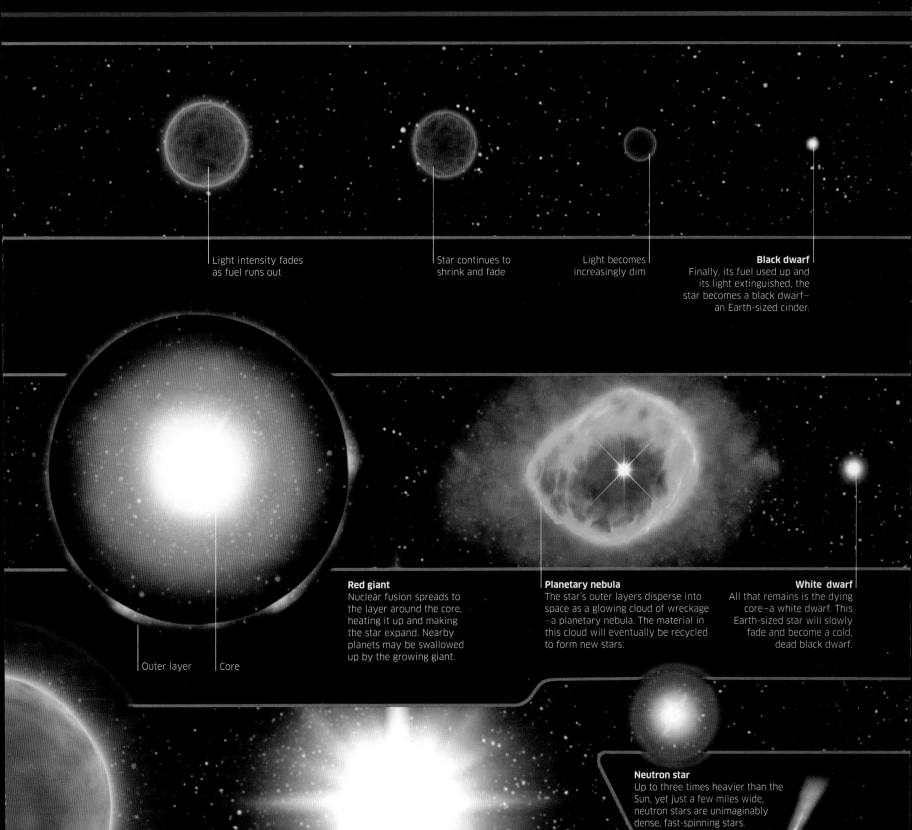

Light intensity fades as fuel runs out

Star continues to shrink and fade

Light becomes increasingly dim

Black dwarf
Finally, its fuel used up and its light extinguished, the star becomes a black dwarf—an Earth-sized cinder.

Outer layer | Core

Red giant
Nuclear fusion spreads to the layer around the core, heating it up and making the star expand. Nearby planets may be swallowed up by the growing giant.

Planetary nebula
The star's outer layers disperse into space as a glowing cloud of wreckage —a planetary nebula. The material in this cloud will eventually be recycled to form new stars.

White dwarf
All that remains is the dying core—a white dwarf. This Earth-sized star will slowly fade and become a cold, dead black dwarf.

Neutron star
Up to three times heavier than the Sun, yet just a few miles wide, neutron stars are unimaginably dense, fast-spinning stars.

Red supergiant
The star has grown into a supergiant. Nuclear fusion carries on inside the core, forcing atoms together to form heavier and heavier elements, until the star's core turns into iron. When this happens, the core no longer generates enough outward pressure to resist the crushing force of gravity, and the whole star suddenly collapses, causing a catastrophic explosion—a supernova.

Supernova
The star self-destructs in an explosion brighter than a billion suns. Its outer layers are blasted into space, but its massive core continues to collapse in on itself. What happens next depends on how massive the core is. A smaller core becomes a neutron star, but a massive core never stops collapsing. It shrinks until it's billions of times smaller than an atom and becomes a black hole.

Black hole
The force of gravity close to a black hole is so intense that nothing can escape from it—not even light. Anything falling inside is torn apart by gravity and then crushed into a point of infinite density.

Loop prominence
Gigantic loops of glowing gas extend high above the Sun's surface, anchored to the star's tangled magnetic field. Called loop prominences, these gas eruptions can last for months.

Spikes of gas
Jets of hot gas rise all the time from the Sun's surface, forming towering spikes that last just a few minutes before collapsing. Called spicules, these formations can reach thousands of miles in height. Seen from above (right), they form shimmering, hairlike patterns around a sunspot.

The Sun

The Sun is a nearly perfect sphere of hot, glowing gas. Its source of power lies buried deep in the central core, where a nuclear furnace rages nonstop, turning matter into pure heat and light.

Slightly bigger than a typical star, the Sun is large enough by volume to swallow 1.3 million Earths. It contains 99.8 percent of all the matter in the Solar System, and the force of gravity generated by this enormous mass keeps the planets trapped in orbit around it. Seen from Earth, the Sun is a life-sustaining source of light and warmth that shines steadily on us. Closer views, however, reveal a world of astonishing violence, its seething surface bursting with vast eruptions that hurl fiery gases into space.

Core
Inside the hot, dense core, the process of nuclear fusion releases energy. Every second, 683 million tons of hydrogen are fused into helium in the core.

Radiative zone
Outside the core is the radiative zone, which is not dense enough for nuclear fusion to take place. Energy from the core seeps very slowly out through this layer.

Convective zone
In the convective zone, vast bubbles of hot gas rise to the surface, cool, and then fall, transferring energy from the Sun's heart to the exterior.

Photosphere
The Sun's apparent surface is called the photosphere. Energy escapes into space from here as light.

Inside the Sun
Scientists divide the Sun's interior into three distinct layers: the core, the radiative zone, and the convective zone. All three are made solely of gas, but the gas gets hotter and denser toward the center. In the core, the temperature soars to 27 million °F (15 million °C) and the gas is 150 times more dense than water.

385 million billion gigawatts—the amount of energy output from the Sun each second.

21

⊕ **SIZE OF EARTH COMPARED TO THE SUN**

Solar flare
A sudden burst of energy from the Sun's surface is called a solar flare. Flares are often followed by a coronal mass ejection (see panel).

Sunspots
Cooler, darker patches on the Sun are called sunspots. The number of sunspots rises and falls over an 11-year cycle.

Grainy surface
The bubbles of hot gas that rise up inside the Sun make its surface look grainy. There are some 4 million granules on the Sun's face, each about 600 miles (1,000 km) wide and lasting for around eight minutes.

Sun statistics

Diameter .... 865,374 miles (1,393,684 km)
Distance from Earth .... 93 million miles (150 million km)
Mass (Earth = 1) 333,000
Surface temperature .... 10,000 °F (5,500 °C)
Core temperature .. 27 million °F (15 million °C)

Energy release

It takes only eight minutes for light from the Sun to reach Earth, but it can take 100,000 years for energy released in the Sun's core to travel to the surface and emerge as light. The journey is slow because the energy is absorbed and reemitted by trillions of atoms as it passes through the dense radiative zone.

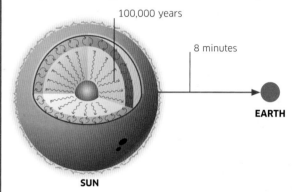

100,000 years

8 minutes

EARTH

SUN

Rotation

Like all objects in space, the Sun rotates. Unlike the Earth, which rotates as a solid object, the Sun is a ball of gas and turns at different speeds in different places. The equator takes 25 Earth days to rotate once, but the polar regions take 34 days.

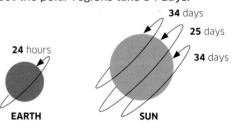

34 days
25 days
34 days

24 hours

EARTH

SUN

Mass ejections

Vast bubbles of superhot gas (plasma), each with a mass of around 1.1 billion tons, erupt from the Sun up to three times a day. Called coronal mass ejections, these bubbles grow millions of miles wide in a few hours and then burst, sending a blast of charged particles hurtling across the Solar System. The blast waves sometimes collide with the Earth, lighting up the polar skies with unusually brilliant auroras.

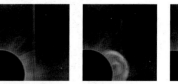

3:23 PM   **6:09 PM**   **6:25 PM**

If the **Sun** were the **size of a basketball**, **Earth** would be a **pea** 270 ft (83 m) away.

If the **Sun** were the **size of a basketball**, **Neptune** would be a **strawberry** 170 miles (270 km) away.

Asteroid

Asteroids are giant space rocks that drift around the inner Solar System. Most lie in a belt between Mars and Jupiter, but some occasionally come dangerously close to the Earth. The smallest are the size of houses, while the largest are big enough to be classified as dwarf planets. Scientists think asteroids are leftovers from the material that formed the planets. All of them together amount to less than a twentieth of the Moon's mass.

Saturn

The second biggest planet is striking for the dazzling system of bright rings that encircle it. It has 62 moons and dozens more moonlets.

Sun

The Sun is like a vast nuclear power station that produces energy by converting hydrogen into helium. It is the only star we can study close up.

Earth

Our home planet is the only place known to support life, thanks to the liquid water on its surface.

Mercury

The closest planet to the Sun, Mercury is also the smallest planet. Its surface is scarred by ancient craters.

Mars

Mars is a bitterly cold, desert world. Like Earth, it has mountains, canyons, and icy poles.

Venus

Though similar in size to Earth, Venus is a hellish world where any visiting astronaut would be crushed and boiled alive.

Orbital distance

The scale bar below shows the relative distances of the planets from the Sun. The distance between one planet and the next increases greatly as we move out through the Solar System.

Sun Mercury Venus Earth Mars

Jupiter

Saturn

500 million miles
(805 million km)

1,000 million miles
(1,609 million km)

Comet
These small, icy bodies can develop spectacular tails of gas and dust when they approach the Sun.

Neptune
The most distant planet, Neptune is a blue giant with 13 known moons. It takes Neptune nearly 164 years to orbit the Sun once.

Kuiper Belt
Thousands, if not millions, of small icy bodies occupy the region beyond the planets. The Kuiper Belt is home to dwarf planet Pluto and is a likely source of comets.

Uranus
Blue giant Uranus orbits the Sun tipped over on its side, perhaps because of a crash with a smaller planet. It has 27 moons.

Jupiter
The largest planet in the Solar System, Jupiter is more massive than all the other planets put together. It has its own family too, with at least 67 moons, some as big as planets.

The Solar System

The force of gravity generated by the Sun's vast mass keeps a family of planets and other bodies trapped in orbit around it. Together, the Sun and all these bodies make up our Solar System.

Our Sun formed from a great cloud of dust and gas around 4.6 billion years ago. Vast amounts of matter were drawn in by the developing star, but not all of it was fully absorbed. A tiny fraction of leftover material—a mere 0.14 percent of the Solar System's mass—formed a disc of gas and dust encircling the newborn star. Over millions of years, the grains of dust in this disc clumped together, growing into ever larger bodies until they grew to the size of planets, pulled into spheres by their own gravity. In the inner Solar System, where the Sun's heat was too intense for gases to condense, planets formed from rock and metal. In the outer Solar System, gases condensed to form much bigger planets.

Today the Solar System has eight planets, more than 100 moons, an unknown number of dwarf planets, and countless millions of comets and asteroids.

The Solar System

The Solar System's planets form two groups. There are four small, inner planets made of rock and metal, and four giant, outer planets made of gas and liquid. Between the two is a belt of rocky bodies called asteroids, and beyond the planets is a zone of icy bodies including dwarf planets and comets. Even farther out is a vast, spherical cloud of more comets—the Oort Cloud. The Solar System has no certain outer boundary.

Orbits

Every major body in the Solar System orbits the Sun counterclockwise. The planets are on near-circular orbits in the same plane as the disc of gas and dust from which they formed. Many smaller objects, such as dwarf planets Pluto and Eris, have stretched orbits tilted to this plane. Comets arrive from all directions.

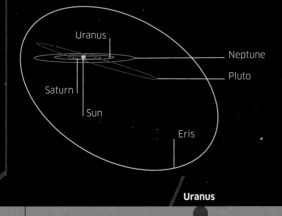

How orbits work

English scientist Isaac Newton was the first person to realize why moons and planets travel in orbits: because they are trapped by gravity. To explain his theory, he drew a giant cannon firing cannonballs off Earth. If a cannonball moved fast enough, the curve of its path as it fell back would be gentler than the curve of Earth's shape, and it would never land—it would stay in orbit.

A slow cannonball falls to the ground.

A very fast cannonball escapes Earth's gravity.

At just the right speed, a cannonball keeps falling but never lands.

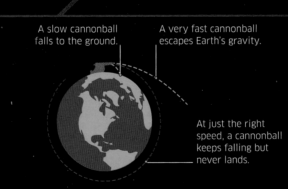

Dwarf planets

Dwarf planets are round in shape but smaller than true planets, and their gravity is not strong enough to sweep their region of space clear of smaller debris. The most famous dwarf planet is Pluto, which was classified as a true planet until 2006.

Ceres
Haumea
Makemake
Pluto
Eris

SIZE COMPARED TO EARTH

Uranus

Neptune

1,500 million miles
(2,414 million km)

2,000 million miles
(3,219 million km)

2,500 million miles
(4,023 million km)

Inner planets

Mercury, Venus, Earth, and Mars are the Solar System's inner planets. On the face of it, they are worlds apart—but underneath the surface, it is a different story.

The inner planets all formed from the same material about 4.6 billion years ago. All are a mix of rock and metal, with interiors that are roughly divided into layers. The heavier metals are concentrated toward the center, while the lighter rock is on top.

Each of these planets was bombarded by asteroids and comets early in the Solar System's history, and each has been affected by volcanic activity too. Mercury's heavily cratered face still bears the scars of the early bombardment, but the surfaces of the other three worlds have changed over time.

This view of Venus's surface was made using radar to see through the planet's thick clouds

Maat Mons is Venus's largest volcano

Smooth plains formed from lava flows in distant past

Brightest craters are the youngest

MERCURY

VENUS

In the Sun's glare

Mercury is the smallest of the Solar System's planets and lies closest to the Sun. It is a lifeless world that has hardly changed in 3 billion years. The planet's entire surface is pitted with craters formed when asteroids crashed into it while Mercury was young. The craters range from small, bowl-shaped ones to the huge Caloris Basin, which is nearly one-third the width of the planet.

Mercury orbits the Sun more quickly than any other planet, but it rotates slowly: for every two orbits, it spins around just three times. So a "day" on Mercury (sunrise to sunrise) takes 176 Earth days. Such long days and nights, coupled with a very thin atmosphere, give Mercury the greatest surface temperature range of all the planets. In the daytime, the surface is hot enough to melt lead, but at night it's cold enough to liquefy air.

Mercury profile

Diameter .... 3,032 miles (4,879 km)
**Average surface
temperature**................333°F (167°C)
One spin on axis .... 58.6 Earth days
One orbit of Sun.........88 Earth days
Number of moons 0

Hot spots
The colors on this heat map of Mercury show the planet's surface temperature. The red region, which is on the equator, faces the Sun and is hottest. Next warmest are yellow areas, then green. The planet's polar regions (blue) are coolest.

Lava land

Venus is sometimes described as Earth's twin because it's almost the same size as our planet and has a similar internal structure. But the two worlds are very different.

Any astronaut who tried to walk on Venus would be killed in seconds. The surface is as hot as the inside of a pizza oven, and the crushing air pressure is 90 times greater than that on Earth.

Venus's deadly surface is hidden from our view by thick cloud cover, but orbiting spacecraft have used radar to see through the gloom, and landers have touched down to take photos. Venus is a world of volcanoes, many thought to be active, and its surface is littered with broken rock from solidified lava. It is permanently overcast, with a sickly yellowish light filtering through the cloud.

Venus spins more slowly than any other planet. It also spins in the opposite direction (clockwise) to every planet apart from Uranus.

Venus profile

Diameter ..7,521 miles (12,104 km)
**Average surface
temperature**................867°F (464°C)
One spin on axis ..... 243 Earth days
One orbit of Sun... 224.7 Earth days
Number of moons 0

Greenhouse effect
Venus is hot because of a process called the greenhouse effect. The Sun's heat passes through the atmosphere and warms the ground, which then reemits warmth. The reemitted warmth is trapped by the atmosphere, much as glass traps heat in a greenhouse.

Sunlight warms the ground

Heat from ground is trapped by atmosphere

Atmosphere is about 50 miles (80 km) deep

2,500 miles (4,000 km)–the **length of** Mars's Valles Marineris canyon.

Mars's **moons Phobos** and **Deimos** were once asteroids.

14 miles (22 km)–the **height of the Olympus Mons volcano** on Mars.

25

Liquid water covers most of Earth's surface

Ice cap at north pole

Like Earth, Mars has a crust made of solid rock

Like all the inner planets, Mars has a core made of red-hot iron

The reddish color comes from iron oxide (rust) in the soil

EARTH

MARS

Living world

Third out from the Sun, Earth is the largest of the inner planets. It's the only planet with liquid water flowing freely on the surface, and it's the only planet in the Universe known to sustain life.

Earth's surface consists of vast oceans (71 percent), continents of land, and two polar ice caps—all supported by a thin, rocky crust. The crust is broken into seven huge segments and many smaller ones. Called tectonic plates, these giant slabs of rock creep slowly over Earth's surface, pushed by churning movements in the softer, hot rock that fills most of Earth's interior. As tectonic plates move, they bump into each other and grind past one another, generating immense forces that thrust up mountain ranges, unleash volcanic eruptions, and trigger earthquakes. These powerful forces continually change Earth's appearance, as do the actions of wind and water— and the planet's 7 billion human inhabitants.

Earth profile

Diameter ..7,926 miles (12,756 km)
Average surface temperature......................59°F (15°C)
One spin on axis .... 23.9 hours
One orbit of Sun...............365.3 days
Number of moons 1

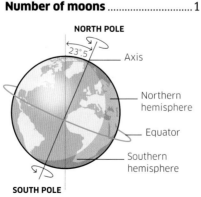

NORTH POLE

23.5°

Axis

Northern hemisphere

Equator

Southern hemisphere

SOUTH POLE

Tilted planet

Earth spins around once a day, but it isn't perfectly upright. Its axis— the imaginary line from pole to pole around which it spins—is tilted by 23.5°. So as Earth travels around the Sun, one hemisphere and then the other is tilted toward the Sun. This is what causes the seasons.

The red planet

The second smallest planet in the Solar System, Mars is half the size of Earth. It's sometimes called the red planet because of its rusty coloring. A vast canyon called Valles Marineris stretches a quarter of the way around this frozen desert world. It formed long ago when the crust of the young planet split open. Elsewhere are dusty plains strewn with boulders and giant, extinct volcanoes, including Olympus Mons–the Solar System's largest volcano.

Mars profile

Diameter .... 4,220 miles (6,792 km)
Average surface temperature..................–81°F (–63°C)
One spin on axis .... 24.6 hours
One orbit of Sun...... 687 Earth days
Number of moons 2

Rocky floodplain

Mars hasn't always been a desert. Dry river beds show that water flowed here long ago. Floods swept rocks across the land and dumped them on floodplains like the one below. Mars may even have been warm and wet enough for life to flourish.

26 space ○ THE UNIVERSE

1,300 The number of times Earth could fit inside Jupiter's volume.

1665 The year Jupiter's Great Red Spot was first seen.

Size of Earth relative to planets

Gas atmosphere
Jupiter's swirling outer atmosphere is 620 miles (1,000 km) thick and consists mainly of hydrogen gas.

Liquid layer
The outer atmosphere merges gradually into a deep layer of liquid hydrogen and helium.

Blue color caused by methane in atmosphere

Great Red Spot
This giant storm is bigger than Earth and has been raging for over 300 years.

JUPITER

Solid core
Jupiter's rocky core is hotter than the surface of the Sun.

Liquid metal layer
Deep inside Jupiter, intense pressure turns hydrogen into a liquid metal.

NEPTUNE

King of the planets

Mighty Jupiter is the fifth planet from the Sun and the largest in the Solar System—so big, in fact, that it's 2.5 times more massive than all the other planets put together. Its strong gravitational pull greatly affects the orbits of other bodies in the Solar System.

Jupiter's fast rate of spin has stretched its surface clouds into bands, with spots (storms) and ripples where neighboring bands swirl together.

Several craft have visited Jupiter, including *Galileo*, which orbited from 1995 to 2003.

Jupiter profile

Diameter .... 88,846 miles (142,984 km)

Average surface temperature .... –186°F (–121°C)
One spin on axis .... 9.9 hours
One orbit of Sun ...... 11.9 Earth years
Number of moons 67

The Jupiter system
Like a king surrounded by his courtiers, Jupiter is circled by a great number of moons. The inner moons, including the four largest, are shown below. Ganymede, the largest, is bigger than the planet Mercury. Most of Jupiter's other moons are probably asteroids captured by the planet's gravity.

Blue planet

Neptune, the eighth and furthest of the planets from the Sun, was discovered in 1846. Astronomers had noticed Uranus wasn't following its expected path—there seemed to be an unseen body, perhaps an undiscovered planet, pulling on it. Two mathematicians—John Couch Adams in England and Urbain Le Verrier in France—calculated where in the sky the undiscovered planet must be. Within days, Neptune was spotted from an observatory in Germany.

Neptune is slightly smaller than Uranus and looks bluer because its atmosphere contains more methane. It has a deep, fluid mantle that is hot and dense and contains water, ammonia, and methane. Neptune also has a barely visible system of rings. Its biggest moon, Triton, resembles Pluto and was likely captured by Neptune's gravity in an encounter billions of years ago.

Neptune profile

Diameter .... 30,775 miles (49,528 km)

Average surface temperature .... –330°F (–201°C)
One spin on axis .... 16.1 hours
One orbit of Sun 163.7 Earth years
Number of moons 13

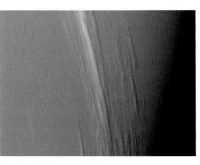

Fastest known winds
When *Voyager 2* flew past Neptune in 1989, it photographed white clouds blown into streaks by winds of up to 1,300 mph (2,100 kph)—the fastest sustained winds in the Solar System. This violent weather is thought to be powered by heat from inside Neptune since the planet is too far from the Sun to absorb much of its warmth.

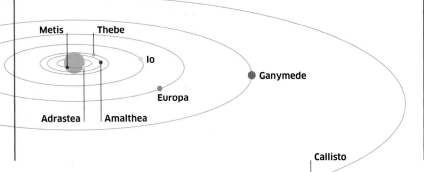

Metis

Thebe

Io

Ganymede

Europa

Adrastea

Amalthea

Callisto

43,000 °F (24,000 °C)—the estimated temperature of Jupiter's core.

150 The number of moons and moonlets observed orbiting Saturn.

27

Outer atmosphere
Although it looks calm, fierce winds whip through Saturn's atmosphere at 1,800 kph (1,120 mph).

Cloud bands
Saturn's clouds form bands around the planet, like those on Jupiter.

Outer planets

Four gigantic planets dominate the outer Solar System. Very different from the rocky, inner planets, these strange worlds are huge globes of gas and liquid, with no solid surface and hundreds of moons.

After the Sun first formed, its heat drove gases out of the inner Solar System, leaving behind heavier compounds such as rock and metal. The rock and metal formed the solid inner planets, while the gases formed the outer planets. Astronomers call the outer planets gas giants, though they consist mostly of liquid and they have solid cores. These four worlds have much in common. All have numerous moons, a deep, stormy atmosphere, and a set of rings made of flecks of rock or ice.

On a roll
Uranus leans so far to one side that it appears to roll along as it travels around the Sun.

Gaps
Gaps in the rings are areas swept clear of ice by the gravity of Saturn's moons.

SATURN

Main rings
The rings consist of billions of sparkling fragments of ice, varying in size from microscopic to as big as a house.

Rings around Uranus
Thirteen rings are known to circle the planet.

URANUS

Lord of the rings

The second-largest planet and the sixth farthest from the Sun, Saturn shines like a bright yellow star. Even a small telescope will reveal its most famous feature: a magnificent ring system. Despite Saturn's size, it is only half as dense as Jupiter. Its clouds form less obvious bands than Jupiter's, but fierce storms blow up every 30 years or so, creating giant white spots.

Saturn's largest moon, Titan, has a dense atmosphere and a rocky surface with seas of liquid methane. The *Cassini* spacecraft has been orbiting Saturn since 2004. It released a probe, *Huygens*, that landed on Titan in 2005.

Saturn profile

Diameter .... 74,898 miles (120,536 km)
Average surface temperature........... −292°F (−180°C)
One spin on axis ....10.7 hours
One orbit of Sun.... 29.5 Earth years
Number of moons 62

Ring system

Saturn's main rings are 220,000 miles (360,000 km) wide, yet they are only 30 ft (10 m) thick. A scale model of the rings made with a sheet of paper would be 2 miles (3 km) wide. Beyond the main rings are hazy outer rings, photographed by *Cassini* while the Sun was behind Saturn (below).

Topsy-turvy world

Uranus, the seventh planet from the Sun, was unknown to ancient astronomers, even though it is just visible with the naked eye in perfectly clear and dark skies. It was discovered by musician William Herschel from his back garden in Bath, England, in 1781.

Uranus is similar to Neptune but has a paler blue, almost featureless face. It is the coldest of all the planets and generates very little heat from within. It orbits on its side—perhaps because it was knocked over by a collision with another planet early in its history. Its extreme tilt gives it very long seasons.

Uranus has a faint set of rings, which were discovered in 1977. The planet's moons are all named after characters in works by William Shakespeare or the English poet Alexander Pope.

Uranus profile

Diameter .... 36,763 miles (51,118 km)
Average surface temperature........−315°F (−193°C)
One spin on axis ....17.2 hours
One orbit of Sun...84 Earth years
Number of moons 27

Outer atmosphere, the cloud layer

Atmosphere (hydrogen, helium, and methane gases)

Core of silicate rock

Hot, liquid mantle

Ice giant

Uranus's pale blue color is due to the methane in its atmosphere. Water and ammonia have also been detected in the clouds. The planet contains less hydrogen and helium than Jupiter and Saturn but has more rock and water.

28 space ○ THE UNIVERSE

18 days—the **time** it would take to fly to the Moon at the **speed of a jumbo jet**.

The Moon

The Moon is Earth's closest neighbor in space and looms larger than any other object in the night sky. Its cratered surface may be cold and lifeless, but deep inside the Moon is a gigantic ball of white-hot iron.

Earth and Moon have existed together in space ever since the Moon formed as the result of a cosmic collision. It orbits around our planet, keeping the same face toward us at all times. As we gaze on its sunlit surface, we look at a landscape that has barely changed since 3.5 billion years ago. Back then, the young Moon was bombarded by asteroids. For millions of years they blasted out surface material and formed craters. The largest of these were then flooded with volcanic lava, creating dark, flat plains that look like seas.

SEA OF SHOWERS (MARE IMBRIUM)

Lunar maria
Dark, flat areas known as maria, or seas, are huge plains of solidified lava.

Gray surface
The Moon's surface is covered in a layer of fine gray dust an inch or so deep.

Moon profile
Diameter .... 2,159 miles (3,474 km)
Average surface temperature .....−63°F (−53°C)
Length of lunar day .... 27 Earth days
Time to orbit Earth .... 27 Earth days
Gravity (Earth = 1) 0.17

How the Moon formed
Scientists think the Moon formed as a result of a collision between Earth and a planet 4.5 billion years ago. The debris was pulled together by gravity and became the Moon.

Impact
A planet smashes into Earth and blasts molten rock into space.

Moon formation
A disc of debris forms. The particles slowly join to form a Moon.

Phases of the Moon
As the Moon orbits the Earth, a changing amount of its face is bathed in sunlight. The different shapes we see are the Moon's phases. One cycle of phases lasts 29.5 days.

NEW MOON   WAXING CRESCENT   FIRST QUARTER

WAXING GIBBOUS   FULL MOON   WANING GIBBOUS

LAST QUARTER   WANING CRESCENT   NEW MOON

The far side
The Moon keeps the same face toward the Earth all the time. The face we never see—the far side—can only be viewed by spacecraft. Its crust is thicker and more heavily cratered than the near side. Elevation (height) maps reveal high and low areas of land.

Height of surface

High

Low

Highlands

South Pole-Aitken Basin

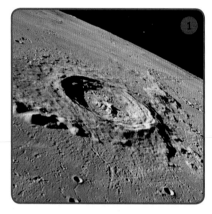

Lunar craters
Craters exist all over the Moon. They range from small bowl-shaped hollows a few miles wide to the vast South Pole-Aitken Basin, which is 1,600 miles (2,500 km) in diameter. Many craters, like Eratosthenes (above), have central hills that formed as the ground rebounded after the asteroid struck.

Man on the Moon
Astronauts landed on the Moon six times during NASA's Apollo program. They found a world of gray, dusty plains and rolling hills under an inky black sky. Below, an astronaut heads back to his rover vehicle parked near Camelot Crater (left), where he had been collecting samples. The large boulders were flung out of the crater when it formed.

Lunar layers
Like Earth, the Moon is made of different layers that separated out long ago, when its whole interior was molten. Lightweight minerals rose to the top, and heavier metals sank to the center. The outermost layer is a thin crust of rock like the rock on Earth. Under this is the mantle—a deep layer of rock that gets hotter toward the center. The bottom part of the mantle is partly molten. In the Moon's center is an iron core heated to about 2,600°F (1,400°C) by energy from radioactive elements. Scientists think the outer core is molten but the inner core is squeezed solid by the pressure of the rock around it.

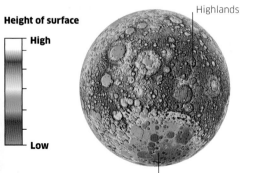

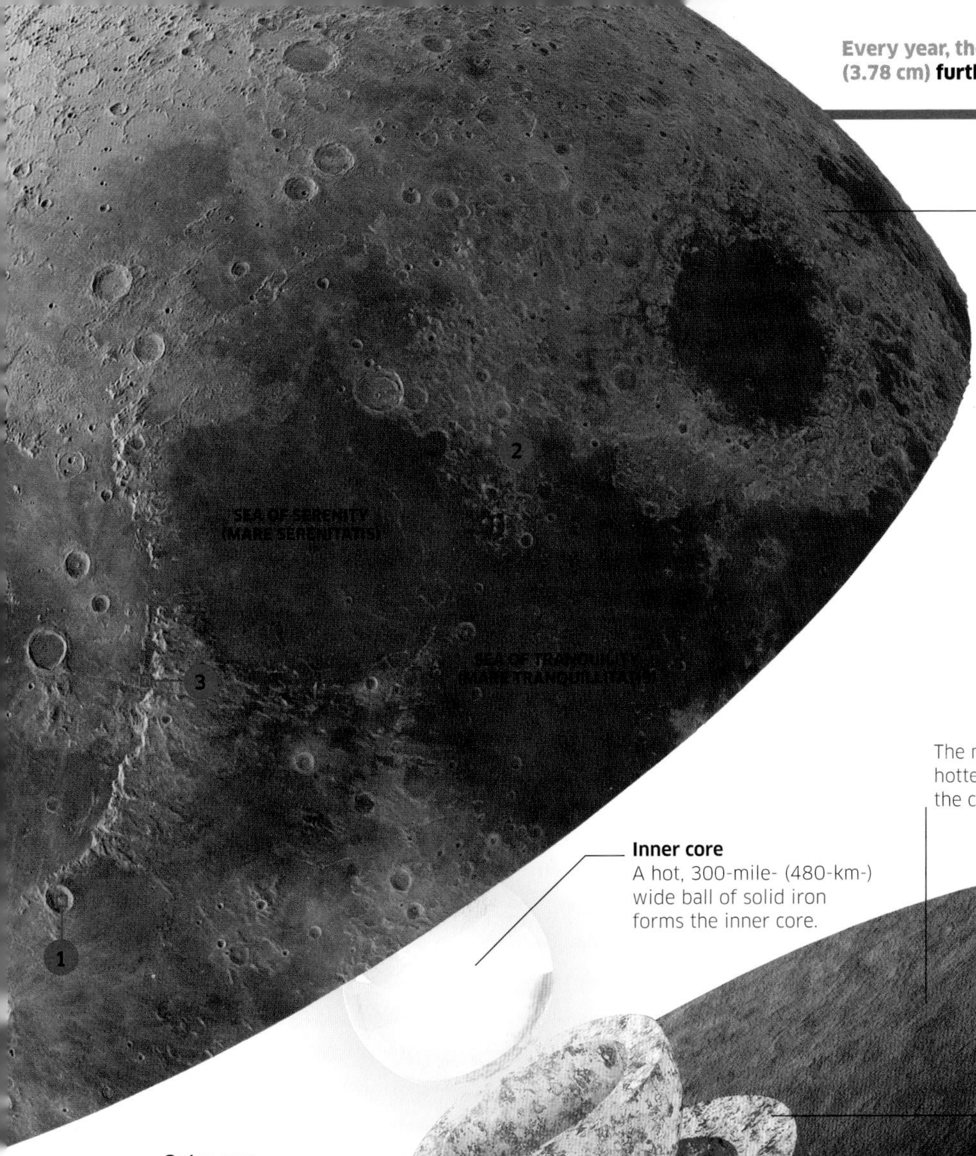

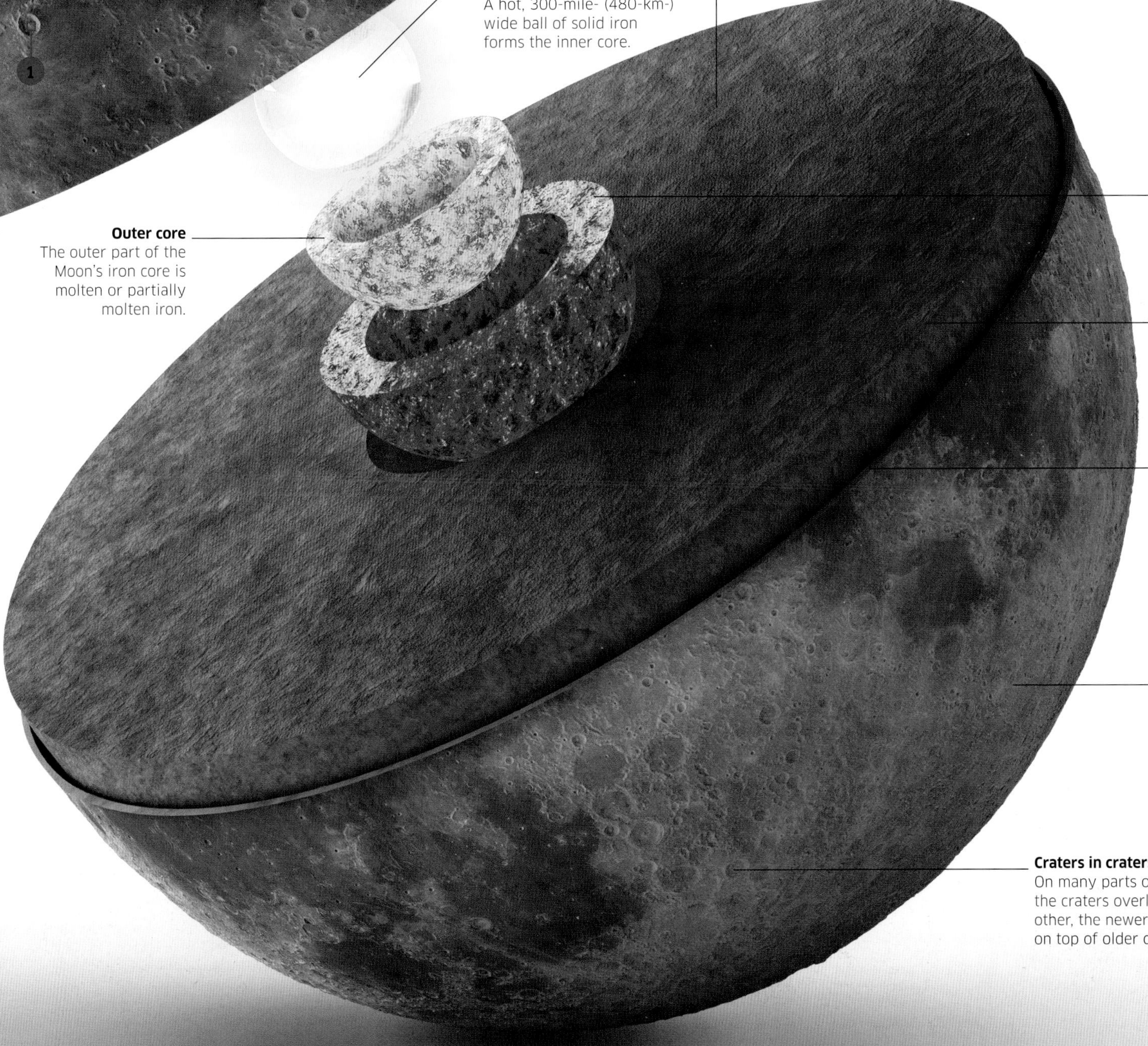

Highlands
All the Moon's hills and mountains are the rims of craters or central peaks in craters.

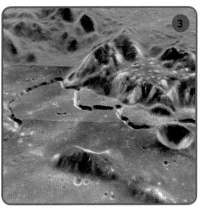

Hadley Rille
A deep gorge named Hadley Rille cuts through flat plains at the edge of the Moon's Sea of Showers, winding for more than 60 miles (100 km). How it formed is a mystery, but it might be an ancient lava channel. In July 1971, Apollo astronauts drove their rover to the edge of Hadley Rille to take photographs and study it.

The mantle gets hotter toward the center.

Inner core
A hot, 300-mile- (480-km-) wide ball of solid iron forms the inner core.

Outer core
The outer part of the Moon's iron core is molten or partially molten iron.

Inner mantle
Heat from radioactive elements has partially melted the inner mantle.

Mantle
The mantle is mainly solid rock and is rich in silicate minerals, which are common on Earth.

Crust
Made of granitelike rock, the Moon's crust is about 30 miles (48 km) thick on the near side and 46 miles (74 km) thick on the far side.

Far side
The Moon's far side, which is not visible from Earth, is covered in craters and has no large maria (seas).

Craters in craters
On many parts of the Moon the craters overlap each other, the newer ones lying on top of older craters.

SEA OF SERENITY (MARE SERENITATIS)

SEA OF TRANQUILITY (MARE TRANQUILLITATIS)

1

2

3

SPACE EXPLORATION

Stars and planets have fascinated people since ancient times, but it wasn't until the 20th century that exploring space became possible. In recent decades we have sent astronauts to the Moon, robotic spacecraft to the outer reaches of the Solar System, and used huge telescopes to peer across the vastness of the Universe.

EXPLORING THE PLANETS

The planets are too far for manned missions, so robotic spacecraft are sent instead. The first to visit another planet was *Mariner 2*, a US craft that flew past Venus in 1962. Since then, and despite a number of early failures, hundreds of spacecraft have visited the Solar System's planets, moons, asteroids, and comets. Most spacecraft either fly past or orbit their target, but some also release landers that touch down on the surface.

Robot explorers

Robotic spacecraft can visit places too far or dangerous for human beings. Launched into space by rocket, they travel vast distances across space and may take years to reach their target. There are various types of spacecraft, each suited to a particular mission.

FLYBY SPACECRAFT
Some spacecraft observe a target as they fly past. NASA's famous *Voyager 1* and *Voyager 2* flew past several planets.

ORBITER
An orbiter flies around a planet repeatedly, giving it plenty of time to study its target. Orbiters have visited the Moon and all the planets except Uranus and Neptune.

OBSERVING THE SKIES

For centuries, astronomers have observed the heavens with their eyes alone or used simple telescopes that magnify the view. But the visible light we see is just one part of a much bigger spectrum of electromagnetic rays that reaches Earth from space. Stars and other objects also emit invisible radio waves, X-rays, infrared, and microwave rays. Modern telescopes can see all of these, and each type of radiation reveals something different.

Capturing light

Telescopes come in many different styles and designs, but basically all do the same thing: collect electromagnetic radiation from space and focus it to create an image. Earth's atmosphere can block or blur the image, so some telescopes are located on high mountaintops or even launched into space.

LAUNCH VEHICLES

Space is only 60 miles (100 km) above the Earth's surface and takes less than 10 minutes to reach in a rocket. Although the journey is short, it takes tremendous power to escape the pull of Earth's gravity. Launch vehicles are built to make the journey only one time, and most of their weight is fuel.

World's largest rockets

Saturn V, which sent astronauts to the Moon, was the largest rocket ever built. Its Soviet rival, the N1, was launched four times but each attempt ended in disaster.

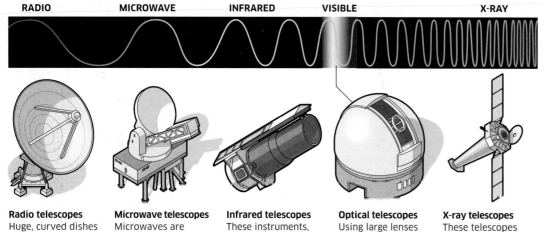

RADIO	MICROWAVE	INFRARED	VISIBLE	X-RAY

Radio telescopes
Huge, curved dishes are used to focus radio waves given out by sources such as galaxies, pulsars, and black holes.

Microwave telescopes
Microwaves are short radio waves. By capturing these rays, telescopes can see ancient radiation from the Big Bang.

Infrared telescopes
These instruments, some of which are sent into space, detect the heat from objects such as clouds of gas and dust.

Optical telescopes
Using large lenses or mirrors, optical telescopes gather faint visible light and can see much further than the human eye.

X-ray telescopes
These telescopes capture high energy rays from extremely hot objects. X-ray telescopes only work in space.

ARIANE 4 (EUROPE)–193 ft (59 m) tall
LONG MARCH 2F (CHINA)–203 ft (62 m) tall
DELTA IV HEAVY (US)–236 ft (72 m) tall
N1 (USSR)–341 ft (105 m) tall
SATURN V (US)–364 ft (111 m) tall

Mapping the stars

Because Earth is surrounded by space, when we look at the night sky it seems as though all the stars are pinned to the inside of a giant sphere. Astronomers call this the celestial sphere and use it to map the positions of stars and planets. Vertical and horizontal lines are used to divide the celestial sphere into a grid, just like the grid of longitude and latitude lines used to map Earth's surface.

Celestial north pole
This is the point directly above Earth's North Pole.

Celestial south pole
This is the point directly above Earth's South Pole.

Declination lines
These split the sky into north–south segments.

Right ascension lines
These divide the sky into east–west segments.

Celestial equator
This imaginary line over Earth's equator divides the sky into north and south hemispheres.

Launch sites

Many countries have spaceflight launch sites. Sites closer to the equator can launch heavier cargo, because rockets there are given a boost by the speed of Earth's spin.

- Baikonur, Kazakhstan
- Cape Canaveral, FL
- Xichang, China

MAJOR LAUNCH SITES

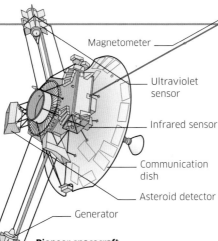

Magnetometer

Ultraviolet sensor

Infrared sensor

Communication dish

Asteroid detector

Generator

Pioneer spacecraft
Pioneers 10 and *11* made flybys of Jupiter and Saturn. They are now heading out of the Solar System into deep space.

ATMOSPHERIC PROBE
This type of craft enters a planet's atmosphere. The *Galileo* probe dove into Jupiter's stormy atmosphere in 2005.

LANDER
Some craft can touch down on the surface of another world. In 1976, *Viking 1* became the first craft to successfully land on Mars.

ROVER
A rover is a robotic lander with wheels that can drive around. Rovers sent to Mars have studied its rocks for signs of ancient life.

PENETRATOR
A penetrator is designed to hit its target at high speed and bury itself. In 2005, *Deep Impact* penetrated the surface of a comet.

12 years and 43 days – the time it took the spacecraft *Voyager 2* to reach Neptune from Earth.

Solar System missions

In little more than 50 years, around 200 spacecraft have left Earth's orbit and headed off to explore the Solar System. More than half the missions have been to Earth's nearest neighbors in space: the Moon and the planets Mars and Venus.

Most visited
This chart shows the number of missions to the major bodies in the Solar System.

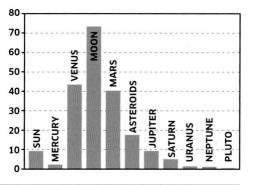

SATELLITES

About 1,000 operational satellites orbit the Earth, carrying out tasks such as beaming TV signals around the world, gathering data for weather forecasters, and spying for the military. Many thousands more pieces of space junk—old satellites, discarded rocket parts, and debris from collisions—also circle our planet. The growing cloud of space debris is a hazard to spacecraft.

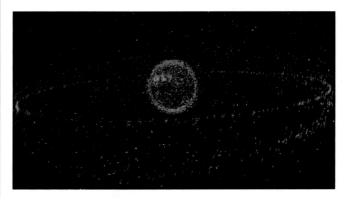

Over 500,000 objects, including satellites and space junk, orbit Earth.

Satellite orbits

Some satellites are a few hundred miles above Earth's surface, but others are much further. Some of the highest ones, such as weather, TV, and phone satellites, have geostationary orbits, which means they stay over a fixed point on Earth. Satellites with lower orbits change position all the time.

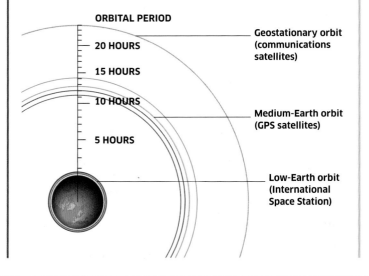

ORBITAL PERIOD

20 HOURS
15 HOURS
10 HOURS
5 HOURS

Geostationary orbit (communications satellites)

Medium-Earth orbit (GPS satellites)

Low-Earth orbit (International Space Station)

LIVING IN SPACE

Astronauts must adapt to a zero-gravity environment when living in space. Although floating weightlessly can be fun, it can also cause medical problems. Space stations are cramped places with few luxuries. Astronauts eat ready-made meals that are either freeze-dried or served in pouches. All water is recycled, including the water vapor from human breath. Astronauts clean themselves with special shampoos and soaps that don't need water, and they use space toilets that suck away waste rather than flushing with water.

Effects on the body

When the human body spends a long time in space, it changes. Without gravity pulling on the spine, the body gets about 2 in (5 cm) taller. Body fluids that flow downward on Earth build up in the head. This gives astronauts swollen faces and blocked noses, making food seem tasteless. When astronauts come back to Earth, the return of full gravity can make them feel extremely weak.

Space stations

A space station is a crewed satellite— a kind of orbiting laboratory in which astronauts and scientists live and work. The USSR launched the first station, *Salyut 1*, in 1971. The US soon followed with *Skylab*, in 1973. Russia's *Mir*, in use from 1986 to 2001, was the most successful station until the US, Russia, and more than 10 other countries joined forces to build the *International Space Station*, in orbit since 1998. China's own space station prototype, *Tiangong-1*, was launched in 2011.

Brain and balance
Without gravity, the inner ear's balance system no longer works, which can make astronauts feel sick.

Heart
Blood flows more easily, so the heart doesn't need to work as hard.

Muscles
Movement is easy when you're weightless, and muscles waste away if not used. Workouts in the onboard gym help to slow this process.

Bones
Bones weaken and become less dense. Regular exercise is essential to keep them strong.

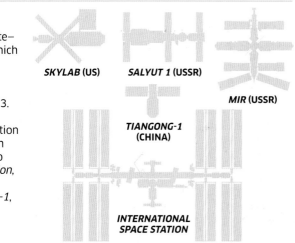

SKYLAB (US)

SALYUT 1 (USSR)

MIR (USSR)

TIANGONG-1 (CHINA)

INTERNATIONAL SPACE STATION

A brief history of astronomy

Many ancient cultures followed the Sun and stars in order to keep track of the time of year, and by Ancient Greek times, astronomers had already worked out that Earth is round. Today, powerful telescopes allow us to peer so far into space that we can look back in time almost to the birth of the Universe.

3000 BCE

Astronomical calendars

Many monuments built by ancient peoples, such as Stonehenge in the UK, align with the Sun. These monuments may have been used as calendars so that farmers knew when to sow crops.

150 CE

Ptolemy

The Greek astronomer Ptolemy cataloged 1,022 stars in 48 constellations. He believed that Earth was the center of the Solar System and Universe, orbited by the Sun, Moon, planets, and stars.

1543

Copernicus

Polish astronomer Nicolaus Copernicus proposed that the Sun, not Earth, is the center of the Solar System. It was a shocking idea since it meant Earth must be flying through space, spinning around.

Earth

1610

Galileo Galilei

Italian scientist Galileo Galilei built a telescope and used it to study the night sky. He saw spots on the Sun, mountains on the Moon, and four moons orbiting the planet Jupiter.

1687

Isaac Newton

English scientist Isaac Newton worked out the laws of gravity—the force that makes objects fall to the ground. He discovered that gravity keeps the Moon in orbit around Earth and keeps the planets in orbit around the Sun.

1990

Modern astronomy

Today, space telescopes such as Hubble, which was launched in 1990, give us breathtaking views of distant objects in space, including the furthest galaxies ever seen.

Astronomy

People have been looking up at the night sky and marveling at its beauty and mystery for thousands of years. Today, a whole branch of science—astronomy—is devoted to studying stars.

Professional astronomers investigate not only stars but everything to do with space—from the meteors that burn up spectacularly as shooting stars in Earth's atmosphere and the planets of the Solar System to distant galaxies billions of light years away. Astronomy makes a rewarding hobby too, and many amateur stargazers enjoy observing the night sky with backyard telescopes or binoculars. Whenever astronomers observe the sky, they are looking back in time. This is because light takes such a long time to reach us from distant objects in space. We see the Moon as it was one and a quarter seconds ago and the stars as they were hundreds of years ago.

The sky at night

Ancient stargazers saw patterns in the stars and named groups of stars after mythical beings and animals. These star patterns, called constellations, look little like the objects they are meant to represent, but we still use the old names. Today, astronomers divide the whole sky into 88 segments, each one named after the constellation within it. Star charts like the one here show which constellations are visible at a particular time and place. This chart shows the stars you can see at midnight in January from the northern hemisphere.

Orion the hunter

One of the best-known and brightest constellations is Orion the hunter, which is visible the world over. Orion includes the red giant star Betelgeuse and the blue-white supergiant Rigel—two of the brightest stars in the night sky.

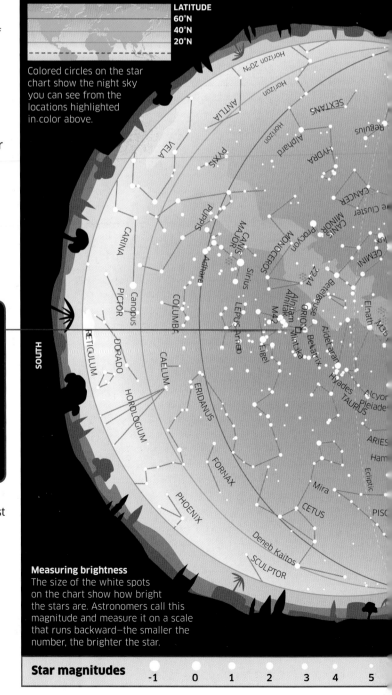

LATITUDE
60°N
40°N
20°N

Colored circles on the star chart show the night sky you can see from the locations highlighted in color above.

Measuring brightness

The size of the white spots on the chart show how bright the stars are. Astronomers call this magnitude and measure it on a scale that runs backward—the smaller the number, the brighter the star.

Star magnitudes	-1	0	1	2	3	4	5

15 million trillion miles (24 million trillion km)—the **distance to the Andromeda galaxy, the furthest object visible to the naked eye.**

2,000 The number of stars visible to the naked eye.

33

How telescopes work

The invention of the telescope revolutionized astronomy. A telescope collects more light from an object than a human eye can. It uses this light to form a magnified image. There are two basic types of telescopes: refracting and reflecting. The refracting telescope has a large convex (outward-curving) lens that gathers and focuses the light. The reflecting telescope uses a curved mirror instead.

Lens

Eyepiece lens magnifies image

Light from star

Focal point

Refracting telescope
A convex lens bends light entering the telescope to focus it, forming an image. At the other end of the telescope, a smaller lens called the eyepiece magnifies the image.

Eyepiece

Focal point

Light from star

Light rays converge

Smaller mirror

Main mirror

Reflecting telescope
A concave (inward-curving) main mirror reflects light on to a smaller, flat mirror. The resulting image is magnified by an eyepiece lens.

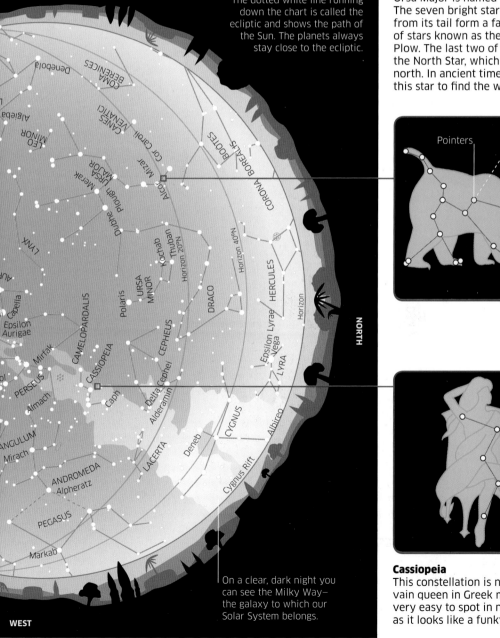

The dotted white line running down the chart is called the ecliptic and shows the path of the Sun. The planets always stay close to the ecliptic.

On a clear, dark night you can see the Milky Way—the galaxy to which our Solar System belongs.

GALAXY   GLOBULAR CLUSTER   OPEN CLUSTER   Star clusters are clouds of stars.

The Great Bear
Ursa Major is named after a bear. The seven bright stars running from its tail form a famous group of stars known as the Big Dipper or Plow. The last two of these point to the North Star, which is always due north. In ancient times, sailors used this star to find the way.

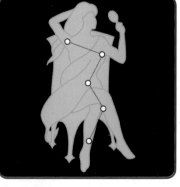

Cassiopeia
This constellation is named after a vain queen in Greek mythology. It's very easy to spot in northern skies as it looks like a funky letter W.

Seeing the invisible

Professional astronomers don't just use visible light to see the night sky. Their telescopes can also create images from wavelengths of light that our eyes cannot see, such as X-rays, radio waves, and infrared rays. The images below all show Kepler's Supernova—the wreckage left by a giant star that exploded in 1604.

X-ray image
This image of Kepler's Supernova is from the orbiting Chandra X-ray Observatory. It shows a cloud of incredibly hot gas that emits high-energy X-rays.

Visible light image
Very little of the object can be seen in visible light, even in this image from the Hubble Space Telescope. The bright areas are clumps of gas.

Infrared image
Taken by the Spitzer Space Telescope, this infrared image shows dust clouds that were heated by a shock wave from the exploding star.

Combined image
Combining all three sources produces a complete image: a shell of supernova debris expanding into space at 1,240 miles (2,000 km) per second.

Escape rocket
(for emergencies during launch)

Command Module
Astronauts stayed in here during launch.

Service Module
This module powered the Apollo spacecraft.

Lunar Module
The Lunar Module was housed in an aluminum cone.

Instrument unit

Third stage
This stage reached low-Earth orbit and then put Apollo on course for the Moon.

Single third-stage engine

Interstage adapter
Covering the third-stage engine, this section linked the rocket's second and third stages.

Second stage
The second stage held a tank of liquid hydrogen fuel and a tank of liquid oxygen.

Second-stage engines

Interstage adapter
This section linked the rocket's first two stages and also covered the second-stage engines.

First stage fuel
The first stage had a tank of kerosene fuel and a tank of liquid oxygen to burn it. The five engines burned 16 tons of fuel per second during the launch.

Five first-stage engines

Engine nozzle
Nozzle for the main engine, which propelled the Apollo craft through space.

Service Module
This module provided life-support systems and power for the crew, and housed the Apollo craft's main engine.

Fuel tanks
Tanks within the Service Module supplied fuel to the main engine.

Astronauts
The crew of three stayed in the Command Module for most of their journey to and from the Moon.

Thrusters
Small thrusters made fine adjustments to the Apollo spacecraft's movements.

Command Module
The Command Module was the only part of the Apollo craft to return to Earth. Its conical shape helped it withstand the heat of reentry into Earth's atmosphere.

Mission to the Moon

Humans have set foot on only one world beyond Earth: the Moon. Just 27 daredevil astronauts have traveled there, of whom 12 walked on its cratered, lifeless surface.

Eight space missions visited the Moon between 1968 and 1972 as part of NASA's Apollo program. Each mission carried three American astronauts inside an Apollo spacecraft, which was launched by a Saturn V rocket. Apollo 8 tested the craft as it orbited the Moon. Then, in a dress rehearsal prior to landing, Apollo 10 flew close to the lunar surface. The first of the six missions that successfully landed on the Moon was Apollo 11 in 1969. Astronauts Neil Armstrong and Buzz Aldrin touched down on the surface in July of that year. As Armstrong took the first historic step, he said, "That's one small step for man, one giant leap for mankind."

Saturn V rocket

The Apollo astronauts were blasted into space inside the nose cone of the largest rocket ever built: Saturn V. Standing nearly 364 ft (111 m) tall, the Saturn V was as tall as a 30-story building. This giant launch vehicle consisted of three rockets in one. The first two parts, or stages, lifted the Apollo craft into space, and the third stage set the spacecraft on course for the Moon.

Apollo spacecraft

The Apollo spacecraft had three parts: the Command, Service, and Lunar Modules. These were all linked together for the 250,000-mile (400,000-km) trip to the Moon. Once there, the Lunar Module took two astronauts down to the Moon's surface, while the third crew member remained in lunar orbit in the combined Command and Service Module (CSM). The top half of the Lunar Module, known as the ascent stage, later returned the two astronauts to the CSM for the journey back to Earth.

21 hours—the length of time Apollo 11 astronauts Neil Armstrong and Buzz Aldrin spent on the Moon. Apollo 17 astronauts spent three days on the lunar surface.

300 The total **number of hours** that astronauts **have spent** on the Moon.

Beef, potatoes, and grape juice—the **first meal** eaten by the **Apollo 11** astronauts in space.

842 lb (382 kg) of **lunar rock and soil** were **brought back** by the **Apollo astronauts.** **35**

There and back

Each of the six Apollo missions that landed men on the Moon took the same route, taking off from Florida, and ending with the astronauts splashing down in the Pacific Ocean.

❶ Saturn V rocket carrying Apollo craft blasts off and positions craft in Earth's orbit.
❷ The rocket's third stage and Apollo craft leave Earth's orbit and head toward the Moon.
❸ Combined Command and Service Module (CSM) separates from the rocket.
❹ CSM turns and docks with

Lunar Module. Third rocket stage is now discarded.
❺ Apollo craft adjusts its course to go into lunar orbit.
❻ Lunar Module transports two astronauts to lunar surface.
❼ Third crew member continues to orbit the Moon in CSM.
❽ Ascent stage of Lunar Module takes astronauts back to CSM,

after which it is discarded.
❾ CSM adjusts its course and heads back to Earth.
❿ Service Module is jettisoned.
⓫ Command Module enters Earth's atmosphere.
⓬ Command Module makes a parachute landing in the sea.

The trip from the Earth to the Moon took about three days.

Landing sites
The Apollo landing sites were on the side of the Moon that faces Earth.

Docking tunnel
Astronauts used this tunnel to move between the Command and Lunar Modules.

Ascent stage
The ascent stage of the Lunar Module was the astronauts' home while they explored the Moon.

Legs and pads
Flexible legs with wide pads on the bottom cushioned the Module's landing and kept it stable on the surface.

Descent stage
This bottom half of the Lunar Module acted as the launch platform when the top half blasted off back into space. The descent stage stayed on the Moon.

Hatch
The astronauts climbed through a hatch to go outside.

Gas tanks
The larger tank contained helium; oxygen was held in the adjacent smaller tank.

Descent engine
This engine was used to slow down the Lunar Module's descent during landing.

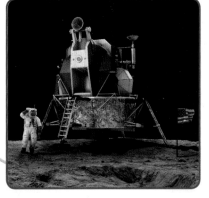

Man on the Moon
The Lunar Module was the only part of the Apollo craft to reach the Moon's surface. Preprogrammed controls maneuvered it into position above the landing site, then an astronaut steered the craft to touchdown. Scientific equipment, a TV camera, and tools and storage boxes for rock collecting were all stored in the bottom half.

Leg ladder
Astronauts used the ladder to climb down to the lunar surface.

Fuel tank
This tank contained fuel for the Lunar Module's descent engine.

Sensing probe
Probes on the legs touched the ground first during landing and sent signals to shut down the engine.

Path to the planets

The paths of spacecraft are often carefully planned to take them close to one or more planets on the way to their final destination. Using the pull of gravity of each planet boosts their speed and saves fuel. *Cassini-Huygens* flew past Venus, Earth, and Jupiter on its way to Saturn.

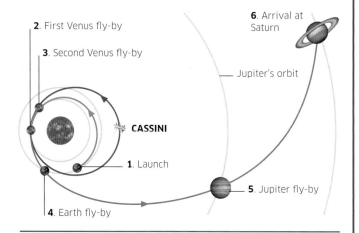

2. First Venus fly-by

3. Second Venus fly-by

Jupiter's orbit

6. Arrival at Saturn

CASSINI

1. Launch

5. Jupiter fly-by

4. Earth fly-by

Landmark missions

Since the first spacecraft to visit a planet was launched in 1962, about 200 craft have explored the Solar System. Some of the most famous missions are shown here.

Descent capsule

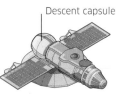

Solar panel

Venera 7
The first craft to touch down on another planet, *Venera 7* landed on Venus in 1970. It lasted 23 minutes before the searing heat destroyed it.

Lunokhod 1
Russian-built *Lunokhod 1* was the first lunar rover. It landed on the Moon in 1970 and spent 322 days exploring, traveling a total of 6.5 miles (10.5 km).

Radio dish

Spectrometer

Voyager 1
Launched in 1977 and still operational, *Voyager 1* is the furthest manmade object from Earth. It visited Jupiter in 1979 and Saturn in 1980.

Sojourner rover
The first rover to explore another planet was *Sojourner*. It reached Mars in 1997 and spent 12 weeks studying the soil and taking photos.

Rovers

A rover is a robotic vehicle built to explore the surface of a planet or moon. Four rovers have landed successfully on Mars. They receive radio commands from Earth but find their way around and carry out tasks independently.

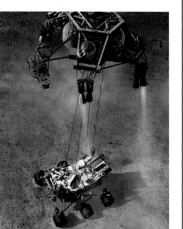

Curiosity lands
The *Curiosity* rover was lowered on to Mars in 2012 by a rocket-powered craft.

Cassini-Huygens spacecraft

Cassini-Huygens is the largest spacecraft to visit another planet. It was launched in 1997 and arrived at Saturn in 2004. It had two parts: the *Cassini* orbiter, designed to orbit Saturn until 2017, and a probe called *Huygens*, which touched down on Saturn's large moon Titan. The main aim of the mission was to discover more about Titan—the only world in the Solar System other than Earth that has a dense, nitrogen-rich atmosphere.

Boom
A 36-foot (11-meter) boom carries instruments to measure Saturn's magnetic field. The long boom reduces interference from other instruments on *Cassini*.

Small radio antenna
This is one of two small radio dishes that serve as backups in case the main dish breaks down.

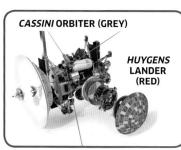

CASSINI ORBITER (GREY)

HUYGENS LANDER (RED)

Large radio dish
The large radio dish communicates with Earth. It is also used to map Titan, which it does by bouncing radio waves off the surface.

98,346 mph (158,273 kph)—the **top recorded speed** of *Cassini-Huygens*.

53 spacecraft have attempted to reach the planet Mars.

27 missions to Mars have ended in failure. **37**

Radio antennas
The three long antennas of the radio and plasma wave science (RPWS) instrument detect radio waves generated by Saturn's outer atmosphere.

Thruster
Cassini has four thrusters. These small engines adjust the craft's flight path precisely.

Plutonium power supply (one of three)

Main engine

Helium tank
Helium gas from this tank pushes fuel from the fuel tanks to the engine.

Fuel tanks
The fuel tanks carry two different liquids that burst into flame when mixed.

Cosmic dust analyzer
This device measures the size and speed of cosmic dust particles in space.

Exploring the planets

While manned spacecraft have ventured no further than the Earth's Moon, robotic craft have visited all the planets in the Solar System—and more than 100 moons.

Robotic spacecraft can visit places that would prove lethal to astronauts, such as the scalding surface of Venus or the deadly radiation belts around Jupiter. Packed with scientific instruments, telescopes, and cameras, they carry out dozens of experiments during their missions and capture thousands of images, which are sent back to Earth by radio.

Triple parachute
Packed under *Huygens*'s back cover were three parachutes that opened in turn to slow the lander's descent onto Titan. *Huygens* discovered a world of freezing, orange-brown plains littered with pebbles of ice.

Front case of *Huygens* probe

Fuel for thrusters

Back cover of *Huygens* probe

Inner body case of *Huygens* probe

Experiment platform
Huygens carried a range of scientific instruments to study conditions on Saturn's moon Titan.

Plasma spectrometer
This device measures charged particles trapped by Saturn's powerful magnetic field.

Heat shield
Without a heat shield, the *Huygens* probe would have burned up like a shooting star when it entered the atmosphere of Saturn's moon Titan. The shield was made of silica fiber tiles able to withstand temperatures up to 2,700°F (1,500°C).

EARTH

Oceans of water, an oxygen-rich atmosphere, and the existence of life make Earth a unique planet. Its surface is continually changing as plates slowly shift and the relentless force of erosion reshapes the land.

PLANET EARTH

Earth formed about 4.5 billion years ago, but it was a very different place then. Its surface was a hot inferno of mostly molten rock, with little or no liquid water and no oxygen in the atmosphere. Since then Earth has developed oceans, continents, an oxygen-rich atmosphere—and life.

THE CHANGING EARTH

Look at a map and it will show you the position of the continents, but in fact our world is always changing. Earth's surface is split up into large slabs called tectonic plates. The plates steadily shift around, carrying continents and oceans with them. When they collide, new mountain ranges are pushed up. Afterward, over millions of years, wind, water, and ice gradually wear the mountains down.

250 MILLION YEARS AGO, EARTH'S CONTINENTS ALL JOINED TOGETHER, FORMING AN ENORMOUS SUPERCONTINENT KNOWN AS PANGAEA.

UNIQUE PLANET

Earth is the only place in the Universe known to support life. It is thought that life developed after water began to collect on the Earth's surface. Eventually, tiny life forms evolved that could survive on water, sunlight, and chemicals in the water. These microbes added oxygen to the atmosphere—an essential step for the development of plants and animals.

Inside our planet

Earth's interior has layers. Scientists discovered this by studying the paths by which earthquake waves pass through the planet.

Thickness

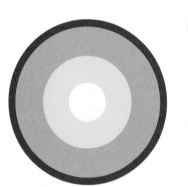

■	3.7–56 miles (6–90 km)
▪	1,790 miles (2,880 km)
▫	1,400 miles (2,255 km)
▫	755 miles (1,215 km)

CRUST
Different types of crust make up Earth's surface and its ocean floor. The crust under the surface is thicker and contains more rock types.

MANTLE
This rocky layer is denser than the crust. It is mostly solid, although it can very slowly deform and flow.

OUTER CORE
The only liquid layer, the outer core is mainly iron but also contains some nickel and small amounts of other substances.

INNER CORE
This is solid, and is mostly iron with some nickel. Its temperature is very hot—about 9,900°F (5,400°C).

Earth's atmosphere

The atmosphere of Earth is made up of several different gases.

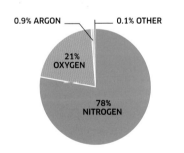

- 0.9% ARGON
- 0.1% OTHER
- 21% OXYGEN
- 78% NITROGEN

NITROGEN – 78%
A gas that can be fixed in the soil as well as loose in the atmosphere. Plants need nitrogen from the soil to survive.

OXYGEN – 21%
Essential for animals to breathe, oxygen was absent until microbes evolved that could use sunlight to turn carbon dioxide and water into carbohydrates, releasing oxygen.

ARGON – 0.9%
An inert gas (one that doesn't react with other substances).

OTHER – 0.1%
These include carbon dioxide (CO_2), which was once abundant, but is now mostly incorporated into materials such as limestone rock.

What's in a layer?

Earth's crust and mantle are mostly made of minerals called silicates, which are a combination of silicon dioxide and metal oxides. The mantle is rich in magnesium-containing silicates, while the two different types of crust have less magnesium and more aluminum and calcium. The core is dominated by metallic iron. No part of it has ever been brought to the surface, but its composition has been worked out by scientific methods such as studying earthquake waves.

Key

- Silicon dioxide
- Aluminum oxide
- Iron and iron oxides
- Calcium oxide
- Magnesium oxide
- Nickel
- Other

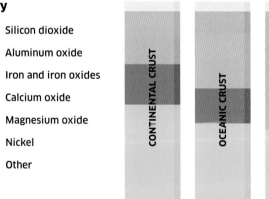

CONTINENTAL CRUST • OCEANIC CRUST • MANTLE • CORE

The oceans

Earth's surface and atmosphere contain the equivalent of 333 million miles³ (1.39 billion km³) of water. There are regions of deep ocean as well as shallow seas that cover areas around the edges of the continents—these are called continental shelves. Earth's surface has not always been as dominated by liquid water. In the past, during ice ages when the polar ice caps were much thicker and more extensive, so much water became locked up in them that sea level was at least 400 ft (120 m) lower than it is today, exposing the continental shelves as dry land.

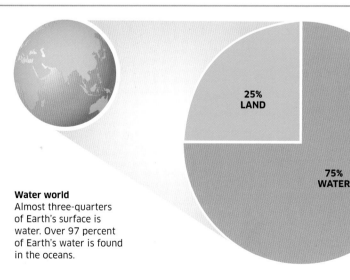

- 25% LAND
- 75% WATER

Water world
Almost three-quarters of Earth's surface is water. Over 97 percent of Earth's water is found in the oceans.

Continental drift

Over millions of years, tectonic plates have moved, shifting around the continents on Earth's surface. Chunks of continents split away and push into each other, creating new land masses and moving the oceans in a process called "continental drift."

200 MILLION YEARS AGO
The supercontinent Pangaea has just begun to break into two main landmasses.

North America, Europe, and parts of Asia are one landmass

130 MILLION YEARS AGO
India has escaped from the southern landmass, and is slowing moving north, toward Asia.

India moves north

Australia is joined to Antarctica

70 MILLION YEARS AGO
South America has split from Africa, while in the north, North America is splitting from Europe.

South America separates from Africa

TODAY
Australia has separated from Antarctica, and India has collided with Asia, forming the Himalayas.

Australia moves into the Pacific Ocean

Plate movement

The continents get rearranged because they are carried along as parts of moving plates. This process has been going on for billions of years, and is thought to be caused by slow, heat-driven movements in Earth's mantle.

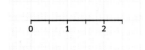

Yearly shift
Plates typically move at a rate of about 1 in (2.5 cm) in a year. That's about as fast as your fingernails grow. Some move faster–up to 4 in (10 cm) a year.

LOOKING AT EARTH

Our planet is far from smooth–its continents and ocean floors are scarred and pitted with marks caused by movement of plates. Earth's place in space also affects its shape, as constantly spinning makes it bulge out around the middle so it is not a perfect sphere. Spinning also creates a magnetic safety field around the planet.

MOUNTAINS
MAKE UP ABOUT
ONE-FIFTH
OF THE EARTH'S
LANDSCAPE.

A spinning planet

Earth's gravity would pull it into the shape of a sphere, but its rotation makes it bulge slightly. This means its diameter at the equator is 25 miles (41 km) more than the distance between its poles.

Bulge at middle

Direction of rotation

Not quite round
At the moment, scientists think that Earth's equatorial bulge is growing at a rate of 0.3 in (7 mm) every 10 years.

Magnetic Earth

Because Earth's outer core is liquid, the planet's rotation stirs it into motion. This motion causes electric currents to develop in the liquid iron itself. Any pattern of electric currents creates a magnetic field, and in Earth's case, the field is similar to what would be produced by a large bar magnet inside the planet. The field protects Earth from damage by harmful, energetic particles that come from the Sun.

The magnetic field
The magnetic poles do not coincide exactly with the geographic (rotational) poles, and they gradually change position over time.

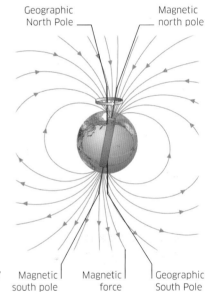

Geographic North Pole

Magnetic north pole

Magnetic south pole

Magnetic force

Geographic South Pole

Earth's surface

The solid surface of the Earth ranges from about 35,750 ft (10,900 m) below sea level in the Challenger Deep (part of the Pacific's Mariana trench) to 29,029 ft (8,848 m) above sea level at the summit of Everest, which may be rising at about 0.16 in (4 mm) per year. The surface of most land areas is less than 1,650 ft (500 m) above sea level.

Elevation

Over 13,125 ft (4,000 m)
6,500-13,125 ft (2,000-4,000 m)
3,300-6,500 ft (1,000-2,000 m)
1,600-3,300 ft (500-1,000 m)
800-1,600 ft (250-500 m)
300-800 ft (100-250 m)
0-300 ft (0-100 m)

Sea depth

0-800 ft (0-250 m)
800-6,500 ft (250-2,000 m)
6,500-13,000 ft (2,000-4,000 m)
Below 13,000 ft (4,000 m)

Mountains and trenches
Earth's solid surface is far from flat. This map shows its elevations and depths–from the highest mountain peaks to the deepest ocean trenches.

Inside the Earth

We can't explore much of the Earth—our deepest mines only travel about a mile into the crust. However, there are scientific ways to find out what it is like inside.

Geologists are able to study rocks from all depths within the Earth's crust, because collisions between continents push up rock that used to be below the surface, forming mountains. In some areas, collisions have even unearthed vast swathes of the mantle. Volcanoes also sometimes erupt lumps of rock from the mantle. Under the mantle is the core, which has never been seen at the surface. However, scientists have used the waves from earthquakes to work out that the core is split into two layers—a liquid outer core and a solid inner core.

Volcanoes in Hawaii
The Hawaiian islands in the mid-Pacific have been built by volcanic eruptions. The rock that formed them was pushed to the Earth's surface by hot rock moving upward in the mantle.

9,900°F

(5,400°C) – the approximate temperature of Earth's inner core.

Layered Earth

Earth is made up of many rocky layers. The top layer is the crust. Below that, uniform and slightly denser rock forms the mantle. The crust and the top of the mantle form a single rigid layer together, which is called the lithosphere. This is broken into sections called tectonic plates. Below the lithosphere is the asthenosphere. Only tiny parts of the asthenosphere are liquid, but it is soft enough to move, pushing around the plates above. Under the mantle lies the core. The outer core is a liquid mix of iron and sulfur, while the inner core is solid iron and nickel.

Continental crust
Thicker and less dense than the oceanic crust.

Rifting
Two tectonic plates pull away from each other, and new land is created between them.

Oceanic crust
Thinner and denser than the continental crust.

Subduction
When two plates meet, one can be pushed underneath the other.

Pacific Ocean

There are **four main layers** inside the Earth. From the outside in, they are the **crust, mantle, outer core,** and **inner core.**

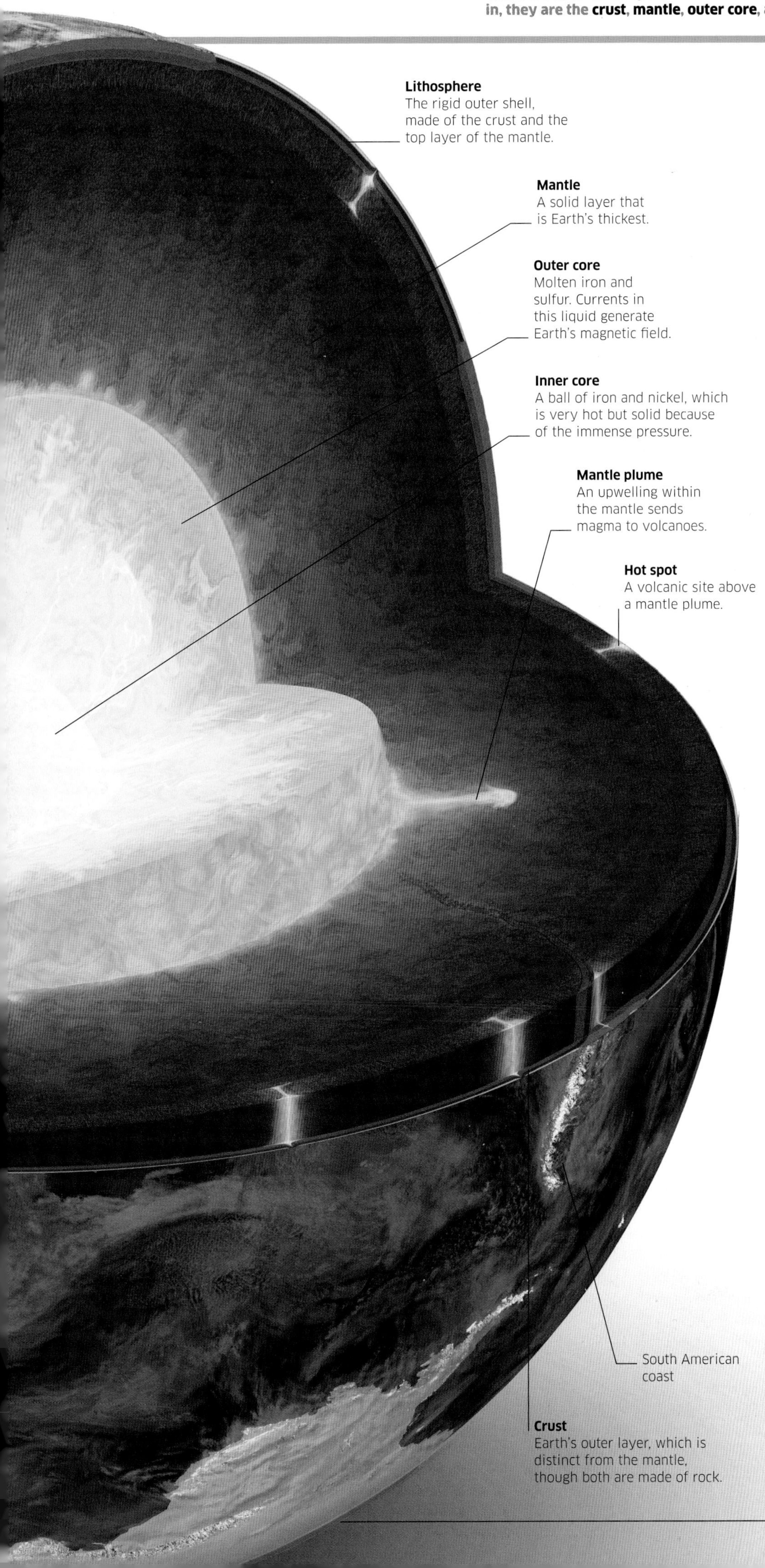

43

Lithosphere
The rigid outer shell, made of the crust and the top layer of the mantle.

Mantle
A solid layer that is Earth's thickest.

Outer core
Molten iron and sulfur. Currents in this liquid generate Earth's magnetic field.

Inner core
A ball of iron and nickel, which is very hot but solid because of the immense pressure.

Mantle plume
An upwelling within the mantle sends magma to volcanoes.

Hot spot
A volcanic site above a mantle plume.

South American coast

Crust
Earth's outer layer, which is distinct from the mantle, though both are made of rock.

The atmosphere

Earth's atmosphere is made up of gases, which are held in place by gravity. There is no clear boundary to the outer edge of the atmosphere–it just fades into space. Outer space is generally thought to begin about 62 miles (100 km) above the surface.

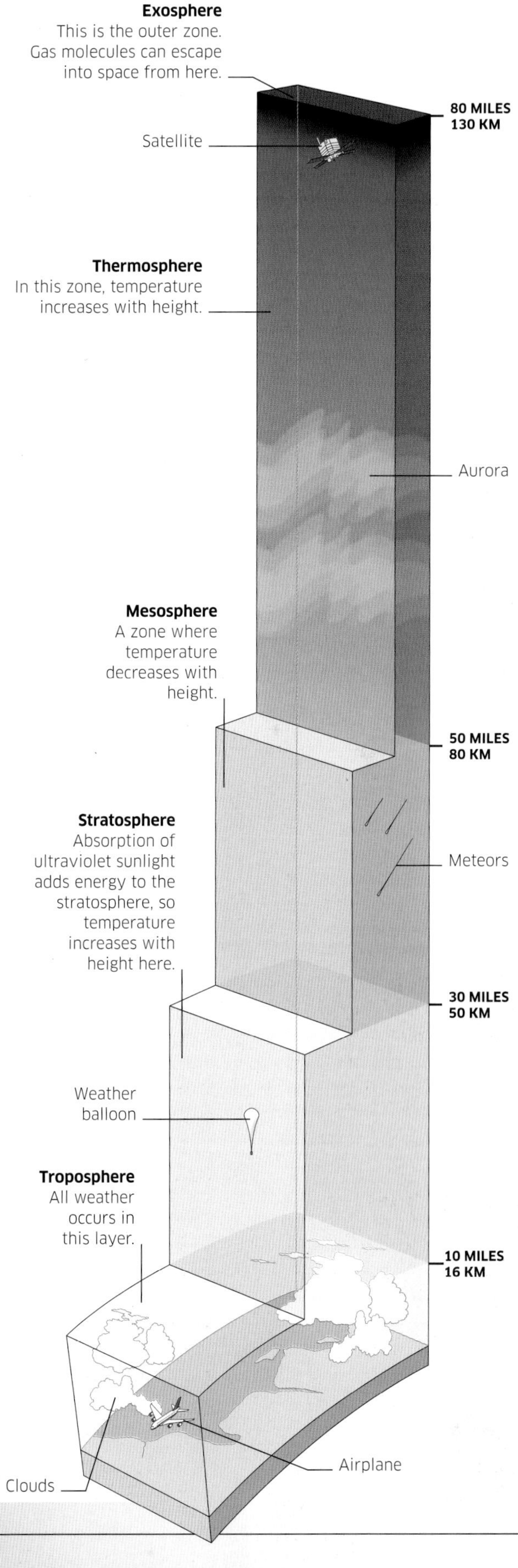

Exosphere
This is the outer zone. Gas molecules can escape into space from here.

Satellite

80 MILES
130 KM

Thermosphere
In this zone, temperature increases with height.

Aurora

Mesosphere
A zone where temperature decreases with height.

50 MILES
80 KM

Meteors

Stratosphere
Absorption of ultraviolet sunlight adds energy to the stratosphere, so temperature increases with height here.

30 MILES
50 KM

Weather balloon

Troposphere
All weather occurs in this layer.

10 MILES
16 KM

Airplane

Clouds

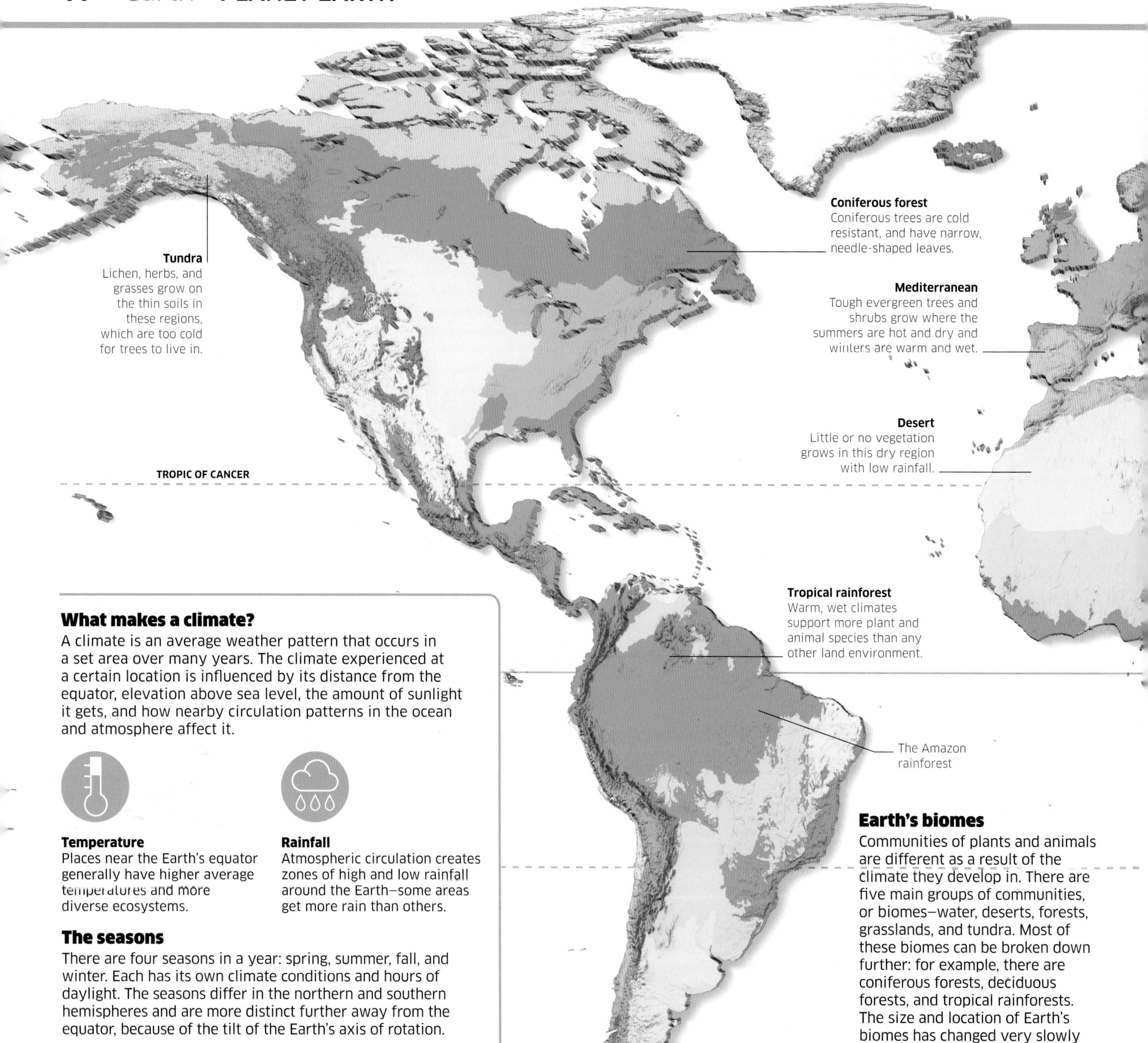

Coniferous forest
Coniferous trees are cold resistant, and have narrow, needle-shaped leaves.

Mediterranean
Tough evergreen trees and shrubs grow where the summers are hot and dry and winters are warm and wet.

Desert
Little or no vegetation grows in this dry region with low rainfall.

Tundra
Lichen, herbs, and grasses grow on the thin soils in these regions, which are too cold for trees to live in.

TROPIC OF CANCER

Tropical rainforest
Warm, wet climates support more plant and animal species than any other land environment.

The Amazon rainforest

What makes a climate?
A climate is an average weather pattern that occurs in a set area over many years. The climate experienced at a certain location is influenced by its distance from the equator, elevation above sea level, the amount of sunlight it gets, and how nearby circulation patterns in the ocean and atmosphere affect it.

Temperature
Places near the Earth's equator generally have higher average temperatures and more diverse ecosystems.

Rainfall
Atmospheric circulation creates zones of high and low rainfall around the Earth—some areas get more rain than others.

The seasons
There are four seasons in a year: spring, summer, fall, and winter. Each has its own climate conditions and hours of daylight. The seasons differ in the northern and southern hemispheres and are more distinct further away from the equator, because of the tilt of the Earth's axis of rotation.

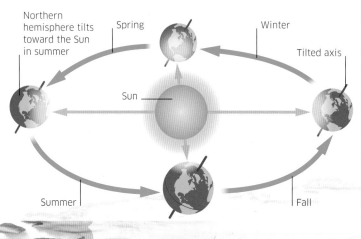

Northern hemisphere tilts toward the Sun in summer

Spring

Winter

Tilted axis

Sun

Summer

Fall

Antarctica

Earth's biomes
Communities of plants and animals are different as a result of the climate they develop in. There are five main groups of communities, or biomes—water, deserts, forests, grasslands, and tundra. Most of these biomes can be broken down further: for example, there are coniferous forests, deciduous forests, and tropical rainforests. The size and location of Earth's biomes has changed very slowly over geological time. The most recent changes have mainly been caused by human activity.

1.5 million species of plants and animals live in tropical rainforests.

0.7 in (2 cm)—**average annual rainfall** in the **Sahara Desert**, compared with **70 in** (180 cm) a year in a **tropical rainforest**.

57°F (14°C)—the average **temperature** on **Earth's surface**.

45

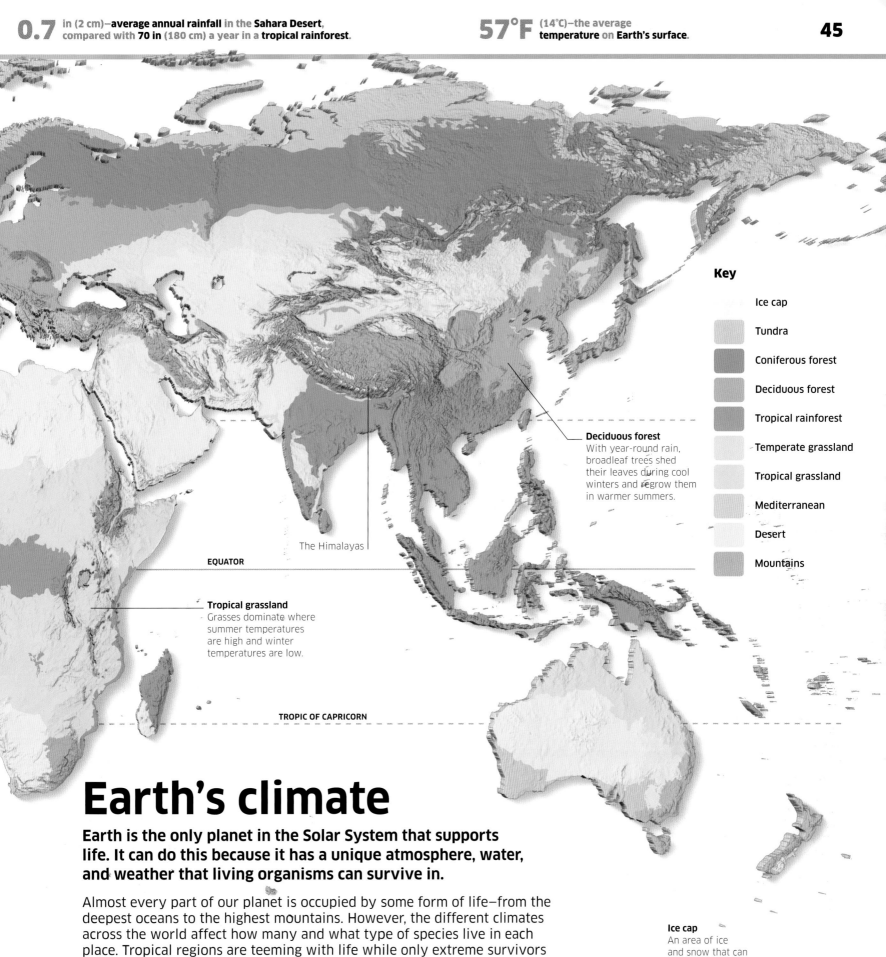

Key

Ice cap

Tundra

Coniferous forest

Deciduous forest

Tropical rainforest

Temperate grassland

Tropical grassland

Mediterranean

Desert

Mountains

Deciduous forest
With year-round rain, broadleaf trees shed their leaves during cool winters and regrow them in warmer summers.

The Himalayas

EQUATOR

Tropical grassland
Grasses dominate where summer temperatures are high and winter temperatures are low.

TROPIC OF CAPRICORN

Ice cap
An area of ice and snow that can cover mountains.

Earth's climate

Earth is the only planet in the Solar System that supports life. It can do this because it has a unique atmosphere, water, and weather that living organisms can survive in.

Almost every part of our planet is occupied by some form of life—from the deepest oceans to the highest mountains. However, the different climates across the world affect how many and what type of species live in each place. Tropical regions are teeming with life while only extreme survivors can live in polar wastes and deserts.

SHIFTING PLATES

Earth's surface appears to be still, but it is actually a collection of plates that is always moving. These plates move around due to currents deep inside the Earth. Plates that are under oceans are much thinner and less dense than those under continents–where they push into each other the oceanic plate gets forced down underneath the continental plate.

Jigsaw planet

Tectonic plates fit together to make up Earth's surface. They move constantly, and can change our planet's features, depending on how they meet. Where they push together, mountains and volcanoes form. Where they pull apart, new ocean floor is created.

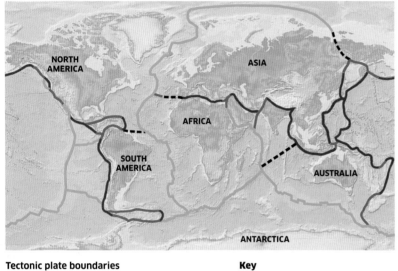

Tectonic plate boundaries
Plate boundaries are classified depending on whether plates are moving together (converging), apart (diverging), or past each other (transform).

Key

▬ Convergent	▬ Transform
▬ Divergent	▬▬ Uncertain

THE LARGEST TECTONIC PLATE IS THE PACIFIC PLATE. IT IS THE ONLY LARGE PLATE THAT DOESN'T CARRY A CONTINENT.

How plates move

No one knows exactly why tectonic plates move, but scientists think it is likely that they shift around on top of currents in the mantle layer underneath. These currents are thought to move in steady loops–rising when an area is heated by processes at the center of Earth, then sinking down again when they are cooled by moving nearer to the surface.

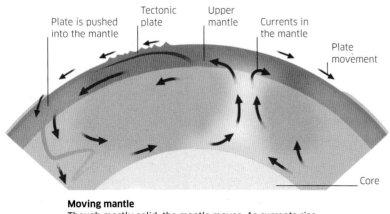

Moving mantle
Though mostly solid, the mantle moves. As currents rise, cool, and sink, they drag the plates around on top of them.

TECTONIC EARTH

The outside layer of the Earth is broken up into giant pieces called tectonic plates. Over millions of years these plates move, bump together, overlap, and slide past each other, in the process making new areas of ocean floor, building mountains, causing earthquakes, and creating volcanoes.

EARTHQUAKES

Most earthquakes happen where tectonic plates rub against each other, in places called faults. Some faults move with a steady, very gradual creep. In other places, a length of fault can remain locked for years, decades, or centuries, before giving way in a few seconds. Earthquakes are caused by the shaking of the ground after a rupture like this. The shallower the depth where the rupture begins, the more severe the shaking is at the surface.

Measuring quakes

The magnitude of an earthquake is a measure of the energy it releases. It can be measured using the Richter scale, where a difference of one point corresponds to a 30-fold difference in energy. The intensity of an earthquake can be measured using the Mercalli Intensity scale (below), which grades earthquakes from I to XII, according to their effects.

I-II	Hardly felt by people, but can be measured by instruments.	VII-VIII	General alarm, cracks appear in buildings, tree branches break.
III-IV	Felt indoors as a quick vibration. Hanging objects swing slightly.	IX-XI	Most buildings destroyed, underground pipes torn apart.
V-VI	Rocking motion felt by most people, buildings tremble.	XII	Almost all buildings destroyed, rivers change course.

Living with earthquakes

Earthquakes can occur anywhere in the world, but the most damaging ones usually happen near plate boundaries. Earthquakes can be very dangerous–buildings can fall down and huge cracks open up in the ground. In earthquake-prone areas, buildings can be designed to sway when there is an earthquake, so that they are not shaken apart. Their foundations must be built in solid rock rather than on sandy or wet ground.

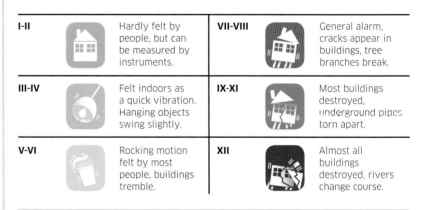

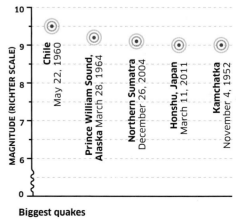

Biggest quakes
There have been many powerful earthquakes in the last 100 years. The largest, in Chile, was strong enough to move rivers.

VOLCANOES

A volcano occurs where molten rock called magma erupts up from under Earth's surface. An exploding volcano is one of the most incredible and dangerous sights on our planet. Volcanoes often form near the boundaries between tectonic plates, but they can also form elsewhere, at hotspots where hot rock moves upward from deep inside the Earth. There are about 550 active volcanoes on land, and more under the sea.

Lava

Hot, molten rock that flows across the ground is called lava. It keeps this name even after it has cooled down and solidified into rock. Lava comes in different forms, depending on what it is made of, how stiff or runny it is, and how fast it flows.

A'a lava
This is a thick lava flow made of basalt. Its surface is made up of loose, broken, and sharp chunks of lava that can tumble down the front of the lava flow as it moves.

Pahoehoe lava
This is a basalt lava with an unbroken surface. As it flows, its surface skin is gradually stretched. The end result can end up looking either smooth or ropelike.

Blocky lava
These chunks of lava form when stiff-flowing lava breaks up into angular blocks. These lava blocks have smoother faces than a'a lava.

Eruption types

Volcanoes can erupt with massive force, a small explosion, or even just a steady dribble. The way each volcano erupts depends on how thick its magma is and how much gas is in the magma. In a gas-rich magma, violent expansion of bubbles can shatter the magma and project volcanic ash into the sky with huge force, creating an ash cloud. More gentle eruptions feed lava flows that ooze slowly down the side of the volcano.

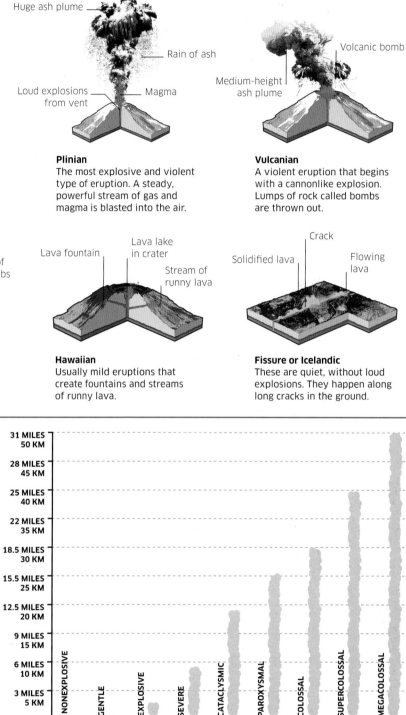

Plinian
The most explosive and violent type of eruption. A steady, powerful stream of gas and magma is blasted into the air.

Vulcanian
A violent eruption that begins with a cannonlike explosion. Lumps of rock called bombs are thrown out.

Strombolian
Short and explosive eruption that creates showers of cinders and lava bombs.

Hawaiian
Usually mild eruptions that create fountains and streams of runny lava.

Fissure or Icelandic
These are quiet, without loud explosions. They happen along long cracks in the ground.

Ash columns

When volcanoes erupt, they can create tall columns of ash. The height of these columns varies, depending on the amount of energy in the eruption, and how much magma is thrown out. The most energetic phase of a major volcanic eruption can last for many hours.

How high?
Column height is one way of estimating how explosive a volcanic eruption is. Eruption types have different names and correspond to different grades of the Volcanic Explosivity Index.

Graph — HEIGHT OF COLUMN vs VOLCANIC EXPLOSIVITY INDEX

Vertical axis: 0, 3 MILES / 5 KM, 6 MILES / 10 KM, 9 MILES / 15 KM, 12.5 MILES / 20 KM, 15.5 MILES / 25 KM, 18.5 MILES / 30 KM, 22 MILES / 35 KM, 25 MILES / 40 KM, 28 MILES / 45 KM, 31 MILES / 50 KM

Categories: 1 NONEXPLOSIVE, 2 GENTLE, 3 EXPLOSIVE, 4 SEVERE, 5 CATACLYSMIC, 6 PAROXYSMAL, 7 COLOSSAL, 8 SUPERCOLOSSAL, 9 MEGACOLOSSAL

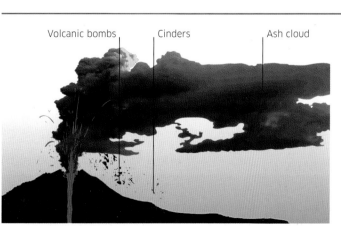

Volcanic fallout

If there is wind, a volcanic ash cloud will be blown to one side of the volcano, so that ash from the cloud falls to the ground in a belt that can extend hundreds of miles away from the volcano. Although it is cold by the time it reaches the ground, ash fallout can strip the leaves from plants and is dangerous to inhale. Aircraft must avoid flying through airborne ash, because it can clog up their engines.

What falls where?
The larger fragments created in an eruption, such as bombs and cinders, fall closest to the volcano. Fine ash travels the furthest.

Plate tectonics

Earth's surface may seem fixed but in fact is made up of lots of huge slabs called tectonic plates. These plates move slowly but constantly, and movements between them create earthquakes and volcanoes.

Most tectonic plates carry both oceans and continents, though a few are almost entirely oceanic. Where two plates pull apart under an ocean, new ocean floor is formed. Where plates are pushed together, dramatic changes to the landscape can occur. If both edges are continental, a huge mountain range will form in the collision zone. If one plate is oceanic and the other continental, the oceanic edge will usually be pushed under its neighbor. Fiery volcanoes occur along the edges of these boundaries, which are called subduction zones.

Earth's plates

The top layer of Earth is like a jigsaw, with seven or eight large plates and dozens of smaller, more fragmented plates. These plates float around, moving on top of the hotter layers below. Their slow, steady movement can change the size of the oceans, and carry continents around the globe.

Key

1	Pacific	20	North Andes
2	North American	21	Altiplano
3	Eurasian	22	Anatolian
4	African (Nubian)	23	Banda
5	African (Somalian)	24	Burma
6	Antarctic	25	Okinawa
7	Australian	26	Woodlark
8	South American	27	Mariana
9	Nazca	28	New Hebrides
10	Indian	29	Aegean
11	Sunda	30	Timor
12	Philippine	31	Bird's Head
13	Arabian	32	North Bismarck
14	Okhotsk	33	South Sandwich
15	Caribbean	34	South Shetland
16	Cocos	35	Panama
17	Yangtze	36	South Bismarck
18	Scotia	37	Maoke
19	Caroline	38	Solomon

Mid-Atlantic Ridge
Most of this ridge lies about 8,200 ft (2,500 m) underwater—Iceland is the only part of it above sea level.

Plate boundaries

The edges of tectonic plates meet up in different ways. The plates move apart, toward each other, or past each other. Earthquakes can occur in any of these circumstances, and studying earthquakes can help us work out where plate boundaries lie. Sometimes there are so many cracks that it is impossible to tell exactly where one plate ends and the next one begins.

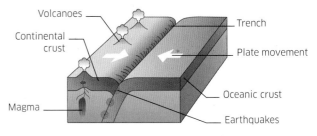

Volcanoes
Continental crust
Magma
Trench
Plate movement
Oceanic crust
Earthquakes

Convergent

Where a plate with oceanic crust moves toward a plate with thicker, continental crust, it will be pushed down, or subducted. The oceanic plate then melts, and can create volcanoes as magma bubbles up to the surface. If two continents collide, they will push up against each other, creating mountain ranges.

40,000 miles (65,000 km)—the length of the **underwater mountain chains** formed by **mid-ocean ridges**.

55 million years ago, the **Indian and Asian plates** crashed together, **creating the Himalayas**.

49

0.75 in (2 cm) per year—the speed of seafloor spreading in the north Atlantic Ocean.

The Challenger Deep
This is the deepest known point on Earth, at 35,800 ft (10,911 m) below sea level.

Continental plate
The Eurasian plate is 85 percent land, with only 15 percent water.

Fresh break
This new rift is causing the African plate to slowly split down the middle, creating two new plates—Nubian and Somalian.

Controversial boundary
Scientists disagree on whether the Indian and Australian plates are separate —some think they are a huge, single, Indo-Australian plate.

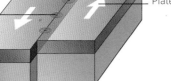

Earthquakes

Plate movement

Ridge

Plate movement

Magma

Transform
When plates slide past each other, they create a transform boundary. Movement at these plate edges is not smooth and gradual—it is very jerky, and earthquakes occur when a sudden shift releases huge amounts of energy. Volcanoes are rare at these boundaries, because little or no magma is created.

Divergent
Where plates pull apart, they create a divergent boundary. When this happens under oceans, rock from the mantle is drawn up into the gap and some of it melts as it rises, creating new oceanic crust. As new crust is formed, other parts of crust are destroyed at convergent boundaries—so Earth stays the same size.

Volcanoes

Where molten rock erupts from an opening on Earth's surface, volcanoes develop. Most of them form near the edges of tectonic plates.

Molten rock called magma is formed in a few places deep in Earth's crust or even in the mantle. If magma reaches the surface it is called lava. Large volcanoes called stratovolcanoes are built by a series of eruptions, with each one adding a layer of solidified lava and ash on top of the last. Volcanoes are classified as active, dormant, or extinct, based on how often they erupt. An active volcano is one that is known to have erupted in recent history. A volcano that has not erupted recently but might erupt again is dormant. A volcano that has stopped erupting altogether is extinct. Some small volcanoes erupt just once, while a large volcano can erupt thousands of times over its lifetime.

75 percent of the world's active volcanoes are underwater.

Lava flow
Some volcanic eruptions produce runny flows of lava instead of explosions with ash clouds. The lava travels steadily downhill away from the volcano, usually moving at a speed slightly slower than a running person.

Mud pool
Hot steam and other gases escaping near a volcano can produce mud pools at the surface. They are not boiling—the bubbles are formed by escaping gases, which can be very smelly.

Farmland
Ash from volcanoes can make the soil nearby very fertile.

Crater lake
Rainwater can fill old volcanic craters to make new lakes.

Fissure
A crack that sometimes leaks lava.

Maar
A crater formed by an explosion, caused by magma interacting with water in the ground.

Volcanic eruption

Magma works its way through solid rock and up toward the Earth's surface. As it rises, gas bubbles in the magma grow, increasing its speed until it erupts to the surface. The violent expansion of these gas bubbles can shatter the magma, shooting it out explosively as ash or bigger lumps called bombs. If there is not an explosion, the magma flows down the side of the volcano in a molten stream called a lava flow.

60 The approximate **number** of **volcanoes** that **erupt** in an **average year**.

The **ash cloud** from a large **volcanic eruption** can be up to **40 miles** (60 kilometers) high.

51

Ash cloud
Explosive eruptions create clouds of sand-sized rock particles, which eventually fall to the ground.

Main vent
The site of most of a volcano's eruptions.

Main conduit
The "pipe" through which magma rises to reach the vent.

Lava bomb
A lump of rock thrown out by an explosive eruption.

Pyroclastic flow
A fast, dangerous flow of hot gas, ash, and rocks.

Secondary vent
Small hole through which magma escapes.

Secondary conduit
A branch off from the main conduit.

Types of volcanoes

The size and shape of a volcano are determined by several factors: the type of magma that erupts from it; the amount of magma that erupts; and whether it produces explosive or non-explosive eruptions.

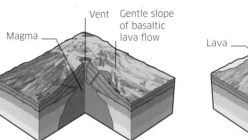

Shield volcano
The biggest but most gently sloping type. Formed mostly by runny lava called basalt.

Stratovolcano
The steepest large volcano, formed of alternating layers of ash and lava.

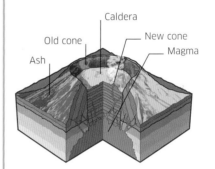

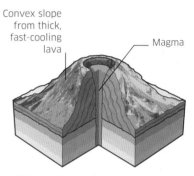

Caldera
The remains of a stratovolcano after a super-eruption empties most of its magma chamber.

Cinder cone
A small, steep mound that grows where very sticky lava has erupted.

Fumarole
Vent in the ground from which hot gas and steam escape—often sulfur-rich and very smelly.

Geyser
A jet of water driven into the sky by expanding steam.

Laccolith
A pocket of magma that has forced the rock around it to move and make space for it.

Dike
A vertical magma seam.

Sill
A horizontal seam of magma, usually between layers of bedrock.

Magma chamber
Magma collects under an active volcano, sometimes over an area many miles wide.

Extinct conduit
The position of the active conduit may change during a volcano's lifetime.

Earthquakes

A natural part of our planet's workings, earthquakes can be terrifying and destructive events. Some trigger powerful ocean waves called tsunamis.

Earth's outer shell is made up of huge slabs called tectonic plates. These plates are constantly moving, and push past each other with hard, jerky movements. In some places, the opposing masses of rock become locked together by friction. In these periods, there is a gradual buildup of strain in the locked-up area. Eventually, the pressure becomes so high that there is a sudden shift between the blocks of rock, or a massive break, usually on or near lines on the Earth's surface called faults. As this happens, energy is released in the form of powerful shock waves, or vibrations, causing an earthquake. When an earthquake happens under the seafloor, it can create a tsunami.

How a tsunami happens

Many types of events can cause tsunamis, including big volcanic eruptions near or in the sea, landslides into the ocean, and even asteroid impacts. However, the most common cause is a huge earthquake under the seafloor, usually where the edge of one tectonic plate rises above another.

Waves in both directions
Waves spread out in opposite directions from a line in the sea surface roughly parallel to the rupture line on the seafloor.

2 Wave origination
At the sea surface, the sudden upthrust of a mass of water from below sets off a series of high-energy waves. These start traveling over the sea surface at a speed of over 500 mph (800 kph).

Uplift
A block of seafloor suddenly shoots up several feet. Elsewhere, other blocks may sink.

Shock waves
These powerful vibrations spread out from the earthquake in all directions.

1 Seafloor rupture
A large rupture below the seafloor causes an earthquake. At the same time, a huge block of seabed is suddenly thrust upward. This in turn pushes up the seawater above, triggering a tsunami wave at the ocean surface.

Epicenter
A spot on the seafloor above the point in Earth's interior where the rupture started.

Even waves
Out at sea, tsunami waves are evenly spaced at distances of up to 120 miles (200 km).

Energy waves
Earthquakes produce massive waves, which can produce shaking, up-and-down movements, and loud noises.

Seawater movements
As each wave passes, there is a circular movement of seawater under it.

Inside a fault
Faults at the boundaries of tectonic plates are prone to earthquakes. Here, two plates move past each other in opposite directions. Occasionally, the movement becomes stuck and stress builds up between the plates. Eventually, the buildup of stress causes a sudden shift or rupture, releasing vast amounts of energy.

Wave height increase
A tsunami wave grows higher as the seafloor under it slopes upward toward the shore.

Epicenter
The point on Earth's surface that is directly above the quake's focus point.

Fault line
A line at Earth's surface, which marks movement between plates.

Focus
The spot in Earth's interior where the quake-producing rupture begins.

Plate movement
These plates are moving past each other side by side, but in some cases one plate moves underneath another.

The **largest earthquake ever recorded** occurred off the
coast of Chile in 1960. It caused a **devastating tsunami**.

0.3 in (1 cm)—the **distance** that the **whole planet vibrates** back
and forth in space **during** the **very largest earthquakes**.

53

Shock waves

Earthquakes produce
two types of shock
waves, called P and
S waves, which travel
through parts of
Earth's interior.
Scientists can
work out where
and when a quake
happened by
detecting these
waves as they arrive
back at the surface.

**Low-height
waves**
In the open
ocean, each
wave has a
low amplitude
(height) and may
pass unnoticed.

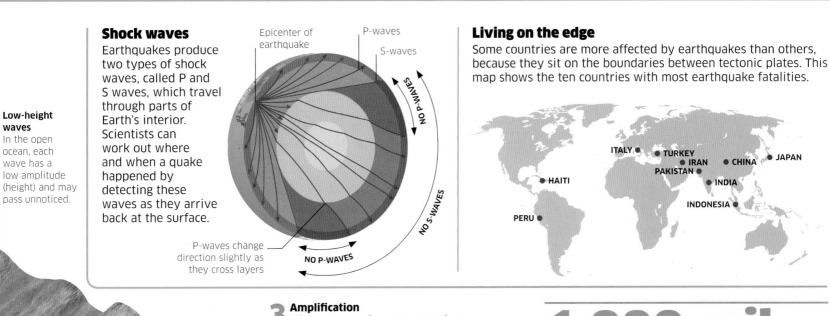

Epicenter of
earthquake

P-waves

S-waves

NO P-WAVES

NO S-WAVES

P-waves change
direction slightly as
they cross layers

NO P-WAVES

Living on the edge

Some countries are more affected by earthquakes than others,
because they sit on the boundaries between tectonic plates. This
map shows the ten countries with most earthquake fatalities.

ITALY

TURKEY

IRAN • CHINA

JAPAN

PAKISTAN

HAITI

INDIA

INDONESIA

PERU

3 Amplification
When a tsunami wave approaches a
shore, it slows down and its height increases.
The upward-sloping seabed creates a resistance
to the water movement—it pushes the
water so that the wave is
amplified (gets bigger).

1,000 miles

**The length of the rupture under
the seafloor that caused the 2004
Indian Ocean tsunami.**

Crest of wave
The top of a large
tsunami wave
usually foams
as it approaches
the shore.

Sea drawback
Sometimes water is drawn
away from the shore a
few minutes before a
tsunami wave arrives.

**Sea becomes
shallower**
As the seabed
shelves upward, it
also slows the
approaching wave.

4 Inundation
When a tsunami wave hits a
shore, it doesn't usually break and
collapse. Instead, it continues to surge
forward for a considerable distance,
flooding the whole coast. The powerful
rush of water can smash buildings and
carry cars and people away.

Buildings in danger
Few buildings can survive
the onslaught of a large
tsunami wave—many are
destroyed or swept away.

EARTH'S RESOURCES

Earth contains many useful and essential natural resources, which have been used heavily by humans in recent centuries. These resources include water and food, fuel and building materials, and the means to make more complex things like metals and plastics. Many resources have a limited supply, and using them has an impact on the environment.

ROCKS AND MINERALS

Over the more than four billion years of Earth's development, thousands of different minerals have formed and combined into hundreds of rock types. Humans have found many uses for these rocks and minerals, from building materials to the manufacture of metals. However, some of the most useful and valuable minerals are rare. Mining and quarrying them is often dangerous and dirty.

Rocks

Humans have used naturally occurring rocks for thousands of years, originally as tools and then for many other purposes, such as the building of houses, factories, and roads.

Rocky landscape
Much of the world around us is made up of rocks. To extract rock, heavy machinery is used, cutting deep into the ground.

Minerals

Earth has thousands of naturally occurring minerals. Many of these, such as metal ores, sulfur, and mica, are used in industry. Other examples include gold, silver, and quartz.

Mineral building blocks
Rocks are made up of natural, nonliving substances called minerals. Most rocks contains several types of minerals.

Gemstones

When minerals are cut and polished, they are known as gems. One useful gem is diamond, famous for its hardness and ability to cut through most other materials. Some other gems have practical uses, but most are valued for their beauty and rarity. Gems can be cut into many different shapes and are typically used in jewelry or other decorative objects.

EMERALD **STEP** **CUSHION**

SQUARE **PEAR** **SCISSORS**

OVAL BRILLIANT **ROUND BRILLIANT** **MIXED**

Cut gems
Gems can be cut into many different shapes. When cut correctly, gemstones reflect light in many directions, making them glitter.

ENERGY

Human life requires energy in the form of light, heat, and food. Earth's energy comes from a variety of sources but mostly from the heat of the Sun and the Earth's hot interior. This is a lot of heat, but capturing, storing, and transporting enough of this energy to meet all our needs is difficult and requires complicated and expensive technology.

Fossil fuels

Fuels such as coal, oil, gas and peat have long been used to heat homes and power machinery. Earth's fossil fuels took hundreds of millions of years to form, but a significant portion of them have been burned up in just a hundred years. Fossil fuels are formed as time, pressure, and heat transform organic plant and animal remains into hydrocarbons—oil and gas.

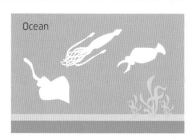
Ocean

1 **500–250 MILLION YEARS AGO**
When ocean animals and microbes died, their remains drifted down to the ocean floor, and were covered with sand and sediment.

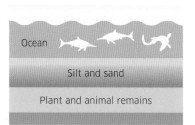
Ocean
Silt and sand
Plant and animal remains
Sand, silt, and rock
Oil and gas deposits

2 **250–0.6 MILLION YEARS AGO**
The plant and animal remains became buried, deep under the ocean. Over time, heat and pressure turned the remains into oil and gas.

3 **TODAY**
Oil and gas deposits are buried deep beneath a layer of sand, silt, and rock. Oil rigs drill through this layer in order to pump out the oil beneath.

Nuclear energy

This energy is produced by the strong force that holds protons and neutrons together inside atomic nuclei. Nuclear energy can be harnessed, and produces low carbon emissions compared to fossil fuels. However, disadvantages include the risk of releasing radiation.

Renewable energy

There are alternative energy sources to fossil fuels, which are more sustainable and better for the environment.

Wind
Wind turbines allow us to harness the power of wind. Turbines work best on high ground.

Geothermal
Earth's internal heat comes close to the surface in volcanic regions and can be used to heat water.

Biofuels
Fuels produced from organic matter such as plants, fats, and waste are called biofuels.

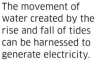

Solar
Light energy created from the Sun can be captured and turned into electricity using solar panels.

Tidal
The movement of water created by the rise and fall of tides can be harnessed to generate electricity.

Hydroelectric
The movement of water through turbines in dams can be used to create power.

Wood
Burning wood for heat and cooking is the most ancient form of energy supply.

AGRICULTURE

Growing food plants and looking after animals that will be eaten is called agriculture. Today, the global population of around seven billion people largely relies on a few cereal crops to provide its essential foods. These crops include corn, wheat, rice, potatoes, cassava, soybeans, and sweet potatoes. Protein from livestock such as fish, cattle, pigs, and poultry makes up less than 20 percent of total global food.

Forestry

Forests provide habitats and food for most of Earth's land-based wildlife, and help control global warming by removing carbon dioxide from the atmosphere. However, forests are also in danger—they are being cut down to supply fuel and lumber for building.

Well-managed forest
Forests can be managed in a way that lets people harvest their produce, such as lumber, without destroying them.

Farming

Farming began 10,000 years ago, in the Middle East. The first farmers grew cereal crops, like wheat, and reared animals for their meat and milk. Modern agriculture has moved on a lot since then. New machine-based techniques let farmers produce much bigger yields from their land. Other innovations include irrigation, pesticides, new plants, new animal breeds, and global transport—farmers can now send their produce all over the world.

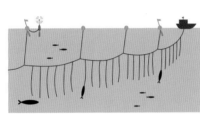

Key

Cattle	Rice
Coffee	Sheep
Pigs	Soybeans
Corn	Tea
Oats	Wheat
Potatoes	Milk

Feeding the world
Food is produced all over the world, both for local consumption and for export. This map shows the top producers of each crop or type of livestock.

MORE THAN HALF THE **WORLD'S POPULATION RELIES ON THREE** GRAINS FOR **THEIR BASIC** FOOD NEEDS **—WHEAT, CORN,** AND RICE.'

Fishing

Fish are one of the most nutritious supplies of protein and have been eaten for thousands of years. Modern fishing techniques allow large quantities of wild fish to be harvested from the world's seas and oceans. Although international limits have been introduced, many popular fish species are now endangered. One solution to overfishing is to rear fish for human consumption in fish farms.

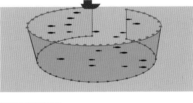

LINE FISHING
Using baited hooks attached to long lines is a very cheap way of fishing. However, animals such as turtles and seabirds can be accidentally killed by this method.

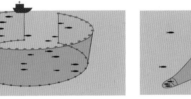

NET FISHING
Net fishing is an ancient method, but its modern form is on an industrial scale, using large synthetic nets that can catch huge volumes of fish at one time.

TRAWLING
Trawling is a form of net fishing where the net is dragged through the water or along the seabed. It can cause damage to the seabed and catches fish of all size and types.

SUSTAINABILITY

Earth's natural resources are limited. If demand for essential resources keeps increasing, they will become rare and expensive. To sustain life as we know it, we must make sure that our resources do not run out.

Human impact

Population growth means that we are using up more and more of the Earth's resources, changing the landscape, and damaging the environment around us. One way to reduce the negative impact people have on the environment is to make sure that as much garbage as possible is recycled, instead of being dumped in a landfill.

LANDFILL SITE

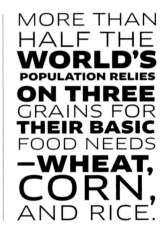

RECYCLING CENTER

Pollution

All over the world, factories, power plants, farms, businesses, and homes produce huge amounts of pollution by releasing chemicals and other substances that pollute, or dirty, the natural environment. As people's use of energy and other resources grows, Earth is becoming more polluted.

The effect of industry
Different countries produce different amounts of pollution. These are the world's top five polluters.

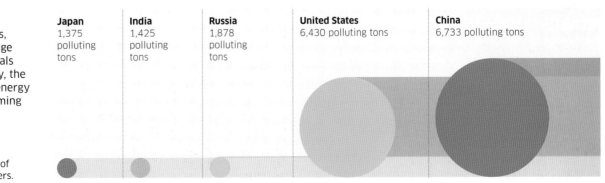

Japan	India	Russia	United States	China
1,375 polluting tons	1,425 polluting tons	1,878 polluting tons	6,430 polluting tons	6,733 polluting tons

Rocks

A rock is a hard natural object made of mineral grains (crystals), held together in a compact structure. There are hundreds of different kinds of rock, but they are grouped into three main types–igneous, sedimentary, and metamorphic–depending on how they were formed.

Igneous
These form when hot liquid rock, called magma or lava, cools down and solidifies.

Sedimentary
These form when particles from other, older rocks are compressed and stick together.

Metamorphic
These rocks form when older rocks are changed by heat and pressure.

GRANITE

SANDSTONE

GNEISS

Minerals

Rocks are made up of minerals. There are thousands of minerals, but only around 30 are found at Earth's surface. Most minerals are crystals–their atoms are arranged in regular patterns, giving them simple geometric shapes. Each mineral has its own chemical composition and physical properties.

Native elements
These minerals each contain a single chemical element, such as sulfur, carbon, or a metal such as copper.

Compounds
These minerals contain two or more chemical elements. For example, Fluorite contains calcium and fluorine.

SULFUR

COPPER

BORNITE

FLUORITE

Measuring hardness
Minerals can be soft, like gypsum, or very hard, like diamond. Different scales are used to express hardness. "Mohs scale" is based on comparing the hardness of ten minerals, while "absolute" hardness is based on precise laboratory testing.

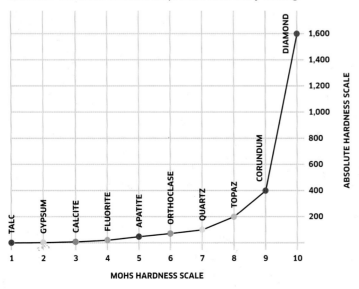

MOHS HARDNESS SCALE

ABSOLUTE HARDNESS SCALE

Extrusion
The escape of magma from a volcano, in the form of lava and ash.

Glacial erosion
When a glacier moves, it transports rocks from under and around it.

Volcano
A typical volcano consists of many layers of solidified lava, with some ash and cinders.

Igneous rock
Rock that forms when magma cools down and solidifies.

Crystallization
When magma cools inside the Earth it solidifies slowly, forming rocks with large crystals, such as granite.

Magma
Hot liquid rock that contains dissolved gas.

Intrusion
A mass of magma inside the Earth.

Melting
When rock is subducted, water escapes from it. Combined with heat and pressure, this makes nearby rock melt.

Metamorphic rock
Heat and pressure deep in the Earth can make any rock change into a different type, called metamorphic rock.

Uplift
Upward movement of rock masses is called uplift.

Subducted rock
Formerly seafloor, the rock at the top of a subducting plate has a high water content.

The rock cycle

Rocks transform from one type into another in an endless cycle. Many factors contribute to this process, both on the Earth's surface and in its interior. On the surface, rock is broken down by weathering, and glaciers, rivers, and winds erode rocks by carrying particles of them away. Sediment made of tiny particles of rock and mud forms in places like lake bottoms, coasts, and seabeds. Inside the Earth, heat, pressure, and melting change sedimentary and igneous rock into metamorphic rock, and volcanoes are formed that create new igneous rock.

1,500 times—the **increase in pressure** above atmospheric pressure needed to create a **new metamorphic rock**.

4,900 The **number of minerals** identified on Earth so far.

57

Glacial deposition
At its end, a glacier dumps rock fragments in piles called moraines.

Precipitation
Snow and rain feed glaciers and streams, which erode rocks.

Weathering
Rain, wind, frost, chemicals, heat, and living things all break down rocks.

Transport
Streams and winds carry particles away from weathered rock.

River erosion
Rivers contribute greatly to the removal of rock fragments created by weathering.

Coastal deposition
Rock particles are transported by river, then settle as sand, mud, or pebbles on the coast.

Marine sedimentation
Tiny rock particles carried into the sea by rivers slowly settle at the bottom of the sea.

Sediment
A layer of fine particles of sand or silt, deposited on the seabed or at the bottom of a lake.

Rocks and minerals

Our planet is mostly made of solid rock. Rock is what gives Earth its features—mountains, canyons, and plains. Minerals are the building blocks of every type of rock.

Most of Earth's rocks are hidden under a layer of soil and vegetation, but in some places they are visible at the surface, in landscape features such as mountains and canyons. Many different types of rock have developed over billions of years, through a variety of processes. These include volcanic activity, which creates rocks at or near the surface, the formation of sediments in places like the seafloor, and changes in form—called metamorphism—brought about by heat and pressure deep within our planet. These processes are linked in a never-ending cycle, known as the rock cycle.

Subduction
When two tectonic plates move toward each other, one plate can be slowly pushed under the edge of the other.

Sedimentary rock
A type of rock that forms when pressure binds particles of sediment together.

Burial and compaction
As new layers of sediment form, deeper layers are pressed together, creating solid sedimentary rock.

WEATHER

The constantly changing condition of Earth's atmosphere creates our weather–clear skies, wind, cloud, rain, and snow. The amount of sunshine we get and how strong it is determines the temperature and pressure in the atmosphere. The amount of moisture it contains determines how high up clouds form and whether they produce mist, rain, or snow, as well as when storms occur. When we study the weather, we can see predictable seasonal patterns around the world, known as climates.

WEATHER SYSTEMS

Patterns of weather depend on the nature of the local air mass and pressure system, which can change over the course of a year. For example, in the summer, continental land surfaces heat up, making warm, dry air rise. This produces a low pressure weather system, which draws in more warm air from the surroundings and can cause storms. In winter, continental land surfaces cool, and colder, dense air sinks down from the atmosphere above.

Pressure fronts

A pressure front divides two different air masses. Air masses with differing moisture content, density, temperature, and pressure do not mix easily, and the front between them is often marked by rising banks of clouds. For example, a low pressure air mass with warm air will rise up above a high pressure air mass with cold air. Any moisture carried by the warm air will condense as the air cools, forming clouds and possibly rain.

Cold front
When cold air pushes into warm air, it forms a cold front, and the warm air is forced to rise up quickly, creating a steep bank of storm clouds with heavy rain.

Warm front
At a warm front, cold air is replaced by warm air, which slowly rises up a shallow slope of cold air, forming clouds followed by rain as the air cools.

Occluded front
An occluded front forms when fast-moving cold air overtakes a slower-moving warm front, lifting the warm air mass up and causing prolonged rain.

Stationary front
A stationary front forms between two air masses that are similar, and does not move much. It can last for several days and often creates prolonged rain.

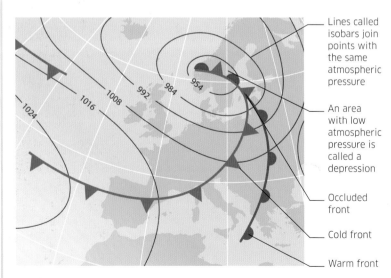

Lines called isobars join points with the same atmospheric pressure

An area with low atmospheric pressure is called a depression

Occluded front

Cold front

Warm front

Weather map
These maps show the main weather of a region. Air pressure is shown by black lines called isobars, which link areas with equal air pressure. Weather fronts on the map show where temperatures will rise or fall.

Monsoons

Monsoon winds are massive seasonal winds that bring heavy summer rain to subtropical regions, such as Southeast Asia and India. In winter, they bring dry, cooler weather. Monsoon winds are strongest in Asia, but they also occur in West Africa, northern Australia, and parts of North and South America. Monsoon winds change direction between summer and winter.

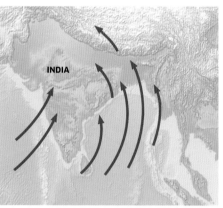

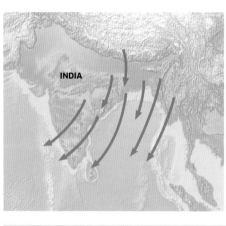

Summer
In summer, the South Asian monsoon blows from the Indian Ocean across India, bringing the torrential rains of the wet season, which are essential for the growth of the continent's staple food crops.

Winter
In winter, the South Asian monsoon reverses, bringing the warm dry winds and fine weather of the dry season across the Indian continent and out into the Indian Ocean.

WEATHER FRONTS ARE BOUNDARIES BETWEEN AIR MASSES OF DIFFERENT TEMPERATURES, MOISTURE, AND PRESSURE.

Hurricanes

A hurricane is a huge, rotating tropical storm with high winds and very heavy rain. These storms start from a cluster of thunderstorms, which develop over warm tropical seawater in late summer, then merge together into a larger, spiral hurricane. Their intense low pressure draws in warm, moist winds, which spiral upward as they spin faster. The rapidly rising air then cools, forming towering storm clouds and torrential rains. When they reach land, hurricanes cause flooding and are highly destructive.

The view from above
A satellite view of a hurricane from above shows its spiral shape and a clear central eye.

PRECIPITATION

Any kind of falling moisture is called precipitation. Precipitation varies widely, from the tiny droplets of clouds or fog to larger drops of rain, hail, or snow. Whether water falls from a cloud as rain or snow depends on how cold the air temperature is.

Types of precipitation

Different types of precipitation can fall from the sky or rise from the ground, depending on the temperature conditions.

Rain
Clouds are made up of tiny droplets of water. Rain falls when these droplets become too heavy to float in the air.

Snow
Snowflakes form when water droplets freeze into crystals, which then stick together as they fall through very cold air.

Sleet
Sleet is a mixture of snow and rain. It forms when rain begins to freeze or when snow begins to melt in air that is above freezing.

Hail
Hailstones are ice pellets that grow from ice crystals in freezing storm clouds. The taller the cloud, the bigger the hailstones.

Fog
Fog forms near ground level, when warm, moisture-laden air is cooled by contact with a cold ground or sea surface.

Cloud formation

When the Sun shines on ponds and lakes, some of the water they hold evaporates into the warm air. This warm water vapor then rises up and away from Earth's surface. As the air rises, it cools. Because cold air cannot hold as much moisture as warm air, the water vapor condenses, and forms clouds. Clouds that form very high in the atmosphere, above 16,500 ft (5,000 m), are made of ice crystals rather than water vapor.

1 MOISTURE RISES Hot sunlight makes moisture from the ground or sea surface rise into the air as water vapor.

2 VAPOR CONDENSES As the vapor rises and cools, it condenses to form visible clouds of tiny water droplets.

3 CLOUDS RISE As water droplets form clouds, they release heat into the surrounding air, lifting the cloud up.

Cloud types

There are three main groups of clouds, though they each have many variations. Cumulus form in bulging heaps, stratus are layered, and cirrus are wispy or fibrous. A cloud's shape reflects the amount of moisture in the atmosphere and how it moves.

Cloud names
Clouds are named according to their shape, size, and how high up they form in the atmosphere.

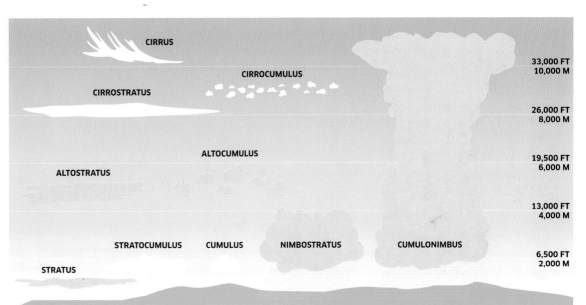

WIND

Winds are common in the Earth's atmosphere. They vary in scale and intensity from gentle breezes to violent storms like tornadoes, and can be daily or seasonal.

What is wind?

Wind is the movement of air from an area of high pressure to an area of low pressure. The greater the difference between the areas of pressure, the faster the wind moves. Wind speed is measured using the Beaufort scale, which ranges from 0 to 12. At 12 on the scale, hurricane wind speeds can reach 300 mph (480 kph).

BEAUFORT WIND SCALE	
0	CALM
1	LIGHT AIR
2	LIGHT BREEZE
3	GENTLE BREEZE
4	MODERATE BREEZE
5	FRESH BREEZE
6	STRONG BREEZE
7	NEAR GALE
8	GALE
9	STRONG GALE
10	STORM
11	VIOLENT STORM
12	HURRICANE

Tornadoes

Tornadoes are rotating columns of air that can be violently destructive. Most have wind speeds of less than 120 mph (200 kph), but they can reach 300 mph (480 kph). Tornadoes are characterized by a central spinning, funnel-shaped column of air, which extends from the clouds to the ground. They have the power to destroy crops and buildings. Tornado formation is associated with summer storms, especially in the US.

1 STEADY SPIN Rising warm air starts to rotate, and the base of the cloud extends down.

2 FUNNEL GROWS Funnel extends down to the ground, draws in hot air, and begins to spin faster.

3 IN PROGRESS Spinning column of air can be several miles wide and very destructive.

4 COLUMN DIES Eventually, the column narrows, and rises back up into the cloud.

Thunderstorms

Thunderstorms form in large cumulonimbus clouds. They carry water vapor high into the atmosphere, where it condenses into hail and ice.

Lightning
The movement of hail and ice in a thundercloud causes an electric charge to build up, which zaps down as lightning.

Over its life, a **hurricane** uses as much energy as **10,000 nuclear bombs**.

2 in (50 mm) per hour—the **rainfall produced** by a **hurricane**.

Hurricanes

Earth's most destructive storms occur in tropical regions, above warm waters. They produce torrential rains and extremely fast winds, which can exceed 155 mph (248 kph).

Hurricanes form in late summer, above warm waters. They begin when clusters of thunderstorms whirl together, evolving into complex structures with vast spiral bands of rain. The low pressure created by these structures draws warm, moist air across the ocean. This air then rises, releasing torrential rains and heat energy. Wind speeds above 74 mph (120 kph) combine with the low pressure to create storm surges of seawater many feet high that flood over coastal regions as the hurricane nears land. When hurricanes pass over land, they are no longer fed by heat from the warm ocean water, and they soon lose force—but often not before they inflict massive damage with their heavy winds, torrential rains, and gigantic waves.

Naming the storm

Hurricanes have the same structure and evolve in the same way wherever they are. However, how they are named depends on the part of the world where they occur. This map shows what they are called in different parts of the world.

ATLANTIC OCEAN

Tropical cyclone

INDIAN OCEAN

PACIFIC OCEAN

Hurricane

Typhoon

Airflows
Warm air from the top of the hurricane spirals out from the eye, then cools and descends as the pressure falls.

Outflow cloud shield
The top of the hurricane is a circular cloud roof of air, flowing out from the eye.

Moving out
Rising pressure pushes the upper clouds outward.

3 Tropical storm
A tropical storm forms when surface winds reach between 38 and 74 mph (61-120 kph). The storm becomes increasingly organized, with clouds rising over 3 miles (5 km) high, and producing torrential rain.

2 Tropical depression
Where tropical storms merge together, the rising air mass produces a low pressure disturbance known as a depression. The low pressure draws warm, moist air in as surface winds, which begin to rotate.

1 Tropical disturbance
In areas with high humidity and light winds, tropical water can become heated. This produces clusters of thunderstorms, which release rain and heat, rising many miles above the surface of the ocean.

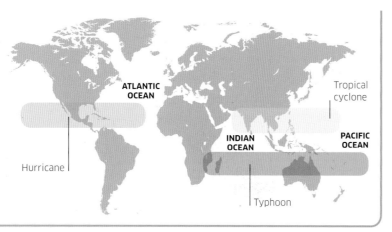

Top of storm spreads outward

Spiraling winds get faster

Winds begin to spin the clouds

Warm, moist air

Towering thunderstorm clouds

Destructive hurricane-force winds can extend up to 100 miles (60 km) away from the eye of the storm.

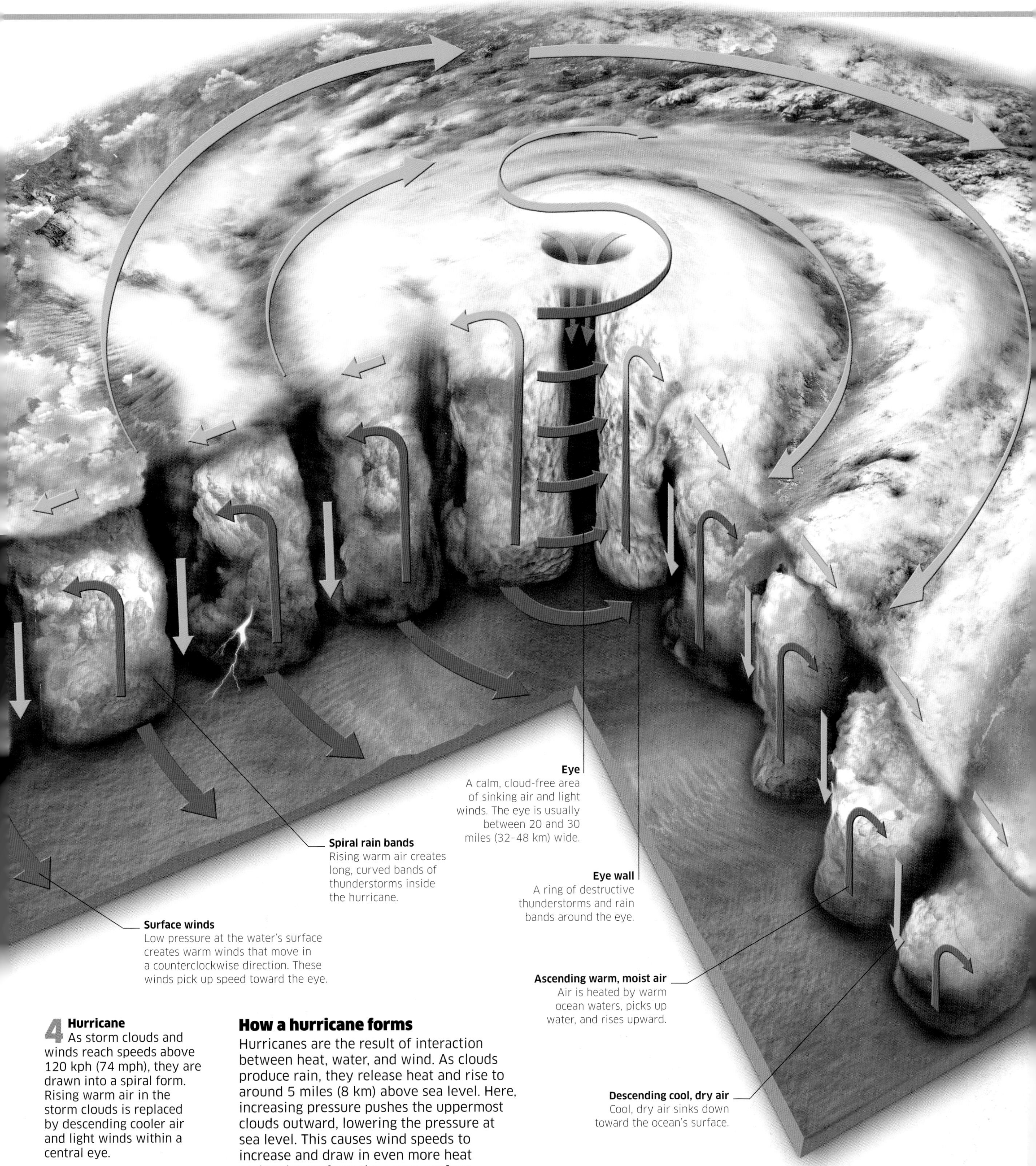

Eye
A calm, cloud-free area
of sinking air and light
winds. The eye is usually
between 20 and 30
miles (32–48 km) wide.

Eye wall
A ring of destructive
thunderstorms and rain
bands around the eye.

Spiral rain bands
Rising warm air creates
long, curved bands of
thunderstorms inside
the hurricane.

Surface winds
Low pressure at the water's surface
creates warm winds that move in
a counterclockwise direction. These
winds pick up speed toward the eye.

Ascending warm, moist air
Air is heated by warm
ocean waters, picks up
water, and rises upward.

4 Hurricane
As storm clouds and
winds reach speeds above
120 kph (74 mph), they are
drawn into a spiral form.
Rising warm air in the
storm clouds is replaced
by descending cooler air
and light winds within a
central eye.

How a hurricane forms
Hurricanes are the result of interaction
between heat, water, and wind. As clouds
produce rain, they release heat and rise to
around 5 miles (8 km) above sea level. Here,
increasing pressure pushes the uppermost
clouds outward, lowering the pressure at
sea level. This causes wind speeds to
increase and draw in even more heat
and moisture from the ocean surface.

Descending cool, dry air
Cool, dry air sinks down
toward the ocean's surface.

The water cycle

Earth's water is always on the move, traveling endlessly around our planet in a process known as the water cycle. Without water, life on Earth would not be possible.

Earth's water is stored in many forms, including oceans, rivers, lakes, glaciers, and groundwater. This water moves around constantly. The water cycle begins when the Sun's heat makes water evaporate into the atmosphere, where it becomes clouds, dew, or fog. This water falls back down to Earth's surface as rain or snow, then streams and rivers carry it to lakes or the sea, where it eventually evaporates and the whole cycle begins again.

The presence of water on the Earth is what gives our planet its wet and warm atmosphere. The atmosphere protects the Earth from the Sun's radiation, which has allowed the evolution and survival of life on Earth. Earth is thought to be the only planet in the Universe to support life.

Water on the move

All water on Earth is included in the constant circulation of the water cycle. Even the snow on mountain peaks or in the ice sheets of the Antarctic is a part of the cycle—eventually, it will melt and be on the move again. Underground water is also involved—it flows in a similar way to rivers, despite being hidden out of sight.

Snow on mountains
Where there are high mountains, moisture in the air falls as snow.

Snowfall
Cold air freezes any moisture it carries, forming snowflakes.

Rainfall
When moisture-carrying clouds cool, they release water as rain.

Snow melt
When air temperatures rise, snow melts, releasing fresh water.

Transpiration
Plants release moisture into the air.

Porous rock
Cracks and holes in rocks allow them to be filled with water.

Freshwater lake
Water collects in hollows in the ground.

Underground water flow
Water can flow downhill underground as well as above ground.

Lake types

Lakes are formed when water fills hollows in the landscape. Most lakes contain fresh water, though they can also be salty. They range in size from ponds to large lakes and even inland seas. The depression lakes are formed in various ways and may be millions of years old or newly man-made. Lakes are not permanent—they can gradually disappear as layers of sediment build up in them.

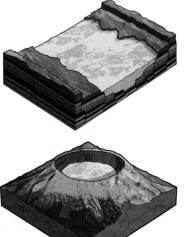

Fault lake
Movement of tectonic plates can create long hollows, which fill with water.

Caldera lake
A circular lake is created when rainwater fills the hole left in a volcano's summit after an eruption.

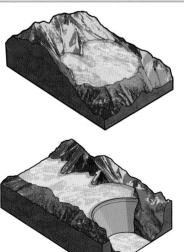

Kettle lake
A steep-sided circular lake, formed when an underground block of ice melts.

Man-made lake
People make lakes to generate hydroelectricity and create reservoirs of clean water.

97 percent of the **world's water** supply is **stored in the oceans**.

A **drop of water** can spend as little as **nine days** or as long as **40,000 years** moving through **the water cycle**.

The world's **largest river** is the **Amazon**, which holds around **20 percent** of the **world's** flowing **fresh water**.

63

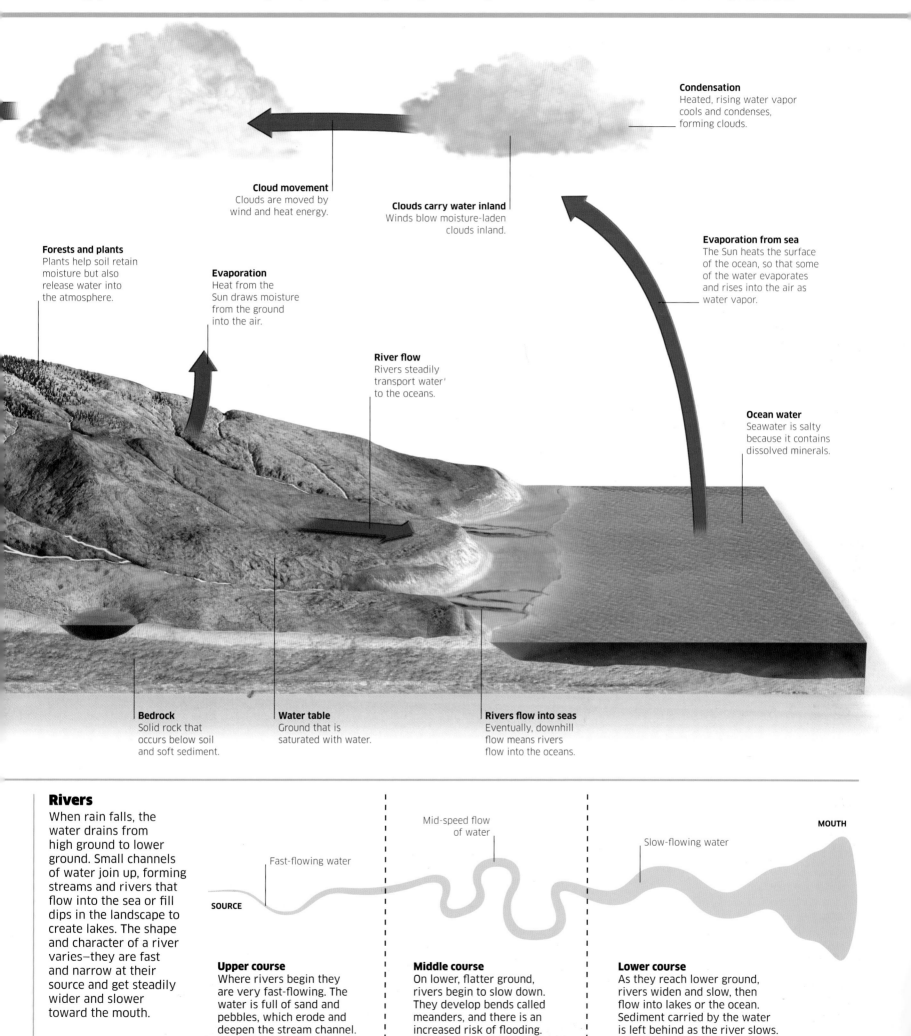

Condensation
Heated, rising water vapor cools and condenses, forming clouds.

Cloud movement
Clouds are moved by wind and heat energy.

Clouds carry water inland
Winds blow moisture-laden clouds inland.

Evaporation from sea
The Sun heats the surface of the ocean, so that some of the water evaporates and rises into the air as water vapor.

Forests and plants
Plants help soil retain moisture but also release water into the atmosphere.

Evaporation
Heat from the Sun draws moisture from the ground into the air.

River flow
Rivers steadily transport water' to the oceans.

Ocean water
Seawater is salty because it contains dissolved minerals.

Bedrock
Solid rock that occurs below soil and soft sediment.

Water table
Ground that is saturated with water.

Rivers flow into seas
Eventually, downhill flow means rivers flow into the oceans.

Rivers

When rain falls, the water drains from high ground to lower ground. Small channels of water join up, forming streams and rivers that flow into the sea or fill dips in the landscape to create lakes. The shape and character of a river varies—they are fast and narrow at their source and get steadily wider and slower toward the mouth.

Mid-speed flow of water

MOUTH

Slow-flowing water

Fast-flowing water

SOURCE

Upper course
Where rivers begin they are very fast-flowing. The water is full of sand and pebbles, which erode and deepen the stream channel.

Middle course
On lower, flatter ground, rivers begin to slow down. They develop bends called meanders, and there is an increased risk of flooding.

Lower course
As they reach lower ground, rivers widen and slow, then flow into lakes or the ocean. Sediment carried by the water is left behind as the river slows.

SHAPING THE LAND

The landscape may look unchangeable, but it has been shaped by the forces of wind and water over millions of years. Together, they break down, or erode, rocks into tiny fragments called sediment, then carry them away. This is usually a very slow process, but extreme events, such as floods and hurricanes, can speed it up.

WIND

You've probably had sand blown in your face on the beach, so you'll know that winds can be strong enough to pick up dust, grit, sand, and soil particles. These sediment particles can be carried over huge distances. Wind erosion and deposition (the laying down of sediment) typically happen in dry places with little vegetation to protect the rocks. Characterized by low rainfall, these environments are known as deserts and often contain sand dunes.

Sand dunes

The more powerful a wind is, the further it can carry sediment particles before dropping them to the ground. As they roll and bounce on the ground, these particles create small, wave-shaped ripples. These ripples sometimes build-up into larger formations, called dunes. With persistent winds, sand dunes can grow to many feet high and several miles long.

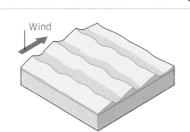

Transverse dunes
Constant winds carrying lots of sand form rows of dunes with crests that lie at right angles to the wind direction.

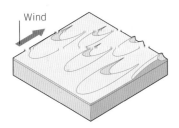

Crescent (barchan) dunes
Winds of varying strength and sand content form crescent-shaped dunes with "horns" pointing downwind.

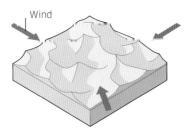

Star dunes
These dunes form when the wind direction constantly changes. They may grow to a considerable height.

Wind erosion

Over time, the constant lashing of winds can wear away at exposed rock surfaces. This wind erosion produces weird-looking and unstable formations, which eventually collapse in most cases. Even very hard rocks may be slowly shaped and polished by sand blasting. Barren landscapes can be created if all the soil in an area is blown away by the wind.

Rocky arch
Sand-blasting can create strange shapes from rocks, such as this natural arch in the Arches National Park in Utah.

COAST

Coasts are constantly being shaped by nature. Where coasts are exposed, the action of powerful ocean currents and waves wears away the landscape to form cliffs and headlands. On more sheltered coasts, sediments build up to form sandy beaches, dunes, mudflats, and salt marshes. Rivers also affect coasts as they lose energy and leave behind the sediments they carry when they approach the sea.

Coastal erosion

Pounding relentlessly, day after day, waves play a key role in shaping the coastline. They break against the shore with immense force, dislodging weak or loose rock material and grinding it into pebbles. Repeatedly hurled back against the shore by the waves, the pebbles themselves increase the waves' erosive action.

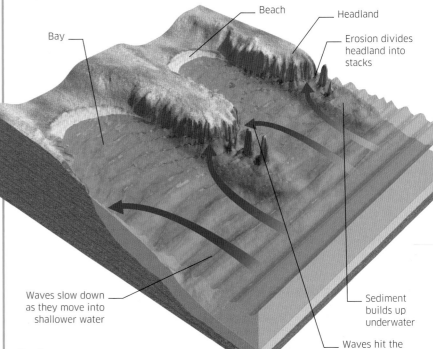

Beach

Headland

Erosion divides headland into stacks

Bay

Waves slow down as they move into shallower water

Sediment builds up underwater

Waves hit the headland

Steady waves
The size of waves—and their power—depends on the strength of the wind and how far the waves travel before they break on the shore.

Deposition

Rivers laden with sediment dump their cargo at river mouths to form wide shallow areas called estuaries. Sea waves and currents wash much of the sediment along the coastline. The mud and sand form beaches, sand dunes, and headlands, which help to protect the coastline from erosion.

Sediment buildup
Sediments can be washed or blown further along the coasts, into offshore waters, and even on to land, where they form dunes.

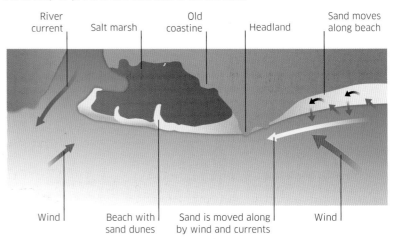

River current

Salt marsh

Old coastine

Headland

Sand moves along beach

Wind

Beach with sand dunes

Sand is moved along by wind and currents

Wind

WATER

The salty waters of the oceans cover about three-quarters of the Earth's entire surface. Heat from the Sun evaporates ocean water, which rises into the atmosphere and forms clouds. This airborne moisture eventually falls to the ground as rain. Some rainwater soaks into the soil or becomes stored in rocks underground. The rest of the water runs off the land to form rivers, which return the water to the sea, completing a process that is known as the water cycle.

Rain

Earth's atmosphere contains tiny particles of moisture in the form of clouds, fog, and steam. Temperature and pressure changes cause the moisture to condense into larger, heavier drops, which fall back down to Earth as rain, hail, or snow. The impact of raindrops hitting the ground can move particles of soil or sand.

Essential water

Rainwater is vital for life—it nourishes all plants and animals that live on land.

RAINDROPS ARE ALWAYS SMALL—THEY'LL **SPLIT INTO TWO DROPS** IF THEY GROW **BIGGER THAN** 0.25 IN (4 MM).

Rivers

Water flows down slopes under the influence of gravity. As a result, Earth's surface water runs off the land as mountain streams, which join to form larger rivers that carve out valleys as they flow down toward the sea. The more powerful the flow of the river, the more loose sediment, such as mud and sand, it can carry.

World's longest rivers

The Nile is the world's longest river, stretching for 4,130 miles (6,650 km). The Amazon, although not as long, carries more water—about one-fifth of all the river water on Earth.

RIVERS		
NILE (AFRICA)		
AMAZON (SOUTH AMERICA)		
YANGTZE (ASIA)		
MISSISSIPPI-MISSOURI (NORTH AMERICA)		
YENISEY-ANGARA (ASIA)		

LENGTH	2,500 MILES (4,020 KM)	3,000 MILES (4,830 KM)	3,500 MILES (5,630 KM)	4,000 MILES (6,440 KM)

Winding river

Where rivers flow slowly over low-lying land and are not hemmed in by valleys, their channels bend sideways into curves known as meanders.

Oxbow lakes

On low-lying land, the course of a river may bend to form snakelike meanders. If a meander curves too much, it will eventually become completely cut off from the main river. The result is a U-shaped body of water known as an oxbow lake.

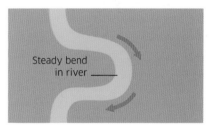

Steady bend in river

1 RIVER WITH MEANDER
A slight curve forms in a river's course as the flowing water erodes the outer bank and deposits sediment on the inner bank. Over time, this action exaggerates the curve and turns it into a meander.

River wears away land

2 BEND TIGHTENS
Continuing erosion and deposition tighten the curve of the meander into a C-shaped loop. The neck of the meander gradually gets narrower and narrower.

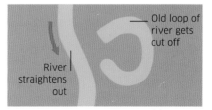

Old loop of river gets cut off

River straightens out

3 BEND IS CUT OFF
The curve grows so tight that the river cuts through the meander's neck to follow a new, straighter course. Sediment seals the ends of the old loop, leaving an oxbow lake.

Waterfalls

The ability of a river to erode its valley depends upon the hardness of the rock over which it flows. Soft rock erodes more quickly than hard rock. In places where the river's course takes it over both hard and soft rock surfaces, the different rates of erosion may gradually lead to the formation of waterfalls.

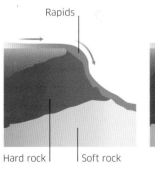

Rapids

Pool forms at base of waterfall

Hard rock | Soft rock

Softer rock is worn away

1 RAPIDS
Where a shallow river flows over a layer of hard rock, its flow is broken up by rapids—rocky outcrops that project above the water's surface.

2 WATERFALL
The river erodes soft rock on the river bed just beyond the rapids, carving out a plunge pool into which the water tumbles freely.

Glaciers

Ice is hard and brittle but it can also flow slowly when under pressure in moving channels of ice called glaciers. Glaciers pick up pieces of grit and rock fragments as they move along, which grind over the landscape, carving out a deep valley underneath the ice.

Glacier on the move

Vast rivers of ice called glaciers flow under the influence of gravity from high mountains to lower ground.

66 earth ∘ **SHAPING THE LAND**

352 miles (563 km)—the length of the **world's longest cave system**—Mammoth Cave System in Kentucky.

Caves

Underground passages and caves are found in rocky landscapes across the world. They are common in areas with a lot of limestone.

Cave systems form when acidic water etches its way through rock. Rainwater becomes acidic when it takes in carbon dioxide from the atmosphere, while groundwater can pick up acids from soil. The water causes existing cracks in the rock to widen into passages, which the water flows through, creating channels. Over time, the flowing water opens up passages and caverns, and more rocks weaken and fall, creating larger caverns. The surfaces of these caverns can become covered with a variety of crystalline deposits, which form when mineral-enriched water evaporates, leaving behind solid structures called stalactites and stalagmites.

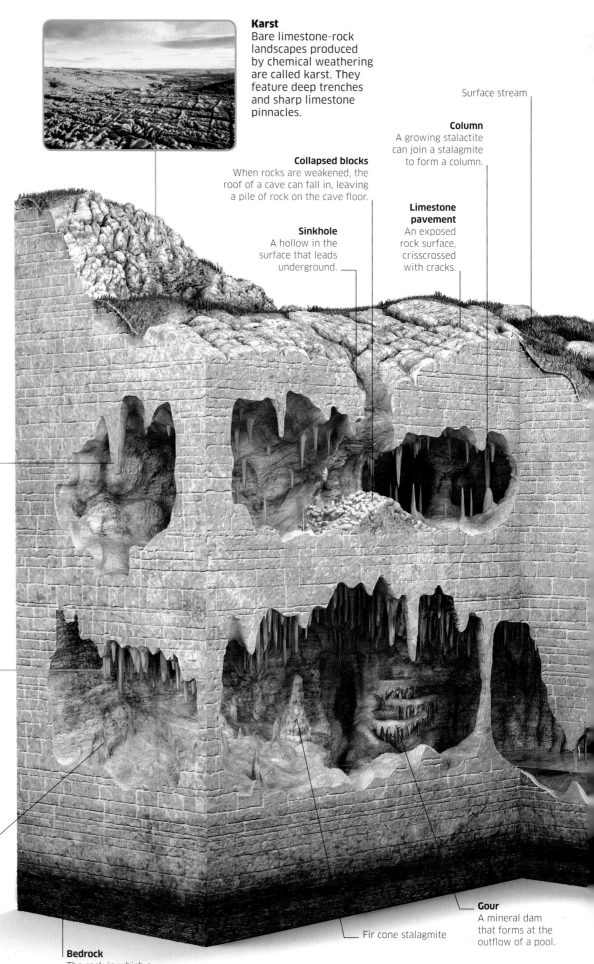

Karst
Bare limestone-rock landscapes produced by chemical weathering are called karst. They feature deep trenches and sharp limestone pinnacles.

Surface stream

Column
A growing stalactite can join a stalagmite to form a column.

Collapsed blocks
When rocks are weakened, the roof of a cave can fall in, leaving a pile of rock on the cave floor.

Limestone pavement
An exposed rock surface, crisscrossed with cracks.

Sinkhole
A hollow in the surface that leads underground.

Stalactite

Stalactite and stalagmite formation
As mineral-saturated water drips from a cave roof, it leaves a mineral residue on the roof and on the floor below. Over time, continued dripping creates pointed deposits hanging from the roof (stalactites) and rising from the floor (stalagmites). Eventually, these can join together to form columns.

Stalagmite

Inside Earth

The gradual weathering of limestone rock by acidic water can create incredible cave systems. Over thousands of years, small caves steadily grow, creating huge caverns, while small cracks in the rock become large tunnels. When these link up, huge interlinked networks are created, filled with thousands of stalactites and stalagmites. With the right safety equipment, these caves can be exciting environments for people to explore.

Bedrock
The rock in which a cave system develops.

Fir cone stalagmite

Gour
A mineral dam that forms at the outflow of a pool.

Tham Hinboum cave in **Laos** has the world's **longest navigable underground river**—it is over 4.5 miles (7 km) long.

92 ft (28 m)—the length of the **world's longest stalactite**, which is in **Gruta do Janelao** cave in **Brazil**.

67

How gorges form

The development of cave systems means large amounts of limestone rock is removed from a landscape. Underground cavities are enlarged by rock falls and form caves. Eventually, the caves roofs collapse, creating sinkholes, which can then merge to form larger sunken regions with steep sides, known as gorges.

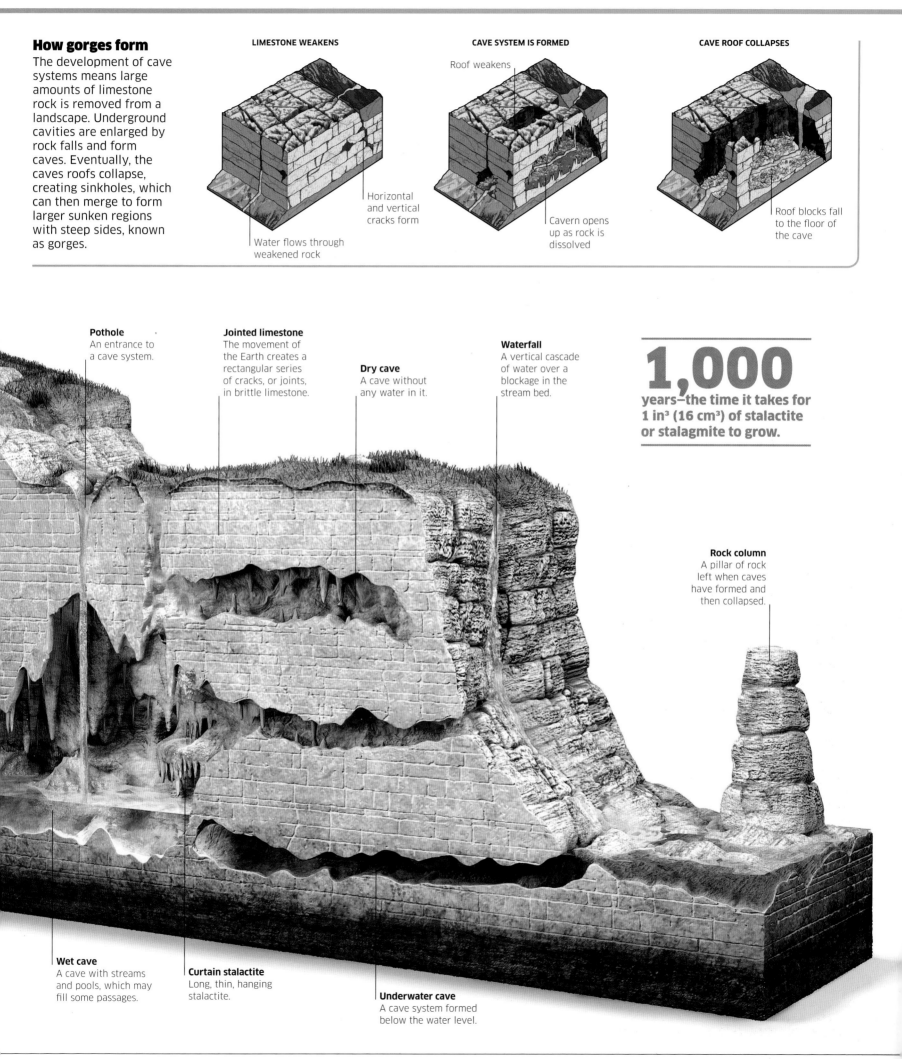

LIMESTONE WEAKENS

Horizontal and vertical cracks form

Water flows through weakened rock

CAVE SYSTEM IS FORMED

Roof weakens

Cavern opens up as rock is dissolved

CAVE ROOF COLLAPSES

Roof blocks fall to the floor of the cave

Pothole
An entrance to a cave system.

Jointed limestone
The movement of the Earth creates a rectangular series of cracks, or joints, in brittle limestone.

Dry cave
A cave without any water in it.

Waterfall
A vertical cascade of water over a blockage in the stream bed.

1,000
years—the time it takes for 1 in³ (16 cm³) of stalactite or stalagmite to grow.

Rock column
A pillar of rock left when caves have formed and then collapsed.

Wet cave
A cave with streams and pools, which may fill some passages.

Curtain stalactite
Long, thin, hanging stalactite.

Underwater cave
A cave system formed below the water level.

10 percent of Earth's land is covered with glacial ice.

If all glacial ice melted, the worldwide sea level would rise by 230 ft (70 m).

Glaciated valley

As a glacier travels through a valley it wears away at the landscape, dragging grit and dirt from the ground and carrying them along with it. Glaciers are not just a mass of solid ice—as well as debris, they are crisscrossed with cracks called crevasses and channels of meltwater.

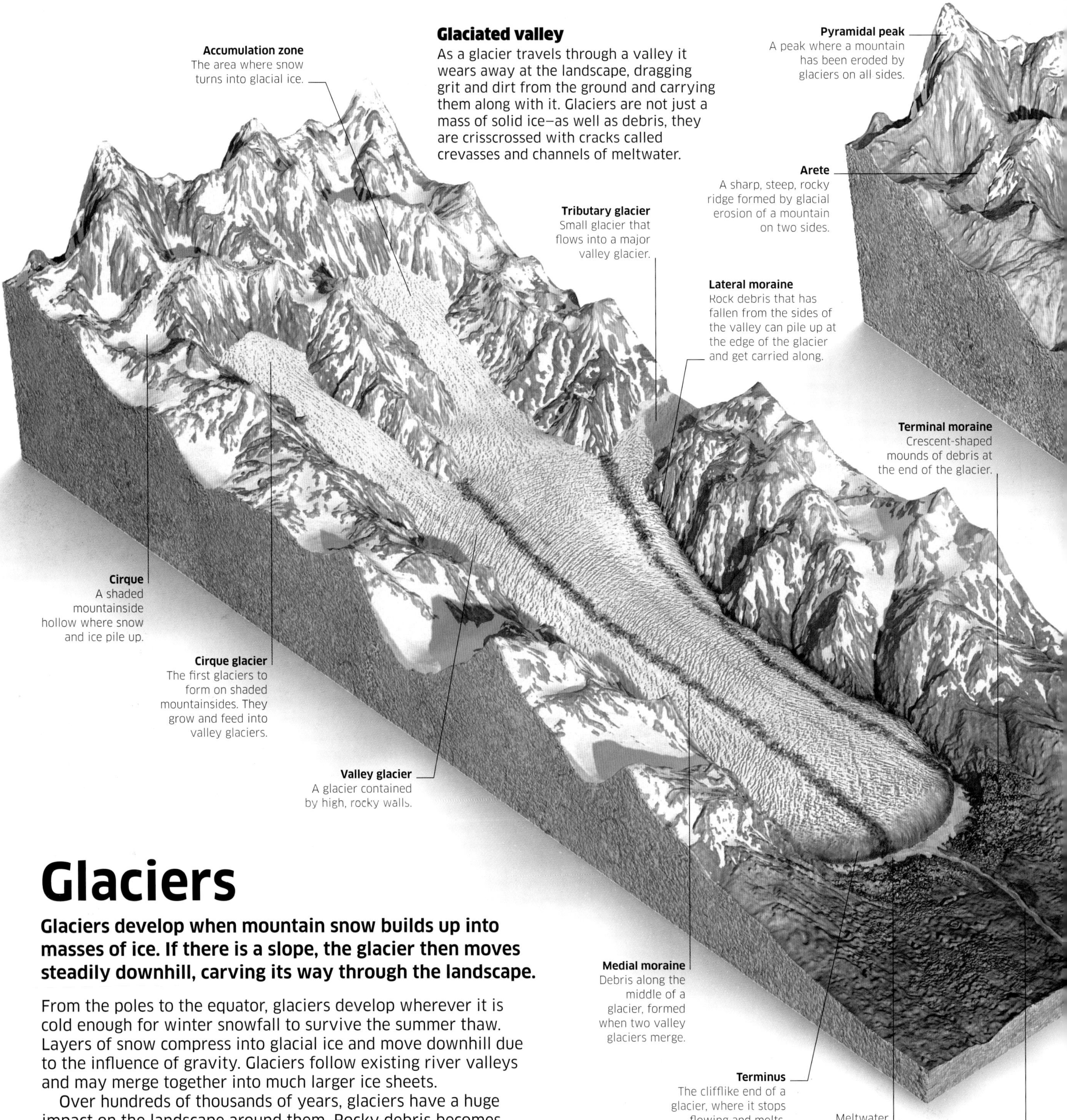

Accumulation zone
The area where snow turns into glacial ice.
Pyramidal peak
A peak where a mountain has been eroded by glaciers on all sides.
Arete
A sharp, steep, rocky ridge formed by glacial erosion of a mountain on two sides.
Tributary glacier
Small glacier that flows into a major valley glacier.
Lateral moraine
Rock debris that has fallen from the sides of the valley can pile up at the edge of the glacier and get carried along.
Terminal moraine
Crescent-shaped mounds of debris at the end of the glacier.
Cirque
A shaded mountainside hollow where snow and ice pile up.
Cirque glacier
The first glaciers to form on shaded mountainsides. They grow and feed into valley glaciers.
Valley glacier
A glacier contained by high, rocky walls.
Medial moraine
Debris along the middle of a glacier, formed when two valley glaciers merge.
Terminus
The clifflike end of a glacier, where it stops flowing and melts.
Meltwater
Meltwater stream
Meltwater flows away from the glacier.

Glaciers

Glaciers develop when mountain snow builds up into masses of ice. If there is a slope, the glacier then moves steadily downhill, carving its way through the landscape.

From the poles to the equator, glaciers develop wherever it is cold enough for winter snowfall to survive the summer thaw. Layers of snow compress into glacial ice and move downhill due to the influence of gravity. Glaciers follow existing river valleys and may merge together into much larger ice sheets.

Over hundreds of thousands of years, glaciers have a huge impact on the landscape around them. Rocky debris becomes embedded in glaciers, and cuts into the landscape, changing the shape of the valleys they move through. This debris is then dumped onto surrounding landscapes wherever the glacier comes to rest and melts.

In some places, **Antarctica's ice sheet** is more than 2.6 miles (4.2 km) **thick**.

32 percent **of land was covered** with **glacial ice** in the **last ice age**.

69

After the glacier

Glaciers leave many signs behind when they have passed through an area. Rock debris called moraine is left in piles. Valleys are gouged into deep U-shapes with close vertical sides, and are often flooded with melt water. Rocks are scratched by other rocks and debris that is carried along by the gritty ice, and even huge boulders can be relocated.

Truncated spur
A mountain ridge that has had its end cut off by a glacier.

Waterfall

Hanging valley
A tributary valley, once occupied by a tributary glacier, whose floor lies high above that of the main valley.

Lateral moraine
A trail of debris along the side of a valley, left when a glacier melts.

70 percent of Earth's fresh water is stored as glacial ice.

Drumlin
A mound of glacial debris that has been molded into an egg shape.

Floodplain
The flat valley floor beside a stream that is periodically flooded.

Tarn
A lake-filled hollow created by a cirque glacier.

V-shaped valley
A river valley that has not been affected by glacial erosion.

U-shaped valley
A steep-sided, flat-bottomed valley, eroded by a glacier.

Ribbon lake
A long, narrow lake.

Stream

Kettle lake
Water-filled hollow formed by the melting of ice that was buried under glacial deposits.

Erratics
Blocks of rock that have been carried away from their original source by a glacier.

How glacial ice forms

Glacial ice forms gradually, when fresh snow is steadily weighed down by the accumulation of newer flakes. Eventually, this compression turns light snow into dense ice with few air bubbles.

Airborne snow
Fresh snow falls, formed of delicate six-sided crystals.

Ground snow
Within days, flakes are broken by the weight of new snowfall.

Granular ice
Within a year, the fragments form round, dense grains.

Firn
The grains steadily get smaller and more tightly packed.

Glacial ice
Firn grains are packed together to create larger ice crystals.

EARTH'S OCEANS

The blue waters of Earth's oceans cover almost three quarters of our planet, dominating its surface. The world beneath the water's surface is Earth's most mysterious and least explored region. Fifty percent of the world's species live in the oceans, which have been home to life since it first evolved, over 4 billion years ago.

THE SEAFLOOR

The ocean floor is just as varied as land. Its features are mainly created by the movement of the plates that make up Earth's crust. Where plates move apart, ridges open and create new ocean floor. Where plates collide, old rock is pushed into Earth's interior, forming deep trenches. Volcanic islands erupt from the ocean floor and some even rise above sea level. They are surrounded by deep, flat abyssal plains and covered with fine-grained sediment.

Ocean features

OCEAN TRENCHES
Where two of Earth's tectonic plates push into each other, one will be forced underneath the other in a process called subduction. Deep, valleylike trenches are formed between the plates—some can be almost 6.8 miles (11 km) deep.

VOLCANIC ISLANDS
The movement of tectonic plates under the ocean causes molten rock (magma) to bubble upward into the water. If there is a lot of magma then it rises and erupts at the surface, forming an arc-shaped series of island volcanoes.

OCEAN RIDGES
These ridges form when two of Earth's tectonic plates pull apart and magma wells up between them, solidifying into new rock. The system of ocean ridges extends over 36,780 miles (59,200 km) around the globe.

HYDROTHERMAL VENTS
The presence of hot rocks beneath spreading ocean ridges produces numerous hot springs, known as hydrothermal vents. The heated seawater is rich in minerals and pours out onto the ocean floor, creating towerlike structures called black smokers. These extreme underwater environments are similar to those in which life first formed.

ABYSSAL PLAINS
The deep ocean floor lies more than 9,843 ft (3,000 m) below sea level. It covers 50 percent of the Earth's surface but is the least explored part of the planet. The rugged volcanic mountain landscape of the seafloor is buried beneath fine-grained, muddy sediment, which forms a dark, featureless, intensely cold and inhospitable environment.

Hidden mountain

Measured from its underwater base to its summit, Mount Kea in Hawaii, is even taller than Mount Everest.

Mount Everest
29,028 ft
(8,848 m)

Mount Kea
33,476 ft
(10,203 m)

13,796 ft (4,205 m) above water

SEA LEVEL

19,680 ft (5,998 m) below water

OCEAN WATER

Most of Earth's water is found in its oceans, which cover much of the planet's surface, with an average depth of around 12,240 ft (3,370 m). Deep ocean waters extend from the north and south poles right around the world to the equator. They vary considerably in properties such as saltiness, temperature, pressure, light penetration, and the forms of life they support.

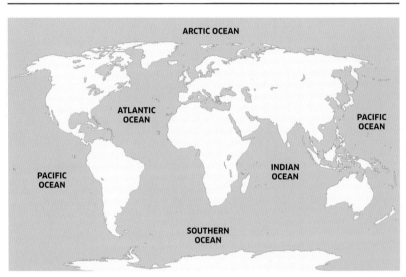

ARCTIC OCEAN
ATLANTIC OCEAN
PACIFIC OCEAN
PACIFIC OCEAN
INDIAN OCEAN
SOUTHERN OCEAN

Oceans and seas

Earth has five oceans and over 50 seas. Oceans are large expanses of open saltwater. Seas still contain saltwater, but they are smaller and partly surrounded by land.

The world's oceans
Oceans are named individually, but they all join up into one global body of water.

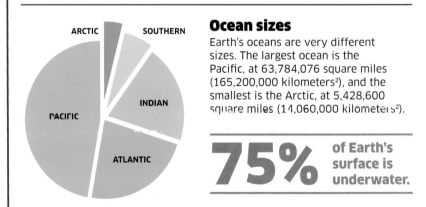

ARCTIC SOUTHERN
PACIFIC
INDIAN
ATLANTIC

Ocean sizes

Earth's oceans are very different sizes. The largest ocean is the Pacific, at 63,784,076 square miles (165,200,000 kilometers²), and the smallest is the Arctic, at 5,428,600 square miles (14,060,000 kilometers²).

75% of Earth's surface is underwater.

IF THE OCEAN WATERS WERE SPREAD OUT EVENLY OVER EARTH'S SURFACE THEY WOULD COVER THE ENTIRE SURFACE TO A DEPTH OF 8,200 FT (2,800 M).

Salty seas

All seawater is salty, but only a small percentage is actually salt. As well as salt, seawater contains over 86 chemical elements and very low concentrations of precious metals such as platinum and gold.

96.5% WATER   3.5% SALT

Sunlight and darkness

Sunlight cannot shine far through ocean water. Only blue light reaches water below 150 ft (45 m), and below 660 ft (200 m) there is no light at all. Ocean waters can be divided into zones depending on how much light reaches them and how cold they are—the water gets colder as it gets deeper. Each ocean zone provides a habitat for different kinds of life. Animals that live in the deeper zones have special adaptations to survive there.

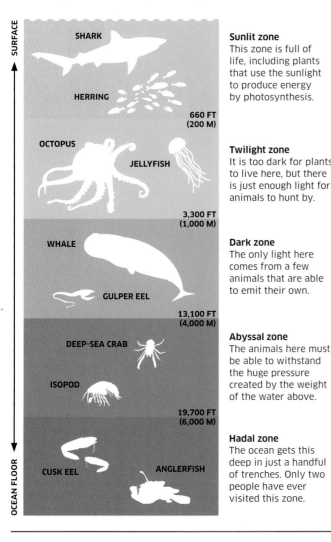

SURFACE

SHARK

HERRING

Sunlit zone
This zone is full of life, including plants that use the sunlight to produce energy by photosynthesis.

660 FT (200 M)

OCTOPUS

JELLYFISH

Twilight zone
It is too dark for plants to live here, but there is just enough light for animals to hunt by.

3,300 FT (1,000 M)

WHALE

GULPER EEL

Dark zone
The only light here comes from a few animals that are able to emit their own.

13,100 FT (4,000 M)

DEEP-SEA CRAB

ISOPOD

Abyssal zone
The animals here must be able to withstand the huge pressure created by the weight of the water above.

19,700 FT (6,000 M)

CUSK EEL

ANGLERFISH

Hadal zone
The ocean gets this deep in just a handful of trenches. Only two people have ever visited this zone.

OCEAN FLOOR

Water temperature

Deep ocean water is always cold, but the temperature of surface waters varies greatly. This means that different ocean habitats exist, with tropical coral reefs in warm areas and cold-loving animals around the north and south poles.

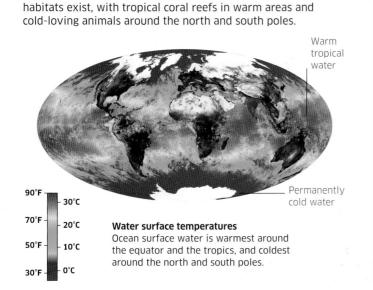

Warm tropical water

Permanently cold water

90°F — 30°C
70°F — 20°C
50°F — 10°C
30°F — 0°C

Water surface temperatures
Ocean surface water is warmest around the equator and the tropics, and coldest around the north and south poles.

WATER ON THE MOVE

Ocean water is in constant motion. Wind on the water's surface creates waves. Gravity between the Sun, Moon, and Earth creates tides. Heat from the Sun generates currents around the world, as the heated water rises to the surface while cold water sinks.

LESS THAN 10% OF THE OCEANS HAVE BEEN EXPLORED.

Waves

Most ocean waves are generated by wind, with wave height, spacing, and direction depending on how strong the wind is and how long it blows. Long-term winds produce giant, widely spaced waves.

Round and round
Water particles do not move forward with waves—they travel in small circles or loops.

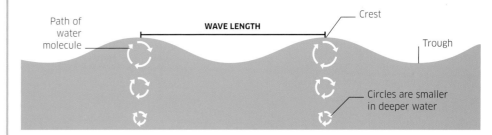

Path of water molecule

WAVE LENGTH

Crest

Trough

Circles are smaller in deeper water

Tides

Regular rises and falls of sea level around the world are called tides. The Moon's gravity produces two high tide bulges of ocean water, on opposite sides of the globe. Between these bulges are the low tides. As Earth rotates, the tides sweep around the globe. As well as this daily cycle, the weaker pull of the Sun produces an additional monthly cycle, with a variation in the heights of the high and low tides.

Low tide
Tides mean the sea level changes through the day. At high tide these boats would be afloat.

Currents

Ocean surface water currents are driven by winds that blow from the hot tropics to cooler northern regions. They form ocean-wide flows called gyres. Oceans also have deeper currents, which are known as the Great Ocean Conveyor. These deep currents are caused by sunlight heating tropical waters. The warm water flows toward cold polar regions, where it cools and sinks, forming a deep current that flows back toward the tropics, where it warms and rises again.

Global currents
There are two sets of currents in Earth's oceans—surface currents on top and deep-ocean currents further down.

→ Warm surface currents
→ Cold surface currents

▮ Warm deep-ocean current
▮ Cold deep-ocean current

72 earth o **EARTH'S OCEANS**

180 million years—the age of the oldest rocks on the ocean floor.

36 °F (2°C) The temperature at the bottom of the ocean.

The ocean floor

The world beneath the ocean surface is as varied as the more familiar one above water, with huge mountains and volcanoes, vast plains, deep canyons and trenches, and massive ridges that snake across the seafloor.

Many seafloor features are the result of melted rock called magma rising up from inside Earth. Where tectonic plates (slabs of Earth's outer shell) pull apart at a mid-ocean ridge, the magma solidifies and creates new seafloor. Older plate is pushed away from the ridge and eventually may move under a neighboring plate. This allows more magma to move upward, creating volcanic islands. Not all seabed features are made by magma—submarine canyons are caused by erosion around the edges of continents, and abyssal fans are created by submarine currents dropping off the silt they were carrying.

Into the depths

Where one tectonic plate dips under another it creates a trench in the seafloor. These are some of the deepest trenches—most are found around the edges of the Pacific Ocean.

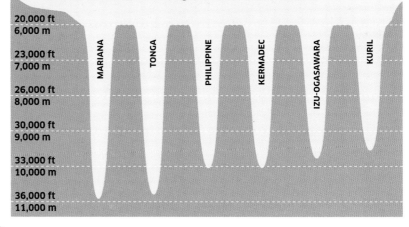

20,000 ft / 6,000 m
23,000 ft / 7,000 m
26,000 ft / 8,000 m
30,000 ft / 9,000 m
33,000 ft / 10,000 m
36,000 ft / 11,000 m

MARIANA TONGA PHILIPPINE KERMADEC IZU-OGASAWARA KURIL

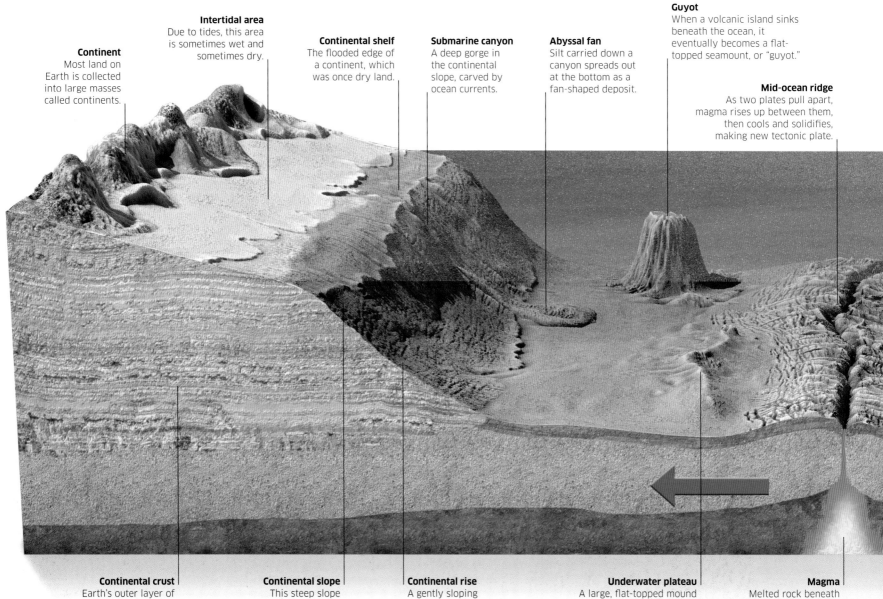

Continent
Most land on Earth is collected into large masses called continents.

Intertidal area
Due to tides, this area is sometimes wet and sometimes dry.

Continental shelf
The flooded edge of a continent, which was once dry land.

Submarine canyon
A deep gorge in the continental slope, carved by ocean currents.

Abyssal fan
Silt carried down a canyon spreads out at the bottom as a fan-shaped deposit.

Guyot
When a volcanic island sinks beneath the ocean, it eventually becomes a flat-topped seamount, or "guyot."

Mid-ocean ridge
As two plates pull apart, magma rises up between them, then cools and solidifies, making new tectonic plate.

Continental crust
Earth's outer layer of rock—can be (43 miles 100 km) thick in continental areas.

Continental slope
This steep slope goes down to about 10,000 ft (3,000 m).

Continental rise
A gently sloping region that extends down from the continental slope.

Underwater plateau
A large, flat-topped mound caused by a few million years of underwater volcanic eruptions.

Magma
Melted rock beneath Earth's surface is called magma. Above Earth's surface it is called lava.

Animals living in **ocean trenches** withstand **pressures** up to 800 times higher than the pressure at sea level.

100,000 The estimated number of **seamounts** in Earth's oceans.

73

Deep-sea smokers

Usually found near mid-ocean ridges, subsea smokers grow where super hot water spurts up from the seabed. Seawater seeps down into the seafloor and gets heated. The hot water rises and surges back into the cold ocean, where minerals dissolved in it turn into solid particles, which look like smoke. The particles also build up to form solid chimneys around the plumes of hot water.

Smoke
Often black but can also be white.

Conduit
A passage that hot water moves through.

Cold seawater
This seeps down through cracks in the oceanic crust.

Super-heated water
Can reach temperatures above 750°F (400°C).

Mineral chimney
Can grow at an incredible 12 in (30 cm) a day.

Tube worms
Unique ecosystems develop in clusters around some smokers.

MANY SUBSEA SMOKERS HAVE NAMES, INCLUDING **MAGIC MOUNTAIN,** LOKI'S CASTLE, **FRED'S FORTRESS, GODZILLA,** HULK, AND **HOMER SIMPSON.**

Hot rock, or magma
This heats water that has seeped into the crust.

Under the sea

The seafloor lies about 2.3 miles (3.7 km) below the surface of the ocean. It is made of a rocky oceanic crust, which is covered in muddy sediment. Tectonic plates are generally made up of this oceanic crust and continental crust, along with part of the mantle layer under it. Erupting magma on the seafloor can create volcanic islands and seamounts.

Seamount
An underwater volcano that may be active or extinct.

Volcanic island arc
A slightly curved line of volcanic islands, found where one plate slides under another at a subduction zone.

Volcanic island
The above-water part of a huge undersea volcano.

Abyssal plain
A flat expanse of mud that covers a vast area of seafloor.

Sea level
The sea surface level, which varies very slightly over time.

Tectonic plate
Each tectonic plate is made of crust and the top layer of the mantle.

Oceanic crust
This type of crust is thinner than continental crust, and made of dark-colored rock.

Ocean trench
This forms where one tectonic plate moves under another.

Magma chamber
A pool of magma beneath a volcano.

Volcano
Forms from a buildup of lava when magma erupts at the surface.

NATURE

Since the first living organisms appeared on Earth 3.8 billion years ago, millions of different species have evolved. Life now flourishes all over the planet, from the highest mountain peaks to the depths of the ocean.

SIGNS OF LIFE

Planet Earth was formed from a cloud of space rock, dust, and gas. For millions of years it was a mass of hot molten rock with a poisonous atmosphere. But eventually its crust cooled to the point where water could form vast oceans. The shallow fringes of these oceans were probably where life began, about 3.8 billion years ago, in a series of chemical reactions that assembled the first living cells.

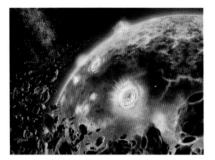

1 EARLY EARTH
For 500 million years Earth was a giant furnace of searingly hot rock, constantly bombarded by asteroids and meteorites. As each lump of space rock crashed into the planet, its energy was converted into more heat. But these impacts also delivered chemical elements that were to be vital ingredients of life.

2 CHEMICAL CAULDRON
As the planet cooled, huge volcanoes filled the air with toxic gases. But they also erupted vast quantities of water vapor that cooled and fell as rain, filling the oceans. Lightning may have then triggered chemical reactions in the water, forming complex molecules that were able to make copies of themselves—the basis of life.

3 FIRST CELLS
The chemical processes that were essential to life needed to occur in a protected place. This was provided by a substance that could form tiny, tough-walled bubbles. These were the first living cells—microscopic packages of life-giving chemicals that became bacteria, the simplest surviving life forms.

4 ENERGY FROM LIGHT
Life needs energy. The first cells used chemical energy, but about 3.5 billion years ago cells called cyanobacteria started using solar energy. They used it to make food from water and carbon dioxide, releasing vital oxygen. Similar cyanobacteria created these stromatolites on the coast of Western Australia.

5 DEEP HEAT
It is likely that the first living cells developed in warm, coastal pools of salty water. However, life may have begun in the deep ocean, around hot volcanic vents that gush energy-rich chemicals from the ocean floor. Simple organisms that still live around these vents are probably very like the earliest living cells.

HOW LIFE BEGAN

Billions of years ago, a chance combination of chemicals somewhere on Earth's surface created a substance that could soak up energy and reproduce itself–the first living organism. This was the beginning of the amazing story of life on Earth.

VARIETY OF LIFE

As soon as life began, it started to change. Living things thrive by making copies of themselves, but the copies are not exact. Over time, the differences generate new forms of life. This process of change, called evolution, has created the diversity of life on Earth.

Evolution

Every living thing is slightly different from its parents. If the difference helps it to survive, it is likely to pass on the advantage to its own young. This is the basis of evolution. Many years later, it may lead to a change that is large enough for the result to be called a different species.

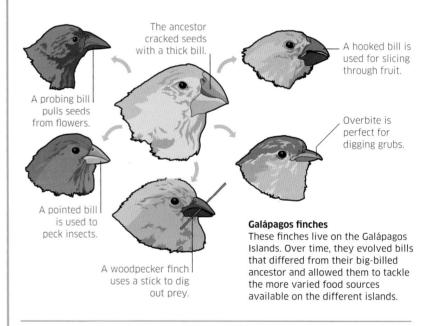

The ancestor cracked seeds with a thick bill.

A probing bill pulls seeds from flowers.

A hooked bill is used for slicing through fruit.

Overbite is perfect for digging grubs.

A pointed bill is used to peck insects.

A woodpecker finch uses a stick to dig out prey.

Galápagos finches
These finches live on the Galápagos Islands. Over time, they evolved bills that differed from their big-billed ancestor and allowed them to tackle the more varied food sources available on the different islands.

Natural selection

The main mechanism of evolution is called natural selection. Life in the natural world is a competition, with losers and winners. Those that survive and breed happen to have a combination of qualities that helps them thrive in their habitat. But if conditions change, the winners may turn into losers.

Survival of the fittest
Most peppered moths have pale wings for camouflage. But a dark form thrived in places with smoke-blackened trees because it was less obvious to birds.

The pale moth is hard to see on the natural tree bark.

The pale moth stands out on the soot-stained tree bark.

WRITTEN IN STONE

We know that life has evolved over time because rocks contain evidence of different life forms that thrived in the distant past. These links with a vanished world are called fossils. Typical fossils preserve the forms of bones, teeth, and shells. By comparing them with those of familiar animals, scientists can piece together the story of evolution. Every new fossil that is discovered makes the picture clearer.

Fossil hunters

The scientists who study fossils are called palaeontologists. They are experts at finding, identifying, and preserving fossils. They can also work out how old each fossil is, and how it fits in with the story of evolution. They often have only fragments to work with, but a single bone can be a crucial clue.

Excavation
Palaeontologists painstakingly uncover a fossil of a 10-million-year-old rhinoceroslike animal in Nebraska.

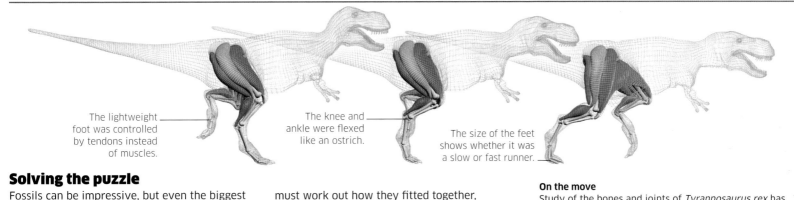

The lightweight foot was controlled by tendons instead of muscles.

The knee and ankle were flexed like an ostrich.

The size of the feet shows whether it was a slow or fast runner.

Solving the puzzle

Fossils can be impressive, but even the biggest and best preserved are just a start. To make sense of a group of fossil bones, palaeontologists must work out how they fitted together, what the living creature might have looked like, and how it might have behaved.

On the move
Study of the bones and joints of *Tyrannosaurus rex* has been used to create this computer simulation, showing that its running action was similar to that of an ostrich.

CHANGING PLANET

The history of life is not a story of steady progress. Living things have faced many global disasters caused by things like asteroid impacts and climate change. Some have left very few survivors, which have had to live in an altered world. This has changed the direction of evolution several times, so new types of animals and plants have evolved while others have become extinct.

Snapshot of life

For about 84 percent of life's 3.8-billion-year history, the largest life forms were microscopic bacteria.

When complex life appeared, the pace of evolution accelerated to create a dazzling variety of species.

EARTH FORMS

In the beginning
For 3 billion years, only the very simplest single-celled forms of life existed on Earth.

Complex life evolves
Multi-celled life—the first animals—only started evolving 600 million years ago (MYA).

TODAY

Mass extinctions

Since life began there have been five mass extinctions—catastrophic events that killed off a large proportion of life on Earth. After each extinction, life recovered slowly, and new types of animals, plants, and other living things appeared. These extinctions were caused by natural forces, but evidence suggests that we are in the early stage of a sixth mass extinction, caused by human activity.

ORDOVICIAN (440 MYA)
This extinction destroyed 60 percent of the species living in the oceans. At the time, there was little if any life on land.

60%

DEVONIAN (358 MYA)
More than three-quarters of the species living in the Devonian Period were wiped out. Life in shallow seas was most badly affected.

75%

PERMIAN (250 MYA)
At the end of the Permian, life suffered a global catastrophe that almost destroyed life altogether. Very few species survived.

96%

TRIASSIC (200 MYA)
The first period of the dinosaur era—the Mesozoic—ended with an extinction that killed off most of the dinosaurs' competitors.

70%

CRETACEOUS (66 MYA)
The mass extinction that destroyed the giant dinosaurs at the end of the Cretaceous was possibly caused by an asteroid impact.

75%

IN THE PAST 500 MILLION YEARS, MORE THAN 90 PERCENT OF ALL LIFE ON EARTH HAS VANISHED.

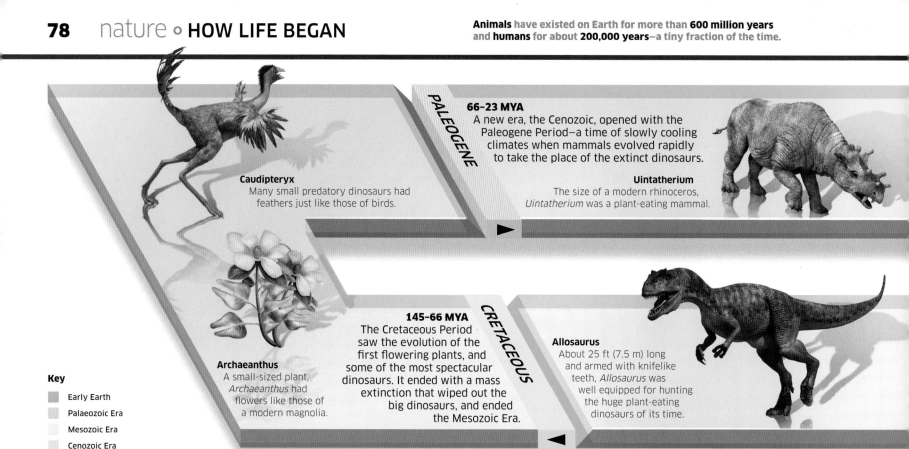

Caudipteryx
Many small predatory dinosaurs had feathers just like those of birds.

PALEOGENE

66–23 MYA
A new era, the Cenozoic, opened with the Paleogene Period–a time of slowly cooling climates when mammals evolved rapidly to take the place of the extinct dinosaurs.

Uintatherium
The size of a modern rhinoceros, *Uintatherium* was a plant-eating mammal.

Archaeanthus
A small-sized plant, *Archaeanthus* had flowers like those of a modern magnolia.

145–66 MYA
The Cretaceous Period saw the evolution of the first flowering plants, and some of the most spectacular dinosaurs. It ended with a mass extinction that wiped out the big dinosaurs, and ended the Mesozoic Era.

CRETACEOUS

Allosaurus
About 25 ft (7.5 m) long and armed with knifelike teeth, *Allosaurus* was well equipped for hunting the huge plant-eating dinosaurs of its time.

Key
- Early Earth
- Palaeozoic Era
- Mesozoic Era
- Cenozoic Era

Timeline of life

Life has existed on planet Earth for 3.8 billion years. Over that time, it has evolved into a dazzling diversity of forms, from microscopic bacteria to giant dinosaurs.

For most of Earth's long history, the only living things were single-celled microbes that lived in the oceans. But around 600 million years ago, the first multicellular animals appeared. This led to an evolutionary explosion of complex oceanic life forms during the Cambrian Period. And once the first simple plants had evolved, life was able to colonize the continents as well as the oceans.

Geological time

The history of life is recorded by fossils preserved in rock layers. Older rocks lie beneath more recent ones, so each layer represents a span of time. Scientists divide this vast stretch of time into eras, and these are further divided into smaller time spans called periods. This geological timescale is the basis of the timeline shown here, measured in millions of years ago (MYA).

Rolfosteus
This long-snouted fish was a late Devonian shellfish-eater.

CARBONIFEROUS

358–298 MYA
Life on land flourished during the Carboniferous, with dense forests of tree-sized primitive plants. Insects and spiders were common, and were hunted by large amphibians.

Drepanaspis
The head of this armored, jawless fish was covered with a broad, flattened shield. It grew to about 14 in (35 cm) long.

419–358 MYA
The Devonian is known as the age of fish because so many new types evolved. Some of these fish gave rise to four-legged amphibians that were the ancestors of all land vertebrates, such as reptiles and mammals.

DEVONIAN

PRECAMBRIAN

4.6 billion to 541 MYA
The huge stretch of time known as the Precambrian Period includes the 3 billion years when only the simplest single-celled life forms existed. The first animals evolved near the very end of the Precambrian.

Early volcanoes
Water vapor erupting from ancient volcanoes created the oceans where life evolved.

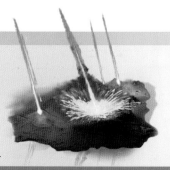

Comets
Space debris bombarded Earth in the early Precambrian, including icy comets that melted into the oceans.

380 million years ago, the first vertebrate animals crawled on to land.

Insects were the **first flying animals**. Today, these thriving life forms make up more than **75 percent of all animal species**.

79

NEOGENE

23–2 MYA
The cooling climate trend continued in the Neogene. Modern types of mammals and birds appeared, and the australopithecine ancestors of humans evolved in Africa.

Australopithecus afarensis
This early hominid could have been the first to walk upright, 4 million years ago.

QUATERNARY

2 MYA to the present
This period of dramatic climate changes has had long ice ages with warmer phases like the one we live in today. Despite this, modern humans–*Homo sapiens*–slowly spread all around the world.

Homo neanderthalensis
These tough, strongly built people were adapted for life in icy climates.

JURASSIC

201–145 MYA
The dinosaurs flourished during the Jurassic Period, rising to become the dominant animals on land. They included gigantic plant-eaters and powerful predators.

Morganucodon
The small, insect-eating *Morganucodon* was one of the first mammals.

Eudimorphodon
One of the earliest pterosaurs, *Eudimorphodon* had wings of stretched skin, and probably flew well.

Plateosaurus
This long-necked dinosaur could reach up to gather leaves high in the treetops.

Meganeura
A dragonflylike insect, *Meganeura* had a 29 in (75 cm) wingspan.

Lepidodendron
Growing to 100 ft (30 m) or more, this Carboniferous tree had bark with a scaly pattern.

PERMIAN

298–252 MYA
The Permian saw the dominance of reptiles and the ancestors of mammals, but ended in a catastrophic extinction.

Dimetrodon
The fossils of this sail-backed carnivore are among the most common fossils of this period.

TRIASSIC

252–201 MYA
Life recovered slowly from the Permian extinction that ended the Palaeozoic Era. But by the end of the Triassic Period, the first of the dinosaurs had evolved, along with the earliest airborne pterosaurs and the first true mammals.

Cooksonia
Found in most parts of the world, *Cooksonia* was one of the oldest plants to have stems.

SILURIAN

443–419 MYA
The Silurian Period saw the appearance of the first bony fish with hinged, movable jaws. Meanwhile, life had spread on to land in the form of simple green plants.

The Precambrian Period makes up 88 percent of the entire history of Earth.

Sacabambaspis
This armored animal had very close-set eyes that faced forward. It had no jawbones, like all the earliest fish.

CAMBRIAN

541–485 MYA
Fossils of complex animals became common in rocks of the Cambrian Period, at the start of the Palaeozoic Era. Many of these creatures had evolved with hard shells, which is why they survived as fossils.

Marrella
About 1 in (2 cm) long, *Marrella* lived on the seabed. It had jointed legs like a crab and spines running along its body.

ORDOVICIAN

485–443 MYA
Life flourished in the oceans during the Ordovician. Many different types of fish evolved during this period along with other animals such as trilobites. But the Ordovician Period ended with one of the biggest extinction events in history.

80 nature ○ **HOW LIFE BEGAN**

80 percent, or more, of **all known dinosaurs** have been **discovered since 1990**.

The dinosaurs

For 165 million years, life on Earth was dominated by the most spectacular animals that have ever existed—the dinosaurs.

The Mesozoic Era was a high point in the history of life, because it was the age of dinosaurs. These fantastic creatures included the biggest, heaviest, and most terrifying of all land animals. They evolved into an amazing variety of forms, ranging from huge, armored leaf-eaters to nimble, feathered hunters, and gave rise to the birds that still flourish today.

Family tree

All the dinosaurs of the Mesozoic Era except the very earliest species belonged to two main groups known as the ornithischians and saurischians. The ornithischians evolved into three main types that were nearly all plant-eaters. The saurischians were divided into the mainly meat-eating theropods and the big, plant-eating sauropodomorphs.

DINOSAURS

Ornithischians
The word ornithischian means "bird-hipped." It refers to the way that the pelvic bones of these dinosaurs resemble those of birds. The ornithischians also had beaks supported by special jawbones. But confusingly the birds themselves are small theropod dinosaurs, part of the saurischian group.

Saurischians
The saurischian dinosaurs of the early Mesozoic Era had pelvic bones that resembled those of lizards, so the word saurischian means "lizard-hipped." But many of the later forms evolved birdlike pelvic bones, which the birds were to inherit. Saurischians also had longer, more flexible necks than the ornithischians.

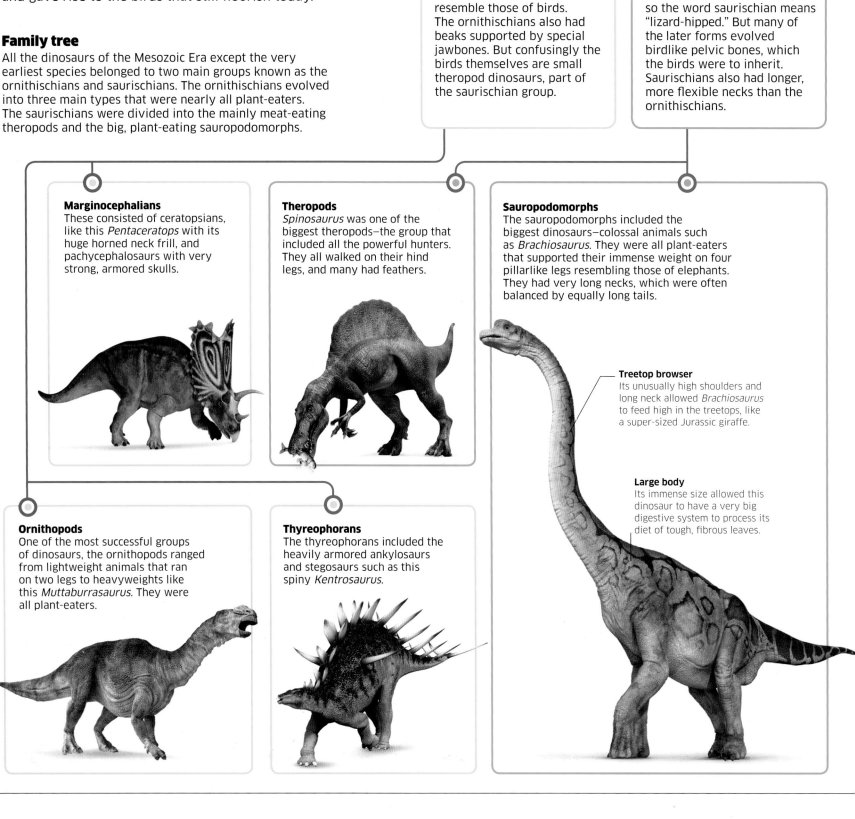

Marginocephalians
These consisted of ceratopsians, like this *Pentaceratops* with its huge horned neck frill, and pachycephalosaurs with very strong, armored skulls.

Theropods
Spinosaurus was one of the biggest theropods—the group that included all the powerful hunters. They all walked on their hind legs, and many had feathers.

Sauropodomorphs
The sauropodomorphs included the biggest dinosaurs—colossal animals such as *Brachiosaurus*. They were all plant-eaters that supported their immense weight on four pillarlike legs resembling those of elephants. They had very long necks, which were often balanced by equally long tails.

Treetop browser
Its unusually high shoulders and long neck allowed *Brachiosaurus* to feed high in the treetops, like a super-sized Jurassic giraffe.

Ornithopods
One of the most successful groups of dinosaurs, the ornithopods ranged from lightweight animals that ran on two legs to heavyweights like this *Muttaburrasaurus*. They were all plant-eaters.

Thyreophorans
The thyreophorans included the heavily armored ankylosaurs and stegosaurs such as this spiny *Kentrosaurus*.

Large body
Its immense size allowed this dinosaur to have a very big digestive system to process its diet of tough, fibrous leaves.

One **fossil site in China** has yielded more than **7,000 dinosaur bones**.

The **biggest sauropod dinosaurs** could weigh as much as **13 elephants**.

800 species of dinosaurs have been named by scientists.

81

Strong legs

Unlike modern reptiles such as crocodiles and lizards, the dinosaurs stood with their legs beneath their bodies in much the same way as mammals. We also know that many of them were warm-blooded, which allowed them to be more active than modern cold-blooded reptiles.

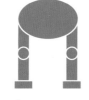

Dinosaur stance
All dinosaurs stood tall on straight legs, so their weight—which could be immense—was fully supported.

Crocodile stance
Modern crocodiles are close relatives of dinosaurs, but their legs do not support their bodies quite as well.

Lizard stance
Lizards usually sprawl with their legs outspread and their bellies close to the ground, which slows them down.

Reptile neighbors

The dinosaurs were not the only giant reptiles living during the Mesozoic Era. They shared their world with marine reptiles such as *Mosasaurus*, and pterosaurs like *Pterodactylus*. These animals were not dinosaurs, although the pterosaurs were close relatives. Most were hunters, and some marine reptiles had massively strong jaws. The pterosaurs were much more lightly built, with small bodies and long, efficient wings of stretched skin.

Mosasaurus
At up to 50 ft (15 m) long, *Mosasaurus* was a powerful predator that lived at the very end of the age of dinosaurs.

Pterodactylus
Like all pterosaurs, *Pterodactylus* was a warm-blooded, furry-bodied animal that probably flew as well as a bird.

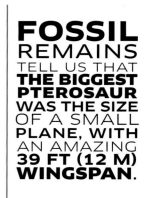

FOSSIL REMAINS TELL US THAT **THE BIGGEST PTEROSAUR** WAS THE SIZE OF A SMALL PLANE, WITH AN AMAZING **39 FT (12 M) WINGSPAN.**

The Mesozoic Era

The age of dinosaurs began 230 million years ago, during the Triassic Period. This was the first of three periods that made up the Mesozoic Era. The earliest dinosaurs had to compete with other types of reptiles, but many of these became extinct at the end of the Triassic, allowing dinosaurs to flourish during the Jurassic Period. The last period, the Cretaceous, saw the evolution of an amazing variety of dinosaurs, including the fearsome tyrannosaurs.

The supercontinent of Pangaea was fringed by a single, immense ocean.

PANGAEA

Pangaea split into Laurasia in the north, Gondwana in the south.

LAURASIA
GONDWANA

The South Atlantic ocean opened up between Africa and South America.

NORTH ATLANTIC
AFRICA
SOUTH AMERICA
SOUTH ATLANTIC

Triassic Earth
From 252 to 201 million years ago, all the continents were joined together in a huge supercontinent with a vast desert at its heart. Most plants and animals lived near the fringes.

Jurassic Earth
The supercontinent split in two near the beginning of the Jurassic Period. The deserts shrank, and the growth of lush forests provided food for huge plant-eating dinosaurs.

Cretaceous Earth
The Jurassic Period gave way to the Cretaceous 145 million years ago. The continents became more fragmented, allowing many different types of dinosaurs to evolve in various lands.

Catastrophe

The Mesozoic Era ended 66 million years ago with a mass extinction event that eliminated all dinosaurs except the birds. It may have been caused by the impact of a giant asteroid in what is now Mexico. At the same time, huge volcanoes were erupting in India, and the combination must have had catastrophic effects on the climate.

Asteroid impact

The asteroid that hit Mexico 66 million years ago was at least 6 miles (10 km) wide. The high-speed impact of such a huge rock would have filled the atmosphere with debris and dust, blotting out the Sun for many years.

SCIENTISTS STILL **DO NOT KNOW** WHAT REALLY **KILLED OFF THE BIG DINOSAURS,** OR HOW BIRDS, **CROCODILES, AND** OTHER ANIMALS **MANAGED TO SURVIVE.**

82 nature ○ **HOW LIFE BEGAN**

28 years—the age of a dinosaur known as Sue,
the biggest **Tyrannosaurus** to be exhibited so far.

Forward-facing eyes
The eyes faced further forward than those of most dinosaurs. This gave *Tyrannosaurus* the binocular vision it needed to judge distances accurately and target its prey.

Air sacs
Air passed right through the lungs and into a network of air sacs before it was pumped out again. This allowed the lungs to absorb more oxygen with each breath.

Lungs
The lungs were like those of birds—super efficient for gathering the oxygen needed to power the hunter's huge muscles.

Ribcage
Strong ribs protected the dinosaur's heart, lungs, and other vital organs from damage.

Lower jaw
The jaws were deep and short, allowing the jaw muscles to exert huge pressure.

Massive neck muscles
The weight of the head was supported by very strong neck muscles. These also helped with tearing prey apart.

Air sac

Shoulder blade

Bone-crushing teeth
Tyrannosaur teeth were bigger and stronger than those of any meat-eating dinosaur found so far. The biggest were at least 8 in (20 cm) long. They were more like spears than teeth—sharp-pointed to pierce thick skin and muscle, yet deep-rooted and very tough to give them the strength to bite clean through the bones of their victims.

Small arms
Each tiny arm had just two sharp-clawed fingers.

Gizzard
Big mouthfuls of meat and shattered bone passed into a muscular, tough-walled gizzard to be ground to a pulp.

Heart
The heart was probably at least ten times the size of a human heart. It needed to be, to pump blood around its colossal body.

Tyrannosaurus rex

The most powerful land predator that has ever existed was a giant theropod dinosaur—a super-sized killer armed with massive jaws and teeth that could bite through solid bone.

The tyrannosaurs were the most deadly hunters of the entire 165-million-year Mesozoic Era—the age of dinosaurs. The biggest and most famous of them, *Tyrannosaurus rex*, evolved only near the end of the era, a few million years before the global catastrophe that wiped out all the giant dinosaurs. It was specialized for killing—inflicting huge bites that crippled its prey or caused it to die of shock. It would then rip its victim apart, biting out great chunks of meat and swallowing them whole.

Birdlike feet
Theropods walked on their toes, like birds. Each foot had three strong, forward-pointing toes, and a small toe at the back.

Tyrannosaurs weighed as much as an adult male African elephant.

More than 30 fossil Tyrannosaurus specimens have been discovered.

60 The number of teeth in a tyrannosaur's jaws.

83

Fact file

When	68–66 MYA (late Cretaceous)
Habitat	North America
Diet	Carnivore
Length	Up to 40 ft (12.4 m)

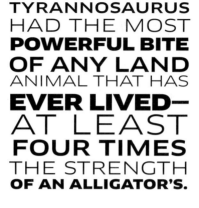

TYRANNOSAURUS HAD THE MOST POWERFUL BITE OF ANY LAND ANIMAL THAT HAS EVER LIVED— AT LEAST FOUR TIMES THE STRENGTH OF AN ALLIGATOR'S.

Intestine
As a dedicated hunter, *Tyrannosaurus* only ate meat. This is easy to digest, so the dinosaur almost certainly had a relatively short intestine.

Backbone
The vertebrae that made up the flexible backbone had tall spines linked to strong muscles, giving excellent back strength.

Tail muscle
Massive muscles flanking the bones of the tail provided strength as well as the weight needed for balance.

Long, heavy tail
Extending well beyond the hips, the long tail balanced the dinosaur's heavy head as it charged into the attack on its hind legs.

3 million years–the length of time that *Tyrannosaurus* may have terrorized the Earth.

Hip bone
Like most theropods, the tyrannosaurs had massive bones extending forward from their hips that helped support their intestines.

Powerful muscular legs
Like all the theropod dinosaurs, *Tyrannosaurus* stood on just two powerful hind legs. These were very muscular at the top, but slim near the ankle for speed.

Stout claws
Each foot was equipped with stout, strong claws to grip the ground. It is possible that this animal could run very well, despite its weight.

Shock tactics

Typical carnivorous dinosaurs had teeth like knife blades, ideal for slicing through skin and flesh. But these bladelike teeth were very slender and likely to snap off if the dinosaur bit into something hard. *Tyrannosaurus* and its relatives were different. Their teeth were sturdy spikes that could punch through virtually anything. This allowed tyrannosaurs to charge straight into the attack on their powerful hind legs. Most of the dinosaurs they preyed upon didn't stand a chance.

How fossils form

Fossils are a window on a lost world. They are our only evidence of spectacular creatures that lived long ago, and of the process of evolution that created them.

A fossil is something that preserves the form or traces of a living thing that died many millions of years ago. When something dies, its remains are usually broken up and attacked by decay organisms that completely destroy it. But some parts are more likely to survive than others, especially the shells, bones, and teeth of dead animals. If they escape destruction for long enough and are buried below ground, they may be replaced by minerals dissolved in groundwater. These can then harden to stone, creating a typical fossil.

Types of fossil

Many fossils are shells or bones that have been turned to stone, but there are other types of fossils. Some are animals that were not turned to stone but simply preserved, like flies in amber. Stony fossils can preserve an impression of something rather than its entire form, such as a footprint. These types of trace fossil can tell us a lot about how long-extinct animals lived.

Preserved in amber
This mosquito was trapped in sticky tree resin millions of years ago, and preserved because the resin hardened into a fossilized form called amber.

A long process

Most of the time, fossilization is a gradual process. After thousands of years, a shell or bone can look as if it has been buried for just a few weeks, especially if it has been frozen. Creating a stony fossil usually takes millions of years as the body tissue of an animal is gradually replaced with the minerals that will eventually turn it to stone. The result often mimics the original in every tiny detail, and this gives scientists vital clues about the animal and how it lived in the distant past.

Conifers
Fossils of needle-shaped leaves and bark show that pines and other cone-bearing trees were common during the dinosaur age.

Flooded landscape
The dinosaurs have died out and the land is now covered by seawater.

Megalodon
A colossal relative of the great white shark, this was the biggest killer in the oceans 20 million years ago.

Triceratops
This leaf-eater lived alongside *Tyrannosaurus*, and was among its main prey.

Tyrannosaurus rex
This famous dinosaur was a bone-crushing hunter that lived at the end of the dinosaur age, about 66 million years ago.

Tyrannosaurus dies

Sediment layers
Different sediments (mud or sand) form layers that vary in color and thickness.

Ammonites
These extinct relatives of cuttlefish and squid had strong coiled shells that are very common as fossils.

1 Deadly battle
Badly injured in a battle with a rival, a *Tyrannosaurus rex* stumbles into a river and dies. Its huge body settles on the riverbed, where its skin and flesh start to decay.

2 Bare bones
Lack of oxygen deep in the river slows the decay process. Eventually, the body of the *Tyrannosaurus* is reduced to a bare skeleton, but the bones stay intact as they were in life.

3 Deep burial
Mud settling on the riverbed buries the skeleton. Then, millions of years later, rising sea level floods the area with seawater, and the mud is covered with a pale layer of marine sediment.

From wood to stone
Plants are fossilized as well as animal remains. Entire tree trunks can be turned to stone (a process known as petrification), which preserves the cell structure of the timber.

Leaving an impression
Sometimes an organism, such as this marine animal *Dickinsonia*, sinks into soft mud that turns to rock, but then dissolves to leave an impression of its shape called a mold.

Natural cast
Minerals dissolved in water can slowly build up inside a mold, re-creating the shape of the original organism. This fossil ammonite was created by such a process.

Trace fossil
This three-toed footprint was left in mud by a predatory dinosaur more than 66 million years ago. A line of such prints shows the animal's stride length and how it moved.

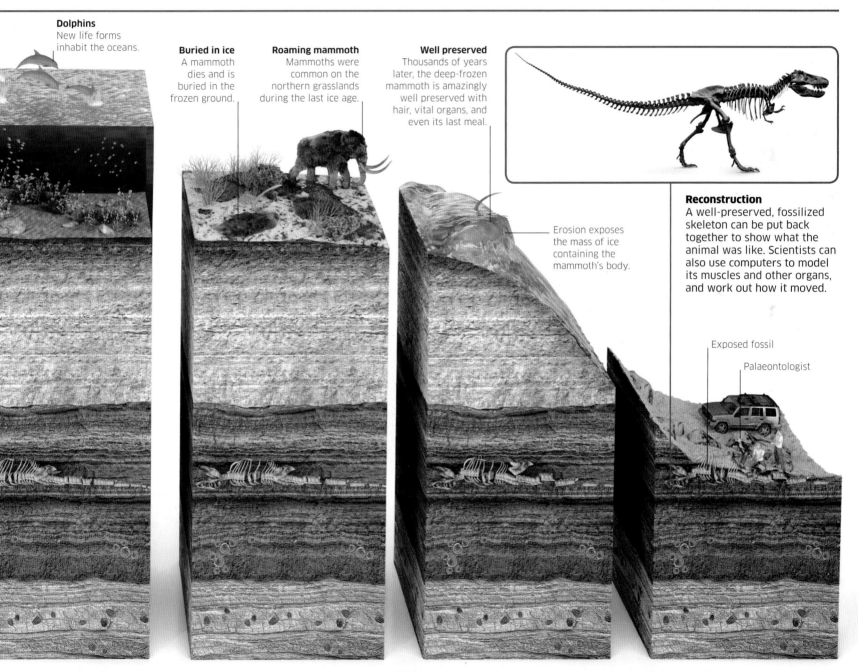

Dolphins
New life forms inhabit the oceans.

Buried in ice
A mammoth dies and is buried in the frozen ground.

Roaming mammoth
Mammoths were common on the northern grasslands during the last ice age.

Well preserved
Thousands of years later, the deep-frozen mammoth is amazingly well preserved with hair, vital organs, and even its last meal.

Erosion exposes the mass of ice containing the mammoth's body.

Reconstruction
A well-preserved, fossilized skeleton can be put back together to show what the animal was like. Scientists can also use computers to model its muscles and other organs, and work out how it moved.

Exposed fossil

Palaeontologist

4 Bone to mineral
As the sediment layers get deeper, dissolved minerals turn them into solid rocks such as chalk and shale. The minerals seep into the buried bones, slowly turning them to stone.

5 Ice age
Closer to our own time, an ice age turns so much water to ice that sea level falls. Mammoths roaming the half-frozen tundra occasionally stumble into swamps, die, and freeze solid.

6 Surface erosion
A river changing its course cuts away the pale chalk rock, exposing the frozen body of the mammoth. But the skeleton of the *Tyrannosaurus* is still hidden deep below ground.

7 Excavation
Long after the end of the ice age, more erosion cuts into the dark shale and reveals the dinosaur fossil. Scientists known as palaeontologists begin a careful excavation.

THE LIVING WORLD

Life has evolved into an incredible variety of forms, with almost 1.8 million known species and many more yet to be discovered. Scientists classify them in six kingdoms. Each kingdom is divided into groups of related living things called phyla, classes, orders, and families. These organisms have evolved different ways of surviving in their particular habitats, but many find it harder and harder to live in a changing world.

LIFE ON EARTH

There is life almost everywhere on Earth, but some regions have many more species than others. Such areas are known as biodiversity hotspots. The warm tropics are the richest – especially tropical rainforests and tropical coral reefs. These habitats offer many ways in which organisms can survive, encouraging the evolution of different types of life.

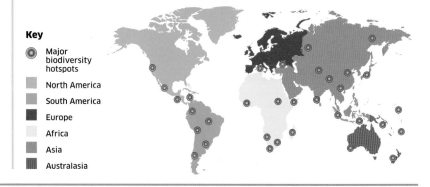

Key
- ⦿ Major biodiversity hotspots
- North America
- South America
- Europe
- Africa
- Asia
- Australasia

LIFE FORMS

Every species of living thing is related to others that evolved from the same ancestors. They form groups of species that are related to other groups in the same way, like a giant family tree. This tree has six main stems—the six kingdoms of life. Three of the kingdoms are made up of organisms that are mostly too small to see without a microscope, but the others consist of the animals, plants, and fungi.

The six kingdoms

1 ARCHAEA
The first life forms to evolve on Earth were the microscopic organisms called archaea. They have a very simple structure—just a single cell enclosing a tiny drop of watery fluid containing the molecules vital to life. Some archaea live in hostile places such as hot, acidic springs.

2 BACTERIA
These are very like archaea, with the same structure. But their chemistry is different, showing that they evolved separately. Some bacteria cause disease, while others are essential to our survival. One type, cyanobacteria, produced nearly all the oxygen in the atmosphere.

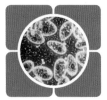

3 PROTISTS
Also known as algae and protozoans, these are mainly microscopic, single-celled organisms. Unlike bacteria or archaea, each cell has a nucleus that contains the main life-giving molecules. There are also other structures within the cell that make food or turn it into energy.

4 FUNGI
Although they seem to grow like plants, fungi feed on other living or dead organisms. Some fungi are single-celled microbes, but most fungi form spreading, multicelled root networks. These produce mushrooms and molds like those that grow on decaying fruit.

5 PLANTS
Green plants are multicelled living things that use the energy of sunlight to make food. In the process, they release oxygen into the air, which is vital to animal life. They mostly live on land or in fresh water, and range from low-growing mosses to magnificent trees.

6 ANIMALS
Like plants, all animals are multicelled organisms. But unlike them, they cannot make their own food, and must eat other organisms instead. Most do so by moving around, using their senses to find the food they need, and this has led to the evolution of intelligence.

How many?

Compared to plants, fungi, and protists, the animal kingdom has the largest total number of named species. Bacteria and archaea numbers run into millions and are impossible to estimate.

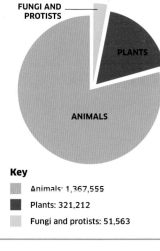

FUNGI AND PROTISTS

PLANTS

ANIMALS

Key
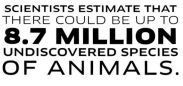
- Animals: 1,367,555
- Plants: 321,212
- Fungi and protists: 51,563

SCIENTISTS ESTIMATE THAT THERE COULD BE UP TO **8.7 MILLION** UNDISCOVERED SPECIES OF ANIMALS.

Classification of life

Each of the six kingdoms of life is divided into several phyla of similar organisms. These are split into classes, orders, and families.

Within each family there are usually groups of closely related organisms, each called a genus. This normally contains several individual species.

Classifying a tiger
The scientific name of an organism is made up of its genus and species. The tiger is in the genus *Panthera*, so its scientific name is *Panthera tigris*.

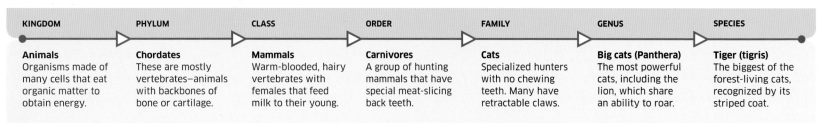

KINGDOM	PHYLUM	CLASS	ORDER	FAMILY	GENUS	SPECIES
Animals Organisms made of many cells that eat organic matter to obtain energy.	**Chordates** These are mostly vertebrates—animals with backbones of bone or cartilage.	**Mammals** Warm-blooded, hairy vertebrates with females that feed milk to their young.	**Carnivores** A group of hunting mammals that have special meat-slicing back teeth.	**Cats** Specialized hunters with no chewing teeth. Many have retractable claws.	**Big cats (Panthera)** The most powerful cats, including the lion, which share an ability to roar.	**Tiger (tigris)** The biggest of the forest-living cats, recognized by its striped coat.

ESSENTIALS FOR LIFE

All living things share certain basic needs. They must have water, for without it the chemistry of life is not possible. The fact that Earth has liquid water on its surface is the main reason why life evolved on this planet.

Living things also need raw materials to build their tissues, and energy to fuel the processes that turn chemicals into living cells. They get these in many ways, often relying on other organisms to supply them.

Living requirements

While all living things need the same essentials, many have more specific requirements. For example, plants and animals get their energy in very different ways–plants need sunlight, while animals need energy-rich food. But few forms of life can manage without most of these basic necessities.

Water
All life is made of cells that contain water, so this is vital. Desert life is able to survive on very little water, but cannot do without it.

Warmth
Few living things can survive in very cold or very hot places. Most live in regions that are always warm, or have warm summers.

Shelter
Many animals live in hostile places where they need shelter from the Sun or cold winds, and even plants may need some protection.

Nutrients
Plants absorb water containing dissolved minerals, using them to build their tissues. Animals get nutrients from their food.

Energy
Plants and many microbes soak up solar energy. They use it to make energy-rich food that supports other forms of life.

Living space
A plant needs soil to take root, and an animal must be able to find enough food. Even a microbe needs its own living space.

Oxygen
Most living things use oxygen to turn food into energy. Luckily, it is constantly being released into the atmosphere by plants.

Energy pyramid

Most natural habitats have many organisms that produce food, and several levels of food consumers. This patch of wild grassland supports several rabbits, which are primary consumers, fewer weasels that prey on the rabbits, and only one fox–the top predator. There are fewer consumers at the upper levels, because at each level some energy is turned into activity and heat instead of food for the next link in the chain. This means that it takes a lot of grass to support one fox, and explains why foxes are much rarer than rabbits.

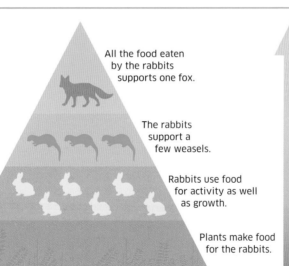

All the food eaten by the rabbits supports one fox.

The rabbits support a few weasels.

Rabbits use food for activity as well as growth.

Plants make food for the rabbits.

DECREASING ENERGY AVAILABLE

Food chain

All living things need energy. Plants and some other organisms gather energy from sunlight and use it to make sugar. Animals eat the plants and turn the sugar back into energy and body tissues. Other animals eat the plant-eaters, so the energy–along with vital nutrients–passes down a food chain. But eventually, the energy and nutrients are turned into a form that can be recycled by plants.

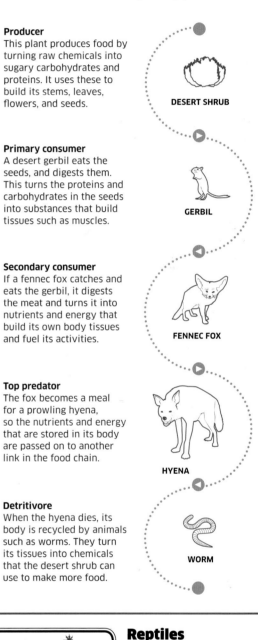

Producer
This plant produces food by turning raw chemicals into sugary carbohydrates and proteins. It uses these to build its stems, leaves, flowers, and seeds.

DESERT SHRUB

Primary consumer
A desert gerbil eats the seeds, and digests them. This turns the proteins and carbohydrates in the seeds into substances that build tissues such as muscles.

GERBIL

Secondary consumer
If a fennec fox catches and eats the gerbil, it digests the meat and turns it into nutrients and energy that build its own body tissues and fuel its activities.

FENNEC FOX

Top predator
The fox becomes a meal for a prowling hyena, so the nutrients and energy that are stored in its body are passed on to another link in the food chain.

HYENA

Detritivore
When the hyena dies, its body is recycled by animals such as worms. They turn its tissues into chemicals that the desert shrub can use to make more food.

WORM

UNDER THREAT

In every kingdom of life there are species that are threatened with extinction. There are many reasons for this, but most of them are the result of human activity. Some animals are deliberately killed, including rare species. Vast areas of wild habitat have been destroyed, denying wildlife its basic needs such as living space and food. But creating wildlife reserves can help save many species.

Plants
The destruction of habitats such as tropical rainforests is threatening the amazing diversity of plant life.

Fish
Although fish are not as threatened as some animals, pollution and overfishing have made many species scarce.

Amphibians
Hardest hit of all are the frogs, salamanders, and other amphibians, with a third of all known species vanishing fast.

Reptiles
Recent research shows that more than a fifth of the reptile species living worldwide are under serious threat.

Birds
Hunting and loss of their natural habitats have made the future uncertain for at least 12 percent of bird species.

Mammals
One in every five mammal species is threatened, including giants such as rhinos and elephants.

Plant life

From creeping mosses to majestic trees, there are plants growing all around us. They create most of the food that supports animal life on land. They also produce most of the oxygen that is in the air we breathe.

Plants are multicelled living things that mostly grow on land or in fresh water. Nearly all plants use the energy of sunlight to turn water and carbon dioxide into oxygen and sugar—a process called photosynthesis. They use the sugar to make the complex materials that form their roots, stems, and leaves. The most primitive types of plants can only grow close to the ground in damp places, but others grow tall and broad, covering the land with green vegetation that provides living space and vital food for animals.

Vital water

All plants need water. Most plants soak it up from the ground, then draw it up through their stems and use it to make sugar. Water pressure inside a soft-stemmed plant holds it up, so if it runs out of water, the plant wilts and collapses. But many plants have strong, woody stems that do not wilt, and their strength allows the biggest trees to spread their leaves high above ground level.

Types of plants

There are two main groups of plants. Nonvascular plants, such as mosses, were the first plants to evolve. Unlike vascular plants, they do not have internal vein systems that allow water and sap to flow all around the plant.

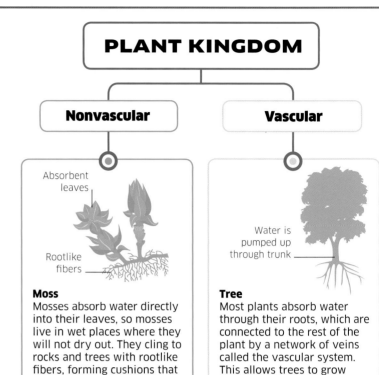

PLANT KINGDOM

Nonvascular

Absorbent leaves

Rootlike fibers

Moss

Mosses absorb water directly into their leaves, so mosses live in wet places where they will not dry out. They cling to rocks and trees with rootlike fibers, forming cushions that soak up water like sponges.

Vascular

Water is pumped up through trunk

Tree

Most plants absorb water through their roots, which are connected to the rest of the plant by a network of veins called the vascular system. This allows trees to grow high above the damp ground.

Flowering plants

Primitive plants, such as mosses and ferns, do not have flowers or seeds. These nonflowering plants are now far outnumbered by flowering plants, which evolved during the dinosaur era around 200 million years ago. Flowers produce pollen, which is carried to other flowers of the same species, fertilizing them so they form seeds.

Wind pollination

Some flowering plants such as grasses and many trees produce a lot of pollen that blows away on the wind. Some of it may land on plants of the same species, and pollinate (fertilize) their flowers. These plants have small, plain flowers.

Pollen

The tiny pollen grains contain the male cells that fertilize the female cells of nearby plants.

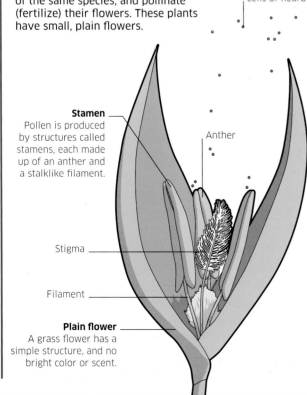

Stamen
Pollen is produced by structures called stamens, each made up of an anther and a stalklike filament.

Anther

Stigma

Filament

Plain flower
A grass flower has a simple structure, and no bright color or scent.

Petals
Brightly colored petals attract insects and birds. But the petals fade once the flower is fertilized.

Stigma
When pollen lands on the stigma, the male cells in the pollen grain fertilize the flower.

Anther is filled with pollen grains

Filament

Bee
Lured by color, scent, and the promise of sweet nectar, a bee picks up some of the pollen.

Style links stigma to ovary

Sepals
Tough green sepals protect the flower bud, splitting apart when the flower opens up.

Ovary
This contains egg cells, or ovules, which turn into seeds when they are fertilized by the pollen.

Animal pollination

Many plants have colorful, often fragrant flowers that contain sugary nectar. The nectar attracts hungry animals, such as hummingbirds, bats, or insects. As they drink the nectar, the animals get dusted with pollen, which they then carry directly to other flowers as they search for more nectar.

Green plants have existed on Earth for at least 400 million years.

379 ft (115.5 m)—the height of a California redwood tree, which makes it the tallest plant on Earth.

10 ft (3 m)—the height of the world's biggest flower—the Sumatran titan arum.

89

How plants grow

When the seed of a flowering plant is warm and moist enough, it sprouts and starts to grow into a seedling plant. A root pushes down into the soil to draw up water that fuels the growth of a stem. In many plants, the stem carries two leaves formed from the two halves of the seed.

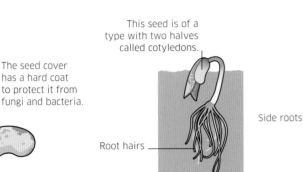
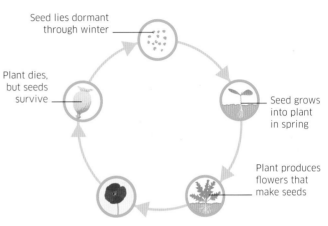

The leaves are the plant's food source.

The cotyledons become a pair of leaves.

Stem

This seed is of a type with two halves called cotyledons.

The seed cover has a hard coat to protect it from fungi and bacteria.

Side roots

Root hairs

1 Germination
A seed has a tough skin that protects it for many months or even years. But eventually, moisture makes the seed swell and split open.

2 Roots
The seed sprouts a root that grows downward. Fine hairs on the root absorb water and dissolved minerals from the soil.

3 Stem
A loop at the top of the shoot pushes up, pulling the two halves of the seed into the light. They become the plant's first pair of leaves.

Evergreen or deciduous

Many tropical plants grow all year round. But other plants must cope with cold winters that stop their growth and could kill them. Some survive by being very tough, but others have evolved ways of shutting down until the warm weather returns.

Evergreen trees
Many conifers, such as these firs, have tough, needle-shaped leaves that can survive freezing. They stay green all winter, so they are always ready to soak up solar energy and make food.

Deciduous trees
Oaks and similar trees have thin, very efficient leaves that make all the food that the tree needs in summer. In winter, the leaves fall off and new ones grow in spring.

Extraordinary plants

Most plants get nearly all their essential nutrients from the soil, stay rooted in one place, and harness the energy of sunlight to make food. But a few plants have evolved other ways of living in places where ordinary plants might struggle to survive.

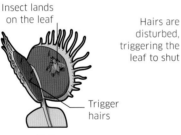

Insect lands on the leaf

Hairs are disturbed, triggering the leaf to shut

Trigger hairs

Venus flytrap
This amazing plant traps insects and digests them. Nutrients from the insect allow the plant to live in places where the soil is poor. When the plant finishes its meal a week later, the leaf opens up again to trap another insect.

Ferocactus
During floods, the cactus's hooked spines catch on floating debris that carries the plant to new places.

Thyme broomrape
This plant cannot make its own food. It lives by attaching its roots to thyme plants and stealing their sap.

Life cycle

Some plants live for many years, flowering every year. They are called perennials. Others, called annuals, live for one growing season and produce tough-skinned seeds that survive the hard times. Many of these short-lived plants grow in places that have very cold winters or scorching summers. Biennials live for two growing seasons, surviving the cold or dry season as energy-packed roots.

Seed lies dormant through winter

Plant dies, but seeds survive

Seed grows into plant in spring

Plant produces flowers that make seeds

Annual
A field poppy produces hundreds of seeds that lie in the ground all winter. In spring, they grow into new plants that flower and produce more seeds. Similar plants grow in deserts, where their seeds survive years of drought.

Seed sprouts to form new plant

Plant dies, but seeds survive

Plant stores sugary food in root

Plant grows flowers that make seeds

Plant lies dormant all winter

Root grows new foliage in spring

Biennial
Some plants have a two-year life cycle. A carrot seed grows and produces leaves that make food. It stores the food in a thick, juicy root that survives the cold winter. In spring, the root produces flowers that scatter seeds.

Oak seed (acorn) forms young tree

Oak tree may live for centuries

Mature tree is ready to flower

Tree loses its leaves in winter

Tree flowers and produces seeds

Perennial
These plants survive for many years, but may lose their leaves in cold or dry seasons. A mature oak tree produces flowers and seeds during each growing season, and the seeds grow into new young trees.

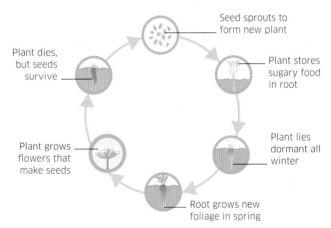

Green energy

Animals must find food, but green plants make their own using energy from sunlight to turn carbon dioxide and water into sugar. This process is called photosynthesis.

A plant's leaves act like solar panels. They soak up solar energy to fuel a chemical reaction that combines carbon, hydrogen, and oxygen to form glucose—a type of sugar. This reaction also releases oxygen into the air. The plant uses the glucose to make cellulose (plant fiber), and combines it with nutrients from the ground to make proteins that are used for growth.

Cross section through a leaf

Inside a leaf are thousands of microscopic cells that act as food factories. Each cell contains tiny structures called chloroplasts that are filled with green chlorophyll— a chemical that absorbs sunlight and turns it into the chemical energy needed for photosynthesis. Other cells form the skin of the leaf, while a network of transport vessels supply the leaf with water and carry away sugar in the form of sugary liquid sap.

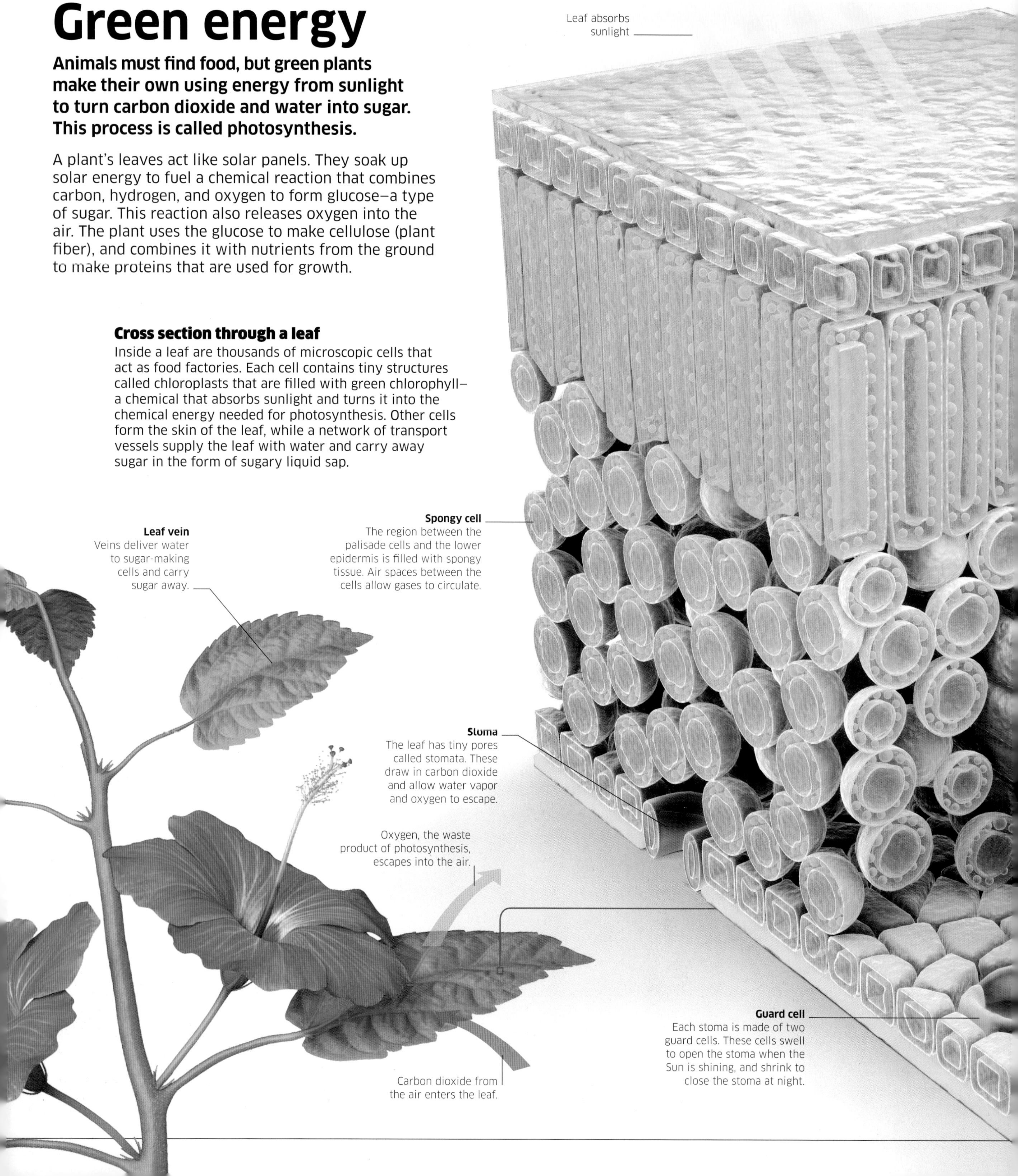

Leaf absorbs sunlight

Leaf vein
Veins deliver water to sugar-making cells and carry sugar away.

Spongy cell
The region between the palisade cells and the lower epidermis is filled with spongy tissue. Air spaces between the cells allow gases to circulate.

Stoma
The leaf has tiny pores called stomata. These draw in carbon dioxide and allow water vapor and oxygen to escape.

Oxygen, the waste product of photosynthesis, escapes into the air.

Carbon dioxide from the air enters the leaf.

Guard cell
Each stoma is made of two guard cells. These cells swell to open the stoma when the Sun is shining, and shrink to close the stoma at night.

The word **photosynthesis** means "putting together through light."

There are up to **500,000 chloroplasts** in every **square millimeter of leaf**.

All the food that **supports life in the oceans is made by tiny drifting algae** using **photosynthesis**.

91

Protective cuticle
A coating of transparent wax forms a waterproof layer on the upper side of the leaf.

Plants only look
green because of the green chlorophyll in their cells.

Upper epidermis
A thin layer of cells forms the upper skin. The cells produce the waxy cuticle that controls water loss by evaporation.

Palisade cell
These tall, cylindrical cells are the main food producers of the leaf. Each palisade cell is packed with chloroplasts that absorb solar energy and use it to make sugar.

Chloroplast
Small green structures called chloroplasts turn sunlight into chemical energy and use this to split water into hydrogen and oxygen. Then they combine the hydrogen with carbon dioxide to form glucose—the plant's food.

Vein
The veins transport liquids to all parts of the plant. Each vein is a bundle of tubular fibers made up of chains of long, hollow cells with walls of tough cellulose.

Lower epidermis
The skin and waxy cuticle of the underside is thinner because it does not face the Sun.

Xylem vessel
Some of the tubes within veins draw water up from the roots of the plant. This root sap contains the dissolved minerals that the plant needs to make proteins.

Phloem vessel
Sugar made in the leaves is dissolved in water and carried to other parts of the plant through the phloem vessels.

Water pathway
In daylight, the stomata in a plant's leaves open up and allow water vapor to escape. The water vapor is replaced by water drawn up though the xylem vessels from the plant stem and roots. This draws more water up from the soil, along with the dissolved minerals that the plant needs to build its tissues. This process is called transpiration.

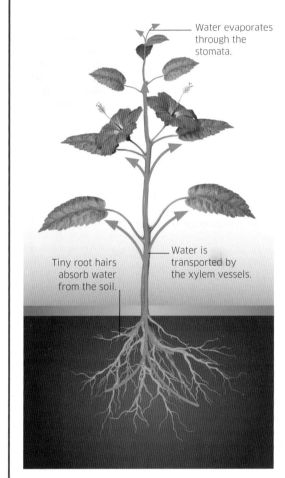

Water evaporates through the stomata.

Tiny root hairs absorb water from the soil.

Water is transported by the xylem vessels.

Oxygen factory
Photosynthesis by plants creates most of the food on Earth and nearly all the oxygen that we breathe. In a single year, one mature tree releases enough oxygen to support ten people.

O₂

NEARLY 40 PERCENT OF THE WORLD'S OXYGEN IS PRODUCED IN THE TROPICAL RAINFORESTS.

INVERTEBRATES

Most of the animals that live around us on land and in the oceans are invertebrates—animals that do not have backbones and jointed internal skeletons like ours. Many have tough external skeletons, while others have hard shells. But many more have soft, muscular bodies with no hard skeletal parts at all.

AMAZING VARIETY

Invertebrates come in every imaginable shape and size, from microscopic worms to giant squid. Some are familiar, like the insects that buzz around our homes, while others can seem like creatures from another planet.

Outnumbered

Most of the biggest, most visible animals on Earth are vertebrates, including humans. But the total number of vertebrate species is suprisingly tiny compared to the amazing diversity of invertebrate species.

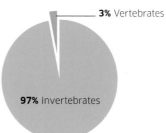

3% Vertebrates

97% Invertebrates

Invertebrate groups

The animal kingdom is divided into 35 major groups, each called a phylum, and each phylum is divided into classes. The vertebrates make up part of just one phylum. Here are a few of the many phyla and classes of invertebrates.

SPONGES
10,000 species
They may look like plants but sponges are the simplest animals of all—they don't even have a nervous system.

CNIDARIANS
11,000 species
Sea anemones, jellyfish, and corals like this one are all aquatic animals armed with stinging tentacles, which they use to catch prey.

ANNELID WORMS
20,000 species
This earthworm belongs to one of several groups of soft-bodied animals that we call worms.

CTENOPHORES
200 species
The comb jellies and their relatives are very simple animals that drift with the ocean currents.

MOLLUSKS
110,000 species
The clams, snails, and cephalopods (octopuses and relatives) form the second-largest group.

INSECTS
1.1 million species
This huge arthropod group outnumbers all the other animal species put together.

CRUSTACEANS
70,000 species
Crabs and other armored sea creatures with jointed legs are the most familiar crustaceans.

ECHINODERMS
7,000 species
Meaning "spiny skin," echinoderms include starfish, sea urchins, and sea cucumbers.

ARACHNIDS
103,000 species
Venomous scorpions, spiders, and their relatives form a class of land-living arthropods.

ARTHROPODS

The biggest invertebrate group consists of the arthropods. They include the insects, spiders and scorpions, and crustaceans. Adult arthropods have tough, jointed external skeletons or exoskeletons, several pairs of jointed legs, and—in the case of insects—wings.

Success story

Arthropods account for more than 80 percent of all known animal species. They are the most successful animals on Earth, conquering land, sea, and air. Scientists discover about 25 new arthropod species every day, and there are countless more waiting to be discovered.

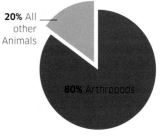

20% All other Animals

80% Arthropods

Inside out

The tough exoskeleton of an adult arthropod is made of chitin, which is similar to the substance that forms your fingernails. In some marine crustaceans such as this lobster, the chitin is reinforced with chalky minerals. Its exoskeleton is a series of rigid segments that enclose the animal's soft tissues. These are linked by thinner, flexible sections, forming joints that allow the animal's body and legs to move.

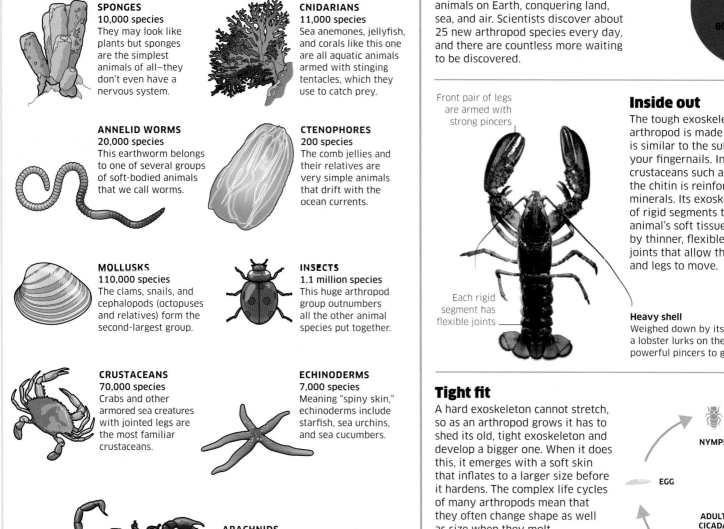

Front pair of legs are armed with strong pincers

Each rigid segment has flexible joints

Heavy shell
Weighed down by its armored exoskeleton, a lobster lurks on the seafloor, using its powerful pincers to grab prey.

Tight fit

A hard exoskeleton cannot stretch, so as an arthropod grows it has to shed its old, tight exoskeleton and develop a bigger one. When it does this, it emerges with a soft skin that inflates to a larger size before it hardens. The complex life cycles of many arthropods mean that they often change shape as well as size when they molt.

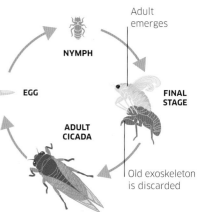

Adult emerges

NYMPH

FINAL STAGE

EGG

ADULT CICADA

Old exoskeleton is discarded

Cicada life cycle
Like many insects, a cicada hatches from its egg as a wingless larva, or nymph, that eventually becomes a winged adult.

TAKING ROOT

Although many invertebrates live on land, the most diverse types live underwater. This has allowed some to evolve a completely different way of life, because instead of having to go in search of food, they can wait for food to drift their way, carried by the water. They don't need legs or fins, and many never move at all. These invertebrates spend their entire adult lives rooted to one spot, more like plants than typical animals.

Snares and stings

Some marine invertebrates, such as sponges, mussels, and many clams, pump water through their bodies and strain it for edible particles. Others spread nets in the water to snare small animals. Sea anemones and corals have crowns of tentacles armed with venomous stinging cells that can even stun and kill small fish.

Deadly crown
The cylindrical body of this sea anemone is crowned with a lethal cluster of stinging tentacles.

Stinging
tentacles

Prey

Mouth

Stomach
cavity

Foot
sucker

MOST INVERTEBRATE ANIMALS ARE TINY, **BUT THE GIANT SQUID CAN GROW TO** AN AMAZING **59 FT (18 M) LONG,** INCLUDING ITS TENTACLES—THAT'S **AS LONG AS** **THREE** **ELEPHANTS.**

WONDERFUL FORMS

Many invertebrates such as insects have the familiar form of a head equipped with a brain and two eyes, attached to a body that has an equal number of legs and even wings on each side. But other invertebrates have a very different body plan.

Stars and suckers

An adult echinoderm such as a starfish has radial symmetry—its body parts are arranged like the spokes of a wheel. It has no head, and its mouth is in the middle of its body. An octopus or a squid has a strange body plan, with muscular, sucker-covered tentacles that sprout from its head and surround its mouth.

Fully armed
Found throughout the world's oceans, octopuses are intelligent animals. They use their strong, suckered tentacles to grasp prey.

Tentacles

Suckers

Protective shells

The soft bodies of many mollusks are protected by shells made from chalky minerals. Snails and similar animals have one shell, while bivalves such as clams have two.

As the animals grow, they add extra layers of minerals to their shells, so the shells grow too. They are often lined with a beautiful, iridescent layer called mother-of-pearl.

CONCH

COWRIE

SCALLOP

LIVING TOGETHER

Many marine invertebrates that spend their lives rooted to one spot live together in large groups known as colonies. Often these are individual animals that settle in the same place because it is an ideal habitat. But other colonial invertebrates are linked to each other, like the twigs of a tree. They share the same body fluid circulation, but each has its own mouth and digestive system.

Mussel colony

These mussels have all settled on this rocky tidal shore because there is so much food for them to eat when they are submerged at high tide. They are not linked to each other—they just need the same conditions to survive.

Underwater garden
Reef corals grow in warm, clear sunlit water on shallow tropical shores, just below the low tide line.

Holding tight
Attached to the rocks by strong threads, mussels close their shells at low tide to avoid drying out.

Reef corals

Each head of coral on this reef is a colony of interlinked animals called coral polyps. They are like tiny sea anemones that feed for themselves, but together they form the distinctive structure of a particular coral species.

Drifting colonies

Some colonial invertebrates look like individual animals, such as the amazing Portuguese man-of-war. It looks like a jellyfish, but it is actually a collection of interconnected animals, each with its own function. One is the float, while others gather food, defend the colony, or produce young.

Stinging tentacles
The Portuguese man-of-war drifts on the ocean surface, trailing long venomous tentacles to ensnare its prey.

Insects

Both in terms of species and sheer numbers, insects outnumber all other animals on Earth. They are the most plentiful creatures on the planet.

More than a million different species of insects have been scientifically named and described, and thousands more are discovered every year. Thanks to their amazing adaptations, they flourish in every land habitat and play a key role in the global ecosystem, recycling dead plants and animals, pollinating flowering plants, and providing food for a host of bigger animals. In fact, insects are so vital to life on Earth that we could not survive without them.

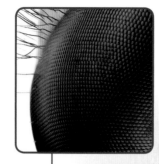

Compound vision
The eyes of adult insects are made up of thousands of tiny lenses, each with its own set of light sensors. Every lens sees a dot of color, and the dots add up to form a mosaic image. The more lenses, the more detail the insects see. This system is very sensitive to movement.

Sensitive bristles
Many fine, touch sensitive bristles on the insect's body help to detect air movement.

Antennae
The long antennae are covered in nerve endings that detect chemical signals. Some insects can pick up scents from more than 1 mile (1.6 km) away.

Head
An insect's head is a strong capsule containing its brain and carrying most of its sense organs. It swivels on a very mobile neck joint.

Insect anatomy

Insects are the most numerous of the arthropods–animals with tough external skeletons and jointed legs. The bodies of all adult insects are divided into three sections–the head, thorax, and segmented abdomen. All adult insects have six legs, and most have one or two pairs of wings. But their young, or larvae, are much more variable.

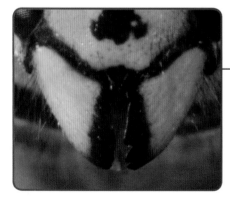

Jaws
This wasp has biting jaws, or mandibles, that pinch together. They have hard, sharp edges that allow the wasp to cut and mash up its prey. Many insects have similar jaws, but the mouthparts of others are highly modified for soaking up liquids, sipping nectar, and even sucking blood.

Claws
Each foot has sharp claws for clinging to surfaces and holding onto prey. Some insects such as blow flies also have sticky foot pads.

Thorax
The central section of an insect's body is called the thorax. It carries the legs and wings, and in most insects it is packed with powerful wing muscles.

Waist
Wasps need to curl their tails forward to use their stingers, so they have narrow, flexible waists.

Legs
Each insect leg is made up of a series of stiff tubes, hinged together with flexible joints and operated by internal muscles.

The **first winged insects** appeared more than 350 million years ago.

A big **dragonfly** may have up to 30,000 tiny lenses in each **eye**.

1,046 The **number of beats** a second a midge flaps its wings.

95

Wings
Most adult insects have wings. These are flat plates of chitin—the tough material that encases the body. They are powered by muscles inside the thorax.

Veins
A network of fine tubes called veins stiffens the wings so they can flex and twist in flight without collapsing under the strain.

Warning pattern
Vivid, contrasting stripes of black and yellow warn birds that this wasp has a stinger in its tail, and help the wasp stay out of trouble.

Abdomen
The segmented, flexible abdomen contains most of an insect's vital organs, such as its stomach.

73 **The percentage of all known animal species that are insects—and** almost half of them are beetles.

Painful sting
Most insects are harmless, but this wasp has a stinger that it uses to kill prey or defend itself and its nest.

Features

Adult insects are very variable in shape and size, but nearly all of them share a few key features.

MOST HAVE WINGS

COMPOUND EYES

EXOSKELETON

THREE BODY SEGMENTS

SIX JOINTED LEGS

Looking at insects

Insects have been classified into about 29 orders, and within each order the insects share the same features. Shown below are some of the major orders.

Dragonflies and damselflies
5,600 species
Large eyes and wings, and slender bodies.

Beetles
370,000 species
Toughened front wings that help protect the hind wings.

Butterflies and moths
165,000 species
Nectar-feeding mouthparts, and overlapping scales on their bodies and wings.

True bugs
88,000 species
Two pairs of wings and long mouthparts that pierce and suck.

Flies
150,000 species
Single pair of functional wings, with small balancing organs called halteres.

Crickets and grasshoppers
25,000 species
Powerful hind legs and chewing mouthparts.

Ants, bees, and wasps
198,000 species
Have narrow waists and many live in colonies.

FOR EVERY HUMAN BEING ON THE PLANET THERE ARE 200 MILLION INSECTS.

The old skin is
bunched up, hiding
the silk pad.

The butterfly is now
fully formed inside its
transparent chrysalis.

The caterpillar
spins a silk pad,
glues it to a twig,
and clings on with
the tiny claws of
its hind legs.

The green chrysalis
is well camouflaged
amid the leaves.

The butterfly's head
is visible at the lower
end of the chrysalis.

4 New skin
A few hours
after attaching
itself to its twig, the
caterpillar sheds its
skin again—but this
time the striped skin is
pushed off to reveal a
bright green chrysalis.

5 Chrysalis
Eventually, the
new chrysalis pushes its
old skin right up to the
top. After reattaching
itself to its silk pad with
a thin black stem, it
wriggles until the old
skin falls away.

6 Metamorphosis
Once the chrysalis is
free of its old skin it gets
shorter, smoother, and
its color changes to a
duller green. Inside, its
body is being completely
rebuilt to become an
adult butterfly.

7 Taking shape
After nine or ten
days, the chrysalis
darkens as the skin of
the butterfly's body
turns black. The vivid
black and orange
pattern of the wings
also becomes visible.

3 Firm grip
After about 14
days, the fully grown
caterpillar crawls up a
twig and attaches itself
by its stumpy back
legs, hanging from
a pad of strong silk.

The butterfly attaches
an egg on the shady
underside of a leaf.

2 Growing caterpillar
The caterpillar spends
its days eating, growing bigger
all the time, and shedding its
skin five times. Toxins in
the milkweed leaf become
concentrated in its body
as it eats, making it
poisonous to birds.

Milkweed plant
Like many butterflies, the
monarch lays its eggs on just
one type of plant—milkweed.
Its caterpillar eats this until
it is ready to become an adult.

Wasplike stripes
warn birds that the
toxic caterpillar is
dangerous to eat.

The strong jaws chew
through the leaf.

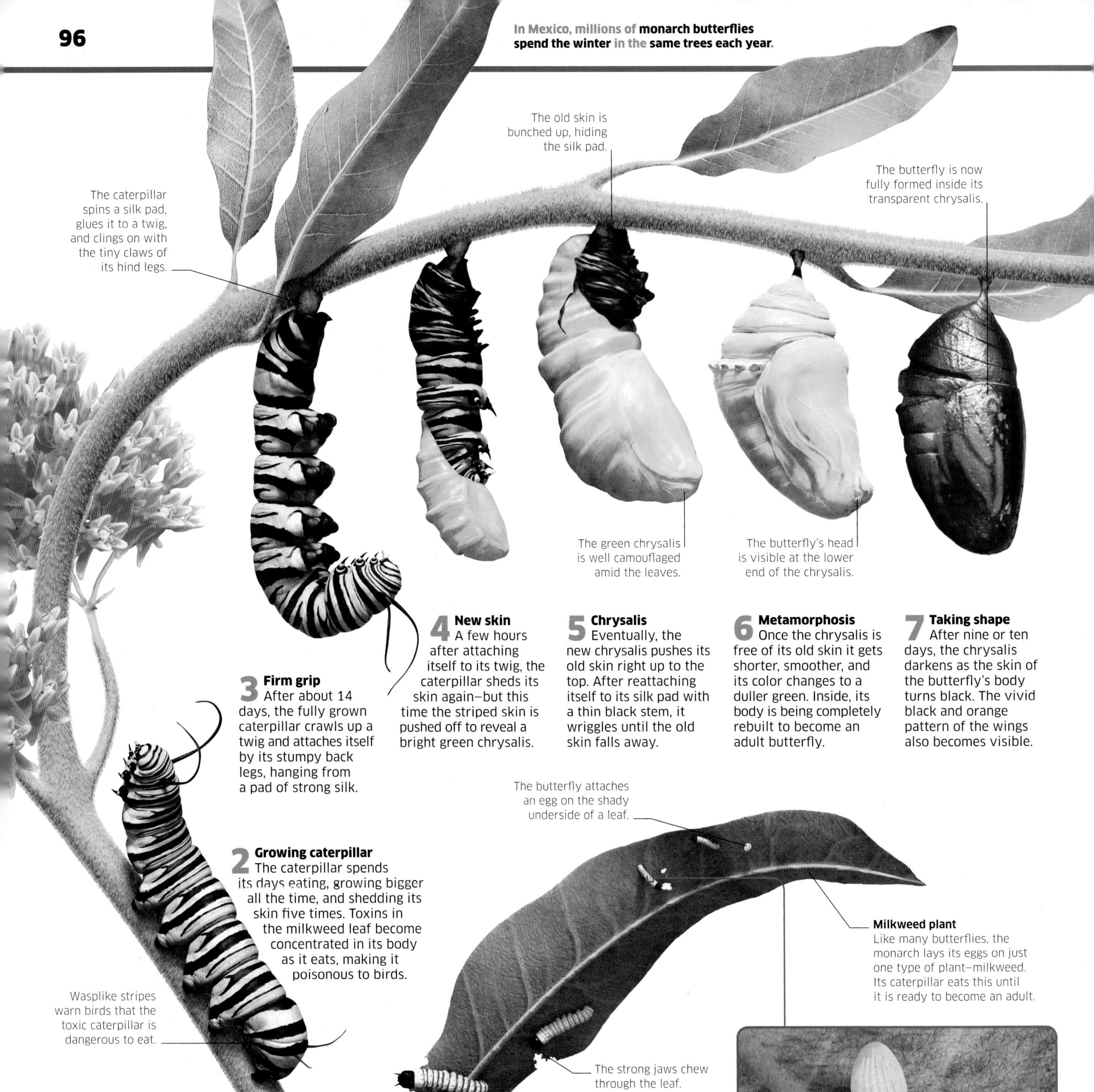

From egg
to butterfly
The metamorphosis
from newly laid egg to
adult monarch butterfly
takes about a month. The egg
hatches as a tiny caterpillar
that eats voraciously for two
weeks, bulking up its body until
it is big enough for the pupa
stage—the ten days that see
it turned into a butterfly.

1 Larva
The female butterfly
lays her tiny pale green
eggs on milkweed plants.
Each egg is the size of a
pinhead, with a beautifully
sculpted shell. Several days
later, the egg develops into
a baby caterpillar that
chews its way out, then
eats the shell before it
starts feeding on the leaf.

20,000 The **number of butterfly species** that live **worldwide**.

3,000 miles (4,800 km)—the **distance** that some **monarchs migrate**.

50 million—the **number of years** that **butterflies** have **existed on Earth**.

97

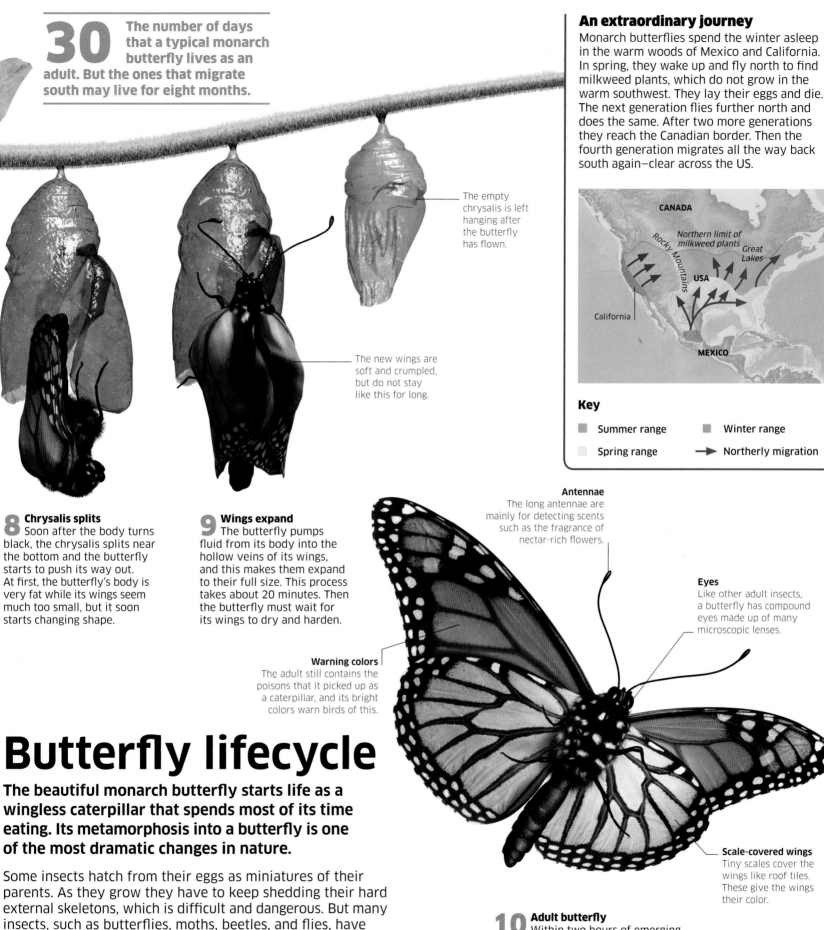

30 The number of days that a typical monarch butterfly lives as an adult. But the ones that migrate south may live for eight months.

The empty chrysalis is left hanging after the butterfly has flown.

The new wings are soft and crumpled, but do not stay like this for long.

An extraordinary journey

Monarch butterflies spend the winter asleep in the warm woods of Mexico and California. In spring, they wake up and fly north to find milkweed plants, which do not grow in the warm southwest. They lay their eggs and die. The next generation flies further north and does the same. After two more generations they reach the Canadian border. Then the fourth generation migrates all the way back south again—clear across the US.

CANADA

Northern limit of milkweed plants

Rocky Mountains

Great Lakes

USA

California

MEXICO

Key

◼ Summer range

◼ Winter range

◼ Spring range

→ Northerly migration

8 Chrysalis splits
Soon after the body turns black, the chrysalis splits near the bottom and the butterfly starts to push its way out. At first, the butterfly's body is very fat while its wings seem much too small, but it soon starts changing shape.

9 Wings expand
The butterfly pumps fluid from its body into the hollow veins of its wings, and this makes them expand to their full size. This process takes about 20 minutes. Then the butterfly must wait for its wings to dry and harden.

Antennae
The long antennae are mainly for detecting scents such as the fragrance of nectar-rich flowers.

Eyes
Like other adult insects, a butterfly has compound eyes made up of many microscopic lenses.

Warning colors
The adult still contains the poisons that it picked up as a caterpillar, and its bright colors warn birds of this.

Butterfly lifecycle

The beautiful monarch butterfly starts life as a wingless caterpillar that spends most of its time eating. Its metamorphosis into a butterfly is one of the most dramatic changes in nature.

Some insects hatch from their eggs as miniatures of their parents. As they grow they have to keep shedding their hard external skeletons, which is difficult and dangerous. But many insects, such as butterflies, moths, beetles, and flies, have evolved a better solution. They do all their growing during a stage of life called a larva—a sausage-shaped creature that can shed its skin easily. When the larva is fully grown, it enters a phase called a pupa, or chrysalis in butterflies. During this stage it is transformed into a winged adult.

Scale-covered wings
Tiny scales cover the wings like roof tiles. These give the wings their color.

10 Adult butterfly
Within two hours of emerging, the butterfly is ready for its first flight. It flexes its wings a few times before launching itself into the air. It will find some sweet nectar to drink, then start looking for a mate so it can breed and create a new generation of caterpillars.

VERTEBRATES

Most of the more obvious animals that live around us are vertebrates—animals with flexible backbones and internal skeletons. They are the mammals (which include humans), birds, reptiles, amphibians, and three types of fish. Compared to the immense diversity of animal life in general, there are relatively few species of vertebrates, but they include the biggest animals now living on land and in the oceans, as well as the largest that have ever lived—the giant dinosaurs.

THREE PERCENT

Scientists classify animal life in 31 major groups, each called a phylum. Just one of these phyla—the Chordata—contains all the vertebrates, which add up to only 3 percent of all the animal species known to science. However, most of the other 97 percent of species, the invertebrates, are very small by comparison, so they can survive in far less living space than is needed by a typical vertebrate.

Vertebrate groups

We generally think of the vertebrates as divided into five main types of animals—mammals, birds, reptiles, amphibians, and fish. But the fish actually consist of three very different groups of animals that happen to live underwater, breathe with gills, and have similar body forms with fins rather than legs. So scientists classify the vertebrates into seven main groups. These make up the vast majority of the phylum Chordata—animals with a spinal nerve cord reinforced by a tough, flexible rod called a notochord. In most vertebrates, the notochord is replaced by a bony spine at a very early stage in the animal's life.

BODY PLAN

Apart from a few primitive jawless fish, all vertebrates have flexible spines made of chains of small bones called vertebrae. They also have strong skulls. Fish have other skeletal elements that support their gills and stiffen their fins. All other vertebrates—even snakes and whales—have evolved from ancestors that were the first four-legged land vertebrates, or tetrapods.

Tetrapods

Modern lungfish and coelacanths belong to an ancient group of fish equipped with four fleshy fins supported by strong bones. About 380 million years ago, some of these lobe-finned fish were living in freshwater swamps, where they started using their fins as legs. Eventually, they crawled right out of the water to become the earliest amphibians.

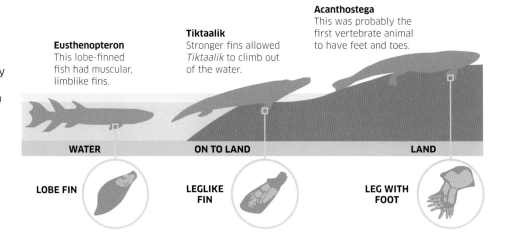

Eusthenopteron
This lobe-finned fish had muscular, limblike fins.

Tiktaalik
Stronger fins allowed *Tiktaalik* to climb out of the water.

Acanthostega
This was probably the first vertebrate animal to have feet and toes.

WATER ON TO LAND LAND

LOBE FIN LEGLIKE FIN LEG WITH FOOT

SUPER-SIZED ANIMALS

All the biggest animals that have ever lived are, or were, vertebrates. This is largely because the strong internal skeleton allows a very heavy creature to support its own weight. Some extinct dinosaurs such as *Argentinosaurus* were probably as heavy as is possible for a land animal. The only known vertebrate that weighs more is the blue whale, which relies on the water for support.

In the lineup
Apart from whales, the largest living vertebrates include the sharks, elephants, hippos, giraffes, bears, and big cats. But these animals would have been dwarfed by some of the dinosaurs that lived in the distant past.

A blue whale can be 98 ft (30 m) long.

The whale shark lives in tropical oceans.

DIPLODOCUS
One of the largest dinosaurs, this 115 ft (35 m) giant was a plant eater. It lived during the Jurassic Period, about 150 million years ago.

BLUE WHALE
This is probably the heaviest animal that has ever existed—weighing anything up to 170 tons. Its heart alone is the size of a small car.

WHALE SHARK
This is the biggest fish in the sea, growing to 39 ft (12 m) long. Although a shark, it feeds on tiny shrimplike creatures and small fish.

GIRAFFE
Its incredibly long neck gives the giraffe a total height of up to 20 ft (6 m). It towers above all other animals—even elephants.

JAWLESS FISH
43 species
Eel-like lampreys do not have bony jaws, and resemble the first vertebrates that evolved.

CARTILAGINOUS FISH
1,200 species
Rays and sharks have skeletons made of flexible cartilage instead of true bone.

BONY FISH
32,300 species
These fish, which include types such as salmon and herring, have skeletons of hard bone.

AMPHIBIANS
6,650 species
Frogs, salamanders, and newts have thin, moist skins and often breed in fresh water.

MAMMALS
5,400 species
Warm-blooded and usually furry or hairy, mammals are vertebrates that feed their young on milk.

REPTILES
9,400 species
These cold-blooded vertebrates have dry, scaly skins. They include crocodiles, lizards, and snakes.

BIRDS
10,200 species
Adapted for flight, birds are warm-blooded, feathered vertebrates that evolved from nonflying dinosaurs.

9% Mammals
19% Birds
48% Fish
15% Reptiles
9% Amphibians

The breakdown
About 64,000 vertebrate species have been scientifically named and described. Around half of these species are various types of fish.

Internal skeletons
The body of a fish such as a shark is supported by the water, so it does not need a weight-bearing skeleton. Its main function is to protect and support delicate organs like the brain and gills, and anchor the muscles. But the skeleton of a land vertebrate such as a dog has to support the weight of the animal, so its bones—especially its leg bones—must be much stronger than those of a fish.

The gills are supported by arches of tough cartilage.

The skeleton serves mainly to anchor the shark's muscles.

The pectoral fin has the strongest skeleton.

Strong bones form the skull and jaws.

The bones of the spine protect the dog's spinal cord.

The ribcage surrounds the dog's heart and lungs.

The leg bones are moved by strong skeletal muscles.

Shark
A shark does not need to support its weight with its fins, so it can have a skeleton of flexible cartilage—the material that stiffens our ears. The "bones" of some fins are not even attached to its spine.

Dog
All the bones of a dog's body are linked to form a strong, weight-bearing skeleton. Other bones protect the dog's vital organs.

DIPLODOCUS REMAINS
INDICATE THAT IT WAS UP TO
118 FT (36 M) LONG—
THIS IS THE LENGTH OF
THREE SCHOOL BUSES.

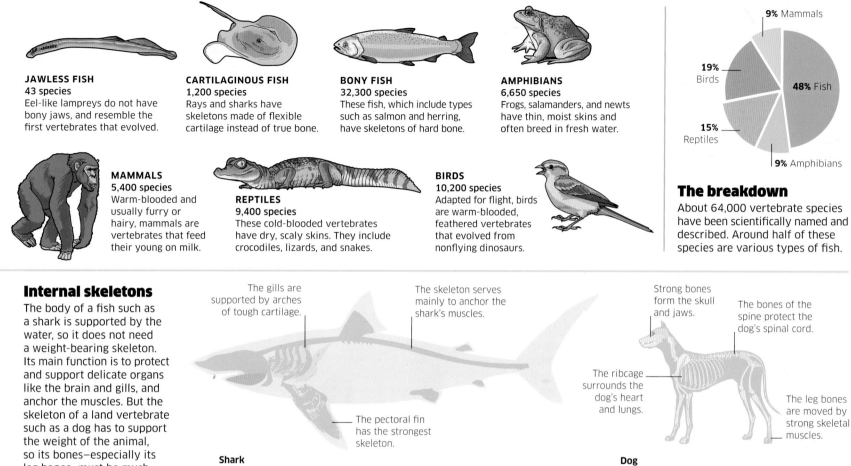

The neck and tail of *Diplodocus* made up most of its immense length.

The only bear that lives by hunting, the polar bear can kill a seal with a swipe of its paw.

Notorious for its bad temper, the hippo is one of the most dangerous African animals.

Most of the surviving tigers live in India, with others in Southeast Asia and eastern Siberia.

AFRICAN ELEPHANT
A big male African elephant can weigh 11 tons, making it the largest living land animal—but smaller than many dinosaurs.

POLAR BEAR
The massively built polar bear is the most powerful carnivorous land mammal, with big males weighing up to 1,500 lb (700 kg).

HIPPOPOTAMUS
One of the largest and heaviest land mammals, the hippo can weigh up to 3 tons. Its closest living relatives are whales.

TIGER
The biggest of all cats, the tiger can grow to 11 ft (3.3 m) long from head to tail. It is a formidable predator, but now very rare.

100 nature ○ VERTEBRATES

Fish have been found living in the deepest parts of the ocean, 7 miles (11 km) below the waves.

Fish

The first vertebrates, or animals with backbones, to evolve were fish. They now make up about half of all vertebrate species, and include many of the most spectacular animals on the planet.

Fish are vertebrates that have always lived underwater, since the evolution of their earliest ancestors around 530 million years ago. Other vertebrates, including whales and seals, also live in the water, but they must breathe air and they have many other features that show their ancestors were land animals. By contrast, a fish's skeleton, internal organs, gills, skin, muscles, and senses are specialized for aquatic life, and they are amazingly efficient.

Key features

Although fish vary greatly in their size, shape, and habits—and even in their basic biology nearly all species of fish share some key features.

VERTEBRATES

SCALY SKIN

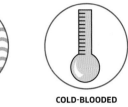

BREATHE WITH GILLS

LIVE IN WATER

COLD-BLOODED

Types of fish

The term "fish" covers three groups of very different, unrelated animals that share the same aquatic habitat and have many of the same adaptations to it. These are the few surviving species of jawless fish, the bony fish such as tuna (which form by far the biggest group), and the cartilaginous fish such as sharks.

Jawless fish
The earliest fish to evolve had muscular mouths with no jawbones. There were many types, but today the jawless fish are reduced to around 43 species of lampreys, which have suckerlike mouths lined with rasping teeth.

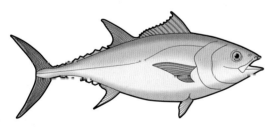

Bony fish
There are at least 32,300 species of fish with skeletons made of hard bone. They include a wide range of body forms—such as eels, flatfish, and seahorses—but most have the streamlined shape of this bluefin tuna.

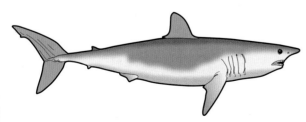

Cartilaginous fish
The 1,200 species of sharks, rays, and chimaeras have skeletons made of flexible cartilage—the same kind of tissue that supports our ears. Many sharks, including this shortfin mako, are highly efficient predators.

Inside a fish

Almost all fish spend their entire lives underwater and extract vital oxygen from the water using gills. Their bodies are supported by the water, so the main function of their muscles and skeleton is movement. Their fins help them swim and steer, and the bodies of typical fish are streamlined so that they use as little energy as possible as they move through the water.

Swim bladder
A bony fish has a gas-filled swim bladder that acts as a float. The fish can rise or sink in the water by adding or removing gas. Sharks and other cartilaginous fish do not have a swim bladder.

Kidney

Eyes
These are specially adapted to suit the way light passes through water.

Brain

Gills
Blood flowing through the delicate, thin-walled gills absorbs oxygen from the water and discards carbon dioxide as waste. Water flows into the fish's mouth, then through the gills and out through a flap or slits at the back of the head.

Heart

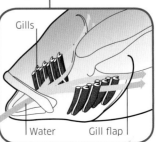

Gills

Water   Gill flap

Stomach

Pelvic fins
This type of fish has two sets of paired fins—pectoral fins near the gills (not shown) and pelvic fins midway along the body. The fish uses them for steering.

9 million—the number of **eggs a female cod** can **produce in a year**, but only a tiny fraction survive.

Flying fish can shoot **out of the water** and glide for **160 ft (50 m)** on **winglike fins**.

68 mph (110 kph) the **top speed** of an **Atlantic sailfish**, as fast as a speedboat.

101

How fish swim

Typical fish swim by flexing their bodies in a series of waves that push against the water. Long-bodied eels wriggle like snakes, but with other fish most of the movement is near the tail. Rays use a different method, "flying" through the water with their winglike pectoral fins. Many small fish swim with their body fins, using them like oars.

S-shaped swimmers

Most fish propel themselves through the water by using their big flank muscles to flex their bodies into "S" shapes. The tail fin makes their swimming more efficient.

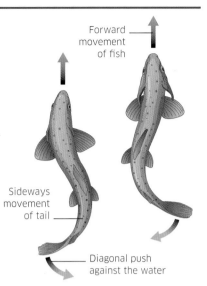

Forward movement of fish

Sideways movement of tail

Diagonal push against the water

Tail fins

Fish tails come in many shapes and sizes. Most sharks have tails with extra-long upper lobes that act as extensions of their flexing bodies. The tail of a typical bony fish, such as a trout, is a symmetrical fan. Tuna and some other fast-swimming fish have tall, narrow, crescent-shaped tails, while the tails of ambush hunters, such as pike, are much broader.

Shark
The extended upper tail is good for steady, long-distance swimming.

Trout
This type of tail helps the fish maneuver in tight spaces.

Tuna
The tuna's slender tail is adapted to sustain high-speed swimming.

Pike
The tail of a pike has a large surface area for bursts of acceleration.

Front dorsal fin
This fish has two dorsal fins, which give stability and help the fish to swim straight. The front fin is spiny for defense.

Lateral line
A fish is able to detect pressure changes in the water around it using a network of sensors called the lateral line. The sensors alert the fish to movements and obstacles in the water and help them to swim close by in schools.

Lateral line

Second dorsal fin

Scales
The fish's delicate skin is protected by tough scales. Each scale is separate, but the scales overlap like tiles on a roof to allow movement.

Intestine

Anal fin
This provides stability as the fish swims.

Skeleton
The skeleton is based on a long, flexible spine with slender ribs projecting from it. Separate bones support the fins and form the fish's skull and jaws.

Flank muscles
Big muscles on each side of the fish's flexible backbone contract to flex its body and power the tail fin, propelling the fish through the water.

Tail fin
The fish sweeps the paddle-shaped tail fin from side to side to drive its body forward through the water.

Eggs and young

Most fish lay hundreds, thousands, or even millions of eggs, spilling them into open water where they drift on the currents. But others lay fewer eggs in secure nests, or even keep them in their bodies. Some fish, including many sharks, give birth to fully formed young.

Safe nursery
After fertilizing the eggs laid by the female, the male gold-specs jawfish gathers them into his mouth and keeps them there until they hatch. This protects the eggs from animals that would otherwise eat them.

Ready to go
Some sharks lay eggs that are secured to coral or seaweed, and the young continue to develop inside their tough-skinned protective egg cases. Others give birth to live young that are already fully developed, such as this lemon shark.

Great white shark

**The most terrifying predator on the planet, the great
white shark combines almost supernatural senses with
a set of teeth that can slice through prey like a chainsaw.**

Most sharks are efficient hunters, but the great white is in a class
of its own. It is much bigger than any other killer shark and far more
powerful. The great white's super-efficient propulsion system drives
it through the water at shattering speed as it charges in for the attack,
and its array of senses enable the shark to target its prey in complete
darkness with deadly accuracy. The shark's broad, razor-edged teeth
are specially adapted for butchering large prey, rather than simply
swallowing small victims whole. Even a single bite can be lethal.

300

The number of teeth that line
the jaws of the great white
shark. Since the teeth are
always being replaced, it may go through
30,000 of them over its entire lifetime.

Backbone
The shark's spine consists
of a long, flexible chain of
vertebrae, made of cartilage
like the rest of its skeleton.

Liver
Occupying almost a quarter
of the shark's body is the liver.
It is rich in oil, which is lighter
than water, and this provides
the shark with buoyancy to
help keep it from sinking.

Lateral line
A line of sensors extending from
head to tail picks up vibrations and
changes in water pressure. It allows
the shark to sense nearby objects
and movements in the water.

Skeleton
As with all sharks and
rays, the skeleton is
made of tough yet
flexible cartilage. This
weighs less than bone
and makes the shark
more agile in the water.

Pelvic fin

Tail (caudal) fin
The tall, crescent-shaped tail
is linked to the body by a
slim, flexible joint, more like
that of a fast-swimming tuna
than a typical shark. It is this
tall tail fin that propels the
shark through the water.

Tail muscle
The tail is driven by two
types of muscle—special
high-stamina red muscle for
steady cruising all day, and
powerful white muscle for
brief, high-speed attacks.

Intestine
The intestine is short,
but food has to pass
around an internal spiral,
slowing its passage for
better digestion.

Built for speed

A typical shark swims by flexing the whole rear part of
its body, but the great white is different. Its body stays
rigid like a torpedo, while its massive flank muscles
drive rapid, powerful strokes of its tail fin—a far more
efficient system. Its body is the ideal shape for slicing
through the water at high speed—broad in the middle
and pointed at each end—and this gives it the ability
to overtake virtually any other fish in the sea.

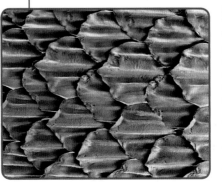

Scales
The shark's skin is studded
with millions of tiny, toothlike,
sharp-edged scales called dermal
denticles. These are covered in
enamel—the same substance that
covers our teeth. The scales not
only act as a flexible coat of
protective armor, but they help
the shark swim efficiently—the
overlapping scales alter the way
the water flows over the shark's
skin, reducing the drag that
makes swimming hard work.

The slightest **movement** made by prey **up to 820 ft (250 m) away** can be **detected** by the great white.

After a **big meal**, a great white can go **without food** for up to **two months**.

3 in (7.5 cm)—the **length** of a mature great white **shark tooth**.

103

Dorsal fin
The tall, pointed dorsal fin helps keep the shark upright and on track as it swims. It is covered with skin and supported by a strong internal skeleton.

Gill arches
Five gill arches on each side support and protect the delicate gills that absorb vital oxygen from the water and release waste carbon dioxide.

Vision
The shark's eyes have internal reflectors like a cat's eyes, increasing their sensitivity to make the most of dim underwater light.

Special sense
All the shark's senses are highly tuned. Most amazing of all is its ability to detect the minute electrical impulses generated by the muscles of other animals. It picks these up with a network of sensors in pores on its snout called the ampullae of Lorenzini—first described by Italian physician Stefano Lorenzini in 1678.

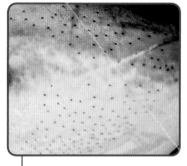

Nostrils
Just below the snout are the super-sensitive nostrils that enable the great white to detect a single drop of blood floating in 10 billion drops of water.

Pectoral fins
The long pectoral fins help with stability and act like wings as the shark swims forward, stopping it from sinking.

Heart
This is heavier than the heart of a typical shark, with thicker muscle to pump blood around the body more efficiently.

Serrated teeth
Each triangular tooth has a serrated knife edge, ideal for shearing through the tough skin, flesh, and bone of the shark's favorite prey—warm-blooded marine mammals such as seals. The great white has up to seven rows of teeth.

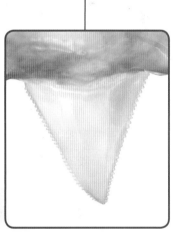

Fact file
Length .... Up to 23 ft (7 m)
Top speed .... 32 mph (50 kph)
Lifespan .... Over 30 years
Prey .... Fish, turtles, and sea mammals

A GREAT WHITE SHARK SOMETIMES RAISES ITS HEAD OUT OF THE WATER TO LOOK AROUND FOR LIKELY PREY.

Lethal jaws
The shark's upper jawbone is only loosely attached to its skull. When it opens its mouth, ready to bite, the jaw pushes forward while the snout bends up out of the way to ensure that it gets a good grip. As its jaws snap shut, the shark jerks its head sideways so its teeth rip through its victim like a saw, slicing out a great mouthful of flesh.

The snout bends back.

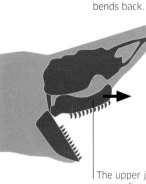

The upper jaw moves forward.

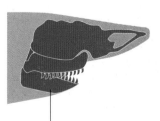

The jaws snap shut upon impact.

Amphibians

Amphibians are best known for the way that many species spend part of their lives in water and part on land. Indeed, the word amphibian means "double life."

Early amphibians were the first vertebrates (animals with backbones) to live on land. They evolved from fish that had developed the ability to breathe air, and they have retained a few key features of their aquatic ancestors. In particular, amphibian eggs do not have tough shells to stop them from drying out, so they usually have to be laid in water. The eggs hatch as aquatic larvae, which eventually turn into air-breathing adults.

Key features

Amphibians have evolved an amazing variety of adaptations to help them survive on land, making them the most diverse group of land vertebrates. Despite this, nearly all amphibians share some key features that have a big influence on their way of life.

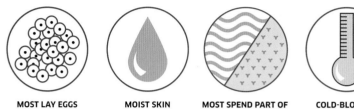

MOST LAY EGGS

MOIST SKIN

MOST SPEND PART OF LIFECYCLE IN WATER

COLD-BLOODED

Types of amphibians

There are three groups of amphibians. The biggest and most familiar group consists of the frogs and toads, which have long hind legs specialized for leaping. The second group includes the salamanders and newts, with their long tails and short legs. The third consists of the legless, burrowing caecilians.

Frogs and toads
5,900 species
Tailless, long-legged frogs and toads live in water, on the ground, and in trees. Most frogs have smoother, shinier skin than toads, but there is no scientific difference between them.

Salamanders and newts
585 species
With their long tails and short legs, there is no real difference between newts and salamanders. Many live entirely on land, while others migrate to water to breed. A few live entirely in water.

Caecilians
190 species
Most of these tropical animals spend their lives under the ground. Legless and almost blind, they have strong skulls to push through soil, and tough skin to protect their bodies from sharp stones.

Evolution

Amphibians evolved from a group of fish with fleshy, leglike fins. These included the ancestors of modern, air-breathing lungfish. Around 380 million years ago, some of these lobe-finned fish began hunting small animals on land. Their descendants have changed into the modern amphibians of today.

Early amphibian
There were many types of amphibians in existence 280 million years ago, including this species, *Diplocaulus*—a four-legged, newtlike animal with a flattened head.

What's inside?

All amphibians are basically four-limbed (tetrapod) vertebrates but, like other animals, they have evolved many different body forms. Salamanders and newts still have the long-tailed, short-legged form of their distant ancestors, but the legless caecilians and leaping frogs are much more specialized.

Eye sockets
These big gaps contain the enormous eyes that frogs use for hunting.

Skull
The broad skull gives the frog a huge mouth, allowing it to swallow its prey in one gulp.

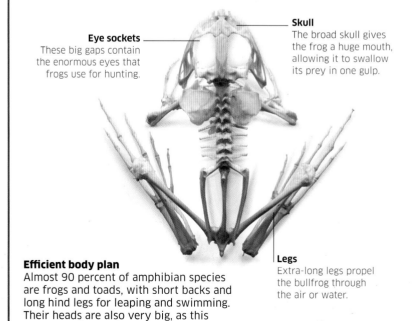

Efficient body plan
Almost 90 percent of amphibian species are frogs and toads, with short backs and long hind legs for leaping and swimming. Their heads are also very big, as this American bullfrog skeleton shows.

Legs
Extra-long legs propel the bullfrog through the air or water.

SOME AMPHIBIANS LAY UP TO 50,000 EGGS EVERY BREEDING SEASON, BUT ONLY A FEW OF THEIR YOUNG SURVIVE LONG ENOUGH TO BREED IN TURN.

Newts have the incredible ability to replace missing limbs and even damaged heart muscle.

The glass frog has almost no color in its skin. It is almost transparent, so you can see its internal organs.

The skin of the golden poison dart frog contains enough poison to kill up to 20 people.

105

Vital oxygen

Like all animals, amphibians need to breathe by taking in oxygen and expelling waste carbon dioxide. The young of many amphibians live in water, and use fishlike gills to take in oxygen. Some aquatic amphibians retain these gills throughout their adult lives, but most species develop lungs for breathing air. Amphibians can also exchange gases through their very thin, moist skin.

By breathing through its skin, the common frog can spend the entire winter asleep underwater.

The gills have very thin skin, allowing oxygen and carbon dioxide to pass through easily.

Gills
The axolotl is a Mexican salamander that lives underwater as an adult. Its feathery gills contain blood, which absorbs oxygen from the water.

The toad's lungs are air-filled bags lined with blood vessels.

Lungs
The toad tadpole has gills to breathe but develops a pair of lungs as it turns into an adult. The toad pumps air into them using its muscular throat.

A newt's breathable skin allows it to live underwater.

Skin
All amphibians, like this newt, gather oxygen and lose carbon dioxide through their moist skin. This process works both in air and underwater.

Cannibal carnivores

All adult amphibians are hunters that catch and eat animals. Apart from caecilians, amphibians hunt mainly by sight, using their big eyes to watch for moving prey. Most eat insects, spiders, slugs, and other small animals, but the biggest frogs may eat small reptiles and mammals. They also eat other amphibians, including smaller frogs of their own species.

157 in (400 cm)—the distance an Australian rocket frog can cover in one leap. This is more than 80 times the length of its body, which is just 2 in (5 cm).

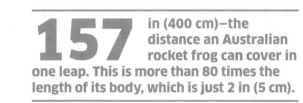

A woodlouse moving on a nearby twig is spotted by the hungry frog.

Large muscles power each part of the frog's long back legs and launch the hunter into the air toward its prey.

The frog's ankle bones are elongated to add extra length to its extended hind limbs.

In a split-second, the frog's long, sticky tongue flips out to seize the woodlouse.

The long back feet are webbed for swimming.

Leaping
Many frogs can make dramatic leaps to escape danger or catch prey. The powerful muscles of their elongated hind legs contract to propel them into the air with explosive force.

The frog's front feet have long toes.

Colors and markings

Nearly all amphibians have poison glands in their skin, which is mostly foul-tasting to predators but sometimes lethal. Many species advertise this with vivid colors that warn their enemies to leave them alone. The color and markings of some amphibians act as camouflage, making the animals hard to see. Others change color with the seasons, becoming brighter when they are ready to breed.

Fire salamander
The dramatic color pattern of the fire salamander is a warning that its skin produces a dangerous poison.

Horned frog
The amazing camouflage of this tropical frog makes it look just like a dead leaf on the forest floor.

Common newts
When these newts are ready to breed, both the male and female develop glowing orange bellies.

A female **common frog** may lay up to 2,000 eggs in the spring.

Frog lifecycle

Most amphibians begin life looking quite unlike their parents. Over time, they change shape until they reach their adult form—a process called metamorphosis.

In early spring, common frogs emerge from their winter sleep and return to the shallow pools where they began their own lives. The females lay their eggs in the water, where they are fertilized by the males and start to develop into embryos. Eventually, these hatch as tadpoles—tiny legless creatures that live underwater like fish. They feed and grow before sprouting legs and becoming more froglike. Then their tails shrink away and they climb out of the water into a new life.

Emperor dragonfly
This big, powerful insect preys on mosquitoes and similar creatures, catching them in midair.

Mosquito

Jelly covering
Each frog egg is protected by a thick coat of tough jelly.

Changing shape

A tadpole passes through several different stages before it turns into a baby frog, and its way of life is transformed in the process. Week by week an aquatic vegetarian turns into an air-breathing hunter that lives mainly on land.

1 Frogspawn
Frog eggs are very like those of fish. They must stay moist, so common frogs lay them in water, in clumps that are called frogspawn. Each female waits until she has a male partner, who clings to her back as she lays her eggs and immediately fertilizes them in the water. Then the pair swim off and leave the eggs to their fate.

2 Tiny tadpoles
When they hatch, the tadpoles are tiny black ribbons of life that cling to the waterweed. But they soon develop obvious heads and wriggling tails, and start swimming. At first, each has a pair of feathery gills, but these become hidden beneath protective flaps. They feed by scraping microscopic edible algae from rocks and plants.

3 Back legs develop
As the tadpoles feed, they get fatter and much bigger. At about five weeks old, a tadpole's body is as big as a small bean, and it grows a pair of back legs. At first, these are too small and weak to be useful, so the tadpole continues on using its powerful tail for swimming. It still feeds mainly on algae, but will eat other scraps.

A **frog's tongue is attached** to the
front of its **lower jaw**, not the back.

A frog **forces food down** its throat by
pulling its eyeballs back into its head.

Frogs hunt by **watching for moving
animals**. Prey is safe if it stays still.

107

13 The number of weeks that
it takes the single cell of a
frog egg to develop into
a leaping, air-breathing froglet capable
of hunting its own prey on land.

Sturdy legs
Powerful hind legs are
used for swimming as
well as leaping.

Special skin
The skin color of the
common frog varies
from yellow to brown
with dark blotches.

Water boatman
This little insect
lives just below the
water's surface and
swims by using its
oarlike back legs.

4 Front legs develop
By about 12 weeks old, the
tadpoles have stopped feeding and
start to change shape. Front legs
grow and its plump body slims
down to a more bony form with a
pointed head and a broad mouth.
It still swims with its tail, but spends
more time clinging to rocks and
plants, breathing air with its
nose out of the water.

5 Froglet
Soon after its body changes
shape, the tadpole's tail begins
to shrivel up. It starts swimming
using its back legs, and is soon
able to hop. It has turned into a
tiny froglet, no bigger than your
fingernail. Now ready to hunt on
land for small animals such as flies,
the froglet climbs out of the water
and finds a safe place to hide.

6 Adult frog
Life is very hazardous for the
little froglets since they have many
enemies. The survivors become
breeding adults in their third year,
and may grow to 4 in (10 cm) long.
They often stay in the water by day,
hunting on land at night when there
is less risk of drying out. They eat
any small animals they can catch
with their sticky tongues.

Dragonfly nymph
The aquatic young of
dragonflies are fierce
hunters that seize
their victims with
hinged, extending
jaws. They can easily
catch and eat tadpoles.

108 nature ○ **VERTEBRATES**

0.7 in (1.7 cm)—the **length of a tiny Caribbean island gecko**, making it the **smallest known reptile in the world.**

Reptiles

With their scaly skins, reptiles seem like relics of a prehistoric age. However, many reptiles are not as primitive as we often think.

Modern reptiles are cold-blooded animals that evolved from amphibians, the first vertebrates to live on land. Reptiles were able to conquer dry land more effectively than amphibians because their tough, waterproof skins stop their bodies from losing vital moisture. They also do not need to find damp places to breed. This allows reptiles to live in some of the hottest, driest habitats on Earth, but very few reptiles can survive in cold places.

Key features

All surviving groups of reptiles share a few key features. The prehistoric dinosaurs were also reptiles, but different because many were warm-blooded.

LAY EGGS

SOME GIVE BIRTH TO LIVE YOUNG

SCALY SKIN

COLD-BLOODED

Family Tree

The earliest reptiles evolved more than 310 million years ago, during the Carboniferous Period of Earth's long history. They were four-legged, cold-blooded creatures that resembled modern lizards. But over time, the reptiles split into different groups. One group gave rise to the crocodilians, dinosaurs, and extinct pterosaurs. The other surviving groups consist of the turtles, tuataras, lizards, and snakes.

Birds
The big dinosaurs became extinct 66 million years ago, but one group of small, feathered, warm-blooded dinosaurs survived—the ancestors of modern birds. Although their closest living relatives are the very reptilian crocodiles and alligators, birds are classified in a group of their own.

With its huge paddlelike flippers, the green sea turtle swims vast distances to reach the remote beaches where it lays its eggs.

REPTILES

Tuataras have been saved from likely extinction by careful conservation.

The American alligator is one of the largest living crocodilians.

Tuataras
2 species
These primitive, lizardlike reptiles belong to a group that flourished 200 million years ago, but which became virtually extinct long before the dinosaurs disappeared. Just two tuatara species survive in New Zealand, where they now live on a few small islands.

Turtles and tortoises
317 species
These animals evolved at about the same time as the first dinosaurs, but in a very different way. Their strong shells provide protection but weigh them down so much that tortoises can only move very slowly. Supported by water, turtles do not have this problem, and many are graceful swimmers.

Crocodilians
24 species
The most powerful modern reptiles are the crocodiles, alligators, gharials, and caimans—large armored predators adapted for hunting in shallow water. They are the nearest modern equivalent to dinosaurs like *Tyrannosaurus*, but their way of life is very different.

The green iguana is a typical four-legged, long-tailed lizard.

Snakes
3,000 species
Snakes evolved from lizards, losing their limbs and developing a specialized jaw arrangement for swallowing their prey whole. Some snakes also have a venomous bite.

This highly venomous coral snake is found in the southeastern US.

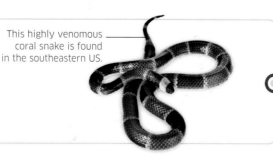

Lizards
4,500 species
The biggest group of reptiles includes a wide variety of creatures ranging from tiny geckos to the colossal Komodo dragon. Most have four legs and long tails, but some are legless. Although they generally prey on smaller animals, a few, such as the iguana, are plant-eaters.

34 ft (10.4 m) long—the **size** of the **biggest snake** in the world, the South American **green anaconda**.

The colossal **Aldabra giant tortoise** weighs up to **794 lb (360 kg)**.

The **Komodo dragon**—a giant lizard—is able to **smell food** from over **2.5 miles (4 km) away**.

109

Waterproof eggs

Unlike the eggs of their amphibian ancestors, reptile eggs have waterproof shells so that they do not dry out. This helps reptiles thrive in dry places, such as deserts. But the eggs need warmth to develop, so some reptiles that live in cooler climates give birth to fully formed young.

1 Egg
Just like birds' eggs, reptile eggs must be kept warm or they will not hatch. Reptiles ensure this by laying them in warm places, such as heaps of green vegetation that heat up as they decay.

2 Hatching
When the baby reptile inside the egg is ready to hatch, it slits the leathery shell open with a sharp, thornlike egg tooth on the end of its snout and pokes its head out to take its first breath of air.

3 Baby snake
Once the baby is able to breathe, it often rests inside the egg for several hours before fully emerging. This baby snake has finally decided to make a move and explore its new world.

The shell of each egg is tough but flexible, like very thin leather.

Hatching is triggered by the baby's need for more oxygen.

Within a few days, the baby will have to fend for itself.

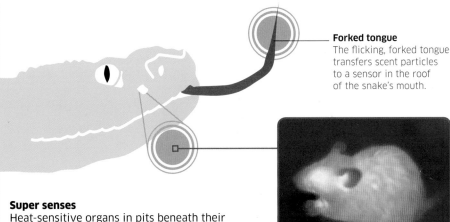

Coiled up tightly within the shell, a baby snake can be seven times longer than the egg.

Scaly skin

All reptiles have a tough outer skin made up of thickened scales linked by thin, flexible hinges. Together, the scales and hinges form a continuous sheet. Reptiles shed this outer skin layer throughout their lives, so any damaged or infected skin is discarded and replaced.

Crocodile
The skin of a crocodile or alligator has plates of bone buried deep within it. These bony plates strengthen the scales and help prevent the animal from getting injured by kicking, struggling prey.

Snake
Many snakes have vividly patterned skin. The color lies deep in the skin, and the outer skin layer is transparent. Snakes shed their outer skin layer in one piece, including the scales that cover their eyes.

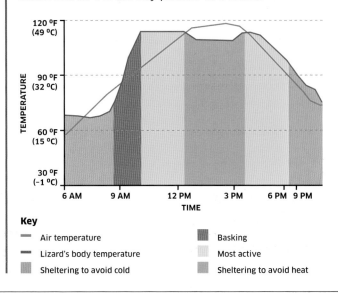

Lizard
The scales of lizards vary greatly. Some species have small, smooth scales while others have big, sharp-edged plates. Unlike snakes, lizards shed their outer skin in large pieces.

Reptile senses

Many reptiles have acute senses, especially hunters such as crocodiles and big monitor lizards. Chameleons have excellent eyesight, with eyes that can move independently to watch for danger or target prey. Snakes hunt by scent, which they gather with their forked tongues. They have no true ears, but are sensitive to vibrations passing through the ground.

Forked tongue
The flicking, forked tongue transfers scent particles to a sensor in the roof of the snake's mouth.

Super senses
Heat-sensitive organs in pits beneath their eyes enable some snakes, such as pit vipers, to locate warm-blooded prey in complete darkness. To a pit viper, the warm body of a mouse seems to glow against the cool darkness of its burrow, making it an easy target.

Cold-blooded creatures

Reptiles rely on their habitats to provide the warmth that their bodies need to function. Since they do not turn energy into body heat, they can survive on far less food than mammals. However, reptiles may have to spend hours basking in the Sun to warm up in the morning, and they often have to seek shade in the middle of the day to keep themselves from overheating. The graph below shows the activity pattern of a lizard.

Key

— Air temperature	▨ Basking
— Lizard's body temperature	▨ Most active
▨ Sheltering to avoid cold	▨ Sheltering to avoid heat

Nostrils
High-set nostrils allow the crocodile to breathe when most of its snout is submerged—a flap seals its windpipe when it opens its mouth underwater.

Pointed snout
Crocodiles have narrow, pointed snouts, and their upper and lower jaws are the same width.

Night vision
A crocodile has eyes like a cat, with big pupils that close to vertical slits in sunlight, but open wide to increase sensitivity at night. They also reflect light like cats' eyes. An extra transparent eyelid flips across each eye to protect it when submerged, but this keeps it from focusing properly underwater.

Super-strong jaws
Powered by massive cheek muscles, the crocodile's jaws snap shut with colossal force, giving its victim no chance of escape.

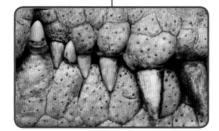

Interlocking teeth
A saltwater crocodile has 64 to 68 stout, pointed teeth that overlap each other when it closes its mouth. New teeth grow inside the old ones, and replace them as they wear out.

Crocodile

Crocodiles are survivors from the age of dinosaurs—powerful, heavily armed reptiles that can devour any animal they seize in their fearsome jaws.

Crocodiles, alligators, and their close relatives are the biggest living reptiles. Although they look rather like lizards, they are actually more closely related to birds, and to the giant dinosaurs that disappeared from the Earth about 66 million years ago. The earliest crocodiles lived alongside the dinosaurs, and probably preyed on them using the same ambush tactics that modern saltwater crocodiles use to kill buffalo. They have not changed much since then, because they have not needed to—they have always been perfectly adapted for their way of life.

Scaly skin
As with other reptiles, the crocodile's skin is covered by tough, waterproof scales made of keratin—the same material that forms your fingernails.

100 The **age in years** that a crocodile can reach.

A crocodile's **stomach acid is** ten times more powerful than a human's.

3,000 The **number of teeth** that a crocodile grows and loses during its lifetime.

111

Fact file

Speed on land..1.9 mph (3 kph)
Speed in water .... 22 mph (35 kph)
Habitat.................... Rivers, estuaries, and saltwater of
....Southeast Asia and Australasia
Diet .... Animals up to the size of a water buffalo
Armed with...............Powerful jaws and pointed teeth
Average length..10–16 ft (3–5 m)

THE SALTWATER CROCODILE IS THE BIGGEST OF ALL CROCODILES, WITH SOME MALES PROBABLY GROWING TO 23 FT (7 M) OR MORE.

Who's who?

There are 24 species of crocodiles and their relatives living in the warmer parts of the world. As well as 15 crocodile species, there are eight species of alligators and caimans, and one species of gharial. Compared to crocodiles, alligators and caimans have broader snouts with wide upper jaws that cover their lower teeth. The fish-eating gharial has a slender snout with 110 sharp teeth, ideal for catching its slippery prey.

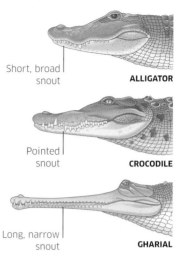

Short, broad snout **ALLIGATOR**

Pointed snout **CROCODILE**

Long, narrow snout **GHARIAL**

Streamlined body
Although a crocodile is relatively clumsy on land, its streamlined body allows it to move alarmingly fast in the water.

Bony armor
The big scales on a crocodile's back are reinforced with bony plates called osteoderms, forming a protective armor.

Powerful tail
A swimming crocodile drives itself through the water with powerful sideways sweeps of its muscular tail, often holding its legs close to its body.

Ambush predator

A crocodile is specialized at hunting in the water. It lurks in ambush, half-submerged, and by simply breathing out it can sink like a submarine. Any prey animal that wades into the water risks being suddenly seized and dragged under to drown. The crocodile then rips the prey apart and swallows it in big chunks, relying on its powerful stomach juices to digest every scrap.

Strong legs
Unlike most reptiles, which walk with their legs splayed out and their bellies close to the ground, crocodiles have strong legs that can support their bodies in an efficient "high walk."

12 The time in months a large crocodile can survive between meals.

112 nature ○ VERTEBRATES

200 mph (320 kph)—**the speed a peregrine falcon** can reach when **diving to attack** other birds.

Birds

With their beautiful feathers, fascinating habits, and amazing flying skills, birds are among the most colorful and intriguing of all animals.

Birds are the most familiar of all wild animals. They live all around us and are easy to watch as they search for food, build their nests, and raise their young. Like us, they use sight as their main sense and have a strong sense of color. But there is something else about birds that makes them particularly interesting. Recent research has proved that they are small, flying dinosaurs, descended from relatives of ancient hunters such as *Velociraptor*. Many of these long-extinct dinosaurs had warm, insulating feathers just like those of birds today, but the birds turned them to even better use—by taking to the air.

Features
Birds are warm-blooded vertebrates. Their bodies are covered with feathers, they lay eggs, and most birds are able to fly.

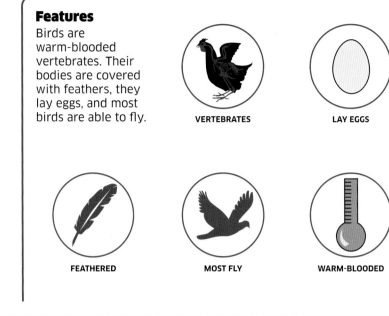

VERTEBRATES   LAY EGGS

FEATHERED   MOST FLY   WARM-BLOODED

Inside a bird
Birds inherited several features from their dinosaur ancestors, such as warm-bloodedness, feathers, and a super-efficient breathing system. But the demands of flight encouraged the evolution of other features too, including a lightweight bill and digestive system, and an extra-strong, yet light, skeleton. Birds also have excellent hearing and vision, and some birds—for example, crows and parrots—are among the most intelligent of all animals.

Vision
All birds have excellent eyesight, especially hunters such as hawks, eagles, and owls.

Bill
The shape of a bird's bill—long, short, straight, or curved—depends on its feeding habits.

Esophagus
Food passes from the mouth to the crop along this tube.

Crop
A bird can eat a lot of food very quickly by storing it in its crop before digesting it.

Heart
This is big compared to the bird's size, and it beats fast to keep the flight muscles supplied with blood.

Liver
The liver processes any toxic substances in the bird's blood and makes them harmless.

Feet and claws
This bird has sharp-clawed feet adapted for perching. Other birds have webbed feet for swimming, extra-long legs for wading, or powerful talons for seizing prey.

Lungs
Fresh air drawn into special air sacs is pumped in only one direction through the lungs, making them more efficient than mammal lungs.

Kidneys
The kidneys remove waste products from the blood, excreting it as solid waste instead of liquid urine.

Air sacs
A bird has seven or nine air sacs. Some draw in fresh air and pump it through the lungs. Others pump the waste air out.

Gizzard
A bird cannot chew its food with its bill. Instead, swallowed food passes into its gizzard—a tough-walled, muscular chamber that grinds the food to a pulp.

Feathers
The bird's feathers protect it, keep it warm, and enable it to fly. Like hair and claws, feathers are made from a flexible but tough protein called keratin.

Intestine
Food processed in the stomach and gizzard passes into the intestine, which absorbs vital nutrients.

Legs
The lower legs are protected by tough scales—a feature that links birds with their reptile ancestors.

Fish-hunting **emperor penguins plunge** to depths of **1,640 ft (500 m)** in the **cold Southern Ocean**.

The bill of the **sword-billed hummingbird** is **longer** than the **rest of its body**.

44,055 miles (70,900 km)—the **distance flown** each year by **migrating Arctic terns**.

113

Eggs and young

All birds reproduce by laying eggs, which vary greatly in size and color. Most birds build nests for their eggs, and use their own body heat to keep them warm until they hatch. The chicks of some birds, such as chickens and ducks, can find their own food right away. But others, including the young of most songbirds, are quite helpless, and need to be fed and kept warm by their parents for several weeks.

1 ostrich egg is the equivalent of **24 chicken eggs**, or an amazing **4,700 eggs** of the world's smallest bird—the **bee hummingbird**.

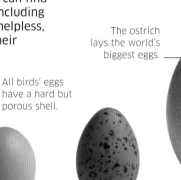

The ostrich lays the world's biggest eggs.

All birds' eggs have a hard but porous shell.

This egg is about the size of a pea.

BEE HUMMINGBIRD   SONG THRUSH   CHICKEN   HERRING GULL   OSTRICH

REED BUNTING NEST

Migration

Many birds nest in the far north in summer, where the days are very long and swarming insects provide a lot of food for their young. At the end of summer, they fly south to spend the winter in warmer regions. Some birds make incredible journeys, flying huge distances across continents and oceans.

Key

■ **American golden plover**
After nesting in the Canadian Arctic, this shorebird flies to the grasslands of Argentina for the winter. Some birds make the flight nonstop.

■ **Arctic tern**
In the northern winter, the Arctic tern hunts in the oceans around Antarctica. It then flies halfway around the world to breed in the far north.

▨ **Short-tailed shearwater**
This ocean bird makes a round trip of 18,600 miles (30,000 km) every year, breeding on the coasts of Australia and then migrating to the Arctic.

■ **Common cuckoo**
Cuckoos spend the winter south of the equator. They return to Northern Europe and Asia in spring to lay their eggs in the nests of other birds.

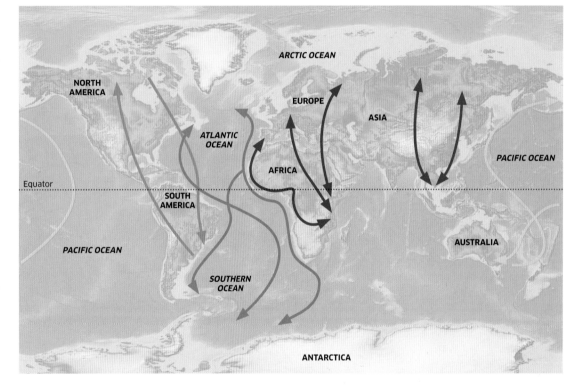

ARCTIC OCEAN
NORTH AMERICA
EUROPE
ASIA
ATLANTIC OCEAN
PACIFIC OCEAN
AFRICA
Equator
SOUTH AMERICA
PACIFIC OCEAN
AUSTRALIA
SOUTHERN OCEAN
ANTARCTICA

Seabirds

Many birds spend most of their lives at sea, where they feed on fish and other sea creatures, such as squid. They stay away from land for months, returning only to lay their eggs and raise their young on remote coasts. Seabirds include gannets, puffins, and seagulls, as well as giant albatrosses that soar over southern seas.

Super-fast divers
Famed for its spectacular plunging dives straight into the sea to catch fish, the northern gannet nests in huge colonies of up to 60,000 breeding pairs. Some gannet colonies cover whole islands.

Flightless birds

Birds are specialized for flight, but despite this some do not fly at all—a feature of birds that have few natural predators. They include strong runners like ostriches and small island birds that have no enemies to escape from. They all have features that show their ancestors could fly, but over thousands of years they lost this ability.

Champion runners
Like all flightless birds, these ostriches have short wings and small wing muscles. Although they can't fly, they can run fast on their long, powerful legs to escape from predators, reaching speeds of up to 45 mph (72 kph).

Flight feathers
The largest wing feathers extend from the back of each wing and are called the primary flight feathers. They provide most of the power for flight. With each wing upbeat the feathers twist to allow air through, then flip back on the downbeat to push against the air.

Wing bones
The bones of each wing are like arm bones, but many of the outer "hand" bones are fused together for strength.

Wing muscles
The muscles within the wing adjust its shape in flight to suit different flying techniques. The bird also uses them when it folds its wings after landing.

Wrist joint

Barbules with hooks

Catches

Hollow shaft

Barb

Feathers
Most of a bird's feathers have stiff filaments called barbs extending from the main shaft. Each barb has rows of smaller barbules that hook on to those of the next barbule. All these barbs zip together to form a smooth, continuous surface, so air flows over the feather and not through it—perfect for forming the wings and tail feathers. Although most birds grow a brand new set of feathers every year, they spend a lot of time looking after them to make sure they stay in shape and do their job well

Wing covert feathers
These small feathers covering the thick front part of each wing smooth out its shape. They also form the aerodynamic profile that makes air flowing over the wing create lift.

Colors
Birds rely on their vision, so color is important to them. Some are vividly colored, like this kingfisher. Others are camouflaged so predators cannot see them.

Spine

Body skeleton
The bones of the body form a strong, lightweight box made up of flattened ribs linked to the keel bone and a very rigid spine. The skeleton needs to be strong to cope with the stresses of flight.

How birds fly

Birds are masters of the air. Other animals can fly, but none can match the sheer speed, agility, and endurance of birds—qualities that have been refined by millions of years of evolution.

Birds can fly faster, higher, and further than any other animal. Many fly vast distances around the world every year, and a common swift may stay in the air for years on end without landing once. Birds have been seen flying high over the summit of Mount Everest, the highest peak on Earth. These feats are possible because a bird is highly specialized for flight. From its feathers to its bones, virtually every part of a bird's body is modified to either permit flight or save weight and make flying easier.

Contour feathers
The bird's body is covered with small overlapping feathers. They give protection, but also form a sleek, streamlined surface that allows air to flow easily over its body while in flight.

Tail feathers
A kingfisher has very short tail feathers, but they are still useful for slowing down in flight, spread wide to act as an air brake.

Feet
The kingfisher's feet are adapted for perching on twigs as it scans the water below for prey. They have long, sharp claws for a secure grip.

A hummingbird may beat its wings **more than 50 times a second** as it **hovers to sip nectar** from a flower.

The powerful **wing muscles** of a bird make up to a **third of its body weight**.

47 mph (76 kph)—the **fastest speed recorded by a bird in level flight**.

115

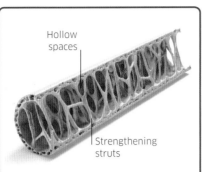

Hollow spaces

Strengthening struts

Hollow bones
Flight uses a lot of energy, and this could make a bird tire very quickly. But the less a bird weighs, the less energy it uses, so every part of its body is adapted to be as light as possible. Many of the bones are incredibly slender, and only just strong enough for the job they have to do. Some of the biggest bones are hollow, but they are reinforced with internal struts to stop them from collapsing under the strain of flight.

Skull
Formed from many bones fused together, a bird's skull is very light. It has an unusually thin cranium—the upper part that protects the bird's brain.

Vision
Like all birds, the kingfisher has excellent vision for navigating at speed in the air. It also targets fish by eye before diving into the water to seize them with its bill.

Hinged jaw
Unlike a mammal, a bird has a movable upper jaw. This allows it to raise the top part of its bill when it wants to open its mouth wide.

Flight muscles
A bird's wings are powered by massive flight muscles, They are attached to the wing bones and anchored to a deep breastbone called the keel bone.

Keel bone

Bill
Instead of heavy jaws and teeth, a bird has a lightweight bill made of keratin—the material that forms our fingernails. It covers a framework of thin bone attached to the skull, and it keeps growing throughout the bird's life as it is worn away at the tip and edges.

Down feathers
Underneath the contour feathers are special down feathers close to the skin that keep the bird warm. Unlike flight feathers, they have loose, soft barbs that do not hook together. This makes the feathers fluffy, forming a layer of insulation against the cold.

Taking flight
Birds are four-limbed animals, like us, and their wings are modified arms. But the area of each wing is made much bigger by the flight feathers rooted in its skin. These overlap to form a broad surface that flexes to push air back with each downbeat, driving the bird forward. Meanwhile, the smooth, curved shape of the wing means that air flowing over it creates lift, just like air flowing over an aircraft wing, and this keeps the bird in the air.

Kingfishers, nectar-feeding hummingbirds, and kestrels have an amazing ability to

hover in midair.
They do this by flying upward just fast enough to push against gravity.

Wing shape
The shape of a bird's wings is related to how it flies. Long, narrow wings are ideal for gliding, while broader wings help a bird soar on rising air currents. Short, rounded wings provide power for a quick takeoff.

Gliding
An albatross has long, slender wings for maximum lift.

Soaring
Eagles have broader wings to catch rising air currents.

Rapid takeoff
The rounded wings of a pheasant enable it to make a fast getaway.

High speed
Pointed wings give a swift speed and agility in the air.

Hovering
A hummingbird's short, triangular wings are ideal for fast wingbeats.

Flying patterns
Birds have different ways of using their wings. Some beat them at a steady rate, either fast or slow. Many other birds use a combination of flapping and gliding, and some barely flap their wings at all.

Fast flapping
Ducks have small wings compared to their heavy bodies, so they use rapid, regular wingbeats.

Slow flapping
Many birds with relatively big wings, such as seagulls, fly with slow, leisurely wingbeats.

Intermittent flapping
Woodpeckers use regular bursts of flapping, which they alternate with brief, swooping glides.

Random flapping
A swallow seems to use a random combination of flapping and gliding as it hunts airborne insects.

116 nature • VERTEBRATES

225 million years ago, the **first true mammals** evolved during the **Triassic Period**.

Mammals

Warm-bodied, often furry mammals are the animals that we find easiest to understand, and for a very good reason. We are mammals too, and share many of the features that have helped them thrive.

The first land mammals evolved from reptilelike ancestors at about the same time as the earliest dinosaurs, near the beginning of the vast span of time we call the Mesozoic Era. But while the big dinosaurs disappeared in the catastrophic extinction that marked the end of that era, around 66 million years ago, the mammals survived. They went on to colonize the entire planet, evolving adaptations that have allowed them to flourish in every possible habitat. There are mammals living everywhere, from the polar ice to the sun-scorched deserts, and from the highest mountain peaks to the deepest oceans.

Key features

All mammals are warm-blooded vertebrates (animals with internal skeletons) that feed their infant young on milk. All 5,400 species give birth to live young, except for the platypus and spiny anteater, which lay eggs.

WARM-BLOODED

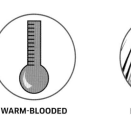

MOSTLY HAIRY

VERTEBRATES

MOST GIVE BIRTH TO LIVE YOUNG

YOUNG FEED ON MILK

Adaptable mammals

All mammals evolved from four-footed (tetrapod) ancestors that lived on dry land. Through millions of years of evolution, this basic body plan has been modified to suit the different ways that mammals live, enabling some to fly and others to survive in the ocean.

Terrestrial
Standing on four legs and with a long tail, the snow leopard has the typical body form of a land mammal. In addition, it is highly specialized for its hunting lifestyle.

Tree-dwelling
Many mammals are adapted for life in the trees, especially those that live in tropical forests. They include primates such as apes, monkeys, and this Madagascan lemur.

Aerial
Bats challenge the birds by flying on wings of skin stretched between greatly elongated finger bones. Most species hunt flying insects at night. Bats make up 20% of all mammal species.

Aquatic
Some mammals, such as seals and this blue whale, have become adapted for living in the sea. Their feet have evolved into flippers, and while seals still have four limbs, whales and dolphins have lost their hind limbs altogether.

Bringing up baby

More than 90 percent of mammal species give birth to live young, which develop to an advanced stage inside the mother's body before they are born. These are known as placental mammals, because the unborn young are supplied with oxygen and food inside the mother through a cord linked to an organ called the placenta. In contrast, the group of pouched mammals, called marsupials, give birth to half-developed young, which crawl into a pouch on their mother's body and stay there until they are fully formed.

Life in a pouch
A newborn marsupial is a tiny pink fleck of life, barely able to move. Despite this, the newborn crawls into its mother's pouch, where it starts drinking an extra-rich form of milk. Here, it grows and develops until it is able to eat solid food.

Red kangaroo
Australia is home to most of the marsupial species, including the red kangaroo—the largest of the marsupial mammals.

Warm and safe
The joey (baby) red kangaroo, develops inside its mother's warm pouch for six months. Once grown, the joey starts to climb out for short periods and, about six weeks later, it leaves the pouch for good.

Small mammals use so much energy keeping warm that some must eat almost their weight in food every day.

The biggest animal on Earth is a mammal: the 98 ft (30 m) blue whale.

Measuring just 1½ in (4 cm), the world's smallest mammal is the bumblebee bat.

117

THE THICK WINTER COAT OF THE ARCTIC FOX KEEPS IT SO AMAZINGLY WARM THAT THE FOX ONLY STARTS SHIVERING ONCE THE TEMPERATURE FALLS BELOW –58°F (–50°C).

Warm-blooded

Mammals depend on the release of energy from food to keep their bodies at an ideal temperature of about 100°F (38°C). This ensures that all their body processes work efficiently, and enables the animals to stay active in cold weather. However, some mammals that struggle to find food in the winter months go into hibernation. They save energy by lying dormant and allowing their bodies to cool down, then they wake up again in the spring.

Sleepy dormouse

A common dormouse may hibernate for up to six months each year, allowing its body temperature to drop below a chilly 39°F (4°C).

The dormouse hibernates in a nest of leaves and moss below the ground.

Senses

Many mammals are most active at night. They rely on their senses of hearing and smell, which are much more acute than ours, and also have a highly developed sense of touch. The eyes of nocturnal mammals are adapted to see in near-darkness and have many sensitive rod cells that react to very dim light. But this means that their eyes have fewer cone cells that detect colour, so these mammals do not see colours as well as we do.

Color blind

The ancestors of dogs hunted at night, so dogs see well in the dark but are not very sensitive to color. Although they see yellow, blue, and gray, dogs are almost blind to red and green.

HOW WE SEE

HOW A DOG SEES

Diet and teeth

Most mammals have several different types of teeth in their jaws—front incisors for biting, pointed canines for gripping, and large cheek teeth for chewing. The teeth are specialized in various ways to suit each mammal's diet and, as a result, the teeth of meat-eating hunters are very unlike those of plant-eaters.

Dolphin
Unlike other mammals, a dolphin's teeth are all the same—simple, sharp spikes, ideal for seizing slippery fish.

Lion
A lion combines long, pointed canine teeth with scissorlike cheek teeth for slicing meat. It cannot chew at all.

Cow
The cheek teeth of a cow are flattened for chewing grass. It has lower incisor teeth, but no sharp canines.

Keeping warm

A warm-blooded mammal uses a lot of energy keeping warm, and this means that it must eat much more than a cold-blooded animal of the same size. The more body heat a mammal can retain, the less food it needs, and this is why many mammals have bodies covered in thick, warm fur. Layers of fat under the skin also keep in body heat. Fur is just thick hair—something that only mammals have, although in some species it is modified to form spines or even scales.

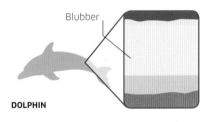

Blubber

DOLPHIN

Blubber
Marine mammals need good insulation to stop cold from draining their body heat. Most have thick fat under their skin, known as blubber. It is full of blood vessels that help regulate temperature.

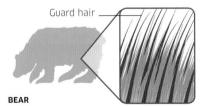

Guard hair

BEAR

Fur
Land mammals that live in cold climates, such as bears and foxes, have extremely thick fur. An outer coat of long, tough guard hair often protects a very warm layer of fine, dense, woolly underfur.

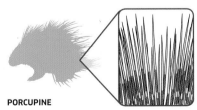

PORCUPINE

Spines
Porcupines, hedgehogs, and some other mammals have spiny coats. The spines are formed from modified hair, making it thick, stiff, and very sharp to protect the animals from their enemies.

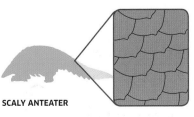

SCALY ANTEATER

Scales
Scaly anteaters are the only mammals with protective scales. These are made of the same material as the animal's hair and claws. Armadillos have a similar type of armor, but in the form of large plates.

African elephant

The biggest and heaviest of all land animals, the magnificent African elephant is a giant plant-eater with an appetite to match its size. It is famous for its intelligence and excellent memory.

With its long trunk, impressive tusks, huge ears, and above all its colossal size, the African elephant is a truly spectacular animal. It is specialized for eating huge quantities of coarse vegetation, including tough grass and tree bark, and will use its enormous strength to push trees over to get at their leaves if it is hungry enough. But the elephant can also be gentle and sensitive, and has a close-knit family life.

Starting life

A baby elephant grows inside its mother's womb for 22 months—almost two years. This gestation time is longer than that of any other mammal, including giant whales. The baby reaches full development during the tropical dry season, and is born at the start of the rainy season when there is plenty of grass for its mother to eat and turn into milk.

Umbilical cord
This supplies the unborn baby with food and oxygen. It is attached to the placenta, an organ that absorbs dissolved nutrients from the mother's bloodstream.

Unborn baby
The baby elephant already has its eyes open, ready for its first view of the world. Unlike most mammals, it is born hind feet first

Baby hair
At first, the baby elephant is covered with bristly black or red-brown hair, but most of this eventually falls out.

Cushion pad
The elephant's foot bones are embedded in a wedge of spongy tissue. This acts as a shock absorber and spreads the elephant's weight so well that it can walk silently, leaving only faint tracks.

Kidneys
The kidneys filter waste products from the blood and pass them to the elephant's bladder.

Backbone
The arched shape of the elephant's backbone helps it support the weight of its body.

Lungs
Big lungs draw in air to extract oxygen. Waste carbon dioxide then passes into the lungs to be breathed out.

Intestine

Heart
Like all mammals, the elephant has a four-chambered heart that pumps blood around its body. Its heart beats about half as fast as a human's.

Legs
The elephant's immense weight is supported on four pillarlike legs, which have very strong bones.

Toenails
Elephants have big toenails. The African elephant has three on each back foot, but four on each front foot.

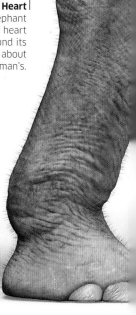

18 hours a day—the time an elephant spends **eating** to **fuel** its **huge body**.

When an **elephant wades** across a **deep river**, it breathes by holding its **trunk** above the surface like a snorkel.

The **tip** of an **elephant's trunk is** as **sensitive** as **our fingertips**, and it uses it in much the **same way.**

119

An African elephant has a flatter head than an Asian elephant.

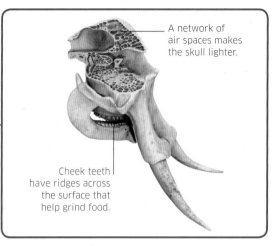

A network of air spaces makes the skull lighter.

Cheek teeth have ridges across the surface that help grind food.

Skull and teeth
The bones of the skull are honeycombed with air spaces to reduce weight. But together with the teeth and tusks, it still makes up almost a quarter of the elephant's total weight. Huge, ridged cheek teeth— one or two on each side of each jaw—grind the elephant's fibrous food to a pulp. Over time, they move forward, like a conveyor belt, so old, worn teeth fall out, and are replaced by new teeth sliding up from behind.

Tusks
The ivory tusks are extended front teeth, used for stripping bark, digging up edible roots, and as weapons. But many elephants are killed for their tusks, because their ivory is very valuable.

Ears
An African elephant's huge ears act as heat radiators, helping the animal shed body heat under the hot African Sun.

Ribcage

Skin
The thick, wrinkly skin is very sensitive, and elephants spray dust on it to protect it from the Sun.

Trunk
The muscular, sensitive trunk is an extension of the upper lip and nose. The elephant uses it for gathering food, drinking, spraying water and dust on itself, and communication.

Fact file
Height	Up to 13 ft (4 m)
Weight	11 tons
Lifespan	70 years
Habitat	African savanna
Diet	Vegetation
Status	Threatened

Elephants keep in touch
by making deep rumbling sounds that can travel through the ground for 5 miles (8 km) or more. They pick up the vibrations through the sensitive soles of their feet.

Family ties
Female elephants and their young live in family groups led by the oldest, wisest female, who knows where to find food and water. They have a close bond, using their trunks to touch and caress each other. When young males reach their teens, they leave to form all-male groups, but they often meet up with the family.

ANIMAL INTELLIGENCE

One of the big differences between animals and other life forms is that animals have evolved networks of nerve cells. Nerves send messages flashing through an animal's body, allowing it to respond instantly to its surroundings. Simple creatures, such as jellyfish and clams, respond automatically. More advanced animals have knots of nerve cells called brains, which allow them to remember what was good and what was bad. They can use this information to make choices about how to behave. This is the basis of intelligence.

Instinct

All animals, including humans, do a lot on instinct. An instinct is a form of behavior that doesn't need any conscious thought. Instincts are inherited from parents. For example, a baby spider is able to spin a web without being taught because, like having eight legs, the web-making instinct is part of its inheritance. For many animals, instinct controls at least 90 percent of their actions.

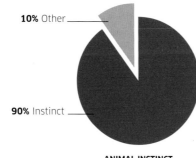

10% Other

90% Instinct

ANIMAL INSTINCT

Smart dolphins
A dolphin's brain is bigger than a human brain, and dolphins are certainly smart. They learn quickly, and some have even been taught a form of sign language.

Memory and learning

The brain of an insect is a tiny bundle of nerve cells, but even insects have memories. A honeybee gathering nectar remembers where the best flowers are, and passes on the information to other bees. The bigger the animal's brain, the more it can store away in its memory. This allows it to use experience to guide its actions, instead of just reacting to what is happening at that moment. Such animals can think and learn—although as far as we know, most of what they learn is practical.

Teaching by example

A few intelligent animals can learn new skills and pass on those skills to others, teaching them by example. Mothers often teach their young in this way, but other animals living in a social group may also learn by imitating a particularly clever individual. Chimpanzees learn how to make tools like this, stripping leaves from twigs so that they can use the twigs to scoop insects out of holes. This sort of learning is known as culture, and it is the basis of human civilization.

Snow monkeys
In the cold, snowy mountains of central Japan, macaques bathe in hot springs to keep warm—a habit learned from the female that first had the idea in 1963.

A DOLPHIN THAT WAS TAUGHT SIGN LANGUAGE AT A RESEARCH CENTER IN HAWAII HAS NOW LEARNED MORE THAN 60 WORDS AND CAN UNDERSTAND MORE THAN 2,000 SENTENCES.

SURVIVAL SECRETS

Animals have a special feature that is not shared by other living things such as plants and fungi—they are active. Most animals look for food, communicate with each other, and have complex patterns of behavior connected with finding mates and producing young. This involves sensing their surroundings, and in some cases making decisions based on past experience. But ultimately, all this activity has just one aim—survival.

ON THE MOVE

Animals are always moving. Some just twitch while staying rooted to one spot, but many others crawl, swim, walk, run, or fly in search of food, shelter, or breeding sites. They may wander almost at random, but others clearly know where they are going. Some of these animals have home territories, and know every rock, tree, and burrow. Many other animals, however, find their way over far greater distances, traveling across the globe to reach their destinations.

Finding the way

Migrating birds cross continents twice a year, while whales and sea turtles cross vast oceans, returning to the same places year after year. Birds may use landmarks, but this does not explain how a whale finds its way across an ocean. It seems to just know where to go. But migrating animals do not follow their instincts blindly. Birds, for example, choose their migration routes with care, and delay their departure if the weather is against them.

Navigation
Birds may use a combination of cues to help them navigate. These may include the Sun, stars, and Earth's magnetic field, as well as landmarks such as coastlines and hills.

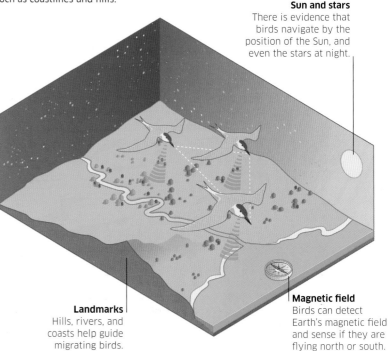

Sun and stars
There is evidence that birds navigate by the position of the Sun, and even the stars at night.

Landmarks
Hills, rivers, and coasts help guide migrating birds.

Magnetic field
Birds can detect Earth's magnetic field and sense if they are flying north or south.

LIVING TOGETHER

Although some animals lead solitary lives, most live with others of the same species. A few live with different animals, or even completely different types of organisms. They form relationships that often make life easier for both partners. This can allow them to survive in difficult habitats where food, shelter, or other necessities of life are hard to find.

Perfect partners

VALET SERVICE
Small coral reef fish called cleaner wrasses make a living by picking bloodsucking lice and bits of dead skin off other fish. Their customers are often big enough to eat them, but don't because they need the service.

FOOD FACTORIES
The corals that build reefs have algae in their tissues that make food using energy from light, and this food helps feed the corals. The giant clams that live on coral reefs have the same arrangement.

APHID FARMS
Small, soft-bodied insects called aphids produce a very sugary fluid called honeydew. Ants love eating this, so they look after aphids as if they were farm animals, defending them from enemies in return for a sweet treat.

HONEYGUIDE
The black-throated honeyguide is an African bird that eats the honeycomb of wild bees. It gets stronger animals to break into the nests, dancing before them to lead them to the site. They get to enjoy some honey too.

MOST BIG ANIMALS HAVE MILLIONS OF MICROBES LIVING IN THEIR STOMACHS THAT HELP THEM DIGEST THEIR FOOD.

COURTSHIP

Finding a mate and reproducing is essential to the survival of a species. Many animals have elaborate courtship routines. Often the males display to females, as with the male chameleons that glow with vivid colors to show they are eager to mate. But pairs may also perform together, like the scorpions that grip pincers and seem to waltz in the sand, and newts that dance together underwater.

Calls and songs

Sound plays an important part in courtship, especially deep in forests, where dense foliage makes it hard for animals to see each other. Male birds and tree frogs often fill the air with songs and calls as they compete to attract females and dominate rival males. The females usually choose to breed with the strongest singers, because they are also likely to be the healthiest.

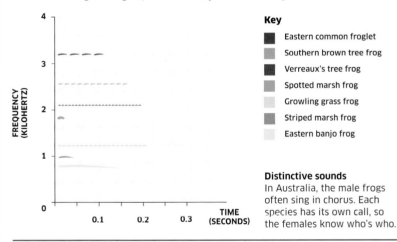

Key
- Eastern common froglet
- Southern brown tree frog
- Verreaux's tree frog
- Spotted marsh frog
- Growling grass frog
- Striped marsh frog
- Eastern banjo frog

Distinctive sounds
In Australia, the male frogs often sing in chorus. Each species has its own call, so the females know who's who.

Ritual dance

Birds put on the most spectacular courtship displays. On European lakes, pairs of great crested grebes engage in wonderfully complex ballets consisting of several dance routines. These are linked together in a strict sequence, which both partners must follow in perfect unison. If the dance goes well, the pair will mate and raise a family.

Head shaking
Courting grebes swim together face to face, shaking their crested heads up and down.

Diving for weeds
They dive and gather beakfuls of weed, then rush toward each other over the lake's surface.

Exchanging gifts
Paddling furiously, they rear up out of the water to present each other with their ritual gifts.

PARENTAL CARE

Many animals, including most fish, produce hundreds or thousands of eggs, because most of the young that hatch from them will not survive. Other animals produce fewer eggs or young, but they look after them for a short while to improve their chances of survival. The parents defend their young and either feed them or show them how to find food. A few animals provide care for many months or even years, during which time they teach their offspring vital life skills.

On its own

This caterpillar of a tropical blue morpho butterfly has just hatched from its egg. Its mother has provided for it by laying the egg on a plant that it can eat, but apart from this, the caterpillar has to fend for itself. It relies on its instincts and a defensive chemical to protect it from hungry birds, but the caterpillar will be very lucky to survive long enough to turn into an adult butterfly.

Gentle jaws

A mother crocodile stays by her nest of eggs for nearly three months, waiting for them to hatch. As soon as she hears the first squeak, she digs them out, helps the babies emerge from the eggs, and carefully carries her young to the water in her jaws. She then guards them for several months while they learn to hunt small animals for themselves.

Long childhood

A young wolf is brought up as part of a family—a wolf pack. At first, the pup is cared for by its mother, who provides nourishing milk. But gradually, it learns to eat meat brought back to the den. When the pup is old enough, it starts hunting with the rest of the pack, copying what they do and learning all the skills that it will need to survive and raise its own family.

122 *nature* ○ **SURVIVAL SECRETS**

1 single oak tree forms a habitat for an amazing variety of wildlife, with hundreds of animals living in its branches.

Habitats

Animals, plants, and all living things are adapted to life in their natural surroundings. These different environments are called habitats.

Every living species on Earth has its own favored habitat, which it shares with others. These different species interact with each other and with their natural environment—be it hot or cold, wet or dry—to create a web of life called an ecosystem. Some ecosystems are very small, but others such as rainforests or deserts cover huge areas. These vast wild habitats are called biomes.

Ecological succession

An ecosystem is constantly changing, as different types of living things move in and push out the species that lived there before—a process known as ecological succession. A bare patch of ground, for example, will be colonized by low-growing plants. Soon bigger plants take root, and then small bushes. Trees move in and grow tall to create a woodland. If the trees are then destroyed by a disaster, the series of changes, or succession, starts over again.

Constant change

Different stages of a succession often occur near each other in the same habitat. Here, new plants are colonizing a forest clearing.

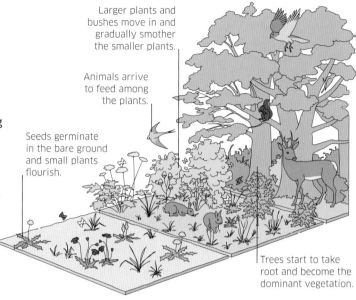

Larger plants and bushes move in and gradually smother the smaller plants.

Animals arrive to feed among the plants.

Seeds germinate in the bare ground and small plants flourish.

Trees start to take root and become the dominant vegetation.

Ecosystems

All animals, plants, fungi, and microbes depend on other forms of life for their survival. These communities of living things provide each other with shelter, food, plant nutrients, and even vital oxygen. All ecosystems are shaped by the climate, which influences the plants that grow. The cacti that grow in deserts, for example, are unlike the trees of a tropical rainforest, and they support different types of animals. The rock type is also important, because this affects the minerals in the soil, and in the water of streams, lakes, and other freshwater habitats. Mineral-rich water is very fertile, so it supports a lot of microscopic algae and water plants. These are eaten by small creatures that feed fish and other animals.

Freshwater ecosystem
A pond is a miniature ecosystem. The plants in the water support the animals, and they, in turn, provide nutrients for the plants to grow.

The Everglades in southern Florida is the biggest freshwater habitat in the world.

Water plants
Submerged plants release oxygen into the water. Other plants float on the surface or grow in the shallows.

Aquatic life
Pond water is full of microscopic algae and tiny creatures, which are eaten by bigger animals such as fish.

Heron
Hunters like this heron prey on fish and frogs. It may visit several ponds—no ecosystem is completely isolated.

All the **habitats on Earth** are part of one huge global ecosystem that we call the **biosphere**.

Some **life forms live inside other living things**—even your body is a habitat for microbes such as bacteria.

3 percent of the original **wild prairie in North America survives.** The rest is now farmland. **123**

Life on land

Different climates create different types of habitats for life on land. Warm, wet places grow lush forests, for example, while hot, dry regions develop deserts. These are just two of the world's principal habitat divisions, or biomes. Each biome consists of many smaller habitats and, in many areas, human activity such as farming has completely changed their character.

Key

■ **Coniferous forest**
Vast areas of Scandinavia, Russia, Alaska, and Canada are the site of coniferous forests—home to moose, beavers, and wolves.

■ **Mountain**
High mountain ranges have arctic climates near the peaks, where few plants grow. Animals must cope in dangerous terrain.

■ **Savanna**
These tropical grasslands with wet and dry seasons support huge herds of grazing animals and powerful predators.

■ **Polar ice**
The ice that forms on cold oceans is a refuge for animals that hunt in the water. The continental ice sheets are almost lifeless.

■ **Tropical rainforest**
The evergreen forests that grow near the equator are the richest of all biomes, with a huge diversity of plant and animal life.

■ **Desert**
Some deserts are barren rock and sand, but many support a range of plants and animals adapted to survive the dry conditions.

■ **Tundra**
These regions on the fringes of polar ice sheets thaw out in summer and attract animals such as reindeer and nesting birds.

■ **Mediterranean**
Dry scrub regions, such as around the Mediterranean, are home to a rich insect life and drought-resistant shrubs and plants.

■ **Temperate grassland**
The dry, grassy prairies with hot summers and cold winters, support grazing herds such as antelope and bison.

■ **Deciduous forest**
In cool, moist regions, many trees grow fast in summer but lose their leaves in winter. The wildlife here changes with the seasons.

Underwater life

The largest biome of all is the ocean, covering almost three-quarters of the planet's surface. It includes a wide variety of marine habitats, ranging from tropical coral reefs to the polar seas and dark ocean floor. Many animals and aquatic plants also live in freshwater habitats, such as rivers, lakes, marshes, and swamps.

The ocean biome is home to the largest and most spectacular animals on Earth.

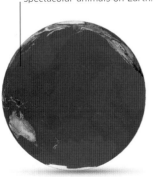

Habitat loss

The greatest threat to the world's wildlife is the loss of their natural habitats. Most living things have evolved to live in a particular ecosystem, and they cannot survive if this is destroyed. Habitat loss is the main reason why many wild species are becoming rare.

Deforestation

Every day, a vast area of wild forest is felled for its lumber, or to clear the land for agriculture.

The Sonoran Desert is one of the world's most diverse deserts, supporting an incredible array of **plants and animals.**

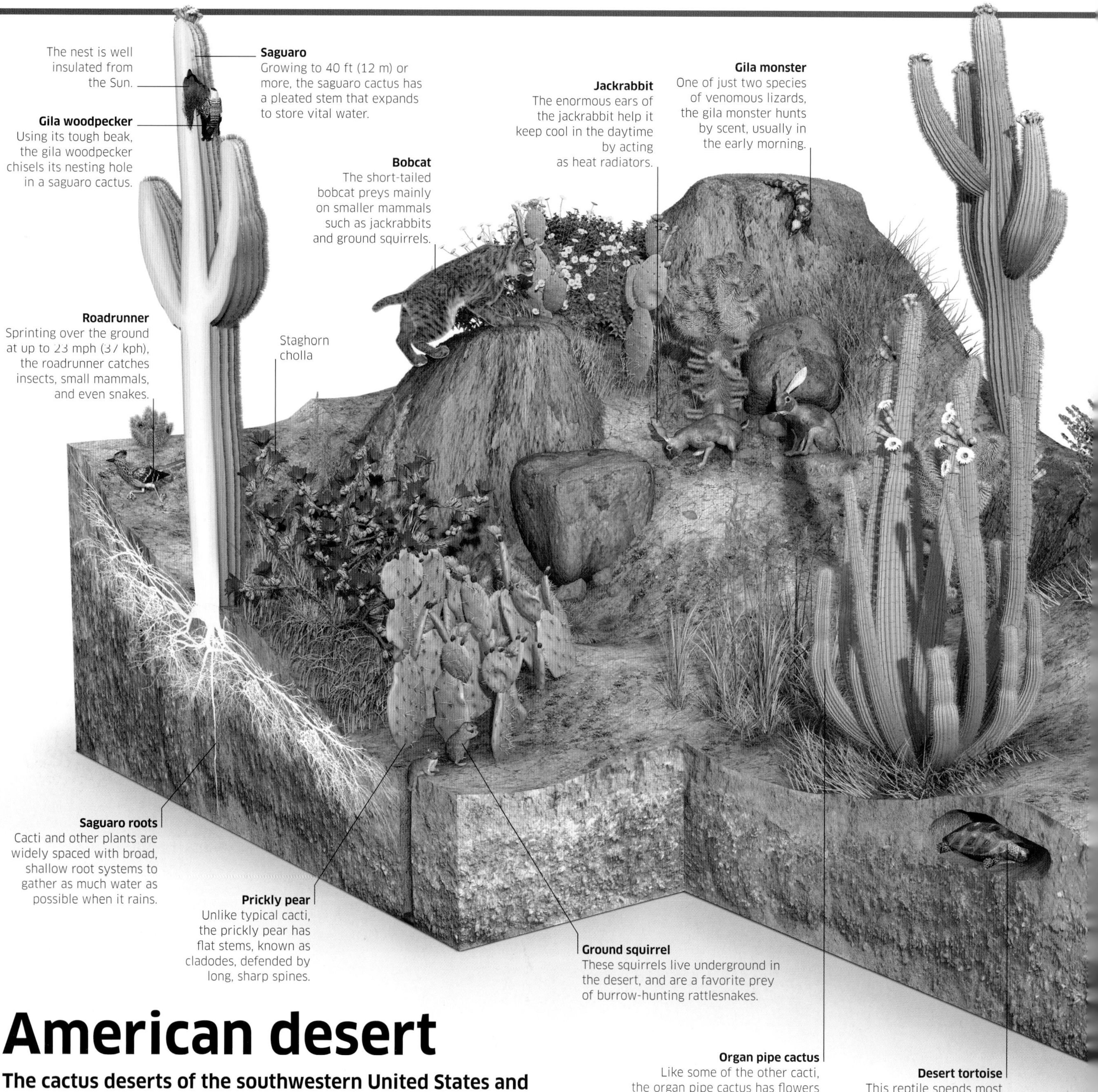

The nest is well insulated from the Sun.

Saguaro
Growing to 40 ft (12 m) or more, the saguaro cactus has a pleated stem that expands to store vital water.

Gila woodpecker
Using its tough beak, the gila woodpecker chisels its nesting hole in a saguaro cactus.

Jackrabbit
The enormous ears of the jackrabbit help it keep cool in the daytime by acting as heat radiators.

Gila monster
One of just two species of venomous lizards, the gila monster hunts by scent, usually in the early morning.

Bobcat
The short-tailed bobcat preys mainly on smaller mammals such as jackrabbits and ground squirrels.

Roadrunner
Sprinting over the ground at up to 23 mph (37 kph), the roadrunner catches insects, small mammals, and even snakes.

Staghorn cholla

Saguaro roots
Cacti and other plants are widely spaced with broad, shallow root systems to gather as much water as possible when it rains.

Prickly pear
Unlike typical cacti, the prickly pear has flat stems, known as cladodes, defended by long, sharp spines.

Ground squirrel
These squirrels live underground in the desert, and are a favorite prey of burrow-hunting rattlesnakes.

American desert

The cactus deserts of the southwestern United States and Mexico are home to a rich variety of plants and animals, all specially adapted to survive the hot, dry climate.

Deserts are the world's driest places. Many are hot while others are bitterly cold. Some may get no rain at all for many years, making them almost lifeless. The climate of the North American deserts, however, is not quite so extreme. The Sonoran Desert, for example, gets regular rain, even if there is not much of it. The rainwater is soaked up by cacti and other plants, which support plant-eating animals such as kangaroo rats, ground squirrels, and jackrabbits. These in turn provide prey for hunting rattlesnakes, owls, and coyotes.

Organ pipe cactus
Like some of the other cacti, the organ pipe cactus has flowers that open at night. These flowers attract nighttime animals such as nectar-feeding bats.

Desert tortoise
This reptile spends most of its life underground, emerging only to feed on grasses and other plants.

Many desert predators are highly venomous, which helps them capture scarce prey.

Kangaroo rats get all the water they need from their food, so they can **survive without drinking** at all.

2,200 lb (1,000 kg)—the **weight of water** that a **big saguaro cactus** can store.

125

Desert life

In the cool of early morning, the Sonoran Desert is alive with activity as animals forage for edible plants and seeds, or search for prey. Many are active throughout the night, relying on their acute senses to guide them in the dark, but as the temperature soars, most of them retreat to underground refuges for shelter from the scorching heat.

Great horned owl
The powerful horned owl usually preys on small mammals, and is big enough to kill and eat a jackrabbit.

Coyote
The versatile coyote will eat fruit and insects as well as taking larger prey.

Brittlebush
Named for its brittle twigs, this low-growing shrub has hairy leaves that trap vital moisture in the air.

Major deserts of the world

Most of the world's hot deserts lie just north and south of the equator. They are created in zones where sinking dry air stops clouds from forming, so there is very little rain. Cooler deserts lie in the center of Asia, far from any ocean, while the coldest desert of all forms the heart of Antarctica.

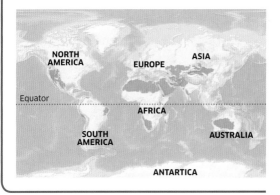

NORTH AMERICA · EUROPE · ASIA · Equator · AFRICA · SOUTH AMERICA · AUSTRALIA · ANTARTICA

Great horned owl nest
A spiny saguaro cactus makes an excellent nest site, since the spines deter many animals that might steal the eggs or the helpless young owls.

Miller's pincushion
The barrel-shaped Miller's pincushion has dark spines with curved points like fish hooks. Its bright pink flowers are followed by vivid red fruit.

Giant desert centipede
About 8 in (20 cm) long, this venomous multilegged predator is big enough to kill lizards and small mammals.

Globemallow
The orange flowers of this tough desert shrub appear in spring, and it often stays in bloom for several months.

Collared lizard
Fast-moving collared lizards chase insects and other small animals, sometimes running on their hind legs.

Octilo

Western diamondback rattlesnake
Heat-detecting organs on its snout enable this venomous snake to target warm-bodied prey at night and in the darkness of their burrows.

Kangaroo rat
The long hind legs of this seed-eater allow it to hop very fast and roam widely in search of scarce food.

Tarantula hawk wasp
This giant wasp feeds its young on spiders, including tarantulas. The wasp lures a spider from its hideaway and paralyzes it with its venomous sting. It then drags the helpless spider back to its burrow and lays an egg on it. When the wasp grub hatches, it has a ready supply of food.

Amazon rainforest

Hot, wet, and teeming with an amazing diversity of plant and animal life, the Amazon rainforest is one of the richest habitats on the planet.

Named after the mighty Amazon River that flows through it, the Amazon rainforest is a vast tract of tropical forest covering an area almost as big as Australia. Its warm, wet climate is ideal for plants, which never have to cope with cold or dry seasons, so they grow fast all year round. Huge evergreen trees soar high above the forest floor, creating an almost continuous canopy of lush green foliage that is alive with insects, tree frogs, snakes, birds, and monkeys.

Scarlet macaw

Toco toucan
This bird uses its huge bill to pick fruit, but it also eats a few small animals.

Blue morpho butterfly
The wings of this dazzling insect flash with iridescent blue as it dances in the dappled light of the forest.

Black caiman
This deadly predator lives in rivers, where it preys mainly on fish but also seizes animals that wade into the water to drink.

High life

Most of the animals that live in a tropical rainforest spend their lives high above the ground, up in the trees. They feed on leaves, fruit, and flowers, which grow all year round, and prey on the swarming insects and other creatures. Far fewer animals live on the shady forest floor, but those that do include all the biggest predators.

Weightlifters
Amazingly strong leafcutter ants can carry pieces of leaf that weigh 20 times their own body weight.

Leafcutter ants

The tiny leafcutter ants live in huge underground nests in colonies of up to 8 million insects. They feed on a special fungus, which grows inside the nest on a compost made from pieces of leaf. The worker ants gather these from the forest, scissoring them out with their sharp jaws and following scent trails to carry them back to the nest.

Paca
Expert swimmers, pacas live in burrows that may be 10 ft (3 m) deep, emerging to feed at night.

Piranha

Giant otter
Around 5 ft (1.7 m) long, this giant otter lives up to its name. It hunts in the water for fish, including the notorious piranhas.

Giant water lily
The floating leaves of this magnificent plant can be over 8 ft (2.5 m) across, with 16 in (40 cm) flowers.

Capybara
The biggest of all rodents, the capybara lives in forest swamps and rivers.

30 million—the estimated **number** of **insect species** living in **rainforests**.

2 percent—the **area of Earth's surface** covered by **tropical rainforests**.

An **area of rainforest** the size of a football field is **destroyed every second**.

127

Blue and yellow macaw
Macaws—big parrots—feed high in the trees on fruit and nuts, which they crack in their powerful bills.

Harpy eagle
The powerful harpy eagle uses its immensely strong talons to rip monkeys and sloths from treetop branches.

Howler monkey
The incredibly loud calls of these leaf-eating monkeys echo through the forest at dawn and near nightfall.

Poison dart frog
Tiny, vividly colored frogs live high in the trees. Their skins ooze powerful poisons, and their colors warn birds that they are deadly to eat. Many rear their tadpoles in the miniature pools that form in plants growing on treetop branches.

Three-toed sloth
Suspended by their long, stout claws, leaf-eating sloths hang upside down from the branches. They are famously slow-moving.

Emerald tree boa
In the rainforest, even snakes live in the trees. This climbing boa seizes prey in its teeth before squeezing it to death.

Jaguar
A powerful predator, the jaguar prowls the forest floor at night in search of prey. It can kill a caiman with a single bite.

Lianas
Many soft-stemmed plants climb toward the light by scrambling up the trunks of tall forest trees.

Kapok tree
Supported by its massive buttress roots, the kapok can grow to 200 ft (60 m), rising well above the main canopy.

Green iguana
Unlike most lizards, iguanas are herbivores, climbing high into the tree canopy to eat leaves, fruit, and flowers.

Tropical rainforests

The world's tropical rainforests lie on and near the equator in South and Central America, Central Africa, Southeast Asia, New Guinea and northeast Australia. They are created by year-round warmth and heavy rain, which falls from huge storm clouds built up by rising warm, moist air.

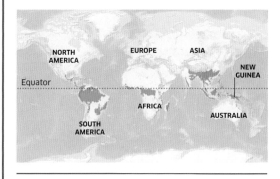

The rainforest canopy

A mature rainforest is a multilayered habitat for wildlife. The main tree canopy is almost continuous, but pierced by very tall emergent trees. Beneath the canopy there is a loose layer of smaller trees, called the understory, and below this lies the ground layer. Few plants grow in the deep shade of the forest floor, and most nonwoody plants are climbers or root themselves high in the trees.

Key

- Emergent trees
- Canopy
- Understory
- Ground layer

AT LEAST HALF
OF ALL PLANT **AND ANIMAL SPECIES** ON EARTH LIVE **IN TROPICAL RAINFORESTS.**

Lions
Powerful hunters, lions rely on stealth, creeping up on their prey before launching a group attack. They spend the heat of the day resting in the shade.

Umbrella acacia
The grasslands are dotted with tall, thorny, broad-topped acacia trees. They can survive many months without rain, and recover quickly from fire.

Wildebeest
Tireless trekkers, wildebeests gather in huge numbers to migrate in search of food. They are prime targets for lions.

African elephants
These giants feed on a wide variety of plants, even pushing trees over to get at their leaves.

White-backed vultures
The remains of a hunter's kill attract keen-eyed vultures that settle to pick the bones clean.

Termite mound
The savanna swarms with termites that live in big colonies. Many build towering nests of sun-baked clay.

Aardvark
Ant-eating aardvarks hunt at night and hide in burrows by day.

Spotted hyenas
Both scavenger and skillful hunter, the hyena is armed with powerful jaws that crush its victims' bones.

Hyenas live in large groups called clans.

Cheetah
Lean, light, and incredibly fast, the cheetah relies on its speed to overtake and kill prey such as gazelles. It hunts alone or sometimes in pairs.

African savanna

The tropical grasslands of Africa are open landscapes of dramatic seasonal extremes. They provide one of the most amazing wildlife spectacles on the planet.

Throughout the tropics, regions that do not get enough rain to support dense forest develop into grasslands. In Africa, these grassy, tree-dotted plains are called savannas. For half the year they are hot, dry, and swept by wildfires, but then the drought gives way to a rainy season that revives the grass. This provides food for the herds of grazing animals that roam the plains, hunted by fearsome predators such as lions and hyenas.

Browsers, grazers, and hunters

At the start of the rainy season a storm fills a dried out pool with rainwater, attracting thirsty animals from a wide area. They include leaf-browsing giraffes that eat the foliage of tall trees, and grazers such as wildebeests and gazelles. Hunters lie in ambush, hoping for an easy kill.

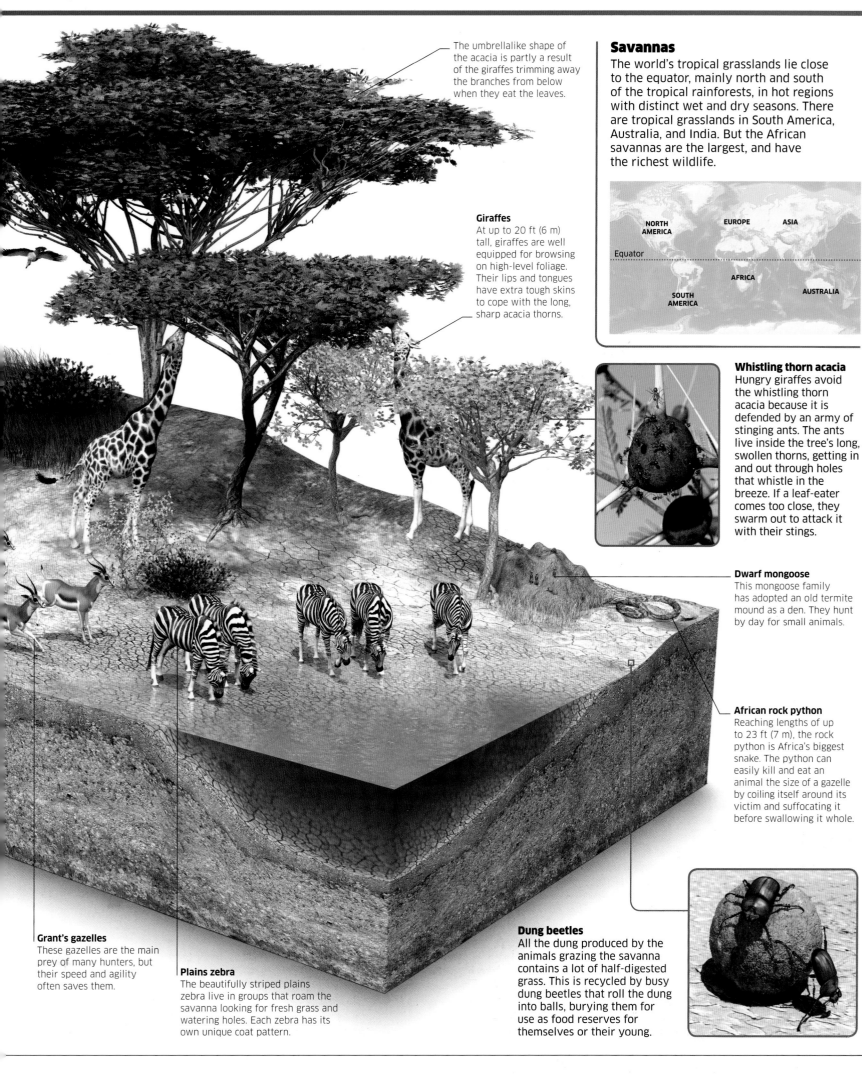

The umbrellalike shape of the acacia is partly a result of the giraffes trimming away the branches from below when they eat the leaves.

Savannas

The world's tropical grasslands lie close to the equator, mainly north and south of the tropical rainforests, in hot regions with distinct wet and dry seasons. There are tropical grasslands in South America, Australia, and India. But the African savannas are the largest, and have the richest wildlife.

Giraffes

At up to 20 ft (6 m) tall, giraffes are well equipped for browsing on high-level foliage. Their lips and tongues have extra tough skins to cope with the long, sharp acacia thorns.

Whistling thorn acacia

Hungry giraffes avoid the whistling thorn acacia because it is defended by an army of stinging ants. The ants live inside the tree's long, swollen thorns, getting in and out through holes that whistle in the breeze. If a leaf-eater comes too close, they swarm out to attack it with their stings.

Dwarf mongoose

This mongoose family has adopted an old termite mound as a den. They hunt by day for small animals.

African rock python

Reaching lengths of up to 23 ft (7 m), the rock python is Africa's biggest snake. The python can easily kill and eat an animal the size of a gazelle by coiling itself around its victim and suffocating it before swallowing it whole.

Grant's gazelles

These gazelles are the main prey of many hunters, but their speed and agility often saves them.

Plains zebra

The beautifully striped plains zebra live in groups that roam the savanna looking for fresh grass and watering holes. Each zebra has its own unique coat pattern.

Dung beetles

All the dung produced by the animals grazing the savanna contains a lot of half-digested grass. This is recycled by busy dung beetles that roll the dung into balls, burying them for use as food reserves for themselves or their young.

130 nature ○ **SURVIVAL SECRETS**

Some of the **coral reefs** we see today are **thousands of years old**—
the **Great Barrier Reef** started forming **500,000 years ago.**

Tropical coral reefs

Coral reefs grow in clear, shallow water on tropical coasts where the water temperature is higher than 64°F (18°C). They are most extensive in the southwest Pacific and nearby Indian Ocean.

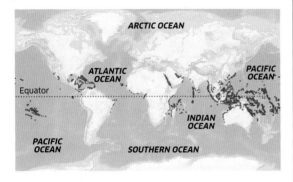

Natural wonder of the world

The Great Barrier Reef off the coast of northeastern Australia is the biggest coral reef in the world, covering an amazing 131,000 sq miles (340,000 sq km)—the size of a small country such as Japan. It comprises more than 2,900 individual reefs, which are home to an extraordinary variety of sea life.

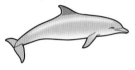

Dolphins
Thirty species of dolphins and whales live in the deeper waters.

Fish
More than 1,500 species of fish live among the coral.

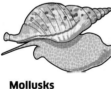

Coral
The reef consists of about 400 different species of coral, all living together in colorful profusion.

Mollusks
As many as 4,000 types of mollusks have been found on the reef, including giant clams.

Turtles
Six of the seven sea turtle species found in the world's oceans breed on the reef.

Starfish
The coral supports about 600 species of echinoderms, including starfish and sea urchins.

THE GREAT BARRIER REEF IS THE LARGEST SINGLE STRUCTURE MADE BY LIVING ORGANISMS, AND IS VISIBLE FROM SPACE.

Banded sea krait
A type of sea snake, the banded krait has a flattened tail that it uses to drive itself through the water in pursuit of fish.

Blue starfish
This starfish creeps over the reef, grazing on seaweed and organic debris.

Cloth of gold cone shell
The cone shell spears its prey with a venomous dart powerful enough to an adult.

Sea grass
This is one of the few true plants able to grow in saltwater. It forms broad underwater meadows in shallow reef lagoons.

Finger coral

Green puller fish

Peacock mantis shrimp
A ferocious hunter, the mantis shrimp uses its armored claws to smash the shells of snails and clams so that it can get at the soft flesh inside.

Staghorn coral
This quick-growing type of coral is very common on the reef, but is fragile and easily damaged by storms. It can be many different colors.

Tube sponge
Sponges are very simple animals that live by pumping water through their bodies, filtering edible particles.

Sea anemones and clownfish

Anemones snare their prey with stinging tentacles, and many can kill fish. Despite this, the clownfish is able to live among the tentacles of certain anemones without being harmed, probably because it has a protective coating on its skin. The stinging tentacles defend the clownfish from bigger fish that might want to attack and eat it.

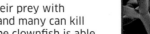

25 percent of all marine animals make their **home in coral reefs**.

Only **tropical rainforests** are home to more **species** of animals **than coral reefs**.

Corals get their **vibrant colors** from the billions of **microscopic algae** within them. **131**

Dazzling coral reef fish
Schools of small, brightly colored fish dart around the reef. Food is in short supply, so to avoid direct competition for the same types of food each species has developed a slightly different way of life. This has led to the evolution of many different species, each with its own special adaptations.

Golf ball sponge

Fox coral

Bird's nest coral

Bicolor angelfish

Weedy scorpionfish
The weedy scorpionfish lurks in ambush, waiting for smaller fish to swim within range. Venomous spines on its back protect it from bigger predators.

Royal angelfish

Moorish idol

Fairy basslet

Coral reef

Tropical coral reefs are the most spectacular of all oceanic habitats, providing homes for an astonishing variety of colorful marine life.

The corals that build reefs are simple animals resembling sea anemones. The individual coral polyps are linked together in colonies that grow in warm, shallow seas. They are supported by limestone skeletons made of minerals absorbed from seawater. When the corals die, their stony skeletons survive, and new corals grow on top. Over centuries, they build up to form a rocky, living reef.

Reef life
Reef corals have microscopic algae in their cells that make food using solar energy. The corals share some of this food, allowing them to live in clear, tropical water that contains very little food of any other kind—although the corals also trap small drifting animals. The reefs that they build support a dazzling diversity of fish and other creatures.

Table coral
Some of the biggest corals are these broad table corals. Each head of coral is a colony of hundreds of small coral polyps that soak up the sunlight they need to make food.

Red sea fan
Like corals but with tough, flexible skeletons, sea fans have spreading branches occupied by tiny polyps that feed by catching edible particles in their tentacles.

Box jellyfish
One of the most deadly animals in the ocean, the box jellyfish has four bunches of long, trailing tentacles, each armed with millions of highly venomous stinging cells.

Limestone rock

Giant grouper
This massively built fish is one of the main predators on the reef. It swallows its prey whole, and has even been known to swallow small sharks.

Bluestreak cleaner wrasse

Sea slug
Colorful sea slugs eat stinging animals such as anemones, but recycle their stinging cells to form their own system of defense.

Blue tang

Brain coral
Like all reef corals this is a colony of animals. They are linked in rows and divided by narrow grooves, giving the coral its amazing brainlike appearance. Each individual coral polyp has tentacles that it uses to snare tiny drifting animals. These supply vital types of food that the algae in the coral cannot make.

Animal architects

Some animals have amazing architectural skills. They use them to build their homes, make temporary nests, or in some cases to create ingenious traps for catching prey.

Many animals dig burrows or make nests, but a few have refined their building skills to create marvels of engineering. Some of the most astounding constructions, such as the monumental fortresses of termites, are built by the simplest of creatures. Over millions of years, they have evolved the ability to create complex structures entirely by instinct. Other animals such as beavers and birds also work mainly on instinct, but they may perfect their skills by trial and error, and by learning from others.

33 ft (10 m)—the height of a big termite mound, from its cool, dark basement deep below ground to the top of its towering chimney.

Termite city

Tiny insects called termites live in huge colonies centered on a single breeding queen. Some of these colonies create astonishing nests that contain royal chambers for the queen, nurseries for her young, and indoor gardens for growing food. They are built by millions of blind worker termites sharing an instinctive master plan that is passed on from generation to generation.

Clay walls
Strong walls keep out enemies, but allow vital oxygen to filter into the nest from the outside.

Central shaft
Heat rises through the tall shaft, helping to cool the living quarters of the colony.

Workers
Small worker termites build the nest, harvest food, tend the queen, and feed the young.

Nursery
The eggs hatch as baby termites called nymphs. Some become workers, while others become soldiers who guard the nest.

Soldiers
Strong-jawed soldiers defend the colony, attacking any intruders such as raiding ants.

Mound entrance

Fungus garden
These particular termites cannot digest plant material. Instead, they chew it up to turn it into compost for growing a special fungus inside their nest, then they eat the fungus.

Queen termite
The queen is far bigger than the tiny blind workers. She lives in a special chamber of the nest, attended by the smaller king termite. She produces thousands of eggs a day, which are taken away and cared for by the workers.

30-60 minutes—the **time** it takes for an orb web spider **to spin its web**.

2,788 ft (850 m)—the **length** of the longest known beaver dam.

300 pairs of **weaver birds** live in some colonies, filling **whole trees with nests**.

133

Beaver lodge

The beavers of northern forests make their nest inside a pile of sticks called a lodge. They protect this from enemies such as wolves by building a dam across a nearby stream so that it forms a lake around the lodge. In winter, the lake freezes over, but since the lodge entrance lies below the ice, the beavers stay safe from hungry hunters.

Icy protection
As winter arrives, the beavers plaster mud over the lodge. This keeps out cold drafts and freezes solid, keeping prowling enemies at bay.

Living chamber
The living area is above water level. Often there is an extra chamber where the beavers can dry off.

Ventilation
There is always a section left free of mud to allow stale air to escape from the living chamber.

Underwater entrance
When the lake freezes, the beavers can still swim in and out of the lodge to gather food previously stored in the cold lake water.

Dam
This is built of mud and trees that the beavers cut down with their teeth.

Water level
As the water level rises behind the dam, the lake gets deeper and broader.

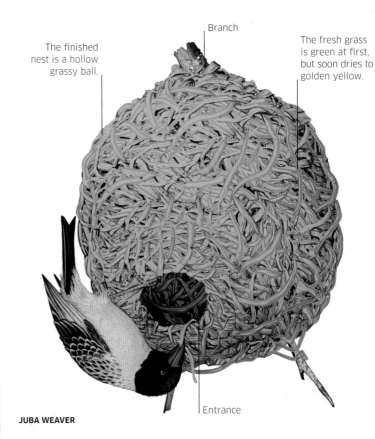

Web spinners

Spiders are experts at using silk to trap their prey. The most spectacular traps are those of orb web spinners. Even tiny newborn spiders can make perfect webs, showing that they work entirely by instinct. Each spider starts by producing a thread of strong silk from its tail end, and letting it stream out on the breeze until the far end catches on something. Once it has bridged a gap with silk, the spider can get on with building its spiral insect trap.

1 Making a start
The spider crawls across the first thread and releases a second looser thread. It drops down the second thread a to make a Y-shape.

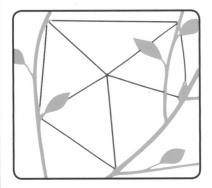

2 Framework
More threads are added from the center to the outside to make a strong framework. The spider tacks this together with a rough spiral.

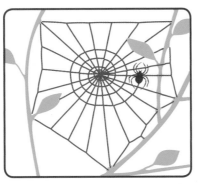

3 Spiral web
Removing the rough spiral as it goes, the spider lays another spiral of special sticky silk around the radial frame to form its finished trap.

Nest weavers

The male juba weaver bird of East Africa makes his nest by using his bill to weave grass blades together. He starts by attaching a woven ring of grass to a branch, then keeps weaving more and more grass onto the ring until it becomes a hollow ball. He leaves a hole near the bottom to use as an entrance.

Branch

The finished nest is a hollow grassy ball.

The fresh grass is green at first, but soon dries to golden yellow.

Entrance

JUBA WEAVER

Predators and prey

Many animals survive by hunting and eating other animals. These predators have special adaptations for finding, catching, and killing their prey, while their victims have evolved defenses that help them escape.

Hunting is difficult and sometimes dangerous, but predators have evolved many ways of improving their chances of success. They have acute senses for detecting their prey, and have ways of ambushing or creeping up on their victims without being detected. Speed, fast reactions, and sheer strength help them catch their meal, and weapons such as sharp teeth, claws, and even venomous fangs help them kill it. But the animals they hunt are not helpless victims. They can avoid detection, run away, confuse their enemies, or even fight back. So predators and prey are often evenly matched in this battle for survival.

Traps and tricks

Stalking and chasing prey is hard work, and it can use a lot of energy. Some venomous snakes avoid it by using lures to tempt animals within range. Other predators rely on traps, such as the spiders that spin webs to snare their prey. Some insects also build elaborate trapss and wait for their victims to fall into them.

Sandy trap
Antlions are the larvae (young) of winged insects that live in warm countries. They dig steep-sided pits in sandy ground and make passing insects tumble in by flicking sand grains at them.

The steep, sandy slope gives no foothold for prey trying to climb out of the trap.

The victim falls into the sharp jaws of the antlion.

Hunting together

Most predators hunt alone. A few, however, have found ways of working together as a group to either outwit their prey or kill animals much bigger than they could bring down alone. These cooperative hunters range from army ants to wolves, hyenas, dolphins, and humpback whales. Recently, scientists have discovered that chimpanzees sometimes band together to hunt small monkeys through the treetops.

Blocker
Chimpanzees in the trees block most of the escape routes, but leave one open.

Ambusher
A chimpanzee leaps out from cover to seize the monkey.

Colobus monkey
The monkey seeks safety in the treetops.

Blocker

Driver
When the hunters are in position, a chimpanzee gets the monkey fleeing for its life.

Chaser
Other chimpanzees chase the monkey to keep it on the run.

Chimpanzee ambush
Troops of chimpanzees hunt colobus monkeys in the forests of tropical Africa. They climb up into the trees, spread out, and hide among the branches and leaves. Then one chimpanzee scares a monkey into trying to escape, and the others herd it toward an ambush.

0.6 mile (1 km)—the **distance** from which a **polar bear** can **smell its seal prey.**

Some **caterpillars** scare off birds by **mimicking venomous snakes.**

To confuse its enemy, a **lizard can shed its own tail.** The twitching tail **distracts the hunter,** letting the lizard escape.

135

Solitary hunters

Lone predators that hunt in the open rely on stealth, speed, and power to catch prey. Hunting uses a lot of energy, so predators must make the chase as brief as possible. If they can, they creep up close before launching a high-speed attack. These lone hunters usually target smaller animals that they can overpower easily.

Super-fast hunters
All these predators use their speed to take their prey by surprise, giving it less chance to escape.

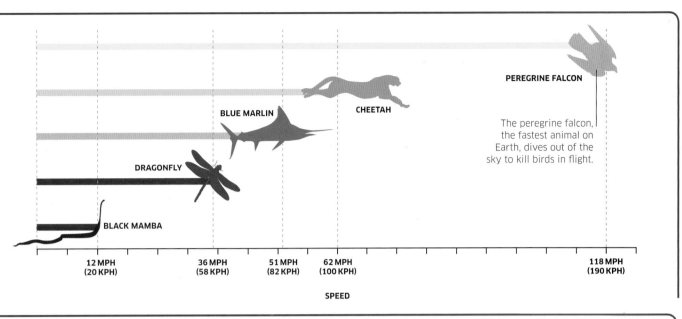

PEREGRINE FALCON

The peregrine falcon, the fastest animal on Earth, dives out of the sky to kill birds in flight.

CHEETAH

BLUE MARLIN

DRAGONFLY

BLACK MAMBA

| 12 MPH (20 KPH) | 36 MPH (58 KPH) | 51 MPH (82 KPH) | 62 MPH (100 KPH) | 118 MPH (190 KPH) |

SPEED

Defense tactics

Some prey animals have armor or spines that make them difficult to attack. Armored animals include armadillos, tortoises, and crabs, while hedgehogs, porcupines, and sea urchins are covered with spines. Amphibians have poison glands in their skin, making them unpleasant or even lethal to eat, and many insects build up poisons in their bodies. Skunks spray their enemies with vile smelling chemicals.

Armored ball
The body and head of an armadillo are protected by plate armor. When attacked, this three-banded armadillo rolls itself into an armored ball that few predators can penetrate.

Southern three-banded armadillos are the only animals in the world that can roll their armored bodies into a
tight, impenetrable ball.

The tough armor is made of rigid, flexibly jointed bony plates.

1 Standing its ground
Instead of running away from danger, the armadillo stays put.

2 Taking no chances
The armadillo curls up, tucking its head and legs inside its shell.

3 Perfect fit
The armored ball has no big gaps for an enemy to pry apart.

Cunning camouflage

Both predators and their prey use camouflage to avoid being seen. By blending in with its background, a hunter can lay a deadly ambush for creatures that wander too close. Other animals rely on near invisibility to protect themselves from predators that hunt by sight, such as birds. Most camouflaged animals have patterns that resemble plants or sand, but some insects even have body shapes that match their habitats.

When the gecko presses itself close to the tree, flaps forming a fringe around its body help it blend in with the bark.

The leaf insect's body has fake leaf veins as well as leaflike legs, making it impossible for predators to spot.

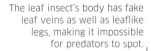

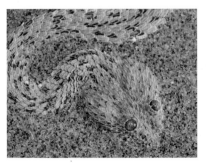

Sand viper
This venomous snake buries itself in the dry sand of Africa's Namib Desert. It waits for small animals to come within striking distance.

Orchid mantis
The body of this tropical predator is shaped and colored like a flower. Insects approaching for a sip of sugary flower nectar are snatched

Leaf-tailed gecko
The night-hunting gecko spends the day crouched on a tree, disguised by its amazing camouflage. Even its eyes are patterned to match the tree bark.

Leaf insect
Few animals are quite as hard to spot as this Malaysian leaf mimic. When it moves, it even sways from side to side like a leaf blowing in the breeze.

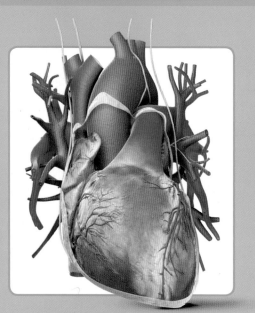

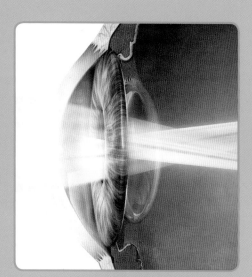

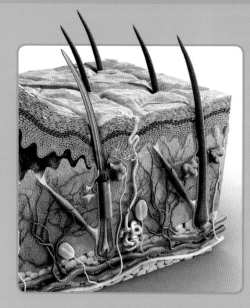

HUMAN BODY

The human body is a fantastically complex machine containing 206 bones, 650 muscles, and 75 trillion parts called cells. Scientists have studied the body in greater detail than any object in history, yet many mysteries remain.

BODY SYSTEMS

The organs and tissues that make up your body are organized into groups that doctors call systems. Each system does a particular job. Your digestive system, for example, breaks down food into nutrients that your body can absorb. Your circulatory system transports these nutrients and other vital chemicals around the body. Some of the main body systems are shown below.

Nervous system
This system allows your body to react with speed. Thousands of nerves run through the body, carrying electric signals to and from the brain. Some nerves bring signals from sense organs to the brain. Others send signals to muscles to make the body react.

Respiratory system
All your body's cells need a supply of life-giving oxygen, which comes from air. Your respiratory system's job is to take in oxygen and pass it to the blood. The main organs in this system are the lungs, which suck in air when you breathe.

Circulatory system
The heart, blood, and a network of blood vessels make up the circulatory system. Its job is to transport vital supplies such as oxygen and food molecules around the body. Blood also carries away waste chemicals for disposal.

Digestive system
Everything you eat passes through your digestive system—a long, complicated tube that runs from your mouth to your anus. The organs of the digestive system break down the large molecules in food into smaller molecules your blood can absorb.

Reproductive system
This body system works only during adulthood and is different in men and women. Its job is to produce babies. Male sex cells from a man's reproductive system join with female sex cells inside a woman's reproductive system and grow into a baby.

Muscular system
Muscles are what make you move. Your largest muscles work by pulling on bones to move your skeleton, allowing you to run, jump, tie your shoelaces, or kick a ball. Muscles also keep your heart beating and churn the food inside your stomach.

Immune system
The immune system's job is to keep you healthy by fighting off germs—microscopic organisms that can cause disease. Any germs that get inside your body are attacked by white blood cells, which patrol the blood and other tissues for invaders.

Skeletal system
The skeleton is a tough, living framework of bones that supports the weight of your body and protects delicate internal organs, such as the brain and heart. The skeletal and muscular systems work together to move your body.

BODY BASICS

The human body is a fantastically complicated machine made from millions of different parts, all packed tightly together beneath the skin. To understand how the body works, we need to look inside and see how the parts fit and work together to make us living, breathing, thinking human beings.

BUILDING A BODY

Just as a building is made from thousands of bricks stacked carefully together, the human body is constructed from simple parts that fit together in an organized way. Small, living units called cells are joined together much like bricks to form larger structures called tissues, which are used in turn to build organs and organ systems.

Atoms and molecules
The smallest individual parts in the body are atoms and molecules. The DNA molecule (left) stores the instructions needed to build and maintain the body.

Cells
Every part of the body is made up of tiny living units called cells. There are 75 trillion cells in the human body. Most are specialized to do specific jobs, from storing fat to carrying nerve signals.

One cell

Tissue
Cells join in groups to form tissues. The wall of the heart, for instance, is made of a special kind of muscle tissue. Other tissues include skin, fat, and bone.

Organ
Tissues join together to form organs, such as the heart, stomach, or brain. Organs perform a specific job. The heart's job is to pump blood around the body.

System
Organs work together in systems. The heart is part of the circulatory system, along with blood vessels and the blood.

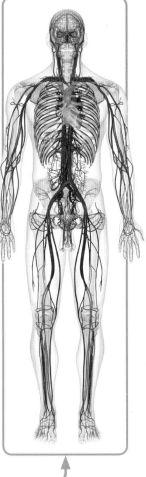

WHAT'S THE BODY MADE OF?

The human body is made almost entirely from just a handful of simple chemical elements. Among the most abundant elements in the body are oxygen and hydrogen, which make up water molecules—our bodies are about 60 percent water. Some elements, including sodium, magnesium, and iron, are essential for life but needed in only very small amounts.

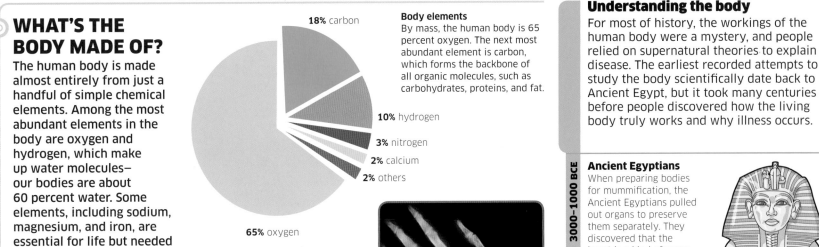

18% carbon

10% hydrogen

3% nitrogen

2% calcium

2% others

65% oxygen

Body elements
By mass, the human body is 65 percent oxygen. The next most abundant element is carbon, which forms the backbone of all organic molecules, such as carbohydrates, proteins, and fat.

LOOKING INSIDE

In the past, doctors could study the inner workings of the human body only by dissecting corpses, and they had no way of looking inside a living person's body to see what was causing their illness. Today, scanning machines and other technologies allow doctors to examine a person's insides in many different ways. These techniques make it possible to spot a disease in the very earliest stages, when it is easiest to cure.

X-ray image
X-rays are a form of electromagnetic radiation, like light, but are invisible to our eyes. They are shone through the body and captured by cameras to make images of bones.

MRI scan
An MRI (magnetic resonance imaging) scanning machine uses powerful magnets to make water molecules in the body give out radio waves. A computer turns the waves into an image, such as the brain scan above.

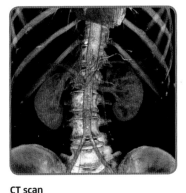

CT scan
In computerized tomography (CT), beams of X-rays are shone through the body from multiple angles and then used by a computer to build a 3-D image. Doctors use the technique to view "slices" through the body.

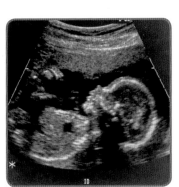

Ultrasound
This technique is used to see babies in the mother's body. High-pitched sound waves that we cannot hear are beamed into the body and bounce off internal organs, producing echoes that a computer turns into images.

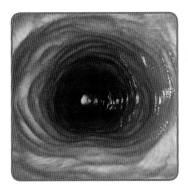

Endoscope
An endoscope is a flexible tube with a tiny camera and a light at the end. It is pushed into the body through either a natural opening, such as the mouth, or a small incision (cut).

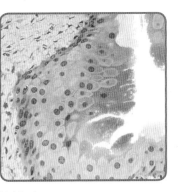

Light microscope
Like telescopes, light microscopes use glass lenses to magnify an image. Doctors use these microscopes to see the body cells in a tissue sample and look for telltale signs of disease.

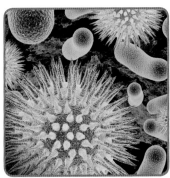

Electron microscope
Much more powerful than a light microscope, an electron microscope can magnify up to 10 million times. This allows us to see tiny germs such as bacteria and viruses in great detail.

Understanding the body
For most of history, the workings of the human body were a mystery, and people relied on supernatural theories to explain disease. The earliest recorded attempts to study the body scientifically date back to Ancient Egypt, but it took many centuries before people discovered how the living body truly works and why illness occurs.

3000–1000 BCE

Ancient Egyptians
When preparing bodies for mummification, the Ancient Egyptians pulled out organs to preserve them separately. They discovered that the heart is a kind of pump that pushes blood around the body.

400 BCE

Father of medicine
The Ancient Greek doctor Hippocrates is known as the father of medicine. He was one of the first people to realize that diseases have natural causes, rather than being punishments inflicted by the gods.

1500s

Dissecting bodies
Flemish professor Andreas Vesalius dissected (cut up) corpses in the 1500s and made detailed drawings of the bones, muscles, and organs. His pioneering work, which he published in a textbook, turned the study of the body into the science of anatomy.

1670s

Discovery of cells
Dutch lens-maker Antonie van Leeuwenhoek built one of the first microscopes. He used it to view blood cells and sperm, and he discovered the microscopic organisms that we now know cause disease.

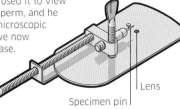

Focusing screw

Lens

Specimen pin

1953

DNA
In 1953, English scientist Francis Crick and his US colleague James Watson figured out the structure of DNA (deoxyribonucleic acid), the molecule that carries the instructions for life as a simple four-letter code.

Building blocks

The human body is a jigsaw made up of around 75 trillion microscopic pieces called cells. Every part of your body is constructed from these tiny building blocks, from your eyelashes to your toenails.

Individual cells are too small to see with the naked eye. The average cell is less than half as wide as a human hair, but some are so tiny that 30,000 could fit inside a period. Cells work as independent units, absorbing food, oxygen, and other basic chemicals from their surroundings, and manufacturing the complex organic compounds they need to grow and function. Some cells, such as blood cells, travel around the body singly. Others are fixed together in sheets to form tissues such as skin or muscle.

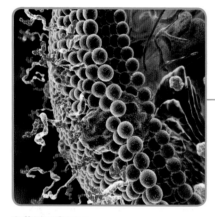

Cell membrane
The outer part of a cell is called the membrane. It consists of two layers of special molecules (phospholipids) that together form an oily film around the cell's watery contents, preventing substances from leaking in or out. Large protein molecules are embedded in the membrane. These act as gates, allowing only certain molecules to enter or leave the cell.

Vacuoles
These bubbles of watery fluid keep various substances separate from the rest of the cell.

Nucleus
The nucleus is the cell's control center. It contains all the instructions needed to operate the cell, stored as code in DNA molecules.

Golgi body
Chemicals manufactured by a cell are packaged by the Golgi body before they leave the cell.

Microvilli
Some cells have tiny, fingerlike extensions to help them contact their surroundings and absorb chemicals from outside the cell.

Secretory vesicle
These tiny bubbles eject substances out of the cell by bursting as they join with the cell membrane.

Inside a cell

Despite their tiny size, cells are immensely complicated inside. Each one is like a factory, packed with machines that carry out particular jobs. The machines inside a cell are called organelles, which means "tiny organs." The most important of these is the nucleus, which controls the rest of the organelles by sending out chemical instructions. Other organelles release energy, manufacture chemicals, and transport substances through the cell.

The **average human cell** is two-thirds the size of a **smartphone pixel**.

1 month–the average lifespan of a **skin cell**.

100 The number of times **your body's cells** would **wrap around Earth** if laid out in a line.

141

Ribosomes
These tiny molecular machines construct large protein molecules by joining small units called amino acids into chains. They use genes as templates to get the order of amino acids correct.

Cytoskeleton
Fine strands of protein form the cell's inner framework.

Mitochondria
Cells get their power from mitochondria, which break down sugar molecules to release stored chemical energy.

Lysosome
This organelle makes powerful chemicals that attack and break down unwanted substances and worn-out cell parts.

Cytoplasm
A jellylike fluid made mostly of water fills the space between the cell's organelles.

Endoplasmic reticulum
Folded membranes form a network of separate compartments in which various chemicals are manufactured, broken down, or stored.

Types of cell

There are more than 200 different types of cells in the human body, each type specialized to do a particular job. Some, such as skin cells and blood cells, last just a few weeks before dying and are continually replaced. Others, such as brain cells, can last a lifetime.

Concave surface

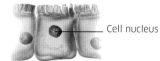
Cell nucleus

Red blood cell
These disc-shaped cells carry oxygen around the body. They are packed with a red pigment called hemoglobin.

Epithelial cell
The inside of the mouth and intestines are lined with these cells. Special toughened epithelial cells form the skin.

Fat globule

0.004 in (0.1 mm)

Fat cell
Body fat is stored in fat cells, which expand like balloons. As well as storing energy, fat cells help keep you warm.

Egg cell
The largest cells in the human body are egg cells. These develop into babies if they are fertilized by sperm cells.

3 feet (1 meter) long.

THE LONGEST CELLS ARE THE NERVE CELLS THAT RUN FROM YOUR SPINE TO YOUR TOES.

Genes and DNA

The nucleus of most cells contains a complete set of your genes, stored as a chemical code in DNA. A single cell contains about 8 ft (2 m) of DNA. When not in use, this DNA is wound up tightly in packages called chromosomes. There are 46 of these in every nucleus.

Making new cells

The human body starts out as a single cell. By dividing in two again and again, it multiplies until there are billions of cells. The most common form of cell division is called mitosis. First, the chromosomes are copied, forming double strands. Next, the chromosome strands are pulled apart, and finally, the rest of the cell divides.

Chromosome

1. Chromosomes form double strands.

2. Chromosomes are pulled apart.

Nucleus

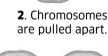

3. Two nuclei form.

4. Cells separate.

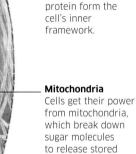

Skull
This protects the brain and houses the eyes and ears. It is made of several bones fused together.

Humerus
This long bone runs from the shoulder to the elbow.

Ribs
Twelve pairs of ribs form a cage around the heart and lungs.

Jawbone
The jawbone holds the lower teeth and connects by hinge joints to the skull.

Backbone
Also known as the vertebral column, the backbone is made of 33 round bones stacked together.

Body framework
The adult human skeleton is made up of 206 bones. Babies are born with more than 300, but some of these fuse together to form single bones as they get older. The largest bones are the two thigh bones (femurs), which support the body's weight. The smallest are tiny ear bones, which are no bigger than grains of rice.

Collarbone
This horizontal bone helps support the shoulder and arm.

Shoulder blade
The arm muscles are anchored to this flat, triangular bone.

Cartilage
The ribs are joined to the middle of the chest by bars of stretchy cartilage that allow the chest to expand

Pelvis
The large bones of the pelvis form a bowl shape, supporting the body's internal organs.

Sacrum
As we grow up, five of the bones in the spine fuse to form a large, triangular bone called the sacrum.

Carpals

The skeleton

Without a framework of bones, your body would collapse into a heap of shapeless flesh. Your skeleton not only holds you up—it also gives your muscles something to pull on, allowing you to move.

Bones are made of living tissue: they can feel pain, they bleed when cut, and they repair themselves if they break. We tend to think of bones as dry and brittle, but living bones are moist and slightly flexible to make them springy. Although smooth and solid on the surface, their insides are riddled with hollows to make them lighter. By weight, about 50 percent of a bone is a white calcium-rich mineral called hydroxylapatite, which is also found in teeth. This hard, crystalline material gives bone the great strength it needs to support the body's weight.

Broken bones
If bones break, the healing process begins immediately. First, a blood clot forms inside the break. Next, tough fibrous tissue grows across it to strengthen the damaged area. New bone cells then replace the blood and fibrous tissue, knitting the broken ends back together. Some broken bones need to be realigned and held in a cast so that they don't heal in a crooked shape.

Blood clot   Fibrous tissue   Spongy bone   Compact bone

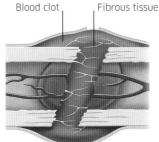 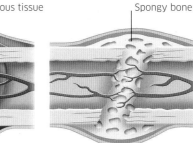 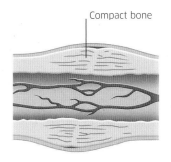

1 Two days
A blood clot fills the break, and fibrous tissue quickly grows through it.

2 Two weeks
Bone-making cells multiply and replace the clot with spongy bone.

3 Three months
Compact bone replaces the spongy bone, and the damaged area is reshaped.

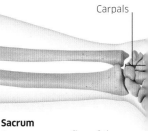

10% of the skeleton is **broken down and rebuilt** every year.

An **adult skeleton** contains more than 2 lbs (1 kg) of **calcium**.

Calcium is the **most abundant metal in the human body.**

143

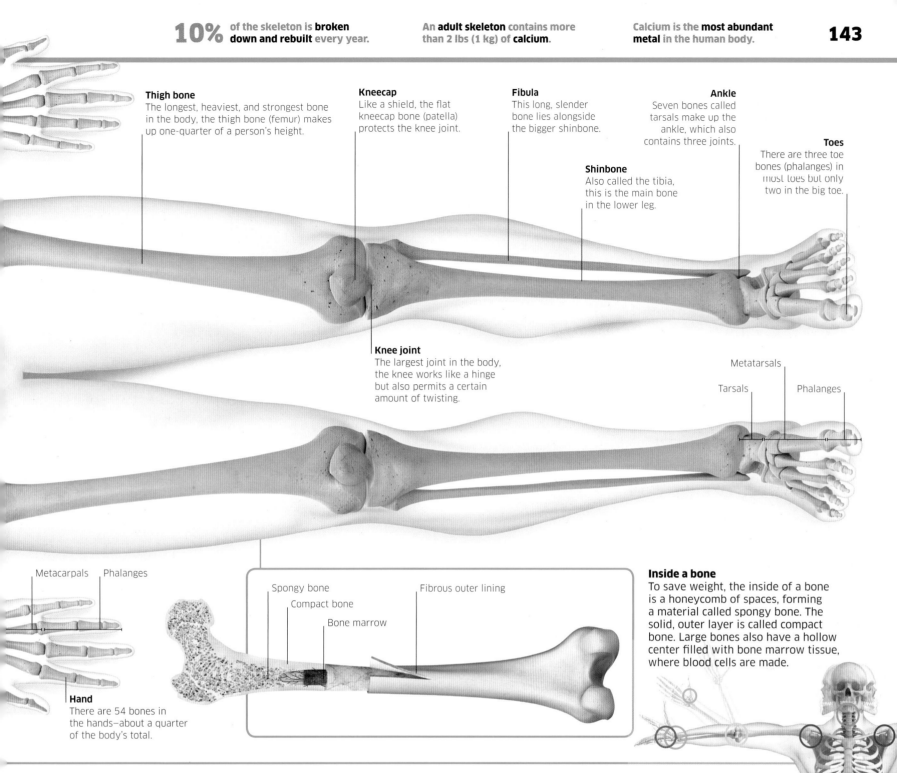

Thigh bone
The longest, heaviest, and strongest bone in the body, the thigh bone (femur) makes up one-quarter of a person's height.

Kneecap
Like a shield, the flat kneecap bone (patella) protects the knee joint.

Fibula
This long, slender bone lies alongside the bigger shinbone.

Ankle
Seven bones called tarsals make up the ankle, which also contains three joints.

Toes
There are three toe bones (phalanges) in most toes but only two in the big toe.

Shinbone
Also called the tibia, this is the main bone in the lower leg.

Knee joint
The largest joint in the body, the knee works like a hinge but also permits a certain amount of twisting.

Metatarsals

Tarsals

Phalanges

Metacarpals   Phalanges

Spongy bone

Compact bone

Bone marrow

Fibrous outer lining

Inside a bone
To save weight, the inside of a bone is a honeycomb of spaces, forming a material called spongy bone. The solid, outer layer is called compact bone. Large bones also have a hollow center filled with bone marrow tissue, where blood cells are made.

Hand
There are 54 bones in the hands—about a quarter of the body's total.

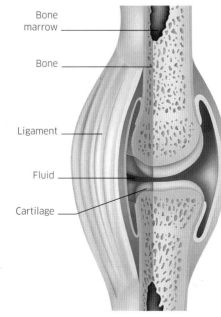

Bone marrow

Bone

Ligament

Fluid

Cartilage

Joints
Bones meet other bones at joints. In some joints, such as those in your skull, the neighboring bones are glued together rigidly. In most, however, the bones don't touch each other but are tied loosely together by tough straps of tissue that allow the bones to move. Joints give your skeleton incredible flexibility.

Inside a joint
To help the two bones in this joint to move, their ends are coated with slippery cartilage and surrounded by a pool of fluid. Tough ligaments tie the bones together.

● **PIVOT JOINT**

● **SADDLE JOINT**

● **HINGE JOINT**

● **ELLIPSOIDAL JOINT**

● **BALL AND SOCKET JOINT**

● **GLIDING JOINT**

Flexible joints
There are six main types of free-moving joints in your body. Each type allows a restricted range of movement, depending on how the bones f it together.

40% of your **weight** is **muscle**.

Each of the **5 million hairs** on the human body has its **own individual muscle**.

Shoulder muscle
This triangular muscle raises the arm.

Facial muscles
There are 43 muscles in the face. We use them to eat, drink, speak, smile, laugh, and frown.

Neck muscle
This sheet of muscle pulls down your jaw to open your mouth.

The muscular system

More than 640 muscles are arranged in crisscrossing layers between the skin and bones of the skeleton. Most are attached to bones by tough fibrous straps called tendons. Muscles, tendons, and bones work together like a system of levers. For example, when the biceps muscle in the upper arm contracts, it pulls on the bone in the forearm and bends the arm at the elbow. In this image, muscles lying just under the skin are shown on one side of the body and deeper muscles are shown on the other.

Chest muscle
The biggest chest muscles are the two pectoralis majors, or "pecs." Push-ups, weight training, and swimming make these bigger.

Biceps
The biceps at the front of the upper arm bends the forearm at the elbow and turns the palm upward.

Abs
The "abs," or rectus abdominis muscles, bend the lower spine and help to maintain posture. Well-developed abs are known as a "six pack."

Muscle power

Muscles allow us to walk, run, jump, and wiggle our fingers. They also move blood around the body and food through our intestines and allow us to speak.

Muscles make the body move. All muscles are made up of tiny fibers that can contract, making a muscle shorter so that it pulls on a part of the body. The largest muscles in the body are connected to the bones. Most of these skeletal muscles are under voluntary control, which means we can move them at will. Other muscles, such as those in the heart and stomach, are involuntary—they work without our having to think. Altogether, there are billions of muscles in the human body, including microscopic muscles on every hair and blood capillary.

Muscle types

There are three types of muscle in the body: skeletal, smooth, and cardiac (heart) muscle. Skeletal muscles are attached to the bones. They are made up of very long, threadlike cells that contract powerfully and quickly, for short periods of time. Smooth muscle occurs in the stomach, intestines, blood vessels, and eyes. It is made up of short, spindle-shaped cells that can contract for longer periods than other types of muscle. Cardiac muscle is found only in the heart. It consists of short muscle cells that contract rhythmically without tiring.

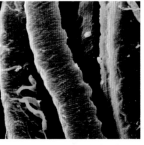
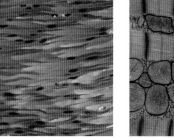
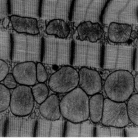

SKELETAL MUSCLE CELLS   **SMOOTH MUSCLE CELLS**   **CARDIAC MUSCLE CELLS**

650 The approximate **number of muscles** attached to the **skeleton**.

200 The **number of muscles** you use when you **walk one step**.

145

Inner thigh muscle
Also called the sartorius, this long, strap-shaped muscle in the inner thigh is the body's longest muscle.

Tendons
Tough bands of fibrous tissue called tendons anchor muscles to bones.

Foot tendons
Long, thin tendons run from your leg muscles to your toes. You use leg muscles to move your toes, and arm muscles to move fingers.

Calf muscle
The muscles in the back of your lower leg let you stand on tiptoe.

Thigh muscle
A four-part muscle called the quadriceps forms the front of the thigh. One of the largest and most powerful muscles in the body, the quadriceps extend your leg when you walk, run, and jump.

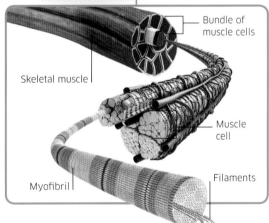

Bundle of muscle cells

Skeletal muscle

Muscle cell

Myofibril

Filaments

Fibers in fibers in fibers
Skeletal muscles, such as those in your legs, consist of bundles of muscle cells, called muscle fibers. Each cell consists, in turn, of a bundle of smaller, rod-shaped fibers called myofibrils, and these are made of even thinner fibers called filaments. The filaments are the parts that create movement. When triggered by a nerve signal, they slide across each other, interweaving to make the cell shorter. All the cells in the muscle contract at once to make the whole muscle shorter.

Working in pairs

Skeletal muscles often work in pairs that pull bones in opposite directions. For example, in the upper arm there are two large muscles: the biceps at the front and the triceps at the back. When the biceps contracts, it bends your arm. When the triceps contracts, it straightens the arm.

Biceps bends the arm

Triceps straightens the arm

Muscle shapes

Muscles come in a wide variety of shapes, depending on their location and role in the body. Some taper to a point at one or both ends to produce maximum pulling force, while others have simple strap shapes. Circular muscles close body openings, such as the mouth and bladder exits.

UNIPENNATE (FINGER)

FUSIFORM (BICEPS)

MULTIPENNATE (SHOULDER)

STRAP (INNER THIGH)

TRIANGULAR (CHEST)

CIRCULAR (MOUTH)

30,000 skin flakes fall off you every minute.

Every **30 days**, you grow a whole new outer **layer of skin.**

Skin deep

Skin consists of two layers. The top layer—the epidermis—is mostly dead and provides protection. The epidermis is paper-thin on the eyelids but about a quarter of an inch (5 mm) thick on the soles of your feet. Under the epidermis is the dermis, a living layer riddled with blood vessels and nerves that can sense touch and pain.

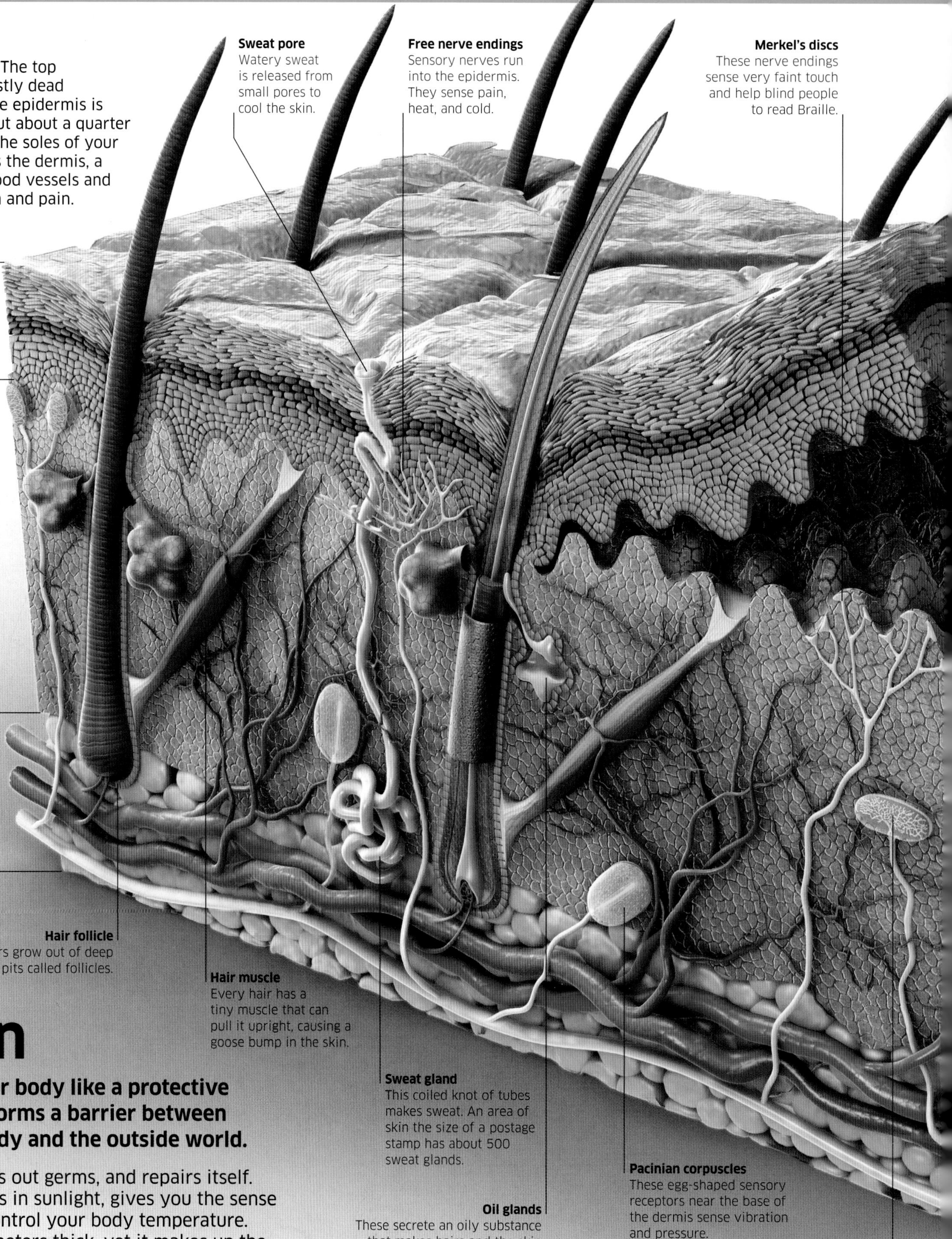

Sweat pore
Watery sweat is released from small pores to cool the skin.
Free nerve endings
Sensory nerves run into the epidermis. They sense pain, heat, and cold.
Merkel's discs
These nerve endings sense very faint touch and help blind people to read Braille.
Epidermis
This tough outer layer is made of flat cells stacked together. New cells are continually made at the base of the epidermis and then pushed upward. As they rise, they fill with waterproof keratin, flatten, and die. Eventually they fall off as skin flakes.
Dermis
This is the skin's living inner layer. It contains blood vessels, sweat glands, roots of hairs, and various types of nerve endings sensitive to touch, pain, heat, and cold.
Fat layer
Beneath the skin is a layer of fat that traps warmth in the body and cushions the body against blows. It also acts as an energy store.
Hair follicle
Hairs grow out of deep pits called follicles.
Hair muscle
Every hair has a tiny muscle that can pull it upright, causing a goose bump in the skin.
Sweat gland
This coiled knot of tubes makes sweat. An area of skin the size of a postage stamp has about 500 sweat glands.
Oil glands
These secrete an oily substance that makes hairs and the skin surface waterproof. Oil glands sometimes get blocked and swell up, creating a pimple.
Pacinian corpuscles
These egg-shaped sensory receptors near the base of the dermis sense vibration and pressure.
Ruffini's corpuscles
These touch receptors sense stretching and sliding. They are common in the fingertips and help us grip things.

The skin

Wrapped around your body like a protective overcoat, your skin forms a barrier between the inside of your body and the outside world.

Skin is waterproof, keeps out germs, and repairs itself. It filters out harmful rays in sunlight, gives you the sense of touch, and helps to control your body temperature.

Your skin is just millimeters thick, yet it makes up the largest organ in the body, accounting for about 16 percent of your weight. Its tough outer surface is designed to wear away, so it continually renews itself from below. Skin also produces hair and nails. Like the outer surface of skin, these protective tissues are made of dead cells hardened by a tough protein called keratin.

18½ ft (5.6 m)—the **world record** for the **longest human hair**.

0.12 in (3 mm)—the **average length** nails grow in a month.

Fingernails grow about **three times faster** than **toenails**.

Skin flakes
Dead cells fall off the skin as flakes.

Dying layer
Cells harden and die in the middle of the epidermis.

Basal layer
The base of the epidermis makes new skin cells.

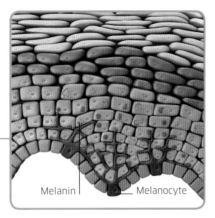

Melanin   Melanocyte

Skin color
Human skin varies from pale to dark brown. The color comes from an inky pigment called melanin, which is made by cells in the base of the epidermis. Called melanocytes, these cells spread packets of melanin into the epidermis, where they burst and release melanin granules. The pigment shields the body from strong sunlight.

Meissner's corpuscles
These receptors sense light touch, but will switch off if stimulated for a long time. That's why we stop feeling our clothes against the skin a few minutes after getting dressed.

Papillae
The top of the dermis is shaped into bumps called papillae. These help bind the epidermis and dermis together.

Fat cells

Nerves
Nerves carry electrical signals from touch and pain receptors to the brain.

Blood vessels
Nutrients and oxygen are brought to the skin by a network of fine blood vessels.

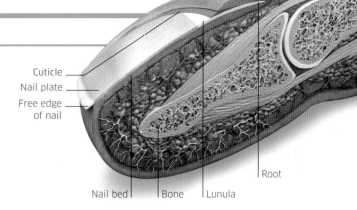

Cuticle
Nail plate
Free edge of nail

Root

Nail bed   Bone   Lunula

Fingernails
Fingernails improve the delicate sense of touch in our fingertips by creating counter pressure when we touch or hold something. They also help us pry and grip very tiny objects. The top part of a nail—the plate—is made of dead cells packed solid with the tough protein keratin. Underneath the plate is the living nail bed—a special type of skin that produces nail cells rather than ordinary epidermis cells. The nail bed contains the most rapidly dividing cells in the human body.

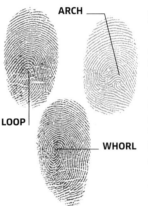

ARCH

LOOP

WHORL

Fingerprints
Look closely at your fingertips and you'll see tiny ridges in swirling patterns. These exist to improve your grip, like the tread on tires. No two people have the same pattern of ridges, which is why police use fingerprints to identify suspects. Fingerprint experts look for distinctive features like whorls (spirals), arches, and loops when they compare prints.

How hair grows
Like nails, hairs are made of dead cells packed with keratin. They grow from living roots in the base of pits called follicles. A typical hair grows for 2–3 years, after which its blood supply is cut off and the root dies. A new hair then starts growing and pushes the old one out. We shed 50–100 old hairs every day.

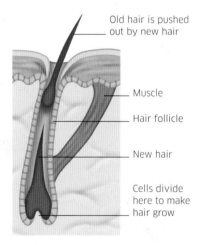

Old hair is pushed out by new hair

Muscle

Hair follicle

New hair

Cells divide here to make hair grow

Straight, wavy, or curly
The shape of your hairs affects the style in which they grow. Hairs that are round in cross section (cylindrical) tend to grow straight. Hairs that are oval in cross section tend to grow in a wavy style, and hairs that are flat tend to grow curly. Curly hair can also be caused by hairs emerging from the skin at a slanted angle.

STRAIGHT HAIR

WAVY HAIR

CURLY HAIR

FUELING THE BODY

Every cell in the human body needs a continual supply of fuel and oxygen in order to stay alive. The fuel comes from the food we eat, while oxygen comes from the air. Inside each cell, food molecules and oxygen are chemically combined to release the energy needed to power the cell's activities. Several body systems work together to supply cells with fuel and oxygen and carry away waste. These include the digestive system, the respiratory system, the circulatory system, and the urinary system.

RESPIRATION

The human body is powered by the same chemical process that powers a car. Inside a car engine, fuel reacts with oxygen to release energy, which turns the wheels. In the human body, food molecules react with oxygen inside cells. The process of obtaining oxygen from the air and then using it in cells is called respiration. The organs that bring oxygen into the body make up the respiratory system.

Respiratory system

The main organs of the respiratory system are the lungs (soft, spongy organs that fill most of the space in the chest) and the airways that lead to the lungs, such as the trachea (windpipe). Inflated by the muscles surrounding them, the lungs suck in air and allow oxygen to pass into the blood, while waste carbon dioxide gas passes in the other direction.

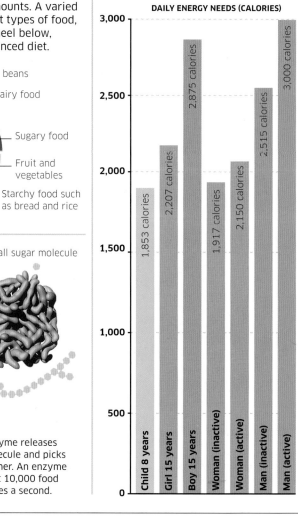

Trachea

Lungs

DIGESTION

Food is a mixture of many different organic compounds, including carbohydrates, fats, and proteins. These compounds are made of long, chainlike molecules that are too big to pass into the blood and enter body tissues. The process of digestion breaks down these large molecules into smaller units that are easy to absorb. Digestion turns carbohydrates into sugars, proteins into amino acids, and fats into fatty acids.

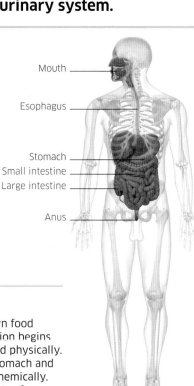

Mouth

Esophagus

Stomach
Small intestine
Large intestine

Anus

Digestive system

The parts of the body that break down food make up the digestive system. Digestion begins in the mouth, which breaks down food physically. Swallowed food then passes to the stomach and intestines, where it is broken down chemically. The intestines also absorb the products of digestion and expel the undigested remains.

Healthy diet

The main nutrients in food are proteins, which help the body build and repair tissues; carbohydrates, which provide energy; and fats, which are used for storing energy. A healthy diet should also include plant fiber, which is indigestible but helps the intestines work, as well as essential chemicals called vitamins and minerals, which are needed in small amounts. A varied mixture of different types of food, as shown in the wheel below, helps ensure a balanced diet.

Meat, fish, eggs, beans

Dairy food

Sugary food

Fruit and vegetables

Starchy food such as bread and rice

Energy from food

Scientists measure the energy in food in calories. The amount of energy you need depends on how active and how old you are. If you eat more calories than you need, the extra energy is stored in your body as fat. Regularly eating too much can make you overweight, which can lead to health problems, especially in later life.

DAILY ENERGY NEEDS (CALORIES)

Child 8 years	1,853 calories
Girl 15 years	2,207 calories
Boy 15 years	2,875 calories
Woman (inactive)	1,917 calories
Woman (active)	2,150 calories
Man (inactive)	2,515 calories
Man (active)	3,000 calories

Enzymes

Digestive organs produce chemicals called enzymes, which break the bonds in food molecules to turn the long chain molecules into smaller units. There are many different enzymes, each one specialized to break down a particular type of food molecule. The enzyme sucrase, for example, breaks down sucrose (table sugar) in the intestines.

Carbohydrate molecule

Molecule splits

Small sugar molecule

Enzyme molecule

ECOLOGICAL LAUNDRY POWDERS USE DIGESTIVE ENZYMES TO BREAK DOWN STAINS ON CLOTHES.

Attach
A carbohydrate molecule attaches to a part of the enzyme molecule called the active site.

Split
The active site breaks bonds in the carbohydrate molecule, splitting it into shorter chains.

Release
The enzyme releases the molecule and picks up another. An enzyme can split 10,000 food molecules a second.

Cellular respiration

Food molecules contain trapped chemical energy, just as gasoline put into a car contains trapped energy. Living cells release this energy through a process called cellular respiration. Molecules such as sugars are made to react with oxygen molecules.

The reaction breaks the chemical bonds in sugar and releases trapped energy. Carbon dioxide and water are produced as by-products. Carbon dioxide is poisonous in large amounts, so the bloodstream carries it away to be breathed out by the lungs.

$$C_6H_{12}O_6 + 6O_2 \longrightarrow 6CO_2 + 6H_2O + energy$$

SUGAR OXYGEN CARBON DIOXIDE WATER

Mitochondria

Cellular respiration takes place in microscopic power plants called mitochondria, which are found in every cell. Some cells have only one or two mitochondria, but a cell that uses a lot of energy—such as a muscle cell—may have hundreds. Each mitochondrion is enclosed by two membranes: a flat outer membrane and a deeply folded inner membrane. The chemical reactions of respiration happen on the inner membrane.

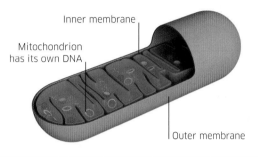

Inner membrane

Mitochondrion has its own DNA

Outer membrane

TRANSPORT

The human body contains thousand of miles of blood vessels, from arteries as thick as your thumb to capillary vessels finer than hairs. Like a network of roads that reach every house in a country, blood vessels deliver vital supplies to every living cell in the body, as well as carrying away waste.

Heart Artery

Vein

Circulatory system

The heart and blood vessels make up the body's circulatory system. With each beat, the heart pumps blood out through thick-walled vessels called arteries. Blood returns to the heart in veins. Between the arteries and veins is a vast network of tiny vessels called capillaries, which have thin walls that let oxygen, food molecules, and other chemicals pass freely across.

How blood works

Blood is a liquid tissue, made up of billions of cells suspended in a watery liquid called plasma. By volume, blood is about 54 percent liquid and 46 percent cells. Oxygen is carried by a protein called hemoglobin in red blood cells. Food molecules, hormones, salt, wastes, and various other chemicals are carried dissolved in plasma.

Red blood cells
These disc-shaped cells pick up oxygen in the lungs and release it everywhere else in the body.

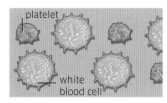

platelet

white blood cell

White blood cells and platelets
Germs that get into the body are destroyed by white blood cells. Platelet cells help blood to clot.

Double circulation

Blood flows around your body in two loops, driven by the heart. The shorter loop (blue arrows, below) runs from the heart to the lungs, where blood picks up oxygen. The longer loop (yellow arrows) takes oxygen-rich blood to the rest of the body. Blood rich in oxygen is bright red, while blood with little oxygen is dark red. In most human body diagrams, however, oxygen-poor blood is shown in blue.

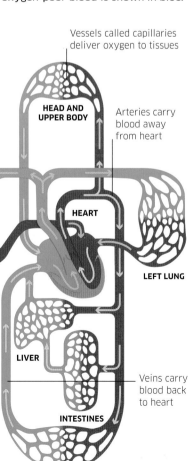

Vessels called capillaries deliver oxygen to tissues

HEAD AND UPPER BODY

Arteries carry blood away from heart

HEART

LEFT LUNG

LIVER

Veins carry blood back to heart

INTESTINES

LOWER BODY

FOOD PROCESSOR

Nutrients absorbed by the intestines are carried by the blood to an organ called the liver. Like a chemical plant, the liver stores hundreds of important chemical compounds and carries out many chemical processes.

Major liver functions
Converts sugar molecules into a substance called glycogen for short-term storage
Removes poisonous compounds from the blood, including drugs and alcohol
Produces a digestive juice called bile, which helps break down fats in the intestine
Stores the vitamins A, B12, D, E, and K and various minerals, including iron and copper
Turns excess protein into fat to provide an energy store

WASTE DISPOSAL

The chemical reactions that happen inside cells produce wastes that would poison the body if allowed to build up. These chemicals are carried by the blood to various organs that destroy or get rid of them, including the kidneys, liver, skin, and the lungs, which breathe out waste carbon dioxide.

Kidneys

Bladder

Urinary system

Many of the wastes in the blood are removed by two bean-shaped organs called kidneys. These filter blood continually, removing excess water and various chemicals, which form a fluid called urine. The urine drains to a storage organ called the bladder, ready to be expelled from the body. The kidneys, bladder, and urine-carrying vessels make up the body's urinary system.

Urine contents

Urine consists mostly of water and a compound called urea, which is produced in the liver when excess proteins are broken down. The other compounds in urine are mostly salts. The amount of water in urine rises if you drink lots of fluid and falls when you're thirsty.

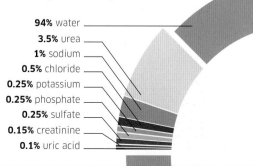

94% water
3.5% urea
1% sodium
0.5% chloride
0.25% potassium
0.25% phosphate
0.25% sulfate
0.15% creatinine
0.1% uric acid

From mouth to stomach

Just the thought or smell of food is enough to get digestive juices flowing in the mouth and stomach. As soon as food enters the body, it's mashed to a pulp and attacked by chemicals that begin to break it down.

Most of the nutrients in food are long, chainlike molecules that are too big to dissolve in water and be absorbed by the blood. The process of digestion turns these giant molecules into tiny units the body can absorb. The first stage of the process is physical: we tear, crush, and mash food as we chew it with our teeth. This physical action helps digestive juices penetrate the food to break it down chemically.

The stomach expands
to as much as 70 times its empty volume when it fills up with food.

Inside the mouth
Unlike cats and dogs, which can wolf down large chunks of food, human beings have to chew food before swallowing it. Inside the mouth, food is mashed by the teeth and mixed with a watery fluid called saliva (spit). Saliva moistens food to make it slippery and easier to swallow. It also contains chemicals called digestive enzymes, which break large food molecules into fragments. The enzyme amylase breaks down starch molecules from foods like bread and rice, turning them into sugar. The enzyme lipase breaks down fat molecules.

Nose
The flavor of food comes largely from our sense of smell. Aromas enter the nose from the back of the mouth.

Food
After being chewed and mixed with saliva, food is molded by the tongue into a soft, squishy mass to make it easy to swallow.

Tongue
This agile and powerful, muscular organ maneuvers food with amazing precision, placing food particles between the teeth to be crushed. It also mixes food with saliva, molds it into a lump, and pushes it into the throat. The tongue also tastes everything it touches.

Teeth
Food is chopped, torn, crushed, and ground into smaller pieces by the teeth.

Salivary glands
Six large salivary glands and around 1,000 tiny ones produce a total of about 2 pints (1 liter) of saliva every day.

Muscular wall squeezes

Muscular wall relaxes

Food

Swallowing
Food doesn't simply fall to the stomach when you swallow it. Instead, it's pushed through a tube called the esophagus by muscle action. The wall of the esophagus contracts behind the food to squeeze it along. A wave of contraction shoots all the way down the esophagus, pushing food to the stomach in 7-8 seconds.

1½ fl oz (45 ml)–the internal **volume** of an **empty stomach**.

6 pints (3 liters)–the maximum internal **volume** of a **full stomach**.

4 hours–the **average time** a large **meal spends** in the **stomach**.

151

How teeth work

Our teeth are the first line of attack in the digestive process, chomping and grinding food into smaller pieces. We have two sets of teeth during our lifetime: 20 milk teeth that last 6–10 years, followed by 32 permanent teeth. There are several different types of teeth. The front teeth (incisors) have thin edges that make them good for snipping and biting into things. The rear teeth (molars and premolars) are broader, with bumpy tops suited to grinding and crushing food. Canines are pointed teeth used for piercing and gripping. Human canines are small, but other mammals have long, sharp canines called fangs.

Canine

Premolars Incisors

Molars

Inside a tooth

Teeth are built to withstand a lifetime of wear and are coated in the hardest substance found in the human body: enamel. Beneath this is a bonelike tissue called dentine, which in turn surrounds a soft center that is highly sensitive to pain.

Crown

Root

Enamel
Calcium minerals make up 96 percent of tooth enamel, making it incredibly hard.

Dentine
This hard tissue is 70 percent mineral. Dentine can feel pain, unlike enamel.

Pulp cavity
The living heart of the tooth contains blood vessels and nerves.

Jawbone
The roots of teeth are cemented firmly into the jawbones.

In the stomach

Like a food processor, the stomach churns and mixes food until it turns into a thick liquid. Glands in the stomach wall secrete acid and enzymes that work together to break down protein molecules in food such as meat and fish. The stomach's wall can't absorb nutrients from food, but it can absorb water and medicines such as aspirin.

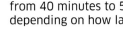

Small intestine

Air space
A space at the top allows gas to collect. The gas is released by burping (eructation).

Elastic wall
Deep folds in the stomach wall allow the stomach to expand like a balloon.

Liquidizer
Food stays in the stomach until it has turned into a soupy liquid free of lumps.

Triple muscle
Three layers of muscle contract in waves to churn food and mix digestive juices into it.

Acid bath

Millions of microscopic pits in the stomach lining (right) release a liquid called gastric acid, which is more acidic than lemon juice. Gastric acid kills germs and activates an enzyme called pepsin, which breaks down proteins. The stomach lining also secretes a layer of protective slime (mucus) to prevent the stomach from digesting itself.

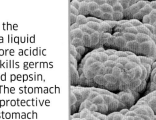
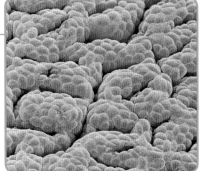

Filling and emptying

The stomach expands like a balloon as it fills. It can comfortably hold about 2 pints (1 liter) of food and drink when full but can expand to three times larger than this. Food spends from 40 minutes to 5 hours in the stomach, depending on how large and rich a meal is.

1 Filling up
The stomach expands and secretes gastric acid as you eat. The food and gastric acid collect in a pool at the bottom of the stomach.

Food mixed with gastric acid

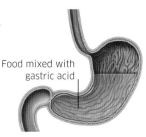

2 Churning
Muscles in the stomach wall contract rhythmically to stir the food and digestive juices together. Enzymes in the gastric acid chemically break down proteins.

Muscles contract

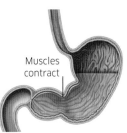

3 Emptying
A ring of muscle (the pyloric sphincter) opens up to let food pass into the intestine. The wall of the stomach contracts to squirt the liquefied food out.

Exit hole opens

Loud rumbling sounds

happen when the stomach is empty and its muscles contract to push unused digestive juices into the intestine.

Chemical attack

As soon as food leaves the stomach and enters the small intestine, it is mixed with powerful digestive chemicals from two nearby organs: the gall bladder and the pancreas. The gall bladder secretes a green liquid called bile, which neutralizes stomach acid and turns fats into tiny droplets that are easier to digest. The pancreas secretes at least seven digestive enzymes. These attack carbohydrate, protein, and fat molecules, breaking them down into smaller units.

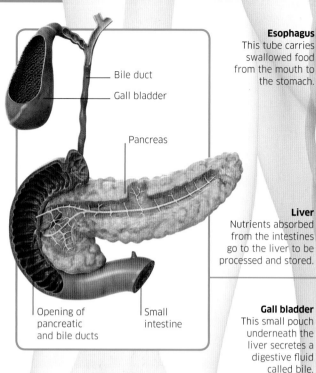

Bile duct

Gall bladder

Pancreas

Opening of pancreatic and bile ducts

Small intestine

Esophagus
This tube carries swallowed food from the mouth to the stomach.

Liver
Nutrients absorbed from the intestines go to the liver to be processed and stored.

Gall bladder
This small pouch underneath the liver secretes a digestive fluid called bile.

Small intestine
Most digestion happens inside this 23 ft (7 m) long tube. The nutrients released when food is broken down are absorbed by blood vessels in the wall.

The intestines

Coiled up in your abdomen, your small and large intestines form a single tube some 28 ft (8 m) long. As food travels through, a collection of chemicals breaks it down into molecules the body can absorb.

The intestines make up the most important part of the digestive system. Here, the process of chemical digestion is completed, and the nutrients released are absorbed into the bloodstream to be carried to other parts of the body. Like the stomach, the intestines have muscular walls that contract to squeeze food along. It takes only a few hours for a meal to pass through the small intestine, by which time nearly all the nutrients are absorbed. The remains then spend up to a day traveling slowly through the large intestine, where water is absorbed and bacteria help digest tough fibrous matter. The journey ends at the anus, where the undigested remains leave the body as feces.

Absorbing food

Lining the inside wall of the small intestine are millions of tiny, fingerlike growths called villi, each about 0.04 in (1 mm) long. Villi absorb the small food molecules produced by digestion, such as sugars and amino acids. These molecules pass into blood vessels in the villi to be carried away. Together, all the villi provide a huge surface area for absorption to take place. If all your villi were stretched out flat, they would cover the same area as a tennis court.

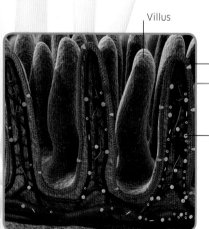

Villus

Blood vessel

Food molecule absorbed by villus

Rectum
When the undigested remains of food fill the rectum, its wall stretches, triggering an urge to go to the bathroom.

Anus
This ring of muscle opens to allow feces (undigested waste) to leave the body.

33 tons—the **total weight of food** processed by the **intestines** in an average **lifetime**.

153

Stomach
Food stays inside the stomach until it has turned into a creamy liquid.

Pancreas
This organ produces enzymes that break down proteins, fats, and carbohydrates.

Small and large intestines

The intestines run all the way from the stomach to the anus. There are two main sections. The first, longer section is the small intestine and does most of the work of digesting and absorbing food. The second section, called the large intestine, is twice the width of the small intestine and a quarter of its length. It receives watery leftovers from the small intestine and turns them into feces.

Large intestine
As food travels slowly through the large intestine, bacteria feed on it and multiply. The bacteria release vitamins and other nutrients, as well as producing odorous waste gases. The large intestine also absorbs water from food, making the undigested remains more solid.

100 trillion bacteria live inside the intestines, outnumbering human cells in the body. These bacteria release extra nutrients from food rich in fiber.

How digestion works

The nutrients in food are locked up in giant molecules that our bodies can't absorb directly. The process of digestion breaks these molecules into smaller molecules that can dissolve in body fluids and enter the blood. The digestive organs produce a range of chemicals called enzymes to break down food. Each enzyme attacks a particular type of food molecule.

Fats
Butter and oil are sources of fat. Enzymes in the small intestine break down fat into glycerol and fatty acid molecules.

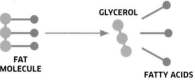

FAT MOLECULE → GLYCEROL / FATTY ACIDS

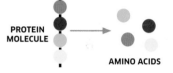

Proteins
Meat and cheese are rich in protein. Enzymes in the stomach and small intestine break protein molecules into amino acids.

PROTEIN MOLECULE → AMINO ACIDS

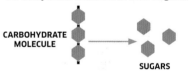

Carbohydrates
Foods rich in carbohydrates include pasta, rice, and bread. Enzymes in the mouth and small intestine split large carbohydrate molecules into sugars.

CARBOHYDRATE MOLECULE → SUGARS

Taking time

Getting all the nutrients from food takes time. From eating a meal to passing out the undigested remains can take between 20 and 44 hours. The speed depends on what you've eaten. Fruit and vegetables pass through the body much more quickly than meat.

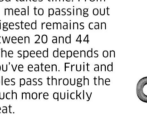

00:00:08
About eight seconds after you swallow food, it arrives in the stomach.

04:00:00
After four hours in the stomach, food is squirted out as a liquid.

07:00:00
Food is now almost completely digested and the nutrients are being absorbed.

09:00:00
The remains leave the small intestine.

15:00:00
Water is absorbed as waste passes along the large intestine.

24:00:00
The undigested leftovers leave the body as feces.

In the blood

Blood is the body's transport system. It carries food, oxygen, hormones, heat, and other vital resources to every living cell in the body, as well as taking away waste.

Blood circulates endlessly around the body, traveling through thousands of miles of tubes called blood vessels. The largest blood vessels are as thick as a garden hose. The tiniest are a tenth as wide as a hair and too small to see with the naked eye. As blood flows through the thinnest vessels, it releases oxygen and nutrients to keep the body's cells alive and functioning. It collects wastes from the same cells and carries them away to be removed from the body. Blood also contains cells that battle against germs and heal wounds. Other roles of blood include transporting chemical messengers called hormones and helping spread heat around the body.

Circulatory system

The heart and blood vessels make up the body's circulatory system. Blood leaves the heart in vessels called arteries (shown in red), which divide into finer and finer branches. It then passes through tiny vessels called capillaries, where it releases nutrients and collects waste. Capillaries join to form larger vessels called veins (shown in blue), which take blood back to the heart.

Vena cava
The largest vein is called the vena cava. It carries blood back to the heart.

Heart
The heart is a muscular pump that pushes blood around the body.

Aorta
As thick as your thumb, the aorta is the body's largest artery.

In the brain
About 20 percent of your blood flow goes to your brain.

Jugular vein
This large vein in the neck carries blood from the head to the heart.

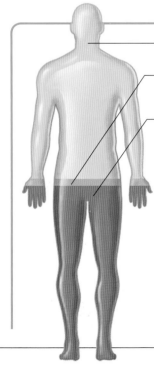

54%
plasma

1%
white blood cells and platelets

45%
red blood cells

What's blood made of?

Blood is a living tissue, consisting of about 20 trillion tiny, living cells floating in a yellowish liquid called plasma. Plasma is mainly water, but it also contains hundreds of vital substances that your body tissues need to stay alive, such as salt, sugar, fat, and protein. It also carries waste chemicals away. An average adult has about 10.6 pints (5 liters) of blood.

Red blood cells
These cells carry oxygen. They make up a quarter of all your body's cells.

Platelet cells
If your skin is cut, these cells make the blood clot.

White blood cells
Germs are killed by white blood cells.

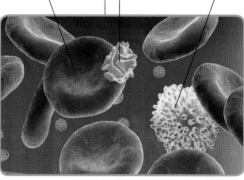

Blood cells

There are three main types of blood cells. By far the most numerous are red blood cells. These bright red, disc-shaped cells have the sole task of collecting oxygen in your lungs and releasing it everywhere else in your body. White blood cells roam through the body hunting for germs and destroying them. Platelet cells are tiny cell fragments that help blood to clot when the body is injured.

7 percent of your body weight is **blood**.

10.6 pints (5 liters)—the **volume** of **blood** in an adult's **body**.

5 million—the **number of red blood cells** in a drop of **blood**.

Arteries
These large blood vessels carry blood away from the heart. They have strong, muscular walls that stretch as blood surges past with each heartbeat. After stretching, arteries shrink back to normal size, which helps push the blood along.

Veins
Blood vessels that carry blood back to the heart are called veins. They have thinner walls than arteries. The force of the heartbeat is much weaker in veins, so veins use one-way valves to keep blood flowing.

Capillaries
Microscopic blood vessels called capillaries carry blood between arteries and veins. There are thousands of miles of capillaries running through almost every part of the body. Their very thin walls allow oxygen and nutrients to pass out of the blood into body tissues, as well as allowing waste to enter the blood.

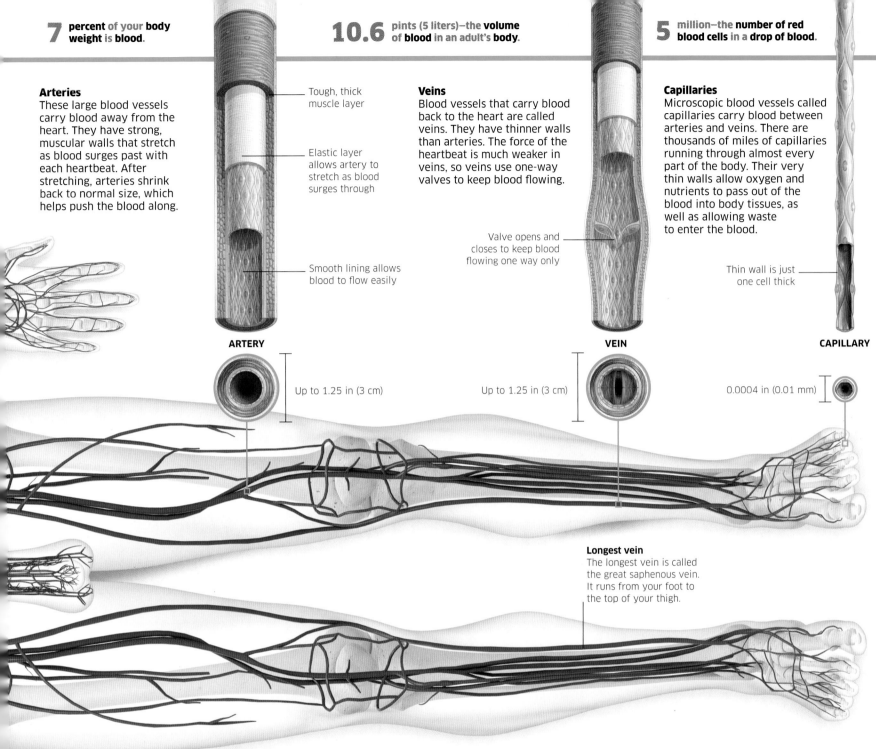

Tough, thick muscle layer

Elastic layer allows artery to stretch as blood surges through

Smooth lining allows blood to flow easily

Valve opens and closes to keep blood flowing one way only

Thin wall is just one cell thick

ARTERY — Up to 1.25 in (3 cm)

VEIN — Up to 1.25 in (3 cm)

CAPILLARY — 0.0004 in (0.01 mm)

Longest vein
The longest vein is called the great saphenous vein. It runs from your foot to the top of your thigh.

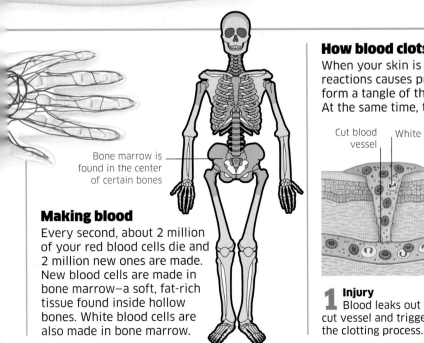

Making blood
Every second, about 2 million of your red blood cells die and 2 million new ones are made. New blood cells are made in bone marrow—a soft, fat-rich tissue found inside hollow bones. White blood cells are also made in bone marrow.

Bone marrow is found in the center of certain bones

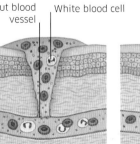

How blood clots
When your skin is cut, a series of chemical reactions causes proteins in blood plasma to form a tangle of threads that trap blood cells. At the same time, the tiny platelet cells in blood change shape, becoming spiky, and then stick together in clumps. These two processes make blood turn solid—it clots. The clotted blood hardens and dries to form a protective scab.

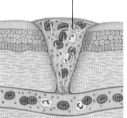
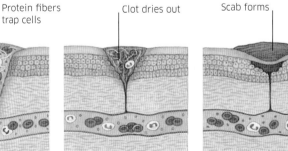

Cut blood vessel

White blood cell

Protein fibers trap cells

Clot dries out

Scab forms

1 Injury
Blood leaks out of a cut vessel and triggers the clotting process.

2 Clot
Protein fibers form a tangled mesh that stops blood flow.

3 Seal
The clot seals the damaged area, stopping further blood loss.

4 Scab
The clot solidifies into a protective scab while the wound heals.

The heart

People once thought the heart was the seat of thought and emotion, but now we know better: it is simply a muscular pump that beats tirelessly to keep blood flowing.

Unlike other muscles in the body, which need to rest and recover after heavy use, the heart is built to work nonstop. It beats 70 times a minute, 100,000 times a day, and 40 million times a year—pumping enough blood in the average lifetime to fill three supertankers. With each beat it squeezes out about a cupful of blood, using sufficient force to keep blood moving through the body's 60,000 miles (100,000 km) of blood vessels. A continual supply of fresh blood is vital to the body's cells because without it, they will die of oxygen starvation in minutes.

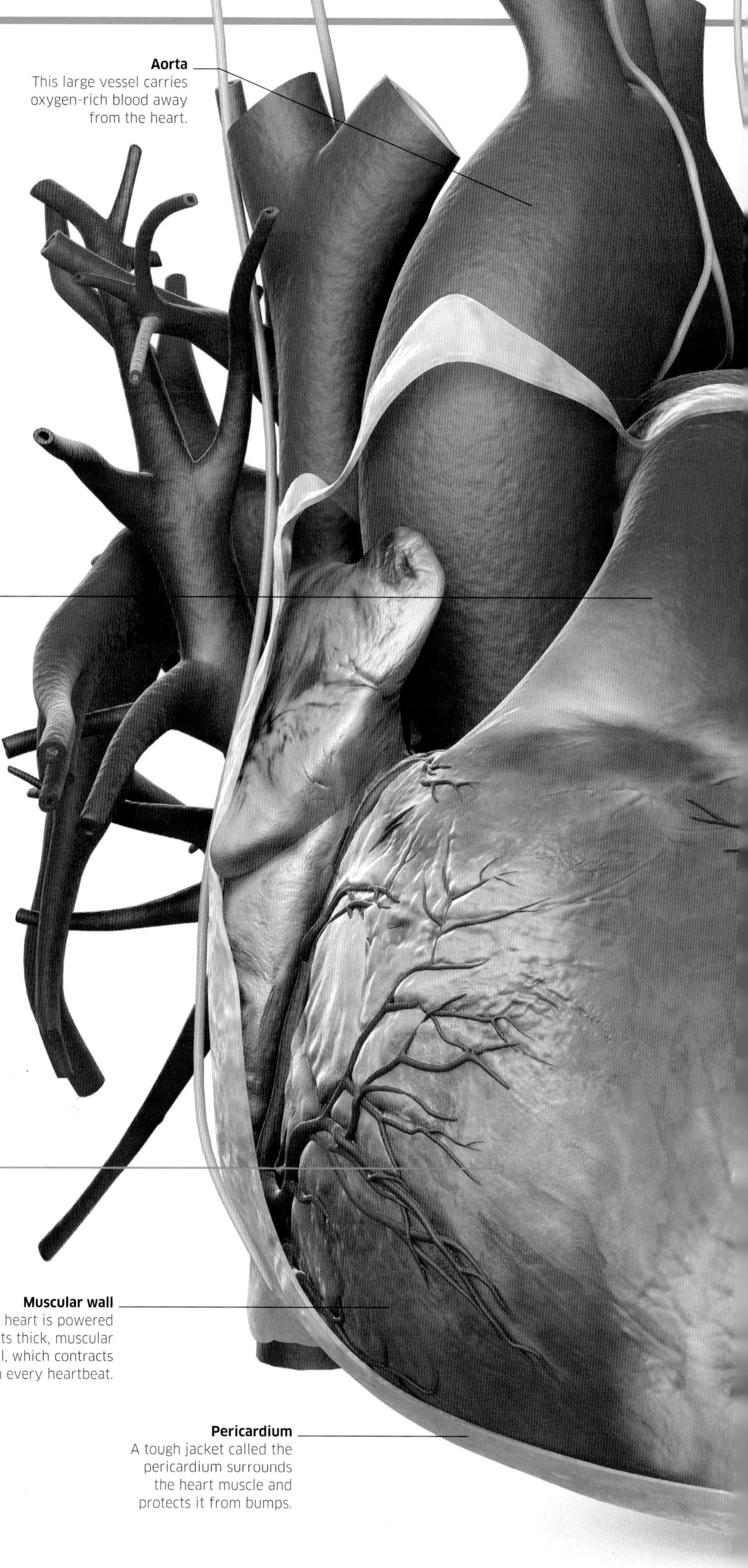

Beating heart

Hollow in the middle and with thick walls of powerful muscle, the heart is about the same size as a clenched fist—and just as strong. The top of the heart is connected to a maze of heavy-duty blood vessels. Blood pours in through vessels called veins, filling the heart's inner chambers. When the heart beats, its muscular wall squeezes and forces the blood out through vessels called arteries.

Mitochondria   Protein fibers

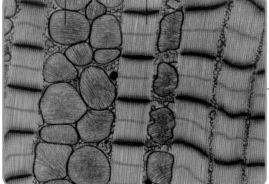

Heart cells

The heart is made of a special type of muscle (cardiac muscle), seen here magnified thousands of times by a microscope. Heart muscle cells burn through energy at a rapid rate and need more fuel and oxygen than other cells. They are fueled by fat, and the energy is released by oval-shaped bodies called mitochondria. Like ordinary muscle cells, they are packed with microscopic protein fibers arranged in parallel. These fibers slide across each other to make the cells contract.

Aorta
This large vessel carries oxygen-rich blood away from the heart.

Pulmonary artery
This blood vessel takes stale blood to the lungs to pick up fresh oxygen.

Muscular wall
The heart is powered by its thick, muscular wall, which contracts with every heartbeat.

Pericardium
A tough jacket called the pericardium surrounds the heart muscle and protects it from bumps.

In one year, the **heart pumps** out enough **blood to fill an** Olympic-size **swimming pool**.

3 billion—the **number of heartbeats** in an average **human lifetime**.

5 hours—the length of time **a heart can survive if removed** from the **body**.

157

14,800 pints (7,000 liters) of blood passes through an average person's heart every day.

Pulmonary vein
After collecting fresh oxygen in the lungs, blood flows back to the heart along the pulmonary vein.

Nerves
Nerves carry signals from the brain to the heart, telling it when to beat faster or slower.

Heart valve
Inside the heart are four large valves that make sure the blood flows one way only. Heart valves have two or three flaps that are forced apart by a surge of blood when the heart pumps. When the blood tries to flow back, it fills the flaps and pulls them together, shutting the valve. The sound of your heartbeat is the sound of your heart valves snapping shut.

Coronary arteries
As well as pumping blood to the body, the heart pumps blood through its own muscular wall. Heart muscle works very hard and needs a generous supply of oxygen-rich blood.

Coronary vein
After delivering oxygen and fuel to the muscular wall of the heart, used blood flows back along veins (shown in blue).

Inside the heart
The heart is divided into two halves, allowing it to work as two pumps in one. The right half pumps stale blood to the lungs to pick up oxygen from air. The left half pumps the oxygen-rich blood to the rest of the body.

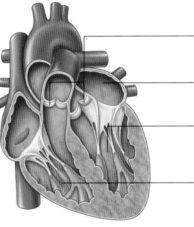

Valves
One-way valves stop blood flowing backward.

Atria
The heart has two small top chambers called atria.

Left ventricle
This large, muscular chamber pumps blood to most parts of the body.

Right ventricle
The smaller right-hand chamber pumps blood to the lungs and back.

Heartbeat cycle
Each beat of the heart involves several carefully timed steps. The whole sequence is controlled by a wave of electricity that sweeps through the heart's muscular wall, triggering the contraction of muscle cells.

1 Filling up
Between heartbeats, blood enters the heart through veins and collects in the top chambers (atria).

Blood returning from the body

Blood returning from the lungs

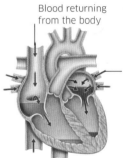

Right atrium contracts   Left atrium contracts

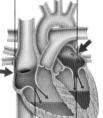

2 Atria contract
The top chambers contract, pushing the blood through valves into the two lower chambers (ventricles).

Blood forced into the ventricles

Blood sent to the body

Blood sent to the lungs

3 Ventricles contract
Finally, the ventricles contract with great force, pushing the blood out to every part of the body.

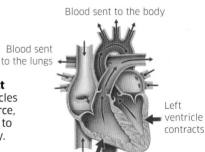

Left ventricle contracts

Right ventricle contracts

Fast and slow
Your heart beats up to 200 times a minute when you're excited or physically active, but the rate falls as low as 60 beats a minute when you're resting or asleep.

Average heart rate:
70-80
beats per minute

Tears
With every blink, watery tears wash dirt and bacteria off the surface of your eyes. Tears also contain lysozyme, a chemical that destroys the cell walls of bacteria.

Saliva
Continually produced by glands in your cheeks and under your tongue, saliva flushes germs out of your mouth and into your stomach, where acid destroys them. Saliva also contains a range of antibacterial chemicals that attack germs.

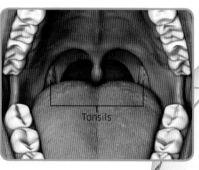

Salivary gland

Tonsils
These soft red areas at the back of the mouth are packed with white blood cells that destroy germs from food or the air. When you have a sore throat caused by viruses or bacteria, your tonsils swell up as they help fight the germs.

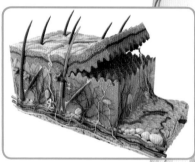

Tonsils

Skin
Your skin forms a thick, protective barrier that germs cannot cross, unless the skin gets cut. Glands in the skin secrete sweat and an oily fluid called sebum, both of which contain chemicals that repel germs.

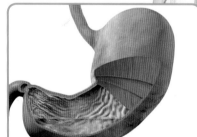

Stomach acid
The lining of the stomach makes powerful hydrochloric acid, which destroys germs in food. It also kills the germs in mucus from the throat, which we swallow regularly to help keep the airways clean.

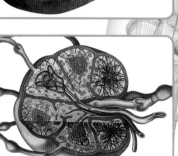

Lymph node
As body fluids flow through the vessels of the lymphatic system, they are filtered through swellings called lymph nodes, which vary from the size of a period to the size of a grape. They are packed with white blood cells that screen the passing fluid for germs and destroy them.

Lymphatic vessels
The vessels of the lymphatic system run through every part of the body.

Lymph nodes
The neck contains around 300 lymph nodes. They swell up when you have an infection.

Into the blood
Having been filtered for germs, fluid from the lymphatic system enters the bloodstream here.

Fighting germs

Your body is under constant attack. Tiny organisms are continually trying to get inside you and multiply, which can make you sick. Fortunately, your body has a powerful immune system to repel the invaders.

The first line of defense against germs is your body's surface, which acts as a barrier. The surface includes not only your skin but also the surface of your eyes and the soft tissues lining your mouth, nose, throat, and stomach. If germs find a break in any part of your body—such as a cut—the damaged tissue reacts immediately by becoming inflamed: it swells and fills with germ-destroying blood cells. Many parts of the immune system work to block all kinds of germs, but others are more specific. Your adaptive immune system identifies new germs and then targets them specifically. It also remembers them for the future, giving you immunity to the diseases they cause.

Filtering germs

Germs that break through the body's barriers and invade internal tissues do not usually survive for long. The human body contains a network of tiny vessels that collect fluid from every organ and carefully filter it for germs, which are swiftly destroyed. This network of vessels is called the lymphatic system. Dotted along its vessels are small filtering units called lymph nodes, which are packed with germ-destroying cells.

Spleen
The largest organ in the lymphatic system, the spleen filters blood for germs, destroys antibody-coated germs, and serves as a store for blood cells.

Germs

Whenever you touch something or breathe in, you pick up tiny organisms too small to see. Most do no harm, but some try to invade your body and feed on you. Harmful microorganisms are called germs. The most common types are viruses and bacteria. Viruses cause colds, warts, and many diseases. Bacteria make wounds swell up and can also cause various diseases.

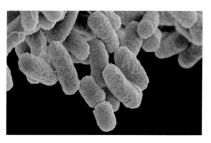

Bacteria
Bacteria are single-celled organisms. They are so tiny that hundreds could fit on the point of a needle.

Defense force

The human body contains about 50 billion white blood cells. These are the body's defenders. They seek out germs and kill them, using a variety of different methods. White blood cells called macrophages kill by swallowing germs whole and digesting them.

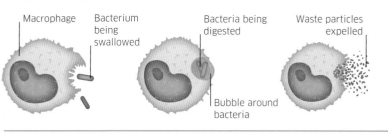

Macrophage | Bacterium being swallowed | Bacteria being digested | Waste particles expelled

Bubble around bacteria

How antibodies work

Antibodies are chemicals that stick to specific kinds of germs, flagging them for destruction. There are millions of different germs, but the human body can manufacture 10 billion different antibodies, ensuring there's one for any germ you encounter. Once an antibody cell has been activated by meeting a matching germ, it makes copies of itself and makes the body immune.

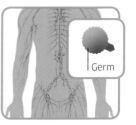

Germ

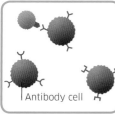

Antibody cell

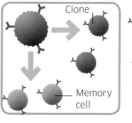

Clone

Memory cell

1 Infect
A new germ invades the body and multiplies. It gets carried by body fluids to a lymph node, where many different white blood cells examine it.

2 Detect
Antibody cells touch the germ to see if it matches molecules on their surface. Eventually, an antibody cell with matching molecules sticks to the germ.

3 Activate
Now activated, the matching cell makes an army of clones. It also makes memory cells, which will stay in the body for years in case the germ returns.

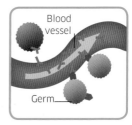

Blood vessel

Germ

4 Seek
The clones make antibodies and release them into the blood. When they find germs, they stick to them.

Macrophage

5 Destroy
The antibodies act as guides to cells called macrophages, which swallow and destroy the germs.

An allergy
occurs when the immune system attacks something harmless, like pollen or household dust.

A vaccine
triggers your body into producing antibodies, making you immune to a disease without having to suffer it.

Waterworks

The bladder's stretchy wall allows it to hold up to 1.48 pints (700 ml) of urine, but the urge to pass urine is triggered when it contains just a quarter of this.

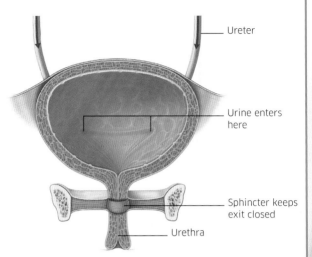

Ureter

Urine enters here

Sphincter keeps exit closed

Urethra

Bladder full

The bladder's muscular wall stretches as it fills up. This activates nerve cells embedded in the bladder wall, which send signals to the brain and trigger the urge to urinate.

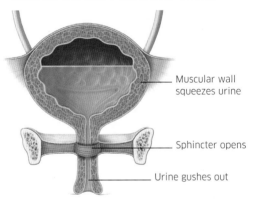

Muscular wall squeezes urine

Sphincter opens

Urine gushes out

Bladder empties

Circular muscles called sphincters normally keep the bladder's exit closed. When you urinate, the sphincters open and the bladder's wall contracts to force urine out through the urethra.

Why is it yellow?

The yellow color of urine is due to a waste chemical produced when the body breaks down old red blood cells. Some foods change the color of urine—beets makes it pink and asparagus makes it green. The amount of water in urine also affects its color.

ENOUGH WATER

SHADES OF YELLOW
Urine is pale when it contains lots of water and dark if it contains little water. If your urine looks dark yellow, you need to drink more water.

DEHYDRATED

Vena cava
This large vein carries blood back up to the heart.

Aorta
This large artery carries oxygen-rich blood from the heart to the body.

Adrenal gland
On top of each kidney is a small gland that makes adrenaline—a hormone that prepares the body for sudden action.

Right kidney
The right kidney is slightly lower in the body than the left kidney to make room for the liver.

Renal artery
This blood vessel carries blood into the kidney.

Renal vein
This blood vessel carries cleaned blood out of the kidney.

Left ureter
Two tubes called ureters carry urine from the kidneys to the bladder.

Urinary system

The urinary system includes the two kidneys, the bladder, and various tubes for carrying urine. The kidneys are reddish-brown organs on either side of the spine, each about the size of a computer mouse. The urine they make trickles constantly down two long tubes called ureters to a stretchy storage organ—the bladder. When this is full, the urine leaves the body through a tube called the urethra.

Right ureter

Urethra
Urine leaves the body through a tube called the urethra.

Bladder
This stretchy, muscular bag stores urine.

450 gallons (1,700 liters)—the amount of **blood cleaned** by the kidneys **every day**.

19 miles (30 km)—the **total length** of **filtering tubes** inside one kidney.

161

Cleaning the blood

The body has its own internal cleaning service called the urinary system, which filters the blood. It removes toxic wastes and excess water from the body, turning them into urine, while keeping back useful substances.

As well as carrying substances like oxygen and food around the body, the blood picks up chemical waste products. These chemicals would poison us if they were left to build up, so they are removed by the urinary system.

Blood is filtered and cleaned in a pair of bean-shaped organs called kidneys, which are located next to the spine. Every day, all the blood in the body passes through the kidneys 300 times. Although we have two kidneys, just 75 percent of one kidney would be enough for us to survive without becoming ill. That's why some people are able to donate one of their kidneys to someone whose own kidneys have been damaged by disease.

Water balance

As well as getting rid of waste chemicals, the urinary system helps us maintain a healthy level of water in the body. When there's too much water in the blood, the kidneys allow a lot of water to pass into the urine. When the water level in the blood is low, the brain releases a hormone that tells the kidneys to reabsorb some of the water from urine. As a result, we produce a smaller volume of darker, more concentrated urine when we're dehydrated.

In and out

Most of our water comes from food and drinks, but a small amount is "metabolic water"—water created by chemical reactions in our cells. We lose water mainly through urine and through breathing.

WATER IN

60% drinks

30% food

10% metabolic water

WATER OUT

60% urine

28% lungs and skin

8% sweat

4% feces

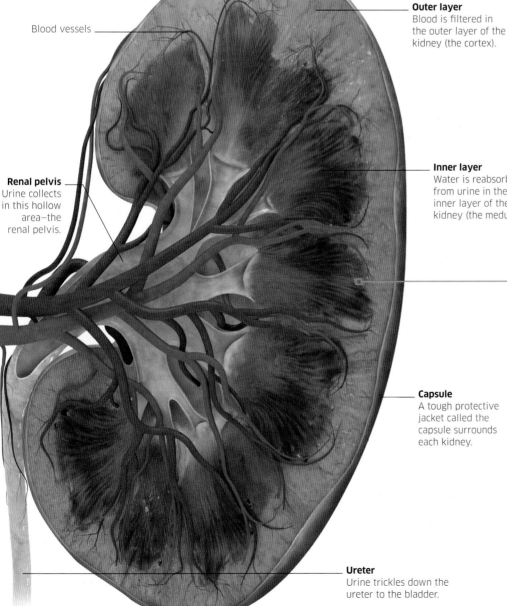

Blood vessels

Outer layer
Blood is filtered in the outer layer of the kidney (the cortex).

Renal pelvis
Urine collects in this hollow area—the renal pelvis.

Inner layer
Water is reabsorbed from urine in the inner layer of the kidney (the medulla).

Capsule
A tough protective jacket called the capsule surrounds each kidney.

Ureter
Urine trickles down the ureter to the bladder.

Inside the kidney

Each kidney contains about one million microscopic filtering units called nephrons. The first part of a nephron is a tiny, tangled knot of blood capillaries that allows fluid to leak out. The fluid then flows along a long, looping tube, from which useful substances and water are reabsorbed. The leftover fluid becomes urine and drains out of the kidney to be stored in the bladder.

Blood filter
In the filtering units of the kidneys, blood flows into knots of tiny blood vessels called capillaries (pink, above). Wrapped around these are cells called podocytes (beige, above). The podocytes act as sieves, allowing small molecules such as water to pass through but stopping cells and larger molecules from leaving the blood.

In medieval times, doctors attempted to diagnose disease by studying urine. They examined its color, smell, and cloudiness—and then tasted a sample.

Air supply

Every minute, without you thinking about it or even noticing, your lungs take in about 15 breaths of air. This vital process of breathing keeps all the cells in your body supplied with the life-giving gas oxygen.

Oxygen is essential for life. Without it, the cells in your body would not be able to release the hidden energy trapped in food molecules. With each gulp of air, fresh oxygen is drawn deep into your lungs. The air is channeled through hollow tubes that branch into finer and finer passages. Finally, it reaches a dead end, formed by millions of tiny, bubble-shaped pockets that swell up like balloons as they fill with air. Oxygen passes through the walls of these air pockets and into the microscopic blood vessels that surround them, to be carried away by red blood cells. The waste gas carbon dioxide travels the opposite direction, from the blood to the air pockets, to be breathed back out.

Inside the lungs

The lungs are spongy, lightweight organs that fill most of the space inside the chest. They are 10 percent solid and 90 percent air, making them so light that they could float on water. The combined surface area of all the tiny air pockets inside the lungs is huge: about 750 sq ft (70 square meters), which is 40 times the surface area of your skin. The surface area needs to be large so that as much oxygen as possible can be absorbed from the air with each breath.

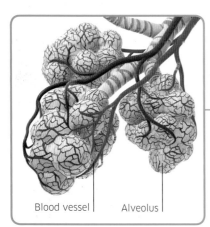

Blood vessel | Alveolus

Air pockets

The tiny air pockets in the lungs are called alveoli. Each single alveolus is just a fraction of a millimeter across and has a network of blood vessels wrapped around it. The walls of the alveoli and blood vessels are so thin that oxygen can pass freely across to enter the blood.

Nose
Most of the air we breathe travels through the nose. Inside the nose, hairs and sticky fluids trap dust and germs, preventing them from reaching the lungs.

Mouth
When we're out of breath, we breathe through the mouth as well as the nose.

Voice box
The flow of air from the lungs creates the sound of our voices when it passes through the voice box.

Windpipe
The main airway to the lungs is called the windpipe, or trachea.

Branching airways
The airways inside the lungs divide into smaller and smaller branches called bronchioles, forming a shape like a tree.

Double lining
Each lung is surrounded by two soft, slippery sheets of tissue (membranes). A layer of fluid between these lets the sheets slide across each other as the lungs expand.

Breathing muscle
Under the lungs is a large sheet of muscle shaped in a dome–the diaphragm. This muscle pulls air into the lungs by flattening as it contracts.

100 mph (160 kph)—the **speed** that **air travels in a sneeze**.

500 million—the **number of alveoli in one lung**.

44 lb (20 kg)—the **amount of dust** you will **breathe in during your life**.

163

Cleaning the lungs

Air contains tiny flecks of dust and germs that could damage our lungs. To get rid of this dirt, the airways make a sticky liquid called mucus, which traps particles. Microscopic hairs lining the surface of the airways beat back and forth to push the mucus upward to the throat, so it can be coughed or sneezed out or swallowed.

Blood vessels

Large blood vessels carry stale blood directly from the heart to the lungs and carry fresh, oxygen-rich blood back to the heart.

Heart

The heart fits snugly in a hollow between the lungs, slightly to the left side of the body.

How breathing works

The lungs have no muscles. To suck in air and push it out again, they rely on the muscles around them. The diaphragm muscle does most of the work, but the rib muscles also help, especially when you breathe deeply.

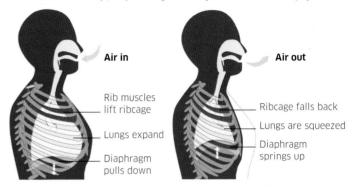

Air in

Rib muscles lift ribcage

Lungs expand

Diaphragm pulls down

Air out

Ribcage falls back

Lungs are squeezed

Diaphragm springs up

Breathing in
The diaphragm contracts and pulls flat, and the rib muscles lift up the ribcage. The chest gets larger, making the lungs expand and suck in air.

Breathing out
The diaphragm relaxes and springs upward, and the ribcage falls back down. The chest gets smaller, squeezing the lungs and pushing out air.

Gas exchange

Because the lungs take oxygen from the air and release waste carbon dioxide, the air you breathe in is different from the air you breathe out. There is also a lot more water vapor in exhaled breath, from moisture in the airways. On a cold day you can see this moisture turn into mist when you breathe out.

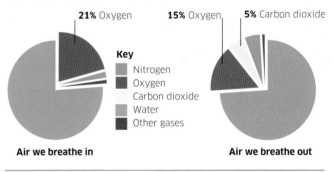

21% Oxygen

15% Oxygen

5% Carbon dioxide

Key
Nitrogen
Oxygen
Carbon dioxide
Water
Other gases

Air we breathe in

Air we breathe out

YOU BREATHE IN ABOUT
21,000 PINTS
(10,000 LITERS) OF AIR EVERY DAY.
THAT'S ENOUGH TO FILL 1,000 BALLOONS.

Lungs and lobes

Your right lung is slightly bigger than your left lung. It has three parts, or lobes, while the left lung has only two. Like many parts of the body, lungs come in pairs. If one becomes damaged by injury or disease, the other acts as a backup, keeping you alive on its own.

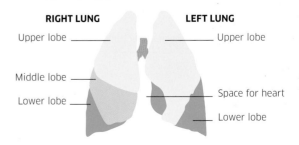

RIGHT LUNG

LEFT LUNG

Upper lobe

Upper lobe

Middle lobe

Space for heart

Lower lobe

Lower lobe

CONTROL CENTER

The brain and spinal cord make up the central nervous system, which serves as the nervous system's control center. In very simple animals, brains do little more than coordinate basic reflexes, a task carried out in humans by the spinal cord. The human brain, however, has evolved into something far more complex, able to generate an inner world and a conscious self that can reflect, plan, and make decisions. How these higher functions work remains a mystery to science.

The human brain

Filling the space inside the skull, the human brain is dominated by a large, folded structure called the cerebrum. Far larger in humans than in other animals, the cerebrum is responsible for conscious thought, planning, social judgment, and language. Beneath the cerebrum is the limbic system, which generates emotions, and the cerebellum, which coordinates movement.

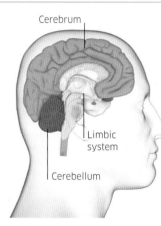

Cerebrum

Limbic system

Cerebellum

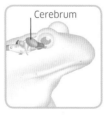

Brain in action

Until recently, scientists could only guess at how the brain creates thoughts. The invention of brain scanners has provided a window on its workings. Functional brain scans reveal that different brain areas specialize in specific tasks, yet mental processes often involve many brain areas working together.

Brain scan
This MRI scan shows the right side of the brain light up as a person moves their left hand.

Brain evolution

The human brain shares many features with the brains of other vertebrates (animals with backbones)—a sign of our shared evolutionary history. Our closest vertebrate relatives are other mammals, which, like us, have a large cerebrum. The thinking part of the brain, the cerebrum allows mammals to learn complex behaviors. The mammal brain also includes a limbic system, which produces emotions such as rage and fear.

Cerebrum

Cerebrum

Cerebrum

Limbic system

Cerebellum

Cerebellum

Frog brain
Frogs have a small cerebrum and rely on preprogrammed instincts more than learned behavior.

Bird brain
The well-developed cerebellum in a bird brain helps to control balance and speed during flight.

Cat brain
Mammals have a larger cerebrum than other animals, making them better able to learn and adapt.

IN CONTROL

Just as an orchestra needs a conductor, so the many organs in the human body need to be coordinated to work together well. The nervous system is the body's main control network. Using high-speed electrical signals, it sends messages along cables called nerves, controlling muscles, glands, and organs. The body also uses chemicals called hormones to send messages via the blood. These act more slowly than nerves.

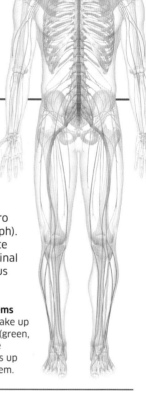

NERVOUS SYSTEM

The brain, nerves, and sense organs make up the body's nervous system. The nervous system carries information around the body in the form of electrical signals. The various parts of the system are in constant communication and continually active. Messages stream into the brain from the senses every split second. At the same time, the brain coordinates the exact tension of hundreds of muscles around the body, from the tiny muscles that move the eyes to the large muscles needed for running.

Control network

Many of the body's nerve cells are bundled together to form cables called nerves. Nerves run to every part of your body, carrying signals to and fro at up to 250 mph (400 kph). Most nerves communicate with the brain via the spinal cord—a column of nervous tissue inside the spine.

Central and peripheral systems
The brain and spinal cord make up the central nervous system (green, above), while the rest of the body's nervous tissue makes up the peripheral nervous system.

Sensing and reacting

The nervous system has three main parts. The first part collects information from sense organs that monitor the outside world and the inner state of the body. The second part—the central nervous system

processes the information and creates a sense of awareness. The third part makes the body react. These three parts work together very quickly, allowing the body to react to a stimulus in a split second.

Stimulus
Sense organs gather information about the world and send signals via sensory neurons to the brain.

Processing
Incoming signals are analyzed in the brain, which decides how the body should react.

Response
Motor neurons carry outgoing signals to muscles, glands, and other organs, producing a rapid response.

Voluntary and involuntary actions

Some of the responses made by our nervous system are under voluntary control, while others are involuntary—they happen without our choice. The voluntary division is called the somatic nervous system, while the involuntary division is called the autonomic nervous system.

Somatic nervous system
This branch of the nervous system controls parts of the body that you control at will, such as the muscles you use to hold this book or kick a ball.

Autonomic nervous system
This part of the nervous system controls organs without you having to think. It makes your heart speed up and slow down, pushes food through your intestines, and controls how wide the pupils in your eyes are.

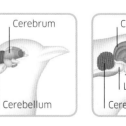

HORMONES

The electric signals that shoot down nerves are not the only messages traveling around the body. Hormones are chemicals that carry messages. They are released into the blood by glands and have powerful effects elsewhere in the body, acting more slowly than nerve signals. Hormones affect only certain target cells, changing the way they work. There are two main ways that hormones can activate their target cells.

Water-soluble hormones

These hormones can dissolve in water but not fat. They are unable to pass through the cell membrane of target cells, which have fatty layers. Instead, they bind to receptors on the cell surface and trigger chemical changes inside the cell.

Fat-soluble hormones

These hormones can dissolve in fat. They pass through the membrane of target cells and bind to receptor molecules inside the cell. The hormone then enters the cell nucleus and switches certain genes on or off. Fat-soluble hormones include sex hormones, such as testosterone.

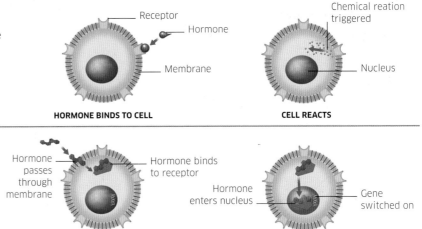

Receptor
Hormone
Membrane

HORMONE BINDS TO CELL

Chemical reation triggered
Nucleus

CELL REACTS

Hormone passes through membrane
Hormone binds to receptor

HORMONE ENTERS CELL

Hormone enters nucleus
Gene switched on

CELL REACTS

Nerve cells

The cells that make up the nervous system are called nerve cells, or neurons. Neurons transmit electric signals along long fibers called axons, which are sheathed by a fatty material called myelin to help the signal travel faster. There are three main types of neurons.

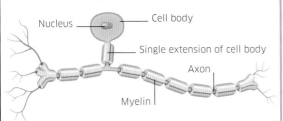

Nucleus
Cell body
Single extension of cell body
Axon
Myelin

Unipolar neurons

These neurons typically carry incoming sensory signals. The cell body has a single extension.

Dendrite carries incoming signal
Axon carries outgoing signal

Bipolar neurons

These neurons are found in the eyes and in muscles. The cell body of a bipolar neuron has two extensions.

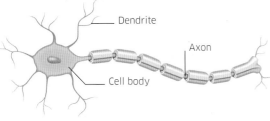

Dendrite
Axon
Cell body

Multipolar neurons

Found in the brain, these are the most common neurons. The cell body has multiple extensions.

THE HUMAN BRAIN CONTAINS ABOUT 100,000 MILES (165,000 KM) OF AXONS.

SENSES

Sense organs gather information about the world and send it to the brain as a stream of electric signals. The brain then decodes this information and uses it to create a feeling of conscious awareness.

Main senses

Five main senses dominate our inner world, with vision being by far the most important. Most of our main senses are created by specialized organs, such as eyes and ears. Large areas of the brain are devoted to processing the incoming signals from these organs.

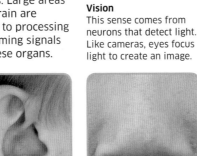

Vision
This sense comes from neurons that detect light. Like cameras, eyes focus light to create an image.

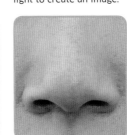

Hearing
Sound consists of invisible waves traveling through air at high speed. Our ears capture and amplify these waves.

Smell
Neurons in the roof of the nose create this sense by detecting thousands of different chemicals in the air we breathe.

Taste
Chemical sensors in the mouth detect five tastes: salty, sweet, sour, bitter, and savory (umami).

Touch
Skin contains a range of different sensory receptors sensitive to different types of touch.

Additional senses

The human body has far more than five senses. Our additional senses help us to move, balance, and detect heat, pain, and the passage of time.

Pain
This sense is a warning that part of the body is damaged and must be left alone while it heals.

Bladder and rectum
Stretch sensors in the bladder and rectum walls trigger the urge to go to the bathroom.

Heat
Heat sensors all over the skin, lips, and mouth can feel warmth or cold, even from a distance.

Muscle sense
Muscles contain stretch sensors that tell the brain about the body's posture, position, and movement.

Gravity
The inner ear contains tiny gravity sensors that tell the brain which way is up, helping us balance.

Time
A clusters of neurons in the heart of the brain works as an inner clock, helping us sense time.

166 human body ∘ IN CONTROL

0.01 seconds—the **time a nerve signal takes** to travel from **your brain to your toe**.

Parts of the nervous system

The nervous system has two main parts. The central nervous system (below, green) consists of the brain and spinal cord. Together, these process incoming signals and decide how the body should react. The peripheral nervous system (yellow) carries signals around the rest of the body, linking the central nervous system to sense organs, muscles, and other parts of the body.

Brain   Spinal cord

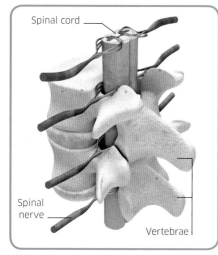

Spinal cord

Spinal nerve

Vertebrae

Spinal cord

Running all the way down the inside of your backbone is your spinal cord—a bundle of nerve tissue containing billions of nerve cells. The spinal cord relays signals between the brain and body, as well as controlling reflex actions (see below). It is protected by a stack of interlocking bones called vertebrae.

Ulnar nerve

This nerve runs under the skin in your elbow. If you bump your elbow, the nerve tingles. People sometimes describe this as "bumping your funny bone."

Nervous system

The human body is controlled by a network of living wires called the nervous system. While man-made wires carry power, the cells that make up the nervous system carry information.

Your nervous system makes it possible for you to react to the world with lightning speed. Every moment, electrical signals from your senses shoot along your nerves, racing toward your brain at up to 250 mph (400 kph). Your brain analyzes the flood of incoming information, decides how to respond, and sends outgoing signals to muscles and other organs, telling them what to do. Much of your nervous system is under voluntary control, which means you can choose how to react. However, many parts of the nervous system work automatically, controlling your internal organs and reflexes without your conscious awareness.

Nerve cells

The nervous system is made up of billions of cells called neurons (nerve cells). These odd-looking cells have many finely branched fibers extending from the main cell body. A typical neuron has one large fiber (an axon) that carries outgoing electrical signals, and a large number of smaller fibers (dendrites) that carry incoming signals. Neurons connect to other neurons at junctions called synapses.

Synapse

Dendrite

Nucleus

Cell body

Axon

Signal is carried to next neuron

Sheath of a fatty substance called myelin insulates axon, making signal travel faster

NEURON

2 billion—the approximate **number of nerve endings** in **your skin**.

100 trillion—the minimum **number of synapses** in your brain.

0 The number of **pain receptors** in your brain.

167

Longest nerve
The sciatic nerve is the longest nerve in the body, running from the spine to the foot.

Tibial nerve
This nerve makes the calf muscle contract, flexing your foot and providing the push that allows you to walk.

Finger nerves
Nerves in your hands carry signals from touch receptors in your fingers to your brain.

If all the nerve cells in your body were laid end to end, they could **wrap around Earth** two and a half times.

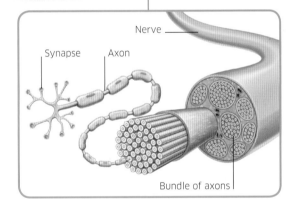

Inside a nerve
Nerve cells have long extensions called axons that can stretch to 3 ft (1 m) in length. Axons running through the body are bundled together to form nerves, much as electric wires are bundled to form cables. Each axon inside a nerve carries a separate electric signal.

Nerve

Synapse Axon

Bundle of axons

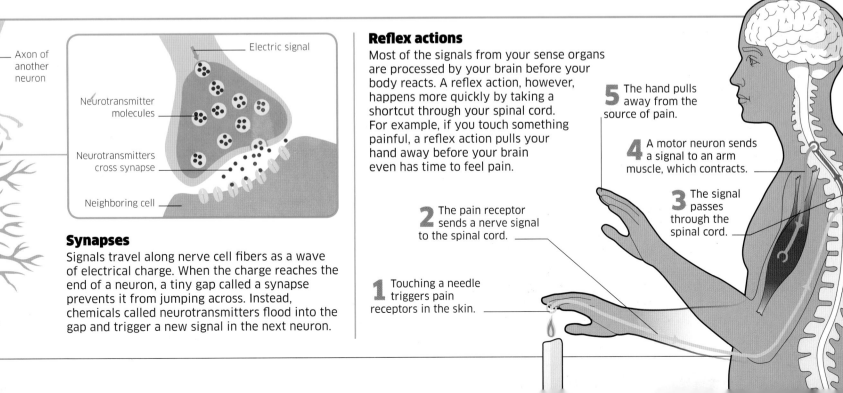

Axon of another neuron

Electric signal

Neurotransmitter molecules

Neurotransmitters cross synapse

Neighboring cell

Synapses

Signals travel along nerve cell fibers as a wave of electrical charge. When the charge reaches the end of a neuron, a tiny gap called a synapse prevents it from jumping across. Instead, chemicals called neurotransmitters flood into the gap and trigger a new signal in the next neuron.

Reflex actions

Most of the signals from your sense organs are processed by your brain before your body reacts. A reflex action, however, happens more quickly by taking a shortcut through your spinal cord. For example, if you touch something painful, a reflex action pulls your hand away before your brain even has time to feel pain.

5 The hand pulls away from the source of pain.

4 A motor neuron sends a signal to an arm muscle, which contracts.

3 The signal passes through the spinal cord.

2 The pain receptor sends a nerve signal to the spinal cord.

1 Touching a needle triggers pain receptors in the skin.

168 human body ○ **IN CONTROL**

100 billion—the **number of neurons** in your brain.

125 trillion—the approximate **number of synapses** in your **brain**.

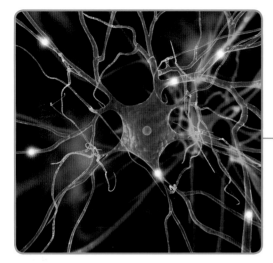

Movement
The top of the cerebral cortex sends signals to muscles to make the body move.

Thinking
The front part of the cerebral cortex is important in conscious thinking, planning, and understanding other people's thoughts.

Speech
Known as Broca's area, this part of the brain is vital in generating speech.

Hearing
Nerve signals from the ears come to the auditory cortex, which creates the sense of hearing.

Brain stem
Situated at the top of the spinal cord, this part of the inner brain controls vital functions such as breathing and the heartbeat.

Brain cells
The brain is made up of cells called neurons, which send electrical signals to each other via thin, wirelike strands that connect at junctions called synapses. A computer chip has about a billion transistors with 3 to 4 connections each, but the human brain has 100 billion neurons with up to 10,000 synapses each. Synapses are more complex than the simple on/off switches in a computer chip. Each one may contain up to 1,000 molecular switches, giving the human brain phenomenal processing power.

Brainpower

Locked safely inside your skull is your brain—the headquarters of your nervous system and your body's control center.

More complex and powerful than the brain of any other animal, the human brain is the most poorly understood organ in the body. Somehow this cauliflower-shaped mass of nerve cells creates a whole inner world of experience and a sense of self. Everything you see, touch, think, dream, and remember is generated within it. In some respects the brain works like a computer, but one that is continually rewiring itself as it learns and adapts. Its basic component is the nerve cell, or neuron—a wirelike cell that sends electrical signals to other neurons, forming complex circuits of activity. Every second, trillions of electrical impulses dart among your brain cells, weaving infinitely tangled paths among an ever-changing maze of connections.

3 lb (1.35 kg)—the **average weight** of an **adult brain**.

78 percent of your **brain** is **water** and 11 percent is **fat**.

20 percent of your **energy intake** is used by your **brain**.

169

Touch
Signals from touch and pain receptors in the skin come to this area, called the somatosensory cortex.

Touch processing
Touch signals pass from the touch area to this part of the brain for further processing, helping us recognize what we can feel.

Learning to speak
Called Geschwind's territory, this part of the brain helps us acquire language skills during childhood.

Vision
The visual cortex receives signals from the eyes and processes them to identify basic shapes and patterns.

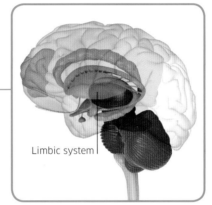

Limbic system

Basic instinct
While the outer part of the brain deals with higher mental processes such as thought, a set of structures deep inside the brain controls basic drives and emotions, such as pleasure, fear, and anger. These structures form what is known as the limbic system.

Visual processing
Basic shapes and patterns identified by the visual cortex are processed further here, helping us recognize objects we see.

Cerebellum
The cerebellum is separate from the rest of the brain. It helps coordinate muscles so they work in perfect sync.

Spinal cord
Nerve signals pass between the brain and body via the spinal cord, a bundle of nerve tissue that runs down the spine.

The thinking brain

The largest and cleverest part of the brain is its outermost layer, the cerebral cortex. Deep folds divide the cortex into distinct areas called lobes, which tend to specialize in different processes, such as speech or vision. However, scans of active brains reveal widespread activity across the cortex during mental tasks, showing that the various areas work together in complex ways.

Brain size

Most of the complex processing happens in the brain's surface—the cerebral cortex, which is packed with synapses. Humans have a far larger cortical area than other animals, giving our brains more processing power.

HUMAN

MONKEY

RAT

Cortical area
If the cortex of your brain were laid out flat, it would cover the same area as four pages of this book. A monkey's cortex is the size of a postcard, and a rat's is the size of a postage stamp.

Sense of touch

The top of the cerebral cortex processes the sense of touch, but some parts of the body have more cortex devoted to them than others. This figure shows how much of the brain receives touch signals from different places, making some parts of the body more sensitive than others.

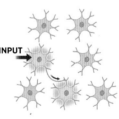

How memory works

The brain stores memories as networks of connections between neurons. Every new experience or new piece of information makes your neurons fire in a particular pattern. When you recall the event or fact, you make the neurons fire in the same pattern again, strengthening the memory.

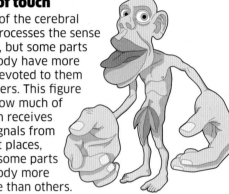

INPUT

1 Experience
A new experience makes neurons send signals in a particular pattern. In reality, hundreds of neurons are involved in the network.

2 Repeating
Repeating the experience or recalling the fact causes new links to form, making the network larger and easier to trigger.

3 Strengthening
Further repetition strengthens the network further, consolidating the memory. Links that are not refreshed tend to fade and are lost.

How vision works

Vision is the most important sense in humans. We gather more information through our eyes than through all our other senses combined.

It takes a fraction of a second for our eyes to take in a scene. They don't simply take a snapshot. Instead, our eyes dart about quickly and instinctively, resting briefly on details that the brain considers important, such as faces, moving objects, and anything that interests us.

The human eye works much like a camera, capturing light rays and focusing them with a lens to form a pinpoint image. Unlike a photograph, the image in our eyes is highly detailed and brightly colored only in the very center. This small, sharp spot in our visual field is created by a tiny pit in the back of the eye called the fovea. Your fovea forms high-definition images of the words in this sentence as you read it.

Inside the eye

The human eye is a hollow ball filled mostly with clear, jellylike fluid that lets light pass through. The light rays are focused partly by the curved front part of the eye—the cornea—and partly by an adjustable lens. A camera autofocuses by moving its lens, but the human eye focuses by changing the shape of the lens. The image is captured by a layer of light-sensitive cells lining the inside of the eyeball—the retina. The retina then sends the image to the brain as electrical code.

Muscle
Each eyeball is attached to six muscles. Working together, they can move the eye in any direction.

Sclera
The white of the eye is the sclera—a tough, protective coat around the eyeball.

Pupil
Light passes through a black hole in the iris, called the pupil.

Cornea
The curved front part of the eye does the bulk of the focusing. Unlike the lens, it cannot change shape.

Lens
Behind the pupil is the adjustable lens. It changes shape to autofocus.

Aqueous humor
A watery liquid called the aqueous humor fills the front part of the eye.

Ciliary muscle
Surrounding the lens is a ring of muscle that pulls on the lens to change its shape.

The iris

The colored part of the eye is called the iris. The iris is a ring of muscle fibers that controls how much light enters the pupil. In bright light, the pupil shrinks to 0.08 in (2 mm) wide. In the dark, it widens to 0.5 in (9 mm). The iris reacts not just to light but also to emotion: if you look at something or someone you like, your pupils widen. The iris's color comes from melanin—the same pigment molecule that gives hair and skin their color.

When the pupil opens from its smallest to its fullest size,

20 times more
light enters the eye.

Retina
Images are captured by the retina, a layer of light-sensitive cells lining the inside of the eyeball.

Cone

Rod

Rods and cones
The light-capturing cells in the retina come in two types: rods and cones. Cones can see color and fine detail, but they need bright light to work. Rods work in dim light, but they see in black and white and pick up less detail. When it's very dark, only your rods work, so the world becomes colorless and blurry. Switch on a light and your cones switch on too, giving you high-definition color vision.

Fovea
In the middle of the retina is a small pit about 0.04 in (1 mm) wide—the fovea. The fovea is very densely packed with cone cells, giving much more detailed vision than the rest of the retina. Half the nerve signals traveling from the retina to the brain come from here.

Optic nerve
Images captured by the retina are carried to the brain by the optic nerve.

Blind spot
Blood vessels and nerves enter and leave the eye here. This part of the retina is called the blind spot because it has no light-sensitive cells.

Jelly
The main part of the eyeball is filled with a jellylike fluid similar to egg white. If you close your eyes, you can see tiny particles floating in this fluid.

8% of males and 0.04% of females are red-green color blind, which means their eyes cannot easily distinguish red from green.

Focusing images
When light rays leave an object, they diverge (spread out). To create a sharp image, the eye must bend the diverging rays so they come back to a point, a process called focusing. The cornea and the lens work together to focus light on the retina. The image this creates is upside down, but the brain turns it upright.

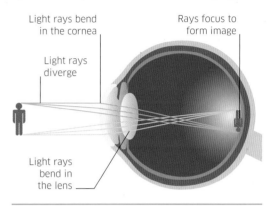

Light rays bend in the cornea

Rays focus to form image

Light rays diverge

Light rays bend in the lens

Near and far
When you look at nearby objects, the muscles around the lens in each eye make the lens rounder, increasing its focusing power. When you look at distant objects, the muscles relax and the lens gets flatter. In some people, the focusing power of the lens is too strong or weak. Wearing glasses corrects this.

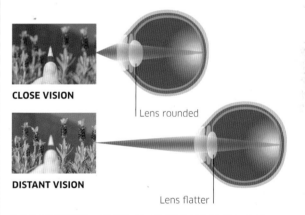

CLOSE VISION

Lens rounded

DISTANT VISION

Lens flatter

Seeing in 3-D
Our two eyes see the world from slightly different points of view, creating different images. These two images are combined in the brain to create a single, 3-D picture. Seeing in 3-D allows us to judge distance.

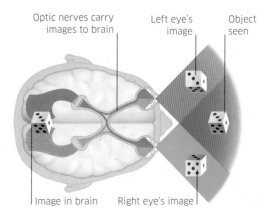

Optic nerves carry images to brain

Left eye's image

Object seen

Image in brain

Right eye's image

Inside the ear

Sound is caused by invisible waves rushing through air at hundreds of miles an hour. Our ears capture and analyze these fast but faint vibrations to create the sense of hearing.

Throw a pebble into a pond and it will make waves that spread out in circles. Sound works in a similar way, spreading through air as spherical ripples that our eyes cannot see. Unlike a wave in the surface of water, a sound wave is a region of higher pressure where air molecules are briefly squashed together. These pressure waves arrive at our ears at a rate of 20 to 20,000 a second. Deep inside each ear is a delicate membrane—the eardrum—that flutters in response to the incoming waves. This incredibly sensitive device can pick up the faintest sound, and it vibrates at the same frequency as the waves, allowing our ears to gauge pitch.

As well as giving us hearing, our ears contain a number of tiny sensory structures that swing back and forth in response to movement and gravity, giving us a sense of posture and balance.

Parts of the ear

The human ear has three different areas: the outer ear, middle ear, and inner ear. The part we can see is the pinna—a flap of rubbery tissue and skin that funnels sound into the ear canal. Its odd shape helps us sense the direction that sound comes from. The ear canal is a hollow tube that runs deep into the skull, carrying sound to the eardrum. Tiny, hinged bones connected to the eardrum transmit the vibrations across the air-filled middle ear to the fluid-filled inner ear.

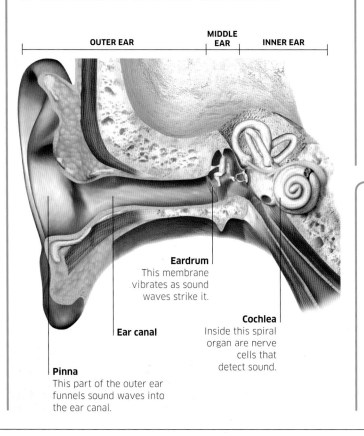

OUTER EAR	MIDDLE EAR	INNER EAR

Eardrum
This membrane vibrates as sound waves strike it.

Ear canal

Cochlea
Inside this spiral organ are nerve cells that detect sound.

Pinna
This part of the outer ear funnels sound waves into the ear canal.

Sensing sound

Vibrations of the eardrum are passed on to and magnified by a chain of three tiny bones (hammer, anvil, and stirrup) in the air-filled middle ear. The final bone in the chain—the stirrup—relays the sound vibrations into the inner ear. The vibrations now travel through fluid into a spiral-shaped organ called the cochlea, which is the size of a pea. Inside the cochlea, the fluid vibrations trigger nerve signals that are sent to the brain.

Ear bones
Three tiny bones transmit sound from the eardrum to the inner ear. They work as levers, magnifying the force of the vibrations.

Smallest bone
The stirrup bone is only 0.13 in (3 mm) long, making it the smallest bone in the body.

Eardrum
This taut, paper-thin membrane is slightly cone-shaped and about 0.4 in (9 mm) wide. It vibrates when sound hits it, matching the frequency of the sound waves. If damaged, the eardrum usually heals itself within a few weeks.

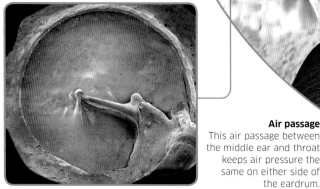

Air passage
This air passage between the middle ear and throat keeps air pressure the same on either side of the eardrum.

Balance organs

Our ears don't just detect sound—they also give us a sense of balance. Inside each inner ear is a complicated set of fluid-filled chambers and tubes, and within these are loose structures designed to swing back and forth. Some swing when you turn your head and make the fluid swirl. Others respond to gravity. All these structures send signals to the brain to keep it updated about your body's position and movement.

Rotation of the head is detected by the semicircular canals.

Up and down motion is sensed by the saccule.

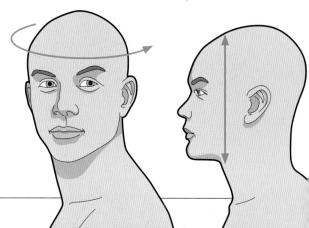

20,000 The number of **sound-detecting hair cells** in the **inner ear**.

6 ft (1.9 m)—the average **wavelength of speech**.

173

We can hear sounds so faint that they make our eardrums move less than the **width of an atom.**

Semicircular canals
These curved, fluid-filled tubes help create our sense of balance.

Nerve
Signals from sound-detecting cells and balance organs are carried to the brain by a nerve.

Hair cells
Inside the cochlea, ripples traveling through the fluid cause a membrane that runs throughout the length of the spiral to wobble. Embedded in this membrane are V-shaped clusters of microscopic hairs (pink, above). When the membrane wobbles, the hairs bend, causing the cells attached to the hairs to send signals to the brain. Very loud noises can damage these hair cells, causing loss of hearing.

Cochlea
Sound travels as ripples inside the snail-shaped cochlea, triggering nerve cells that send signals to the brain.

Tilting movements are detected by the utricle.

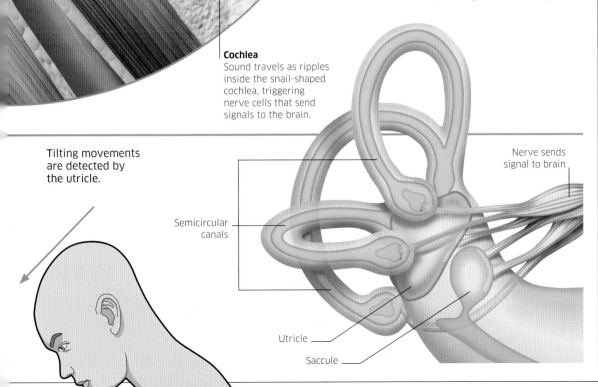

Nerve sends signal to brain

Semicircular canals

Utricle

Saccule

How pitch works

Our ears detect sounds with wavelengths from about 0.7 in (1.7 cm) long to 56 ft (17 m) long. Sounds with short wavelengths have a high frequency (thousands of waves per second) and sound high-pitched. Long wavelengths have a low frequency (dozens of waves per second) and sound low-pitched.

Spiraling in
Sound waves enter the outer part of the cochlea first and work their way around toward the center. High-pitched sounds are detected at the beginning, while deeper sounds are detected farther in.

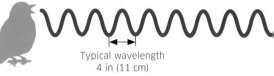

Typical wavelength 4 in (11 cm)

❶ High pitch
The outer cochlea detects high-pitched sounds, such as birdsong. A typical song might include sounds with a frequency of about 3,000 waves per second and a wavelength of about 3 in (8 cm). Sounds higher than 20,000 waves per second are too high for most human ears.

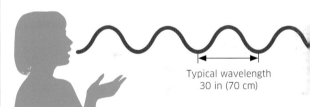

Typical wavelength 30 in (70 cm)

❷ Medium pitch
Speech contains a complex mixture of different sounds, with frequencies between 100 and 1,000 waves per second and wavelengths between 1 ft (30 cm) and 10 ft (3 m). These are detected in a wide stretch of the cochlea.

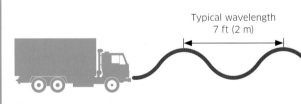

Typical wavelength 7 ft (2 m)

❸ Low pitch
The deep rumbling of a large truck passing by includes frequencies of 100–200 waves per second, which are detected near the center of the cochlea. Human ears can't hear sounds deeper than 20 waves a second, though we can sometimes feel these vibrations in our bones.

BATS CAN DETECT SOUNDS **10 TIMES HIGHER** THAN HUMAN EARS CAN, **BUT THE HUMAN VOICE** IS TOO DEEP FOR THEM TO HEAR.

The human tongue has around
10,000 taste buds,
each containing up to 100 taste receptor cells.

Olfactory bulb
A part of the brain called the olfactory bulb receives smell signals from the nose.

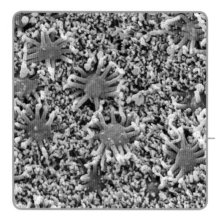

Smell cells
High up inside the nose is a small patch of tissue, no bigger than a postage stamp, called the olfactory epithelium. This is where the sensation of smell begins. Odor molecules from air dissolve in the sticky fluid that covers the epithelium and activate tiny hairs (shown in pink above) on smell-detecting cells. The cells then send smell signals to the brain.

Nasal cavity
Behind the nose is a large air space called the nasal cavity.

Odor in air
As we breathe in, odor molecules are sucked up through the nostrils into the nasal cavity.

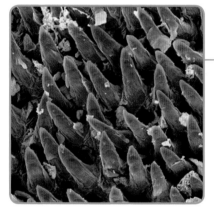

Surface of the tongue
The surface of your tongue feels rough because it's covered with hundreds of tiny, fingerlike bumps called papillae, which help the tongue grip food. The largest of these papillae also help create the sense of taste. Embedded in the surface of each one are dozens of microscopic pits called taste buds. These contain sensory cells that detect chemicals like salt and sugar.

Tongue
The tongue's warmth helps release odors from food held in the mouth.

Odor molecules

Taste and smell

The human nose can detect around 10,000 odors, but our mouths react to only five different tastes. These two senses combine in the brain to give the food we eat an infinite variety of flavors.

Fresh food
Very fresh food has a distinctive odor that our noses can detect in an instant.

Taste and smell work in similar ways. Both are "chemosenses," which means they work by detecting particular chemicals. The distinctive taste of our favorite foods, from pizza to fresh orange juice, is created by both senses working together. In fact, up to 75 percent of what we experience as taste is actually smell—which is why food tastes bland when your nose is blocked. Our senses of taste and smell conjure up pleasurable sensations that tell us when food is rich in energy and safe to eat. They also warn us when something is dangerous by triggering an intense feeling of disgust.

Nose and mouth
The sense of taste comes mainly from your tongue, but there are also taste buds in the roof of the mouth, the throat, and even the lungs. The sense of smell comes only from the nose. When food is in the mouth, smell molecules travel around the back of your mouth and into your nose, giving the food its complex flavor.

Amygdala
This part of the brain screens signals from the nose for signs of danger, such as a burning smell.

Air flow
Air can flow from the mouth to the nose, carrying odors.

The tongue

A complicated bundle of eight different muscles, the tongue is an amazingly strong and agile organ. It can reach and manipulate food anywhere in the mouth, and its rough surface keeps the mouth clean. As well as being the main organ of taste, it is also vital for speech.

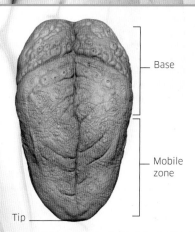

Base

Mobile zone

Tip

How taste buds work

Chemicals from food dissolve in the saliva that covers the tongue, and the saliva then enters taste buds through pores (holes) in the papillae. Inside the pores, tiny hairs on the tips of taste receptor cells detect any of the five basic tastes (see below), triggering signals. These signals travel at high speed to the brain, which creates the conscious experience of taste.

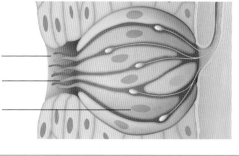

Pore (hole) in side of a papilla

Taste hairs detect tastes

Receptor cells send signals

Five tastes

Taste buds respond to only five kinds of chemicals, giving us just five main tastes.

Salty
Taste buds sensitive to salt trigger a very powerful, salty sensation.

Sweet
Sweet foods trigger taste buds that detect sugars.

Sour
A sour taste comes from taste buds that detect acids, such as lemon juice.

Bitter
Poisonous or inedible foods trigger taste buds that create a bitter sensation.

Savory (umami)
Some taste buds react to the deep, savory flavor of cooked foods.

Smell and memory

Smells sometimes unlock powerful memories—perhaps the smell of the ocean brings back vivid memories of a happy vacation. Scientists suspect this happens because the part of the brain that recognizes smells has strong links to an area called the amygdala, which plays a key role in emotion and memory.

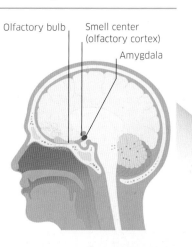

Olfactory bulb

Smell center (olfactory cortex)

Amygdala

The endocrine system

The endocrine system consists of a number of hormone-producing glands and tissues scattered throughout the body. The hormones they produce are secreted directly into the bloodstream. Along with the nervous system, the endocrine system keeps the body working in a coordinated way. It plays a vital role in a process known as homeostasis—the maintenance of a stable internal environment within the body.

Stomach
The lining of the stomach produces hormones that trigger the release of digestive enzymes.

Pancreas
This gland produces insulin, which controls blood sugar levels.

Thyroid gland
This gland regulates your metabolic rate—the rate at which the body's cells use energy.

Adrenal glands
These glands on top of the kidneys produce adrenalin, which prepares the body for sudden action.

Pineal gland
The hormone melatonin from the pineal helps control the daily sleep-wake cycle.

Hypothalamus
This part of the brain controls the pituitary gland.

Pituitary gland
The pituitary gland secretes hormones that control many other hormone-secreting glands.

Heart
Produced by the heart, the hormone atriopeptin reduces blood volume and blood pressure.

Kidneys
Erythropoietin secreted by the kidneys stimulates bone marrow to make red blood cells.

Control chemicals

Every second of every day, powerful chemicals called hormones course through your bloodstream. Hormones are made in your body and target specific organs, controlling the way they work.

Hormones are complex chemical substances that regulate body functions such as growth, water balance, and sexual development. They are made and released into the blood by organs called endocrine glands. Hormones work more slowly than the electrical impulses that flash through nerves, but they usually have longer-lasting effects.

Hormones reach every part of the body via the blood, but they only affect specific target tissues and organs. When they reach their destination, they trigger major chemical changes inside cells, sometimes switching particular genes on or off to change the way a cell operates. Many hormones are controlled by other hormones, and some hormones work in pairs to keep levels of body chemicals such as sugar in balance.

Master gland

The pea-sized pituitary gland at the base of the brain is often called the master gland because it is such an important part of the endocrine system. It secretes nine different hormones, five of which control major body functions directly, while four trigger other glands to release hormones of their own. Parts of the body targeted by pituitary hormones are shown below.

8 ft 11 in (2.7 m)

The height of Robert Wadlow, the tallest person in history, who suffered from gigantism—an excess of growth hormone.

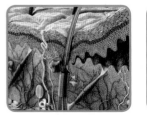

Skin
Melanocyte-stimulating hormone makes skin cells produce melanin, a pigment that tans (darkens) the skin.

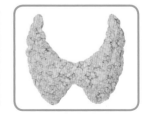

Adrenal gland

Kidney

Adrenal glands
The hormone ACTH causes glands on the kidneys to secrete hormones that help the body cope with stress.

Thyroid gland
The hormone TSH tells the thyroid gland to release thyroxine, a hormone that speeds up body chemistry.

Ovaries

In females, the two ovaries secrete estrogen and progesterone. These hormones trigger the development of adult sexual features in girls. In adults, they control the monthly reproductive cycle.

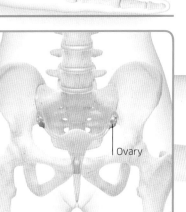

Ovary

Testes

In boys, the sex hormone testosterone, made by the testes, causes adult features such as facial hair to develop.

Intestines

Endocrine cells in intestinal tissue secrete a range of hormones that help the digestive process.

Sugar balance

Hormones act to keep levels of body chemicals balanced. For example, two hormones released by the pancreas—insulin and glucagon—control sugar levels in your blood. Glucose, a simple sugar, is the fuel that provides energy for all body activities. Insulin reduces blood glucose levels, while glucagon increases them. If there's too much glucose in the blood, more insulin is produced; if there's too little, more glucagon is secreted. These two hormones work together to keep glucose levels constant.

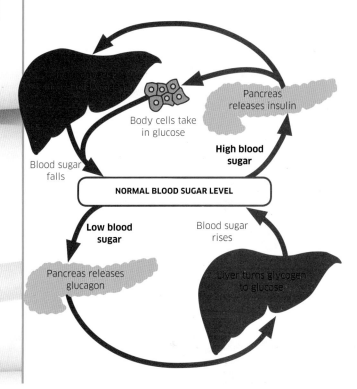

Pancreas releases insulin

Body cells take in glucose

High blood sugar

Blood sugar falls

NORMAL BLOOD SUGAR LEVEL

Low blood sugar

Blood sugar rises

Pancreas releases glucagon

Liver turns glycogen to glucose

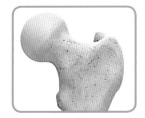

Milk production

The pituitary hormone prolactin triggers a woman's body to start making milk after giving birth.

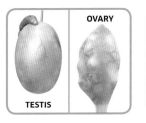

Uterus

Uterus

During birth, oxytocin triggers muscle contractions in the uterus, forcing the baby from the womb.

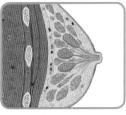

Kidney tubules

The hormone ADH tells the kidneys to reabsorb more water from urine, helping the body retain water.

Bones

Growth hormone stimulates the growth plates in bones, making the body grow larger during childhood.

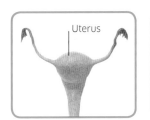

OVARY

TESTIS

Sex organs

Two pituitary hormones trigger activity in the testes and ovaries and make them release sex hormones.

Milk release

When a baby suckles at the breast, the pituitary secretes oxytocin, which stimulates the release of breast milk.

Adrenalin

When you're scared or excited, your heart pounds and your breathing gets deeper. These are two of the effects of adrenalin, a fast-acting hormone released by the adrenal glands. Adrenalin is called the fight or flight hormone because it prepares the body for sudden action in emergencies. By making the heart and lungs work harder, it helps get extra oxygen and fuel to body muscles.

Adrenalin sports

In sports that involve high-speed action and risky maneuvers, such as wakeboarding, adrenalin increases in response to the excitement, risk, and stress of competition.

LIFE CYCLE

The human life cycle begins as a single cell barely visible to the eye. Programmed by the genes it has inherited, this speck of life divides and multiplies to form a mass of cells, and a new human body begins to grow. We continue growing and developing for around 20 years, by which time we are old enough to have babies ourselves. Like all living things, from the tiniest virus to the tallest trees, human beings strive to create offspring before growing old—a process known as reproduction.

SEXUAL REPRODUCTION

Like most other animals, human beings reproduce sexually, which means that two parents are needed to create offspring. Sexual reproduction mixes up the genes from both parents. Doing so combines characteristics from both parents and makes every child (except identical twins) unique. The parents produce special cells called sex cells. Male and female sex cells fuse inside the mother's body to form an embryo. Over the following nine months, in the protective environment of the mother's uterus, the embryo develops into a baby ready for life in the outside world.

Sperm and egg

Male sex cells are called sperm, and female sex cells are called eggs. Both carry a single set of genes, stored on structures called chromosomes. When sex cells join, the two sets of chromosomes combine, giving the new individual a full set of genes. Egg cells are far larger than sperm because they contain a supply of food.

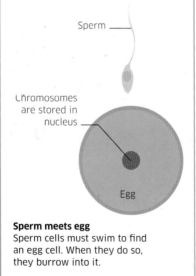

Sperm

Chromosomes are stored in nucleus

Egg

Sperm meets egg
Sperm cells must swim to find an egg cell. When they do so, they burrow into it.

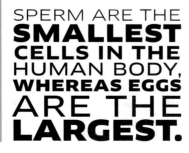

SPERM ARE THE **SMALLEST CELLS IN THE HUMAN BODY, WHEREAS EGGS** ARE THE **LARGEST.**

Making sex cells

Sex cells are produced by a special kind of cell division called meiosis. During meiosis, genes are shuffled about between chromosomes, and the total number of chromosomes is halved.

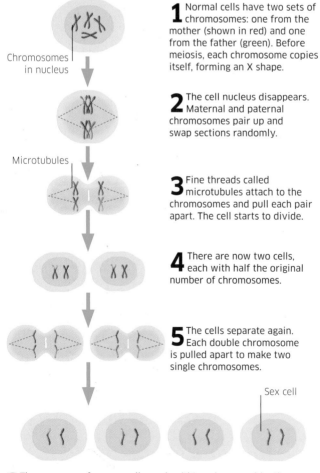

Chromosomes in nucleus

Microtubules

Sex cell

1 Normal cells have two sets of chromosomes: one from the mother (shown in red) and one from the father (green). Before meiosis, each chromosome copies itself, forming an X shape.

2 The cell nucleus disappears. Maternal and paternal chromosomes pair up and swap sections randomly.

3 Fine threads called microtubules attach to the chromosomes and pull each pair apart. The cell starts to divide.

4 There are now two cells, each with half the original number of chromosomes.

5 The cells separate again. Each double chromosome is pulled apart to make two single chromosomes.

6 There are now four sex cells, each with a unique combination of genes and half the normal number of chromosomes. When two sex cells join, the full number of chromosomes is restored.

REPRODUCTIVE SYSTEM

The parts of the body dedicated to creating babies make up the reproductive system. The male and female reproductive systems are very different. Both produce sex cells, but the female reproductive system must also nourish and protect the growing baby.

Male reproduction system

Male sex cells (sperm) are made nonstop in a man's body—at a rate of 50,000 a minute—inside organs called testes. These hang outside the body within a bag of loose skin called the scrotum. Sperm are delivered into a woman's body in a liquid called semen after passing through the penis. Sperm cells make up about five percent of this liquid.

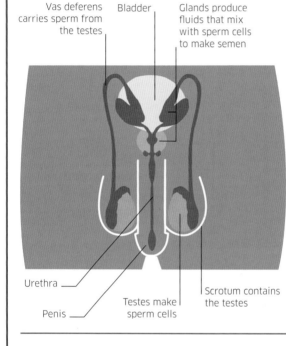

Vas deferens carries sperm from the testes

Bladder

Glands produce fluids that mix with sperm cells to make semen

Urethra

Penis

Testes make sperm cells

Scrotum contains the testes

Female reproduction system

Female sex cells are made inside a girl's body before she is born and stored in organs called ovaries. In a woman's body, an egg cell is released from one of the ovaries every month and travels along a tube toward the uterus. If the egg cell meets a sperm cell, fertilization occurs and the resulting embryo implants itself in the uterus and grows into a baby.

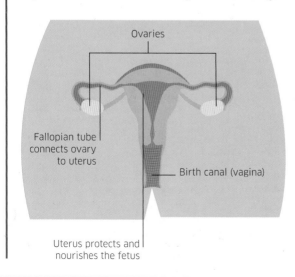

Ovaries

Fallopian tube connects ovary to uterus

Birth canal (vagina)

Uterus protects and nourishes the fetus

GENES AND DNA

All living cells carry a set of instructions that control the chemical activity inside the cell. These instructions, called genes, are stored as a four-letter code by the molecule DNA (deoxyribonucleic acid). Human cells contain about 20,000 genes. These genes direct the process of development that turns a single-celled embryo into a fully functioning human body made of trillions of cells.

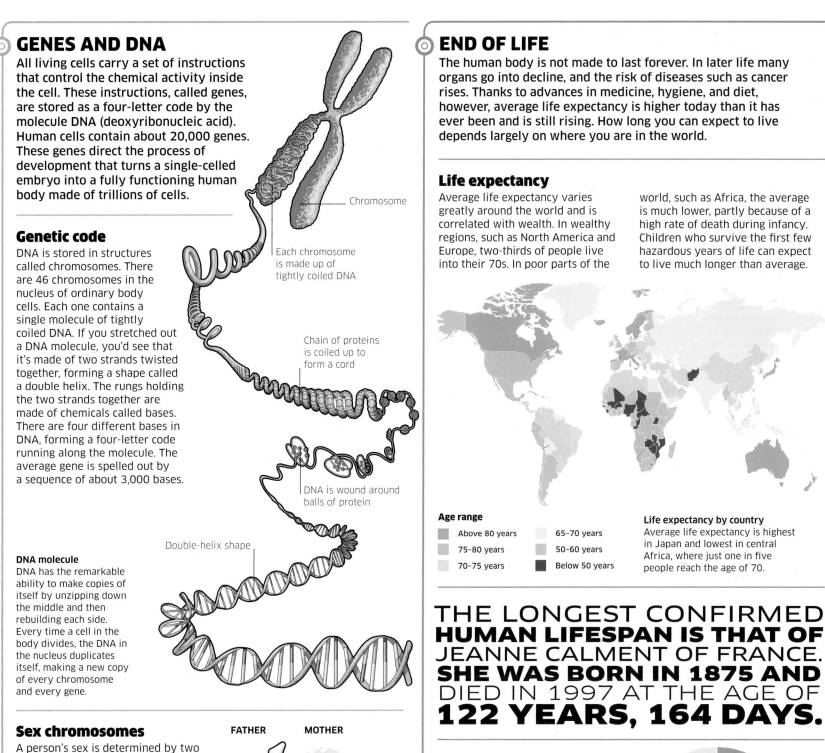

Chromosome

Each chromosome is made up of tightly coiled DNA

Chain of proteins is coiled up to form a cord

DNA is wound around balls of protein

Double-helix shape

Genetic code

DNA is stored in structures called chromosomes. There are 46 chromosomes in the nucleus of ordinary body cells. Each one contains a single molecule of tightly coiled DNA. If you stretched out a DNA molecule, you'd see that it's made of two strands twisted together, forming a shape called a double helix. The rungs holding the two strands together are made of chemicals called bases. There are four different bases in DNA, forming a four-letter code running along the molecule. The average gene is spelled out by a sequence of about 3,000 bases.

DNA molecule
DNA has the remarkable ability to make copies of itself by unzipping down the middle and then rebuilding each side. Every time a cell in the body divides, the DNA in the nucleus duplicates itself, making a new copy of every chromosome and every gene.

Sex chromosomes

A person's sex is determined by two particular chromosomes, called X and Y after their shapes. Females have two X chromosomes, while males have an X and a Y chromosome. The Y chromosome is much smaller than the X and contains fewer genes—less than 100, compared to the 2,000 genes on the X chromosome. A mother's egg cells always carry an X chromosome, while a father's sperm can carry either an X or a Y chromosome.

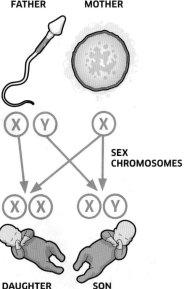

FATHER   MOTHER

X Y   X

SEX CHROMOSOMES

X X   X Y

DAUGHTER   SON

Determining gender
As a mother always passes on an X chromosome to her children, it's the father's sperm that determines the sex of a baby. If a sperm carries an X chromosome the baby will be a girl. If it carries a Y chromosome, the baby will be a boy.

END OF LIFE

The human body is not made to last forever. In later life many organs go into decline, and the risk of diseases such as cancer rises. Thanks to advances in medicine, hygiene, and diet, however, average life expectancy is higher today than it has ever been and is still rising. How long you can expect to live depends largely on where you are in the world.

Life expectancy

Average life expectancy varies greatly around the world and is correlated with wealth. In wealthy regions, such as North America and Europe, two-thirds of people live into their 70s. In poor parts of the world, such as Africa, the average is much lower, partly because of a high rate of death during infancy. Children who survive the first few hazardous years of life can expect to live much longer than average.

Age range

Above 80 years	65–70 years
75–80 years	50–60 years
70–75 years	Below 50 years

Life expectancy by country
Average life expectancy is highest in Japan and lowest in central Africa, where just one in five people reach the age of 70.

THE LONGEST CONFIRMED **HUMAN LIFESPAN IS THAT OF** JEANNE CALMENT OF FRANCE. **SHE WAS BORN IN 1875 AND** DIED IN 1997 AT THE AGE OF **122 YEARS, 164 DAYS.**

Cause of death

In developing countries, infectious diseases such as HIV/AIDS and malaria are among the main killers. Babies and young children are at particular risk of dying from malnutrition (poor diet) or from diarrhea, which is often spread by germs in unclean water. In wealthy countries, where health care, sanitation, and diet are all better, the main causes of death are diseases related to aging, such as heart disease and cancer. Lung diseases are a common cause of death worldwide. Many are linked to smoking. Scientists estimate that smoking causes about one in ten of all adult deaths.

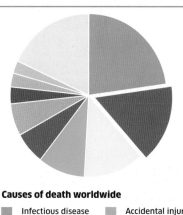

Causes of death worldwide

Infectious disease	Accidental injury
Heart disease	Digestive disease
Cancer	Deliberate injury
Stroke	Brain disease
Lung disease	Other causes

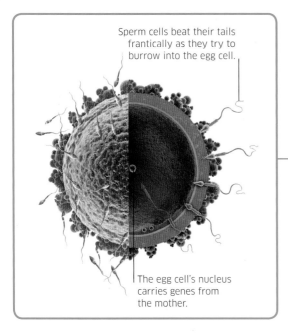

Sperm cells beat their tails frantically as they try to burrow into the egg cell.

The egg cell's nucleus carries genes from the mother.

Egg meets sperm

A new embryo forms when a sperm cell successfully burrows into an egg cell to deliver its genes—a process called fertilization. Around 300 million sperm cells are released into a woman's body during sex, but only one of these will win the race to fertilize the egg. Sperm cells have tails, which they lash like tadpoles to swim through body fluids.

Unfertilized egg

A woman's ovaries release a new egg cell about once a month. Egg cells are packed with nutrients, making them the largest cells in the human body.

Embryo

The fertilized egg cell is now an embryo and begins to divide.

Fallopian tube

It takes nearly a week for an egg cell to travel along this long tube connecting the ovary to the uterus.

Ovary

Women have two egg-storing organs called ovaries. The egg cells inside them have already formed by the time a baby girl is born.

A new life

We start life as a single cell about half as wide as a period. Directed by the genes inside it, and nourished by its mother's body, this tiny speck of life soon transforms into a unique human being made of trillions of cells.

A new life begins when two sex cells join and pool their genes together. Male sex cells (sperm) from the father and female sex cells (egg cells) from the mother join inside the mother's body to form an embryo. In the first few days an embryo looks nothing like a human body, but by four weeks it has a head, the beginnings of eyes, arms, and legs, and its heart has started beating. The images on these pages show what happens in the first month of an embryo's life. The following pages show what happens in the months leading up to birth.

The growing embryo

A newly formed embryo goes through a series of incredible changes. In the first week, it doesn't grow. Instead, it divides into two cells, then four, then eight, and so on, until it becomes a cluster of cells that looks like a berry. Most of the cells in this cluster will grow into structures that support and nourish the growing baby, but a few form a flat sheet destined to become the body. Within a period of only two weeks or so, this sheet grows into a recognizably human form, with head, arms, legs, eyes, a beating heart, and internal organs.

0 days old

At first the embryo consists of a single cell. Protected by a thick coat, it drifts slowly down the fluid-filled fallopian tube, pushed along by the tiny, beating hairs (cilia) that line the inner surface.

ACTUAL SIZE → (look closely)

4 days old

About a day after fertilization, the cell divides in two. Twelve or so hours later, it divides again. After four days the embryo is a ball of 32 small cells and looks like a berry.

ACTUAL SIZE →

1 week old

The embryo has now entered the uterus and attached itself to the inner wall, anchoring itself with fingerlike growths that will help nourish it from the mother's blood.

ACTUAL SIZE →

The uterus

Babies develop and grow in a protective organ inside the mother's belly—the uterus. After first entering the uterus, an embryo embeds itself in the soft lining and grows fingerlike extensions that collect nutrients from the mother's blood. The muscular wall of the uterus is very stretchy, allowing the organ to expand as the baby grows.

Cluster of cells
The embryo is 4 to 5 days old when it reaches the uterus. It is now a ball-shaped cluster of cells.

Inside the uterus
The growing embryo bursts out of the thick coat that covered the egg cell. Doing this will help it stick to the wall of the uterus.

Muscular wall
The wall of the uterus is made of powerful muscles that contract to push the baby out during childbirth.

2 weeks old

A week later, the embryo has developed a yolk sac (yellow) and a fluid-filled space called an amnion (blue). Inside the amnion is a layer of cells—the embryonic disc—that will develop into a baby.

ACTUAL SIZE ➤ •

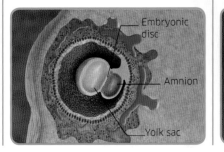

Embryonic disc

Amnion

Yolk sac

3 weeks old

The embryonic disc grows rapidly and folds into a curved shape. Within a matter of days, it develops a head, tail, blood vessels, and the beginnings of major internal organs.

ACTUAL SIZE ➤ ●

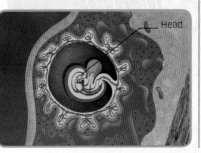

Head

4 weeks old

Now the size of a bean, the embryo has the beginnings of arms and legs, and its heart has started beating. Nerves and muscles develop, and eyes begin to form, at first without eyelids.

ACTUAL SIZE ➤

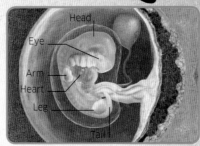

Head

Eye

Arm

Heart

Leg

Tail

Implanting
Like a seed planted in the ground, the embryo implants in the soft inner lining of the uterus and begins to get fed by the mother's tissue.

Life in the womb

Nourished by its mother's blood and protected by her body, an unborn baby (fetus) develops rapidly inside the womb, doubling in weight every four to five weeks.

Although we can't remember the period of life before birth, our brains and sense organs had already started working. In the late stages of pregnancy, an unborn baby can see the pinkish glow of light filtering through its mother's skin and can hear her voice, her booming heartbeat, and the noisy sloshing of fluid in the uterus. Using its hands and feet, it explores the watery world around it and feels its own body. It can't breathe while submerged in liquid, but it practices by sucking in the liquid and swallowing. For nine months, the womb provides a safe, warm, and comfortable environment, while the mother's bloodstream supplies the growing baby with all the oxygen and nutrients it needs.

Ready for birth

Toward the end of pregnancy, the fetus positions itself head downward, ready for birth. Its digestive system is now capable of processing food, but it continues to draw nutrients from the mother's blood via a bundle of blood vessels called the umbilical cord. A layer of fine hair grows all over the fetus's body late in pregnancy but usually disappears before birth.

The eyes open when the fetus is six months old, but it can only see light and dark.

Placenta
Oxygen and food pass from the mother's blood to the baby's blood inside the placenta.

Mother's blood vessels in placenta

Baby's blood vessels in placenta

Umbilical cord
This lifeline carries oxygen and nutrients from the mother, via the placenta, to the fetus.

The growing fetus

All the major organs appear during the first nine weeks of life, when the developing baby is known as an embryo. From nine weeks onward, it is called a fetus. Over the next seven months, the fetus grows rapidly. Complex tissues and body systems form, strengthen, and begin to work. A skeleton comes together, made at first of rubbery cartilage tissue instead of bone. The brain develops and so do the senses—a fetus can see, hear, smell, taste, and feel long before it's born.

4 weeks old

At four weeks old, the embryo is the shape of a shrimp and has a tail. Its arms and legs are little more than buds. Eyes and ears are forming, and the heart starts to pump blood, working at a rate of 150 beats a minute—twice the adult rate.

LENGTH: 0.4 IN (11 MM)

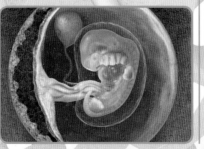

6 weeks old

The face is taking shape and the hands and feet are forming. They look like paddles at first because the fingers and toes are joined together by webs of skin. Parts of the fetus's cartilage skeleton begin hardening into bone.

LENGTH: 0.6 IN (1.6 CM)

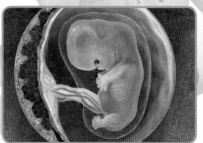

10 weeks old

The fetus has eyelids but they will remain fused shut for the next three months. It can swallow and begins to urinate into the amniotic fluid. Elbow and wrist joints have formed, allowing it to make simple arm and hand movements.

LENGTH: 2.1 IN (5.4 CM)

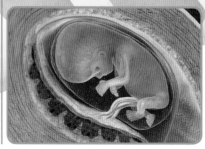

69 The **largest number of children** born to **one mother**.

9 The **largest number of babies** born in a **multiple birth**.

183

Uterus
The wall of the uterus stretches as the baby grows.

Skin
The skin is covered by a cheesy white substance called vernix, which provides waterproofing to stop the skin from absorbing amniotic fluid.

A baby's heart
starts beating when its body is the size of a lentil.

Birth canal
The baby must squeeze through a tight passage called the birth canal, or vagina, during birth.

Amniotic fluid
The fetus floats submerged in a watery liquid that cushions it from bumps.

Changing proportions
Because the brain and nervous system develop quickly in early pregnancy, the head grows faster than the rest of the body. By nine weeks it takes up half of the baby's length and looks enormous. The rest of the body catches up in the later months of pregnancy.

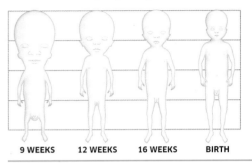

9 WEEKS   12 WEEKS   16 WEEKS   BIRTH

Multiple births
Sometimes more than one baby grows in the uterus at the same time. About one in 80 pregnancies are twins and about one in 8,000 are triplets. Twins can form from two different eggs (fraternal twins, who look different) or a single egg that splits (identical twins, who look the same).

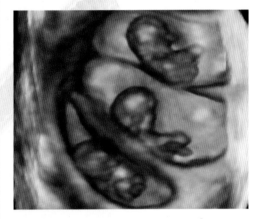

Triplets
This ultrasound scan shows triplets growing in the same uterus. Each fetus is surrounded by its own amniotic sac.

15 weeks old
The fetus is now the size of a hamster, with a huge head and tiny body. Facial features are well formed, and it practices making facial expressions, including smiles and frowns. It swallows amniotic fluid and hiccups so strongly the mother can feel it.

LENGTH: 5 IN (13 CM)

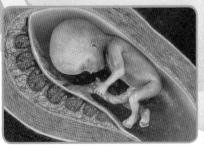

22 weeks old
Just over halfway through pregnancy, the baby can now move its fingers, which have developed fingerprints. It responds to sound and is easily startled by loud noises. The mother begins to feel the fetus kicking inside her.

LENGTH: 12 IN (30 CM)

34 weeks old
The fetus is nearly fully developed. It spends about 90 percent of the time sleeping and has dreams. It practices breathing by inhaling fluid about 40 times a minute. It can smell its mother's meals and recognize her voice.

LENGTH: 19 IN (47 CM)

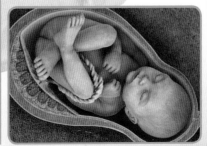

Birth
After the umbilical cord is cut, a baby takes its first breath. Fluid drains out of its lungs and they fill with air. The baby will now get its oxygen from the air in its lungs rather than from its mother's blood via the placenta.

LENGTH: 21 IN (53 CM)

Growing up

Our bodies and brains are transformed as we grow up. The most dramatic changes happen in infancy and during the teenage years, but we continue changing throughout life.

A newborn baby weighs only 7 lb (3 kg) or so. Unable to walk, feed itself, or see further than a few inches, it is completely dependent on its parents. By the age of 20, we weigh perhaps 20 times as much and are capable of leading independent lives. The process of development that transforms a baby into an adult is continuous, but two major growth spurts occur during childhood. One takes place in the first six months, when a baby doubles in weight. The second is during puberty, when the release of sex hormones triggers the emergence of adult features. Growing up is not just a physical process. We also grow emotionally and intellectually, our brains changing as we slowly acquire complex knowledge and social skills needed to navigate the adult world.

Growing bones

As you grow taller and broader, your bones become longer and wider too. Bones are too hard to simply stretch in length, but they contain areas of soft tissue near the ends where new bone cells are laid down. Called growth plates, these look like gaps on X-rays. When you reach adulthood and your bones stop growing, the growth plates fill with solid bone and disappear.

CHILD'S HAND

In a 10-year-old's hand, growth plates in the finger bones look like gaps in the X-ray.

ADULT'S HAND

In a 20-year-old's hand, bones have stopped growing and the growth plates have filled in.

The changing body

The human body changes continuously throughout life. In the first 18 years, a person develops from a helpless baby needing its parents for survival to an independent adult, capable of raising his or her own children. In their 20s and 30s, men and woman are in their physical prime. From the mid-30s onward, however, the body slowly begins to decline. The rate of deterioration varies widely from person to person and depends on lifestyle factors such as diet and exercise, as well as genes.

Adult teeth begin to replace baby teeth

Facial hair develops in young men

Bones in face continue to change with age

Brain is almost adult size

Most babies crawl before they learn to walk

Infancy
Babies have a large head in proportion to the body and short limbs. By 12–18 months, they develop the strength and balance needed to take their first steps.

Early childhood
The growth of the limbs begins to catch up with that of the head. Young children learn to walk and run, and become skilled at using their hands to manipulate objects precisely.

Childhood
Steady growth continues and height increases by about 2½ in (6 cm) each year. During these years, children master physical skills such as cycling, swimming, climbing, and playing sports.

Puberty
Height increases significantly and adult features begin to appear in response to sex hormones. Emotional changes such as mood swings are common during puberty.

Early adulthood
Adult height has been reached and the body is near peak fitness. Men and women are now capable of having their own children, but still need a few years to mature emotionally.

Adulthood
The human body is in its prime between the ages of 20 and 35. Bones are at their strongest and all body systems run smoothly. This is the ideal age to have and raise children.

3 in (8 cm) per year—the **peak growth rate** during **puberty**.

16 The **age** at which **girls** typically reach their **full adult height**.

18 The **age** at which **boys** typically reach their **full adult height**.

185

Brain development

At birth, a baby's brain is about a quarter the size of an adult's, but it has almost the same number of cells (about 100 billion). The brain grows rapidly until about age 6, when it reaches 90 percent of adult size. In early childhood, brain cells form a dense web of connections to each other, giving the brain great potential to learn new skills. Later, connections that haven't been used are pruned away, and the remaining ones are strengthened.

DURING EARLY **PREGNANCY, A BABY'S BRAIN** PRODUCES 250,000 **NEW BRAIN CELLS** EVERY MINUTE.

Child's brain

At around three years of age, a part of the brain called the hippocampus matures, allowing vivid memories to form. Changes in an area called the reticular formation allow a child to pay attention for longer. Language skills improve and social skills develop as the brain's parietal cortex and prefrontal cortex begin to mature.

The teenage brain

The part of the brain that generates emotions (the amygdala) is mature by the teenage years, but the area involved with thinking and planning (the prefrontal cortex) is not. As a result, teenagers are prone to act on sudden impulses without thinking. Neural circuits that aren't used much are pruned away in the teenage years.

The adult brain

In adulthood, the prefrontal cortex matures, allowing more thoughtful perceptions and dampening the influence of the amygdala. Unused circuits have been pruned away, making the brain less able to acquire new skills. Apart from an area called the hippocampus, most parts of the brain cannot generate new brain cells.

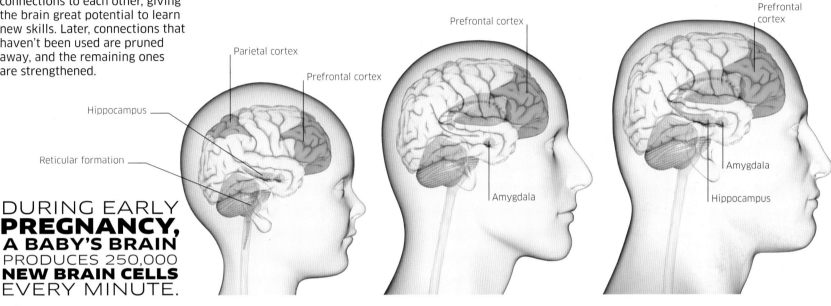

Parietal cortex

Prefrontal cortex

Hippocampus

Reticular formation

Prefrontal cortex

Amygdala

Prefrontal cortex

Amygdala

Hippocampus

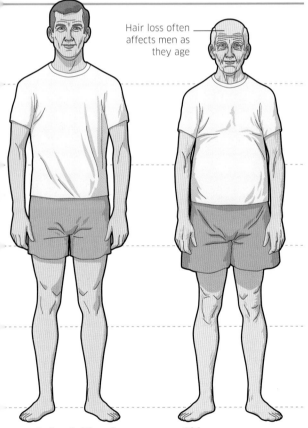

Hair loss often affects men as they age

Late adulthood
By the 50s and 60s, the skin loses its stretchiness and wrinkles appear. Muscles become smaller, and vision and hearing begin to deteriorate. Women lose the ability to have children.

Old age
As bones, joints, and muscles weaken, height is lost. Joints also stiffen, slowing movement. The brain shrinks by about 10 percent by age 90, senses worsen, and the heart is less efficient.

Puberty

Around the age of 10 to 14 in girls and 11 to 15 in boys, the body goes through a period of rapid growth and sexual development known as puberty. Sex hormones are released by the testes in boys and by the ovaries in girls. These cause many physical changes, such as growth of body hair and facial hair, development of breasts and the menstrual cycle, and changes in height and body shape. The physical changes are accompanied by emotional and behavioral changes as the brain matures—a slow process that lasts well into the 20s.

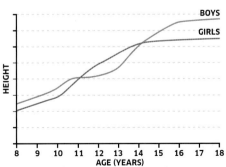

BOYS
GIRLS

HEIGHT

8 9 10 11 12 13 14 15 16 17 18
AGE (YEARS)

Growth spurts
Bones grow more quickly in puberty, causing a sudden increase in height. Girls reach puberty earlier than boys and overtake them in height at about age 11. Boys catch up by about age 14 and reach a greater average adult height than girls.

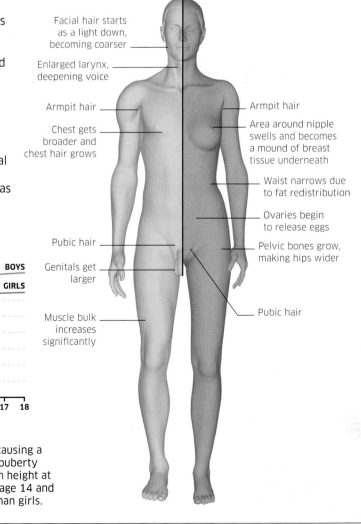

MALE BODY FEMALE BODY

Facial hair starts as a light down, becoming coarser

Enlarged larynx, deepening voice

Armpit hair

Chest gets broader and chest hair grows

Pubic hair

Genitals get larger

Muscle bulk increases significantly

Armpit hair

Area around nipple swells and becomes a mound of breast tissue underneath

Waist narrows due to fat redistribution

Ovaries begin to release eggs

Pelvic bones grow, making hips wider

Pubic hair

Genes and DNA

Packaged inside every cell nucleus in your body is a set of instructions that controls the way your body works and develops. These instructions, known as genes, are stored as a four-letter code by the molecule DNA.

Unless you're an identical twin, you have a unique set of genes that makes you different from anyone else. Half your genes came from your father and half came from your mother. These two sets joined to form a complete set, or genome, with a maternal and a paternal version of every gene. Your genome controls most of your physical characteristics, from the color of your eyes to the shape of your body. It also influences your abilities and personality, though your experiences in life affect these too.

If you unraveled all the DNA from every cell in your body, there would be enough to stretch to the Sun and back **400 times.**

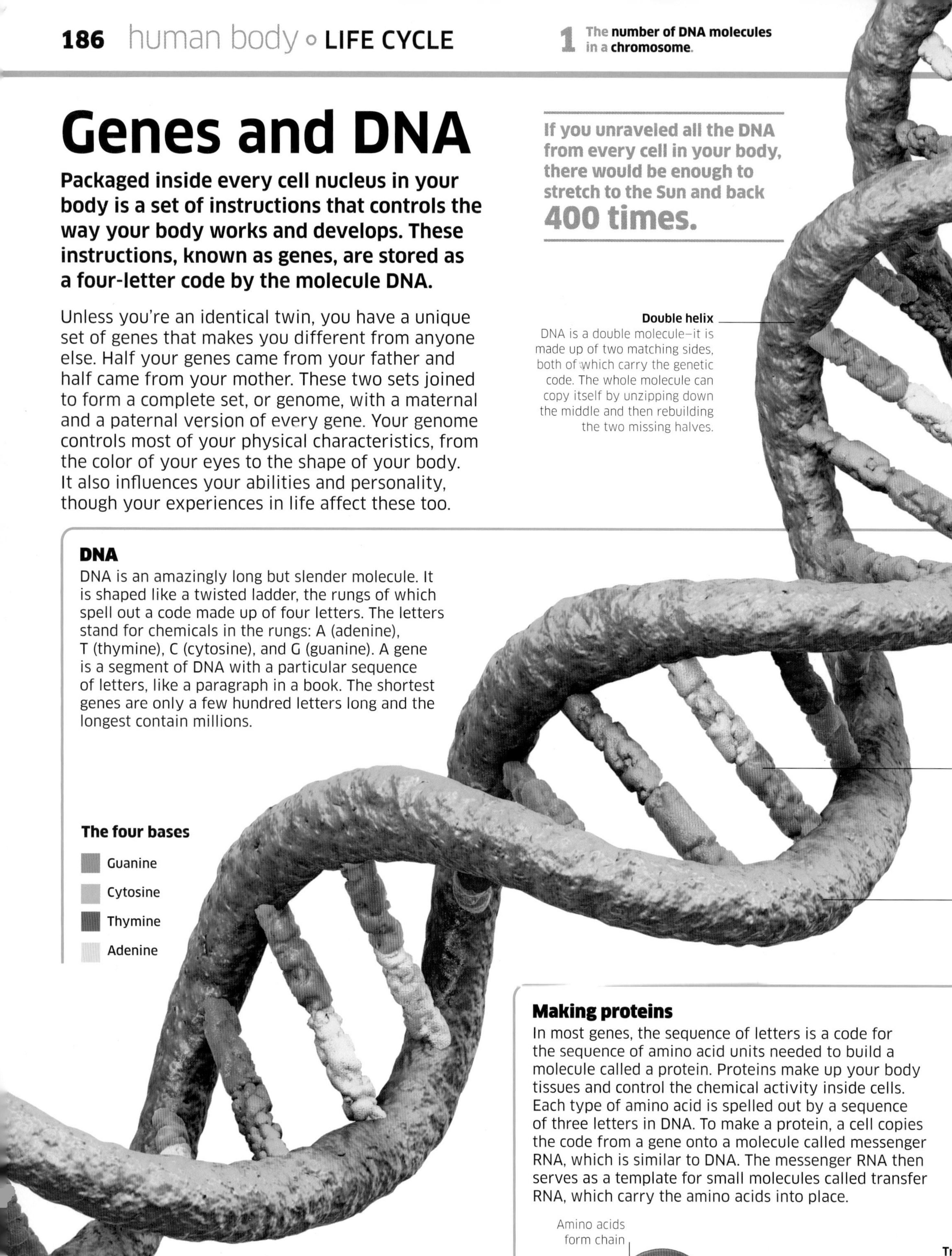

Double helix
DNA is a double molecule—it is made up of two matching sides, both of which carry the genetic code. The whole molecule can copy itself by unzipping down the middle and then rebuilding the two missing halves.

DNA

DNA is an amazingly long but slender molecule. It is shaped like a twisted ladder, the rungs of which spell out a code made up of four letters. The letters stand for chemicals in the rungs: A (adenine), T (thymine), C (cytosine), and G (guanine). A gene is a segment of DNA with a particular sequence of letters, like a paragraph in a book. The shortest genes are only a few hundred letters long and the longest contain millions.

Base pairs
Each rung is made of two bases paired together. Adenine always pairs with thymine, and cytosine always pairs with guanine.

Backbone
The backbone of DNA is made of alternating sugar and phosphate units joined in a chain.

The four bases

- Guanine
- Cytosine
- Thymine
- Adenine

Making proteins

In most genes, the sequence of letters is a code for the sequence of amino acid units needed to build a molecule called a protein. Proteins make up your body tissues and control the chemical activity inside cells. Each type of amino acid is spelled out by a sequence of three letters in DNA. To make a protein, a cell copies the code from a gene onto a molecule called messenger RNA, which is similar to DNA. The messenger RNA then serves as a template for small molecules called transfer RNA, which carry the amino acids into place.

Protein molecule
All protein molecules consist of a chain of units called amino acids.

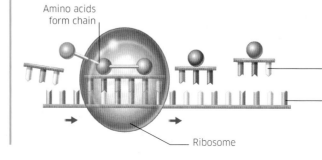

Amino acids form chain

Transfer RNA
These short RNA strands carry single amino acids around inside a cell.

Messenger RNA
This molecule carries the genetic code from a gene to a ribosome (protein-making site).

Ribosome

1.7 in (44 mm)—the **average length of the DNA molecule** in a chromosome.

2.2 million—the **number of letters** in the **longest known gene**.

25 percent—the amount of **DNA** that **humans share with daffodils**.

187

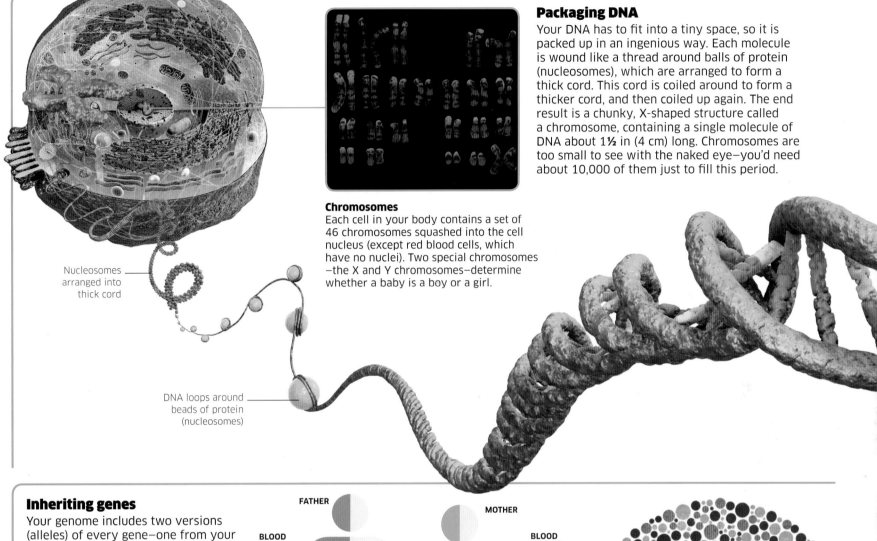

Packaging DNA

Your DNA has to fit into a tiny space, so it is packed up in an ingenious way. Each molecule is wound like a thread around balls of protein (nucleosomes), which are arranged to form a thick cord. This cord is coiled around to form a thicker cord, and then coiled up again. The end result is a chunky, X-shaped structure called a chromosome, containing a single molecule of DNA about 1½ in (4 cm) long. Chromosomes are too small to see with the naked eye—you'd need about 10,000 of them just to fill this period.

Chromosomes

Each cell in your body contains a set of 46 chromosomes squashed into the cell nucleus (except red blood cells, which have no nuclei). Two special chromosomes —the X and Y chromosomes—determine whether a baby is a boy or a girl.

Nucleosomes arranged into thick cord

DNA loops around beads of protein (nucleosomes)

Inheriting genes

Your genome includes two versions (alleles) of every gene—one from your mother and one from your father. Some gene versions are dominant, which means they always have an effect on the body, no matter what the other version is. Others are recessive, which means they have no effect when paired with a dominant gene. A recessive gene has no effect unless you have two copies—one from each parent.

Blood groups

Your blood group depends on which combination of three alleles (A, B, and O) you carry. Alleles A and B are both dominant genes, while allele O is recessive. Only people with two O genes have blood group O.

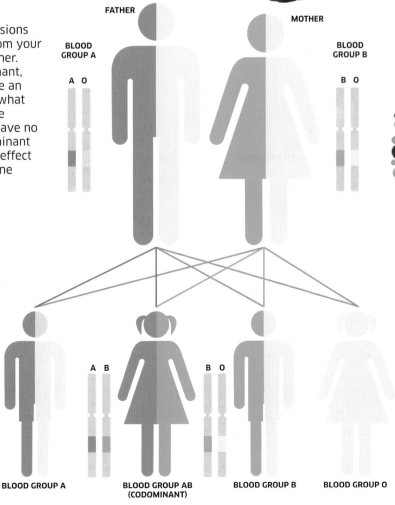

FATHER

MOTHER

BLOOD GROUP A

BLOOD GROUP B

A O

B O

A O

A B

B O

O O

BLOOD GROUP A

BLOOD GROUP AB (CODOMINANT)

BLOOD GROUP B

BLOOD GROUP O

Key

A allele

B allele

O allele

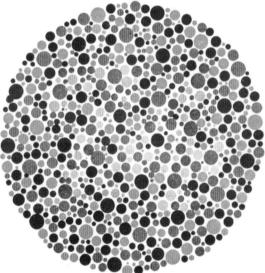

X-linked genes

Some genes are carried by the X chromosome. Since boys have only one X chromosome while girls have two, faulty genes are more likely to cause problems in boys than girls. Such conditions are known as X-linked disorders. A common example is color blindness, which is tested by images like the one above. If you can't see the number 74 in the image, you might have the gene for color blindness. Color blindness affects 8 percent of males of European descent but only 0.5 percent of girls.

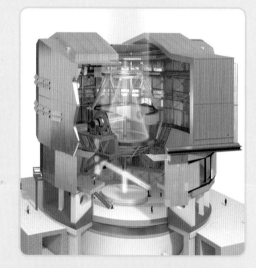

SCIENCE

Science is the search for the hidden laws that govern the way everything in the Universe works, from atoms and light to gravity and magnetism. Technology is how we apply this knowledge to create ever more complex machines and devices.

Atoms and molecules

All the matter in the Universe that we know of is made of tiny, invisible particles called atoms. Atoms are crammed into everything you can see—from the skin on your fingers to the words in this book—and things you can't see too, such as the air you breathe and the cells rushing through your blood.

The idea of atoms is one of the oldest in science. Some Ancient Greek philosophers thought atoms were the smallest possible bits of matter and couldn't be broken down further. They chose the name atom because it means "uncuttable" or "indivisible." This early concept of atoms lived on for thousands of years, until, in the early 20th century, ingenious scientists "split the atom," smashing it apart into even tinier particles.

When atoms combine, they make bigger clumps called molecules. Although there are only about 100 types of atoms, together they can form millions of different types of molecules.

Proton
Protons have a positive electric charge, and are attracted to electrons.

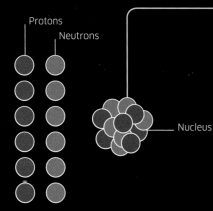

Protons
Neutrons

Nucleus

The nucleus
A cluster of protons and neutrons make up the nucleus of an atom. It makes up most of an atom's weight, but only takes up a tiny amount of its volume. Outside the nucleus, more than 99.99 percent of an atom is just empty space. If an atom were the size of a football stadium, the nucleus would be the size of a pea in the center of it, and the electrons would be zooming around the outer stands.

Neutron
These are around the same size as protons. Neutrons are neutral, which means they don't have an electric charge and aren't attracted to electrons or protons.

The **nucleus** is **10,000 times smaller** than the **atom** it fits inside. **Electrons** are **10,000 times smaller again**.

In 1911, physicist Ernest Rutherford **"split the atom"** by firing parts of atoms at other atoms, and subsequently **discovered the nucleus**.

193

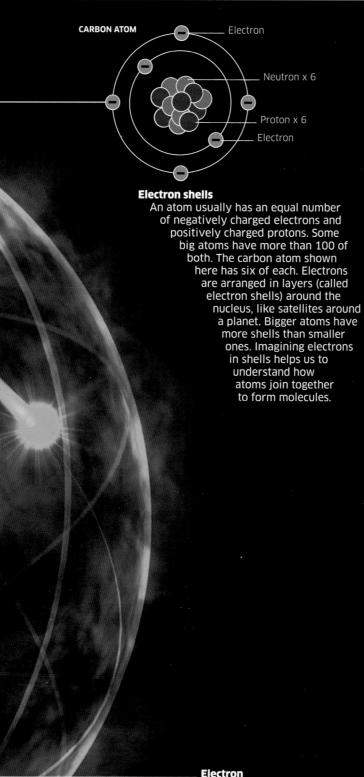

CARBON ATOM

Electron

Neutron x 6

Proton x 6

Electron

Electron shells
An atom usually has an equal number of negatively charged electrons and positively charged protons. Some big atoms have more than 100 of both. The carbon atom shown here has six of each. Electrons are arranged in layers (called electron shells) around the nucleus, like satellites around a planet. Bigger atoms have more shells than smaller ones. Imagining electrons in shells helps us to understand how atoms join together to form molecules.

Making molecules
Atoms can join together–or bond–to make molecules. A molecule can be made of the same atoms or different ones. Gases such as hydrogen have simple molecules made of just two atoms, while plastics can be made from endlessly repeating molecules made up of thousands of atoms joined together in very long lines.

Water (H_2O)
A molecule of water is made from two hydrogen atoms joined to one oxygen atom.

Carbon dioxide (CO_2)
A carbon dioxide molecule is made from two atoms of oxygen joined to one atom of carbon.

How atoms bond
Atoms bind together to make molecules using their electrons, which they give, take, or share with each other. Three main types of bonds hold atoms together.

Ionic bond
One atom gives electrons to another. The first atom becomes positively charged and the second atom becomes negatively charged, so the atoms attract and lock.

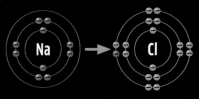

Covalent bond
Two atoms share their outer electrons by making their outer electron shells overlap.

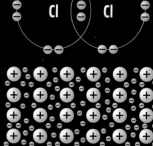

Metallic bond
Metals bond into what's called a crystal lattice by sharing their outer electrons in a giant cloud.

Electron
These particles are about 2,000 times lighter than protons and neutrons, and orbit the nucleus at almost the speed of light. They have a negative electric charge.

The structure of an atom
Inside an atom are even tinier particles of matter called protons, neutrons, and electrons. Protons and neutrons are found in the center of an atom, which is called the nucleus, and are locked tightly together by powerful forces. Electrons spin up, down, and around outside the nucleus within areas called electron shells.

Quarks and strings
If the nucleus of an atom is built from protons and neutrons, what are these things made of? It seems that each consists of three even smaller particles called quarks. Some scientists believe that everything is really made from vibrations of matter or energy called strings. But so far, no one knows what, if anything, strings are made of.

String

Quark

Proton

ATOM

The Large Hadron Collider

This gigantic machine runs for 17 miles (27 km) in a circular tunnel buried 330 ft (100 m) underground. It whizzes two beams of atomic particles around the tunnel, in opposite directions, at up to 99.9999999 percent the speed of light, and then diverts them so that they smash together. These blistering particle collisions are studied using four detectors spaced around the loop called Alice, Atlas, CMS, and LHC-b.

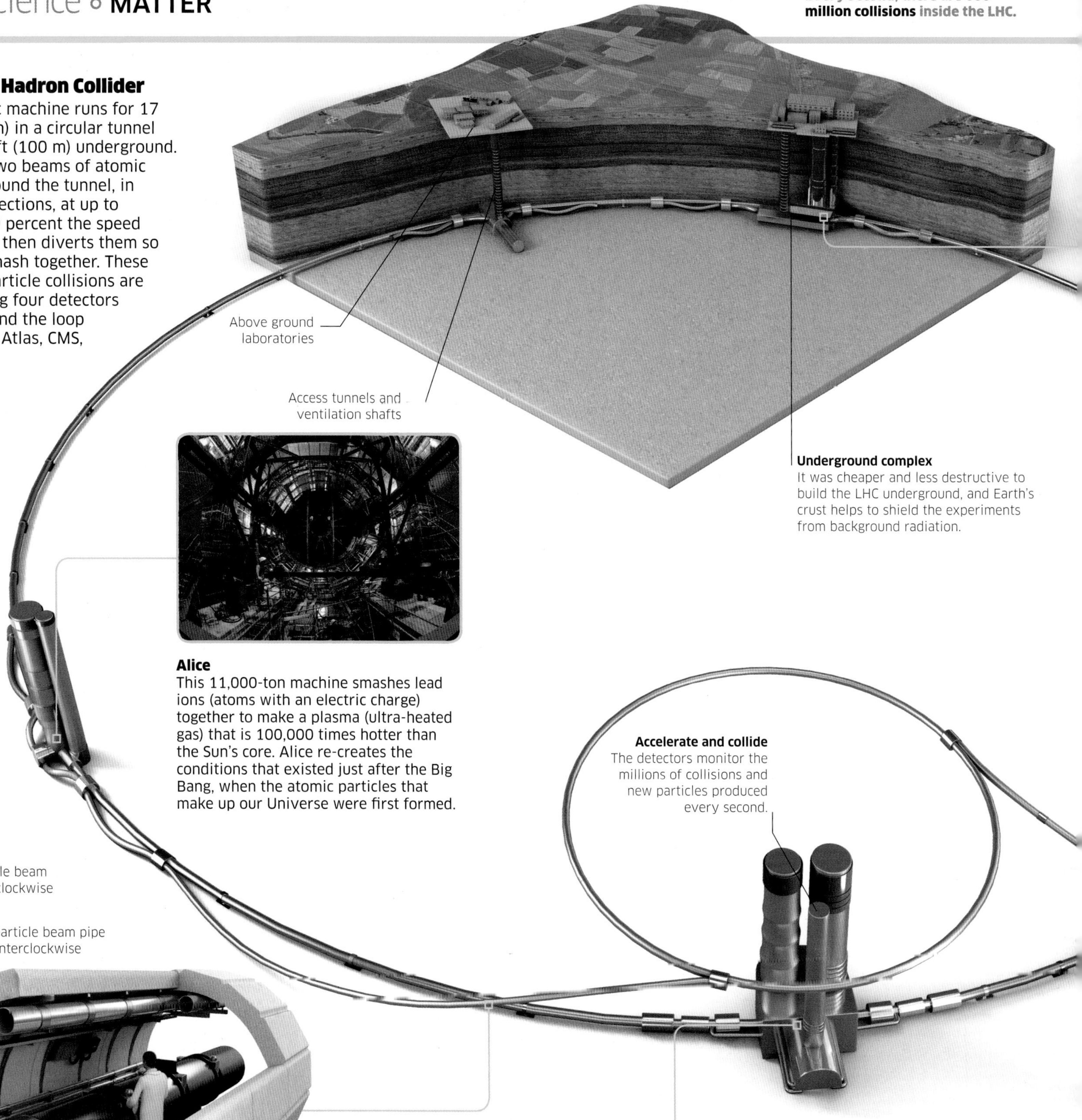

Above ground laboratories

Access tunnels and ventilation shafts

Underground complex
It was cheaper and less destructive to build the LHC underground, and Earth's crust helps to shield the experiments from background radiation.

Alice

This 11,000-ton machine smashes lead ions (atoms with an electric charge) together to make a plasma (ultra-heated gas) that is 100,000 times hotter than the Sun's core. Alice re-creates the conditions that existed just after the Big Bang, when the atomic particles that make up our Universe were first formed.

Accelerate and collide
The detectors monitor the millions of collisions and new particles produced every second.

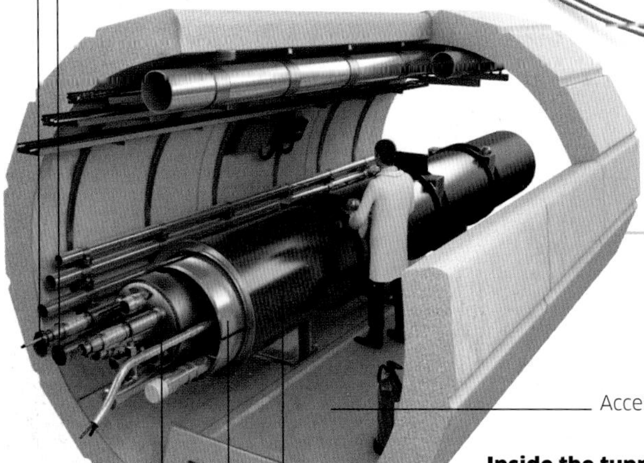

First particle beam pipe goes clockwise

Second particle beam pipe goes counterclockwise

Access tunnel

Powerful magnets

Heat insulation

Vacuum outer case

Inside the tunnel

The tunnel contains a thick blue pipe with two thinner pipes inside it that carry the particle beams in opposite directions. Wrapped around the thin pipes are more than 1,600 magnets, which bend the particle beams, steer them, and then squeeze them together so they collide.

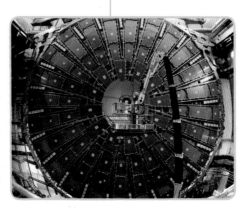

Atlas

This detector uses a huge doughnut-shaped system of magnets clamped around a beam pipe to watch collisions between protons. It's looking for a mysterious particle called the Higgs boson. If scientists find it, they hope it will help them to understand how other particles come to have their mass.

10,000 The **number of scientists**, from **100 countries**, involved in the project.

The **super powerful magnets** in the LHC's tunnel contain enough cable to **wrap around Earth six times.**

195

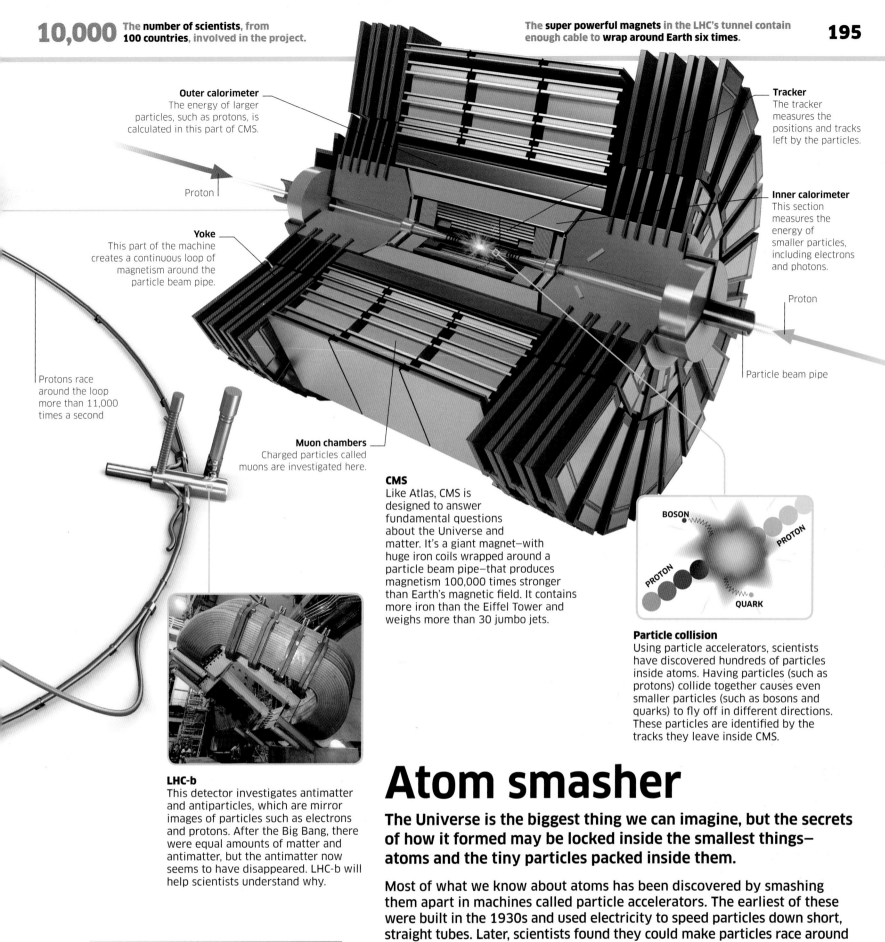

Outer calorimeter
The energy of larger particles, such as protons, is calculated in this part of CMS.

Proton

Tracker
The tracker measures the positions and tracks left by the particles.

Inner calorimeter
This section measures the energy of smaller particles, including electrons and photons.

Yoke
This part of the machine creates a continuous loop of magnetism around the particle beam pipe.

Proton

Protons race around the loop more than 11,000 times a second

Particle beam pipe

Muon chambers
Charged particles called muons are investigated here.

CMS
Like Atlas, CMS is designed to answer fundamental questions about the Universe and matter. It's a giant magnet—with huge iron coils wrapped around a particle beam pipe—that produces magnetism 100,000 times stronger than Earth's magnetic field. It contains more iron than the Eiffel Tower and weighs more than 30 jumbo jets.

BOSON
PROTON
PROTON
QUARK

Particle collision
Using particle accelerators, scientists have discovered hundreds of particles inside atoms. Having particles (such as protons) collide together causes even smaller particles (such as bosons and quarks) to fly off in different directions. These particles are identified by the tracks they leave inside CMS.

LHC-b
This detector investigates antimatter and antiparticles, which are mirror images of particles such as electrons and protons. After the Big Bang, there were equal amounts of matter and antimatter, but the antimatter now seems to have disappeared. LHC-b will help scientists understand why.

The LHC's tunnel is the world's
largest refrigerator—
cooled to a temperature lower than that in outer space—with a vacuum pump that keeps air out.

Atom smasher

The Universe is the biggest thing we can imagine, but the secrets of how it formed may be locked inside the smallest things— atoms and the tiny particles packed inside them.

Most of what we know about atoms has been discovered by smashing them apart in machines called particle accelerators. The earliest of these were built in the 1930s and used electricity to speed particles down short, straight tubes. Later, scientists found they could make particles race around tracks until they reached incredibly high speeds. When the particles crashed together, they shattered apart in spectacular collisions, splitting into a storm of smaller bits that could then be captured and studied.

Today, the world's biggest particle accelerator is located in an international laboratory called CERN on the French-Swiss border. CERN is currently running the boldest and most expensive science experiment ever devised. Known as the Large Hadron Collider (LHC), it's attempting to reproduce the conditions that existed when the Universe was formed in the Big Bang, almost 14 billion years ago.

Solids, liquids, and gases

Place an ice cube on the palm of your hand and you will soon have a pool of water. Leave it for long enough and the water will evaporate and disappear. What makes water appear as ice rather than a vapor? What makes it change between solid, liquid, and gas?

Every substance is made up of atoms or molecules that jiggle around in constant motion. Depending on how hot or cool it is, and how much "squeezing" (pressure) a substance receives from its surroundings, its atoms or molecules move quicker or slower, spring together or bounce apart. It's the strange dance of atoms inside a substance that makes it shift between solid, liquid, gas, or plasma—the four main states of matter.

Although the solid, liquid, or gas forms of a substance contain the same number of atoms, they have different inner structures. Ice, water, and water vapor look very different and behave in amazingly different ways—all because of the patterns their atoms take up inside them.

Solids

When something is cooled or put under pressure, its atoms or molecules lock tightly together to form the strong bonds of a solid. These powerful links between atoms make solids difficult to bend or reshape. Some materials form orderly solids called crystals, while others form more random (amorphous) solids.

Strong bonds between atoms keep a solid's shape from changing

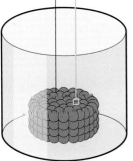

Water in a solid state
Most substances contract (shrink) when they freeze, but water is different. It expands as it freezes, making ice slightly less dense than water. This is why ice floats and why water pipes can burst when they freeze.

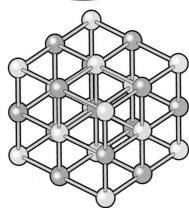

Crystalline solid
If you cool a liquid slowly, it has time to arrange its atoms and molecules into a very regular form called a crystal. Many metals are like this.

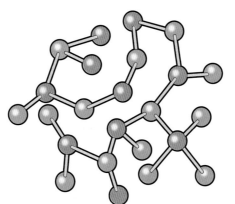

Amorphous solid
Some materials cool and snap together into a more random structure. Glass is like this—a mix between an orderly solid and a chaotic liquid.

Liquids

Liquids are usually hotter and less compressed than solids, so their atoms and molecules are slightly further apart from one another. The forces between the particles are weaker, so they can move around more freely. This is why liquids have no fixed shape, but spread out to line the container in which they are placed.

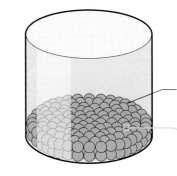

Atoms and molecules in liquids are packed almost as closely as those in solids, but with weaker bonds between them

Water in a liquid state
Life exists on Earth because there is water. It's a liquid at everyday temperatures and pressures, which means it's easy to transport and recycle, and just as easy for plants and animals to absorb.

Viscosity
The weaker bonds between atoms and molecules in liquids allow liquids to flow as you pour them. A liquid's viscosity means how slowly or quickly it flows.

Honey is very viscous, and flows slowly

Oil is less viscous, and does not splash much

Water has very low viscosity, and drips and splashes easily

60 percent of a **man's body** is water, compared to **55 percent of a woman's body**, and **78 percent of a baby's**.

Tungsten has the **highest melting point** of any metal (6,192°F or 3,422°C), which is why it's **used to make** the **filaments in light bulbs**.

197

Gases

In gases, atoms and molecules are not bonded together but move quickly and freely and have enough energy to flow all by themselves. Constantly bumping into one another, they spread out to fill whatever container they are inside.

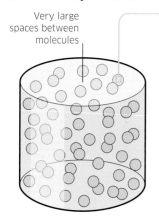

Very large spaces between molecules

Water in a gaseous state
Gases are normally hotter than their liquid forms, which is why steam is hotter than water. Gases can also form when the pressure is low. In clouds, water is a cold gas (water vapor), due to the low air pressure high above Earth.

Plasma

Heat a gas or lower its pressure enough, and the atoms come apart to form a cloud with an electric charge, called a plasma. Plasmas are made of charged particles, called electrons, and ions (atoms missing electrons), so they behave in strange ways when electricity and magnetism are nearby.

Aurora
The northern lights (Aurora Borealis) happen when plasma from the Sun hits Earth's atmosphere and bends in its magnetic field.

Changing states of matter

Boil a kettle and you will transform water from a liquid to a gas (steam). Freeze food and you will change the water inside it into a solid (ice). It's easy to make water change states because its solid, liquid, and gas forms can exist at everyday temperatures and pressures. It's harder to change materials like metals into liquids or gases, since much higher temperatures and pressures are needed.

GAS

HEAT

Steam takes up about
1,600 times
as much space as the same amount of water.

Evaporation
When you heat a liquid, the atoms and molecules gain much more energy. They collide more often and start to push apart. Some have enough energy to escape from the liquid, forming a gas (vapor) directly above it.

Sublimation
You can change a solid into a gas without making liquid first. The dry ice used to make smoke in concerts is made from frozen lumps of carbon dioxide. Once exposed to the air, it heats up rapidly and forms a cold gas.

Deposition
Gases can turn directly into solids without first becoming liquids. If water vapor in the air is cooled enough, it condenses and freezes to form snow in clouds, or frost on the ground.

Condensation
If you cool a gas or lower its pressure, it will turn into a liquid. Water vapor inside your home will often condense on your windows on cold days if the outside temperature falls low enough.

Freezing
As liquids lose energy, their atoms and molecules move about more slowly and gradually come together. Bonds form between them and they lock in a rigid structure, making a solid.

Melting
Solids change to liquids by melting. For instance, ice cream quickly soaks up heat from the atmosphere. Water molecules in the ice gain energy and move apart, becoming liquid.

SOLID

LIQUID

Platinum (Pt) is one of the most expensive elements. A man-sized mass of platinum would cost about $4.5 million.

The most recently discovered element, ununseptium (Uus), was created in a laboratory in 2010.

The elements

Elements are the basic chemical building blocks of matter, and atoms are the basic unit of an element. Snap together atoms of a few chemical elements and you can make anything on Earth, from the smallest beetle to the tallest skyscraper.

You could build living things from a handful of elements based on carbon, and you could make the water that covers most of our planet from just two elements—hydrogen and oxygen. But to make everything on Earth you would need about 100 elements in total. Most elements occur naturally—they are locked in rocks or drifting around in the atmosphere. But since elements are made from protons, neutrons, and electrons glued together by strong forces, it's also possible to build brand new ones. Scientists have done just this in laboratories, pushing the total number of known elements to 118.

Growing atoms
Atoms get bigger and heavier as we move down each column (group) of the table. This is because there are more protons in the nucleus and more electrons in the shells (rings) around it. A shell is added each time we move another step down a group.

One shell

Two shells

Shrinking atoms
As we move along each row (period) of the table, atoms gain more protons and electrons. Each atom has the same number of electron shells, but there are more positively charged protons pulling the shells inward. This shrinks the atom, and makes it more tightly packed.

One electron in outer shell

Two electrons in outer shell

The Periodic Table
If we sort the elements into a grid according to their atomic structure, patterns emerge. Elements that behave in similar ways group together, so we can predict how an element will behave from its place in the grid. This idea is called the Periodic Table, and it was created by a Russian chemist called Dmitri Mendeleev in 1869.

Transuranic elements
Elements with a greater number than uranium (92) are called transuranic. Unlike elements 1-92, these aren't found in nature and have to be created in particle accelerators or nuclear reactors, which makes them very expensive to use.

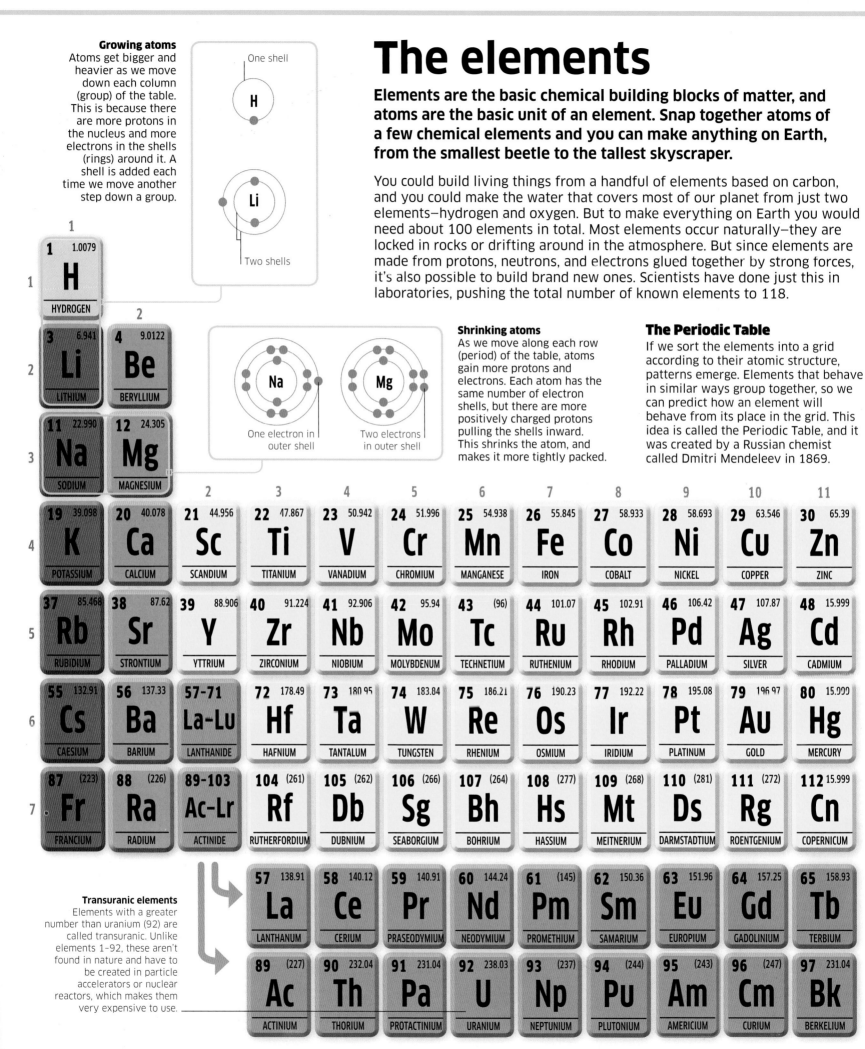

4.4 lb (2kg)–how much a **tennis ball** would weigh if it was made of **plutonium** (Pu), one of the **heaviest natural elements**.

In 1811, French chemist Bernard Courtois **accidentally discovered** the element **iodine** while he was **making explosives from seaweed**.

199

Periodic Table Key

- Alkali metals
- Alkali earth metals
- Transition metals
- Rare earth metals
- Other metals
- Metalloids
- Other nonmetals
- Halogens
- Noble gases
- Unknown

Under everyday conditions, two of the elements—mercury and bromine—are liquids, 11 are gases, and the **rest are solids**.

Helium
This gas makes up about a quarter of the entire mass of the Universe.

Carbon
This is the fourth most common element. Both plants and animals are about 18 percent carbon.

12	13	14	15	16	17
					2 4.0026 **He** HELIUM
5 10.811 **B** BORON	6 12.011 **C** CARBON	7 14.007 **N** NITROGEN	8 15.999 **O** OXYGEN	9 18.998 **F** FLUORINE	10 20.180 **Ne** NEON
13 26.982 **Al** ALUMINUM	14 28.086 **Si** SILICON	15 30.974 **P** PHOSPHORUS	16 32.065 **S** SULFUR	17 35.453 **Cl** CHLORINE	18 39.948 **Ar** ARGON
31 69.723 **Ga** GALLIUM	32 72.64 **Ge** GERMANIUM	33 74.922 **As** ARSENIC	34 78.96 **Se** SELENIUM	35 79.904 **Br** BROMINE	36 83.80 **Kr** KRYPTON
49 114.82 **In** INDIUM	50 118.71 **Sn** TIN	51 121.76 **Sb** ANTIMONY	52 127.60 **Te** TELLURIUM	53 126.90 **I** IODINE	54 131.29 **Xe** XENON
81 204.38 **Tl** THALLIUM	82 207.2 **Pb** LEAD	83 208.96 **Bi** BISMUTH	84 (209) **Po** POLONIUM	85 (210) **At** ASTATINE	86 (222) **Rn** RADON
113 284 **Uut** UNUNTRIUM	114 289 **Uuq** UNUNQUADIUM	115 288 **Uup** UNUNPENTIUM	116 293 **Uuh** UNUNHEXIUM	117 294 **Uus** UNUNSEPTIUM	118 294 **Uuo** UNUNOCTIUM

66 162.50 **Dy** DYSPROSIUM	67 164.93 **Ho** HOLMIUM	68 167.26 **Er** ERBIUM	69 168.93 **Tm** THULIUM	70 173.04 **Yb** YTTERBIUM	71 174.97 **Lu** LUTETIUM
98 (251) **Cf** CALIFORNIUM	99 (252) **Es** EINSTEINIUM	100 (257) **Fm** FERMIUM	101 (258) **Md** MENDELEVIUM	102 (259) **No** NOBELIUM	103 (262) **Lr** LAWRENCIUM

What is an element?

The elements are different substances (solids, liquids, and gases) made from atoms that have different inner structures. If two atoms have the same number of protons, they are atoms of the same element. An atom is the smallest amount of an element you can have.

Atomic number
This is the number of protons inside the nucleus of the atom. The metal titanium has 22 protons and an atomic number of 22.

Atomic mass
This is the total number of protons and neutrons in an atom.

22 47.867 **Ti** TITANIUM

Name
The name of an element often describes its properties. Titanium is named after the Titans, Ancient Greek gods of incredible strength.

Chemical symbol
This is a shortened way of representing an element. Some elements have symbols made up from their names.

96% OF YOUR BODY IS MADE OF JUST FOUR ELEMENTS: OXYGEN, CARBON, HYDROGEN, AND NITROGEN.

Building blocks

The Periodic Table is made up of rows called periods and columns called groups. As we move across each period, the elements change from solid metals (on the left) to gases (on the right).

Period
The elements in a period all have the same number of electron shells.

Group
The elements in groups are similar because they have the same number of electrons in their outer shell.

Series

Within the table are bigger blocks of elements that behave in similar ways. On the left are reactive metals such as sodium (Na). Most everyday metals occur in the middle of the table in a set called the transition metals. Nonmetals are mostly on the right of the table. Rare earth metals are all soft metals.

REACTIVE METALS

MAINLY NONMETALS

TRANSITION METALS

RARE EARTH METALS

Chemical reactions

When you watch a display of fireworks shooting, screeching, and banging their way across the sky, you are seeing the power of chemistry bursting into action.

The world often seems unchanging, but in fact, little stays the same for very long. Atoms and molecules are constantly rearranging themselves—breaking down old things and building up new ones. Chemistry helps to explain how this happens through step-by-step changes called chemical reactions.

In a reaction, elements join together to make bigger units called compounds, or compounds split back into their original elements. Many reactions are silent and invisible. Others, like an exploding firework, are energetic and violent. Reactions are the amazing transformations that drive many of the things around us. When candles flicker and cakes rise in your oven, reactions are rearranging atoms into new and different forms.

2 The outer shell explodes
Once the firework is safely in the sky, the time-delay fuse burns to its outer shell and sets fire to the stars inside. These burst into dozens of small separate explosions as they race through the sky.

Symmetry
Fireworks usually explode symmetrically, with equal amounts of energy fired in all directions.

Bright lights
Shell fireworks produce the most colorful, and often the loudest, displays.

What is a firework?
A firework is a missile packed with explosive chemicals that shoots high into the sky before shattering in a series of carefully controlled and very colorful reactions. In most chemical reactions, the end products are what matter most—how they are produced isn't important. A firework display is the opposite—the chemical reaction itself is what we want to see.

Firework trail _____

Stars
Tiny packets of explosives.

Report charge
A firework exploding doesn't always make a loud noise, so a report charge is added to create an impressive bang.

Black powder
Tightly packed gunpowder is used to explode the inner and outer shells.

Inner shell
The stars in the inner shell are released during the final explosion.

Outer shell
Stars in the outer shell are released while the firework is still climbing into the sky.

1 Launch
Most chemical reactions need to be kick-started using what's called activation energy. When a firework is launched, an electric spark lights its fuse. A small, explosive charge at the bottom of the firework starts burning, and then the firework is blasted out of its tube.

Inside a shell firework
The fireworks used in a big display are formed as a shell that explodes twice or more in the sky. A fuse burns through their middle, setting off an outer shell of explosives and then, seconds later, an inner shell.

Lift charge
The main explosive that launches the firework into the sky.

Time-delay fuse
A fuse that safely sets fire to the lift charge, followed by the shells.

Mortar stand
Fireworks are stored in separate tubes that can be aimed at precise points in the sky.

What is a chemical reaction?
In a chemical reaction, one ingredient (called a reactant) combines with a second one. During the reaction, the bonds that hold together the atoms or molecules of the reactants split apart. The atoms then rearrange themselves and new bonds form between them to make a different set of chemicals called the product.

Lit fuse
Each tube is connected to one or more others. As one tube fires, it triggers the next in the sequence.

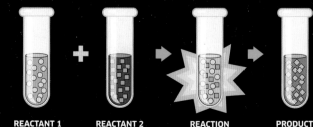

REACTANT 1   REACTANT 2   REACTION   PRODUCT

The **biggest fireworks** can be **launched more than 1,000 ft (300 m)** into the air.

201

Beautiful shapes
The pattern the firework makes in the sky depends on how the stars are arranged inside the shell.

3 The final explosion
The time-delay fuse burns at a precise rate, so the final explosion happens when the firework has reached its highest point in the sky. Most of the explosive is packed into the middle of the firework so the final explosion is the biggest and most spectacular.

MAGNESIUM

COPPER SALTS

STRONTIUM NITRATE

The chemistry of colors
Chemical reactions give off light when atoms are heated up and emit energy. Different sized atoms absorb and give out different amounts of energy, which makes different colored light. In a firework, each color is produced by a separate metal compound.

BARIUM NITRATE

SODIUM SALTS

IRON

Types of chemical reaction

Although the products can be very different from the reactants, no atoms are created or destroyed. So, no matter how the reaction takes place, there are always the same number of each kind of atom after a reaction as there were before it. There are three main types of chemical reaction.

SYNTHESIS REACTION—TWO OR MORE REACTANTS JOIN TOGETHER

DECOMPOSITION REACTION—ONE REACTANT BREAKS APART INTO TWO PRODUCTS

DISPLACEMENT REACTION—ATOMS OF ONE TYPE SWAP PLACES WITH THOSE OF ANOTHER, FORMING NEW COMPOUNDS

Combustion

Car engines, power stations, and home heating are three common things powered by a chemical reaction called combustion (burning). The reactants are a fuel (perhaps gas or coal) and oxygen from the air. Adding heat (setting fire to the fuel) provides activation energy that starts the reaction and releases more energy as fire.

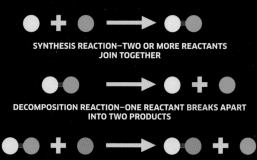

OXYGEN

HEAT

FUEL

202 science ○ **MATTER**

2011 The year **engineers in Kuwait** built the world's **biggest ever** sculpture from recycled materials—a gigantic hat **87 ft (27 m)** long.

Choosing materials

Although materials such as wood and plastic have many uses, no single material can do everything. When we're choosing a material, we have to consider carefully what it will need to do. Should it be hard or soft? Does it need to be strong and long lasting, or weak enough to break down quickly in a landfill site?

Ceramics

Materials such as pottery and brick are examples of ceramics. They're made from clays dug from the Earth, which are shaped and then fired so that they harden. They can survive high temperatures and insulate against electricity, but are brittle and fragile.

Glass

A unique, see-through ceramic, glass is inexpensive, easy to shape when it's being made, and can withstand high temperatures. Although it's fragile, it can be toughened by laminating it (sandwiching it between layers of plastic).

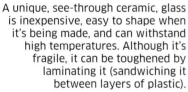

Plastic

Plastics are cheap, easy to mold, and come in any color (as well as clear). There's a huge range, from tough ABS plastic (hard enough to make car bumpers) to light and flexible polyethylene, which is used for drink bottles.

Synthetic fabrics

Natural fibers such as wool are warm, but they're not waterproof or easy to clean. That's why many of us wear plastic-based fabrics such as nylon, polyester, and Lycra. These fabrics are particularly good for sports clothes.

Composites

Composites are made by combining two or more materials to make a better one. A surfboard, which needs to be strong, reasonably light, buoyant (able to float), and waterproof, is best made from a tough composite such as fiberglass (plastic reinforced with glass).

A STRAWBERRY-SIZED CUBE OF GRAPHENE AEROGEL, THE LIGHTEST SOLID ON EARTH, **CAN BALANCE ON A BLADE OF GRASS.**

Material world

There are reasons why clothes aren't made from concrete, books from metal, or bikes from glass. Every material does some things well, and materials science is all about putting the right material in the right place by understanding the structure of the atoms and molecules inside it.

What stops a rocket from tearing itself apart as it blasts into the sky? Why do rubber tires make a bicycle so much more comfortable to ride? Study materials through a microscope and you'll find the answers to these questions hiding inside. In the tough steel alloys of a space rocket, atoms are locked together tightly. In the rubber of a bike tire, molecules will stretch far apart, making a soft and spongy cushion. Understanding the secret stories of matter helps us to pick the perfect material for every job—and develop even better materials in the future.

New materials

After thousands of years of inventing, you might think we have all the materials we will ever need. But scientists are constantly developing better ones that improve on traditional materials such as wood, glass, and metal.

Bioplastics

Plastics are hard to recycle and take up to 500 years to break down in the environment, so they cause a lot of pollution. Scientists have developed bioplastics from natural materials, such as cornstarch, which break down in soil in just weeks or months. They're perfect for use as garbage bags.

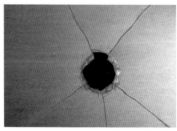

Self-healing materials

Wouldn't it be great if your car's paintwork repaired its own scratches? Self-healing materials do just this. They have built-in repair capsules containing glues that leak out to fill any cracks. There are even aerospace materials that will automatically fill in bullet holes.

Color-changing plastics

Forehead thermometers and battery tester strips are made from thermochromic plastics, which change color as they get hotter or colder. Inside, they have layers of molecules that absorb and give out different frequencies (colors) of light as their temperature rises and falls.

Nanotechnology

If we could move atoms and molecules around under a microscope, we could theoretically use them to build any material we choose. This idea is called nanotechnology and will revolutionize the way materials are developed in the future.

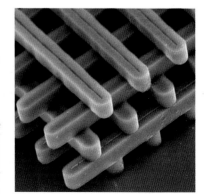

Atomic building site

Nanotechnology will let us build tiny structures thousands of times smaller than a human hair. Layer by layer, we could build new medicines, body parts, tiny machines, or anything else we need.

The **oldest material** discovered on Earth is **4,568.2 million years old**. It was found **in a meteorite** in Morocco in 2004.

Kevlar is just a plastic, but 30 layers of it **can stop a handgun bullet** traveling at **975 mph (1,570 kph)**.

203

Material teamwork

When professional cyclists speed along roads, they're powered by the latest advances in materials science. High-tech materials such as alloys and composites give cycling athletes an edge on the competition. Using a strong composite material for your bike will make it lighter and faster, while energy-absorbing plastics in your helmet and clothes will keep you safer if you crash.

Molecules lock together on impact

D30 helmet
This plastic is soft if you press gently, but upon impact its molecules lock together and turn it rock hard. It's ideal for absorbing bumps in a crash.

Nitrogen gas bubbles

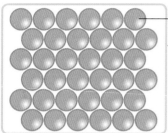

Neoprene cycling shorts
Neoprene (artificial rubber) has tiny nitrogen gas bubbles locked inside it, which makes it good for absorbing impacts and great for keeping you warm.

Carbon rods

Molecules

Brakes
Brakes slow you down by clamping blocks against your wheels. Some use Kevlar, a bulletproof plastic built from tightly packed carbon rods. This material is five times stronger than steel.

Small atoms between big atoms

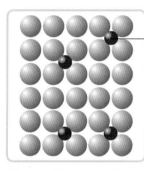

Alloy pedals and cranks
Alloys are mixtures of metals and other elements. They're stronger because the small atoms of the other materials sneak between the big metal atoms, making a tougher overall structure.

Carbon fiber

Nylon plastic

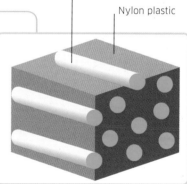

Carbon-fiber frame
Carbon-fiber composites are strong and light. They're often made from tiny fibers of aerospace carbon set in a backing of nylon plastic.

Strong bonds between molecules

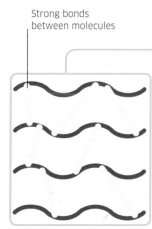

Chromium skin

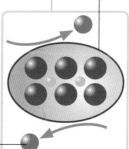

Stainless-steel spokes
Rustproof parts of a bike are made from stainless steel, an alloy of iron and chromium. The chromium forms a skin around the iron that keeps out water and keeps rust off.

Water is repelled

Tires
In its natural form, rubber (latex) is stretchy and weak. Cooking it with sulfur forms strong bonds between the molecules, producing vulcanized rubber that's tough enough for tires.

FORCES

Whenever planes hurtle overhead or cars screech to a halt, forces are working hard behind the scenes. On a larger scale, gravitational forces span the Universe, causing stars to cluster into galaxies and keeping planets whirling in orbit around the Sun. At the other end of the scale, atoms cause forces like sticking and friction.

WHAT IS A FORCE?

A force is a push or pull that makes something happen. When you kick a ball, your foot supplies the force that makes the ball fly into the air. Forces are usually invisible. Gravity is the invisible force that pins us to the ground, while magnetism is another hidden force that makes a compass spin. Simple forces can change an object's shape, alter its direction, or change its speed.

Changing shape
If you bend something, you push and pull on the atoms inside it and alter its shape.

Changing direction
Hitting the ground applies force to the ball to make it move in a different direction.

Changing speed
The harder you kick a ball, the more force you use, and the further the ball travels.

Balanced forces

If two equal forces act in opposite directions, they cancel each other out and there's no movement or change of any kind. Architects design buildings so that the downward pull of gravity is balanced by upward forces inside the buildings.

Tension in cables pulling up

Weight of bridge pulling down

Supporting a bridge
You might think there are no forces acting on a suspension bridge. In fact, huge forces are perfectly balanced. The deck (road) should plunge into the river, but its weight is supported by giant cables.

Simple machines

Levers, wheels, pulleys, and gears all magnify forces and make jobs easier to do. These force magnifiers are called simple machines. If you sit on a seesaw, you can lift someone heavier by moving further from the balancing point. The seesaw works as a lever and multiplies your lifting force. You press down with a small force and the lever makes a bigger lifting force at the other end. Machines such as cranes are built from many simple machines working together.

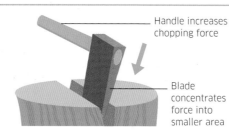

Handle increases chopping force

Blade concentrates force into smaller area

Focusing force
Axes combine two simple machines. The handle is a lever that gives your swing more speed. The blade is a wedge. It concentrates your force on the thin blade edge, so that it cuts more easily.

MAKING MOVEMENT

Three rules explain how forces make movement: 1. Objects will stay still or go on moving steadily unless a force acts on them; 2. When a force acts, it moves something faster or changes its direction; 3. When a force acts, there's always a force just as big acting in the opposite way.

Velocity and acceleration

An object's speed in a certain direction is its velocity. If it speeds up or changes direction, its velocity changes. A change in velocity is called an acceleration. Force is needed to accelerate an object.

Increasing velocity
When a car speeds up, its engine produces more force to make the vehicle accelerate.

Changing direction
As a car turns, it accelerates, even if it keeps the same speed, since the change in direction changes the car's velocity.

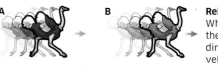

Decreasing velocity
When the driver brakes, force is applied to the wheels, slowing the car. This is called deceleration, or negative acceleration.

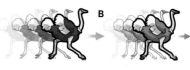

Relative velocity

The difference in speed between two moving objects is called their relative velocity. Because velocity is speed in a particular direction, you have to take account of the direction in which the objects are moving when you calculate their relative velocity.

Relative velocity zero
When two object move at the same speed in the same direction, their relative velocity is zero.

Catching up
When one object moves faster than the other, their relative velocity is the difference in their speeds.

Heading for collision
If two objects move equally fast in opposite directions, their relative velocity is the sum of their speeds.

What's faster?

Machines with powerful engines, such as rockets, usually go fast because their engines produce enormous forces to push them forward at high speed. Objects can travel even faster in space as they move away from the downward pull of Earth's gravity.

HELIOS SPACE PROBE: 157,083 mph (252,800 kph)
APOLLO SPACECRAFT: 24,854 mph (40,000 kph)
LANDSPEED CAR – THRUST SSC: 763 mph (1,228 kph)
SPORTS CAR – MCLAREN F1: 217 mph (349 kph)
CYCLIST: 167 mph (269 kph)
TOWED CARAVAN: 139 mph (224 kph)
CHEETAH: 62 mph (100 kph)
TANK: 50 mph (82 kph)
SUBMARINE: 46 mph (74 kph)
DRAGONFLY: 36 mph (58 kph)
PERSON: 27 mph (43 kph)

GRAVITY AND THE UNIVERSE

The force of gravity holds everything in the Universe together like a mysterious, invisible spider's web. Gravity is also the force of attraction between your body and Earth that, quite literally, keeps your feet on the ground.

The pull of gravity

Everything in the Universe that is made of matter (and so has mass) pulls on everything else with gravitational force. The bigger and closer the objects are, the greater the pull of gravity between them. Earth's gravity is the reason that we do not float off into space, and why objects fall down to the ground. Without air resistance to slow them down, all objects—from feathers to pool balls—would fall at the same rate.

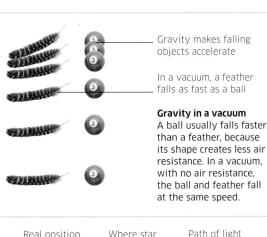

Gravity makes falling objects accelerate

In a vacuum, a feather falls as fast as a ball

Gravity in a vacuum
A ball usually falls faster than a feather, because its shape creates less air resistance. In a vacuum, with no air resistance, the ball and feather fall at the same speed.

Gravity and relativity

The gravity from a massive object, such as the Sun, still pulls at vast distances and never disappears entirely. It affects light as well as physical objects. According to a theory called relativity developed by German-born physicist Albert Einstein (1879–1955), the gravity of a body like the Sun actually bends space and time, rather like a heavy weight setting on a rubber sheet. Because space-time is bent, things moving near the Sun will curve toward it as though being pulled inward.

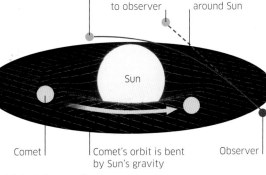

Real position of star

Where star seems to be to observer

Path of light from star is bent around Sun

Sun

Comet

Comet's orbit is bent by Sun's gravity

Observer

Distorted space-time
The Sun's heavy mass bends space-time and makes things curve toward it. A comet orbiting the Sun is pulled inward, as are rays of light from distant stars.

FRICTION

Friction is a dragging force that occurs when one object moves over another. You may not realize it, but you use this force whenever you walk down the street. Friction helps your shoes grip the pavement so that you don't slip.

A rough force

When one object moves over another, the rough surfaces of the two objects catch against one another and stick. This sticking process makes it harder to move the objects, producing a force between them that we call friction. In general, the rougher a surface is, the more friction it produces. But even polished surfaces that look and feel smooth will have microscopic bumps and ridges that produce some friction. One way to reduce friction is to make objects as smooth as possible, so they slide past one another more freely. Another way is to use lubrication.

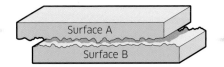

Surface A
Surface B

How friction works
As two rough surfaces slide over each other, their surfaces catch together, slowing the sliding down by converting kinetic (movement) energy into heat.

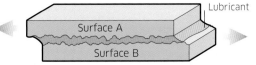

Lubricant
Surface A
Surface B

Lubrication—overcoming friction
Put a slippery substance, such as oil, between two surfaces and they will move past one another more freely. Oil is a lubricant—a thin, easily flowing liquid.

Water resistance

It's harder to move through water than through air, because water is a thick liquid. Water pulls against the front of a fish, slowing it down with what's called drag. The streamlined body shape of a fish reduces drag, allowing it to swim at higher speeds.

PRESSURE

The same force can have very different effects. If you stand on snow in ordinary shoes, the force of your weight makes you sink. But if you wear skis, your weight is spread over a larger area. You don't sink because you produce less pressure. Pressure depends on the size of the force and the area it acts over. The bigger the force or the smaller the area, the greater the pressure.

$$PRESSURE = \frac{FORCE}{AREA}$$

Larger area, lower pressure
You can't push a thick bar into a wall. If you press with a certain force on the far end, the same force travels down the bar but can't penetrate the wall.

Same force applied at wall

Force applied

Wall

Smaller area, higher pressure
Sharpening the end of the bar focuses the force into a smaller area, increasing the pressure so the bar pierces the wall. This is why nails taper to a point.

Concentrated force creates larger pressure

Force applied

Water pressure

Water exerts pressure on anything submerged in it. The deeper you go, the more water pushing down on you, and the greater the water pressure.

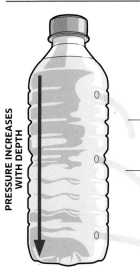

PRESSURE INCREASES WITH DEPTH

A weak jet shoots out near the top, because there's little water above

Midway down there's more water pressure, creating a stronger jet

At the base, lots of water pushes down and makes a powerful jet

Jet pressure
Fill a carton with water, poke holes at different heights, and watch pressure in action!

MAGNETISM

A magnet is surrounded by an invisible field of magnetic force that is strongest at the north and south poles of the magnet. Magnets will push and pull on other objects with magnetism. Earth's iron core is a huge magnet with its own magnetic field. A compass has a magnetic pointer that is attracted to Earth's magnetic poles.

COMPASS

206 science ○ FORCES

40 The number of times per second that a **dragonfly flaps its wings**, producing a **huge force** that speeds it through the air.

Laws of motion

No matter how quiet or calm it might seem, nothing in our world is ever still. Deep inside every object, even in the air that surrounds us, atoms and molecules are restlessly moving.

All motion—even the random dance of atoms—is caused by forces pushing and pulling. Forces act logically, so most things in the world move in ways we can understand and predict. For this, we use the three laws of motion: a simple set of scientific rules first thought up over 300 years ago.

Isaac Newton
The laws of motion were first published in 1687 by English physicist Isaac Newton (1642-1727). Often called Newton's laws, they are part of his book *Principia Mathematica*, one of the greatest scientific works of all time. Although Newton worked alone, he built his discoveries on the earlier work of scientists such as Galileo. He once said: "If I have seen farther than others, it is because I have stood on the shoulders of giants."

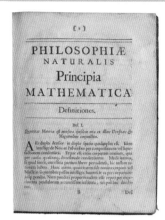

NEWTON'S *PRINCIPIA MATHEMATICA*

First law of motion
All things will either stay still or move with a steady speed unless a force acts on them. This idea is called inertia. The more mass something has, the more inertia it has too—so it will be more likely to stay still or resist changes to its motion.

MOTION

Ball is slowed by a force that opposes its motion

Foot brings ball to a stop

FORCE

Ball is motionless

Foot applies force to ball

FORCE

At rest
A soccer ball rests on the ground because there is no overall force acting on it. Its weight is perfectly balanced by the ground, and there is no sideways force.

Force applied
When you kick the soccer ball, you apply a force to one side. There's nothing to counteract or balance this force so it makes the ball move.

Motion stopped
The ball shoots through the air or rolls across the ground with a fairly steady speed until it hits something, such as your foot. When your foot applies a force, the ball stops moving.

Second law of motion
When a force acts on something, it makes it accelerate (go faster, slower, or change direction). The amount of acceleration depends on the size of the force and the mass of the object. The bigger the force or the lighter the object, the more it accelerates.

Amount of matter an object contains (in kilograms)

Acceleration is how fast speed (meters per second) is changing over time (per second). It is measured in meters per second per second (ms⁻²)

Product of mass and acceleration (in newtons (N))

Force = Mass × Acceleration

Small mass, small force
Kick a ball lightly (with a small force) and it accelerates at a steady rate. The acceleration is equal to the size of the force divided by the mass of the ball.

SMALL FORCE

1 N

Ball has a mass of 1 kg (2.2 lb)

Acceleration is 1 ms⁻² (3.3 fts⁻²)

Small mass, medium force
Kick the same ball with twice the force and you get twice the acceleration. If it flies in a straight line, it accelerates to twice the speed in the same time.

MEDIUM FORCE

2 N

Ball has a mass of 1 kg (2.2 lb)

Acceleration is 2 ms⁻² (6.6 fts⁻²)

Double mass, large force
A heavier ball needs a bigger force to get it moving. If you use eight times your original force and the ball is twice as heavy, you get four times the original acceleration.

LARGE FORCE

8 N

Ball has a mass of 2 kg (4.4 lb)

Acceleration is 4 ms⁻² (13 fts⁻²)

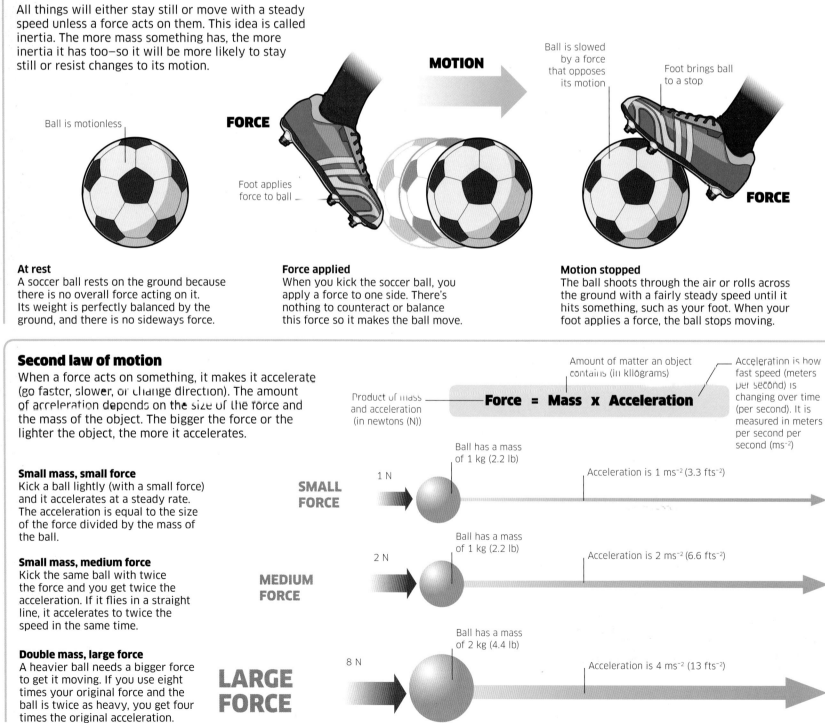

2.3 seconds—the time taken for the **world's fastest-accelerating road car**, the Ariel Atom, **to go from 0–60 mph** (0–100 kph).

Bullets accelerate at up to 3.3 **million feet** per second every second.

207

Third law of motion

Newton's third law says that when a force acts on something, there is always another force just as big acting in the opposite direction. If the original force is called the action, the opposite force is called the reaction. That's why the third law is often written in a shortened form: every action has an equal and opposite reaction.

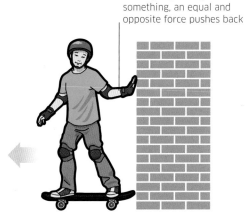

When you push against something, an equal and opposite force pushes back

Action

Imagine you're on a skateboard and you push against a wall (action). The wall pushes back with a reaction force, causing you to roll away from the wall.

People move apart with the same velocity

Wheels help to overcome friction

Reaction

If you push a friend, who is also on a skateboard, your force (action) moves them away from you. The reaction force makes you move in the opposite direction at the same speed as your friend.

Blast off

Newton's laws of motion proved that rockets would work long before anyone tried to make one. Robert Hutchings Goddard (1882–1945) was the father of the modern rocket, but when he first suggested building a spacecraft, in 1916, people thought he was crazy. They believed a rocket could never fly in space because there was no air to push against. The laws of motion proved that Goddard was right.

First law
When a rocket sets on the launch pad with its engines switched off, there's no overall force acting on it. Inertia keeps it in place so it goes nowhere.

Third law
The action (the exhaust gas firing down) produces an equal and opposite reaction (the rocket shoots up). The rocket doesn't push against the air: it moves up because the exhaust blasts down, so it can fly even in the emptiness of outer space.

Second law
The main engines and booster rockets fire out hot, high-speed exhaust gas. This creates a huge downward force that accelerates the rocket upward.

A SPACE SHUTTLE'S MAIN ENGINE PRODUCES A FORCE OF 2 MILLION NEWTONS.

With over a **billion cars** in the world, there's at least **one engine for every seven people** on the planet.

Engines

Whenever you travel by car, plane, ship, or even spaceship, you're powered by fire-roaring flames or carefully controlled explosions happening inside the engine.

Fossil fuels such as oil, coal, and gas still provide about 80 percent of the power we use every day. Gasoline (made from oil) packs huge amounts of energy into a tiny volume of liquid, so it is particularly good for use in vehicles. Engines are the machines that release this energy, using a chemical reaction called combustion. When fuels burn with oxygen from the air, their molecules smash apart and release their energy as heat. Engines capture this heat and convert it into a force that powers us down roads, over waves, or through the sky.

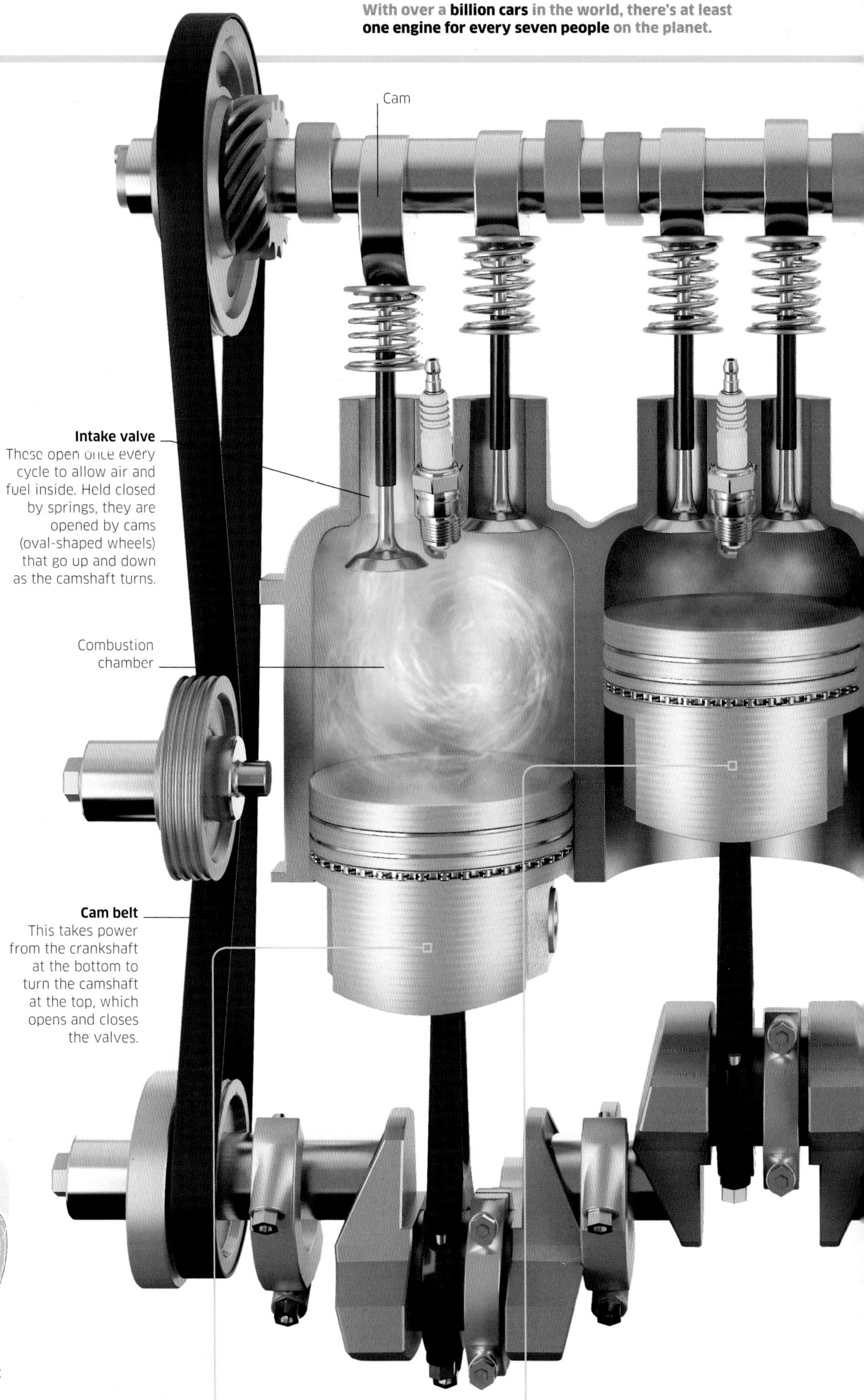

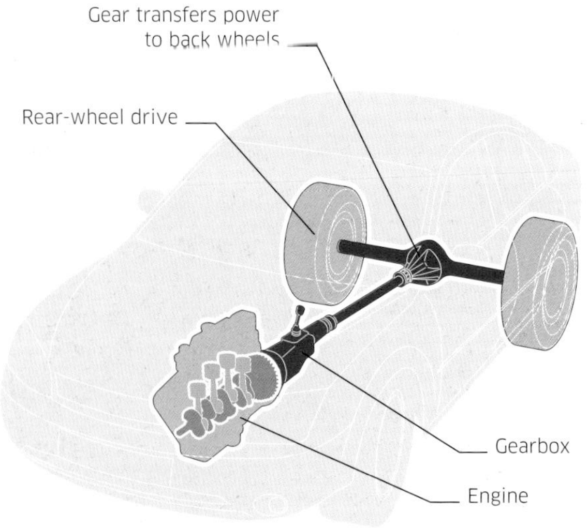

Cam
Intake valve
These open once every cycle to allow air and fuel inside. Held closed by springs, they are opened by cams (oval-shaped wheels) that go up and down as the camshaft turns.
Combustion chamber
Cam belt
This takes power from the crankshaft at the bottom to turn the camshaft at the top, which opens and closes the valves.

Internal combustion engine

In car engines, fuel (gasoline or diesel) explodes inside sturdy metal cylinders, pushing pistons up and down to generate the power that drives the wheels. Piston engines go through four simple steps, called a four-stroke cycle, which repeat over and over again, moving the car along.

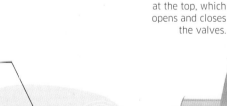

Gear transfers power to back wheels
Rear-wheel drive
Gearbox
Engine

Inside a car
Engines work best when their pistons pump quickly, but cars themselves may need to move slower or faster than this. The gearbox between the engine and the wheels alters the engine's power so the wheels turn at the speed the driver needs—slowly and with more force for climbing hills, or quickly and with less force for driving on a flat road.

1 Suck
The cycle begins when the intake valve opens at the top of the cylinder. The piston moves down, and fuel and air are sucked in through the open valve. They swirl together to make a highly explosive mixture.

2 Squeeze
The valve closes and the piston rises, squashing the mixture into about a tenth of the space and heating it up. The more the mixture is compressed, the more energy it will release when it burns and expands.

50 The number of **explosions** that happen **every second** in a **sports car engine** while driving at high speed.

The world's **smallest internal combustion engine** is the size of a penny.

209

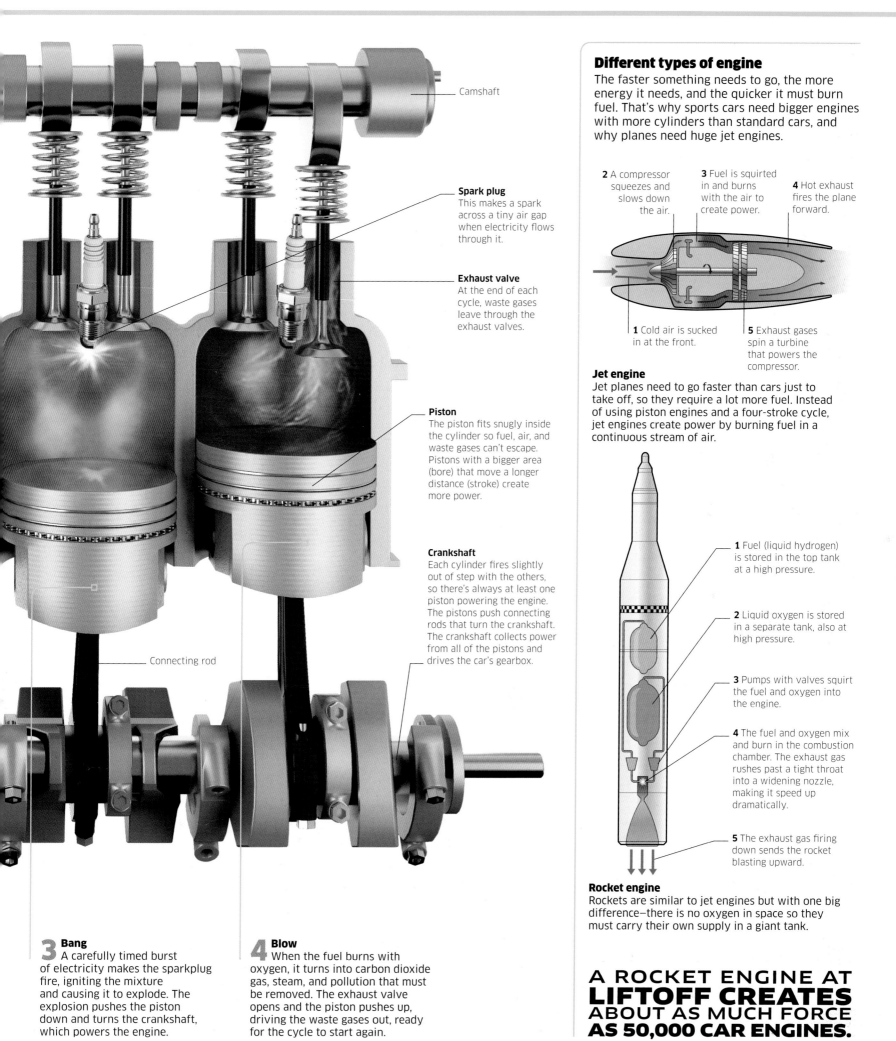

Camshaft

Spark plug
This makes a spark across a tiny air gap when electricity flows through it.

Exhaust valve
At the end of each cycle, waste gases leave through the exhaust valves.

Piston
The piston fits snugly inside the cylinder so fuel, air, and waste gases can't escape. Pistons with a bigger area (bore) that move a longer distance (stroke) create more power.

Crankshaft
Each cylinder fires slightly out of step with the others, so there's always at least one piston powering the engine. The pistons push connecting rods that turn the crankshaft. The crankshaft collects power from all of the pistons and drives the car's gearbox.

Connecting rod

3 Bang
A carefully timed burst of electricity makes the sparkplug fire, igniting the mixture and causing it to explode. The explosion pushes the piston down and turns the crankshaft, which powers the engine.

4 Blow
When the fuel burns with oxygen, it turns into carbon dioxide gas, steam, and pollution that must be removed. The exhaust valve opens and the piston pushes up, driving the waste gases out, ready for the cycle to start again.

Different types of engine
The faster something needs to go, the more energy it needs, and the quicker it must burn fuel. That's why sports cars need bigger engines with more cylinders than standard cars, and why planes need huge jet engines.

2 A compressor squeezes and slows down the air.

3 Fuel is squirted in and burns with the air to create power.

4 Hot exhaust fires the plane forward.

1 Cold air is sucked in at the front.

5 Exhaust gases spin a turbine that powers the compressor.

Jet engine
Jet planes need to go faster than cars just to take off, so they require a lot more fuel. Instead of using piston engines and a four-stroke cycle, jet engines create power by burning fuel in a continuous stream of air.

1 Fuel (liquid hydrogen) is stored in the top tank at a high pressure.

2 Liquid oxygen is stored in a separate tank, also at high pressure.

3 Pumps with valves squirt the fuel and oxygen into the engine.

4 The fuel and oxygen mix and burn in the combustion chamber. The exhaust gas rushes past a tight throat into a widening nozzle, making it speed up dramatically.

5 The exhaust gas firing down sends the rocket blasting upward.

Rocket engine
Rockets are similar to jet engines but with one big difference—there is no oxygen in space so they must carry their own supply in a giant tank.

A ROCKET ENGINE AT LIFTOFF CREATES ABOUT AS MUCH FORCE AS 50,000 CAR ENGINES.

210 science ∘ FORCES

Thanks to **gears and wheels**, a bicycle uses about **3–5 times less energy** than walking.

The **Singapore Flyer ferris wheel** is the biggest wheel in the world, and is about **250 times bigger** than a bike wheel.

Simple machines

You can't lift a car, crack a nut, or split logs just using your bare hands, however strong you might be. But you can do all these things relatively easily with the help of tools that multiply the force you can make with your own body.

In science, any device that increases force is called a simple machine. Most of the tools we use around the house are devices of this sort, including hammers, drills, and screwdrivers. Even our own bodies have the simplest of all machines—levers—built into them in the form of our arms and legs. We generally use tools because they boost our body force. But some simple machines help us increase our speed as well. These include wheels and gears, which enable bicycles and cars to achieve amazing speeds our bodies can never hope to match.

Wheels and axles

A heavy load is hard to push across the ground because you have to work against the force of friction. If you put the load on a cart with wheels, the only friction is a tiny amount of rubbing between each wheel and its axle (the rod passing through the center of the wheel). This makes pushing a heavy load much easier.

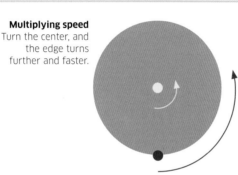

Multiplying speed
Turn the center, and the edge turns further and faster.

Multiplying force
Turn the edge, and the center turns around with more force.

How a wheel works
Wheels can increase force just like levers. They can also increase speed. Racing bikes have large wheels to help boost the speed from the pedals.

Ramps, wedges, and screws

Ramps help you raise heavy objects. Instead of lifting something straight up, you push it up an incline, moving it a greater distance but with less effort. Wedges, such as axe blades, are similar. When you chop wood, it splits along the ramp of the blade.

How a screw works
A screw behaves like a ramp wrapped around in a spiral. The large head and spiral thread make it easier to drive a screw into the wall.

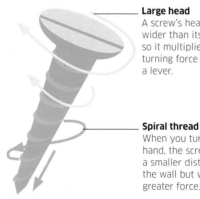

Large head
A screw's head is wider than its shaft, so it multiplies your turning force like a lever.

Spiral thread
When you turn your hand, the screw moves a smaller distance into the wall but with greater force.

Levers

Levers are rods that turn a pushing or pulling force (effort) into a bigger force (load) with the help of a pivot (fulcrum). The longer the lever, the more it multiplies force. There are three types of levers, with the effort, load, and fulcrum arranged in different ways.

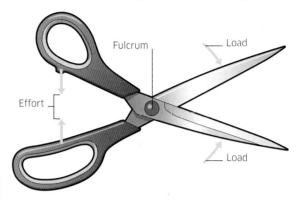

Fulcrum — Load
Effort
Load

Class one lever
Scissors have long handles, so they multiply your pressing force when you squeeze them.

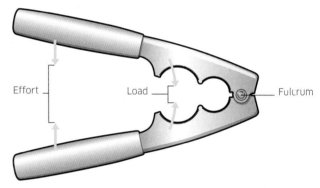

Effort — Load — Fulcrum

Class two lever
With the fulcrum right at the end of the nutcrackers, it produces a large squeezing force in between the arms.

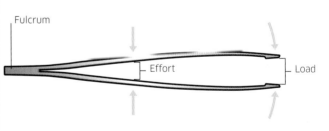

Fulcrum
Effort — Load

Class three lever
With the effort near the fulcrum, tweezers and tongs reduce your squeezing force but give you better control.

Pulleys

You can lift much heavier weights using a system of ropes and wheels called pulleys. The more wheels and ropes there are, the less force you need to lift something, but the further you have to pull the rope. Although a pulley reduces the lifting force, making it easier to lift the weight, you have to use just as much energy as you would without it (sometimes even more).

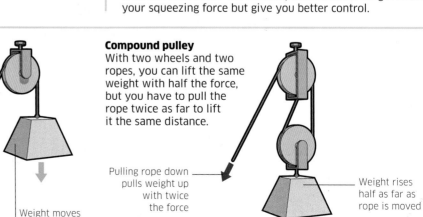

Single pulley
With one wheel and one rope, you can lift a weight with a certain amount of force.

Pulling rope down pulls weight up with same force

Weight moves exactly the same distance as rope

Compound pulley
With two wheels and two ropes, you can lift the same weight with half the force, but you have to pull the rope twice as far to lift it the same distance.

Pulling rope down pulls weight up with twice the force

Weight rises half as far as rope is moved

300 quadrillion (trillion trillion) miles—the **length of the lever** you would need to **lift Earth by hand**.

The **world's biggest screwdriver** is over 3 ft (1 m) long and its **shaft is 1 in (25 mm) thick**.

211

Gears

Two wheels touching work like two connected levers, and are called gears. With teeth around the edge to stop them from slipping, they turn together to give an increase of either speed or force.

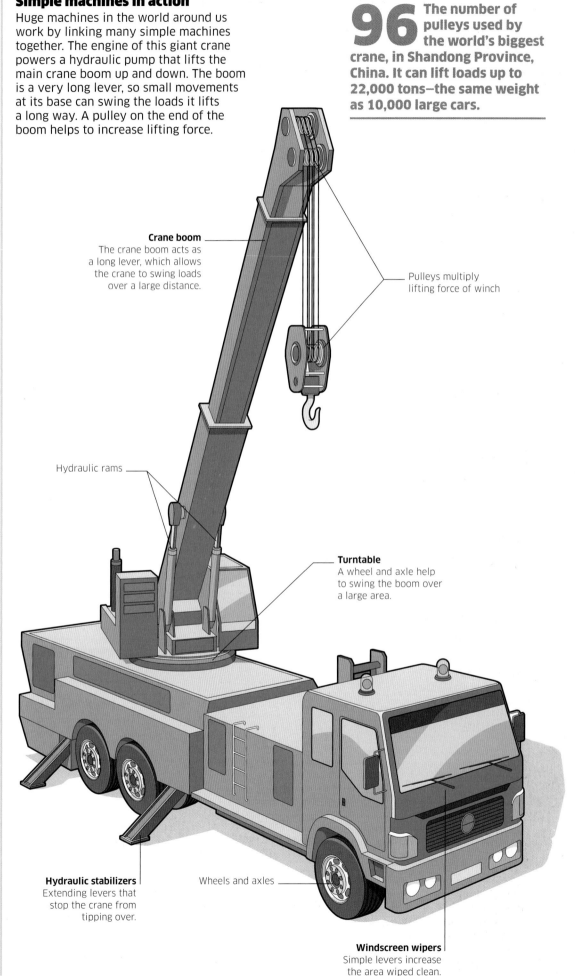

More force

More speed

Gear ratio

If a large gear turns a small one, the small one spins faster but with less force. If a small gear turns a large one, the large one turns slower but with more force.

Hydraulics

Liquids are almost impossible to squeeze into less space, so if you fill a pipe with liquid, you can use it to transmit a force. If the pipe is wider at one end than the other, the force increases, but you have to push the liquid farther. This idea is called hydraulics—and it's used to power rams, cranes, and diggers.

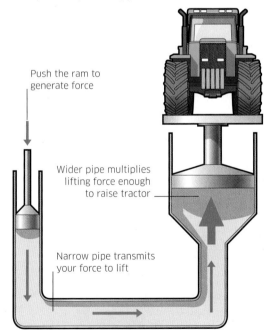

Push the ram to generate force

Wider pipe multiplies lifting force enough to raise tractor

Narrow pipe transmits your force to lift

How a hydraulic ram works

When you push the ram, liquid flows along the pipe and up to the lift. Because the lift pipe is wider than the ram pipe, you can raise the tractor with less force. However, you have to pump down farther than the tractor lifts up.

Simple machines in action

Huge machines in the world around us work by linking many simple machines together. The engine of this giant crane powers a hydraulic pump that lifts the main crane boom up and down. The boom is a very long lever, so small movements at its base can swing the loads it lifts a long way. A pulley on the end of the boom helps to increase lifting force.

Crane boom
The crane boom acts as a long lever, which allows the crane to swing loads over a large distance.

Pulleys multiply lifting force of winch

Hydraulic rams

Turntable
A wheel and axle help to swing the boom over a large area.

Hydraulic stabilizers
Extending levers that stop the crane from tipping over.

Wheels and axles

Windscreen wipers
Simple levers increase the area wiped clean.

96 The number of pulleys used by the world's biggest crane, in Shandong Province, China. It can lift loads up to 22,000 tons—the same weight as 10,000 large cars.

Submarines can zip along **2.5 times** faster underwater than on the surface.

$2.5b The cost of a Virginia class submarine.

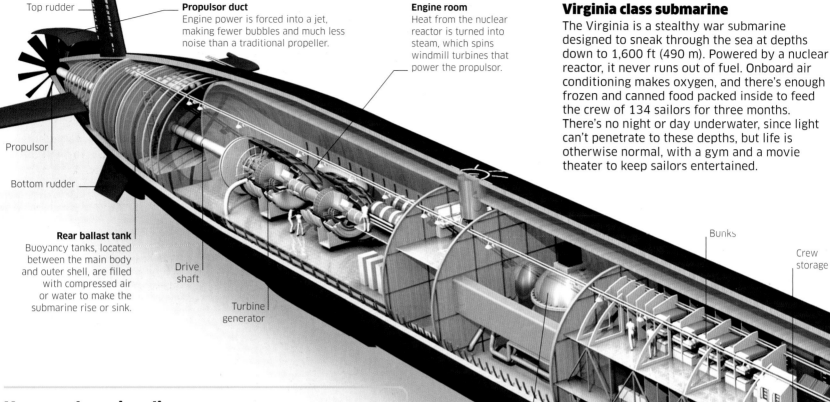

Top rudder

Propulsor duct
Engine power is forced into a jet, making fewer bubbles and much less noise than a traditional propeller.

Engine room
Heat from the nuclear reactor is turned into steam, which spins windmill turbines that power the propulsor.

Propulsor

Bottom rudder

Rear ballast tank
Buoyancy tanks, located between the main body and outer shell, are filled with compressed air or water to make the submarine rise or sink.

Drive shaft

Turbine generator

Bunks

Crew storage

Virginia class submarine

The Virginia is a stealthy war submarine designed to sneak through the sea at depths down to 1,600 ft (490 m). Powered by a nuclear reactor, it never runs out of fuel. Onboard air conditioning makes oxygen, and there's enough frozen and canned food packed inside to feed the crew of 134 sailors for three months. There's no night or day underwater, since light can't penetrate to these depths, but life is otherwise normal, with a gym and a movie theater to keep sailors entertained.

How a submarine dives

Water is heavy, so the deeper you dive underwater, the bigger the weight squashing down on you. This is what gives water its pressure, which is what makes objects float or sink. We can swim because the force of the water pressure pushing up from underneath us balances our weight pushing down. Although ships and submarines weigh much more, they float for the same reason. Submarines can either float or sink by pumping water in and out of huge buoyancy tanks to change their weight. If their weight equals the force pushing upward on them, they float—either on the surface or at any depth beneath.

Nuclear reactor
An energy source that produces as much power as 100 sports cars.

Dining area

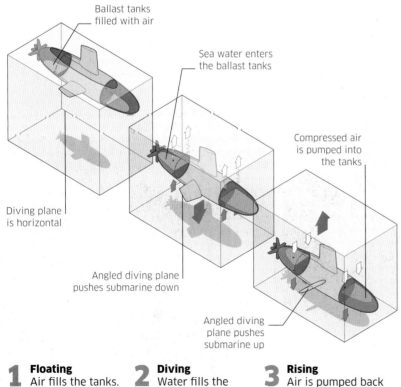

Ballast tanks filled with air

Sea water enters the ballast tanks

Compressed air is pumped into the tanks

Diving plane is horizontal

Angled diving plane pushes submarine down

Angled diving plane pushes submarine up

1 Floating
Air fills the tanks. The submarine weighs relatively little, so the water pressure underneath is enough to support its weight.

2 Diving
Water fills the tanks, and the craft gains weight. The force pushing upward is less than the weight of the vessel, so it sinks.

3 Rising
Air is pumped back into the tanks. The submarine loses weight, so the upward force due to water pressure pushes it to the surface.

Combat control

Ship control

Fiberoptic cables

Operations center
The ultra-modern Virginia has a photonics mast (a periscope with night vision and a zoom lens) linked electronically to a control room. Giant displays show radar maps (on the surface), sonar (underwater), and satellite navigation. Control desks manage the torpedoes and try to ensure the submarine avoids enemy detection.

Modern submarines have a **maximum crush depth** of about **2,400 ft (700 m)**, where water pressure **crunches their sturdy steel hulls**.

1620 The year the **first submarine was built**—an egg-shaped rowboat waterproofed with leather and wax.

213

Flotation

Ships struggle through waves whipped up by the wind. Submarines, on the other hand, sneak stealthily underwater by adjusting their buoyancy to maneuver up and down.

Whether things float or sink is not about how big or heavy they are, but how much they weigh compared to the water they displace (push out of the way). Heavy ships are able to float because they displace a colossal amount of water. Submarines, like the US Navy's Virginia class, float or sink at will, using buoyancy tanks to change their weight.

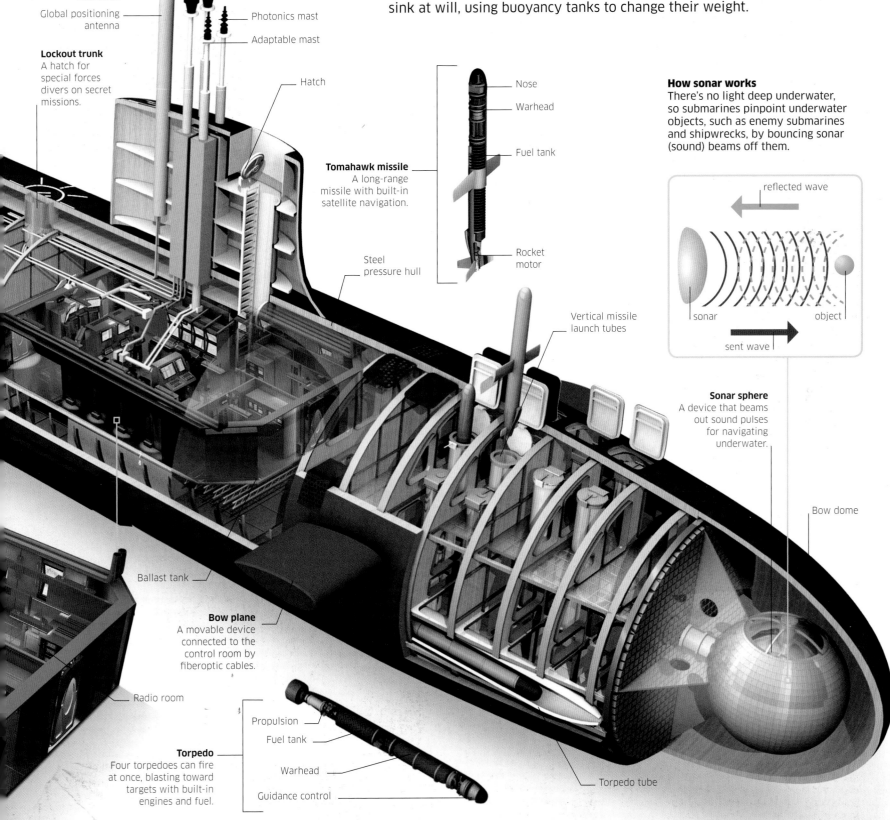

Masts
Slimline, powerful radio antennas gather information from satellite navigation systems, radio, and radar.

High data rate mast

Global positioning antenna

Multifunction mast

Photonics mast

Adaptable mast

Lockout trunk
A hatch for special forces divers on secret missions.

Hatch

Tomahawk missile
A long-range missile with built-in satellite navigation.

Nose

Warhead

Fuel tank

Rocket motor

Steel pressure hull

Vertical missile launch tubes

How sonar works
There's no light deep underwater, so submarines pinpoint underwater objects, such as enemy submarines and shipwrecks, by bouncing sonar (sound) beams off them.

reflected wave

sonar

object

sent wave

Sonar sphere
A device that beams out sound pulses for navigating underwater.

Bow dome

Ballast tank

Bow plane
A movable device connected to the control room by fiberoptic cables.

Radio room

Propulsion

Fuel tank

Torpedo
Four torpedoes can fire at once, blasting toward targets with built-in engines and fuel.

Warhead

Guidance control

Torpedo tube

Magnetism

Magnets helped discover the world as we know it. Earth is like a giant magnet, and its steady pull spun the compasses that pointed explorers like Christopher Columbus across the oceans. Compasses powered navigation, turning the unexplored, ancient world into a modern globe people could understand.

Like gravity, magnetism is an invisible force that streams through our world. But while we can see gravity at work, magnetism is harder for people to detect. Animals find magnetism much more useful: the hidden lines of magnetic fields that bend around the Earth help creatures such as pigeons and turtles to find their way home.

Although magnets seem to push and pull things almost by magic, the strange things they do are actually powered by electrons spinning inside atoms. This is why magnetism is so closely linked to electricity, which is also driven by the movement of electrons. Working together, electricity and magnetism whirl the generators and motors that power almost everything in our modern world, from electric trains to vacuum cleaners.

Discovering magnetism

People discovered magnetism when they found rocks inside the Earth that naturally attracted things. Ancient Greek, Roman, and Chinese people realized they could make compasses by magnetizing needles with these rocks and suspending them over circles marked with directions.

Ship's lodestone
Lodestones were carried aboard ships to remagnetize compasses.

Natural magnet

Lodestone (magnetite) is a naturally magnetic material made from iron oxide. Magnets get their name from Magnesia (now called Manisa, in Turkey), where lodestone was first discovered.

Magnetic forces

Magnets have two different ends called poles, which they use to pull things toward them (attract) or push things away (repel). Although we can't see magnetism, we can watch its effects if we place two magnets close to one another. If the same ends (like poles) of two magnets are placed together, they repel. If opposite ends are placed together (unlike poles), they attract.

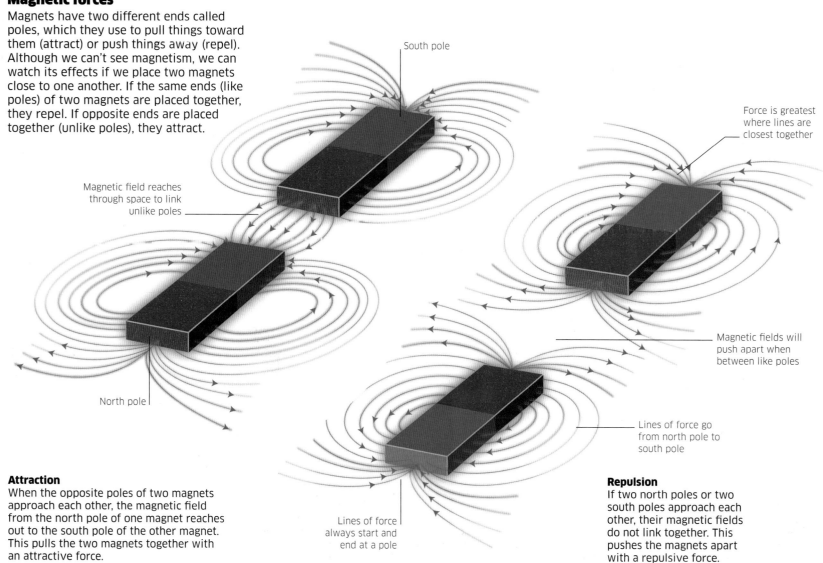

South pole

Force is greatest where lines are closest together

Magnetic field reaches through space to link unlike poles

Magnetic fields will push apart when between like poles

North pole

Lines of force go from north pole to south pole

Lines of force always start and end at a pole

Attraction

When the opposite poles of two magnets approach each other, the magnetic field from the north pole of one magnet reaches out to the south pole of the other magnet. This pulls the two magnets together with an attractive force.

Repulsion

If two north poles or two south poles approach each other, their magnetic fields do not link together. This pushes the magnets apart with a repulsive force.

Magnetotactic bacteria line themselves up along Earth's magnetic field lines, like **living compass needles**.

215

Magnetic materials

Most things that are magnetic are generally made from iron and its compounds or alloys (mixtures of iron with other elements). Magnets themselves are usually made from iron, nickel, cobalt, or other elements in the Periodic Table called the rare earth metals (especially neodymium and samarium).

Magnetic objects
Steel is an alloy of iron, and is used to make food cans, cutlery, and safety pins. Some coins contain nickel.

METAL SPOON   SAFETY PINS   COIN

Nonmagnetic objects
These objects don't respond to magnetic fields or repel them. Plastics aren't magnetic, nor are aluminum drink cans or brass instruments.

PLASTIC BOTTLE   ALUMINUM CANS   BRASS INSTRUMENT

Homing pigeon
Small magnetite crystals above the beak work like a compass.

Animal magnetism
How do creatures find their way home without compasses or a GPS? Scientists have long believed that animals such as pigeons, newts, and turtles navigate using Earth's magnetic field. Pigeons have small magnetite crystals positioned in their heads, just above their beaks. Like a mini compass, these help them find their position and follow an accurate course.

Electromagnetism

Electricity and magnetism are closely linked: each can create the other. British scientist Michael Faraday (1791–1867) was the first person to see how useful this could be. In 1821, he fed electricity into a wire and made it spin around a magnet, inventing the electric motor. Ten years later, he showed that an electrical conductor moving through a magnetic field could make electricity, inventing the electricity generator. Faraday's work led to our modern world of electric power.

Using electromagnets
Electromagnets can be used to pick up scrap metal. Turning the current on creates a strong magnetic field that picks up the metal. When the current is turned off, the magnetism disappears and the metal is dropped.

Loops make rings of magnetic field

South pole

Magnetic field   Electric current

Rings overlap to make overall field like bar magnet

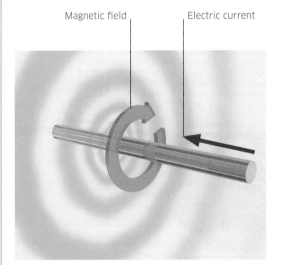

North pole

Electric current flows through wire

Magnetic field around a wire
When an electric current surges through a wire, it generates rings of magnetic field lines all around it. You can see this by placing a compass near a wire carrying a current. The bigger the current, the stronger the magnetism.

THE STRENGTH OF EARTH'S MAGNETIC FIELD AT ITS SURFACE IS VERY WEAK. A TYPICAL **FRIDGE MAGNET** IS 200 TIMES STRONGER.

Magnetic field around a coiled wire
When a current flows through a coiled wire, it creates a more complex magnetic field. Each loop makes a field like a single wire and these fields combine, making an overall field pattern similar to one from a bar magnet.

If you weigh **165 lb (75 kg)**, **your weight on the Sun** would be over **4,400 lb (2,000 kg)**—heavier than most cars on Earth.

On the Moon, the world's best **long jumper** could leap almost **160 ft (50 m)**—the **length of 3.5 school buses**.

Gravity

When the Earth spins on its axis, people on the equator hurtle round at about 1,000 mph (1,600 kph), but they don't fly off into the sky. Gravity is the force that pins us to the planet, and it also keeps the stars spinning endlessly in space. Gravity is the pull of every object on everything else and it holds the Universe together like a giant, invisible spiderweb.

Earth's gravitational pull is lower the further you go from the center of the planet, so you weigh slightly less at the top of a mountain than you do down a mine. But, no matter how high up you go, even if you take a rocket to the stars, there is no escape from gravity altogether because it extends to an infinite distance. The only way to fight gravity is to balance it with another force. Planes and helicopters fight gravity by using lift to shoot into the sky. Not everyone wants to fight gravity, however. Skydivers embrace gravity by jumping out of planes and using the force to hurtle at great speeds toward the ground.

Mass and weight

The words mass and weight are often used to mean the same thing, but they are different. Mass is the amount of matter an object has, and weight is the force pulling on matter because of gravity. Your mass is always the same, but your weight varies from place to place because gravity varies across Earth.

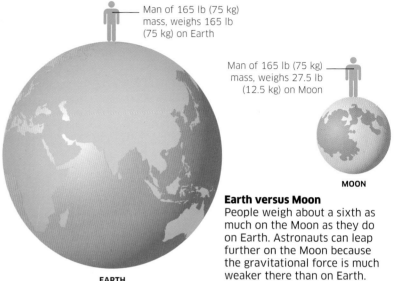

Man of 165 lb (75 kg) mass, weighs 165 lb (75 kg) on Earth

Man of 165 lb (75 kg) mass, weighs 27.5 lb (12.5 kg) on Moon

MOON

EARTH

Earth versus Moon
People weigh about a sixth as much on the Moon as they do on Earth. Astronauts can leap further on the Moon because the gravitational force is much weaker there than on Earth.

Force of attraction

Gravity is a force of attraction—always a pull and never a push. This is different from magnetism and other forces, which can either pull (attract) or push (repel). The gravitational pull between two things depends on their mass and the distance between them. The bigger the mass and shorter the distance, the greater the pull.

Falling pear
Gravity makes an pear and the Earth pull each other with the same force. The pear falls to the ground because the Earth has a greater mass and accelerates far less than the pear.

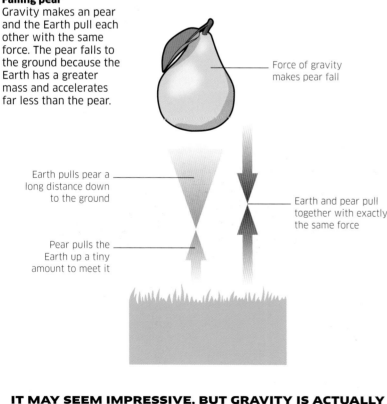

Force of gravity makes pear fall

Earth pulls pear a long distance down to the ground

Earth and pear pull together with exactly the same force

Pear pulls the Earth up a tiny amount to meet it

Pull of the tides

The Moon is smaller and lighter than Earth, and about 240,000 miles (384,000 km) away. Even so, it is big enough to pull on the Earth's oceans as it spins around our planet, and this is what causes tides. The Sun, which is further away, also affects the tides. Twice a month, when the Sun and Moon line up, we get higher and lower tides than usual because of their combined pull.

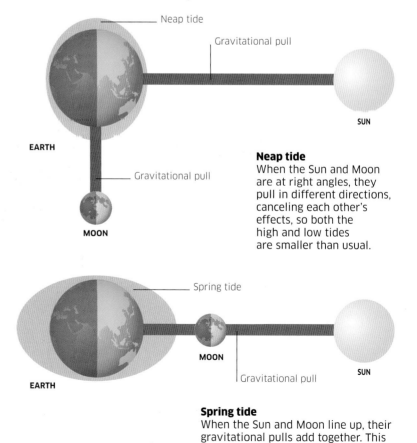

Neap tide

Gravitational pull

SUN

EARTH

Gravitational pull

MOON

Neap tide
When the Sun and Moon are at right angles, they pull in different directions, canceling each other's effects, so both the high and low tides are smaller than usual.

Spring tide

MOON

SUN

Gravitational pull

EARTH

Spring tide
When the Sun and Moon line up, their gravitational pulls add together. This makes high tides higher, and low tides lower, than usual.

IT MAY SEEM IMPRESSIVE, BUT GRAVITY IS ACTUALLY
THE WEAKEST FORCE
IN THE UNIVERSE.

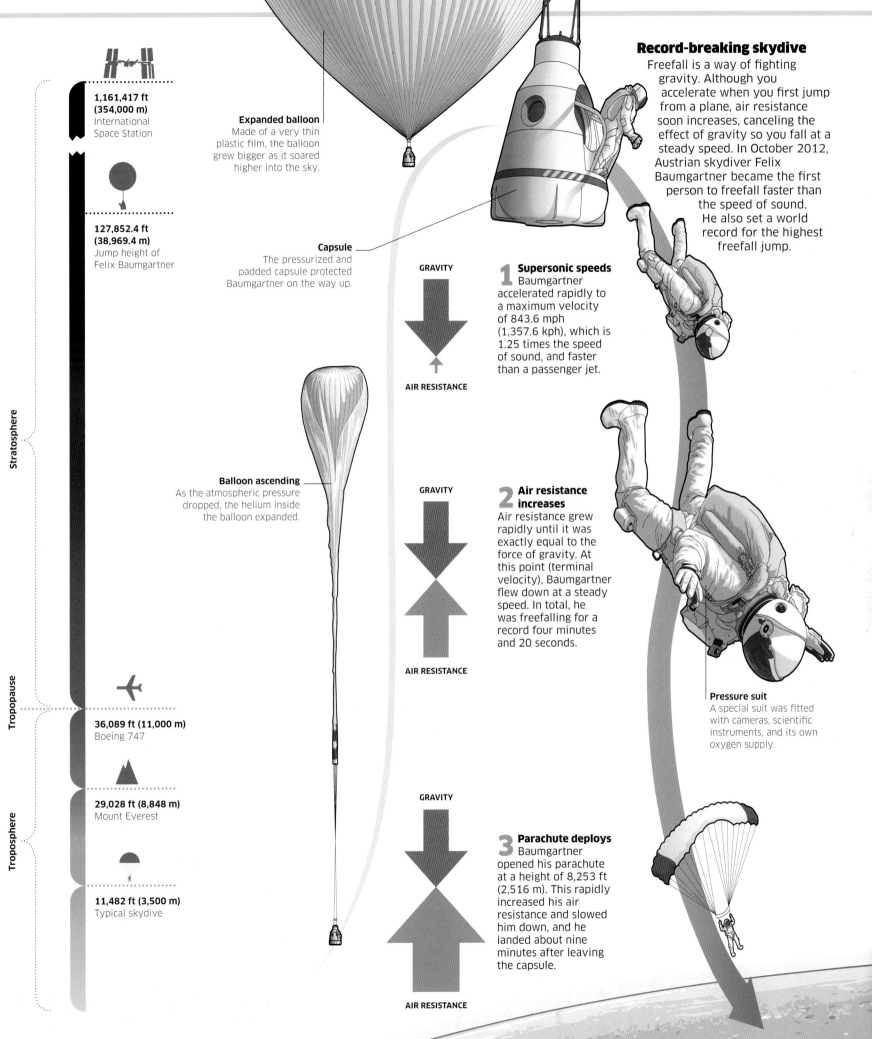

1,161,417 ft (354,000 m)
International Space Station

127,852.4 ft (38,969.4 m)
Jump height of Felix Baumgartner

Stratosphere

Tropopause

36,089 ft (11,000 m)
Boeing 747

29,028 ft (8,848 m)
Mount Everest

Troposphere

11,482 ft (3,500 m)
Typical skydive

Expanded balloon
Made of a very thin plastic film, the balloon grew bigger as it soared higher into the sky.

Capsule
The pressurized and padded capsule protected Baumgartner on the way up.

Balloon ascending
As the atmospheric pressure dropped, the helium inside the balloon expanded.

GRAVITY

AIR RESISTANCE

GRAVITY

AIR RESISTANCE

GRAVITY

AIR RESISTANCE

Record-breaking skydive
Freefall is a way of fighting gravity. Although you accelerate when you first jump from a plane, air resistance soon increases, canceling the effect of gravity so you fall at a steady speed. In October 2012, Austrian skydiver Felix Baumgartner became the first person to freefall faster than the speed of sound. He also set a world record for the highest freefall jump.

1 Supersonic speeds
Baumgartner accelerated rapidly to a maximum velocity of 843.6 mph (1,357.6 kph), which is 1.25 times the speed of sound, and faster than a passenger jet.

2 Air resistance increases
Air resistance grew rapidly until it was exactly equal to the force of gravity. At this point (terminal velocity), Baumgartner flew down at a steady speed. In total, he was freefalling for a record four minutes and 20 seconds.

Pressure suit
A special suit was fitted with cameras, scientific instruments, and its own oxygen supply.

3 Parachute deploys
Baumgartner opened his parachute at a height of 8,253 ft (2,516 m). This rapidly increased his air resistance and slowed him down, and he landed about nine minutes after leaving the capsule.

218 science

The Sikorsky X2, the **world's fastest helicopter**, can **travel at speeds** of up to **300 mph (480 kph)**.

Tail rotor blade

Tail rotor
When the main rotor spins one way, the body of the helicopter tries to turn the other way. The tail rotor stops this from happening by pushing sideways with a counterforce.

Rotor blades
The rotor blades stretch 53 ft (16 m) tip to tip, but fold automatically, making the craft just $10^2/_3$ ft (3.3 m) wide for easy parking on ships.

Stabilator
A mechanism used to provide stability and help control the helicopter when landing.

Engine exhaust pipe

Magnetic Anomaly Detector
A device used to detect submarines.

Storage pod

Forces of flight

Airplanes and helicopters move when forces push or pull them in a certain direction. Four forces act on an aircraft as it flies through the sky. Thrust from the engines pushes it forward, while drag (air resistance) pulls it back. Lift from the wings or rotors shoots it upward, while gravity tugs it back down to Earth. When an airplane accelerates at a steady height, lift balances gravity, but thrust is bigger than drag, so it speeds forward. However, in a hovering helicopter, lift and gravity exactly balance, as do thrust and drag, so it can stay in the same spot in the air.

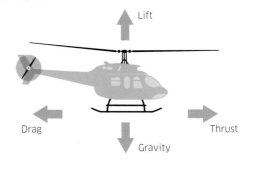

Lift

Drag

Thrust

Gravity

Generating lift

The curved shape of a wing or rotor blade is called an airfoil, and it generates lift in two ways. First, air has to go further over the curved top than the straighter bottom, so it speeds up. Speeding air has a lower pressure than slower air, so an upward force is created. Airfoils also create lift because they are tilted slightly back. Air sweeps up and over, then down and behind the wings. An airplane flies up because its wings force air down.

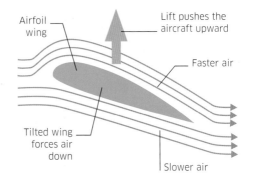

Airfoil wing

Lift pushes the aircraft upward

Faster air

Tilted wing forces air down

Slower air

How the rotor blades turn
The Seahawk is powered by two turboshaft engines. Air entering the engine is compressed and then mixed with fuel, which is burned to make a powerful shaft rotate. Gears (wheels with interlocking teeth) connect the horizontal engine to the vertical spinning rotor.

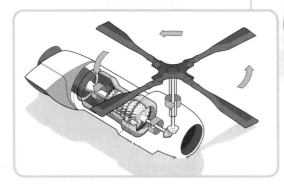

Flight

Forces normally pin us to the ground, but if used in the right way they can sweep us high into the sky. If you want to fly, you need lift—an upward force—greater than your weight. Airplanes and helicopters create lift using wings and rotors to move vast quantities of air.

An airplane has large, fixed wings that generate lift as air gusts around them. Its engines simply power it forward, pushing the wings through the air. It's the wings that launch an airplane into the sky. The bigger the wings and the faster they move, the greater the airflow and subsequent lift. Unlike airplanes, helicopters, such as the United States Navy's Sikorsky Seahawk, don't need to fly forward to generate lift. A helicopter's rotors are tiny compared to an airplane's wings, but they spin hundreds of times a minute, generating enough lift to push the craft up into the air.

Airplanes can glide for a time without their engines: as long as they move forward, their wings will continue to generate lift. If the engines in a helicopter fail, it can freewheel its rotors in order to make a safe landing.

1901 The year **Igor Sikorsky** built his **first helicopter**, a model **made from rubber bands**.

The **rotor** of a large helicopter **blows enough air** each second **to fill** an Olympic-size **swimming pool**.

219

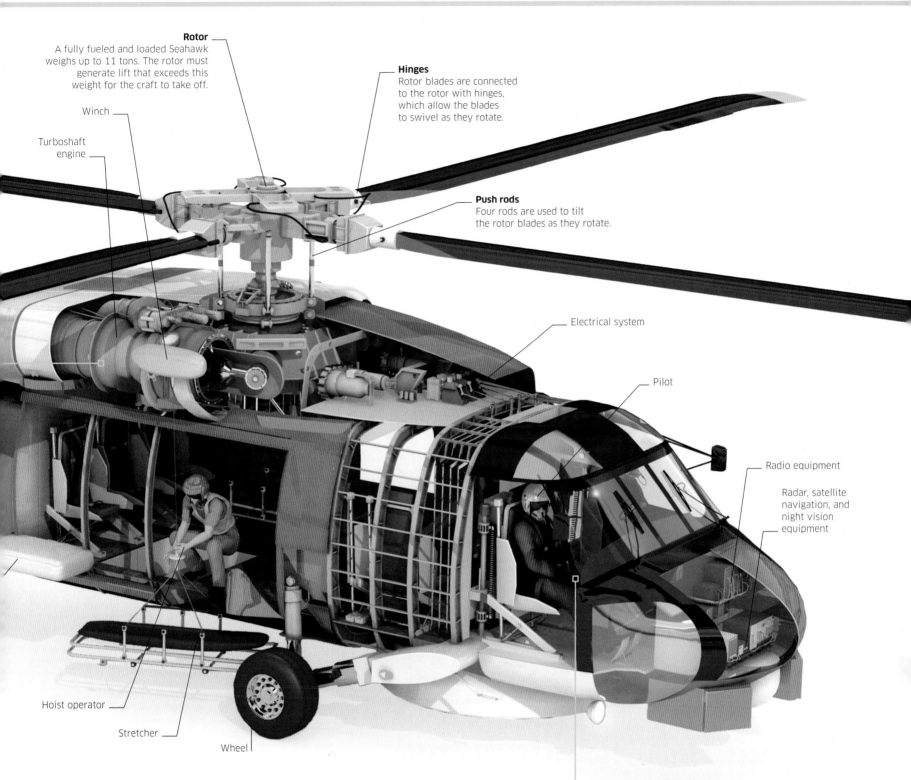

Rotor
A fully fueled and loaded Seahawk weighs up to 11 tons. The rotor must generate lift that exceeds this weight for the craft to take off.

Winch

Turboshaft engine

Hinges
Rotor blades are connected to the rotor with hinges, which allow the blades to swivel as they rotate.

Push rods
Four rods are used to tilt the rotor blades as they rotate.

Electrical system

Pilot

Radio equipment

Radar, satellite navigation, and night vision equipment

Hoist operator

Stretcher

Wheel

Seahawk helicopter

One of the Seahawk's main jobs is flying search and rescue missions at sea. The nose of the helicopter is packed with electronic radar and radio equipment for finding objects, as well as night vision cameras. Meanwhile, sonar (sound-detecting) kit on the side can locate objects underwater. The wide cargo doors, and a cabin big enough to hold several stretchers, are specially designed to rescue casualties at sea.

Primary flight display

Navigation display

Cyclic stick

Yaw pedals control the tail rotor

Navigation computer

Collective lever

Cyclic stick

Cockpit
The Seahawk's cockpit has four computer screens that display crucial information to the pilots. Dual controls allow either the pilot or copilot to fly. The collective lever is used to lift the helicopter into the air, while the cyclic stick is like a joystick— it increases the lift on one side so that the helicopter slides in the opposite direction.

ENERGY

Every second of every day, the Sun pumps energy toward Earth, firing our planet with light and life. Though you can't always see it, energy is everywhere you look. It's locked in the atoms bouncing inside things, and it keeps the heart that pumps blood through your veins beating steadily. It shoots comets through space and makes trees reach for the sky. Energy is the secret power behind everything in our world.

WHAT IS ENERGY?

Things happen because forces push and pull, and whenever forces are at work, energy is needed to power them. Mass (the ordinary matter around us) is another kind of energy. Tiny amounts of mass can be converted into huge amounts of energy.

LIGHTNING
There are few more spectacular examples of energy than a lightning strike. A typical bolt delivers about a billion joules of energy—as much as a power station makes in a second.

Measuring energy

We measure energy in units called joules (J), named after English physicist James Joule (1818–89), who investigated energy forms.

Work into energy
You use one joule lifting the lemon, and the lemon gains one joule of potential energy.

ONE JOULE
When you lift a lemon weighing 3 oz (100 g) up in the air to a height of 3 ft (1 m), you use one joule of energy to work against the force of gravity.

Converting energy

There's a fixed amount of energy in the Universe. When we think we're using energy, we're really just converting it into a different form. The total energy before something happens is exactly equal to the total energy afterward.

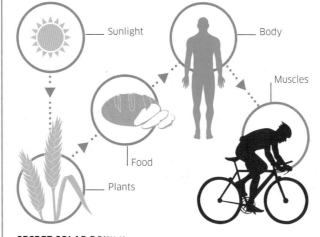

Sunlight

Body

Muscles

Food

Plants

SECRET SOLAR POWER
Almost all action on Earth, even cycling, is ultimately powered by sunlight. As you pedal a bike, your muscles use energy from food—the fuel we get from animals and plants. Animals also eat plants, which absorb energy from the Sun as they grow.

Types of energy

Energy can exist in many different forms, most of which can be converted into other forms. When you burn a lump of coal, you change the chemical energy locked inside the coal into heat. If you do this in a power station, you can convert the heat energy into electricity. Once energy is in electric form, it's easy to change it into movement, light, heat, sound, or virtually any other kind of energy.

Kinetic energy
Moving things have kinetic energy. The heavier and faster they are, the more kinetic energy they have.

Electrical energy
Electricity is energy carried by charged particles called electrons moving through wires.

Heat energy
Hot things have more energy than cold ones, because the atoms inside them move around more quickly.

Light energy
Light travels at high speed and in straight lines. Like radio waves and X-rays, it is a type of electromagnetic energy.

Chemical energy
Food, fuel, and batteries store energy within the chemical compounds they're made of.

Potential energy
This is stored energy. Climb something, and you store potential energy to jump, roll, or dive back down.

Sound energy
When objects vibrate, they send energy waves traveling through the air, which we hear as sounds.

Nuclear energy
Atoms are bound together by energy, which they release when they split apart in nuclear reactions.

Dark energy
Most of the Universe's energy is in the form of mysterious dark energy. No one really knows what it is.

ENERGY WAVES

When energy moves through materials such as air and water, it travels as waves. We can see waves on water, but we can't see light waves or seismic waves carrying earthquakes underground.

Different types of waves

Up-and-down oscillation

Direction of wave

Compression

Direction of wave

Rarefaction

TRANSVERSE WAVE
Ocean waves are transverse. As energy races over the surface, the water moves up and down while traveling forward.

LONGITUDINAL WAVE
As you bang a drum, the air is squeezed (compressed) and stretched (rarefied) as the sound waves race toward your ears.

AN AVERAGE MAN'S BODY MASS CONTAINS AS MUCH ENERGY AS A NUCLEAR POWER PLANT CAN PRODUCE IN 90 YEARS.

Measuring waves

Energy waves have an up-and-down pattern of crests and troughs. We can measure waves in three ways. The height of a wave is its amplitude. The distance from one wave crest to the next is the wavelength. The number of crests passing in one second is the frequency.

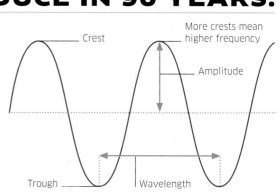

Crest

More crests mean higher frequency

Amplitude

Trough

Wavelength

ENERGY SOURCES

Cooking, heating, traveling, and making things—all these need energy. Prehistoric people relied on fire for their energy needs, but today we use a wide range of energy sources. Some energy sources, such as the fuel that powers our cars, are in limited supply. Renewable energy comes from unlimited natural sources, including sunlight, wind, and waves.

Timeline of energy

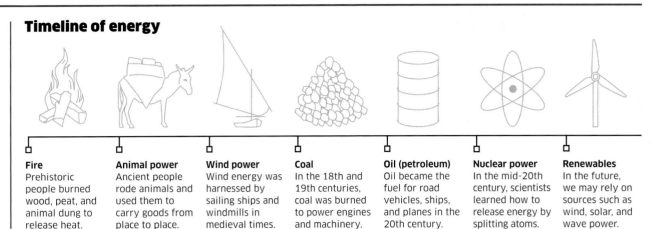

Fire
Prehistoric people burned wood, peat, and animal dung to release heat.

Animal power
Ancient people rode animals and used them to carry goods from place to place.

Wind power
Wind energy was harnessed by sailing ships and windmills in medieval times.

Coal
In the 18th and 19th centuries, coal was burned to power engines and machinery.

Oil (petroleum)
Oil became the fuel for road vehicles, ships, and planes in the 20th century.

Nuclear power
In the mid-20th century, scientists learned how to release energy by splitting atoms.

Renewables
In the future, we may rely on sources such as wind, solar, and wave power.

Pollution

More than 80 percent of our energy comes from fossil fuels (coal, gas, and oil). The problem with these fuels is that burning them causes pollution—releasing toxic waste that harms the environment. Other forms of energy, such as nuclear power, also have an impact on the climate.

AIR POLLUTION
Exhaust fumes from car engines and harmful gases from power stations and factories cause air pollution, which can lead to health problems such as asthma.

ACID RAIN
Sulfur dioxide gas escaping from power stations mixes with rain and makes it acidic. This acid rain can damage trees, poison lakes, and kill fish.

RADIOACTIVE WASTE
Nuclear power stations produce radioactive waste that is difficult to dispose of safely. It can leak into rivers and seas and travel a long way as water pollution.

REEF EROSION
Gases released by burning fossil fuels are causing the planet to get hotter. One result is damage to coral reefs, which die and turn white in water that is too warm.

NOISE POLLUTION
Cars, planes, and machines all waste some of their energy by making noise. Noise pollution disturbs people and animals, causing stress and anxiety.

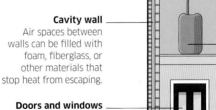

OIL SPILLS
Accidental spills from tankers, rigs, and refineries release huge amounts of oil into the sea, which can be deadly to seabirds, fish, and other marine life.

World energy use

As the world's population has grown and we've invented gas-guzzling cars and built fuel-hungry homes, our energy needs have increased too. Total worldwide energy use has increased by about 14 times since the early 20th century.

Energy type

- Nuclear
- Hydroelectricity
- Natural gas
- Oil
- Coal
- Biofuels

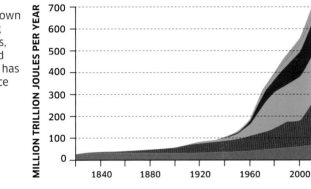

WORLD ENERGY CONSUMPTION

(y-axis: MILLION TRILLION JOULES PER YEAR — 0, 100, 200, 300, 400, 500, 600, 700)
(x-axis: 1840, 1880, 1920, 1960, 2000)

Energy equivalents

One reason cars are so popular is because oil is rich in energy, so it carries vehicles a long way. Uranium, which makes electricity in nuclear power stations, is packed with even more energy. Although coal contains a lot of energy, it's difficult to transport and creates pollution. Natural gas is easy to send through pipelines, but it takes a huge amount to produce the same energy that you get from a few barrels of oil or a pile of coal.

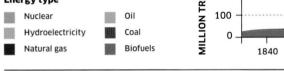

1 URANIUM PELLET
(shown actual size)

3.5 BARRELS OF OIL
(147 gallons/556 litres)

1,789 lbs COAL
481 M

17,000 Ft³ NATURAL GAS
(481 M³)

Heat loss and insulation

If your house were perfectly sealed, you could heat it once at the start of winter and it would stay warm until spring. In reality, all houses leak heat. Energy is expensive, so it pays to insulate homes using materials that keep heat in and cold air out.

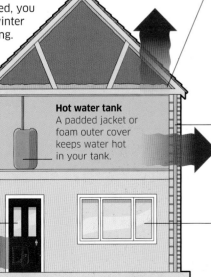

Attic insulation
A quarter of the energy you pump into your home vanishes through the roof. Thick layers of attic insulation reduce this effectively.

Hot water tank
A padded jacket or foam outer cover keeps water hot in your tank.

Cavity wall
Air spaces between walls can be filled with foam, fiberglass, or other materials that stop heat from escaping.

Leaky walls
About 30 to 40 percent of the heat in your home escapes through the walls.

Doors and windows
A porch cuts heat loss from your door when you go out, and heavy curtains trap insulating air next to windows.

Double glazing
Trapping air (a good insulator) between two panes of glass creates a barrier to reduce heat loss.

Electromagnetic spectrum

As the Sun sends its rays to Earth, it lights up our world. But there's more to the world than the things we can see with light alone.

As light races through space, it makes electricity and magnetism ripple down its path like waves on the sea. Light is not the only energy that behaves like this: there's a whole collection of similar waves called the electromagnetic spectrum. Some of these waves are very long, with large spaces from one peak to the next. Others are extremely short and close to each other. Different waves have different uses, depending on their length.

Although we can't see most electromagnetic waves, they are incredibly useful, helping us with everything from spotting broken bones to watching TV shows.

Where electromagnetic radiation comes from

Light is made when atoms flash on and off like fireflies. If you heat an iron bar, it glows red hot. The atoms inside absorb heat energy, but it makes them unstable. To return to normal, they have to get rid of the energy again, and do so by giving off a flash of light. Other kinds of electromagnetic waves are made in the same way.

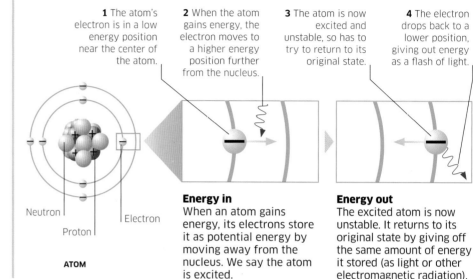

1 The atom's electron is in a low energy position near the center of the atom.

2 When the atom gains energy, the electron moves to a higher energy position further from the nucleus.

3 The atom is now excited and unstable, so has to try to return to its original state.

4 The electron drops back to a lower position, giving out energy as a flash of light.

Neutron

Proton

Electron

ATOM

Energy in
When an atom gains energy, its electrons store it as potential energy by moving away from the nucleus. We say the atom is excited.

Energy out
The excited atom is now unstable. It returns to its original state by giving off the same amount of energy it stored (as light or other electromagnetic radiation).

On your wavelength

The longest waves on the electromagnetic spectrum are radio waves, which can be thousands of miles long from the top of one wave to the next. At the other end of the spectrum, gamma rays are even smaller than atoms, and are packed full of energy. The shortest waves have the most energy and the highest frequency (meaning they vibrate the fastest), while the longest waves vibrate more slowly and have less energy. As you travel along the spectrum you can see how different wavelengths are used for a variety of useful tasks.

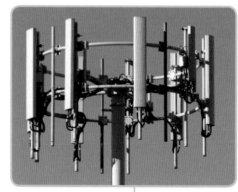

Microwaves
One microwave is typically about as long as a pen. Like other electromagnetic waves, they race along at the speed of light, which makes them perfect for carrying phone calls and Internet data.

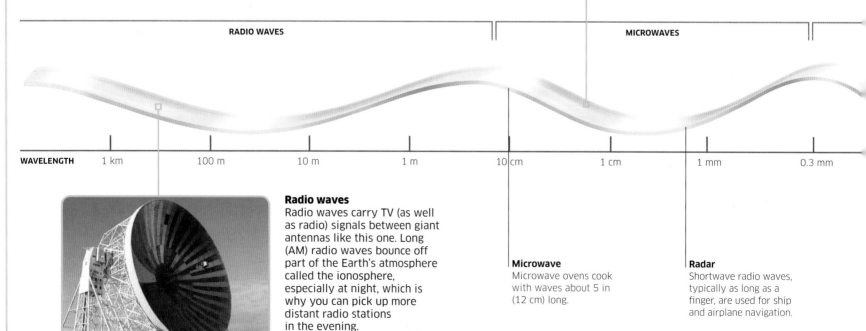

| RADIO WAVES | | | | MICROWAVES | | |

| WAVELENGTH | 1 km | 100 m | 10 m | 1 m | 10 cm | 1 cm | 1 mm | 0.3 mm |

Radio waves
Radio waves carry TV (as well as radio) signals between giant antennas like this one. Long (AM) radio waves bounce off part of the Earth's atmosphere called the ionosphere, especially at night, which is why you can pick up more distant radio stations in the evening.

Microwave
Microwave ovens cook with waves about 5 in (12 cm) long.

Radar
Shortwave radio waves, typically as long as a finger, are used for ship and airplane navigation.

10 The number of seconds a **gamma ray burst** takes to **equal the energy** put out by the Sun over its **10-billion-year lifetime.**

Scientists can still pick up the **microwaves** left over from the **Big Bang** at the birth of the Universe.

223

The visible or color spectrum

The light that looks white to our eyes is really a mixture of different colors. We can see this by firing a light beam through a wedge-shaped piece of glass called a prism, which causes light to spread into the spectrum. Rainbows work in exactly the same way. As sunlight shines through rain, each water droplet acts like a miniature prism.

7.5 The number of times that light can go around the world in one second. It travels at a blistering 186,000 miles (300,000 km) per second.

White light contains all colors

Original white beam has dispersed (spread out) into a broad color spectrum

Light bends again as it moves back from glass to air

Light bends as it moves from air to glass

Blue rays bend more than red rays, so always appear on the inside of rainbows

Red
Orange
Yellow
Green
Blue
Indigo
Violet

Infrared rays
We feel the heat that things give off when the atoms in our bodies absorb a kind of hot light called infrared radiation. Although invisible, infrared radiation shows up on thermal (heat-sensitive) cameras, like the one that photographed this elephant.

Gamma rays
The smallest electromagnetic waves are like super-energetic X-rays, but do much more damage to the human body. They're made when atoms split apart in nuclear explosions.

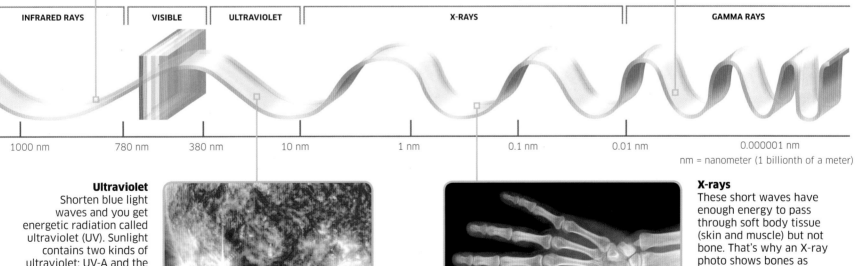

| INFRARED RAYS | VISIBLE | ULTRAVIOLET | X-RAYS | GAMMA RAYS |

1000 nm   780 nm   380 nm   10 nm   1 nm   0.1 nm   0.01 nm   0.000001 nm

nm = nanometer (1 billionth of a meter)

Ultraviolet
Shorten blue light waves and you get energetic radiation called ultraviolet (UV). Sunlight contains two kinds of ultraviolet: UV-A and the more harmful UV-B. Small amounts of UV give a nice suntan; in bigger doses, it ages skin and causes cancer.

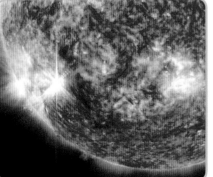

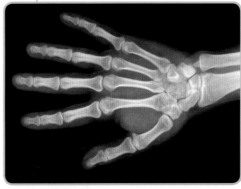

X-rays
These short waves have enough energy to pass through soft body tissue (skin and muscle) but not bone. That's why an X-ray photo shows bones as shadows. High doses of X-rays can be very harmful.

$400 million (£260 million)—the cost of the **Intelsat 27 satellite**, accidentally destroyed in February 2013 on its way to space.

Signals from space

Whether you're scrambling up Mount Everest or trekking the Sahara Desert, you're never more than a few seconds from your friends. That's because telephones and the Internet, linked by space satellites, can zap messages from any place on Earth to anywhere else at the speed of light.

Earth might seem huge, but no two places are more than half its circumference (12,400 miles or 20,000 km) apart—and a beam of light can cover that distance in less than a tenth of a second. When you chat to friends in faraway countries by phone or online, the sound of your voice, the image of your face on your webcam, or the message you type is bounced across the Earth in less than a second via satellites in space. Signals from space satellites can also tell us exactly where we are. Thanks to technology like GPS (Global Positioning System), getting lost has now become almost impossible.

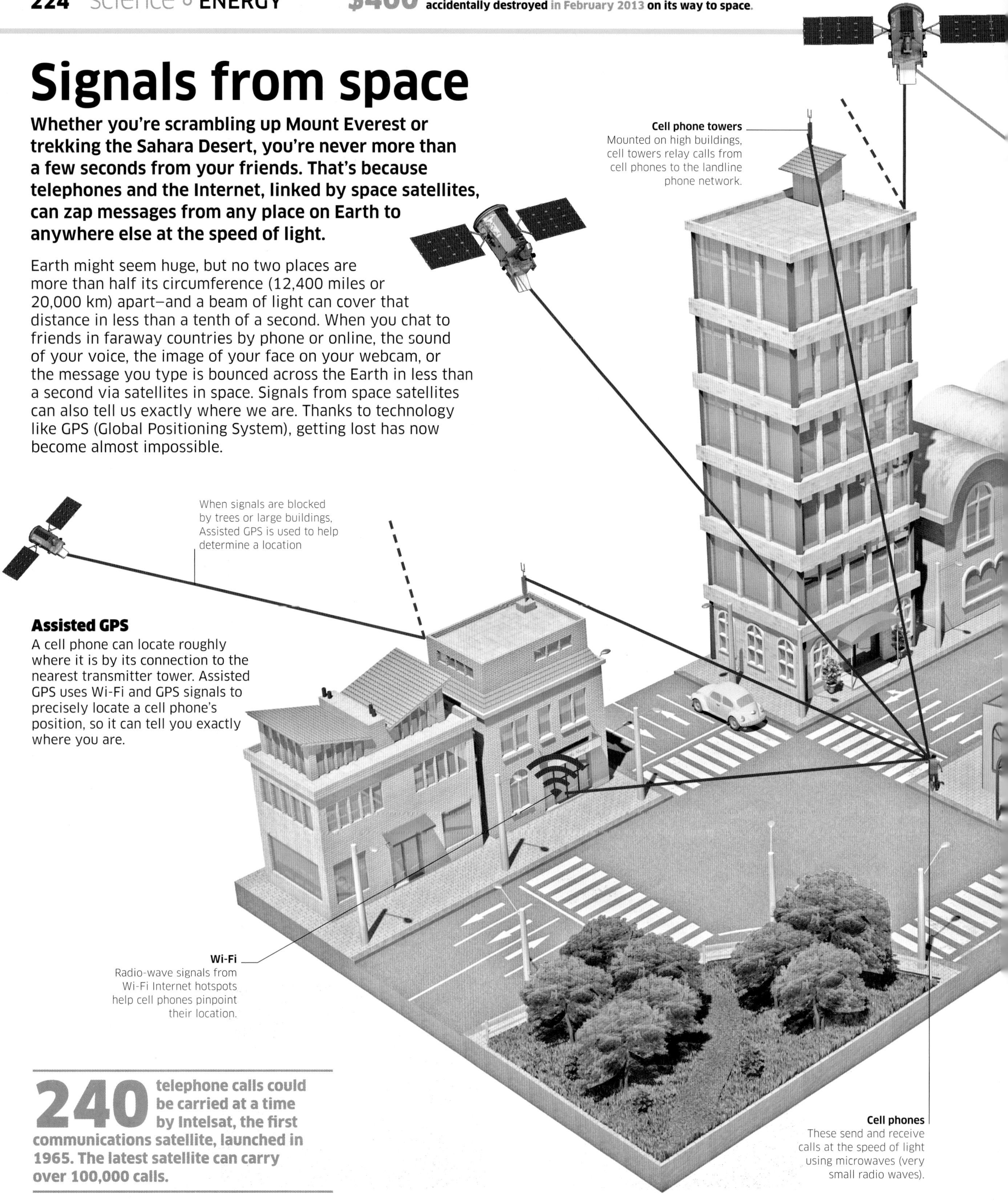

Cell phone towers
Mounted on high buildings, cell towers relay calls from cell phones to the landline phone network.

When signals are blocked by trees or large buildings, Assisted GPS is used to help determine a location

Assisted GPS

A cell phone can locate roughly where it is by its connection to the nearest transmitter tower. Assisted GPS uses Wi-Fi and GPS signals to precisely locate a cell phone's position, so it can tell you exactly where you are.

Wi-Fi
Radio-wave signals from Wi-Fi Internet hotspots help cell phones pinpoint their location.

240 telephone calls could be carried at a time by Intelsat, the first communications satellite, launched in 1965. The latest satellite can carry over 100,000 calls.

Cell phones
These send and receive calls at the speed of light using microwaves (very small radio waves).

2.5 million **pictures of Earth** have been **taken by Landsat 5,** a survey satellite, since it was **first blasted into space in 1984.**

225

Large solar panels generate electric power from the Sun

Satellite
GPS satellites catch signals from Earth and send new signals straight back.

GPS signals

GPS satellites work differently from ordinary communications satellites. Each beams out two coded signals toward the Earth. A short signal travels fast and lets people locate themselves fairly accurately. A more precise signal helps the military to fire missiles with pinpoint accuracy.

GPS satellites

No single satellite could cover every place on Earth at once. That's why the GPS system has a network of at least 24 separate spacecrafts. No matter where you are, at least four of them are sending signals to your phone.

GPS satellites orbit at about 12,400 miles (20,000 km) above Earth

The satellites are kept in a precise orbit by small rocket thrusters

Finding your position

It takes less than a second for a GPS signal to reach Earth from space, traveling at the speed of light. Knowing how long the signal took, a GPS receiver calculates how far away the satellite is. Using signals from at least three satellites (preferably four), it's possible to calculate your precise location.

Radius of sphere is your distance from satellite

You are somewhere on this sphere

1 One satellite
If the satellite is a certain distance away from you, your position must be somewhere on a sphere with that distance as its radius.

You must be here

You are somewhere on this line

2 Two satellites
If there are two satellites, your location must be in the area where their signals overlap.

3 Three or more satellites
There is only one place on Earth's surface where three signals meet. This is your precise location.

Satellite navigation

A car's navigation system uses a stored database of maps linked to GPS satellite positions. As you drive along, a GPS receiver detects your changing position. A computer in the system calculates how fast you are moving and continually redraws the map to show your progress.

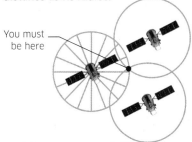

226 science ○ **ENERGY**

99.9999 percent–the amount of light that the most accurate scientific mirrors will reflect back. An ordinary mirror reflects less than 90 percent.

Light

Light is a type of radiation that moves through space. Animals such as humans have eyes sensitive to light to see and understand the world around them.

Although light seems special, it's really just another kind of electromagnetic energy, like microwaves and radio waves. Light normally travels in straight-line rays, and reflects and refracts (bends) in very precise ways as it speeds through the world. Most of the light we see with our eyes is very weak because it has already reflected off things. Not all light is so weak, however: light beams made by lasers are super concentrated and can be powerful enough to slice through metal.

Refraction

Light rays travel slower in more dense (thicker) substances such as water and glass than in air. The change in speed causes light to bend (refract) as it passes from air to glass and back. Lenses use refraction to magnify things–as the lens bends the light, the rays seem to be coming from a point closer to us, making objects appear bigger.

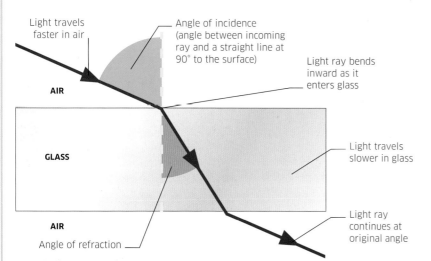

Changing direction

Light rays slow down and bend inward as they pass from air to glass, and speed up and bend outward as they go from glass to air.

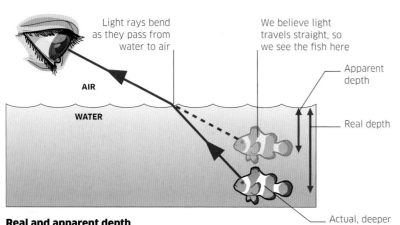

Real and apparent depth

Refraction makes fish appear nearer to the surface. Because our brains assume light rays travel in a straight line, rather than bend, we see the fish higher up than they really are.

Reflection

We see things because light bounces off them into our eyes. If a surface is smooth, like a mirror, the light rays all bounce off at the same angle to make a single beam. This is called specular reflection. If the surface is rough, the rays bounce off randomly in different directions. This is called diffuse reflection.

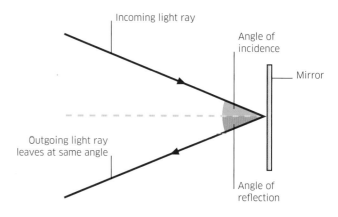

The law of reflection

A light ray shooting at a mirror bounces off again at exactly the same angle. In more scientific terms, we say the angle of incidence is equal to the angle of reflection.

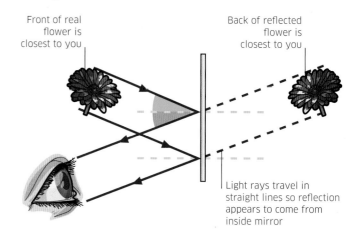

How a mirror reverses things

Mirrors don't reverse things left to right–writing looks reversed in a mirror because you've turned it around to face the glass. Mirrors actually switch things from back to front, along a line through the mirror.

Reflection in action

Still water acts like a flat (plane) mirror. It reproduces what's above it through specular reflection. When the water ripples, light bounces off at random angles so the reflection becomes blurry.

A **light wave** is about **5.5 million times smaller** than an **FM radio wave**.

When the **Channel Tunnel** was dug between Britain and France, **laser beams** helped to ensure **the two ends met beneath the sea to within 0.8 in (2 cm)**.

227

Interference

When two or more light rays, water waves, or sound waves meet, they combine to make interference. In some places, the waves add together (interfere constructively) and in others, they subtract or cancel out (interfere destructively). The result is a new wave that's bigger in some places and smaller in others. This explains why an ocean wave can be followed by another wave that may be much bigger or smaller.

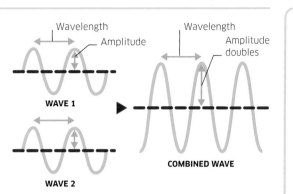

Wave 1 — Wavelength, Amplitude
Wave 2
COMBINED WAVE — Wavelength, Amplitude doubles

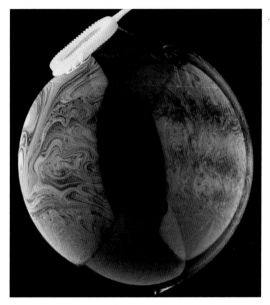

Colorful soap bubbles

Interference makes soap bubbles swim with color. The soapy film varies in thickness over the bubble. As light rays shoot into a bubble and reflect off its inner and outer surfaces, they add or subtract to make waves of different colors.

Constructive interference

When two waves of the same length and height (amplitude) overlap exactly in step (in phase), they add together. The new wave they make has the same wavelength, but twice the height. If two light waves added together like this, it would make light twice as bright.

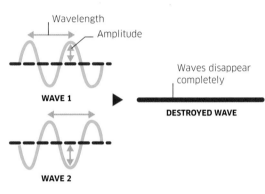

Wavelength, Amplitude
WAVE 1
WAVE 2
Waves disappear completely
DESTROYED WAVE

Destructive interference

When two identical waves add together, but are moving out of sync (out of phase), they cancel out altogether. The wave they make has zero amplitude. If two light waves added together like this, they would make darkness.

Diffraction

Light waves spread out when they pass through tiny gaps or holes. The smaller the gap, the more spreading (diffraction) that occurs. You can see diffraction for yourself if you squint your eyes almost closed and stare at a streetlight. As you close your eyes, you'll see the light spreading out as it diffracts through the gaps between your eyelashes.

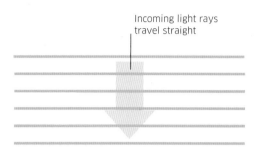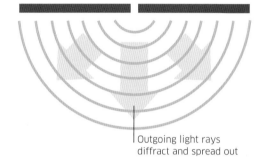

Incoming light rays travel straight

Outgoing light rays diffract and spread out

Diffraction through a narrow gap

For diffraction to work, the gap has to be about the same size as the wavelength of the waves. Sound waves also diffract, which is why we can hear through open doorways and around corners into other rooms.

Lasers

Lasers make very powerful beams of light. Unlike in normal lamps, the light waves from lasers are in sync and add together (constructive interference). This is why laser light is strong enough to travel incredible distances and why the most powerful lasers (carbon dioxide lasers) can weld metal or slice right through it.

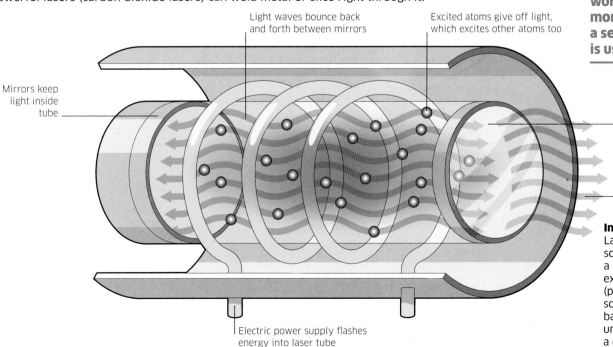

Light waves bounce back and forth between mirrors

Excited atoms give off light, which excites other atoms too

Mirrors keep light inside tube

Light emerges from partial (half-silvered) mirror

Laser beam is powerful and concentrated

Electric power supply flashes energy into laser tube

192 beams are emitted from the NIF, the world's biggest laser. It creates more power, for a fraction of a second, than the entire US is using at that same moment.

Inside a laser

Lasers make light when a power source flashes energy through a central tube. The atoms become excited, give out flashes of light (photons), and excite other atoms so they flash too. The light bounces back and forth between two mirrors until it emerges from one end as a concentrated beam.

Telescopes

Most of what we know about the Universe comes from large, professional telescopes, some of which are as big as office blocks. They use lenses and mirrors to catch and bend light, making distant stars snap crisply into focus.

Giant mirrors can be heavy and expensive to build, so several telescopes can be linked together to work as one. The world's biggest optical (light-based) telescope is the Very Large Telescope (VLT) in Chile. It can link together two or three telescopes, each with mirrors 27 ft (8.2 m) wide, to make a single instrument that can create clearer images of bright objects than individual telescopes are able to.

Laser guiding
Stars twinkle because their light is being distorted by Earth's atmosphere, and this makes images blurry. A powerful laser beam is fired into the atmosphere to create an artificial star, which is used to monitor the effect of the atmosphere. A computer can then counteract the blurring effect.

Paranal Observatory
The VLT consists of four giant telescopes fixed in place, four small auxiliary (additional) telescopes that shuttle along rails to different positions, and about 20 scientific instruments for analyzing the light these telescopes capture. The large telescopes are named Antu, Kueyen, Melipal, and Yepun (the names for the Sun, Moon, Southern Cross, and Venus in one of Chile's native languages).

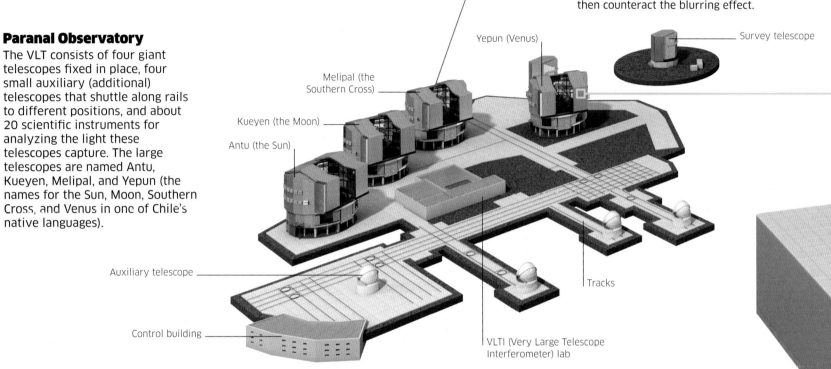

Yepun (Venus)

Survey telescope

Melipal (the Southern Cross)

Kueyen (the Moon)

Antu (the Sun)

Auxiliary telescope

Tracks

Control building

VLTI (Very Large Telescope Interferometer) lab

Images of outer space

With two or three telescopes working together, the VLT can reveal tiny details no other telescope on Earth can hope to capture. Since it started operating in 2000, the VLT has taken some incredible images of stars, galaxies, and nebulas that have helped to enhance our understanding of the Universe. Recently it has taken images of exoplanets (planets outside our Solar System).

Sombrero Galaxy
It takes about 30 million years for light to reach the VLT from the Sombrero Galaxy, which is shaped like a Mexican hat. Altogether, the galaxy weighs as much as 800 billion Suns. It has an outer ring of stars, gas, and dust, and a dense central nucleus of mature stars.

Crab Nebula
The Crab Nebula is the remains of a huge star that exploded into a supernova. Captured by the VLT, this image shows a blue region at its center made of high energy electrons spiraling around in a magnetic field. The Crab Nebula is about a thousand years old and five light years in diameter.

N70 Nebula in the Large Magellanic Cloud
Virtually the neighbor of our own Milky Way galaxy, the Large Magellanic Cloud is 160,000 light years from Earth. Ancient astronomers thought it looked like a fuzzy cloud or hazy mountains. N70 Nebula is a giant bubble of gas within the Large Magellanic Cloud.

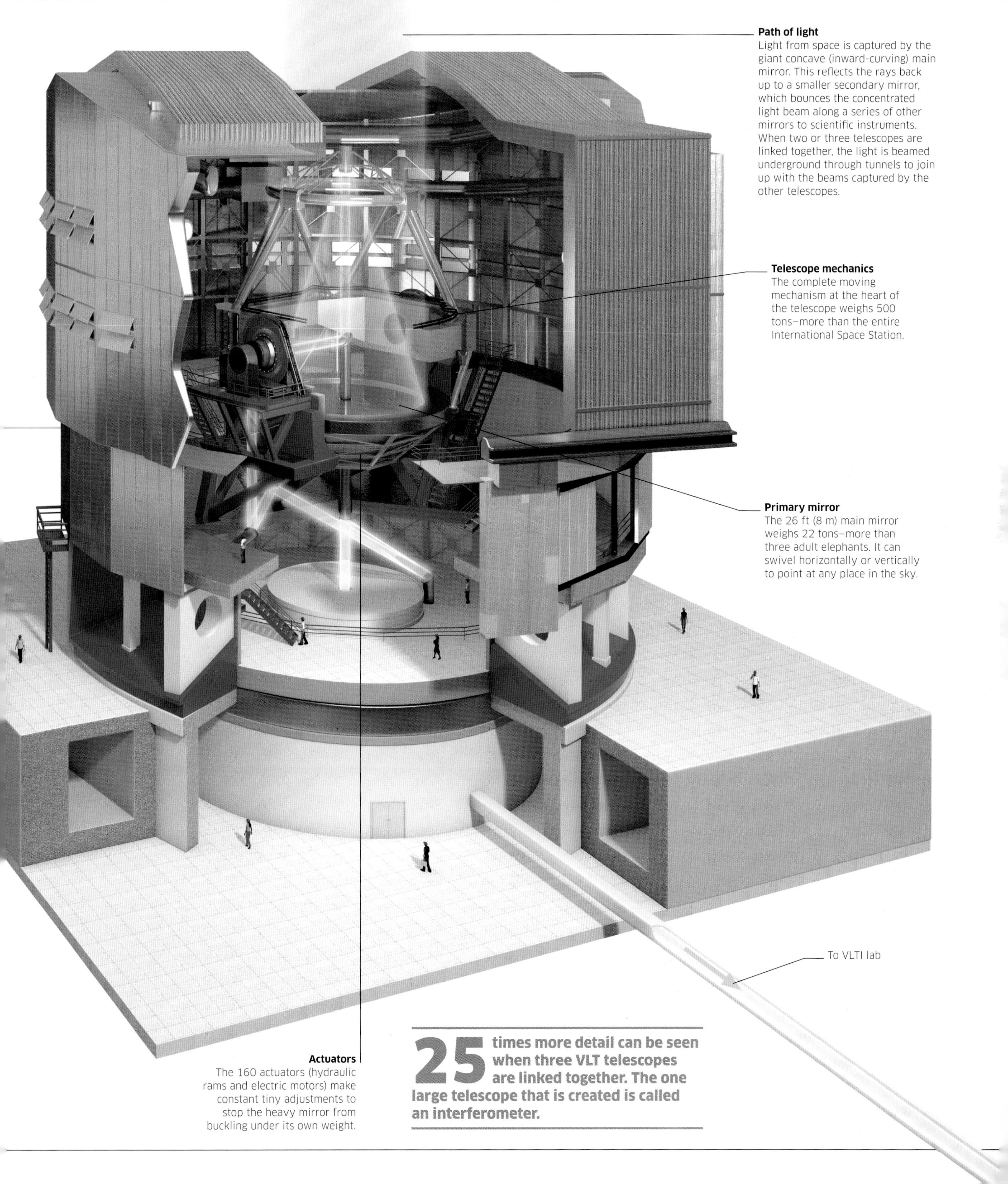

Path of light
Light from space is captured by the giant concave (inward-curving) main mirror. This reflects the rays back up to a smaller secondary mirror, which bounces the concentrated light beam along a series of other mirrors to scientific instruments. When two or three telescopes are linked together, the light is beamed underground through tunnels to join up with the beams captured by the other telescopes.

Telescope mechanics
The complete moving mechanism at the heart of the telescope weighs 500 tons—more than the entire International Space Station.

Primary mirror
The 26 ft (8 m) main mirror weighs 22 tons—more than three adult elephants. It can swivel horizontally or vertically to point at any place in the sky.

To VLTI lab

Actuators
The 160 actuators (hydraulic rams and electric motors) make constant tiny adjustments to stop the heavy mirror from buckling under its own weight.

25 times more detail can be seen when three VLT telescopes are linked together. The one large telescope that is created is called an interferometer.

Sound

When someone shouts hello, billions of molecules push and shove through the crowded air between you, speeding the sound to your ears. If we could watch this happen, we'd see that sounds are waves of energy that squeeze and stretch the air as they travel.

All sounds travel in waves, and what makes one sound different from another is simply the shape of its waves. Unlike waves on water, which snake up and down as they move forward, sound waves push and pull in the same direction that they travel.

Sound is ultimately just another type of energy, like light or heat, but it's special to us because it carries words and music at high speed. Without sound we wouldn't be able to listen to birds singing in the trees or the latest hit songs on the radio. It has the ability to affect our emotions and stir up our interest in the world around us.

How sound travels

If you bang a drum, its skin vibrates, shaking the air molecules around it. These push on nearby molecules, which shake others, and the sound quickly ripples outward, spreading energy in all directions. When the energy finally reaches our ears, it makes the air inside them vibrate too and we hear sounds.

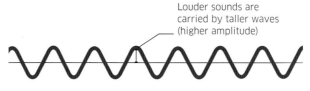

Louder sounds are carried by taller waves (higher amplitude)

Quieter sounds are carried by shorter waves (lower amplitude)

Loudness
It takes more energy to make louder sounds. The harder you beat a drum, the more its skin shakes up and down. That makes the air molecules push and pull harder, producing a louder sound in your ears.

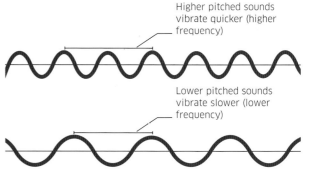

Higher pitched sounds vibrate quicker (higher frequency)

Lower pitched sounds vibrate slower (lower frequency)

Pitch
The pitch (frequency) of a sound comes from how often it vibrates. A tight drum skin vibrates more than a loose one, making higher pitched (higher frequency) sounds. These vibrate more often than lower frequency sounds.

Speed of sound

We see lightning flash several seconds before we hear thunder claps, because light travels much faster than sound. At ground level, at an air temperature of about 68°F (20°C), sound travels at 1,125 feet per second (768 mph or 1,235 kph). However, it doesn't move at the same speed in every material. Because sound moves by shaking energy through atoms or molecules, its speed depends both on the inner nature of a material—how close together its atoms are—and the temperature.

SPEED OF SOUND (m/s)

- STEEL: 6,000
- WATER: 1,500
- AIR: 343

Speed of sound in different materials
You can walk faster through air than through water, so you might expect sound to do the same. But sound waves travel fastest in solids (since the atoms are closest together), slower in liquids, and slower still in gases. Sound travels over 17 times faster in steel than in air.

Supersonic motion

By the time you hear a jet plane screaming overhead, it's already shot past. Flying faster than the speed of sound, it leaves its own noise far behind. Supersonic planes make so much noise because they ram and squeeze the air in front of them, trailing huge shock waves behind.

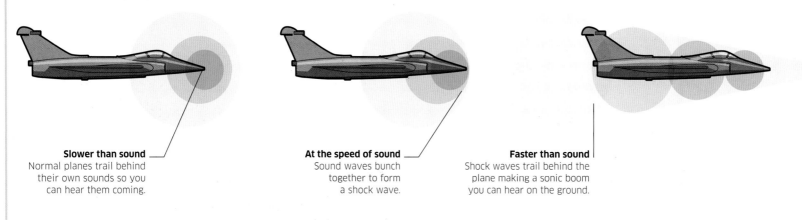

Slower than sound
Normal planes trail behind their own sounds so you can hear them coming.

At the speed of sound
Sound waves bunch together to form a shock wave.

Faster than sound
Shock waves trail behind the plane making a sonic boom you can hear on the ground.

Cracking whips and bursting balloons sound so loud because they make **shock waves faster** than the **speed of sound**.

1,000 miles (1,600 km)—the distance blue whales can hear.

231

The Doppler effect

When an ambulance hurtles toward you, its siren sounds high-pitched. This is because the ambulance is driving forward into the sound waves sent out by the siren, so the waves get closer together and arrive at your ears more frequently, giving them a higher pitch. After the siren passes, you hear a sudden drop in pitch. This is because the ambulance is moving away in between the sound waves, so they grow further apart, and therefore sound lower pitched. This is called the Doppler effect after the physicist who discovered it.

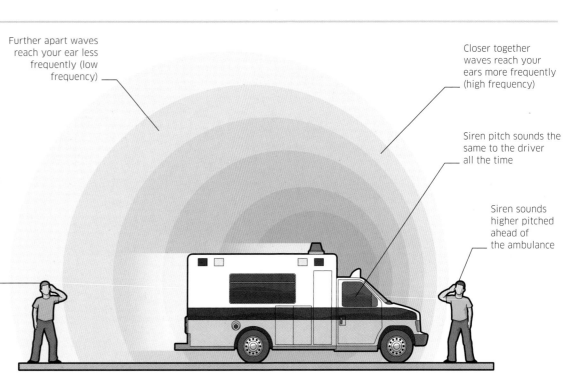

Further apart waves reach your ear less frequently (low frequency)

Closer together waves reach your ears more frequently (high frequency)

Siren pitch sounds the same to the driver all the time

Siren sounds higher pitched ahead of the ambulance

Siren sounds lower-pitched behind the ambulance

Shifting sirens
The pitch of a siren is helpful in working out if an ambulance is moving toward or away from you. In the moment the ambulance passes you, you will hear its siren exactly as the driver hears it.

Musical sound

Our brains instantly spot the difference between noise and music. Musical notes are made from sound frequencies connected in precise ways. If you play the eight notes in an octave (musical scale), the highest has exactly twice the frequency of the lowest. If you play the same note on different instruments, you make complex waves that have the same frequency but different shapes.

Smooth, even sound wave

Tuning fork
Bang a tuning fork and it makes a simple, regular, up-and-down sound wave pattern called a sine wave. Each fork produces only one note (frequency) and you need different forks to make other notes.

Spiky sound wave

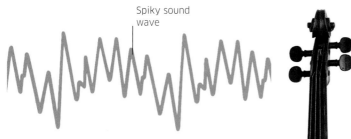

Violin
When you play a violin, the strings vibrate, setting the air moving inside the hollow wooden case. A violin's sound wave is a sharp and spiky wave.

Air inside wooden case amplifies string sounds

Complex, even sound wave

Flute
Flutes make sounds when you blow into them, vibrating and making waves inside the pipe. The sound waves are similar to the sine wave from a tuning fork, but slightly more complex.

Bigger cymbal vibrates greater volume of air and sounds louder

It's possible for a powerful singer **to shatter a crystal** wine glass by singing at the same note or frequency that the glass makes when clinked.

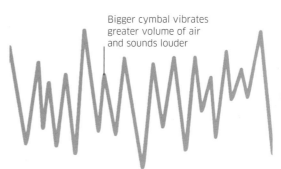

Cymbal
Percussion instruments make sounds when you hit them. Their sound waves are more like a short burst of random noise (white noise) than the precise wave shape of a tuning fork.

Heat

When an ice cream cone dribbles down your hand, blame science. Heat (kinetic energy hidden inside things) moves around our world in very distinct ways according to rules that cannot change.

Heat is a type of energy stored when atoms and molecules move around inside objects. Hotter objects contain more heat than colder ones because their atoms and molecules move faster. Heat doesn't always stay in one place—if something hot is near something cold, it passes heat on until the two temperatures are equal. When the hot object cools down, it loses a certain amount of energy to the cold one, which gains exactly the same energy and heats up.

Kinetic theory

The hotter a gas, the faster its atoms and molecules move around. The faster they move, the more they collide with the container, making pressure. If you heat or squash a gas, the particles move faster and collisions happen more often, increasing the pressure and temperature. This idea is called kinetic theory.

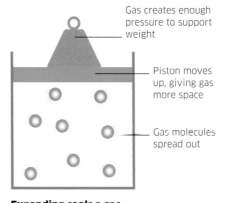

Gas creates enough pressure to support weight

Piston moves up, giving gas more space

Gas molecules spread out

Expanding cools a gas
Atoms in the gas have more space to move. The overall heat energy is spread over a bigger space, so the gas is cooler.

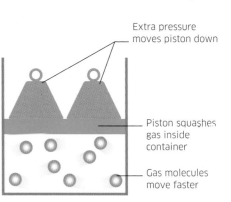

Extra pressure moves piston down

Piston squashes gas inside container

Gas molecules move faster

Compressing heats a gas
As the piston moves in, the atoms are squashed closer so they collide more often with the container, and heat it up.

Temperature

The temperatures that people experience on Earth fall within a tiny range of less than 150 degrees. The maximum possible range of temperatures, from absolute zero (the coldest possible) up to the high temperature inside the Large Hadron Collider, is about 2 trillion degrees.

0K or -273°K

1/1000,000,000K (a millionth to a billionth of a Kelvin): Temperature of a typical black hole

184K (-128°F): Coldest (ambient) temperature ever recorded on Earth, at Vostok Station, Antarctica, 1983

273K (32°F): Freezing point of water

330K (134°F): Hottest (ambient) temperature ever recorded on Earth, at Death Valley, CA, 1913

373K (212°F): Boiling point of water

0K

100K

Range of temperatures on Earth

Absolute zero
At the coldest possible temperature, the atoms and molecules inside things stop moving and lock down. We call this absolute zero. No one has yet made anything this cold, although scientists have gotten to within fractions of a degree of this temperature.

How heat travels

Like other forms of energy, heat tends to spread out evenly. Hot objects pass energy to colder ones nearby by three processes, called conduction, convection, and radiation. Often, more than one of these processes happen at the same time. A radiator in your room might pass heat to the wall and floor by conduction (direct contact), convection (warm air currents), and radiation (beaming heat directly to your body).

Conduction
When something hot touches something cold, the atoms in the hotter object are moving faster and agitate their colder neighbors. The colder atoms do the same—and soon the heat flows all along the object.

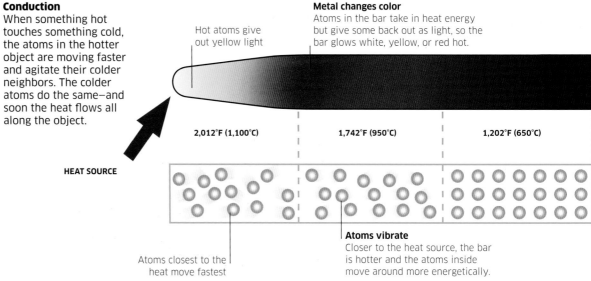

Hot atoms give out yellow light

Metal changes color
Atoms in the bar take in heat energy but give some back out as light, so the bar glows white, yellow, or red hot.

HEAT SOURCE

2,012°F (1,100°C)   1,742°F (950°C)   1,202°F (650°C)

Atoms closest to the heat move fastest

Atoms vibrate
Closer to the heat source, the bar is hotter and the atoms inside move around more energetically.

Gallium metal will **melt in your hand**—its melting point (85.6°F or 29.8°C) is less than **body temperature**.

Scientists have **cooled** things to within **0.000000001** degrees of **absolute zero**.

233

Measuring heat

Temperature measures how hot or cold something is, but not how much heat energy it has. An iceberg is enormous so, even though it seems cold, all its moving atoms and molecules contain lots of heat energy. A cup of coffee, though hotter, is much smaller than an iceberg and therefore contains less heat energy overall.

Different measurements

We measure temperature with three different scales. Fahrenheit is the official scale in the US and a few other countries. Celsius is the most common unit of measurement, while Kelvin is mostly used by scientists.

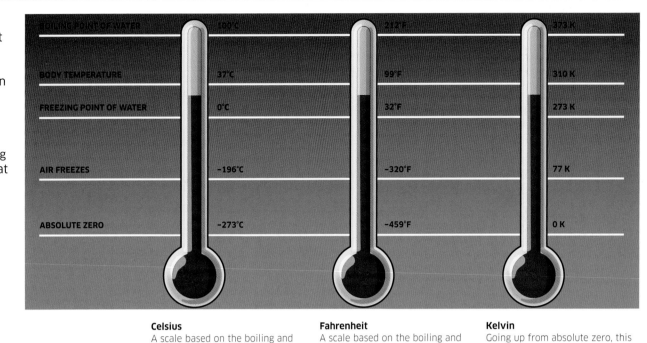

	Celsius	Fahrenheit	Kelvin
BOILING POINT OF WATER	100°C	212°F	373 K
BODY TEMPERATURE	37°C	99°F	310 K
FREEZING POINT OF WATER	0°C	32°F	273 K
AIR FREEZES	−196°C	−320°F	77 K
ABSOLUTE ZERO	−273°C	−459°F	0 K

Celsius
A scale based on the boiling and freezing points of water, with 100 degrees in between.

Fahrenheit
A scale based on the boiling and freezing points of water, with 180 degrees in between.

Kelvin
Going up from absolute zero, this scale has degrees the same size as the Celsius scale.

Absolute maximum

The hottest temperature scientists can imagine is 140 million trillion trillion degrees K (known as the Planck temperature). The Universe is believed to have been this hot a fraction of a second after the Big Bang, but nothing has been anywhere near this temperature since then.

1,673K (2,552°F): Melting point of steel

14,000,000K (25.2 million °F): Temperature at the center of the Sun

1,000,000,000K (1.8 billion °F): Temperature 100 seconds after the Big Bang

1.6 trillion K: Temperatures achieved inside the Large Hadron Collider (LHC)

1,000K   10,000,000K   1,000,000,000K   1,000,000,000,000K

Convection

Convection is the way heat circulates through flowing liquids and gases (fluids). When you heat water in a kettle, the rising hot water and sinking cold water gradually warm the entire liquid.

Handle stays cool because plastic conducts heat poorly

Colder water is pushed out of the way

Hotter water becomes less dense and rises

Kettle passes heat to water by conduction

Radiating heat

Like light, heat beams out from hot objects and can even travel through a vacuum. The more surface area something has, the faster it radiates heat and cools down.

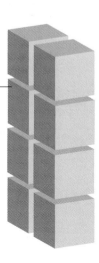

Cooling quickly
Object made of eight blocks with 28 sides of surface area radiates heat faster.

Cooling slowly
Object made of eight blocks with 24 sides of surface area radiates heat slower.

Electricity

Leaping bolts of lightning are fueled by electrons. These tiny charged particles that whiz around inside atoms are about the smallest things we can imagine. Yet everything electric is ultimately driven by them.

From heating and lighting our homes to powering trains, electricity can do a remarkable range of things. When electrons march through wires, they carry energy from place to place, making what we call an electric current. Electric currents power everything that plugs into a socket at home and, through batteries, fuel cell phones and laptops when we are on the move. When electrons build up in one place, they make static electricity. It's static electricity that crackles when you take off your sweatshirt—and static buildup that causes lightning bolts to zap back to Earth.

What happens when a current flows?

When you plug a lamp into an outlet or turn on a light switch, electrical energy flows along the wire. The atoms in the wire stay put, while electrons flow all around them, each one carrying a tiny amount of electricity called a charge. Although each electron moves slowly, the wire is packed with them. That's why electricity takes no time at all to flow from its source to where it's used. The lamp lights instantly.

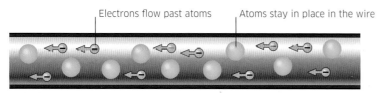

Electrons flow past atoms   Atoms stay in place in the wire

Current flowing
When the power is switched on, electrons that are already inside the wire start to move. The bigger the voltage, the more electrons are pushed through the wire and the bigger the electric current.

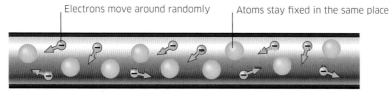

Electrons move around randomly   Atoms stay fixed in the same place

No current flowing
When you switch off the power, there's nothing to push the electrons along in the same direction. They stop flowing in a current and dance around more randomly.

How a battery works

Batteries are portable power supplies that make electricity using chemistry. They have a negative terminal (the metal case and plate at the bottom), a positive terminal (the metal knob on top), and an electrolyte (chemical mixture) in between. When you connect a battery into a circuit, chemical reactions start up inside it, generating electrons and positive ions (atoms missing electrons). The positive ions drift through the inside of the battery. The electrons flow around the circuit outside, powering whatever the battery is connected to.

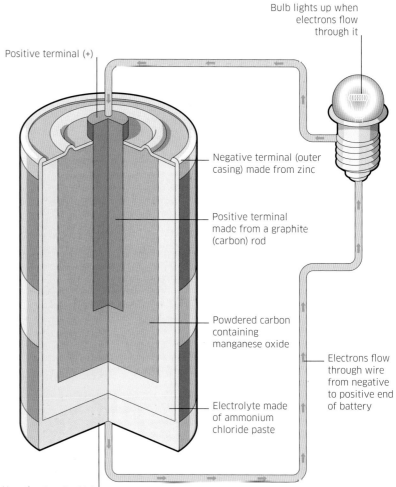

Bulb lights up when electrons flow through it

Positive terminal (+)

Negative terminal (outer casing) made from zinc

Positive terminal made from a graphite (carbon) rod

Powdered carbon containing manganese oxide

Electrons flow through wire from negative to positive end of battery

Electrolyte made of ammonium chloride paste

Negative terminal (−)

Battery
The simplest batteries have a negative terminal made from zinc and a positive terminal made from carbon (graphite) and can only be used once before being thrown away. Rechargeable batteries use materials that allow reversible chemical reactions inside them and so can be reused hundreds of times.

Electric circuits

The path that electrons flow along is called a circuit. An electric circuit carries energy from a power source (such as a battery) to something that uses power (such as a lamp) and back again. Electricity only flows if a circuit forms a complete (closed) loop. If the loop is broken somewhere along the line, electrons can't get across the gap and the electric current stops flowing. Switches work by breaking circuits in this way.

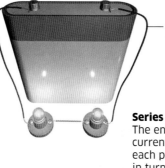

Components are connected by a single loop of wire

Series circuit
The entire electric current flows through each part of the circuit in turn. Exactly the same current flows through each lamp.

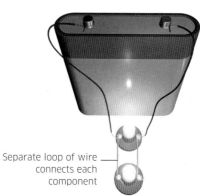

Separate loop of wire connects each component

Parallel circuit
The electric current has to split to flow through different parts of the circuit. Only half the current flows through each lamp.

Sharks **are a million times more sensitive** to electricity than humans and can **detect minute electric currents** in water.

65 million trillion **electrons** flow into an **electric toaster** every single **second**.

235

Static electricity

We usually think of electricity as flowing through something, but when electrons build up with no circuit for them to flow along they create static electricity. Static electricity is what makes your hair stand on end when you pull on a polyester T-shirt, or a balloon stick to the wall after you have rubbed it on your sweatshirt. The surfaces of things like balloons steal electrons from other surfaces and the extra electrons make them negatively charged.

Lightning can heat the air surrounding it to a temperature that is more than

five times hotter

than the Sun's surface.

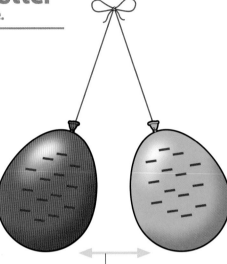

Negative charge

If you rub a balloon on your sweatshirt, the balloon develops a negative charge. If you hold the balloon up to a wall, it pushes away negative electrons and makes the wall's surface positive.The balloon sticks in place.

Negatively charged electrons on balloon push negative electrons deeper into the wall

Unlike charges attract
Negative and positive charges attract, so the balloon sticks to the wall.

Repulsion

When you rub two balloons on your sweatshirt, one after another, they both become negatively charged. If you try to hold the balloons together, their negative charges push apart.

Like charges repel
Two negative charges repel each other, so the balloons push apart.

Plasma spheres

The swirling streams inside this clear glass sphere, filled with a mixture of gases, are produced by static electricity. When the rod in the middle is charged to a high voltage, atoms of gas inside the ball are pulled apart to make a plasma (a soup of atoms split into ions and electrons). Electricity builds up in the center and then zaps through the ions and electrons to the outer edge, making streams of mini lightning bolts.

Plasma sphere
A glass ball filled with a low pressure gas such as neon or argon.

Electric currents
Light streams are electric currents flowing from the center to the edge of the sphere.

High-voltage center
The Inner rod and ball feeds high-voltage electricity into the middle of the sphere.

Lightning bolts speed through the air at around

200,000,000 mph

(322,000,000 kph).

From source to the home

Electricity surges through a complex grid network linking the power stations and generators that produce it to the many things that use it. How much electricity we use rises and falls through the day, but the many different forms of electricity generation can be balanced to meet demand, so we never run out of power.

Fossil fuels
Fuels such as coal and oil have to be burned in giant furnaces to release the energy they contain.

Hydroelectric power
Water from a dammed river rushes through a turbine, spinning a generator and creating electricity.

Solar power
Large glass-coated panels convert the energy in sunlight directly into electricity.

Nuclear power
Large atoms release heat energy when they split up. This heat is used to make the steam that generates electricity.

Geothermal power
Cold water is piped underground, captures heat, and returns as hot water that is used to generate electricity.

Step-up station
Voltage is increased to 400,000 volts to reduce power losses.

Pylons

Substation
Voltage is reduced to 50,000–150,000 volts for heavy industry and large factories.

Wind power
Giant rotors turned by the wind have gearboxes and generators inside that produce electricity automatically. A single large turbine can produce enough electricity for over 1,000 homes.

Industry
Factory machines are powered by large electric motors that are highly efficient, quiet, and don't cause any pollution.

Power network

Chunks of coal, gusts of wind, raging rivers, and shattering atoms—these are some of the things we use to make electricity, our most versatile form of energy.

Before the first electric power stations were developed in 1882, people had to make energy by burning fuels such as wood and coal, which was often dirty and time-consuming. Large-scale electricity generation solved these problems. Electricity could be made in one place, then sent hundreds or thousands of miles down wires to where it was needed. Coal and wood can only provide heating, while gasoline only powers vehicles. But electricity can be used in many different ways—for heating, lighting, and powering motors that drive everything from tiny electric toothbrushes to huge electric trains.

1 Generation
Traditional power stations generate electricity by burning fuels to release heat. This is used to boil water and produce jets of steam, which spin windmill-like machines called turbines. The turbines turn generators, which are like electric motors in reverse—they convert mechanical energy into electrical energy.

2 Distribution
Only a third of the energy in the original fuel becomes useful electricity. The rest is lost during generation and in the power lines that carry the electricity to its destination. Transmitting power at a very high voltage helps to cut energy losses. Substations along the route reduce the voltage back to low levels.

442 The number of **nuclear power stations** and **reactors** currently **operating worldwide**.

In 1903, the **inventor** Thomas Edison **electrocuted an elephant** to prove that a rival's **electricity generating system** was unsafe.

237

Sources of electricity

Most countries make the majority of their electricity from fossil fuels (coal, natural gas, and oil). In some countries, like France and Japan, nuclear power generates a lot of electricity too. Wind and solar are the best-known types of renewable energy. Even so, most renewable energy is actually produced with hydroelectric power.

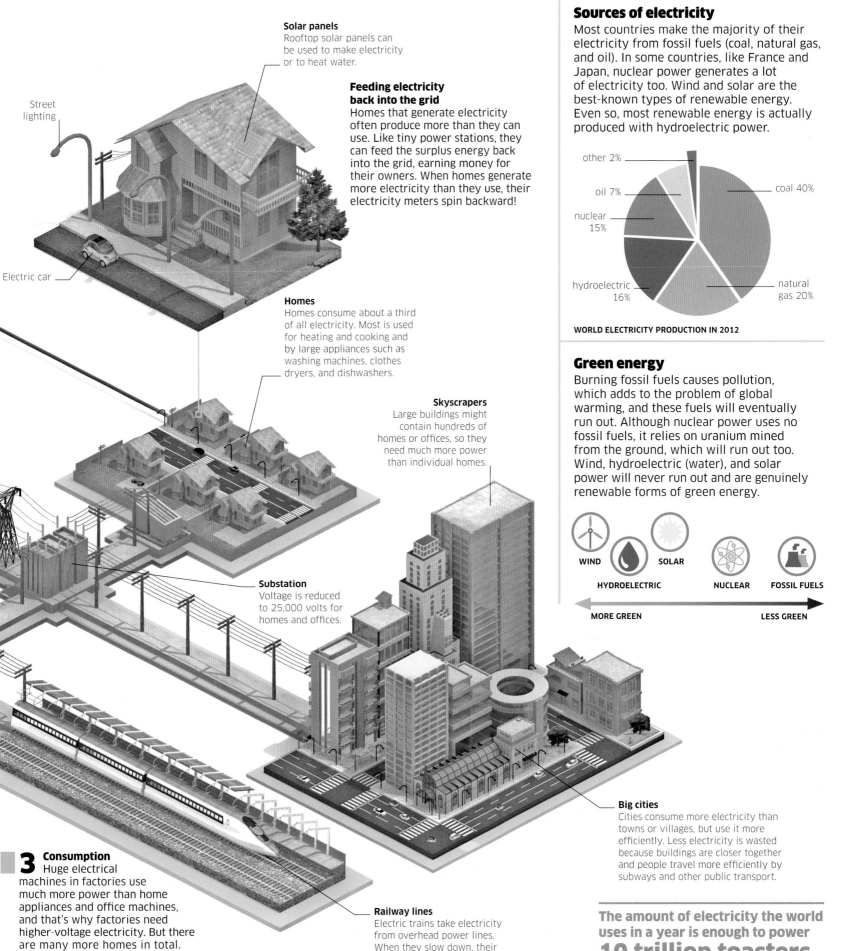

- other 2%
- oil 7%
- nuclear 15%
- hydroelectric 16%
- coal 40%
- natural gas 20%

WORLD ELECTRICITY PRODUCTION IN 2012

Green energy

Burning fossil fuels causes pollution, which adds to the problem of global warming, and these fuels will eventually run out. Although nuclear power uses no fossil fuels, it relies on uranium mined from the ground, which will run out too. Wind, hydroelectric (water), and solar power will never run out and are genuinely renewable forms of green energy.

WIND
SOLAR
HYDROELECTRIC
NUCLEAR
FOSSIL FUELS

MORE GREEN ← → **LESS GREEN**

Solar panels
Rooftop solar panels can be used to make electricity or to heat water.

Street lighting

Feeding electricity back into the grid
Homes that generate electricity often produce more than they can use. Like tiny power stations, they can feed the surplus energy back into the grid, earning money for their owners. When homes generate more electricity than they use, their electricity meters spin backward!

Electric car

Homes
Homes consume about a third of all electricity. Most is used for heating and cooking and by large appliances such as washing machines, clothes dryers, and dishwashers.

Skyscrapers
Large buildings might contain hundreds of homes or offices, so they need much more power than individual homes.

Substation
Voltage is reduced to 25,000 volts for homes and offices.

3 Consumption
Huge electrical machines in factories use much more power than home appliances and office machines, and that's why factories need higher-voltage electricity. But there are many more homes in total. Overall, homes, offices, and factories each use just under a third of the total electricity produced.

Railway lines
Electric trains take electricity from overhead power lines. When they slow down, their brakes feed energy back to the power lines instead of wasting it as heat.

Big cities
Cities consume more electricity than towns or villages, but use it more efficiently. Less electricity is wasted because buildings are closer together and people travel more efficiently by subways and other public transport.

The amount of electricity the world uses in a year is enough to power
10 trillion toasters
for a whole hour.

238 science ∘ ENERGY

If you could **wire a nuclear power station** up to an electric kettle, you could **boil the water** for a cup of tea in **50-millionths of a second.**

Types of radiation

Unstable atoms break up to release three types of radioactivity—alpha, beta, and gamma. Alpha and beta radiation are made from bits of the broken atoms. Gamma rays are a type of electromagnetic radiation, similar to light but more energetic and highly dangerous.

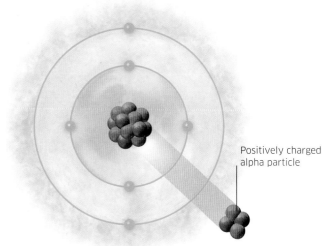

Positively charged alpha particle

Alpha radiation

The slowest and heaviest forms of radioactivity are called alpha particles. Each alpha particle has two protons and two neutrons (the same as the nucleus of a helium atom).

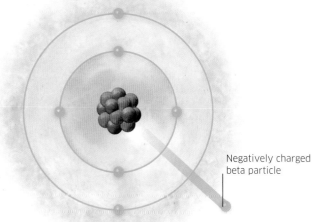

Negatively charged beta particle

Beta radiation

Beta particles are smaller and faster forms of radiation. In fact, they are just streams of electrons that unstable atoms shoot out at about half the speed of light.

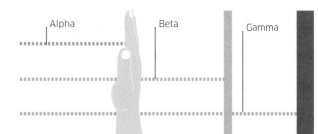

Alpha   Beta   Gamma

Penetrating power

Alpha, beta, and gamma radiation can go through different amounts of matter because they have different speeds and energy. Alpha particles can't even get through paper. Beta particles can get through skin, but not metal. Gamma rays can only be stopped by very thick lead or concrete.

Radioactivity

Nuclear power stations make electricity by smashing atoms apart. Atoms are locked together by huge forces, and they release massive amounts of energy when they disintegrate.

Many elements have atoms with slightly different forms, called isotopes. Some of these are very unstable (radioactive) and naturally break apart to turn into more stable forms, releasing energy. Atoms can also be forced to split apart artificially, in nuclear power stations and atomic bombs. Although radioactive atoms are dangerous enough to kill people, they can help to save lives as well. Radioactive particles are used in smoke alarms, and they help to preserve foods by killing harmful bacteria. They are also used to treat and detect life-threatening illnesses such as cancer.

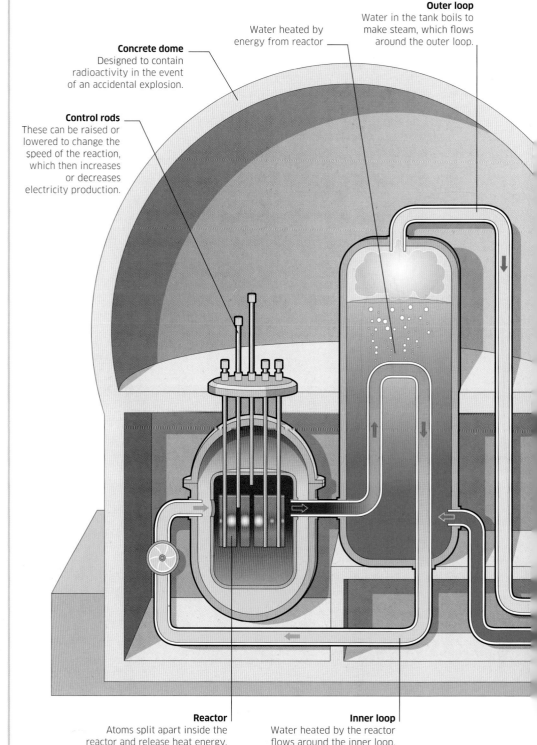

Outer loop
Water in the tank boils to make steam, which flows around the outer loop.

Water heated by energy from reactor

Concrete dome
Designed to contain radioactivity in the event of an accidental explosion.

Control rods
These can be raised or lowered to change the speed of the reaction, which then increases or decreases electricity production.

Reactor
Atoms split apart inside the reactor and release heat energy.

Inner loop
Water heated by the reactor flows around the inner loop.

17,000 The number of **nuclear weapons** stockpiled **around the world**.

Our bodies contain enough **natural radioactivity** to produce **120,000 beta particles** every minute.

239

Energy from atoms

Atoms release energy in two ways. When large, unstable atoms (such as uranium) split into smaller atoms, they give off heat. This process is called fission (splitting). It creates heat because the total energy in the smaller atoms is less than the energy in the original atom. A second process is called fusion (joining), when small atoms (hydrogen isotopes) smash together, combine, and release energy. All of the world's nuclear power stations currently work by fission, but scientists hope to build fusion stations because they will be much cleaner.

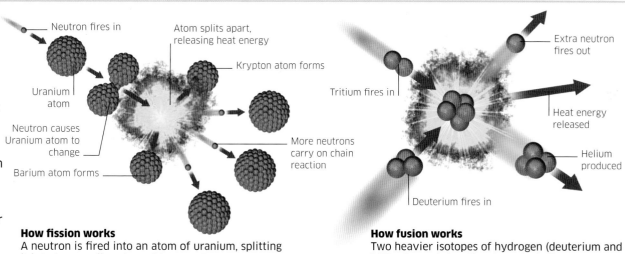

Neutron fires in

Uranium atom

Neutron causes Uranium atom to change

Barium atom forms

Atom splits apart, releasing heat energy

Krypton atom forms

More neutrons carry on chain reaction

Tritium fires in

Extra neutron fires out

Heat energy released

Helium produced

Deuterium fires in

How fission works
A neutron is fired into an atom of uranium, splitting it into two smaller atoms. More neutrons are released in the process, producing a chain reaction.

How fusion works
Two heavier isotopes of hydrogen (deuterium and tritium) smash together to make helium. A spare neutron is fired out and heat energy is released.

How nuclear power works

In a nuclear power station, the heat that boils steam to make electricity isn't made by burning coal or gas, but by splitting atoms inside a giant nuclear reactor and capturing their energy. The amount of power can be controlled by raising and lowering rods to speed up or slow down the nuclear reactions.

13% of the world's electricity is now generated using nuclear energy, and its use is gradually increasing.

Other uses of radioactivity

From archaeological digs to making bombs, radioactivity has lots of uses, many of them medical. Heart pacemakers once used tiny nuclear power units, because they lasted decades longer than batteries. Medical scans often involve people swallowing or being injected with safe radioactive substances. Scanning equipment outside of their body detects the radiation and creates detailed images of their illness. Radioactivity can also treat cancer. Radiotherapy treatment bombards tumors with gamma rays, killing the cancer and stopping it from spreading.

Nuclear weapons

Most atomic weapons use nuclear fission and need pure uranium or plutonium so their chain reactions continue over and over. Hydrogen (H) bombs are even more powerful and work through nuclear fusion.

ATOMIC BOMB (REPLICA)

Radiometric rock dating

Rocks on Earth contain unstable radioactive atoms (such as uranium) that are constantly changing into more stable atoms (such as lead) at a precise rate. If we compare the amount of uranium and lead in a piece of rock, we can work out how old it is.

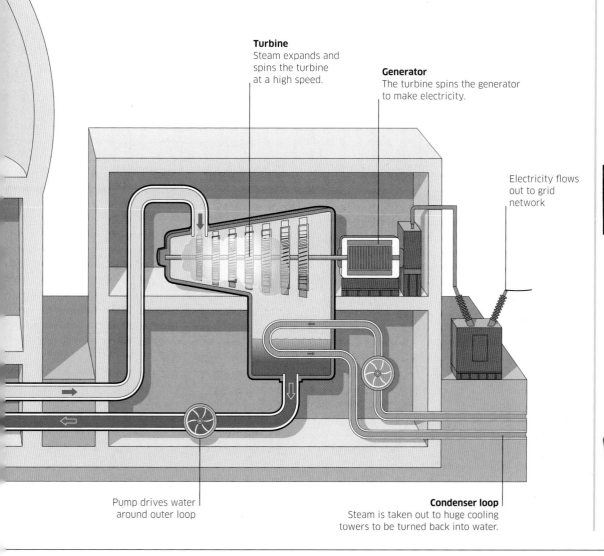

Turbine
Steam expands and spins the turbine at a high speed.

Generator
The turbine spins the generator to make electricity.

Electricity flows out to grid network

Pump drives water around outer loop

Condenser loop
Steam is taken out to huge cooling towers to be turned back into water.

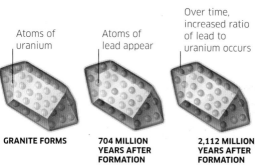

Atoms of uranium

Atoms of lead appear

Over time, increased ratio of lead to uranium occurs

GRANITE FORMS

704 MILLION YEARS AFTER FORMATION

2,112 MILLION YEARS AFTER FORMATION

ELECTRONICS

Electrons traveling through circuits can play your favorite songs, turn your television on and off, or capture digital photos of your friends. When gadgets use electrons in this way, we say they're electronic—they use electricity in a way that's more precise and finely controlled than the kind that powers simple home appliances. Electronics is the secret power behind calculators, computers, robots, and the Internet.

WHAT IS ELECTRONICS?

It takes quite a lot of electricity (large electrical currents) to boil water or heat a home. Electronics uses carefully controlled electric currents thousands or millions of times smaller, and sometimes just individual electrons, to do useful things.

Circuits
Electronics uses complex circuits, but these circuits only need tiny currents. Because they don't consume much energy, many electronic appliances can be battery-powered.

Controlling

We can use electronics to switch things on and off. When you press a button on a TV remote control, an electronic circuit detects what you want and sends an invisible beam to the TV set. The TV detects this and another circuit responds.

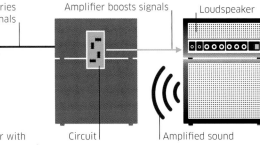

Remote control

Circuit detects button presses | Infrared beam | TV

Amplifying

Electronic circuits can boost tiny electric currents into bigger ones. An electric guitar uses electromagnets to convert the movement of the strings into electric currents. These are boosted in an electronic amplifier, which powers a loudspeaker.

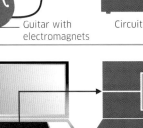

Cable carries signals | Amplifier boosts signals | Loudspeaker

Guitar with electromagnets | Circuit | Amplified sound

Processing information

The electronic circuits in computers digest information. When you type, electronic circuits decode the keys you press, understand what you are typing, and work out where to display the letters.

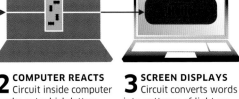

1 KEYBOARD DETECTS Electric or electronic switches in the keyboard detect the keys you press.

2 COMPUTER REACTS Circuit inside computer works out which letters you are typing.

3 SCREEN DISPLAYS Circuit converts words into patterns of light on the screen.

Communication

In cell phones, electronic circuits convert our speech or text into a form that can be beamed through the air using invisible radio waves. They can also convert radio waves from other phones back into spoken words or text messages.

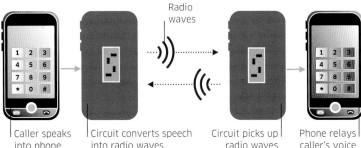

Radio waves

Caller speaks into phone | Circuit converts speech into radio waves | Circuit picks up radio waves | Phone relays caller's voice

COMPONENTS

An electronic circuit is made of building blocks called components. A transistor radio might have a few dozen components, while the processor and memory chips in a computer could have billions. Four components are particularly important and appear in almost every single circuit: resistors, capacitors, diodes, and transistors.

Resistors

Resistors reduce an electric current so it's less powerful. Some have a fixed size, while others vary. The volume on a TV set is a variable resistor. As you move it, its resistance rises or falls, altering the current, and making the sound quieter or louder.

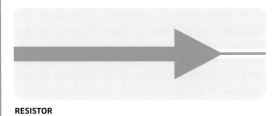

RESISTOR

Capacitors

Capacitors store electricity in a sandwich of metal foil separated by air or plastic. It takes a precise time for them to charge up, so they are often used in circuits that work as timers. Capacitors are also used to detect key punches on cell phone and tablet touchscreens.

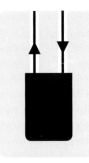

CAPACITOR

Diodes

A diode is the electronic version of a one-way street: a current can only flow along it in one direction. Diodes are often used to convert electricity that flows in both directions (alternating current) into electricity that flows only one way (direct current).

DIODE

Transistors

Transistors can switch electric currents on and off or convert small currents into bigger ones. Most transistors are used in computers. A powerful computer chip contains a billion or more transistors.

TRANSISTOR

INTEGRATED CIRCUITS

Electronic components such as transistors are about as big as a pea, so a computer with a billion of them would be enormous. It would also be difficult to make, unreliable, and power hungry. In 1958, two US engineers named Jack Kilby and Robert Noyce found ways of shrinking electronic components and their connections into a tiny space. This idea became known as an integrated circuit, or chip.

Printed circuit boards

Electronic circuits are often made in the millions for cell phones or TVs. To save money and reduce mistakes, machines wire components into ready-made printed circuit boards (PCBs). Each is unique to a particular device. The circuit is made from metal connections (tracks) that crisscross the board, linking the components. There are no moving parts, so PCBs are very reliable.

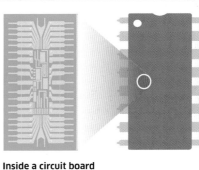
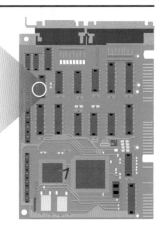

Inside a circuit board
A circuit board is made from interconnected chips. Each chip has an integrated circuit inside it, containing millions or billions of components.

Making chips

Chips are intricate and have to be made in ultraclean, dust-free conditions. Many chips are made at once on the surface of a thin wafer sliced from a crystal of silicon (a chemical element found in sand).

Testing, testing
Each chip has to be tested to make sure it is wired up and working correctly. Once this is done, the individual chips are cut from the wafer and sealed in cases with connecting pins, ready for their circuit boards.

Moore's law

Engineers are constantly finding new ways to add more components into chips. This graph shows that the power of computers (number of transistors on a chip) has doubled roughly every two years since the first single-chip computer appeared in 1971. This is called Moore's law, named after Gordon Moore (1929-), a founder of the Intel chip company.

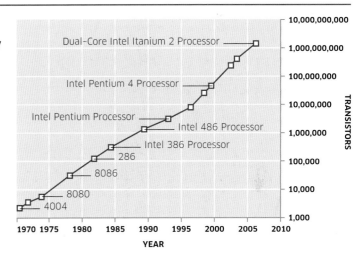

DIGITAL ELECTRONICS

Most of the gadgets we rely on every day use digital technology: they convert information into numbers (digits) and process the numbers instead of the original information. Digital cameras turn pictures of the world into patterns of numbers (digital photos), and cell phones send and receive calls not as sounds but as long strings of numbers. Gadgets like these use integrated circuits to convert, store, and process information in digital form—a technology known as digital electronics.

Analog and digital

Ordinary information, like the sound waves made by a guitar, is called analog information. If you use an oscilloscope (an electronic graph-drawing machine) to draw these sound waves, they look exactly like the sounds you can hear—the waves rise and fall as the sound rises and falls. Digital technology converts this analog information into numbers through a process called sampling.

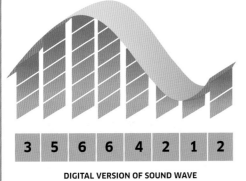

| 3 | 5 | 6 | 6 | 4 | 2 | 1 | 2 |

DIGITAL VERSION OF SOUND WAVE

Sampling
To convert music into a digital MP3 file, sound waves have to be turned into numbers. The size of the waves is sampled (measured) at different times and its value recorded, making a string of numbers. The more often the wave is sampled, the better the result.

Logic gates

Computers process digital information with circuits called logic gates. These compare two numbers (0 or 1) and produce a third based on the result. The main types are AND, OR, and NOT.

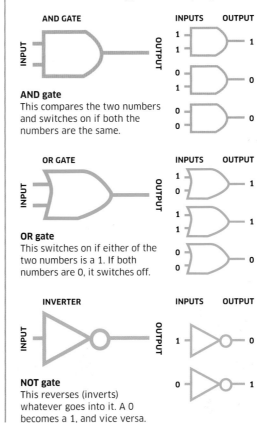

AND gate
This compares the two numbers and switches on if both the numbers are the same.

OR gate
This switches on if either of the two numbers is a 1. If both numbers are 0, it switches off.

NOT gate
This reverses (inverts) whatever goes into it. A 0 becomes a 1, and vice versa.

Calculators

Calculators use logic gate circuits to add and subtract numbers. Dividing is done by subtracting repeatedly; multiplying is done by adding a number over and over again.

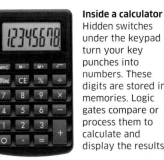

Inside a calculator
Hidden switches under the keypad turn your key punches into numbers. These digits are stored in memories. Logic gates compare or process them to calculate and display the results.

Memory

Computers store information as well as process it. This happens in memories made from transistors. To store a word, a computer converts it into a pattern of zeros and ones called binary code. Each zero or one is stored by its own transistor, switched on or off.

1010101010101000010100010101010100001000010101010100111001001010101010101001111

BINARY CODE

242 science ○ ELECTRONICS

Facebook has over a billion users—more than the individual populations of **every country in the world** except China and India.

Digital world

What's better, a computer or a brain? Computers can rattle through billions of equations every second and tell you the name of every king and queen that has ever lived. But the fastest supercomputer on the planet is less powerful than a mouse's brain and takes up a million times more space.

Computers are electronic machines we can use to do many different things just by changing the instructions (programs) stored inside them. The first computers were little more than giant calculators. Later, people found that computers had superb memories: they could store more information much more reliably than the human brain. Many people now use their computers as communication tools to make friends, send emails, and share the things they like. This is possible because virtually all of the world's computers are connected together in a giant worldwide network called the Internet. Part computer and part human brain, the online world of the Internet brings us the best of both.

Early Computers

Computers are based on calculators that simply add numbers. The first mechanical calculators appeared in the 17th century. When people found ways to make calculators automatic, computers were born. The first electronic computer that could be programmed to do different jobs was ENIAC, completed in 1946. It was bigger than a delivery truck and had more than 100,000 separate parts.

Difference Engine
Mathematician Charles Babbage (1791–1871) was the first person to design a computer that worked by itself. Babbage never finished the Difference Engine in his lifetime, but this impressive replica was built after his death.

How a computer works

Computers are electronic machines that take in information, record it, work on it in various ways, and then show the results of what they've done. These four stages are called input, storage, processing, and output, and they're carried out by separate pieces of equipment. You can input information using a keyboard, mouse, touchscreen, or microphone. The information is usually stored in either a hard drive or memory chips. Processing is done by the main processor chips. The results are output on a screen or spoken through speakers.

Processor chip
Also known as a microprocessor, this is a complex integrated circuit that carries out all of the computer's main operations. The more powerful the microprocessor, the faster it can work through problems.

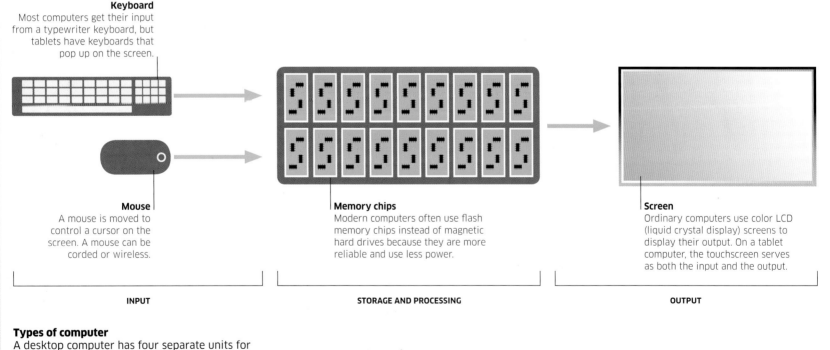

Keyboard
Most computers get their input from a typewriter keyboard, but tablets have keyboards that pop up on the screen.

Mouse
A mouse is moved to control a cursor on the screen. A mouse can be corded or wireless.

Memory chips
Modern computers often use flash memory chips instead of magnetic hard drives because they are more reliable and use less power.

Screen
Ordinary computers use color LCD (liquid crystal display) screens to display their output. On a tablet computer, the touchscreen serves as both the input and the output.

INPUT   **STORAGE AND PROCESSING**   **OUTPUT**

Types of computer
A desktop computer has four separate units for the keyboard, mouse, processor, and screen. Laptops have all of these things built into a single, portable unit. Tablet computers squeeze the same parts into even less space by building the keyboard and mouse into the screen.

THERE ARE MORE MOBILE DEVICES CONNECTED TO THE INTERNET THAN THERE ARE PEOPLE ON EARTH.

90 percent of the **data in the entire world** has been created within **the last two years**.

70 percent of people in **developed countries** have **access to the Internet**, compared to only 24 percent in **developing countries**.

243

How the Internet works

The Internet is a worldwide network that links together virtually every computer on the planet—well over a billion of them. Each computer has its own address (Internet Protocol, or IP, address) so that any other machine on the network can instantly send emails or messages to it or receive them from it.

1 Sender's computer breaks photo into many tiny digital packets.

2 Each packet is labeled with the destination address.

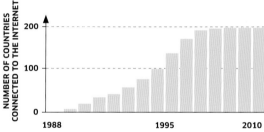

3 Separate packets travel across different routes over the Internet.

5 Receiver sees the final picture as though it traveled in one piece.

4 Pieces are reassembled at the end.

Packet switching
When you email a photo, it doesn't travel over the Internet in one big lump. Instead, it's broken into tiny packets. Each one is given the final IP address and travels separately. This makes data stream across the Internet very efficiently.

Supercomputers

Some scientific problems are so huge and complex that an ordinary home computer might take years to solve them. For intricate problems, such as weather forecasting, we need more powerful computers that work a different way. Some of them have tens of thousands of processors all working on a problem at once.

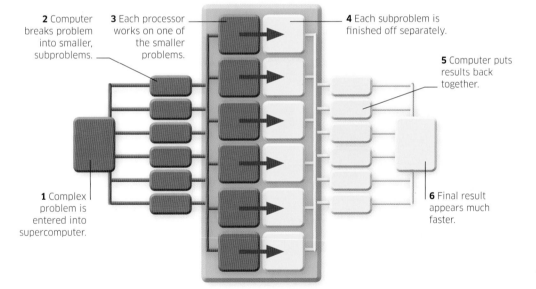

1 Complex problem is entered into supercomputer.

2 Computer breaks problem into smaller, subproblems.

3 Each processor works on one of the smaller problems.

4 Each subproblem is finished off separately.

5 Computer puts results back together.

6 Final result appears much faster.

How supercomputers work
Most giant supercomputers use a system called parallel processing, where problems are broken up into small bits and tackled by separate processors. Although it takes time to break up and reassemble problems, overall it's much faster to work this way.

NASA supercomputer
The American space agency NASA runs this powerful supercomputer called Pleiades. It has 112,896 individual processors arranged inside 185 separate workstations.

150 billion—the estimated number of **emails sent across the Internet every day.**

Getting online

Well over half the world's population is now online. People in richer countries, such as the US, were first to get connected in the mid-1990s, but even people in some of the poorest developing countries are now online. Having access to up-to-date information is expected to make it easier for people in poorer countries to gain a decent education.

NUMBER OF COUNTRIES CONNECTED TO THE INTERNET

200

100

0

1988   1995   2010

Number of countries online
After the World Wide Web was invented in 1989, lots of countries went online. By the early 2000s, people in virtually every nation were connected.

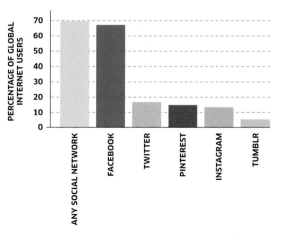

PERCENTAGE OF GLOBAL INTERNET USERS

70
60
50
40
30
20
10
0

ANY SOCIAL NETWORK | FACEBOOK | TWITTER | PINTEREST | INSTAGRAM | TUMBLR

Social networks
Many people use their computers for chatting with friends and sharing photos or news. Popular websites such as Facebook and Twitter have hundreds of millions of regular users.

244 science ∘ **ELECTRONICS**

1966 The year the **first-ever factory robot**, Unimate, appeared on a TV show, where it **hit a golf ball**, **poured a glass of beer**, and **conducted an orchestra**.

Robotics

Ingenious inventors have dreamed up machines that can do almost anything, from playing chess to exploring Mars. But there's no single robot that can do everything—yet.

Part mechanical and part electronic, robots are automated machines that clank, scuttle, and whiz around doing dirty and dangerous jobs that people prefer not to. Robots sniff out bombs, drag survivors from earthquakes, and can even make nuclear explosions safe.

Most robots that exist today can't think for themselves, and have to be reprogrammed every time they do something new. In the future, robots might become autonomous—with built-in computer brains, they will think for themselves, learn from their mistakes, and possibly do things even better than humans.

Digital camera

Four microphones
These pick up spoken commands and help to locate where sound is coming from.

Sonar sensors
These detect nearby obstacles so NAO can avoid them.

Moving limbs
Gears attached to electric motors control limb movements precisely.

Eyes
Behind the eye sockets, two detectors fire out beams of infrared radiation and pick up the reflections. NAO uses these infrared sensors to communicate with other devices, such as TVs. It also has two digital cameras mounted in its head, taking photos that enable it to recognize objects such as faces and balls.

Stereo speakers play music and speak

NAO robot

This robot, built by Aldebaran Robotics in France, is determined to be your friend. It can recognize your face, hear what you're saying, speak back in 19 languages, and even dance. Like a person, it senses things around it, thinks about them, and responds. Unlike a person, it does these things with 50 electronic sensors, a microprocessor (computer chip) brain, and limbs moved by 25 electric motors.

Chest
NAO's chest is a busy hub filled with electronic circuit boards that are used to control its different joints and sensors.

Prehensile hands
Fingers with knuckles can grasp things firmly but gently.

Factory robots that are built for welding can **join metal together** about **three times faster** than humans.

The world's **smallest robot** is less than **half the size of a comma.**

245

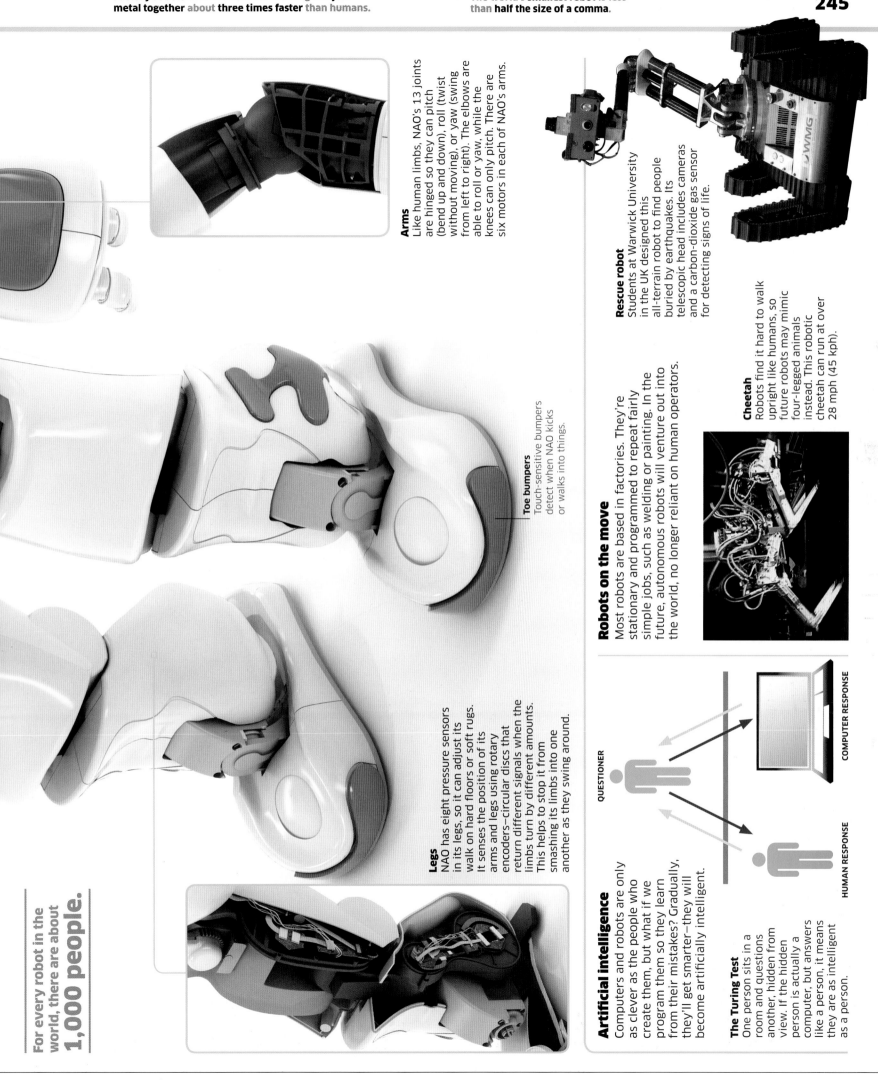

For every robot in the world, there are about **1,000 people.**

Arms

Like human limbs, NAO's 13 joints are hinged so they can pitch (bend up and down), roll (twist without moving), or yaw (swing from left to right). The elbows are able to roll or yaw, while the knees can only pitch. There are six motors in each of NAO's arms.

Toe bumpers
Touch-sensitive bumpers detect when NAO kicks or walks into things.

Legs

NAO has eight pressure sensors in its legs, so it can adjust its walk on hard floors or soft rugs. It senses the position of its arms and legs using rotary encoders–circular discs that return different signals when the limbs turn by different amounts. This helps to stop it from smashing its limbs into one another as they swing around.

Rescue robot

Students at Warwick University in the UK designed this all-terrain robot to find people buried by earthquakes. Its telescopic head includes cameras and a carbon-dioxide gas sensor for detecting signs of life.

Robots on the move

Most robots are based in factories. They're stationary and programmed to repeat fairly simple jobs, such as welding or painting. In the future, autonomous robots will venture out into the world, no longer reliant on human operators.

Cheetah

Robots find it hard to walk upright like humans, so future robots may mimic four-legged animals instead. This robotic cheetah can run at over 28 mph (45 kph).

Artificial intelligence

Computers and robots are only as clever as the people who create them, but what if we program them so they learn from their mistakes? Gradually, they'll get smarter–they will become artificially intelligent.

The Turing Test

One person sits in a room and questions another, hidden from view. If the hidden person is actually a computer, but answers like a person, it means they are as intelligent as a person.

QUESTIONER

COMPUTER RESPONSE

HUMAN RESPONSE

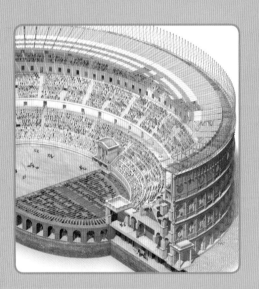

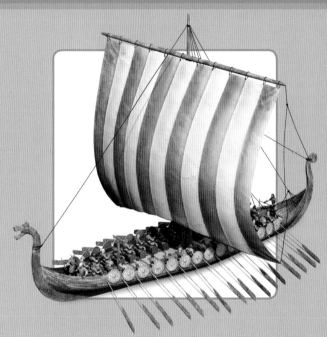

HISTORY

Human history includes terrible wars and disasters, but also amazing advances in culture and technology. From the Stone Age to the Space Age, great civilizations have risen and fallen, shaping the world we live in today.

THE ANCIENT WORLD

The story of humanity begins with our earliest human ancestors, hardly distinguishable from apes, who appeared in Africa around 7 million years ago. The first modern humans only developed about 200,000 years ago. They spread throughout the globe, starting out as isolated bands of hunters, but eventually settling in farming villages, and later founding small towns and cities. Stone tools were replaced by metal, and around 8,000 years ago, villages began to grow into cities. By 500 BCE, the Classical period had begun, in which advanced cultures across the globe created great empires with cities full of magnificent buildings, and made enormous strides in human knowledge.

THE RISE OF THE EMPIRES

The first cities emerged around 4000 BCE in Mesopotamia (modern Iraq) and Egypt. The great rivers of these areas made the land fertile and prosperous, providing enough food to support larger communities of people living together. The rulers of some of these early cities became wealthy and powerful, taking control of surrounding lands to build the first kingdoms. Some sent their armies to conquer neighboring states, creating the first empires.

First cities

The first cities of Mesopotamia were built by a people called the Sumerians. They grew rich thanks to new farming methods and more productive crops. This allowed them to build temples and palaces in mini-kingdoms (or city-states) such as Uruk, Ur, Nippur, and Lagash. They were soon followed by cities in other regions such as Egypt. The invention of writing around 3100 BCE made it easier for rulers to keep records and for merchants to trade.

Ruins of Karnak Temple Complex, Egypt
The Ancient Egyptians were capable of creating elaborate, large-scale buildings, as the vast ruins at Karnak show.

THE STONE AGE

Around 2.6 million years ago, one humanlike species, *Homo habilis*, began to use stones as tools. For more than 2.5 million years after this, people lived in small groups, hunting with stone axes and spears, and gathering roots, berries, and other plants. They lived in caves or shelters made of branches, and used fire to cook.

Cave art
Early humans created the world's first art: paintings on the walls of deep caves that showed the animals they hunted.

Early humans

Modern humans (*Homo sapiens*) spread from Africa across the globe. Their most successful migration began around 60,000 years ago, when much of the Earth was in the grip of an ice age. Highly intelligent and adaptable, they replaced the Neanderthals (a humanlike species) in Europe, built boats to reach Australia, and crossed the frozen ocean to North America in about 15,000 BCE. These early humans developed sophisticated stone tools, invented the bow and arrow, and created the first musical instruments.

First villages

About 8,000 years ago, humans began to form larger groups and settle in villages. They built houses out of whatever materials were available nearby. Most villagers farmed the surrounding land. Since time previously spent hunting was freed up, specialists, such as potters, builders, and priests, appeared.

Çatalhöyük, Turkey
Mud brick houses built close together.

Khirokitia, Cyprus
Round houses built of stone.

Scotland
Long family houses made of wood and sod.

Orkney, Scotland
These stone houses even had stone beds.

From stone to metal

People began to make simple metal tools around 7000 BCE. Copper was used first, and later alloyed (mixed) with tin to make bronze—a harder metal suitable for armor and weapons. From around 1000 BCE, blacksmiths learned how to make iron, which was even stronger.

- **8000 BCE** Cold working (hammering of gold or copper) is the first type of metalworking.
- **5500 BCE** Copper smelting (heating of ores to extract pure metal) appears in the Middle East.
- **3200 BCE** Metal casting, the molding of molten metal, is first used in Mesopotamia.
- **3000 BCE** Bronze is created by adding tin to copper in a smelting furnace to make harder tools.
- **1300 BCE** In Egypt, furnaces with bellows create the heat needed for iron smelting.

HUMANS' DISTANT ANCESTORS FIRST USED STONE TOOLS MORE THAN 2.6 MILLION YEARS AGO.

Agriculture

Farming began around 11,000 BCE when communities in the Fertile Crescent, an area of the Middle East, began to sow and harvest wild rye seeds. Gradually, farmers developed more productive crops, and also tamed animals such as cattle and sheep. As the food supply became more reliable, larger villages and small towns appeared.

Yoke attaches to shoulders of beasts such as oxen

Stone or metal blade for cutting through the soil

An early plow
Plows were developed to cut furrows in the soil, so that seeds could be sown. This was far easier than breaking up the ground with hoes, and allowed more land to be used for farming.

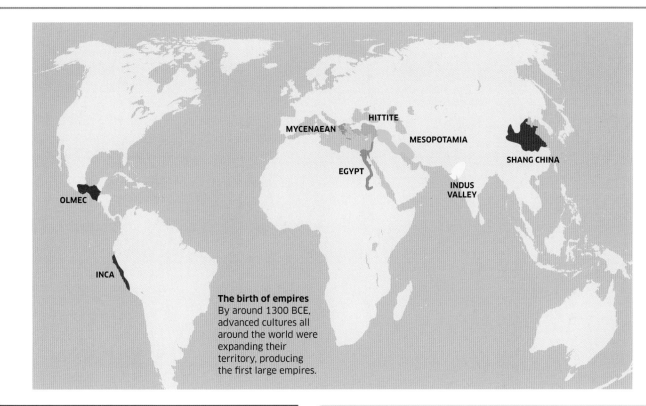

The birth of empires
By around 1300 BCE, advanced cultures all around the world were expanding their territory, producing the first large empires.

The early kingdoms

Early civilizations varied widely. Some were empires united by a strong ruler, others were alliances of city-states.

- **The Egyptians** Around 3100 BCE, Ancient Egypt was united to create an advanced civilization that would last for 3,000 years.

- **The Indus Valley** Around 2600 BCE, large cities arose on the River Indus. They shared a system of trade and writing, but did not form an empire.

- **Mesopotamia** Sargon of Akkad united rival city-states around 2300 BCE, founding the first great empire of the Middle East.

- **The Hittites** Anatolia (modern Turkey) was ruled by the Hittites, fierce enemies of the Egyptians, from 1800 to 1200 BCE.

- **Shang China** The Shang ruled China from 1766 to 1122 BCE, fighting off raiders from the north and rival kingdoms to the east.

- **The Olmec** Giant pyramid temples, built from about 1500 BCE, mark Olmec cities on the coast of Mexico.

Megaliths

Around 5000 BCE, people began building megaliths (large monuments made from huge pieces of stone), mainly in northern and western Europe. Their exact purpose is unknown, but many may have functioned as a type of calendar, measuring out the seasons and the passage of the sun and moon.

Important megaliths

1 GÖBEKLI TEPE, TURKEY
The earliest known megalith, built around 8000 BCE, is a hilltop temple with massive pillars of limestone that may originally have supported a roof.

2 CARNAC, FRANCE
This series of over 3,000 standing stones (menhirs) was set up between 4500 and 3000 BCE. The rows, or alignments, may have had some astronomical significance.

3 STONEHENGE, ENGLAND
A series of large bluestones formed the first circle at Stonehenge in around 2500 BCE. Giant sandstones, along with huge stone crosspieces, were added 200 years later.

4 NEWGRANGE, IRELAND
This tomb, built around 3200 BCE, consists of a room with a massive stone roof, topped by an earth mound. The dark interior of the tomb is lit up once a year by the rays of the rising sun shining down the connecting passageway.

THE CLASSICAL WORLD

From around 500 BCE, the great civilizations of Greece, Rome, Persia, India, China, and Central America reached new levels of sophistication and power. They developed scientific ideas, and rich forms of art and writing. New religions emerged, such as Buddhism and Christianity. Larger empires were able to support larger armies, which led to long and bitter wars, such as those between Rome and Carthage, and Greece and Persia.

Conquering the world

Wealth, organization, and ambition drove Classical civilizations to build empires far bigger than the world had seen before. Some, like the Persian Empire, ruled vast areas of wilderness lined with important trade routes. Others, such as the Roman Empire, expanded into busy, populated areas, spreading their culture in the form of laws, art, buildings, and religion.

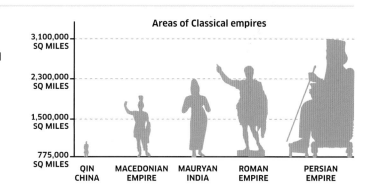

Areas of Classical empires

3,100,000 SQ MILES	
2,300,000 SQ MILES	
1,500,000 SQ MILES	
775,000 SQ MILES	QIN CHINA — MACEDONIAN EMPIRE — MAURYAN INDIA — ROMAN EMPIRE — PERSIAN EMPIRE

THE FIRST EMPEROR OF CHINA, QIN SHI HUANG,
IS BURIED IN A TOMB GUARDED BY AN ARMY OF MORE THAN 8,000 TERRA-COTTA SOLDIERS.

New thinking

During the Classical period, the first philosophers and scientists emerged, as well as new ideas in astronomy, mathematics, physics, medicine, and architecture.

Math
Greeks such as Pythagoras and Archimedes established key principles of math, while the Chinese developed tools such as the abacus for calculating.

Politics and law
Classical Athens saw the world's first democracy, in the 5th century BCE. In China at around the same time, Kong Fuzi (Confucius) laid out an ethical system for the law.

Medicine
Early texts of the Ayurveda (Hindu medicine) appeared in India in the 6th century BCE. Hippocrates turned medicine into a science in Greece in the 5th century BCE.

Philosophy
Great thinkers across the world began to ask questions about who we are and how we should live. Plato, Aristotle, and Socrates are some of the most famous.

Homo neanderthalenis
Homo neanderthalensis (Neanderthal man) evolved around 200,000 years ago in southern Europe. They were heavily built, with bulky bodies that resisted the cold of the ice age well. Their brains were large and there is evidence they buried their dead.

Sharp flint blades
Early humans learned how to make sharper blades, like this one from 300,000 years ago, by striking the shape of blade they wanted off a larger flint stone (rather than by chiseling a blade out of the larger stone).

Rise of the modern human
The last million years have seen dramatic advances in human evolution. Our own species, *Homo sapiens*, appeared. All other humanlike species became extinct, while modern humans flourished and civilization began.

1 MILLION YEARS AGO

Homo erectus
Homo erectus lived between 1.9 million and 200,000 years ago. They are thought to be the first species to build shared fireplaces (hearths) for cooking food.

The first humans

The earliest humanlike animals, our ancestors, evolved from apes millions of years ago. Many different species rose up and died out before modern humans appeared.

Around 5 to 8 million years ago (MYA), the line that would lead to modern humans split off from chimpanzees—the living animals most similar to us today. Over millions of years, these ancestors (or hominins) gradually evolved, developing legs suitable for walking upright, smaller jaws, and larger brains.

Varied diet
These teeth belonged to a hominin known as *Paranthropus boisei*, which lived between 2.3 and 1.4 MYA. Their large back teeth were adapted for chewing tough plant material such as roots and nuts.

The course of human evolution

Scientists have discovered the remains of many different hominins. We can learn a lot from these skeletons, such as how a particular species walked (whether on two legs or on all-fours) and what they ate.

Olduvai settlement
Olduvai Gorge in Tanzania was the site of an ancient lake. Several species of hominins lived here from 2.6 MYA, and the site was inhabited for almost 2 million years. Some of the earliest known stone tools were found here.

7 MILLION YEARS AGO

From tree to ground
Hominins developed from apes living in trees on the edge of African forests. Some began to spend more time on the ground and eventually learned how to walk on two legs.

Sahelanthropus tchadensis
Sahelanthropus lived about 7 MYA in the grasslands and forests of western Africa. They probably walked on two legs, had smaller canine (cutting) teeth than apes, and brains not much larger than a chimpanzee's.

Walking upright
This femur (thigh bone) belongs to a species called *Orrorin tugenensis*, which lived about 6.2 MYA. The bone's shape and thickness suggest this may have been one of the earliest hominins to walk on two legs.

40 in (1 m)—the **average height** of *Homo habilis*.

17,000 The **number of years** ago *Homo floriensis*, the **last** surviving **human** species, apart from ours, **became extinct.**

251

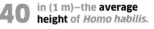

Homo sapiens
Our species developed in Africa around 200,000 years ago and began to spread about 100,000 years later. With large brains and able to use spoken language, *Homo sapiens* were very adaptable and learned to make advanced tools.

Cave painting
Around 40,000 years ago, early humans began to make paintings deep inside caves, evidence they had developed the idea of art. Paintings often show animals these early people hunted and may have had a magical meaning.

Agriculture, pottery, writing
Humans made rapid advances after the last ice age ended 11,000 years ago. Agriculture and pottery were invented and people began to live in farming villages. Around 6,000 years ago, the first towns appeared and writing developed.

Paleolithic hand axe
A stone called flint was used to make early tools, since it can be chipped into sharp edges. One common tool was a hand axe, like this one from 1.7 MYA, made by striking chunks off a large piece of flint using another stone.

Homo ergaster
Originally seen as a separate species, *Homo ergaster* is now thought to be a variety of *Homo Erectus*. They had larger brains than earlier hominins, and used more complex tools than *Homo habilis*.

Homo habilis
Homo habilis lived between 2.4 and 1.4 MYA. They are the earliest species known to have used stone tools—the first step on the long road to civilization.

2 MILLION YEARS AGO

Out of Africa
The earliest hominins all lived in Africa. It wasn't until just less than 2 MYA that new species began to spread to other parts of the world. They developed new tools and settled as far away as East Asia.

▶

3 MILLION YEARS AGO

The first humans
Around this time, the first hominins belonging to the genus *Homo* (the group of species that includes modern humans) appeared in East Africa. Stone tools came into use around 2.6 MYA, marking the beginning of the Palaeolithic Age, or Early Stone Age.

Australopithecus africanus
Like many early species, these hominins had prominent ridges above their eyes. They lived in grassy areas and probably ate tough plant material and soft fruit. Scientists know they were bipedal from the shape of their hip and leg bones.

◀

Lighter bodies
Between 4 and 2 MYA, a group of species called australopithecines were the most successful hominins. They had larger brains than our previous ancestors, and they were less heavily built than apes.

4 MILLION YEARS AGO

Australopithecus afarensis
This species lived from 3.9–2.9 MYA. Their fingers were long and powerful, good for grasping but not suitable for delicately moving small objects. They were also bipedal (they walked on two legs).

◀

252 history ○ **THE ANCIENT WORLD**

Stone Age rituals included **coating the skulls of the dead in clay** to make new faces.

7500 BCE—the date of the earliest known **manufactured cloth.**

The first towns

During the late Stone Age, nomadic tribes of hunters began to settle down. They planted crops instead of gathering food from the wild, and built farms and houses instead of living on the move.

Farming offered a more reliable food source than hunting and gathering. Farmers could grow the most fruitful crops and breed the fattest and most peaceful livestock, so that they could produce more food every year. Extra food could be stored in case of later famine, and permanent houses made of brick or sometimes stone provided a base to store food and tools.

Staying in one place made these settlers vulnerable to raiders, who could steal livestock and stores. Townspeople had to be able to defend themselves—for example, by building walls around their homes. They also exchanged spare food and goods with other tribes, sometimes over long distances, marking the beginnings of global trade.

Stone Age tools

The earliest settlements grew up during the Stone Age, before humans had begun to use metal. Their inhabitants made tools from whatever materials they could find. The most useful were hard substances that were easy to carve or chip into shape. Wood could be used for bows, spears, or axe handles. Stone such as flint and obsidian (volcanic glass) was chipped into sharp edges, to make arrowheads, knives, and hammers. Bones from animals could be carved into fine points to make needles and combs.

WOOD

FLINT

BONE

OBSIDIAN

Çatalhöyük

This settlement, in modern Turkey, is one of the largest early towns yet discovered. Up to 8,000 people lived here from 7400–6000 BCE. The houses were packed together with only small spaces in between, so that any attackers would find it hard to gain access.

Rooftop culture
The town's roofs were the main streets. Many daily activities took place outside.

Animal skins
Hunting was still a vital source of food, and also provided skins for clothing, and bones and antlers for making tools.

Woven cloth shelter

Wooden beams

Mud brick walls
Mud from the nearby marshes was formed into bricks, which were hardened by drying in the sun.

Roof made of dried reeds

Useful cattle
Wild oxen were tamed later than sheep, but provided larger quantities of milk and meat.

Sheep and goats
Domesticating these animals offered a steady supply of milk, meat, and wool.

Shared spaces
The areas between houses were mostly used to pen livestock and dump garbage. They may also have been used as gardens.

Hunters sometimes **embedded bones and horns in** the walls of houses **as trophies**.

20 football fields—the **area of** Çatalhöyük at its height.

Holes in the roofs of Çatalhöyük houses acted as **chimneys, windows, and doorways** all in one.

253

Weaving
The invention of the loom provided strong, colorful cloth for clothing, blankets, and decoration.

Main entrance on roof

Gathering food
Although farming provided a regular food supply, people still needed to gather fruit, nuts, and berries.

Beasts of burden
Cattle could be used for labor such as carrying burdens and plowing.

Hunting scene
The walls of some houses were painted with scenes from everyday life, such as hunting.

Wall paintings

Grave site
At Çatalhöyük, the dead were buried under clay platforms in the floors of the houses.

The people of Çatalhöyük slept on clay platforms under which they buried their ancestors' bones.

Animal helper
Animals were not just tamed for food. Dogs helped with hunting and herding, and protected livestock.

Working in clay
Permanent fireplaces were used to bake clay into hard terra-cotta. This allowed people to make durable pots and dishes, as well as decorative objects, such as this statue. It was found in a food store at Çatalhöyük, and is thought to be a religious idol.

10 football fields could fit inside the area occupied by Nebuchadnezzar's palace.

Early empires

As early towns grew, they had to develop new systems of government, new means to store and distribute food, and new ways to protect themselves. The strongest settlements expanded their territory by conquering their neighbors, creating the first empires.

One of the most powerful early empires belonged to the Babylonians. In the 18th century BCE, they conquered a large area in what is now the Middle East, but were then defeated by their rivals, the Hittites. They rose to power again in the 6th century BCE, and their capital city, Babylon, became one of the richest and most magnificent in the ancient world.

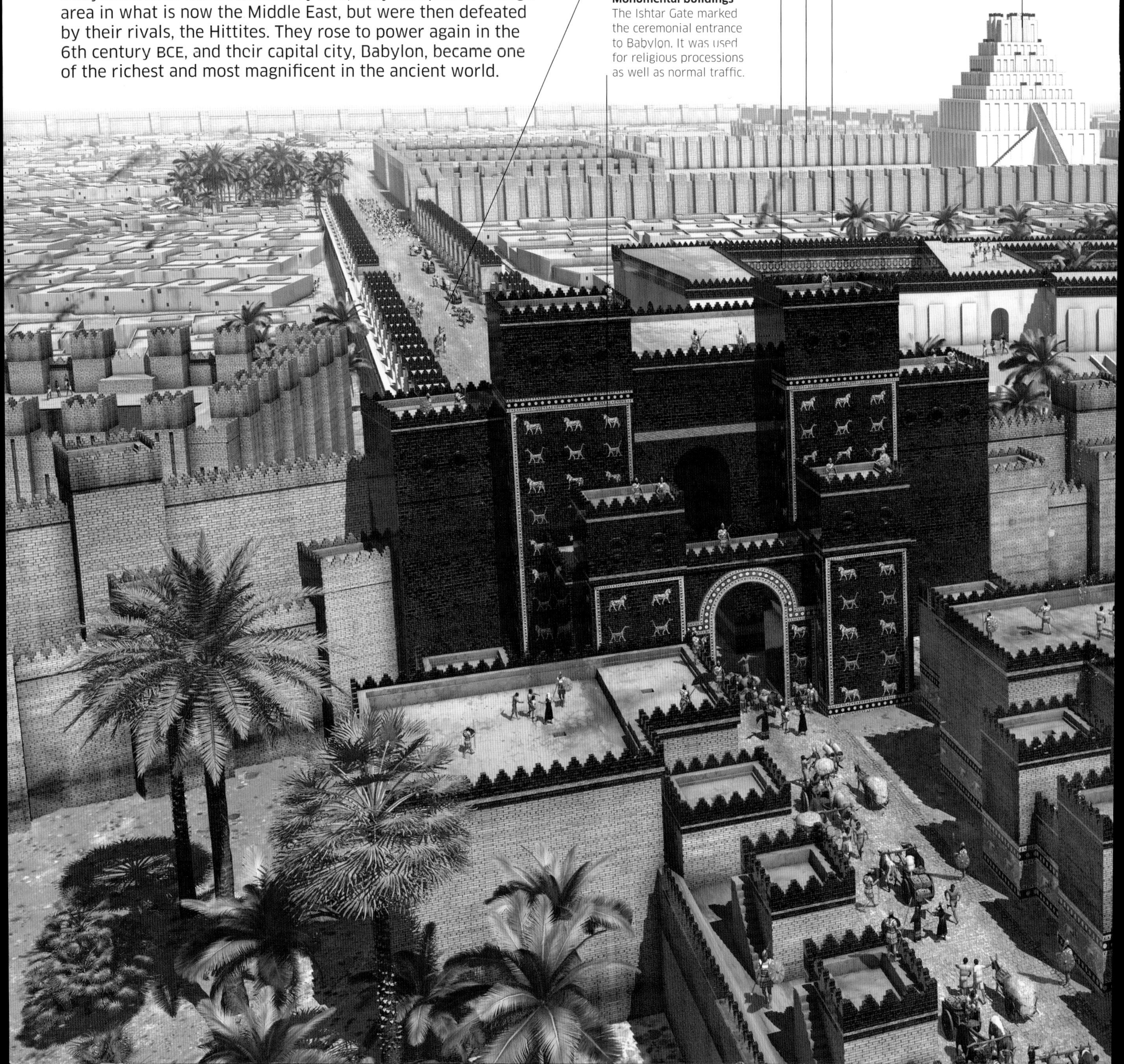

Public spaces
The processional way ran through the city, lined with blue patterned tiles. It was used for public gatherings and religious rituals.
Temple enclosures walled off
Organized religion
The Etemenanki Ziggurat was a temple dedicated to Marduk, the patron god of the city.
Private houses
Ordinary houses were built of mud bricks, with a central courtyard. They are thought to have had no windows, to keep out the desert heat.
Tiled wall patterns
Monumental buildings
The Ishtar Gate marked the ceremonial entrance to Babylon. It was used for religious processions as well as normal traffic.

43 major **religious shrines** were sited in the **city of Babylon**.

100 years—the **time to rebuild Etemenanki** after it was **destroyed by invaders**.

15 million bricks are said to have been used to build the **walls of Babylon**.

255

The city of Babylon

This great city sat at the heart of the Babylonian Empire. The huge buildings were constructed around 580 BCE by King Nebuchadnezzar II, who wanted his capital to be the most magnificent city in the region.

Royal palace
The lavish royal palace was the symbol of the king's power, designed to inspire awe in his subjects and enemies.

Large courtyards in palace complex

City walls
Wealthy cities were targets for raiding nomads and enemy armies. Babylon was defended by strong walls of mud brick.

Wonders of the World
The Hanging Gardens of Babylon were one of the Seven Wonders of the World. Nobody knows for sure where they stood, but the foundations of terraced gardens were found in Babylon in the early 20th century.

Defensive technology
Babylon was famously well defended. Soldiers on the walls could rain rocks, spears, and arrows down on any attackers.

River Euphrates
Early cities depended on water supplies for drinking and fertile soils for farming. The Euphrates provided both, as well as a vital trade route for boats.

Cradle of civilization

Mesopotamia, the land between the Tigris and Euphrates Rivers, had very fertile soil, making it ideal for farming. As a result it was home to a number of settlements, some of which, such as Nineveh, Ur, and Babylon, became very powerful. The first empire in the region was the Akkadian Empire, founded by Sargon the Great in around 2330 BCE. Sargon built a new city, Agade, as his capital. Its location is not known, but is thought to be near Babylon.

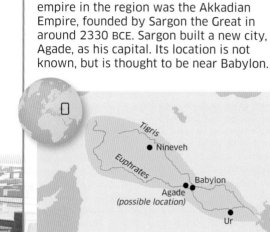

Monumental buildings

The rulers of new empires often ordered their subjects to build great monuments. This was a good way to demonstrate their power and wealth, and impress their enemies and rivals. The great Etemenanki Ziggurat in Babylon is thought to have been 300 ft (90 m) tall—that's twice the height of the Statue of Liberty in New York City. However, it was dwarfed by the Great Pyramid at Giza, which rose to 479 ft (146 m) and was the tallest building in the world for more than 3,700 years.

490 FT (150 M)

| GREAT PYRAMID | ETEMENANKI ZIGGURAT | STATUE OF LIBERTY |

Code of law

As empires grew, their people required detailed written laws to resolve disputes and protect property. The Babylonian king Hammurabi created a detailed system of laws in about 1750 BCE, with brutal punishments if they were broken.

"BRING ABOUT THE RULE OF RIGHTEOUSNESS IN THE LAND, **DESTROY THE WICKED** AND THE EVILDOERS, SO THAT THE **STRONG SHOULD NOT HARM THE WEAK"**
HAMMURABI'S CODE OF LAW

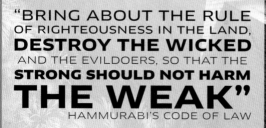

Ancient Egypt

For more than 3,000 years, Egypt was home to one of the most advanced civilizations of the ancient world. They left behind many clues about their way of life, from religious texts to huge, mysterious pyramids.

The Ancient Egyptians were ruled by kings called pharaohs, who were thought to be the children of the gods. Their complex society had strict layers—from priests, governors, and mayors to soldiers and peasants—and they developed a detailed system of writing to keep records of wealth and ownership.

Egyptian life was full of ritual. They worshipped hundreds of gods and goddesses, and the pharaohs and priests performed complex rituals to ensure good crops, keep away disease, and bring success in war. They also built massive tombs for their dead, many of them stuffed with gold and treasure.

Words in pictures

Ancient Egyptian writing used pictures called hieroglyphics. Each symbol could represent a sound, a word, or an action. Instead of paper, the Egyptians used flattened sheets of a type of reed called papyrus. Inscriptions could also be pressed into clay, painted on pottery, or carved in stone. Writing was seen as a gift from Thoth, the god of wisdom, and only priests and specially trained scribes were taught how to read and write.

Famous names

The names of important figures, such as kings and queens, were written inside an oval called a cartouche, as a symbol of eternal life.

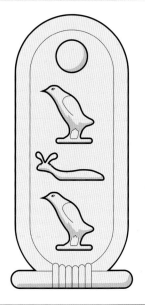

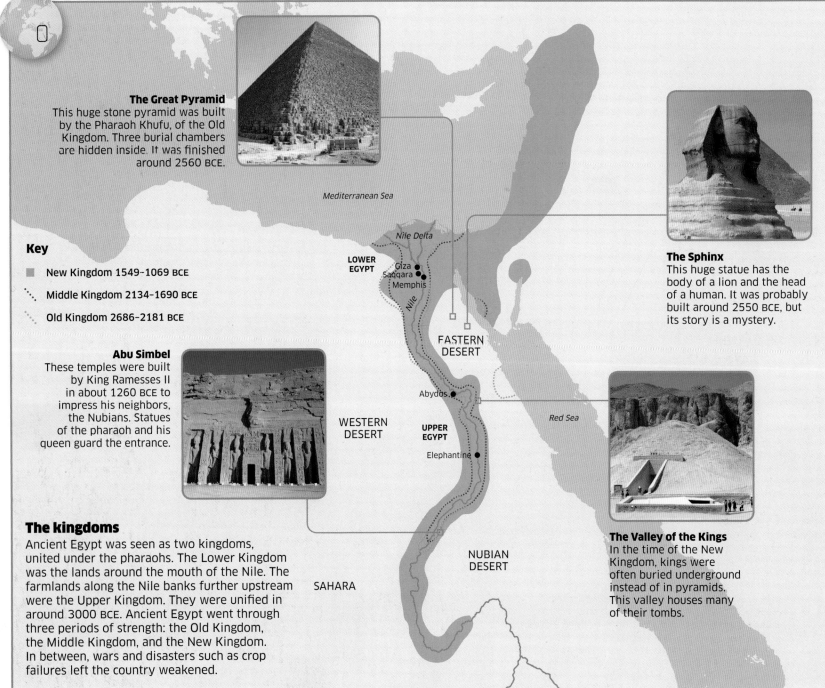

The Great Pyramid
This huge stone pyramid was built by the Pharaoh Khufu, of the Old Kingdom. Three burial chambers are hidden inside. It was finished around 2560 BCE.

The Sphinx
This huge statue has the body of a lion and the head of a human. It was probably built around 2550 BCE, but its story is a mystery.

Mediterranean Sea

Nile Delta

LOWER EGYPT

Giza
Saqqara
Memphis

Nile

FASTERN DESERT

Abydos

Red Sea

WESTERN DESERT

UPPER EGYPT

Elephantine

Key

■ New Kingdom 1549–1069 BCE

∴ Middle Kingdom 2134–1690 BCE

∴ Old Kingdom 2686–2181 BCE

Abu Simbel
These temples were built by King Ramesses II in about 1260 BCE to impress his neighbors, the Nubians. Statues of the pharaoh and his queen guard the entrance.

The Valley of the Kings
In the time of the New Kingdom, kings were often buried underground instead of in pyramids. This valley houses many of their tombs.

NUBIAN DESERT

SAHARA

The kingdoms

Ancient Egypt was seen as two kingdoms, united under the pharaohs. The Lower Kingdom was the lands around the mouth of the Nile. The farmlands along the Nile banks further upstream were the Upper Kingdom. They were unified in around 3000 BCE. Ancient Egypt went through three periods of strength: the Old Kingdom, the Middle Kingdom, and the New Kingdom. In between, wars and disasters such as crop failures left the country weakened.

10 loaves of bread–the daily wage of Egyptian laborers.

The Ancient Egyptians made **boats** out of **dried reeds to sail** up and down **the Nile**.

2,000 The approximate number of **Egyptian gods and goddesses**.

257

Journey of the dead

The Egyptians believed that the soul of a dead person undertook a perilous journey to another world. After death, the soul wandered the underworld until it could be judged by the gods. The god Anubis would weigh their hearts to measure their worth. Good people were rewarded with a happy afterlife, but bad people were devoured by Ammit, a fearsome beast with the head of a crocodile, the chest of a lion, and the torso of a hippopotamus.

Scales of judgment
The dead person's heart sits on the left side of the scales. On the other side is the feather of truth. An evil person's heart will be heavier than the feather.

The gods bear witness
The soul of the dead person would also have to swear before the gods that they had not sinned.

God of the dead
The jackal-headed god Anubis makes sure the scales are even.

Terrible fate
Ammit waits ready to devour the souls of people who have lived an evil life.

God of wisdom
Thoth, the ibis-headed god of wisdom, records the judgment.

Life on the Nile

Egypt is surrounded by desert, so the ancient kingdom depended entirely on the River Nile. Every year the river flooded, submerging the farmland along its banks. The floods washed rich soil down from the highlands to the south. The Egyptians built ditches and low walls to trap the mud and water in fields along each side of the river, giving them fertile soil in which to grow crops such as wheat, barley, grapes, and vegetables. The whole kingdom depended on the floods. In a dry year, many people would starve.

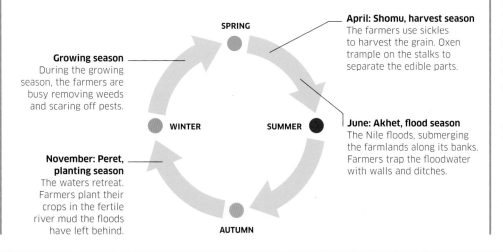

April: Shomu, harvest season
The farmers use sickles to harvest the grain. Oxen trample on the stalks to separate the edible parts.

Growing season
During the growing season, the farmers are busy removing weeds and scaring off pests.

June: Akhet, flood season
The Nile floods, submerging the farmlands along its banks. Farmers trap the floodwater with walls and ditches.

November: Peret, planting season
The waters retreat. Farmers plant their crops in the fertile river mud the floods have left behind.

SPRING

SUMMER

WINTER

AUTUMN

Gods and goddesses

The Egyptians worshipped a large number of gods, often in the form of animals and natural forces. The greatest god was Ra, the sun god, who created the universe. Cow-headed Hathor was goddess of motherhood. The god of wisdom, Thoth, had the head of an ibis, while Sobek, god of the Nile, was shown as a crocodile. The goddess Nut arched her body over the earth to form the sky.

Symbols of Ra
The god Ra journeys across the sky as the sun. The disc on his head produces light. He stands on a boat that sails across the sky from morning until night.

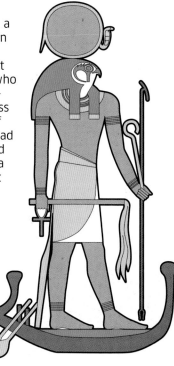

Entrance hall
A short entrance corridor sloped downward into the tomb.

Gold-covered couches with animal heads

Rock-cut walls
The walls were bare rock, chiseled to a smooth finish.

Four full-size chariots

Steps to surface
The tomb was cut into the rock of the valley floor. It was reached by a flight of 16 stone steps.

The pharaohs

Ancient Egypt was ruled by the pharaohs, powerful kings who were worshipped as gods. They are most famous today for their great pyramids and temples, and the priceless treasures found in their tombs.

An Egyptian pharaoh wielded enormous power. He could write laws, set taxes, lead the army into battle, and judge legal cases. However, he also had many responsibilities. He was thought to control the flooding of the River Nile, which was essential for growing the kingdom's food. If disaster or famine struck, the pharaoh had to beg the gods for assistance, and might be blamed by the people if the situation did not improve.

After death, pharaohs and other important figures were mummified to preserve their bodies in the afterlife. Some of the earliest kings of Egypt were laid to rest in huge pyramids, while later kings were buried in underground tombs.

Doorways
After the funeral, these entrances were sealed with plaster to deter robbers.

Bales of cloth
Rich fabrics would provide clothes for the dead king in the afterlife.

Model boats
These models were believed to grow to full size in the afterlife.

Companion mummies
Two smaller mummies were found here, thought to be children of the king who died when they were young.

Treasury
This room contained the king's most valuable treasures.

Tutankhamun's tomb

Tutankhamun became pharaoh at the age of nine. He died suddenly, just nine years later, in 1327 BCE. He was buried in an underground tomb in the Valley of the Kings, on the west bank of the River Nile. Although grave robbers stole some of his burial treasure, thousands of precious artifacts lay undisturbed for more than 3,000 years before archaeologists rediscovered the tomb in 1922.

Storing organs
As part of the process of mummification, the internal organs were removed from the dead body. They were kept in containers called canopic jars and housed in a shrine.

Shrine for organs
The jars containing the king's organs were enclosed in a wooden shrine covered in gold.

296 lb (110kg) of **pure gold** was used to make Tutankhamun's **inner coffin**.

5,000 The approximate number of **artifacts** found in **Tutankhamun's tomb**.

259

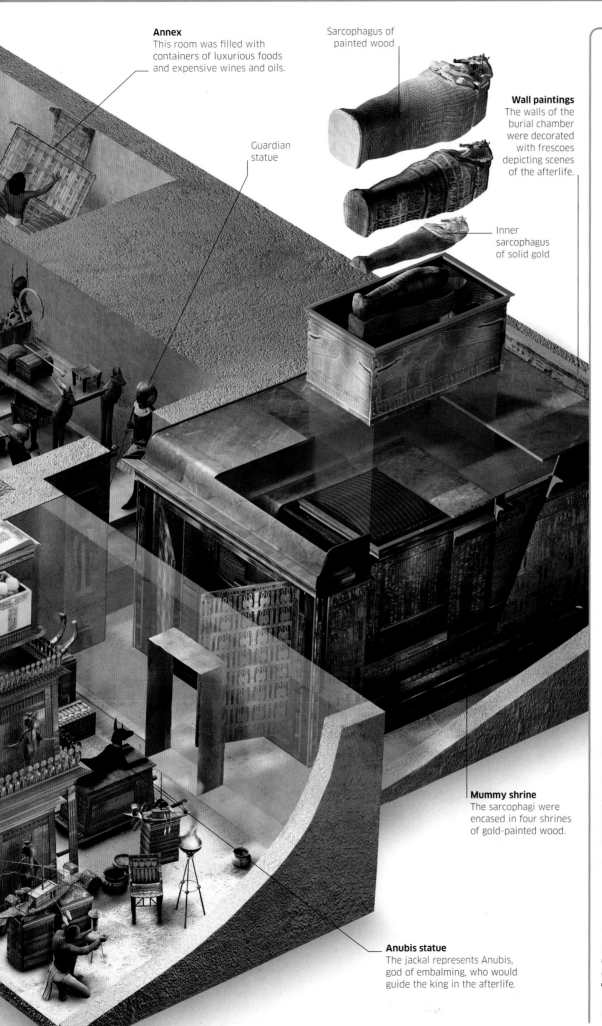

Annex
This room was filled with containers of luxurious foods and expensive wines and oils.

Sarcophagus of painted wood

Guardian statue

Wall paintings
The walls of the burial chamber were decorated with frescoes depicting scenes of the afterlife.

Inner sarcophagus of solid gold

Mummy shrine
The sarcophagi were encased in four shrines of gold-painted wood.

Anubis statue
The jackal represents Anubis, god of embalming, who would guide the king in the afterlife.

Making a mummy

The Ancient Egyptians believed that if your dead body rotted or was damaged in this world, your spirit would suffer in the afterlife. Rich Egyptians arranged for their bodies to be preserved after death. Their techniques worked so well that many of these mummies are still intact to this day.

1 Removing organs
After washing the body with wine, priests removed the internal organs. Special hooks were used to pull the brain out through the nostrils. The heart was left behind, since the Ancient Egyptians believed it was the home of the soul.

2 Drying out the body
The hollowed-out body was packed with bags of natron, a natural salt that drew water out of the flesh. It was left like this for 40 days while the natron did its work.

3 Washing the corpse
Once the body had completely dried out, it was washed in wine to remove the salt, then packed with sawdust or resin-soaked linen. The skin was rubbed with oils and perfumes, and often painted with resin for extra protection.

4 Wrapping in bandages
The next stage was to wrap the mummy in layers of bandages. Amulets (pieces of jewelry with magical powers) were included to keep the spirit safe on its journey to the next world. The finishing touch was a decorated mask.

5 Into the coffin
The mummy was placed in a coffin, or sarcophagus, which was painted or carved with a likeness of the dead person. The mummies of rich people were enclosed in several coffins, which in turn sat inside large wooden shrines.

6 The funeral
Exactly 70 days after death, the mummy was laid to rest. A procession would carry the coffin and burial goods to the tomb, often sealing them away so that robbers could not break in.

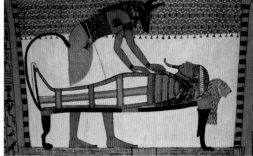

Priests of the dead
The process of mummification was a religious ritual and was carefully supervised by priests. One would wear a jackal mask to represent Anubis, the god who guided spirits of the dead.

MOST TOMBS IN THE VALLEY OF THE KINGS HAVE PAINTED WALLS. **ONLY THE BURIAL ROOM IN TUTANKHAMUN'S TOMB IS PAINTED, SUGGESTING IT** WAS PREPARED IN A HURRY.

Ancient Greece

From math masters to playwrights, great philosophers to military conquerors, Ancient Greece produced some of the most famous figures in western civilization.

Greek culture began on islands in the Eastern Mediterranean around 2000 BCE, with trading empires such as the Minoan civilization on Crete. As time went on, power shifted to the mainland, in warlike city-states such as Mycenae. As these city-states grew more sophisticated, they gave rise to great thinkers, builders, and writers, and the first democracy, in Athens. They also defeated the armies of the powerful Persian Empire to the east. Greek power reached its peak with Alexander the Great, a military genius whose empire stretched all the way to India.

Gods and goddesses

The Greeks believed in many gods, and the stories told about them have been remembered in art and literature to this day. The main gods, who were seen as behaving in very human ways, lived on Mount Olympus, ruled over by Zeus and his wife, Hera. On Earth, the deeds of great heroes, such as Heracles and Odysseus, and warriors, such as Achilles and Hector (who fought in a war over the Greek city of Troy), formed part of many stories.

POSEIDON, GOD OF THE SEA

Ancient Priene

The polis, or city-state, was the main kind of Greek settlement. Each one centered on a powerful city, which controlled an area of the surrounding countryside. The most important city-states, such as Athens, Corinth, or Sparta, owned large areas of territory and grew very rich. Priene (now in southwestern Turkey) was a typical Greek city-state. It was originally founded around 1000 BCE, but was completely rebuilt in about 350 BCE.

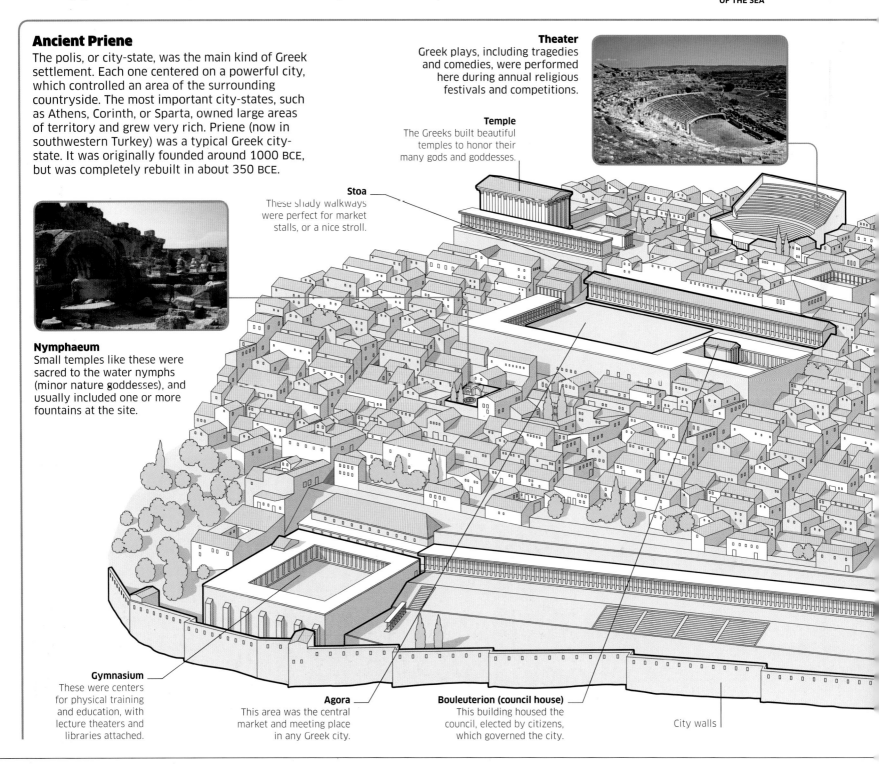

Theater
Greek plays, including tragedies and comedies, were performed here during annual religious festivals and competitions.

Temple
The Greeks built beautiful temples to honor their many gods and goddesses.

Stoa
These shady walkways were perfect for market stalls, or a nice stroll.

Nymphaeum
Small temples like these were sacred to the water nymphs (minor nature goddesses), and usually included one or more fountains at the site.

Gymnasium
These were centers for physical training and education, with lecture theaters and libraries attached.

Agora
This area was the central market and meeting place in any Greek city.

Bouleuterion (council house)
This building housed the council, elected by citizens, which governed the city.

City walls

42 ft (13 m)—the height of the **statue of Zeus** at **Olympia**, one of the **Seven Wonders of the Ancient World**.

500 The number of people on the **ruling council** of Athens.

261

ZEUS, KING OF THE GODS

ARTEMIS, GODDESS OF HUNTING

ATHENA, GODDESS OF WISDOM

THE HERO HERACLES KILLS A GIANT SNAKE

ONLY MEN COULD BE CITIZENS OF A CITY-STATE AND TAKE PART IN ELECTIONS —WOMEN, SLAVES, AND CHILDREN WERE EXCLUDED.

The Olympic Games

The Greeks held regular athletic contests in honor of their gods. The most important of these were the Olympic Games, founded in 776 BCE and held (like the modern version) every four years. The athletes who took part had to be Greek citizens, but they competed individually, not for their home cities. Victors were rewarded, not with valuable prizes or medals, but with wreaths of wild olive leaves. The games began as a single day of events but were later extended to five days.

Five days of Olympic events

Day 1
The first day was marked with a religious procession. Athletes swore before the gods that they would compete without cheating, while judges swore not to be biased.

Day 2
The pentathlon, held on the second day, involved five events: long jump, discus, javelin, running, and wrestling. In later years, chariot racing also took place on day two.

Day 3
Younger athletes competed in running, wrestling, and boxing. On this day, 100 oxen were sacrificed to Zeus, and the best meat burned before his temple.

Day 4
The fourth day was for adult wrestling, boxing, and *pankration*—a brutal sport combining wrestling and boxing. A foot race in full armor also took place.

Day 5
The last day of the festival saw olive wreaths presented to all winning athletes. A banquet of meat from the oxen sacrificed on the third day concluded the celebrations.

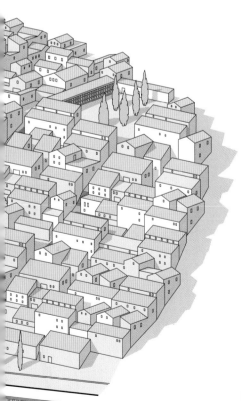

Stadium
Used for athletic contests and games, the stadium included a running track, which gave its name to the Greek unit of distance, the stade.

"WE SWEAR WE WILL TAKE PART IN THE **OLYMPIC GAMES** IN THE SPIRIT OF CHIVALRY, FOR THE HONOR OF OUR COUNTRY, AND FOR **THE GLORY OF SPORT**"
1920 OLYMPIC OATH INSPIRED BY ANCIENT GREECE

From island to empire

For centuries, Greece was made up of many small rival states. They were united by shared traditions and language, and sometimes allied together to face common enemies such as the Persians. Greece was united under Alexander the Great and his father, Philip. But when Alexander died, his empire fell apart and Greece came under the power of the Romans.

2000 BCE – 1500 BCE

Minoan period
From 2000 BCE, the Minoans of Crete built up a trading empire. They became very wealthy, allowing the building of great palaces such as Knossos. Around 1500 BCE, earthquakes, revolts, and invasions caused the Minoan culture to collapse.

LATE MINOAN VASE WITH SQUID MOTIF

1600 BCE – 1100 BCE

Mycenaean period
Around 1600 BCE, new tribes began to settle in centers such as Mycenae and Tiryns. A warlike people, they conquered Crete and engaged in pirate raids as well as trading. Around 1200 BCE, new invaders destroyed most of the Mycenaean cities.

GOLD FUNERAL MASK OF MYCENAEAN KING

1100 BCE – 750 BCE

Homeric period
From about 1100 BCE, Greece entered a Dark Age, about which little is known. Around 800 BCE Greek civilization began to recover and many small city-states emerged, with a common language and alphabet. The poet Homer wrote of this time in the *Iliad*, his epic poem.

BRONZE HELMET

750 BCE – 336 BCE

Archaic and Classical periods
City-states grew in size and spread to colonies abroad. Greece was invaded twice by huge armies from the Persian Empire, but defeated both attacks. This era also saw wars between city-states, especially Athens and Sparta.

VASE SHOWING ONE OF HERACLES'S LABORS

336 BCE – 146 CE

Hellenistic period
In 338 BCE, after decades of war, Philip, king of the state of Macedon, conquered all of Greece to create one kingdom. His son, Alexander the Great, invaded Persia in 335 BCE and conquered it. Greek civilization spread to this vast area, creating a new Hellenistic culture.

COIN DEPICTING ALEXANDER THE GREAT

A defensive wall **4 miles (6 km) long** protected Athens' access to the **sea**.

220 lb (100 kg)—estimate for the weight of **gold** in Phidias's **statue of Athena**.

Ancient Athens

In the fifth century BCE, the Greek city of Athens was home to some of history's most brilliant artists, philosophers, and politicians. Its citizens formed the world's first known democracy, and their writings and ideas are still famous today.

In the early part of the century, Greece was invaded twice by vast armies from the empire of Persia to the east. Athens played a significant role in defeating both invasions, at the land battle of Marathon in 490 BCE, and the sea battle of Salamis in 480 BCE. These victories brought the city great wealth and power, and its citizens built beautiful temples, theaters, and public buildings. Toward the end of the century, Athens began a long and costly war with neighboring Greek states such as Sparta. After military defeat and a terrible plague, Athens was eventually conquered by the Spartans in 404 BCE.

22,000 tons
of marble are estimated to have been used to build the Parthenon and the gateway to the Acropolis.

Wooden beam

Statue of Athena
The statue was made by the sculptor Phidias. It was covered in gold and ivory.

Pediments
The sculptures on this side told the story of the birth of Athena. On the other side, they showed the contest between Athena and Poseidon for control of Athens.

Nike
The goddess of victory sat in Athena's palm.

Inner frieze
Sculptures around the inner walls showed a procession of citizens in honor of Athena.

The Parthenon

The religious center of Athens was the Parthenon. This great temple was dedicated to Athena, the goddess of wisdom and courage in battle, who was believed to be the city's special protector. It was also the city's treasury, where tribute was stored.

100 cows were **sacrificed** to Athena at the annual Panathenaia festival.

6,000 The **minimum number** of citizens needed for a **vote to be valid.**

The walls of the **Odeon of Pericles** were made from the wood of defeated **Persian ships.**

263

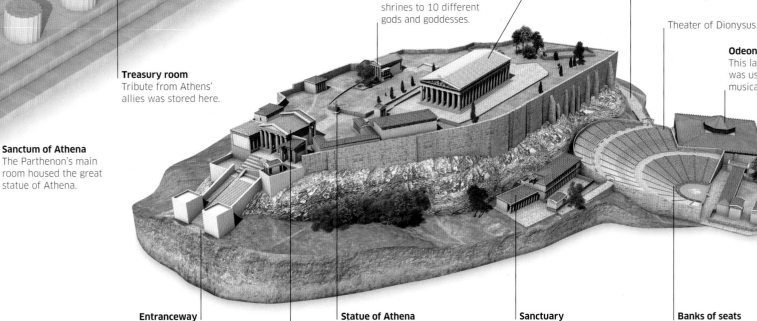

Roof ornament

Marble tiles
The roof was made of marble tiles, carefully cut to keep out the rain.

Marble columns

Treasury room
Tribute from Athens' allies was stored here.

Sanctum of Athena
The Parthenon's main room housed the great statue of Athena.

The first democracy

All political decisions in Athens were taken by popular vote. However, voting was restricted to male citizens, who only made up about 12 percent of the population.

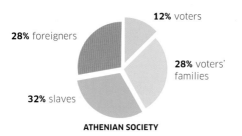

12% voters

28% foreigners

28% voters' families

32% slaves

ATHENIAN SOCIETY

Enemy neighbors

Sparta was a Greek city-state with a very different culture. It was ruled by kings instead of a democracy, and its people valued fighting ability above all else. Young boys underwent harsh military training. The Spartans allied with Athens against the Persians, but later became fierce enemies.

"FOR NO MAN EVER PROVES HIMSELF **A GOOD MAN IN WAR** UNLESS HE CAN ENDURE TO FACE THE **BLOOD AND THE SLAUGHTER,** GO CLOSE AGAINST THE ENEMY AND **FIGHT WITH HIS HANDS."**
TYRTAEUS, SPARTAN POET

The Acropolis

The Parthenon stood on a hill, or Acropolis, at the center of ancient Athens. Originally a defensive fort, the Acropolis became a place of worship as Athens grew more secure. Within its walls were several temples and holy sites, while outside was a theater dedicated to the god Dionysus, used for festivals of drama.

Erechtheum
This temple included shrines to 10 different gods and goddesses.

Parthenon

Processional way

Theater of Dionysus

Odeon of Pericles
This large hall was used for musical contests.

Entranceway
A staircase 66 ft (20 m) wide brought visitors to the top of the hill.

Monumental gateway, or *propylea*

Statue of Athena
This huge bronze statue stood guard over the city.

Sanctuary
These buildings were dedicated to Asclepius, the god of healing.

Banks of seats
The curve was designed so that actors' voices could be heard in the back row.

264 history ○ **THE ANCIENT WORLD**

The Romans had one of the **first fire brigades** under Augustus's reign.

25 The **number of years** a soldier had to **serve in the Roman army**.

The legacy of Rome

The Romans are still remembered today, for good reason. Their politics and philosophy inspired Western thinking for many centuries. Many of their amazing buildings, supported by advanced engineering skills, still stand today. Roman words crop up in many modern languages, and even some modern laws follow Roman examples.

Law and learning

Roman authors produced great works of history, poetry, politics, and philosophy. Copies of these were spread all over the empire. The library of Celsus at Ephesus in modern Turkey (above) contained about 12,000 scrolls.

Architecture and engineering

The Romans were astonishing engineers. They used concrete to build strong, watertight structures, and they invented stone arches. This aqueduct at Pont du Gard in France is just one of many great Roman landmarks still standing today.

A connected empire

The Romans built a huge network of roads, allowing armies, messengers, and traders to move quickly around the empire. Combined with careful record-keeping, roads helped the Romans to control a huge and prosperous empire.

> ## "IT IS BETTER TO CREATE THAN TO LEARN! CREATING IS THE ESSENCE OF LIFE."
> JULIUS CAESAR, ROMAN DICTATOR, REIGNED 49–44 BCE

The Roman Empire

From its beginnings as a small village in central Italy, the city of Rome came to rule over one of the largest and most prosperous empires in history. Its armies were seemingly unstoppable, conquering most of Europe, North Africa, and the Middle East.

Rome was founded in 753 BCE, and at first was ruled by kings. In 509 BCE, the kings were replaced by a republic and control of the city fell to consuls chosen by the Senate (ruling council). The Senate, and later the emperor, also appointed generals to lead Rome's armies in wars of conquest. They divided the captured regions into provinces controlled by Roman governors and guarded by Roman soldiers. They built new cities and roads, and imposed Roman laws on their conquered subjects. Although they could be cruel, especially to people who rebelled against them, the Romans spread wealth, stability, and valuable new ideas all across their empire.

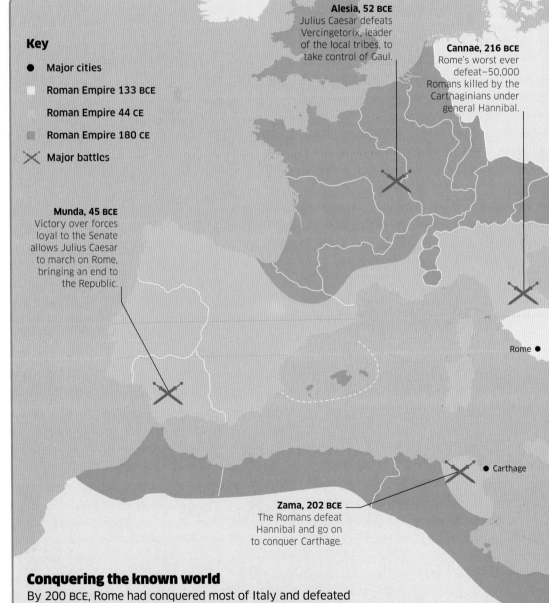

Alesia, 52 BCE
Julius Caesar defeats Vercingetorix, leader of the local tribes, to take control of Gaul.

Cannae, 216 BCE
Rome's worst ever defeat—50,000 Romans killed by the Carthaginians under general Hannibal.

Key
- ● Major cities
- ☐ Roman Empire 133 BCE
- ☐ Roman Empire 44 CE
- ☐ Roman Empire 180 CE
- ✕ Major battles

Munda, 45 BCE
Victory over forces loyal to the Senate allows Julius Caesar to march on Rome, bringing an end to the Republic.

Rome ●

● Carthage

Zama, 202 BCE
The Romans defeat Hannibal and go on to conquer Carthage.

Conquering the known world

By 200 BCE, Rome had conquered most of Italy and defeated the powerful city of Carthage in North Africa. Between 262 and 146 BCE, Rome gained Sicily, Sardinia, Spain, and North Africa. Gaul (France) was conquered by 50 BCE, as well as much of Turkey and the Middle East. Britain was invaded in 43 CE. The empire was at its largest around 117 CE, when it held Dacia (Romania) and parts of modern Syria and Iraq.

355 The number of days in the **Roman calendar year** before Julius Caesar reformed it.

23 The number of times **Julius Caesar was stabbed**, when he was **assassinated by senators** who called him a tyrant.

265

Rome's rise and fall

As the Roman army grew stronger, its generals became more powerful than the Senate. After a series of civil wars between military leaders, the Republic collapsed and Julius Caesar became sole ruler. His adopted son, Augustus, became the first Roman emperor. In 395 CE, the empire was split. The western part was ruled from Rome, but a new emperor ruled the eastern half from the city of Constantinople (or Byzantium). The west gradually lost territory to barbarian tribes, and the last emperor was deposed in 476 CE.

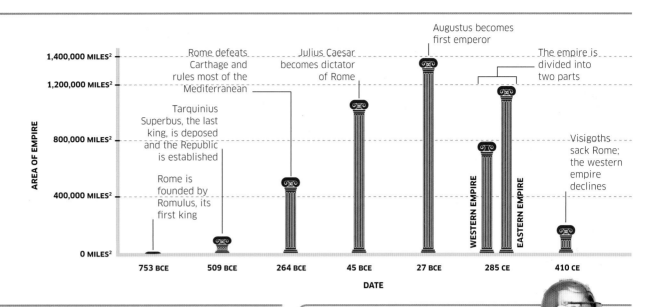

AREA OF EMPIRE

- 1,400,000 MILES²
- 1,200,000 MILES²
- 800,000 MILES²
- 400,000 MILES²
- 0 MILES²

753 BCE — Rome is founded by Romulus, its first king

509 BCE — Tarquinius Superbus, the last king, is deposed and the Republic is established

264 BCE — Rome defeats Carthage and rules most of the Mediterranean

45 BCE — Julius Caesar becomes dictator of Rome

27 BCE — Augustus becomes first emperor

285 CE — The empire is divided into two parts (WESTERN EMPIRE / EASTERN EMPIRE)

410 CE — Visigoths sack Rome; the western empire declines

DATE

53,000 Gauls were sold
into slavery when Julius Caesar defeated their armies and captured their territory.

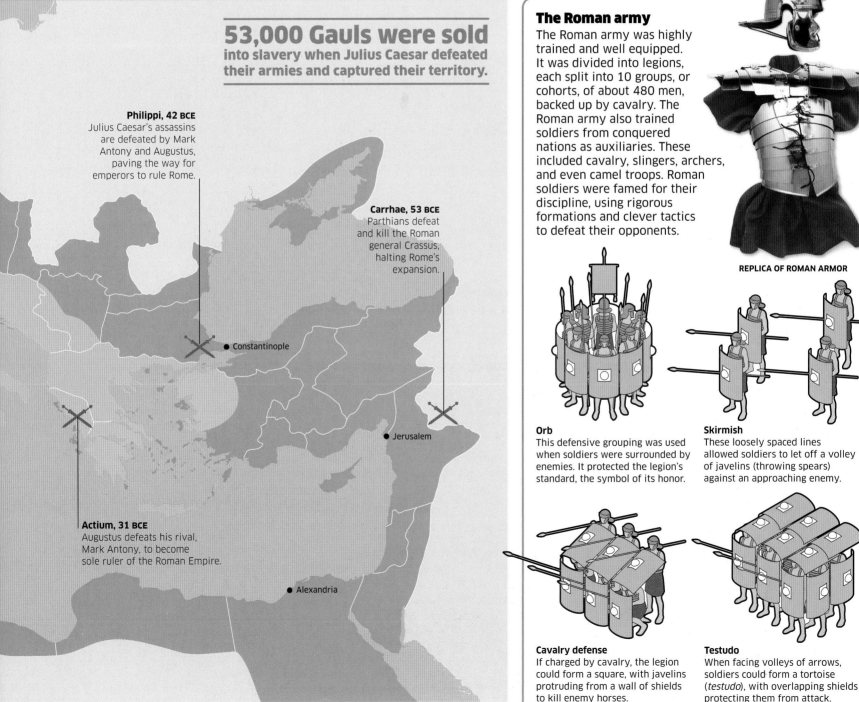

Philippi, 42 BCE
Julius Caesar's assassins are defeated by Mark Antony and Augustus, paving the way for emperors to rule Rome.

Carrhae, 53 BCE
Parthians defeat and kill the Roman general Crassus, halting Rome's expansion.

● Constantinople

● Jerusalem

Actium, 31 BCE
Augustus defeats his rival, Mark Antony, to become sole ruler of the Roman Empire.

● Alexandria

The Roman army

The Roman army was highly trained and well equipped. It was divided into legions, each split into 10 groups, or cohorts, of about 480 men, backed up by cavalry. The Roman army also trained soldiers from conquered nations as auxiliaries. These included cavalry, slingers, archers, and even camel troops. Roman soldiers were famed for their discipline, using rigorous formations and clever tactics to defeat their opponents.

REPLICA OF ROMAN ARMOR

Orb
This defensive grouping was used when soldiers were surrounded by enemies. It protected the legion's standard, the symbol of its honor.

Skirmish
These loosely spaced lines allowed soldiers to let off a volley of javelins (throwing spears) against an approaching enemy.

Cavalry defense
If charged by cavalry, the legion could form a square, with javelins protruding from a wall of shields to kill enemy horses.

Testudo
When facing volleys of arrows, soldiers could form a tortoise (*testudo*), with overlapping shields protecting them from attack.

Roman society

The city of Rome stood at the heart of the Roman Empire. For more than 500 years it was the most powerful city in the western world.

Rome was in many ways like a modern city. It had paved roads, underground sewers, and even multistory apartment buildings. Food was imported from across the empire to feed the populace, and aqueducts brought in fresh water from the surrounding countryside. The rulers of Rome, emperors and powerful politicians, filled the streets with great monuments to demonstrate their power. The heart of the city was the Forum, an open space for public meetings and celebrations. Around it were built great arenas, temples, bathhouses, theaters, markets, and palaces, many of which are still standing thousands of years later. As the empire grew, the city of Rome became richer and its population swelled. It is thought that 1,200,000 people lived there at the empire's height around 100 CE, as many as in modern-day Dallas, Texas.

Professional fighters

There were more than 20 types of gladiator, each with different weapons and armor. The Romans enjoyed watching gladiators of different kinds fighting each other, to see which styles and equipment were most effective. Gladiators were slaves, but if they fought well enough they could sometimes win their freedom. The most successful ones became celebrities to their adoring fans.

Gladiator helmet
This bronze helmet was used by a *murmillo*, a heavily armed gladiator who carried a short sword and large, rectangular shield into battle.

Social sitting

The seating levels in the Colosseum mirrored the social classes in Roman life. The front rows were reserved for richer and more important people, while the less fortunate sat further back. The emperor had a private box reserved for him and his guests. Slaves attended the circus only to serve their masters.

SOCIAL CLASSES OF ANCIENT ROME

Emperor
The ruler of the empire, often threatened by enemies.

Senators
Politicians whose power depended on the emperor.

Equestrians
Aristocratic families, often wealthy and influential.

Plebians
Working people, such as merchants and laborers.

Foreigners
Visitors from other parts of the empire.

Slaves
Treated as property, slaves had no rights and had to obey their masters.

Arena floor
The arena floor was made from wooden boards covered in sand.

Cage can be winched up to release the lions

Underground lift
Wild beasts such as lions, wolves, and elephants fought against each other and against trained hunters. The animals were kept in cages underground. They were brought up to the surface in elevators and released into the arena through trapdoors.

The Colosseum

This huge arena was the site of elaborate public shows called circuses. They included acrobats, wild beast fights, public executions, and battles between professional warriors called gladiators.

Retractable shade
A huge awning could be extended to protect spectators from the heat of the sun.

Awning masts
A special group of sailors from the Roman navy was assigned to operate the awning ropes and masts.

Entrance to upper level

Crowd of thousands
Circuses were paid for by the emperor as a gift to the people, and huge crowds attended.

Famous faces
The outside was decorated with statues of generals and politicians.

Many exits
Spectators entered through the 80 archways spaced around the outside.

Gladiator gate
The gladiators entered the arena through two large gateways, at the north and south.

Delivery tunnels
Supplies were brought in from outside through underground passages.

Gladiators
Once the beast fights were finished, the gladiators entered the arena. This was the most popular part of the show. They would fight in pairs around the ring. Although most gladiators were slaves, they could win their freedom if they fought well in the arena.

Emperor's box
The emperor and his guests sat in their own special box. When a gladiator was wounded and unable to fight on, he could appeal for mercy. The emperor would then decide whether the beaten gladiator should be spared or killed by his opponent.

THE MEDIEVAL WORLD

In the 5th century CE, the Roman Empire in Europe collapsed, splitting into smaller kingdoms that were poorer and less advanced than the Romans had been. A huge Arabian empire arose in the Middle East, which preserved and built on the knowledge of the Ancient Greeks and Romans. In China and India, new empires discovered scientific advances that would not be matched in Europe for hundreds of years.

THE FALL OF ROME

In the 4th century CE, the Roman Empire split between east and west. The Western Empire, ruled from Rome, became weaker, because its armies could not defend against the barbarian raiders from Germany. By the end of the 4th century, it had lost much of its territory, and in 476 CE, the last emperor of Rome lost his throne.

The Byzantine Empire

The Eastern Roman Empire (or Byzantine Empire) survived longer than the Western Empire. Emperor Justinian recaptured Italy and North Africa in the 6th century, but the empire was invaded by Muslim armies soon after. The Ottoman Turks conquered the empire's capital, Constantinople, in 1453.

A Christian city
This mosaic shows two Byzantine emperors dedicating Constantinople to Jesus and the Virgin Mary.

Barbarian raiders

By around 450 CE, barbarian tribes had set up kingdoms in land previously owned by the Romans. The new kings took up some Roman customs, such as giving out written laws.

Saxon helmet
This decorated helmet was found buried inside a ship, along with the body of a 7th-century Germanic king.

- **HUNS**
  This tribe from Germany mounted devastating raids on the Roman Empire in the 5th century.

- **GOTHS**
  The Goths sacked Rome in 410. They later split into the Visigoths (Spain) and Ostrogoths (Italy).

- **ANGLES AND SAXONS**
  These raiders from north Germany conquered former Roman lands in England, setting up new kingdoms.

- **MAGYARS**
  From Central Asia, the Magyars raided Eastern Europe from 850 CE, settling in Hungary in 900.

- **VIKINGS**
  Fierce Viking warriors raided European coasts from 793 for 200 years, taking land in France, Ireland, and Britain.

The Holy Roman Empire

In Germany, Christian rulers took on the power and lands of the Western Roman Empire, 400 years after it fell. In 800 CE, a king called Charlemagne crowned himself emperor and set about rebuilding a Christian empire in Europe. By 900, his empire had fallen apart, but ambitious German princes took on the title of Holy Roman Emperor for centuries afterward.

CHARLEMAGNE'S EMPIRE

The Holy Roman Empire
Charlemagne conquered large areas of Europe before his death in 814. By 843, his empire had split into three kingdoms.

CHANGING EUROPE

Everyday life in medieval Europe was dominated by the Church on the one hand and powerful kings on the other. France was conquered by the Franks, a Germanic tribe, but went on to become the most powerful country in Europe, fighting a Hundred Years War with England in 1337–1453. The Moors, an Islamic people from North Africa, conquered Spain in the 8th century. They were driven out in a series of wars lasting until 1492. Most devastating of all was the Black Death, a plague that killed millions as it swept across Europe.

AN ESTIMATED 45 PERCENT OF THE POPULATION OF EUROPE DIED OF THE BLACK DEATH.

Feudalism

Under the feudal system that arose in Europe, noblemen became the followers (vassals) of a king by swearing loyalty (fealty) to him and promising to support him in time of war. In exchange, the vassal was given land to rule as he saw fit.

King
The king was at the head of feudal society and the chief nobles (known as tenants-in-chief) were his vassals, and given land in return.

Vassal
Nobles sometimes had their own vassals, such as knights, who received smaller portions of land in return for service (normally military).

Peasant
The lowest members of society, peasants also swore fealty to a lord, but worked his land instead of doing military service.

Church and state

The Christian Church grew more powerful during the medieval period. Most people paid a tithe of one-tenth of their income as a tax to the Church, and huge new cathedrals sprang up in cities across Europe. The head of the Church was the Pope, based in Rome, and his power often made other rulers resentful.

CHARTRES CATHEDRAL, FRANCE

WARS OF FAITH

In the early 7th century, the tribes of the Arabian Peninsula were united under a new religion, Islam, led by the Prophet Muhammad. Arab Muslim armies took Christian Byzantine land in North Africa, Palestine, and Syria, and captured Jerusalem, a city holy to both Islam and Christianity. From the 11th to the 13th century, Christian armies tried to take Jerusalem back in a series of Crusades, invading the Holy Land and even setting up kingdoms there for a short time.

Arab learning

Islamic learning was often much more advanced than medieval European ideas. Muslim armies occupied Persian and Byzantine lands, where they rediscovered Ancient Greek and Roman manuscripts, and Arab scholars made great advances in math and medicine.

Astrolabe
This device is used in astronomy. Arab scholars developed it from ideas found in Ancient Greek writings.

The rise of Islam

The Prophet Muhammad began preaching in around 610, and by the time he died in 632, Muslim armies had conquered most of the Arabian Peninsula. Under the leaders who followed after Muhammad's death (the caliphs), the Islamic caliphate (empire) grew beyond Arabia, until it included Egypt (in 641), Persia (in 640), and most of Syria and Palestine. Under the Umayyad dynasty, which ruled from 661, Muslim armies invaded the rest of North Africa and, from 711, captured most of Spain. In the east, the borders of the Islamic caliphate extended to Afghanistan and northern India.

Key
- Muslim lands by 634
- Muslim lands by 656
- Muslim lands by 756

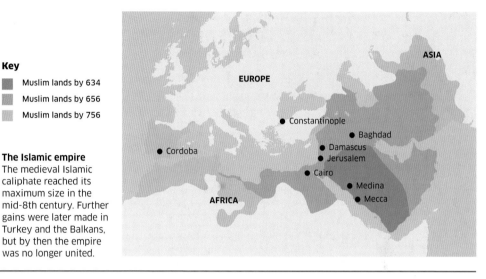

The Islamic empire
The medieval Islamic caliphate reached its maximum size in the mid-8th century. Further gains were later made in Turkey and the Balkans, but by then the empire was no longer united.

The Islamic world

As the Islamic empire grew, its cities expanded, housing the palaces of rulers as well as great mosques, hospitals, and libraries. They also became centers of trade and learning.

MEDINA
This was the first powerful Muslim city, after the Prophet Muhammad moved there with his early followers in 622.

DAMASCUS
This city in Syria became the capital of the Umayyad dynasty in 661. It is one of the oldest continuously inhabited cities.

JERUSALEM
Jerusalem was taken by Muslim armies in 637. It is one of the holiest cities in Islam, and site of one of the first great mosques.

BAGHDAD
Founded in 762, this center of learning was the capital of the Abbasid dynasty, which replaced the Umayyads in 750.

CAIRO
Cairo, founded in 969, lay near Memphis, the Ancient Egyptian capital. By 1325, it was the largest city in the world.

ISTANBUL
The former Byzantine capital, Constantinople, was captured by the Ottoman Turks in 1453. It remained their capital for 450 years.

EMPIRES OF ASIA

The greatest empires of the medieval period were in Asia. India, China, and Japan had courts and governments that were far more advanced than those in Europe. Between the 12th and 15th centuries, however, China was conquered by the Mongols, a nomadic people from Central Asia, Japan was engulfed in civil wars, and India was invaded by tribes from the north.

Tang China

China, divided for many centuries into warring kingdoms, was reunited under the Tang dynasty in 618 CE. The Tang capital at Chang'an lay at the end of the Silk Road, a trading route from Asia to the Mediterranean, which brought fabulous wealth to China. Under Tang rule, Chinese armies captured many oasis towns and reached the borders of Persia. A huge uprising in 755 led by An Lushan weakened the later Tang, and in 907 China fell apart.

Tang monument
The Great Wild Goose Pagoda in Xian (once Chang'an), China, was built in 652 under the Tang.

India

From around 320 CE, much of India came under the rule of the Gupta Empire, famous for its wealth and advances in literature, art, and science. After almost 150 years of peace, the Gupta Empire fell apart around 570. North India came under the rule of the Harsha Empire, but when its leader died in 647, India broke up into smaller kingdoms, only reuniting in the 13th century.

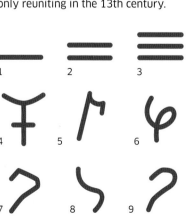

Brahmi numerals
This ancient number system was adapted and expanded by Indian mathematicians in the 5th and 6th centuries. It is the basis of our modern system of counting.

The Mongol Empire

In 1206, the nomadic tribes of Mongolia were united under one ruler, Genghis Khan. He conquered a vast empire, including much of Central Asia, Persia, and China. The Mongols were famous as astonishing archers, master horsemen, and brutal warriors.

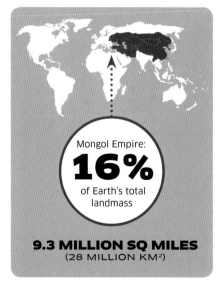

Mongol Empire:
16%
of Earth's total landmass

9.3 MILLION SQ MILES
(28 MILLION KM²)

Mongol expansion
By 1279, the Mongols controlled around a sixth of the Earth's entire land surface. Their last major conquest was China.

Viking raiders

From the late 8th century CE, fierce warriors from Scandinavia terrorized coastal settlements across northern Europe. The Vikings attacked without warning, killing anyone who resisted them and carrying off treasure and slaves.

The Vikings may have had a fearsome reputation, but they were more than just brutal raiders. They were also champion shipbuilders, whose ships traveled quickly and safely across the roughest seas. They were bold explorers, reaching the Americas centuries before anyone else from Europe. They built settlements in northern Europe, Iceland, and Greenland, where their culture influenced local life for centuries.

Raiding party
Viking raiders traveled in longboats—fast, sleek ships that could strike anywhere along coasts and rivers. They carried large, square sails, and oars for use when the wind was against them.

Dragon figurehead
At the front of Viking raiding ships was a fierce monster head, perhaps representing a warlike spirit.

Setting sail
Large, square sails were made out of woolen cloth. The material was so valuable it was sometimes used as currency.

Viking helmets
Like metal armor, helmets were difficult to make and very expensive. Steel was hammered into plates, which were riveted together with metal strips. The helmet was lined with cloth padding inside, and leather straps held it on the owner's head.

Viking clothes
Vikings wore tunics made of linen or leather stuffed with horse hair.

Deck boards had storage space underneath

Slim hull
Longboats had narrow hulls (bodies) and sat high in the water, so that they could sail up shallow rivers to raid inland.

Double-edged longsword

Deep keel
A deep keel (a beam sticking out from the hull) kept the ship stable in rough seas.

Weapons of war
Vikings were skilled at metalworking. Their weapons included broad axes that were swung with two hands, and large-bladed knives called saxes, which doubled as tools for everyday use.

Planks overlap to keep out water

Chest containing rower's belongings

Expensive armor
Wealthy warriors could afford chain mail armor and helmets made out of steel plates.

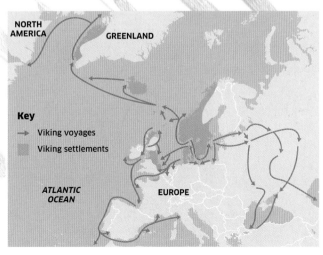

Strong ties
Ropes were made from fibers that stayed strong when wet, such as horsehair, walrus hide, or a plant called hemp.

Carved wooden decoration at stern

Keel decorated with carvings

Steering oar
A special, extra-long oar was attached to the back of the ship to act as a rudder.

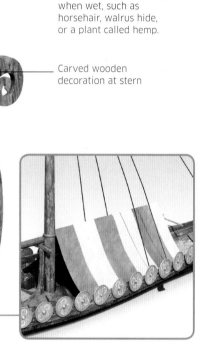

Sleeping quarters
The sail on a Viking ship could also be used for shelter. By hanging it across the beam that held the sail up, and tying it to the sides of the boat, voyagers could turn the sail into a tent to protect them from storms.

Shield wall
The warriors mounted their shields on the sides of the boat, to protect the rowers and intimidate enemies.

Oars about 15 ft (4.5 m) long

Great explorers

As well as fierce warriors, the Vikings were bold explorers. From their homes in Scandinavia, Viking ships traveled for thousands of miles in every direction. Vikings were the first Europeans to land in the Americas, almost 500 years before Christopher Columbus. The remains of a Viking settlement have been found in Newfoundland, Canada. They also traveled widely across Europe, sailing or rowing around coasts and along rivers, and even carrying their ships over land when they could not continue by water.

NORTH AMERICA

GREENLAND

Key
→ Viking voyages
▢ Viking settlements

ATLANTIC OCEAN

EUROPE

Skilled craftsmen

Viking craftsmen produced fine leatherwork and intricate metal jewelry. At first their work mostly featured monsters and giants from their traditional legends. However, around the 11th century, many Vikings converted to Christianity, and crucifixes began to replace the old symbols.

CRUCIFIX   DRAGON BROOCH

In some sieges, attackers **launched dead bodies** over **castle walls**, trying to **cause disease** inside.

Fortresses

With towering stone walls bristling with arrow slits, murder holes, and other defenses, castles were a formidable obstacle to any medieval invader.

Castles were built all across the world, ranging from simple wooden enclosures to vast stone palaces. A large number were built by feudal lords in Europe, who needed a place to keep their families and treasures safe from rivals while they were away at war. The Crusaders depended on castles to protect their settlements in the Holy Land, where they might come under attack at any time.

At the center of the castle was the keep, a tall tower where the lord and his family made their home, and which could be defended even if the rest of the castle fell. Around the keep were wards, open areas where the castle's other inhabitants lived and worked, all protected by stone walls.

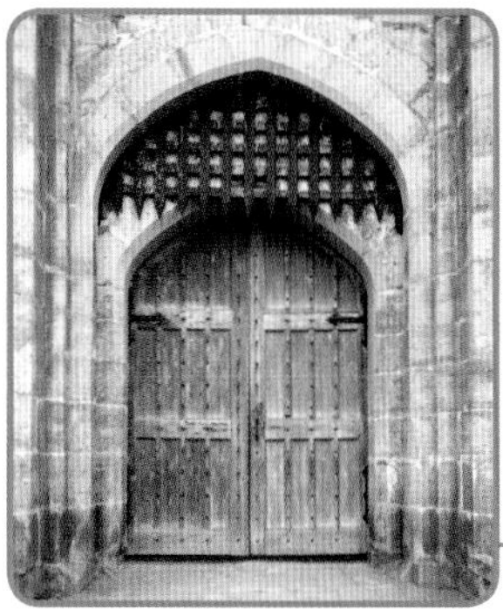

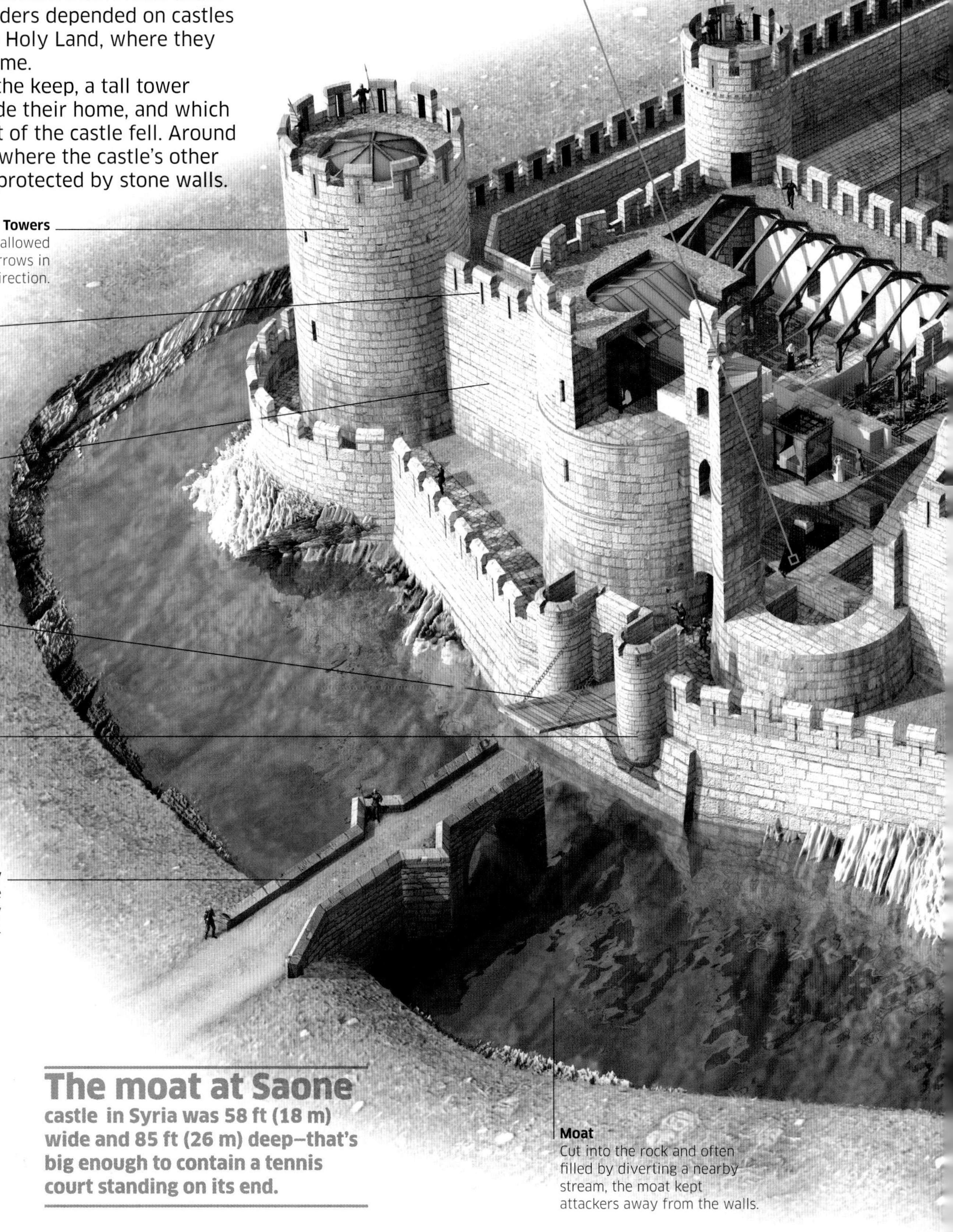

The gatehouse
The castle entrance was heavily defended. It was often built as a narrow tunnel with wood or iron gates at either end. Holes in the ceiling (murder holes) could be used to pour boiling oil or water on attackers in the tunnel.
Lord's chambers
The lord and his family had private rooms in the strongest part of the castle, known as the solar.
Towers
Circular towers allowed defenders to fire arrows in any direction.
Battlements
Defenders standing here could bombard attackers while staying sheltered.
Curtain wall
Thick stone walls kept the castle's inhabitants safe from attack.
Drawbridge
This wooden bridge could be raised to cut off access to the gate.
Gatehouse towers
Towers on either side of the gatehouse allowed defenders to rain arrows, stones, or boiling water on anyone attacking.
Entranceway
A single narrow entrance meant attackers could only approach one at a time.
Moat
Cut into the rock and often filled by diverting a nearby stream, the moat kept attackers away from the walls.

Life in a castle

During peacetime, a castle like this 13th-century concentric fortress was home to the lord, his family and servants, and guards known as men-at-arms. Many castles were like little villages inside, with kitchens, blacksmiths, gardens, stables, and a chapel. If they were attacked, the people inside had everything they needed to survive until help came.

The moat at Saone castle in Syria was 58 ft (18 m) wide and 85 ft (26 m) deep—that's big enough to contain a tennis court standing on its end.

During a **long siege**, when supplies ran low, **defenders** might have to **eat horses, dogs**, and even **rats**.

3,500 soldiers defended **Rhodes** against a besieging army of **70,000 Ottoman Turks** in 1480.

273

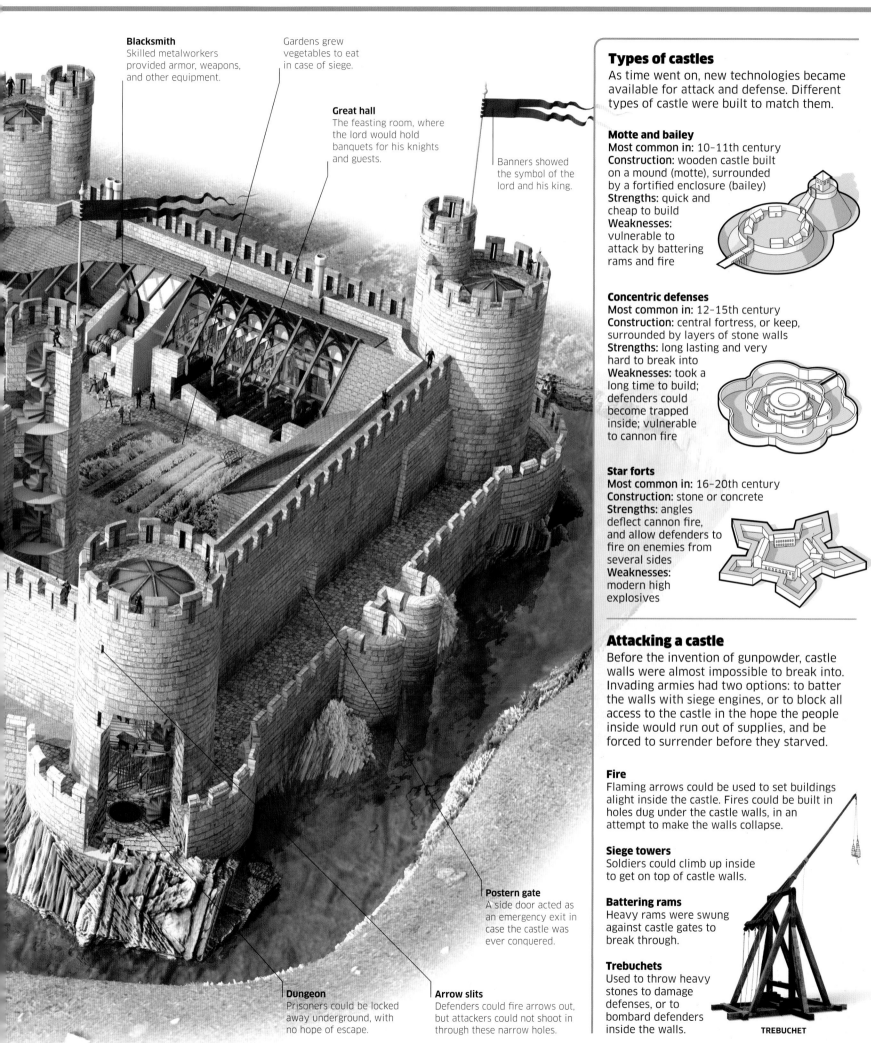

Blacksmith
Skilled metalworkers provided armor, weapons, and other equipment.

Gardens grew vegetables to eat in case of siege.

Great hall
The feasting room, where the lord would hold banquets for his knights and guests.

Banners showed the symbol of the lord and his king.

Postern gate
A side door acted as an emergency exit in case the castle was ever conquered.

Dungeon
Prisoners could be locked away underground, with no hope of escape.

Arrow slits
Defenders could fire arrows out, but attackers could not shoot in through these narrow holes.

Types of castles

As time went on, new technologies became available for attack and defense. Different types of castle were built to match them.

Motte and bailey
Most common in: 10–11th century
Construction: wooden castle built on a mound (motte), surrounded by a fortified enclosure (bailey)
Strengths: quick and cheap to build
Weaknesses: vulnerable to attack by battering rams and fire

Concentric defenses
Most common in: 12–15th century
Construction: central fortress, or keep, surrounded by layers of stone walls
Strengths: long lasting and very hard to break into
Weaknesses: took a long time to build; defenders could become trapped inside; vulnerable to cannon fire

Star forts
Most common in: 16–20th century
Construction: stone or concrete
Strengths: angles deflect cannon fire, and allow defenders to fire on enemies from several sides
Weaknesses: modern high explosives

Attacking a castle

Before the invention of gunpowder, castle walls were almost impossible to break into. Invading armies had two options: to batter the walls with siege engines, or to block all access to the castle in the hope the people inside would run out of supplies, and be forced to surrender before they starved.

Fire
Flaming arrows could be used to set buildings alight inside the castle. Fires could be built in holes dug under the castle walls, in an attempt to make the walls collapse.

Siege towers
Soldiers could climb up inside to get on top of castle walls.

Battering rams
Heavy rams were swung against castle gates to break through.

Trebuchets
Used to throw heavy stones to damage defenses, or to bombard defenders inside the walls.

TREBUCHET

70,000 The number of people said to have been killed when the Crusaders took Jerusalem in 1099.

German princes
As well as French and British crusaders, several armies set out from the Holy Roman Empire and states in what is now Germany.
Crusader knights
European knights wore heavy armor and fought mainly on horseback. They were supported by foot soldiers called men-at-arms.
LONDON
MAINZ
SPEYER
CLERMONT
VENICE
GENOA
ZARA
MARSEILLE
ROME
London
King Richard I (called the Lionheart for his bravery) set out for the Third Crusade soon after he was crowned in London in 1189. He managed to defeat the great Muslim leader Saladin, but could not retake Jerusalem.
Rome
The popes, based in Rome, dreamed of restoring Jerusalem to Christian rule. They called for each Crusade, asking European rulers to provide knights and men-at-arms to go to war in the Holy Land.
Journey to the Holy Land
Some Crusaders traveled overland to the Holy Land, but it was a long journey through Muslim-controlled territory. It was far safer to go by sea.

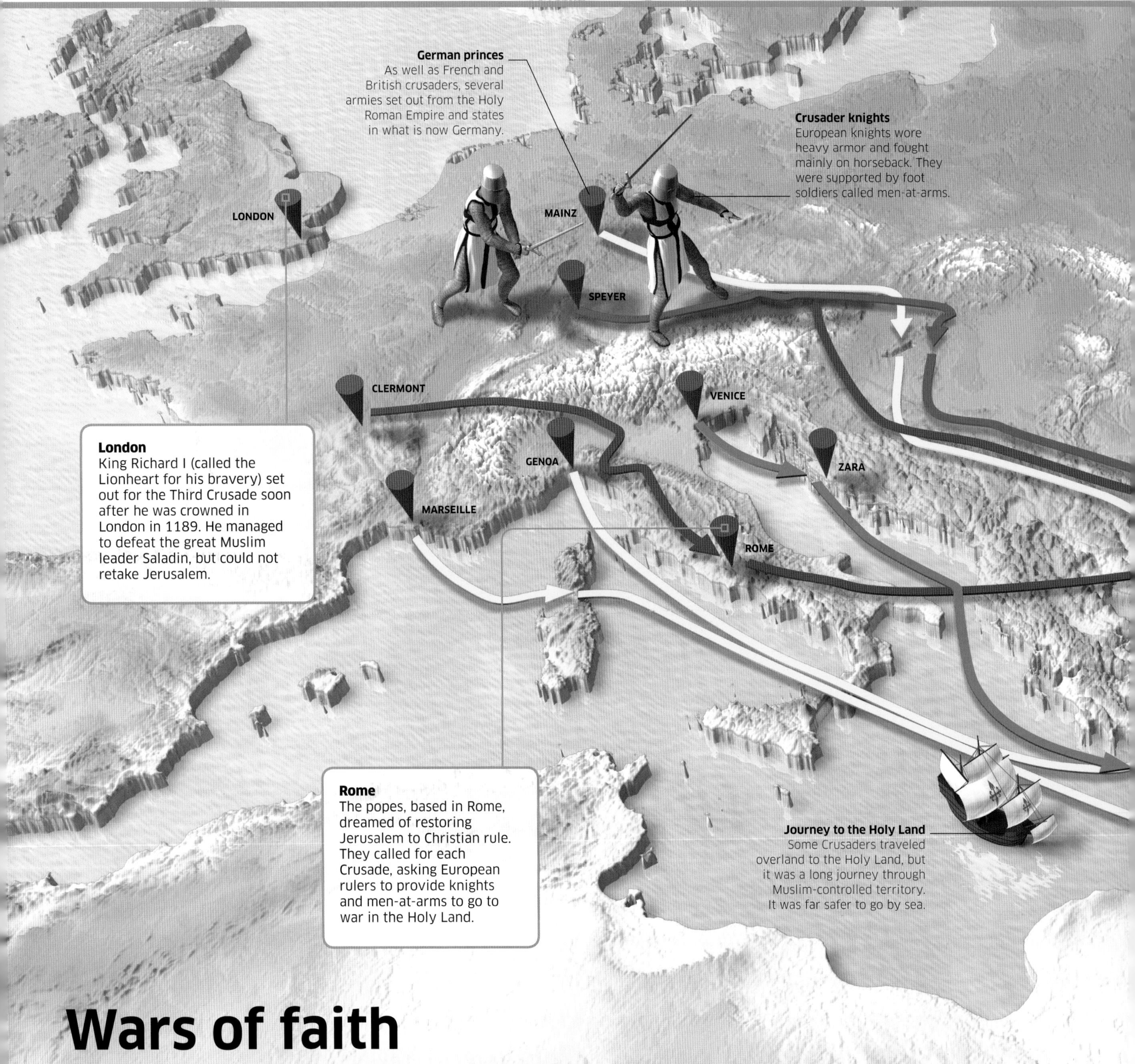

Wars of faith

Between 1095 and 1271, European armies set out on a series of Crusades. These were military expeditions to retake Christian holy sites, which had been in Muslim hands since the 7th century.

The First Crusade began in 1095, after Pope Urban II called on Christian knights to "take the cross" and pledge to capture Jerusalem. Thousands responded and, with the Muslim rulers of the Holy Land divided, they were able to take the city. The Crusaders set up small states and built castles, often defended by orders of religious knights such as the Templars. But when rulers such as Saladin and Baybars united the Muslims, the Crusaders slowly lost ground. The Muslims took Jerusalem in 1187, and in 1291 the last Crusader fortress fell.

The first four Crusades

Since they involved the largest armies and the biggest battles, the first four Crusades, between 1095 and 1204, are sometimes called the Principal Crusades. Apart from these, there were five Minor Crusades in the later years, as well as many other expeditions in between.

Key

- First Crusade
- Second Crusade
- Third Crusade
- Fourth Crusade

200 The **number of ships** in the fleet that **carried the English knights** of the Second Crusade in 1147.

1,000 The approximate **number of Crusader knights** left in **Acre** when it **fell to Sultan Baybars** in 1291.

275

Constantinople
The Byzantine Empire was made up of Christians descended from the Eastern Roman Empire. They were not always trusted by the Crusaders, and often quarreled with them. In 1204, a Crusading army heading for Jerusalem attacked and looted the Byzantine capital, Constantinople.

Saracen horsemen
The Crusaders called their Muslim opponents Saracens. They wore armor of interlinked metal rings and were excellent archers.

CONSTANTINOPLE

ANTIOCH

EDESSA

DAMASCUS

JERUSALEM

CAIRO

Jerusalem
A holy city to Christians and Muslims, Jerusalem became the capital of a Christian kingdom after the Crusaders captured it in 1099. However, they did not have enough knights to defend it for the long term.

Egypt
Some later Crusades landed in Egypt, hoping to defeat the Muslim sultans who ruled from Cairo. In 1250, the Mamluks, a new Muslim dynasty, took over in Egypt. Their ruler, Sultan Baybars, seized many of the remaining Crusader forts in the 1270s.

Centuries of conflict
The First Crusade captured lands in the Middle East, founding Christian kingdoms. But as years went on, the Muslims fought back, and the Crusaders were driven out.

November 1095
Pope Urban II preaches the First Crusade at Clermont in France, calling on Christian knights to take back holy sites in Palestine.

June 1097
The armies of the First Crusade defeat the Turks after a hard-fought battle, opening a way across Turkey.

July 1099
The Crusaders capture Jerusalem after a short siege. Many inhabitants (Muslims, Jews, and local Christians) are massacred.

December 1144
Edessa, a Crusader kingdom in Syria, is captured by the Muslim leader Zengi. The Second Crusade sets out to take it back.

November 1147
One of the armies of the Second Crusade, led by Otto II of Germany, is defeated by Seljuk Turks.

July 1148
The remaining armies of the Second Crusade besiege the Muslim city of Damascus, but are defeated.

July 1187
Crusaders living in the Holy Land lose almost all their territory to the Muslim leader Saladin. The Third Crusade is launched in response.

May–June 1191
King Philip Augustus of France and King Richard I of England arrive with Crusading armies at the city of Acre, near Jerusalem.

September 1191
Richard defeats Saladin, helped by Crusader knights from the Templar and Hospitaller orders.

October 1202
The army of the Fourth Crusade gathers in Venice and sails across the Adriatic in Venetian ships supplied by Doge Enrico Dandolo.

October–November 1202
In exchange for the use of the Venetian fleet, the Crusaders attack Venice's enemies in the Christian town of Zara.

April 1204
The Crusaders sack the Christian city of Constantinople after a quarrel over money with the Byzantine emperor, Alexius IV.

1217
Armies of the Fifth Crusade fail to take Jerusalem, invading Egypt instead. They are defeated outside Cairo in 1221.

1228–29
Emperor Frederick II of Germany leads the Sixth Crusade, which retakes most of Jerusalem.

1248–54
The Seventh Crusade invades Egypt, but ends when the Sultan of Egypt captures its leader, King Louis IX of France.

1291
Sultan Baybars captures Acre, the last major stronghold of the Crusaders.

World religions

Millions of people around the world worship a greater power that gives meaning to their lives. For many, religion is an intrinsic part of their very existence.

A religion is a set of beliefs that deal with every aspect of life, from birth to death, joy and sorrow, good and evil. Some people worship a god or gods, others follow a religious teacher. Religion includes not just beliefs themselves, but the religious rituals and ceremonies that are the outward expression of those beliefs. Religion can bind a small community, or offer people membership of a huge global organization. There are six major religions in the world: Christianity, Judaism, Islam, Hinduism, Buddhism, and Sikhism. These account for 85 percent of all the world's believers. Millions of others belong to religions old and new, making religion a rich, diverse, and sometimes controversial aspect of human history.

World religions

Apart from the followers of the six largest religions, about 12 percent of people belong to other faiths, sects, and cults. Pagans, for example, including witches and druids, revere nature. All religions share a quest to understand the world and make sense of our existence.

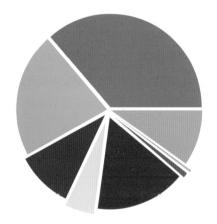

World religions by percentage

- ■ Christianity (33%)
- ■ Islam (21%)
- ■ Hinduism (13%)
- ■ Buddhism (6%)
- ■ No religious belief (14%)
- ■ Sikhism (0.5%)
- ■ Judaism (0.2%)
- ■ Other religions (12.3%)

Judaism

The religion of Jewish people, Judaism centers on the first Jew, Abraham, who taught Jews to worship one God. There are around 14 million believers today, but there are different forms of Judaism, including Orthodox and Liberal. Jews worship in synagogues, observe many rites of passage, and have a day of rest, called the Shabbat (Sabbath). They have struggled against hatred—in World War II, more than 6 million Jews were killed in the Holocaust. Most Jews now live in the United States and Israel.

Torah scroll
The most holy Jewish book is the Torah, which contains the rules for everyday life. In the synagogue, the Torah is read from precious scrolls.

Islam

Followers of Islam are called Muslims. There are 1.5 billion Muslims in the world, divided into Sunni and Shi'a. Their faith is based upon the Five Pillars: belief, worship, fasting, alms-giving, and pilgrimage. They follow a Holy Scripture known as the Qur'an, the word of God as told to the Prophet Muhammad.

Mosque
Many Muslims visit a mosque daily to say their prayers, but on Fridays all attend to listen to the Imam (teacher). Larger mosques have libraries and classrooms.

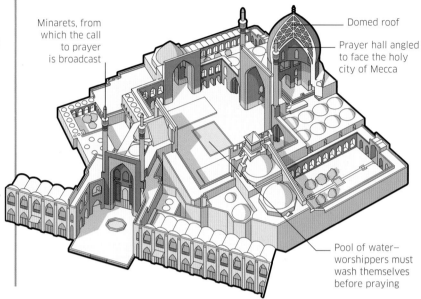

Minarets, from which the call to prayer is broadcast

Domed roof

Prayer hall angled to face the holy city of Mecca

Pool of water—worshippers must wash themselves before praying

Christianity

Christians follow the teachings of Jesus Christ, believing he was the Son of God. There are about 2.1 billion Christians worldwide, and they are united in the belief in one God, the Bible as a holy text, and the use of prayer in worship. However, different branches of Christianity—Protestant, Catholic, and Orthodox—have different ideas about how their faith should be practiced.

Protestant	Catholic	Orthodox
No official leader	Led by the Pope in Vatican City	Led by Patriarchs
Began with Martin Luther, a 16th-century scholar who rejected Catholic teaching	Believe that popes inherit their authority from Saint Peter, one of the 12 apostles of Jesus	Formed in 451 CE after Christians in Rome and Constantinople disagreed over the Church's teachings
Found across the world, but chiefly in Northern Europe, North America, New Zealand, Australia, and parts of Africa	Found across the world, but especially in Southern Europe, Eastern Europe, and South America	Found mainly in Greece, the Balkans, Russia, the Middle East, and North Africa
Emphasize simple worship in language everyone can understand	Use elaborate ceremonies, sometimes in Latin, to glorify God	Use elaborate ceremonies in different languages, including Greek and Syriac, to glorify God
Do not generally have monasteries, but use churches or cathedrals	Have monasteries for men and women	Have monasteries for men and women
Believe everyone can speak directly to God through prayer	Believe most people can speak to God only through the help of a priest or saints	Believe most people can speak to God only through the help of a priest or saints

99 The number of **names** used to describe **God** in the **Qur'an**.

613 The number of **commandments**— "dos" and "don'ts"—in the **Torah**.

277

Hinduism

To the 900 million Hindus worldwide, Hinduism is quite a varied religion. Hindus believe in a great spirit called Brahman who cannot be seen, but is present everywhere. They worship a wide range of gods and goddesses, each depicting a different aspect of Brahman's power. The three most important gods are Brahma, the creator; Shiva, the destroyer; and Vishnu, the protector. According to Hinduism, every person has a soul, which lives on after a person dies. The soul takes on a new form and begins a new life, and this cycle continues. This is known as reincarnation. For Hindus, the aim is to escape this cycle and gain freedom to be with Brahman. Each good deed takes them a step closer. A bad deed takes them further away. This is the law of karma.

Brahma
The creative aspect of Brahman, Brahma is depicted with four arms, and four faces, each reciting one of four holy texts.

Shiva
The force of destruction and transformation, Shiva can be both kindly and fearsome. As Nataraja, he dances inside a ring of flames.

Vishnu
Blue-skinned Vishnu is charged with upholding the *dharma*–the law that maintains the Universe.

Lakshmi
The goddess of luck and wealth, Lakshmi is one of the most widely worshipped Hindu deities. She is often seen sitting on a lotus.

Hanuman
A monkeylike being (or *vanara*), Hanuman is best known for aiding the hero Rama in his war against the demons.

Ganesh
Elephant-headed Ganesh is the patron of wisdom, writing, art and science, and new endeavors.

Buddhism

Buddhism originated in India 2,500 years ago when a man called Siddhartha Gautama gained enlightenment and became the Buddha ("the Enlightened One"). Buddhism gradually spread from India to other countries. Today, about 376 million people across the world follow the teachings of the Buddha–the *dharma*, which seeks to end suffering (*dukkha*) and find answers to the true meaning of life. By respecting the Eightfold Path, including right thoughts and deeds, keeping Five Promises, and repeating three prayers (Three Jewels), Buddhists hope to attain a state of peaceful enlightenment called nirvana.

"WE ARE WHAT WE THINK. ALL THAT WE ARE ARISES WITH OUR THOUGHTS. WITH OUR THOUGHTS, WE MAKE THE WORLD."
BUDDHA

Statue of Buddha meditating
Buddhists worship by meditation (*dhyana*), trying to clear their minds of earthly distractions in order to perceive the Universe more clearly.

53,840 The number of **janissaries** under Sultan Mehmed IV in **1670**.

737 The number of **imperial tailors** in 1670.

The Ottoman Empire

For more than 600 years, the Muslim Ottoman Turks ruled one of the largest empires ever seen. It stretched across the Middle East, central and southern Europe, and Africa. Powerful emperors called sultans ruled this huge territory with the help of the janissaries, a personal army of slave-soldiers.

The Ottoman Empire began as a tiny state in the northwest of present-day Turkey. The Ottomans were skillful warriors, and they quickly increased their territory. In 1453, they captured Constantinople, which had been the capital of the Eastern Roman (Byzantine) Empire for 1,100 years. Renamed Istanbul, it became the center of their Islamic empire, and its rulers, the sultans, were leaders of the Muslim world.

In the 15th and 16th centuries, the empire became very powerful and wealthy. The sultans built grand mosques and palaces, many of which can still be seen today. The different cities became famous for the beautiful decorative arts practiced by their craftsmen: Iznik for ceramics, Bursa for silks and textiles, Cairo for carpets, and Baghdad for calligraphy.

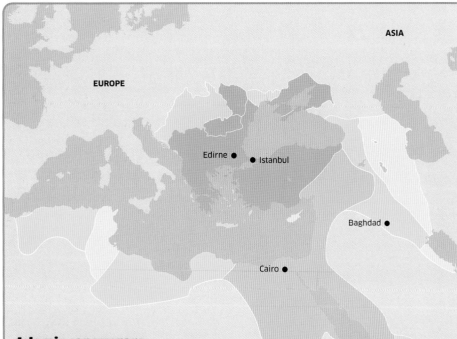

ASIA

EUROPE

Edirne ● ● Istanbul

Baghdad ●

Cairo ●

AFRICA

Islamic conquerors

The Ottoman Empire was founded by invaders from Central Asia, who carved out a homeland in northwest Turkey around 1300. They soon began to expand, and conquered territory across Europe and the Middle East. However, they were slow to adapt to new military tactics, and after 1700 they started to lose territory to Europe and Russia. A series of weak sultans and corruption in government caused further damage, and the empire collapsed in 1919 shortly after being defeated in World War I.

Ottoman conquests

▪ The empire in 1512

▪ The empire in 1520

▪ The empire in 1566

▪ The empire in 1639

City of Islam

When the Ottomans captured the city of Constantinople, they renamed it Istanbul and set about remodeling it as their new capital. They built magnificent mosques, and filled the streets with beautiful gardens, *hans* (markets), and grand tombs. A luxurious complex called the Topkapi Palace was constructed as the center of government and home of the sultans.

Minarets (towers for calling Muslims to prayer) added by Ottomans

Religious conversion

The church of Hagia Sophia stood at the center of Constantinople under the Byzantine Emperors. The Ottomans converted it into a mosque, adding minarets and painting over the Christian images inside.

Ottoman art and design

The religion of Islam does not allow realistic pictures of humans and animals to be shown in public places. Instead, the Ottomans created beautiful patterns based on plants, flowers, or Arabic script to decorate their mosques and other buildings. At Topkapi Palace in Istanbul, the most talented artists, designers, weavers, and calligraphers gathered in workshops to produce official products for the sultan and his household. Their designs were the height of fashion across the empire.

Wall tile from Iznik

The Ottoman town of Iznik, in northwestern Turkey, was famous for its beautiful ceramic tiles.

145 The number of **ships in the Ottoman fleet** in 1453.

1,700 The number of **slaves owned by Rüstem Pasha**, Süleiman the Magnificent's **vizier** (chief minister).

279

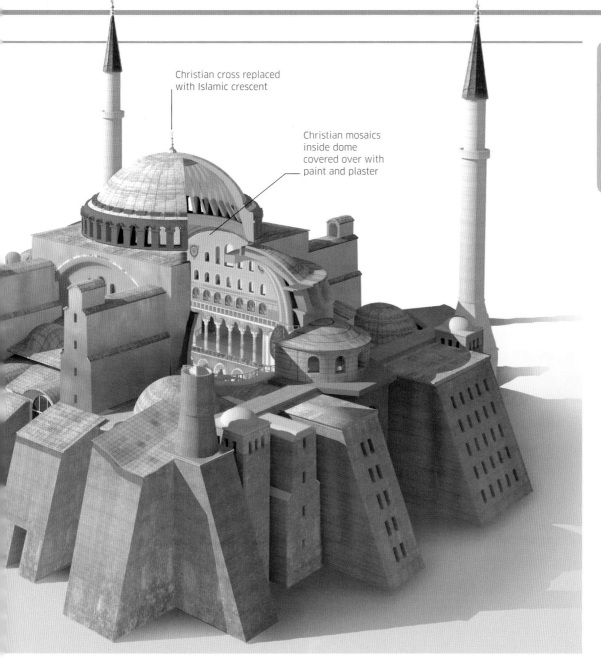

Christian cross replaced with Islamic crescent

Christian mosaics inside dome covered over with paint and plaster

The sultans

The Ottoman Empire was ruled by the descendants of a single family for 600 years. The early sultans were warriors who fought to gain more land. Under them, life in the empire was mostly peaceful and secure. Later sultans were less ambitious, and the Empire was overtaken by rivals in Europe.

Orhan
reigned 1300–1362

The second Ottoman sultan inherited a tiny state from his father, Osman I, and spent his life expanding it into an empire. He fought wars with the Christian Byzantine Empire and seized much of northwest Turkey from them, making the city of Bursa the first Ottoman capital. It was during Orhan's reign that Ottoman armies first invaded Europe.

Murad I
reigned 1362–1389

Under Murad the empire expanded even further into Europe, conquering Macedonia, Bosnia, and Bulgaria. Murad moved the Ottoman capital city to Edirne (Adrianople), in northwestern Turkey, and fought off local Muslim rivals to the empire. He reorganized the janissaries into a paid army in the service of the sultan, and created the *devshirme* recruiting system.

Mehmed II
reigned 1444–1481

Also known as "the Conqueror," Mehmed II was just 21 years old when he led his army to capture the Byzantine capital, Constantinople. As well as a fierce warrior, he was a patron of culture, science, and law. Some of Europe's best artists and scholars visited Mehmed at his palace, and he invited people of different races and religions to live in the capital.

Süleiman I
reigned 1520–1566

Known as "the Magnificent," Süleiman was one of the greatest Ottoman sultans. Under his rule, the empire became a world power. Süleiman was a brave military leader who personally led his army into battle, but he also loved the arts and wrote poetry.

SULTAN SÜLEIMAN I

Structure of an empire

Although the empire was made up of many different races and had several major cities, it was organized from Istanbul by the sultan and his government. The sultan was both the political leader and the *caliph*, or religious head, of the Muslim world. He was assisted by a grand vizier, or chief minister, and other court officials and military commanders. Soldiers who volunteered for the army received land in return for service. The sultan's top troops were the janissaries, a tough, highly trained army of foot soldiers willing to lay down their lives for their ruler.

Slave army

The Ottomans had a system called the *devshirme* (gathering), which took male children from Christian families as slaves. The boys were converted to Islam and brought up to be loyal to the sultan. Most became janissaries, while some became scribes or clerics. The very brightest became personal aides to the sultan, and could become wealthy and powerful.

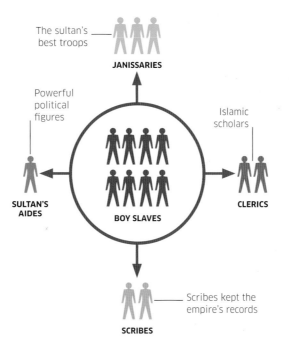

The sultan's best troops

JANISSARIES

Powerful political figures

SULTAN'S AIDES

Islamic scholars

CLERICS

BOY SLAVES

Scribes kept the empire's records

SCRIBES

"MY WOMAN OF THE **BEAUTIFUL HAIR,** MY LOVE OF THE **SLANTED BROW, MY LOVE OF EYES** FULL OF MISCHIEF, **I'LL SING YOUR PRAISES ALWAYS."**

SULTAN SÜLEIMAN I, POEM WRITTEN TO HIS WIFE

4,000 silk tunics—the **ransom** given to the Visigoths not to sack **Rome** in 408 CE.

The Silk Road

For more than a thousand years the great overland trading route known as the Silk Road carried precious goods between China and the Middle East and Europe.

When the Han dynasty of China conquered Central Asia around 200 BCE, it became possible to travel safely all the way to the borders of Persia and then westward to the Mediterranean Sea. Merchants who transported goods such as silk and gold along this route could make large profits, and the places they stopped at along the way often became rich cities. The Silk Road was at its height in the time of the Chinese Tang dynasty (618–907 CE) and then under the Mongols (13th–14th century).

Europe
Silk reached Europe from China as early as the 1st century CE. However, few Europeans traveled the other way to China until the 13th century, when the Venetian merchant Marco Polo visited the court of the Mongol ruler Kublai Khan.

VENICE

CONSTANTINOPLE

SAMARKAND

ISFAHAN

The Arab world
In the 7th century, the Arabs conquered the entire area from the shore of the Mediterranean Sea to the eastern borders of Persia. Damascus and Baghdad, the capitals of the Arab caliphs (rulers), grew prosperous from Silk Road trade.

ARAB SILVER VASE

Profitable exchange
Merchants on the Silk Road did not just carry silk. Traders heading toward the Arab world and Europe also brought other Chinese products, such as jade, lacquer, pottery, and bronze objects, which were highly prized in the west. Trading caravans heading toward China carried gold (to pay for the silk) and goods that were rare in China, such as ivory and glass.

Valuable trade items
The Chinese did not know how to make glass until the 5th century, and the Arabs and Byzantines only learned how to manufacture silk in the 6th and 7th centuries, so both these trade items were very valuable.

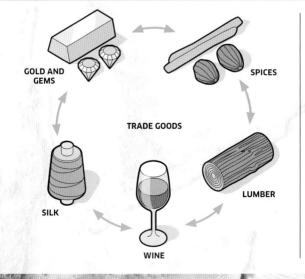

GOLD AND GEMS

SPICES

TRADE GOODS

SILK

LUMBER

WINE

A perilous journey
As trade increased along the Silk Road, nomads such as the Xiongnu people began to attack the caravans in which the merchants traveled. The Chinese were forced to take control of the Central Asian oases, and stationed soldiers there to protect the trade. Some sections of the route traveled through perilous landscapes such as the Lop Nur salt desert, and groups not carrying enough water faced dying of thirst. The places where merchants stopped turned into towns, and artistic and religious ideas moved along the Silk Road with the travelers. This resulted in a great spreading of ideas, such as the introduction of Buddhism from India into China in the 2nd century CE.

30,000 craftsmen were **deported by Genghis Khan** to **Mongolia** after he captured **Samarkand** in 1220.

30 days—the time it took **Marco Polo** to cross the **Lop Nur Desert**.

281

Mongol raiders
For centuries, Mongol horsemen raided Silk Road caravans. In 1206, led by Genghis Khan, they conquered most of Central Asia and northern China, taking control of the eastern Silk Road.

Kashgar
This ancient oasis town lay at the point where the northern and southern routes of the Silk Road joined.

MING BUDDHA STATUE

China
Until the 6th century, the Chinese were the only people who knew how to manufacture silk. The Silk Road flourished as China took control of the oases of Central Asia, providing safe passage for traders to the west.

KARAKORUM

DUNHUANG

BEIJING

KASHGAR

XI'AN

Central Asia
This region was dominated by blistering deserts and towering mountains. In the 8th century, Arab conquests spread Islam to the region giving rise to great Muslim empires that contributed to Silk Road trade. The Timurids conquered a swathe of territory in the 14th and 15th centuries, leaving behind beautiful cities such as Samarkand. To the south, the Mughal Empire spread across India in the 16th century.

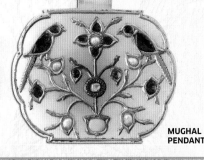

MUGHAL PENDANT

DELHI

Constantinople
The capital of the Byzantine Empire, Constantinople, was the meeting point between European and Asian traders. A rich and powerful city, it controlled one of the main crossing points over the Bosphorus, the strip of water separating Europe from Asia.

Isfahan
As the Silk Road passed out of Central Asia and into Persia, it passed through Isfahan, a city famous for its wealth. The city became so important that in 1598 it became the capital of Persia under the Safavid dynasty.

Samarkand
Also known as Maracanda, this was one of the main cities on the northern section of the Silk Road. It changed hands many times between Chinese, Arabs, and Huns before it was conquered by the Mongols in 1220.

Dunhuang
The westernmost point of Chinese territory, Dunhuang was an important stopping point before travelers set out on the month-long crossing of the Lop Nur Desert. A treasure trove of important Buddhist manuscripts was found here in 1900.

Xi'an
Chang'an (now Xi'an) was the capital of China in Han and Tang times, and the setting-off point for merchants traveling westward along the Silk Road. It became very wealthy, and in the 8th century was the world's largest city, with about a million inhabitants.

Beijing
The city was the winter capital of the Mongol rulers of China in the 13th century, and it was here that Marco Polo visited their ruler Kublai Khan in 1275. The journey from Venice took Polo more than three years.

New samurai **sword blades** were **tested** by using them to **cut through dead bodies**—or condemned **criminals**.

Samurai warriors

Japan in the Middle Ages was ruled by an emperor but governed by military generals called *daimyo*, who often fought among themselves. At the head of their armies were some of the most fearsome warriors of all time: the samurai.

The samurai lived at the top of a strictly layered society. While the emperor and his family held the most respect, the samurai controlled the wealth and political power. Rich and influential *daimyo* gave their samurai supporters gifts of land, and the samurai would fight for the *daimyo* in exchange. Peasants working on the land paid taxes in food and money to support their masters.

Although most famous for warfare, the samurai valued music, poetry, and art. Many were attracted to Zen Buddhism, which teaches that perfect understanding of the universe lies through meditation and escaping from the self, which can be achieved just as well through painting as swordsmanship.

220 **years—the length of time Japan isolated itself from the outside world, from 1633–1853. No foreigner could enter on pain of death.**

Weapons and armor

Samurai favored hand-to-hand combat using razor-sharp swords. Their fighting style depended on nimble movement, so their armor had to be light enough not to slow them down. Samurai did not have shields; they used the sides of their swords to block enemy attacks.

Kabuto **(helmet)** These often featured impressive crests, as well as cheek and neck protectors.

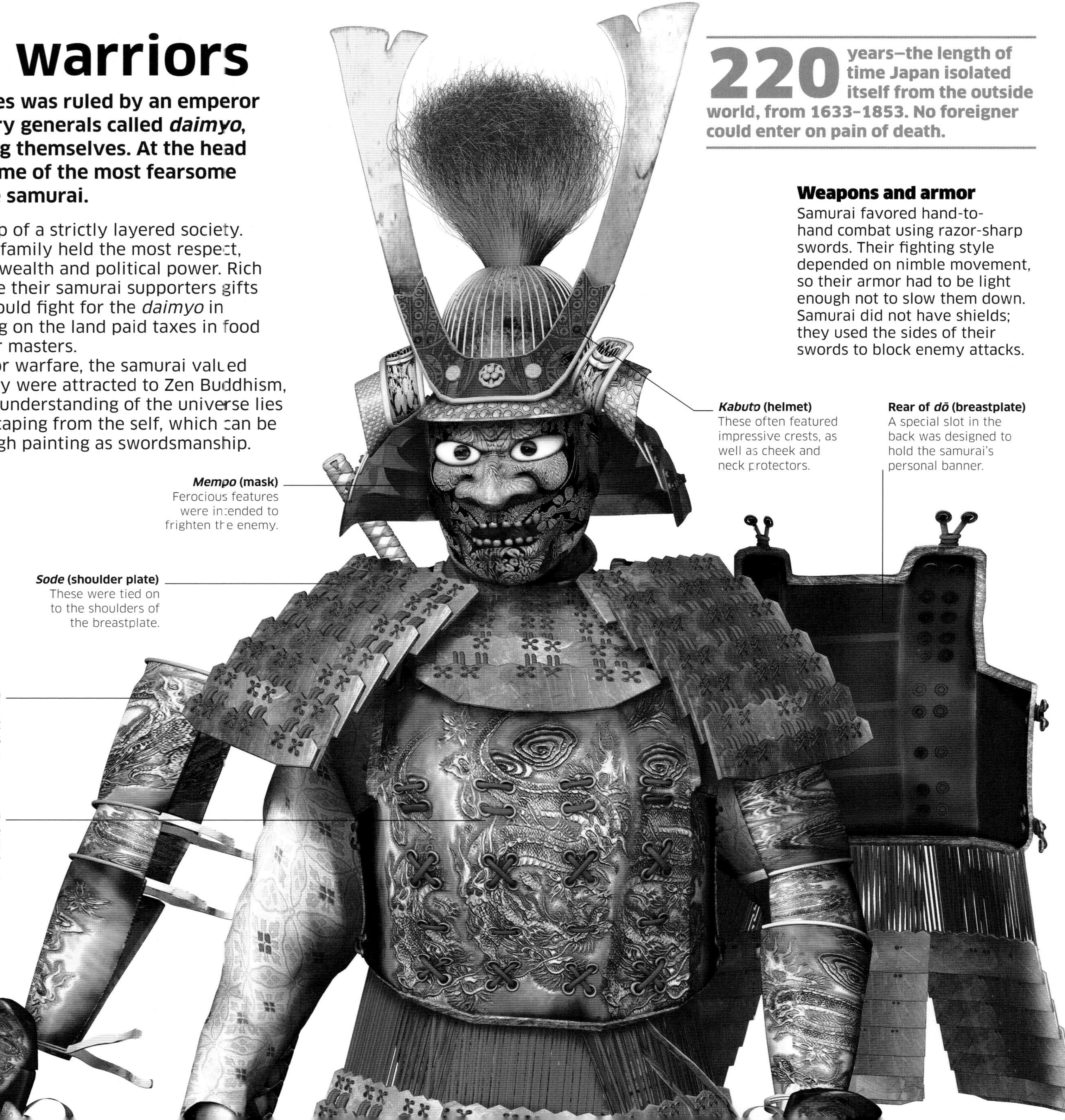

Rear of *dō* **(breastplate)** A special slot in the back was designed to hold the samurai's personal banner.

Mempo **(mask)** Ferocious features were intended to frighten the enemy.

Sode **(shoulder plate)** These were tied on to the shoulders of the breastplate.

Kote **(arm guard)** Sections of lacquered metal sometimes had chain mail at the elbow and other joints so the arm could bend freely.

Dō **(breastplate)** Early versions were made of wood and leather, but later armor used steel plates.

Tekko **(glove)** Protection even extended to the samurai's thumbs.

1 million—the number of **layers of steel** in a samurai **sword blade**.

28 in (70 cm)—the usual **length** of a **katana blade**.

2,370 º F (1,300º C)—the **heat** of the **furnaces** used to **forge samurai swords**.

283

Saya (scabbard)

***Kusazuri* (skirts)**
Attached to the breastplate with silk cords, these protected the samurai's thighs.

***Suneate* (greaves)**
These protected the samurai's calves.

***Tabi* (sock)**
These had special toe holes for sandal straps.

Sword cross-section
Samurai swords are famous for their incredible strength and sharpness. Swordsmiths achieved this by allowing different parts of the blade to cool at different rates. The edge of the blade was hard and sharp, but the body was soft and flexible, and so less likely to snap.

Soft, flexible core

Hard cutting edge

Strong sides for blocking

***Katana* (long sword)**
The samurai's main weapon was wielded with two hands.

Armor layers
Samurai armor needed to be strong but light to match their nimble fighting style. It was made of thin strips of metal covered with varnish called lacquer and bound together with silk. In the 16th century, with the arrival of guns, samurai started to include plates of steel to cover vulnerable areas such as their chests.

An honorable death
To be a perfect warrior, a samurai must always behave with honor, even toward his enemies. Battles were often fought according to strict rituals, starting with an exchange of bow shots between generals, followed by a volley of arrows from both sides, and then single combat between swordsmen. Samurai were completely loyal to their lords and unafraid of death. Dishonored samurai would undergo *seppuku* (ritual suicide) rather than live in shame. The preferred method was *hara-kiri*: the samurai would cut open his own stomach before being finished off with a chop to the neck by a friend.

White Heron Castle
Powerful samurai lords built castles as homes, fortresses, and symbols of their power. This one was built in the city of Himeji in the 17th century.

Warring states
The samurai began as bodyguards to the emperor, but by the 12th century they had become the real rulers of Japan. Although the emperor was still officially in charge, true power rested with the *shogun*, the head of the most powerful samurai clan. Many battles were fought between rival *daimyo* for the honor of becoming *shogun*. The greatest of these took place between 1550 and 1600, the Sengoku period, during which all of Japan was plunged into civil war. The victor was Tokugawa Ieyasu, who ushered in a peaceful age known as the Edo period. In 1868, a new government replaced the Tokugawa rulers. To modernize Japan, they abolished the samurai.

THE AGE OF DISCOVERY

The world experienced huge changes between 1450 and 1750. A wave of new ideas swept across Europe as explorers founded new colonies and trading networks all across the world. European rivals often went to war with each other, and with the powerful empires of Asia, in the scramble for new territory.

NEW WAYS OF THINKING

In the medieval period, the Christian Church controlled art and learning in Europe. This changed around 1450 when important works by Greek and Roman authors were rediscovered and became popular. Scholars such as Erasmus (1466-1536) created a new movement called humanism, teaching that art and science should be based on experiment and observation rather than old traditions.

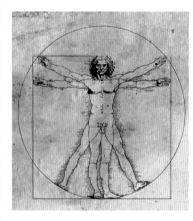

The Renaissance

A great deal of Roman art and architecture survived in Italy around 1400. It inspired artists, such as Michelangelo, Leonardo da Vinci, and Raphael, and architects, such as Brunelleschi, to produce daring new works of their own. Their artistic movement is called the Renaissance, and it soon spread across Europe.

Vitruvian Man
Renaissance artists such as Leonardo da Vinci studied human anatomy carefully to make their art as realistic as possible.

The Reformation

In 1517, a German priest called Martin Luther attacked the wealth of the Church and the right of the Pope to decide what people should believe. This movement—the Reformation—created a split between traditional Christians (Catholics) and supporters of Luther, called Protestants.

"WHY DOES THE POPE NOT BUILD [CHURCHES] WITH HIS OWN MONEY, RATHER THAN WITH THE MONEY OF POOR BELIEVERS?"
MARTIN LUTHER

Scientific thinking

The invention of the printing press by Johannes Gutenberg meant that books could be produced quickly, and knowledge could spread more rapidly. New ideas emerged, including the notion that the Earth orbits the Sun, proposed by Polish astronomer Copernicus in 1543, and Isaac Newton's theory of gravity, published in 1687.

Scientific instruments
Isaac Newton invented a new model of telescope in 1678. It used a series of mirrors to create a better-quality image.

GLOBAL AMBITIONS

Spices such as pepper and nutmeg were very expensive in Europe in the 15th century, because they could only be obtained by trade with East Asia. Land routes such as the Silk Road were controlled by Islamic empires, so European explorers sought sea routes, founding colonies and outposts in India, Southeast Asia, and the Americas.

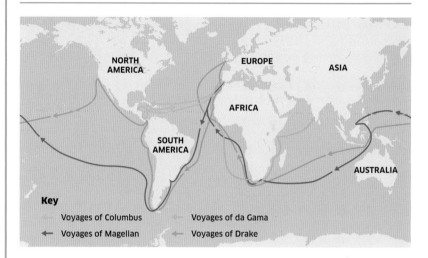

NORTH AMERICA
EUROPE
ASIA
AFRICA
SOUTH AMERICA
AUSTRALIA

Key
← Voyages of Columbus
← Voyages of Magellan
← Voyages of da Gama
← Voyages of Drake

Voyages of discovery

Christopher Columbus reached America in 1492. Portuguese captain Vasco da Gama rounded southern Africa to reach India in 1498. Spaniard Ferdinand Magellan led the first voyage around the world in 1519-21, followed by Englishman Sir Francis Drake in 1577-80.

Rival explorers
Many brave explorers set out to map new sea routes and claim new territories. Some achieved great fame, but many were lost at sea.

OF 237 MEN WHO JOINED MAGELLAN ON HIS VOYAGE AROUND THE WORLD ONLY 18 RETURNED ALIVE.

Trading empires

Trade with Asia and colonies in America brought great wealth to the European powers. Spanish and Portuguese ships carried huge quantities of gold and silver from the Americas, often harassed by pirates and privateers encouraged by rivals such as Britain.

Vast riches
Spanish mines in the Americas produced 100 tons of silver every year—the weight of 10 buses.

European powers

The influx of new wealth made some European states very powerful. Wars and rivalry were common, but the new empires also saw scientific advances and flourishing new movements in art and literature.

ELIZABETHAN ENGLAND
England grew rich during the reign of Elizabeth I (1558-1603), despite conflict between Protestants and Catholics and the threat of war with Spain.

FRANCE UNDER LOUIS IV
France became the most powerful country in Europe during the long reign of Louis XIV (1643-1715), famous for his strong army and cultured court.

FERDINAND AND ISABELLA OF SPAIN
The rulers of Spain, Ferdinand of Aragon and Isabella of Castile, took control of new territories in the Americas, thanks to a treaty with Portugal in 1494.

RISE OF THE HABSBURGS
This family of minor nobles gained control of much of central Europe. They went on to become kings of Spain and rulers of the vast Holy Roman Empire.

THE NEW WORLD

Before the arrival of European explorers, the people of the Americas had built civilizations and empires. However, they did not have gunpowder, and even large armies could be defeated by the guns of Spanish soldiers. The Europeans also brought new diseases that killed huge numbers of indigenous Americans.

IT IS ESTIMATED THAT UP TO 90 PERCENT OF THE INDIGENOUS POPULATION OF CENTRAL AMERICA WAS WIPED OUT BY DISEASE AND WARFARE FOLLOWING THE ARRIVAL OF THE SPANISH.

Incas, Aztecs, Mayans

The most advanced peoples the Spanish encountered were the Incas (in Peru) and the Aztecs (in Mexico), both of whom controlled large empires. The Spanish attacked the Aztecs in 1519 and the Incas 1531 and soon captured their capital cities.

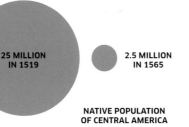

25 MILLION IN 1519

2.5 MILLION IN 1565

NATIVE POPULATION OF CENTRAL AMERICA

European colonies

The Spanish soon had to face competition from other European powers, who were quick to take land in the Americas. The Portuguese settled in Brazil around 1500. The French and English took islands in the Caribbean, but concentrated mainly on North America, where the English set up their first colony at Jamestown, Virginia, in 1607.

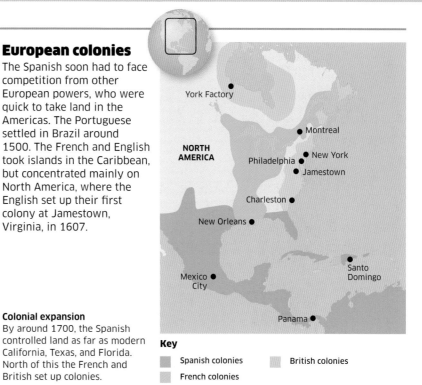

Colonial expansion

By around 1700, the Spanish controlled land as far as modern California, Texas, and Florida. North of this the French and British set up colonies.

Key

Spanish colonies

British colonies

French colonies

EASTERN POWERS

In Asia, great empires continued to fight off European competition, but often suffered internal turmoil. In China, the Ming dynasty collapsed in 1644 and was replaced by the Qing, who made China strong again. Japan sealed itself off from European influence, banning foreigners for more than 200 years. Two Muslim empires, the Mughals in India and the Ottomans in Turkey, gained great power, before growing stagnant and collapsing.

Ottoman expansion

The Ottoman Empire, based in modern Turkey, quickly expanded to fill the space left by the collapse of the Byzantine Empire. They took control of the Middle East, ruling much of the Arab world. Their advance on Europe was halted by the Poles and Habsburgs on land, and in the Mediterranean by rich Italian city-states such as Venice.

SIEGE OF CONSTANTINOPLE

In 1453, the Ottoman sultan Mehmed II captured Constantinople, the capital of the Byzantine Empire. He used huge cannons to break down the strong walls. He then made the city his capital.

BATTLE OF MOHÁCS

In 1526, Sultan Süleiman the Magnificent defeated and killed the Hungarian king Louis II in a battle at Mohács. The Ottomans then took over much of Hungary. Süleiman's armies also conquered large areas of the Balkans, the Middle East, and North Africa.

BATTLE OF LEPANTO

The Ottomans captured Cyprus in 1570. A strong Spanish and Italian fleet was sent to take it back. They defeated the Turks at Lepanto, off the Greek coast, in 1571. Their victory ended Ottoman dominance in the Mediterranean.

SIEGE OF VIENNA

In 1683, an Ottoman army that had been trying to capture the Habsburg capital of Vienna (Austria) was defeated by an army led by King Jan Sobieski of Poland. The Ottomans never again reached so far west.

AMUR

OUTER MONGOLIA

MANCHURIA

XINJIANG

Mukden

Beijing

TIBET

Nanjing Suzhou

Lhasa

Chongqing

Changsha Fuzhou

Taiwan

Guangzhou

Macao

Key

Qing Empire in 1660

Qing Empire in 1770

Qing China

In 1644, the Ming dynasty was overthrown by a series of peasant revolts. The new rulers, the Qing, came from Manchuria in northeast China. They tried to make people adopt Qing customs, like the wearing of a ponytail, but this proved very unpopular. Nevertheless, they overcame opposition and increased Chinese territory.

Greater empire

The Qing conquered new territory to make China larger than ever. The new territories included Taiwan and Mongolia.

Mughal India

In 1526, a Muslim prince from central Asia called Babur captured Delhi and founded the Mughal Empire. The Mughals expanded steadily from northern India, making their greatest gains under Sultan Akbar (1556–1605). The Mughal court was a rich one, famous for its magnificent works of art and beautiful buildings.

Combining cultures

Mughal buildings, such as the tomb of Sultan Humayun, who died in 1556, combined Islamic tradition with Indian culture to create a new style.

Tokugawa Japan

In Japan, a period of civil war ended when powerful general Tokugawa Ieyasu declared himself shogun (military ruler). He moved the capital to Edo (Tokyo) and reduced the power of the daimyo (warlords) who had previously dominated Japan. The Tokugawa family ruled Japan until 1868, and isolated it from the outside world.

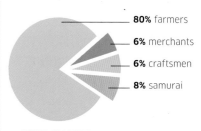

80% farmers

6% merchants

6% craftsmen

8% samurai

SOCIAL CLASSES IN TOKUGAWA JAPAN

Samurai society

Warrior nobles called samurai were the most honored class in Japanese society. Merchants and craftsmen may have been wealthy, but they were less respected than poor peasant farmers.

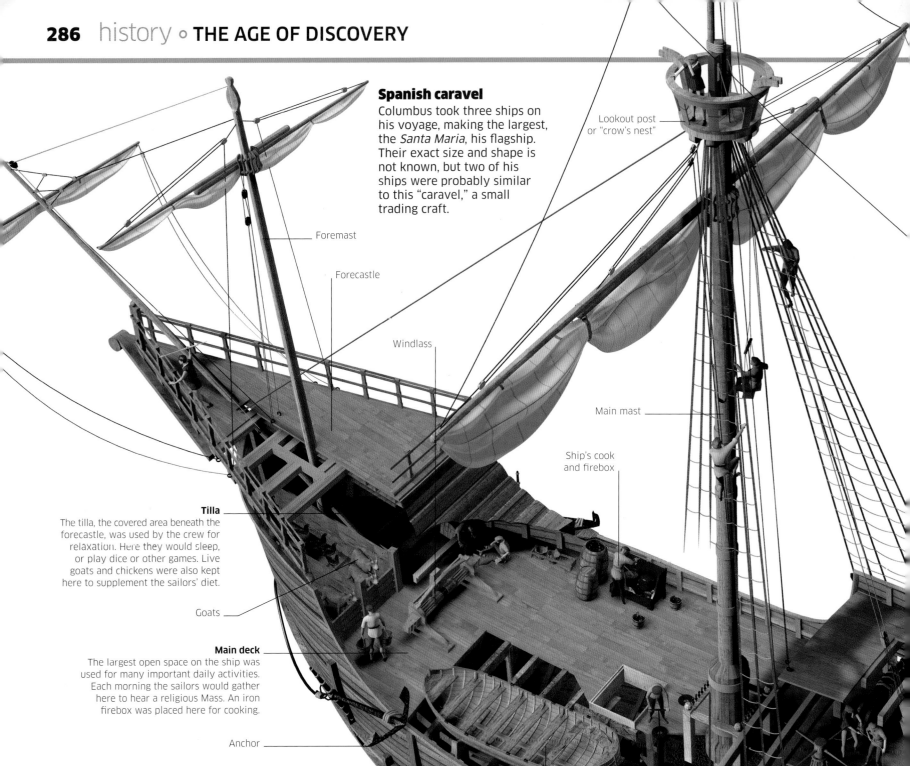

Spanish caravel
Columbus took three ships on his voyage, making the largest, the *Santa Maria*, his flagship. Their exact size and shape is not known, but two of his ships were probably similar to this "caravel," a small trading craft.

Foremast

Forecastle

Windlass

Lookout post or "crow's nest"

Main mast

Ship's cook and firebox

Tilla
The tilla, the covered area beneath the forecastle, was used by the crew for relaxation. Here they would sleep, or play dice or other games. Live goats and chickens were also kept here to supplement the sailors' diet.

Goats

Main deck
The largest open space on the ship was used for many important daily activities. Each morning the sailors would gather here to hear a religious Mass. An iron firebox was placed here for cooking.

Anchor

Voyage to the Americas

For centuries the people of Europe and Asia had no idea the Americas existed, until 1492 when Christopher Columbus led a voyage across the Atlantic Ocean.

Columbus did not know of the existence of the Americas. He intended to discover a new route from Western Europe to East Asia. He was astonished to discover a new land, and he and his wealthy sponsors, King Ferdinand and Queen Isabella of Spain, were quick to exploit the new territory. Explorers brought back gold, silver, and new plants such as tobacco. They established colonies in the new land, taking advantage of fertile soil to grow sugar and cotton. However, for the indigenous peoples living in the area, the arrival of European explorers was catastrophic, bringing disease, war, slavery, and death.

Long boat

Hold
The main storage area was below decks. The floor was covered with river pebbles, which kept the boat upright. The hold was filled with supplies: barrels of wine and water, beans and biscuits for food, as well as spare wood, sailcloth, and rope.

Capstan
This huge winch was pushed by eight sailors. It was used to hoist heavy loads such as supplies and the ship's anchors.

40 The **number of men** in the *Santa Maria's* **crew**.

70 days—the time it took **Columbus** to reach the **Americas** on his **first voyage** from Spain.

1,500 The **number of men** who joined **Columbus's second voyage**.

287

"At two o'clock in the morning the **land was discovered,** at two leagues' distance...they found themselves near a small island, one of the Lucayos, called in the Indian language Guanahani."
Log of Christopher Columbus, October 12, 1492

Flag of the King and Queen of Spain, Columbus's sponsors

Afterdeck and aftcastle
The open space above the quarterdeck was known as the afterdeck. Two small cannons were mounted here. The space above the admiral's cabin was called the aftcastle, and with a clear view on all sides was an ideal place to take navigational readings.

Aftcastle

Admiral's cabin
Columbus shared this tiny cabin with three other officers and a servant boy.

Tiller for steering

Quarterdeck
The area under the afterdeck housed the tiller, used to steer the ship. Next to it were a compass and hourglass for navigation. Pallets were laid around the walls for sailors to sleep on.

Rudder

Columbus's voyages

Columbus undertook four voyages to the Americas. On his first, he visited islands in the Caribbean, where his second voyage established colonies a year later. It wasn't until his third visit, in 1498, that he set foot upon the American mainland, touching the coast of what is now Venezuela. His last voyage, begun in 1502, took him along the coast of Central America, seeking a passage through to the Pacific Ocean beyond.

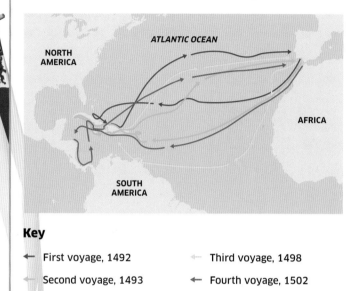

Key

← First voyage, 1492

← Third voyage, 1498

← Second voyage, 1493

← Fourth voyage, 1502

Finding your way

Explorers like Columbus often had no maps, and had to navigate by other means. They used a compass to measure the direction the ships were moving in, and an hourglass to keep track of the time. They also used a device called a quadrant, to calculate their latitude by measuring the angle of the sun and stars.

Sighting tube for aiming the quadrant

Dial marked with numbers to measure the angle of the stars

QUADRANT

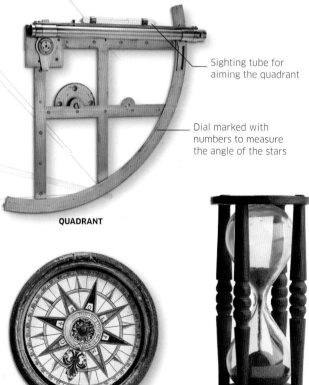

COMPASS

HOURGLASS

Human sacrifice

The Aztecs believed that the blood of human victims was needed to feed the Sun to make sure that it did not go out. Many people sacrificed to the Sun were captured in wars. The priest would plunge a sharp knife into the victim's chest and then pull out his still-beating heart.

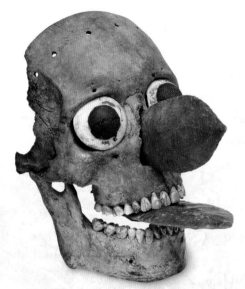

Death mask
This mask was made from the skull of a sacrificial victim and was probably worn by an Aztec priest who performed sacrifices.

The Incas

Between 1438 and 1500, the Inca people conquered a large empire in what is now Peru. Their capital was the mountain city of Qusqu. They built a road network to connect their territory, and grew rich and powerful, but the empire was destroyed by Spanish invaders in the 1530s.

● QUSQU

Key

▢ Inca Empire

▢ Mayan Empire

▢ Aztec Empire

Tenochtitlán
This giant Aztec city was built on an island in Lake Texcoco. Its Great Temple was dedicated to the rain god Tlaloc. The heads of sacrificial victims were hurled down its steps.

STATUE OF TOLTEC WARRIOR

Toltecs
A warlike people, the Toltecs ruled in central Mexico before the Aztecs, from around 950 to 1150 CE. Not much is known for sure about their history, but the Aztecs are thought to have inherited aspects of their culture.

Teotihuacan
A holy site, this ancient city-state was one of the most powerful in the region, until it was destroyed and abandoned in 700 CE under mysterious circumstances.

Ancient Americas

From about 3000 BCE until 1500 CE, a series of advanced cultures dominated South and Central America. Centered on powerful city-states, they were often at war with one another.

The first cities were built by the Chavín people (in South America) and the Olmecs (in Central America) in around 1000 BCE. Both of these cultures constructed huge, pyramid-shaped temples, which became a feature of the cities that were built in the region over the next 2,000 years. Different cultures rose and declined over the centuries, until most of the city-states had become part of the Inca Empire (in Peru) or the Aztec Empire (in Mexico). However, both of these empires were eventually conquered by European invaders in the early 16th century.

60,000 The population of the **Mayan city of Tikal** at its height.

500 The aproximate number of **glyphs** in the **Mayan writing system.**

1697 Date of the **conquest of the last Mayan city** by the Spanish.

289

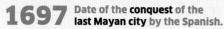

Mayans

Mayan cities in Guatemala and the Yucatan peninsula of Mexico were at their most powerful between 300 and 900 CE, but were then abandoned, probably due to overpopulation. The Mayan writing system of glyphs tell us a lot about their history.

MAYAN RAIN GOD STATUE

Cortés

The Spanish adventurer Hernán Cortés arrived in 1519. His army took over the Aztec Empire.

Chichen Itza

This city became important after Mayan centers further south were abandoned in around 900 CE.

Palenque

The most powerful of Palenque's kings, K'inich Janaab Pakal, was found buried in a tomb under the Temple of Inscriptions.

Tikal

The pyramid temples of Tikal are among the most magnificent in the Mayan world.

Aztecs

From 1375, the Aztecs conquered a large empire based around their capital, Tenochtitlán, attacking their neighbors to capture prisoners to sacrifice to their gods. Although they were fierce warriors, the Aztecs were conquered by Spanish invaders in 1521.

GOLD AZTEC LIP ORNAMENT

The Renaissance

An explosion of new ideas transformed Europe in the 15th century, bringing revolutionary works of art, science, and invention. This period has gone down in history as the Renaissance, or "rebirth."

The Renaissance began in Italy in around 1400, where scholars rediscovered the writings of Greek and Latin mathematicians, artists, and philosophers. The ideas in these texts gave rise to a school of thought called humanism, which prized experiment and experience as the sources of knowledge, in contrast to the tradition and superstition of the medieval era. This new way of thinking spread across Europe, inspiring a generation of artists, architects, and philosophers. Perhaps the most famous was Leonardo da Vinci, an ingenious scientist, artist, and inventor who represented the ideal humanist, or "Renaissance man."

New artistic techniques

One of the techniques that Renaissance scholars rediscovered was perspective—a way to give depth to paintings and drawings. Objects that are further away look smaller and shorter than objects up close. The Romans used mathematical formulas to mimic this effect in drawings. Renaissance artists copied the Roman technique to make their paintings astonishingly lifelike.

Drawing distance

Artists using perspective show distant objects as smaller. The artist sets one or more "vanishing points," where objects are too far away to see.

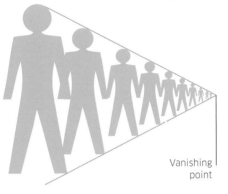

Vanishing point

Painting

Renaissance painters tried to show their subjects as realistically as possible. They wanted their paintings to look like a window onto another scene, rather than a flat plane filled with characters. They used techniques such as perspective to give their images depth, and they painted people in a lifelike manner. They also covered a greater variety of subjects: medieval art mostly showed religious scenes and portraits, but Renaissance artists also painted scenes from history, Greek and Roman myths, and everyday life.

The School of Athens (1510)

This painting was created for the Pope by Raphael, one of the most admired artists of the Renaissance. It depicts Ancient Greek philosophers, painted to resemble Renaissance thinkers such as Leonardo da Vinci, Michelangelo, and Raphael himself.

140 years—the **time** it took to **build Florence Cathedral**, from laying the foundations to **completing the dome**.

47.8 million dollars—the **highest price paid for a work** by a **Renaissance artist** (*Head of a Young Apostle* by Raphael).

291

Architecture

Many Italian cities contained ruins of Roman buildings, and the architects of the Renaissance were determined that their creations should be just as grand and beautiful. They studied Roman writings on architecture and geometry to make the shapes of their buildings more harmonious, and they copied Greek and Roman styles of columns and arches for decoration.

Florence Duomo (1436)

The rulers of the city of Florence wanted their new cathedral (*duomo*) to be the envy of all their rivals. By 1413, it was almost complete, but nobody had worked out how to build its huge dome. Architect Filippo Brunelleschi solved the problem, designing a dome with two layers using lightweight bricks.

The Dome
The dome is octagonal in shape, with an inner layer of bricks supporting the light roof.

Facade
The front of the cathedral has three arched doorways with mosaics over the doors.

Bell Tower
The bell tower is decorated with numerous sculptures by 14th and 15th century Florentine carvers.

Renaissance rulers

In the 15th century, Italy was made up of city-states ruled by wealthy merchant families. Their dukes and princes acted as patrons, paying for artists and thinkers to create artworks, monuments, and inventions to impress rival rulers. New political ideas arose. These were most famously summed up by a diplomat named Niccolò Machiavelli, who advised nobles to be unjust or even cruel in order to achieve noble ends.

Medici coat of arms
The Medici family ruled Florence from 1434. The balls on their coat of arms may represent coins, showing their origins as traders and bankers.

> "MEN ARE DRIVEN BY TWO IMPULSES,
> **LOVE AND FEAR... IT IS MUCH SAFER TO BE FEARED THAN LOVED."**
> NICCOLÒ MACHIAVELLI, *THE PRINCE*, 1513

The Northern Renaissance

From Italy, the ideas of the Renaissance quickly spread to Northern Europe. Rich kings such as Francis I of France and wealthy merchants in Belgium and the Netherlands, were eager to benefit from the new ideas. Their artists followed the techniques of the Italian Renaissance, and developed new styles of their own. Scholars such as Dutchman Desiderius Erasmus translated Greek and Roman texts into versions that could be widely read.

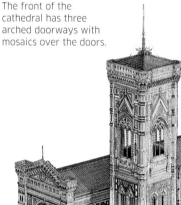

Sculpture

Like the painters of the era, Renaissance sculptors tried to make their works as lifelike as possible. Inspired by Greek and Roman sculptures, they showed their subjects in natural poses, and brought out details such as hairs and folds of cloth. Many artists studied human anatomy so that their works copied the shapes of limbs, muscles, and veins exactly as they appear in real life.

Renaissance doctors and artists studied human **anatomy by dissecting** (cutting open) the bodies of dead criminals.

Michelangelo's *David* (1504)

Michelangelo was one of the greatest painters and sculptors of the Renaissance. His sculpture of David, biblical King of Israel, is regarded as one of the most perfect human figures ever carved in marble.

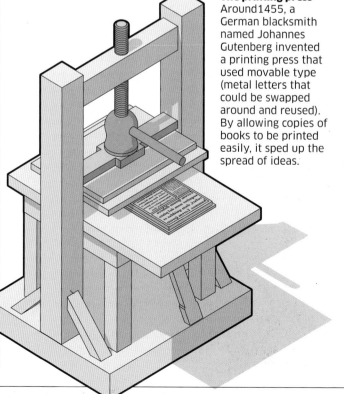

The printing press
Around 1455, a German blacksmith named Johannes Gutenberg invented a printing press that used movable type (metal letters that could be swapped around and reused). By allowing copies of books to be printed easily, it sped up the spread of ideas.

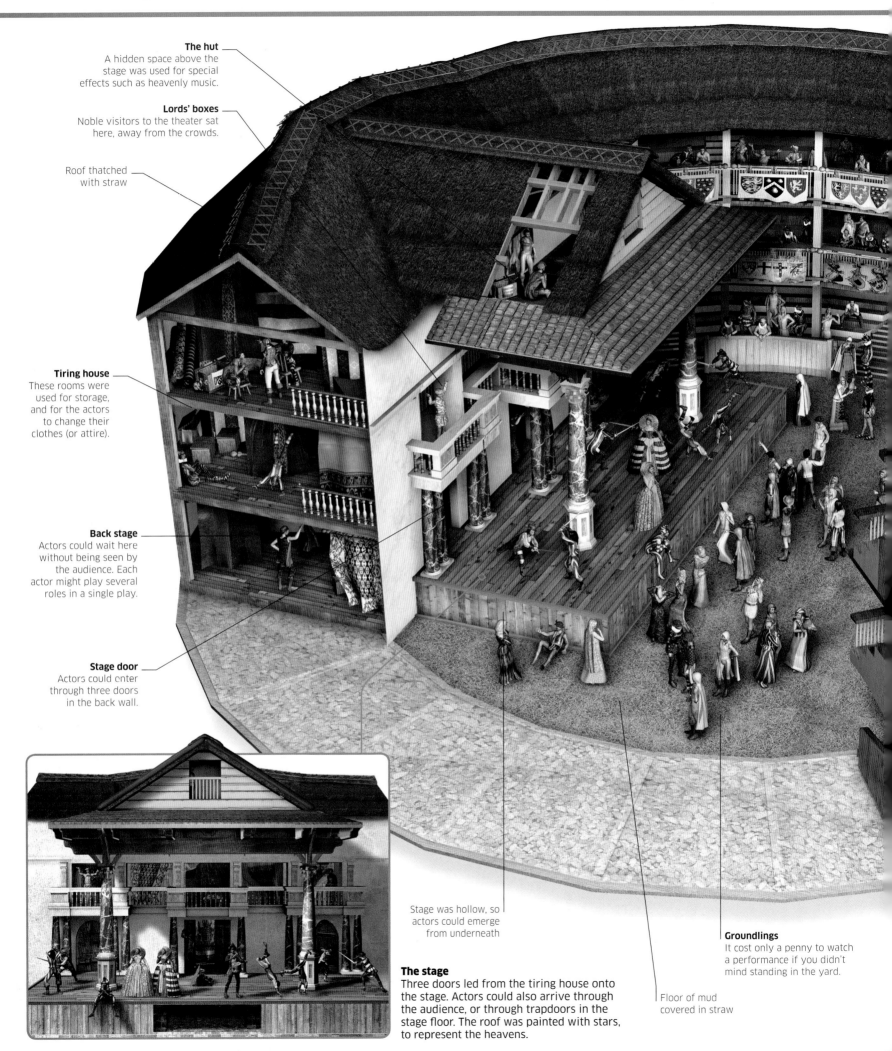

The hut
A hidden space above the stage was used for special effects such as heavenly music.

Lords' boxes
Noble visitors to the theater sat here, away from the crowds.

Roof thatched with straw

Tiring house
These rooms were used for storage, and for the actors to change their clothes (or attire).

Back stage
Actors could wait here without being seen by the audience. Each actor might play several roles in a single play.

Stage door
Actors could enter through three doors in the back wall.

Stage was hollow, so actors could emerge from underneath

The stage
Three doors led from the tiring house onto the stage. Actors could also arrive through the audience, or through trapdoors in the stage floor. The roof was painted with stars, to represent the heavens.

Groundlings
It cost only a penny to watch a performance if you didn't mind standing in the yard.

Floor of mud covered in straw

1,700 The estimated **number of new words** invented by Shakespeare that are in **common use today**.

1613 The Globe Theater **burned down** in this year when a **stage cannon** set the thatched **roof on fire**.

293

Entranceway
Three entrances led under the galleries to the street outside.

Shakespeare's theater

Painting and sculpture were not the only arts to be revolutionized by the Renaissance. Theater also changed, not least with the arrival of the period's most famous playwright, William Shakespeare.

In Europe, medieval theater was mostly morality plays and stories from the Bible, which followed a fixed formula. Around the middle of the 16th century, new plays began to present stories of romance, tragedy, and adventure based on Classical myths, history, and even current events. The new plays were extremely popular. Everyone from poor laborers to rich merchants and nobles flocked to the new theaters, and the most famous actors were even invited to court to perform for royalty.

Seated spectators
Those who could afford it bought seats in the galleries, so they could watch in comfort.

"All the world's a stage, And all the men and women merely players."
As You Like It, by **William Shakespeare**

Outer walls plastered with a mixture of lime, sand, and goat hair

Shakespeare's Globe Theater
The late 16th and early 17th centuries saw many great playwrights emerge. By far the most famous is English writer William Shakespeare. His plays were so successful that, in 1599, his theater company was able to build a permanent playhouse in London: the Globe Theater. A copy of his theater stands near the original site today.

Staircase access to upper levels

Stories on stage

For thousands of years, human beings have used theater to share stories and ideas. The Ancient Greeks built some of the earliest theaters. They divided plays into two types.

Tragedy
Serious stories in which the heroes and heroines suffer and often die at the end are called tragedies. They often explore the way honor, justice, or fate can force us to go against our personal feelings.

Comedy
These plays use humor to tell a story, although not always a happy one. Some versions, known as satire, use comedy to point out weakness or bad behavior, especially in those in power.

Theater design

Plays can be performed almost anywhere, from open streets to tiny studios. Most take place in buildings designed to allow the audience to see and hear the actors, and to make the scene seem as realistic as possible.

Ancient Greek theater
This design uses a curve of seats to reflect sound. Even a whisper from the stage can be heard by the whole audience.

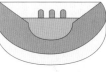

In the round
Traveling actors in medieval Europe often set up a stage surrounded by the audience on three or even four sides.

Proscenium arch
Modern theaters often have an arch to frame the action on stage and keep the audience separate.

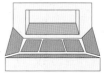

The Great Wall

For centuries, China's greatest threat came from the north, where warlike tribes mounted swift, fierce raids on unprotected settlements. To keep them out, the Chinese emperors built a series of walls stretching thousands of miles.

Signal tower
Often built on high points to be easily seen, these towers were used to send signals along the wall.

Signal cannon
The noise of the cannon could be used to signal at night, when smoke could not be seen.

Brazier for sending smoke signals

Garrison
Small numbers of troops were stationed at regular intervals along the wall to watch for invaders.

Bamboo supports

Rubble filling
The inside of the wall was filled with broken stones and mud.

Stone layers
The outsides of the wall were built of stone and fired bricks.

25 ft (7.5 m)—the **thickness** of the **wall** at its **widest**.

13,170 miles (21,196 km)—the **length** of the **Great Wall**.

9,999 Said to be the **number of rooms** in the **Forbidden City**.

295

Imperial China

At its height, China was the most powerful empire in the world. Its emperors controlled wealth and influence beyond the wildest dreams of European monarchs.

China is one of the world's oldest civilizations, with written records going back almost 3,500 years. Its history includes long periods of civil war and conflict with its neighbors. Despite all this, Chinese imperial society was generally extremely stable and well organized. From the 1st century BCE, the government was run by a civil service, which later on could only be entered by passing difficult exams. Chinese explorers established trade routes as far as Africa and Arabia, and Chinese craftsmen created some of the most important inventions in human history, including paper, gunpowder, and porcelain.

The surface of the wall acted as a road

Imperial families

Several different dynasties rose to power over the centuries. Some brought war and famine, while others saw incredible advances in philosophy, technology, and art. The first ruling dynasty began in the 16th century BCE under the Shang, but they controlled only a part of the vast empire that would follow.

Zhou dynasty
1050–256 BCE

The Zhou conquered their neighbors to build an empire across China. Great sages lived under their rule: Laozi, founder of Tao philosophy, and Kong Fuzi (Confucius), whose code still influences Chinese culture today.

CHARIOT DECORATION

Warring States period
475–221 BCE

Rival states formed after the decline of the Zhou. Their rulers fought for land and power, using strict military organization to raise and control their armies.

LEATHER ARMOR

China united
221 BCE

The Warring States period ended with victory by the Qin kingdom, reuniting China after centuries of war. Qin Shi Huangdi became emperor. He built new roads and canals, and introduced consistent weights and measures across the empire.

Death of an emperor
210 BCE

Qin Shi Huangdi died 11 years after becoming emperor. He was buried in a vast tomb complex guarded by an army of thousands of terra-cotta warriors, complete with weapons and armor.

Han dynasty
206 BCE – 220 CE

Qin Shi Huangdi's son ruled for only four years, and died during a popular rebellion. Liu Bang, a peasant who had risen to become a powerful general, took control of the empire, founding the Han dynasty.

HAN LACQUER BOWL

Tang and Song dynasties
618–1279

After centuries of turmoil, China returned to peace under the Tang and Song dynasties. Art, literature, and invention flourished as the empire expanded and China became very wealthy.

TANG MODEL HORSE

Ming dynasty
1368–1644

After the fall of the Song, China was ruled by Mongols from the north for many years. They were overthrown by rebel Zhu Yuanzhang. His descendants, the Ming emperors, ruled from a huge palace called the Forbidden City.

MING VASE

The last emperor
1912

By the 19th century, China had come into conflict with European powers. The emperors were weakened and, in 1912, a military revolt deposed the Qing rulers and founded the Republic of China.

Key

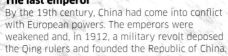

- Ming China
- Path of the Great Wall

Beijing

The path of the wall

The earliest parts of the wall were built in the 7th century BCE, to protect Chinese farmland from nomadic raiders to the north. They were first joined together in the 3rd century BCE under Qin Shi Huangdi. Successive Chinese emperors fortified and extended these walls, and they reached their greatest extent in the 16th century, under the rule of the Ming emperors.

Rulers of India

The Mughals were warrior horsemen from Central Asia who swept through northern India in the 16th century. Their rulers built a great empire in which Hindu and Muslim people lived side by side in relative peace.

The Mughals invaded India in 1526 under the command of the warrior Babur. They captured the important northern Indian city of Delhi, and Babur became the first Mughal emperor. Within 150 years, his descendants had expanded their empire to include most of India.

The Mughals ruled over 150 million people. A Muslim people, they were tolerant toward the religion of their Hindu subjects. The emperors were lavish patrons of the arts, and their craftsmen built many beautiful buildings. Yet only a century after reaching the height of its power, the Mughal Empire had lost most of its territory.

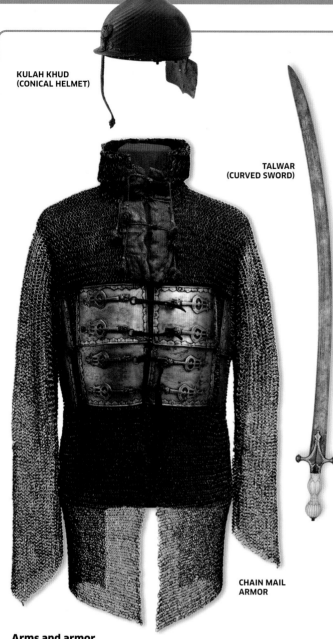

KULAH KHUD (CONICAL HELMET)

TALWAR (CURVED SWORD)

CHAIN MAIL ARMOR

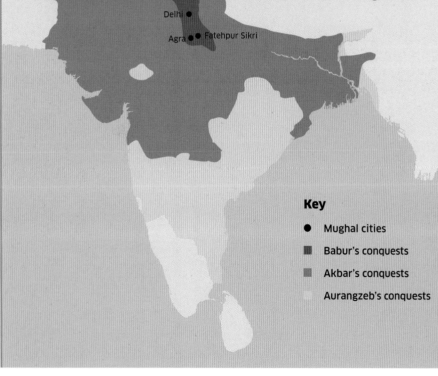

Finding an empire
Zahir-al-Din Babur, known as Babur, was the founder of the Mughal Empire. A descendant of Genghis Khan, he originally ruled a small state around Kabul in Afghanistan. He was known as a lover of poetry and gardens, and also as a fierce warrior. In 1526, he defeated the Sultan of Delhi and made the city his new capital. His son, Humayun, was expelled from India in 1540, but returned to continue Mughal rule.

Key
- ● Mughal cities
- ■ Babur's conquests
- ■ Akbar's conquests
- □ Aurangzeb's conquests

Arms and armor
Mughal warriors mostly fought on horseback. They wore chain mail over their lower neck, arms, body, and upper legs, with an iron breastplate for extra protection. Their armies were also well equipped with guns and cannons.

Battle and conquest
The Mughal Empire was founded after a great battle at Panipat near Delhi in April 1526, where Babur's army of just 12,000 defeated an enemy force of 100,000 men and 1,000 elephants. Babur's men had the advantage of gunpowder weapons (cannons and handguns), which their opponents lacked. The Mughal army went on to conquer other Indian kingdoms, and absorbed their warriors into its ranks, gaining well-trained heavy cavalry and eventually amassing 100,000 men.

Mughal lords
From the mid-16th century, the Mughal Empire entered a golden age during which its rulers established a strong government and conquered new territories. They grew wealthy and powerful, leaving behind great monuments, many of which survive to this day.

Akbar "The Great" (1556–1605)
The third emperor, Akbar, is considered one of the greatest rulers of all time. He was fierce to his enemies, defeating the Afghans and Uzbeks, and conquering Gujarat and Bengal. But he was wise and gentle with his subjects, allying with the Hindu Rajput kings, who joined his empire, and promoting peace and religious tolerance across the empire.

Jahangir (1605–27)
Akbar's son, Jahangir, focused more on managing the empire than conquering new territory. But he did defeat the last of the Rajputs who had refused his father's alliance. Jahangir was a great patron of the arts. During his reign, Mughal painters developed an exquisite new style based on carefully recording the world around them.

Shah Jahan (1627–58)
Shah Jahan, who had rebelled against his father, Jahangir, took the throne on his father's death. He expanded the Mughal Empire further and built a new city, Shahjahanabad, as his capital. Shah Jahan was an active patron of religion and the arts. Mughal architecture flourished under his rule, and he ordered the Taj Mahal built as a mausoleum for his wife.

6 square miles (15 km²)—the **area** of **Akbar's capital** at **Fatehpur Sikri.**

86 The number of **tigers killed** by **Jahangir** while hunting.

141,053 The number of **war elephants** in the **Mughal emperors' army.**

297

The end of the empire

Shah Jahan's son, Aurangzeb, conquered new provinces in the south of India, expanding Mughal territory by a quarter. But the empire came under attack from a new power, the Maratha Confederacy. Constant wars drained the Mughal treasury and the empire began to crumble. Aurangzeb was also unpopular with Hindus and other non-Muslim subjects. After he died in 1707, the empire fell apart, with weak rulers unable to defend it from its enemies. In 1739, the Persian ruler Nadir Shah invaded, sacking the city of Delhi and carrying off many Mughal treasures. By 1857, the Mughals ruled only central Delhi. Emperor Bahahdur Shah joined a rebellion against the British in 1857. He was deposed and the Mughal Empire came to an end.

1.2 MILLION SQUARE MILES (3.2 MILLION KM²)

386 SQUARE MILES (1,000 KM²)

1700   **1737**

SIZE OF MUGHAL EMPIRE

27 years— the length of the war between the Maratha Confederacy and the Mughal Empire.

Mughal art

Art and architecture flourished under the Mughals. Manuscripts with delicate paintings were especially prized. These now provide us with lots of information about the Mughal court. The emperors ordered new cities full of wonderful buildings to be constructed, such as Fatehpur Sikri and Shahjahanabad. Some of their buildings, such as the Taj Mahal at Agra, are world famous to this day.

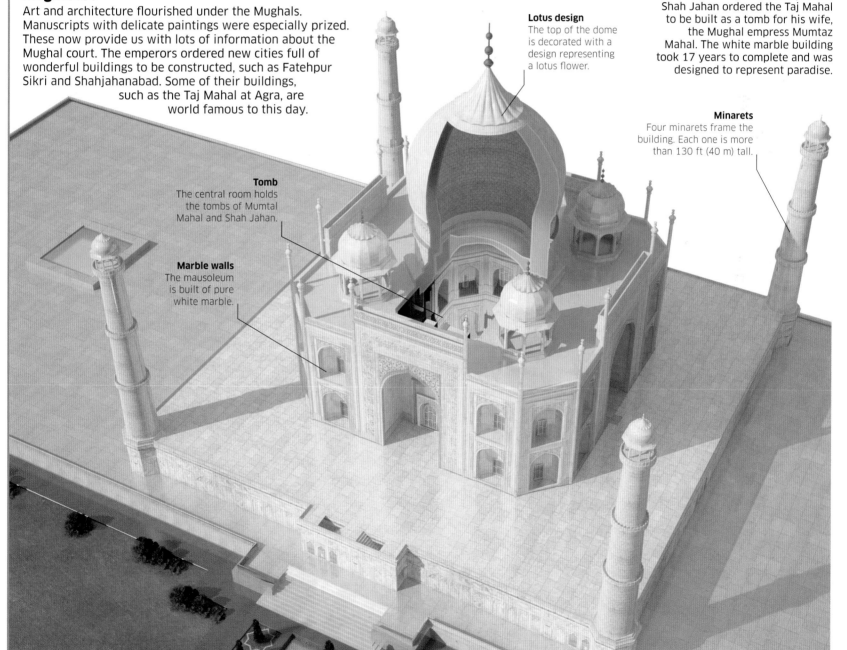

The Taj Mahal
Shah Jahan ordered the Taj Mahal to be built as a tomb for his wife, the Mughal empress Mumtaz Mahal. The white marble building took 17 years to complete and was designed to represent paradise.

Lotus design
The top of the dome is decorated with a design representing a lotus flower.

Minarets
Four minarets frame the building. Each one is more than 130 ft (40 m) tall.

Tomb
The central room holds the tombs of Mumtal Mahal and Shah Jahan.

Marble walls
The mausoleum is built of pure white marble.

THE MODERN WORLD

The years since 1750 have seen huge turbulence in every area of life. Globe-spanning empires arose in the 19th century, and fell apart as the balance of power shifted from nobles and emperors to everyday citizens. New technology transformed agriculture, industry, transport, and warfare, and a digital revolution changed communications and entertainment forever.

THE AGE OF REVOLUTION

From around 1750, new political movements called for kings and governments to grant more freedom to the people. At the same time, colonies began to seek independence from their ruling countries. When rulers and colonial powers refused these demands, the populace rose up in rebellion. The USA won their independence from Britain by force in 1783, inspiring other revolutions.

The French Revolution

In 1789, the French people rebelled. King Louis XVI was deposed and executed. The Revolution became a bloodbath, as the new leaders turned on each other in an era of violence known as the Terror.

Napoleon Bonparte
After the French Revolution, a popular general named Napoleon became Emperor of France, and began a long and bloody war of conquest across Europe.

The arrival of communism

In the 19th century, German philosopher Karl Marx proposed a new theory of government called communism. It argued that the wealth of a country should be shared equally among all its citizens. In 1917, revolutionaries in Russia overthrew the emperor (or tsar) to establish the world's first communist state. It would go on to become the USSR, one of the superpowers of the 20th century.

Key
- Spanish colonies 1810
- Portuguese colonies 1810

Liberation in Latin America

Between 1813 and 1822, revolutionary movements led by Simón Bolivar and José de San Martin freed most of South America from Spanish control. Mexico, too, became independent after a revolution headed by Miguel Hidalgo.

Vladimir Lenin
After the overthrow of the tsar, Lenin declared himself leader of the people. He was the head of the communist government until his death in 1924.

AGE OF IMPERIALISM

During the 19th century, European countries expanded their overseas colonies into vast empires. European armies were well trained and armed with guns, and were easily able to overcome resistance to their expansion. This policy of acquiring new colonies, known as imperialism, spread European rule over much of Africa, Australasia, and large parts of Asia by 1900.

Dividing the world

By 1914, a few powerful countries had control over almost every part of the world. The largest empire belonged to the British. Their colonies were guarded by a powerful navy, which controlled seas and oceans around the world.

Territories and empires

British	Portuguese	Italian
Ottoman	Swedish	Russian
French	Dutch	Japanese
Danish	German	Chinese
Spanish	Austrian	USA

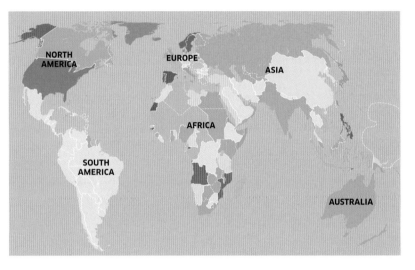

Imperial rivals

Wars in this period became ever larger and more bloody as rival empires threw their full might against each other.

Seven Years War (1756-63)
The world's first global war was fought mainly between the empires of Britain and France over colonies in India and North America.

Napoleonic Wars (1803-15)
Napoleon Bonaparte proclaimed himself Emperor of France and waged a war of conquest, but was defeated at Waterloo by an alliance of European powers.

Crimean War (1853-56)
Russia's attempts to capture land from the Ottoman Empire were halted when Britain and France allied against them.

Opium wars (1839-60)
The Chinese tried to stop British merchants from trading in opium, sparking two wars with Britain. The fighting ended with the Chinese forced to open 14 ports to European trade.

Russo-Japanese War (1904-05)
Japan's powerful, modernized army and navy inflicted a shock defeat on Russia in a war over territory in China and Korea.

A postcolonial world

European colonies in Asia and Africa found it harder to win independence than those in America. However, two World Wars greatly weakened the European empires. India and Pakistan won their independence from Britain in 1947, after mass popular protests led by a lawyer named Gandhi. In Africa, Ghana was the first colony to win independence in 1957, and many others soon followed.

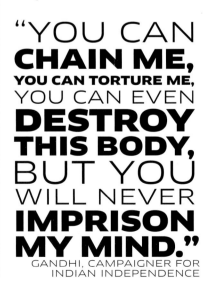

"YOU CAN **CHAIN ME, YOU CAN TORTURE ME,** YOU CAN EVEN **DESTROY THIS BODY,** BUT YOU WILL NEVER **IMPRISON MY MIND."**
GANDHI, CAMPAIGNER FOR INDIAN INDEPENDENCE

A CENTURY OF CONFLICT

The first half of the 20th century saw two of the bloodiest wars in human history. Each started with conflicts in Europe, then spread to countries all across the world. World War I (1914–18) saw millions of fighting men killed in bitter trench warfare. World War II (1939–45) brought battles between armies of tanks and aircraft, and the development of the atomic bomb. When the dust had settled, the world's most powerful nations were the US and the communist USSR. They fought a Cold War, backed by vast nuclear arsenals.

World War I

In 1914, the killing of Archduke Franz Ferdinand of Austria in Sarajevo caused a war between the German-led Central Powers and the Allies (led by the French and British). Much of the fighting happened on the Western Front in France and Belgium, where attempts to capture heavily defended trench systems caused massive casualties. Only in 1918 did the Allies break through and defeat Germany.

World War I cemetery
Nearly 10 million soldiers died during World War I. Many of them were buried in graveyards near where they fell.

World War II

In 1933, Adolf Hitler became leader of Germany. His campaign to conquer neighboring countries set off a new global conflict in 1939. German armies were victorious at first, but were defeated in 1945 by their Allied enemies. Japan joined the war in 1941, but was forced to surrender after the US attacked with atomic bombs in 1945.

4 percent

A terrible cost
World War II caused between 60 and 80 million deaths, estimated to be around 4 percent of the entire population of the world before the war.

The Cold War

Although the US and USSR had been allies in World War II, they became enemies once it was over. They did not fight directly, but fought a "Cold War" by other means, such as overthrowing governments friendly to the other side. The Cold War was especially dangerous since both sides had nuclear weapons that could have killed many millions of people.

IN 1982, THE USSR AND US BETWEEN THEM HAD MORE THAN 20,000 NUCLEAR WARHEADS **WITH A COMBINED EXPLOSIVE POWER ESTIMATED** AT MORE THAN 12,000 MEGATONS, OR 1 MILLION TIMES THE ENERGY RELEASED BY THE BOMB THAT DESTROYED HIROSHIMA.

A TRANSFORMED WORLD

While wars and revolutions brought political changes, advances in science and technology transformed society. Developments in medicine created cures for diseases that had killed millions. The Industrial Revolution brought new machines that could do the work of dozens of workers. These new societies brought much greater equality, and the old order was overturned, as women and nonwhite people fought to win equal rights.

Workers in US employed in agriculture

1800 — 80%

1900 — 35%

The rise of industry

The Industrial Revolution brought great new advances, but also new problems. Goods and household items became cheaper as they were mass-produced in factories instead of being made by hand. However, many workers were badly paid and lived in terrible poverty, especially in cities.

Equal rights

Before the 20th century, women, African-Americans, and nonwhites in European colonies were often denied basic freedoms. It took the determination of many brave campaigners to ensure that basic rights such as voting and education were available to all.

1893
New Zealand becomes first country to grant women the right to vote in national elections.

1920
19th Amendment to the United States Constitution grants women the vote.

1948
South Africa begins passing legislation discriminating against nonwhites. This policy is called apartheid.

1964
The Civil Rights Act makes it illegal in the USA to deny black people equal access to education and housing.

1965
Voting Rights Act (US) removes obstacles to African-Americans voting.

1994
South Africa holds first elections in which adults of all racial groups can vote, ending apartheid.

Science and medicines

The 20th century saw scientific advances beyond anything in human history. Antibiotics cured untreatable diseases, and cars and airplanes reduced journeys that would have taken days or weeks to a few hours. Human beings discovered ever more about the universe, their history, and themselves.

"ANYONE WHO HAS NEVER MADE A MISTAKE HAS NEVER TRIED ANYTHING NEW."
ALBERT EINSTEIN

Environmental challenges

The 19th and 20th centuries saw a rapid rise in the world's population, and a huge increase in the resources human beings use. Supplies such as coal, oil, and even fresh water may become scarce. Many natural habitats have been damaged by pollution or human exploitation. Rising global temperatures threaten to disrupt vast areas of farmland and human living space across the world.

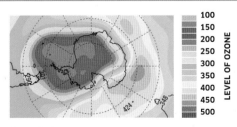

100
150
200
250
300
350
400
450
500
LEVEL OF OZONE

Ozone hole
In the 1990s, air pollution led to a breakdown in the ozone layer, a part of the atmosphere that protects the Earth from harmful radiation. At its biggest, the hole, situated above Antarctica, was twice the area of Europe.

300 history • THE MODERN WORLD

115 The number of **gallons of rum** that could be **exchanged for a male slave** in 1756.

North America
Around 650,000 African slaves were taken to plantations in what is now the southern US. In the north, which was more industrial, merchants sometimes took the place of Europe in the triangular slave trade, selling manufactured goods directly to Africa in exchange for slaves. The international slave trade was banned by the US in 1808.

NORTH AMERICA

ATLANTIC OCEAN

IRON TO BRAND SLAVES

Slave plantations
Most slaves transported to the Americas were brought to work on cotton, sugar, and tobacco plantations in the Caribbean, southern US, and Brazil. Conditions were harsh—the slaves were often branded or shackled, and overseers, those who organized the work on the plantations, were cruel.

SOUTH AMERICA

The slave trade

European settlers in America needed laborers to work on plantations. Between 1500 and 1900, this led to 12 million African slaves being taken to the Americas.

The slave trade is often called the "Triangular Trade" because it had three stages. Goods from Europe were traded in Africa for slaves, who crossed the Atlantic in a journey known as the Middle Passage. These slaves were then exchanged for crops to be sold in Europe. Many slaves died on the journey to the Americas, and those who survived faced appalling working conditions on the plantations. An international campaign banned the Atlantic slave trade in the 19th century.

39 The **percentage of slaves** carried on the Middle Passage who **went to Brazil**.

4 million—the estimated **number of slaves in the US** at the time of **abolition in 1865**.

301

EUROPE

AFRICA

European traders

Until around 1640, Portugal was the only European country trading slaves in the Americas, but Britain, France, the Netherlands, Spain, Sweden, and Denmark later joined in. European merchants took manufactured goods such as textiles, beads, guns, and ammunition to their colonies in Africa, and sold them to local traders in exchange for slaves at colonial forts along the African coast.

Terrible conditions

On the voyage across the Atlantic, which could last from six weeks to six months, slaves were crammed together below deck in the ship's hold, with little fresh food or water. Male slaves were chained together to prevent them from attacking the crew.

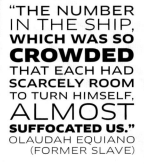

Slave ship

To make the most profit possible, the traders packed slaves into very small spaces, sometimes less than 12 in (30 cm) high. One infamous slave ship, the *Brooke*, carried as many as 600 slaves, shackled together in pairs.

> "THE NUMBER IN THE SHIP, **WHICH WAS SO CROWDED** THAT EACH HAD SCARCELY ROOM TO TURN HIMSELF, ALMOST **SUFFOCATED US.**"
> OLAUDAH EQUIANO (FORMER SLAVE)

A deadly voyage

Cramped conditions and lack of food and water meant that 1.8 million slaves died of disease or starvation while voyaging to the Americas on the Middle Passage. Their bodies were thrown overboard.

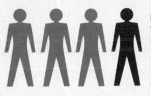

Death toll

The death rate for slaves reached as high as one in four on the worst Atlantic voyages.

Calling for an end

Calls to put an end to the inhumanity of the slave trade led to its abolition in Britain in 1807. Other countries soon followed, until the final country to end the trade, Brazil, did so in 1831.

> "**NEVER, NEVER** WILL WE DESIST TILL WE HAVE WIPED **AWAY THIS SCANDAL FROM THE CHRISTIAN NAME,** RELEASED OURSELVES FROM THE LOAD OF GUILT, UNDER WHICH **WE AT PRESENT LABOR,** AND EXTINGUISHED EVERY TRACE **OF THIS BLOODY TRAFFIC.**"
> WILLIAM WILBERFORCE (ANTISLAVERY CAMPAIGNER)

SLAVE SHIP SHACKLES

African slaves

The vast majority of slaves were taken from the coastal regions of western Africa between modern Senegal and Angola. They were captured in war or taken by kidnappers and exchanged for trade goods from Europe.

302 history ∘ **THE MODERN WORLD**

72,000 The approximate number of articles in Diderot's *Encyclopédie*.

The Enlightenment

The 18th century was a time of revolution. The power of governments, religious beliefs, and scientific principles were all challenged by a wave of new thinkers determined to replace outdated traditions.

The Renaissance had brought new ways of thinking about science and philosophy, but they were still based on old traditions: the teachings of the Church and writings of the Ancient Greeks and Romans. The thinkers of the Enlightenment wanted to replace these sources of wisdom with individual observation, experiment, and logic–the rule of reason. Their radical ideas would bring wars, revolutions, and the beginnings of modern science.

Revolution of ideas

In the 18th century, people who wanted to know about the world studied natural philosophy, which included all the sciences and maths. At the time, a flood of new information was spreading across Europe, helped by new discoveries of explorers in Asia, Africa, and the Americas, and by the printing press. A group of natural philosophers in Paris, led by Denis Diderot and Jean d'Alembert, compiled an *Encyclopédie*, a giant, 28-volume work summing up everything they knew about art, science, and crafts. Their message was that reason and science could be applied to almost any subject, and their ideas spread across Europe and America. German philosopher Immanuel Kant summed up the new way of thinking as: "Dare to know. Have courage to use your own understanding."

The *Encyclopédie*
Diderot's great work covered not only art and science but everyday professions, such as music, cooking, and even farming.

Isaac Newton

One of the founding figures of the Enlightenment was the English scientist Isaac Newton (1642–1727). He is most famous for working out the laws of gravity and motion, which showed how the movements of the Moon and stars follow the same laws as the movements of objects on Earth. He also made vital discoveries about the nature of light and heat, and was one of the first to formulate a mathematical process called calculus. His curiosity about the world sometimes led him to do strange things. For example, he pushed a blunt needle into his eye socket to see how changing the shape of his eyeball affected his vision, as part of his studies into how light moves.

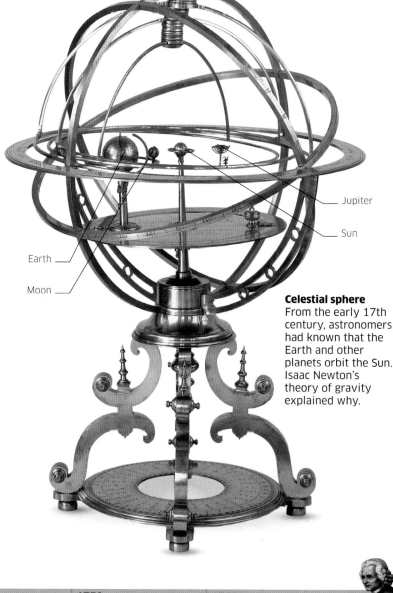

Jupiter

Sun

Earth

Moon

Celestial sphere
From the early 17th century, astronomers had known that the Earth and other planets orbit the Sun. Isaac Newton's theory of gravity explained why.

Rights of Man–and Woman

As well as scientific advances, the Enlightenment was marked by new ideas about society. From around 1750, a group of radical philosophers in France began to spread ideas that questioned traditional thinking. They argued that kings, nobles, and clergymen did not deserve special rights and privileges over other people. Other thinkers such as Jean-Jacques Rousseau and Mary Wollstonecraft produced powerful arguments calling for all human beings to be treated equally, while writers such as Voltaire and Montesquieu wrote satires (mocking imitations) of corrupt institutions and outdated opinions.

1748
A French thinker named Charles-Louis de Secondat, known as Montesquieu, published *Spirit of the Laws*, which called for political power to be divided between the monarchy, parliament, and the courts of law– a system known as the "separation of powers."

1759
Candide, a satirical novel by French philosopher Voltaire, highlighted the hardships and injustices suffered by many people around the world. Voltaire wrote that, for people to be truly free, they had to be able to use the power of reason, and they had to know and defend the basic rights of all human beings.

1762
Swiss philosopher Jean-Jacques Rousseau proposed that governments should only rule with the consent of the people. In *The Social Contract*, he wrote, "Man is born free, and everywhere he is in chains."

87 percent—the drop in value of South Sea Company stocks when the venture collapsed in 1720.

9 The number of symphonies written by Romantic composer Ludwig van Beethoven.

303

Revolution of wealth

Among the new concepts to develop at this time was the science of economics, or the study of wealth and money. Great empires grew rich by trading goods across the world. Banks offered a safe place for the wealthy to deposit their money, and gave loans to people who needed funds to start new businesses. Ordinary people were also encouraged to invest in money-making projects. Financial projects sometimes went disastrously wrong: for example, in 1720, when the British South Sea Company collapsed, taking with it millions of pounds (dollars) of investors' money.

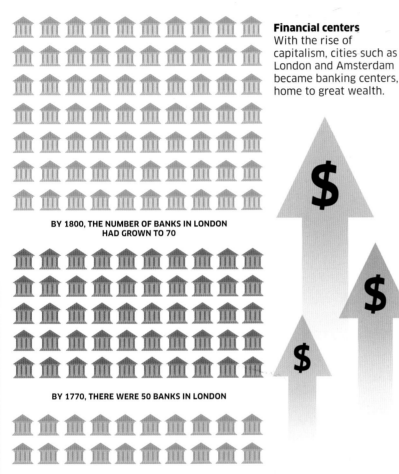

Financial centers
With the rise of capitalism, cities such as London and Amsterdam became banking centers, home to great wealth.

BY 1800, THE NUMBER OF BANKS IN LONDON HAD GROWN TO 70

BY 1770, THERE WERE 50 BANKS IN LONDON

IN 1750, THERE WERE JUST 20 BANKS IN LONDON

"LABOR WAS THE FIRST PRICE, **THE ORIGINAL PURCHASE-MONEY THAT WAS PAID FOR ALL THINGS. IT WAS NOT BY GOLD OR BY SILVER, BUT BY LABOR, THAT ALL THE WEALTH OF THE** WORLD WAS ORIGINALLY PURCHASED."
ADAM SMITH, SCOTTISH ECONOMIST, 1776

1776
English-American Thomas Paine published a pamphlet, *Common Sense*, which supported America's independence from Britain. His later work, *Rights of Man*, argued that people should overthrow the government if it abuses their rights.

1792
Englishwoman Mary Wollstonecraft called for women to receive the same education and opportunities as men in *A Vindication of the Rights of Women*. She imagined a society based on the rule of reason, which respects all human beings.

Romantic rebellion

The ideals of the Enlightenment spread quickly, but by the late 18th century they had already inspired a backlash, especially among artists, musicians, and poets. A new movement, Romanticism, arose, arguing that total reliance on reason ignored the values of emotion and natural beauty. Famous Romantics include the composer Beethoven, writers such as John Keats and Edgar Allan Poe, and painters such as Eugène Delacroix.

Burning of the Houses of Lords and Commons
Romantic artists such as Englishman Joseph Turner painted images depicting the power of natural forces. This painting shows a fire that swept through the British Houses of Parliament in 1834.

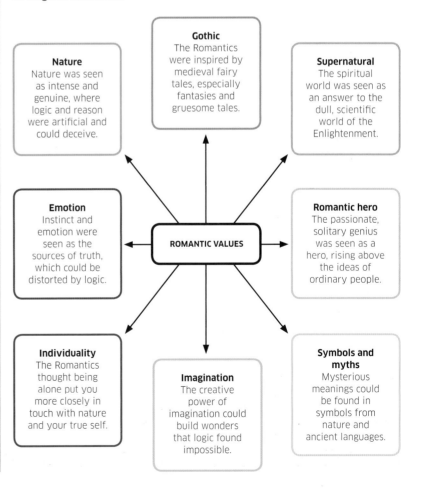

Nature
Nature was seen as intense and genuine, where logic and reason were artificial and could deceive.

Gothic
The Romantics were inspired by medieval fairy tales, especially fantasies and gruesome tales.

Supernatural
The spiritual world was seen as an answer to the dull, scientific world of the Enlightenment.

Emotion
Instinct and emotion were seen as the sources of truth, which could be distorted by logic.

ROMANTIC VALUES

Romantic hero
The passionate, solitary genius was seen as a hero, rising above the ideas of ordinary people.

Individuality
The Romantics thought being alone put you more closely in touch with nature and your true self.

Imagination
The creative power of imagination could build wonders that logic found impossible.

Symbols and myths
Mysterious meanings could be found in symbols from nature and ancient languages.

The American Revolutionary War

In the 18th century, Britain ruled 13 colonies along the east coast of North America. From 1770, these colonies began to rebel against British control and, 13 years later, they won their independence.

Britain's colonies in North America were governed from London. Their inhabitants were British citizens, but were not given full rights: they could not vote and had no one representing their views in parliament. The colonists were angry about this unfair treatment, but the British ignored their concerns, passing unpopular laws and putting high taxes on everyday goods such as sugar, tea, and paper.

In 1775, tensions erupted into war. A large, well-trained British army invaded from Canada in 1777, to support British troops stationed in the colonies, but they were outmaneuvered by skillful American commanders led by George Washington. The war ended with the British defeated, and the creation of a new independent country: the United States of America.

The Continental Army

From 1775, the American forces began to organize their volunteer troops into a regular army. George Washington was determined to train a force to rival the well-trained British soldiers, and formed the Continental Army. For much of the war the men were poorly paid and equipped, but they nevertheless achieved a number of stunning victories.

Disciplined volley

One of the key skills an army needed was the ability to fire their muskets all together in a volley. This required training and discipline, so that the soldiers did not fire too early as the enemy advanced.

Lead-up to the war

Britain had run up huge debts during the Seven Years War (1756–63), and urgently needed money to pay them off. The government planned to raise the money by taxing its American colonies. The colonists protested against this taxation without representation, and the revolutionary idea of becoming free of British rule spread. In 1773, the British imposed a harsh new tax on tea, and colonists in Boston took action. They boarded a ship in the harbor and threw chests of British tea into the sea. This event, famous as the Boston Tea Party, lit the fuse for the war. The British responded by imposing restrictive new laws on the colonies, and especially on Boston. The Continental Congress—a group of representatives of the 13 colonies—called these laws intolerable acts and sent messages of protest to the king.

AT THE BOSTON TEA PARTY,
**COLONISTS DESTROYED
342 CHESTS OF TEA**
WITH A VALUE OF
ABOUT $15,000.

The new nation

At the end of the war, the 13 colonies that had fought for independence became the first states of the US. They signed a peace treaty with Britain in 1783, which also granted them ownership of substantial territory to the west.

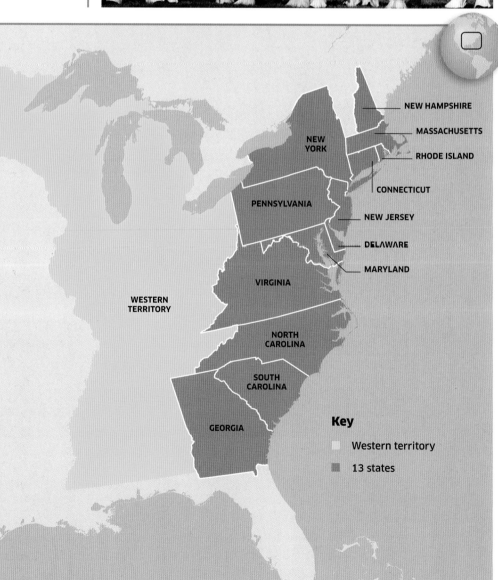

NEW HAMPSHIRE

MASSACHUSETTS

RHODE ISLAND

CONNECTICUT

NEW YORK

PENNSYLVANIA

NEW JERSEY

DELAWARE

MARYLAND

VIRGINIA

WESTERN TERRITORY

NORTH CAROLINA

SOUTH CAROLINA

GEORGIA

Key

☐ Western territory

■ 13 states

2.5 million—the **population of the colonies**, less than one-third of Britain's.

Boys as young as **10 fought** in the **American army**, and **women** served as **nurses, cooks, and even spies.**

305

The Declaration of Independence

The 13 rebel colonies formed their own government, the Continental Congress, which soon decided to seek complete independence from Britain. A lawyer from Virginia named Thomas Jefferson was given the task of drafting a Declaration of Independence to formalize their position. The argument of the Declaration was based on four key points, listed below. On July 4, 1776, representatives of the 13 colonies signed the Declaration to form a new nation: the United States of America.

1 Right to rebel
That colonies must be allowed to sever their connection with their rulers as long as they have good reasons and can explain them.

2 Legitimate government
That the only acceptable form of government is one that tries to do the best for its people and respects their rights.

3 Crimes of the king
That the British king had ruled the colonies without respecting the rights and interests of the people who lived there.

4 Declaration of independence
That, therefore, the colonies had a right to throw off the government of the British and rule themselves, and were no longer part of the British Empire.

"WE HOLD THESE TRUTHS **TO BE SELF-EVIDENT,** THAT ALL MEN ARE CREATED **EQUAL, THAT THEY ARE ENDOWED BY THEIR CREATOR** WITH CERTAIN **UNALIENABLE RIGHTS,** THAT AMONG THESE ARE **LIFE, LIBERTY AND THE PURSUIT OF HAPPINESS."**
DECLARATION OF INDEPENDENCE

Commander-in-chief

George Washington was a tobacco farmer and trained surveyor from Virginia who gained military experience fighting against the French in North America during the Seven Years War. His opposition to Britain's treatment of its American colonies led to his appointment as commander-in-chief of the rebel American army. Washington turned his men into a professional fighting force. He held them together during tough times and lost battles, and led them to victory. In 1789, he was elected as the first President of the United States of America.

Statue of Washington
Washington is often referred to as the father of the nation because of his leadership and influence in the founding of the United States.

The two sides

The American forces relied heavily on militia—local groups who organized themselves into fighting units. The Continental Army was also supported by French and Spanish troops, and some Native Americans. The "redcoats" of the British army were assisted by Loyalists (colonists who wanted to remain part of the British Empire), German mercenaries, and Native Americans, who wanted to protect trading and territory agreements with the British. The British navy controlled the coast, but could not affect the war inland.

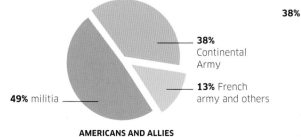

38% Continental Army
13% French army and others
49% militia

AMERICANS AND ALLIES

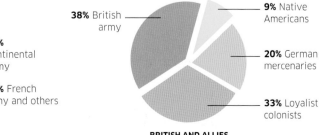

38% British army
9% Native Americans
20% German mercenaries
33% Loyalist colonists

BRITISH AND ALLIES

The march to independence

Nearly all of the early battles of the American Revolutionary War ended in a draw. The British forces were too powerful for the Americans to defeat outright, while the colonial forces used local support and knowledge of the land to escape attacks by the British. As the war went on, however, stronger leadership and assistance from foreign allies tipped the balance in favor of the Americans, and the British suffered crushing defeat.

1773

The road to rebellion
After the colonists destroyed shiploads of British tea in Boston harbor, the British tightened their control on the colonies by passing laws to limit their freedoms. It was the final straw, and two years later, the first shots of the Revolutionary War were fired.

BELT OF A LOYALIST SOLDIER, WITH ROYAL INSIGNIA

April 1775

The first battle
British troops marched to Concord, Massachusetts, to raid the colonists' store of weapons. The colonists sent a force to resist them. Although they were forced to withdraw, the Americans succeeded in blocking the British and protecting their supplies.

Autumn 1777

Battle of Saratoga
More than 6,000 British soldiers were surrounded and forced to surrender by the Continental Army. This resounding American victory encouraged the French to join the war on the American side, followed by the Spanish and the Dutch.

Winter 1777

Valley Forge
With foreign support on the way, the American army sought shelter in a defensive camp at Valley Forge, near Philadelphia. Although safe from British attack, they suffered from harsh conditions and lack of supplies throughout the winter months. An estimated 2,000 men died of disease and starvation.

October 1781

Victory for the colonists
After several further defeats, the British were forced to retreat to the east coast. As the American army and the French navy closed in, the British were trapped at Yorktown, Virginia, and surrendered. The war was over and the Americans had won.

1783

Peace treaty
After long negotiations, a peace treaty was finally agreed in Paris in September 1783. Britain handed over large areas of territory to the US, and also signed separate treaties with the Americans' European allies, France, Spain, and the Netherlands.

PROPOSED MODEL FOR THE FIRST UNITED STATES SILVER DOLLAR, 1777

French Revolution

In 1789, the French monarchy was overthrown in a bloody revolution. The rebels created a government run by the citizens rather than the nobility, but rivalry between its members brought chaos and bloodshed.

At the end of the 18th century, France was nearly bankrupt after a series of costly wars. To make matters worse, a bad harvest in 1788 left much of the population short of food. While the country faced starvation, King Louis XVI and the nobility lived in luxury, and rumors spread that they were hoarding grain that the poor desperately needed. The French people had heard how the Americans overthrew the rule of the British king in 1776, and as the poor grew more dissatisfied, they demanded change. In 1789, a sharp rise in the price of bread caused riots on the streets of Paris, and when the king demanded a rise in taxes that same year, the people took action and the French Revolution began.

An unequal society

French society was split into three classes, called Estates. The First Estate, the clergy, and the Second Estate, the nobility, were extremely wealthy. Although they made up only 3 percent of the population, they owned 40 percent of the land and paid almost no taxes. The remaining 97 percent of the population made up the Third Estate, common people ranging from merchants and craftsmen to poor country farmers. Their taxes paid for the wealthy lifestyle of the rich. All three Estates had representatives in the government assembly, the Estates General. On June 17, 1789, the representatives of the Third Estate decided to set up their own government, the National Assembly.

Key

■ First Estate, clergy

■ Second Estate, nobles

■ Third Estate, commoners

POPULATION   LAND OWNERSHIP

The end of the monarchy

The new National Assembly promised to give power to the people, leaving the king as only a figurehead. When rumors spread that the king had ordered the army to close down the new government, the citizens formed a National Guard to fight back. Their first target was the Bastille, a prison where enemies of the old government were held, which they stormed on July 14, 1789. Many of the king's supporters fled or joined the revolution, and the king himself was imprisoned in the Tuileries Palace in Paris. He tried to regain favor with the people by agreeing to their demands for reform, but remained a hated figure. On August 10, 1792, his palace was stormed by the mob and the king was sent to prison. In 1793, he was found guilty of plotting against the French people and sentenced to death by beheading.

The Taking of the Tuileries Palace, 1792
On August 10, 1792, a mob stormed the Palace of Tuileries, where the king and queen were living, and arrested them, ending the French monarchy. This painting depicts the overwhelming numbers of the revolutionaries, who far outnumbered the Swiss Guards protecting the palace.

The Bastille
was nearly empty when it was stormed. Only seven prisoners were rescued, but 98 revolutionaries died in the attack.

Timeline

The French Revolution saw France change from a monarchy, ruled by the king, to a Republic, in which power was held by the people, although suspicion and brutality left many living in fear. The end of the Revolution saw the rise of a new emperor.

June 14, 1789
The King of France, Louis XVI, asked the government to approve an increase in taxes. Already angered by a national food shortage and unfair taxes, representatives of the Third Estate (the working people) broke away from the other two Estates. They announced their intention to govern the country themselves, and formed a National Assembly.

July 14, 1789
Rumors spread that the king had called for the army to shut down the new National Assembly. Angry mobs began to riot throughout Paris, bringing chaos to the city. A crowd stormed the Bastille prison, liberating seven inmates. This date came to be known as the beginning of the Revolution, and July 14 is celebrated as a national holiday in France to this day.

October 5, 1789
A crowd of about 7,000 women marched on the royal palace at Versailles, outside Paris, to protest over the shortage of bread. According to later rumor, when she heard the people lacked bread, the French queen, Marie Antoinette, said "Let them eat cake." This was taken as a symbol of how little the monarchy understood the sufferings of the people.

10 The number of **days in a week** in the new **revolutionary French calendar**.

1.6 million—the **number of soldiers** in **Napoleon's army** at its height.

307

The Terror

After the death of the king in 1793, the National Assembly was headed by a group called the Jacobins, a political club led by Maximilien de Robespierre. They believed that France was full of spies sent by foreign powers who wanted to bring back the monarchy. The Jacobins began to execute anyone they suspected of working against them. Around 40,000 people were killed in Paris alone during this bloody period, known as The Terror, which only ended when Robespierre himself was sent to the guillotine in 1794.

The guillotine

This gruesome machine was used during the French Revolution to execute people as quickly and efficiently as possible.

THE GUILLOTINE WAS NICKNAMED THE **"NATIONAL RAZOR" AND WAS USED TO EXECUTE** UP TO 20 PEOPLE A DAY.

The ideals of the Revolution

The new Republic of France was influenced by the United States, which had won independence from Britain in 1776. Like the Americans, the French Revolutionaries wrote out a document, the "Declaration of the Rights of Man and the Citizen," which would underpin the new government. It proclaimed that all men and women are born equal, so kings and nobles have no right to rule over those of common birth, and that people should be allowed to govern themselves by democratic vote. These ideas remain important to theories of democracy and human rights to this day.

Maximilien de Robespierre
French lawyer Maximilien de Robespierre was at the forefront of the Revolution. He believed passionately in equal rights and government by the people. However, he betrayed his own beliefs by deciding the only way for the Revolution to succeed was by the deaths of those who opposed it. Tens of thousands of so-called "enemies of the Revolution" were executed on the orders of Robespierre and his allies.

The Napoleonic Wars

After the Revolution, France was left without a strong leader and surrounded by enemies. In 1800, Napoleon Bonaparte (1769–1821), a young general, became a hero to the people after a series of stunning military victories. In 1804, he made himself Emperor of France, and began a campaign of conquest across Europe. From 1805–1807, his armies defeated Austria, Russia, and Prussia until his empire covered most of Europe. He was finally defeated in 1815 at the Battle of Waterloo by an alliance of the nations of Europe.

UNIFORM

MUSKET

French infantryman's uniform
Napoleon's soldiers were the most feared in Europe. They were superbly trained and operated in tight formations. Their uniform consisted of white breeches, dark blue jacket, and a hat, or shako, decorated with a red plume. Each man was armed with a large, heavy gun called a musket.

June 25, 1791	1792–1801	Spring 1793	December 2, 1804
The king and queen attempted to flee the country in disguise. They were spotted and taken back to Paris, where they were held under guard in the Tuileries Palace. They were moved to prison in 1792 and, in 1793, they were executed by guillotine after being accused of helping Austria, the queen's homeland, which was at war with Revolutionary France.	France's neighbors were outraged by the overthrow and death of King Louis. They also hoped to gain control of French lands in the confusion of the Revolution. Wars broke out between France and other European countries such as Austria, Italy, and Britain, and in French overseas territories such as Haiti. The French armies emerged victorious.	A Committee of Public Safety was founded by Maximilien de Robespierre to fight back against agents of the old government, thought to be secretly undermining the Revolution. The Committee ran out of control, accusing many innocent people of betraying the Republic. As many as 40,000 people were executed during this Reign of Terror.	Napoleon Bonaparte proclaimed himself Emperor of France and was crowned in Paris. A military genius, he had become enormously popular among the French people after winning a stunning series of victories during the wars of 1792–1801. After his coronation, Napoleon's armies begin a war of conquest across Europe, winning great success at first.

The Industrial Revolution

Between 1760 and 1860, an age-old way of life based on farming and crafting by hand was transformed, as people moved to towns and goods were produced by machines in factories.

This transformation began in Britain, where ingenious inventors and engineers applied new scientific ideas to the old methods of farming, mining, and manufacturing. Britain also had a ready supply of raw materials, such as coal and iron ore, to power the new inventions, and a rapidly growing population eager to work in the factories and buy the new goods they produced. The Industrial Revolution transformed our way of life, bringing incredible wealth to some, but crushing poverty to many others.

Faster travel

Industrial factories depended on being able to bring in large quantities of raw materials (such as coal and cotton fiber) and send out large quantities of finished products. The old methods of transportation—such as wagon trains and sailing ships—could not move materials quickly enough or in large enough amounts. Industrial countries built huge networks of canals, where barges carrying up to 33 tons were pulled along by horses. Rail networks and steam engines allowed people and goods to travel quickly over long distances. Steam ships made ocean journeys far quicker and more reliable.

Steam locomotives

The railway became one of the greatest symbols of the Industrial Revolution. From around 1840, the US led the world in producing fast, reliable steam locomotives, such as this one built in 1863 by the Baltimore and Ohio Railroad.

New machines

The backbone of the Industrial Revolution came from new machines. Cotton making, for example, had been a lengthy process involving hours of hard work. Inventions such as the Spinning Jenny (1764), and the Spinning Mule (1779) could do the work automatically in a fraction of the time. At first, these bulky machines were powered by water wheels, and so were built-in factories next to rivers. The first water-powered cotton mill was built by entrepreneur Richard Arkwright in 1771 in Derbyshire, England. Over time, water wheels were replaced by steam engines, and factories moved into towns.

Water-powered cotton mill

Cotton is made by combing out fluffy fibers and spinning them into thread. Before the Industrial Revolution, this was done by workers in their own homes. Cotton mills could process much larger amounts of cotton far more quickly.

Reeling and winding
These machines wind the cotton on to tapered rods called bobbins.

Carding machines
These machines comb and untangle the raw cotton to separate out the fibers.

Water wheel
Flowing water turns the huge wheel's paddles to power the machines.

River

Water frame
Water-driven spinning frames are used to spin the cotton into thread.

55 million tons—the amount of coal mined in 1850 in Britain.

The new **spinning machines** produced cotton **1,000 times more quickly** than a human worker.

4,000 miles (6,400 km)—the length of new canal built in Britain from 1760-1840.

309

NO. 117 THATCHER PERKINS LOCOMOTIVE

Poverty in towns

Industrial progress brought great wealth to factory owners and entrepreneurs, and made basic goods such as food and clothing cheaper than ever before. However, it also created a new kind of poverty. Large numbers of people moved to the cities in search of work, where they were packed into crowded, dirty housing. Many were unemployed and ended up in prison for debt, or forced to move into harsh lodgings called workhouses, where they performed hard labor for no pay. Those who did have jobs worked in unsafe conditions. They were often paid poorly, and many families struggled to afford basic essentials.

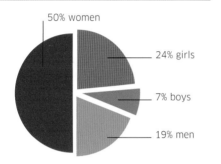

- 50% women
- 24% girls
- 7% boys
- 19% men

Workers in a cotton mill, 1859
A third of workers in the mills were children, aged as young as five. Some worked for 12 hours a day, and dangerous accidents were common.

Rise of the machines

The changes brought by industry quickly gathered momentum across Europe and North America. New factories created cheap goods and jobs for poor laborers. At the same time, mechanized farming left many rural workers unemployed, and forced them to move to cities to work in factories. With so many people looking for work, factory owners offered low wages, which meant laborers looked for even cheaper goods. Scientists and entrepreneurs used their profits to built new machines and factories, bringing prices down and creating more jobs.

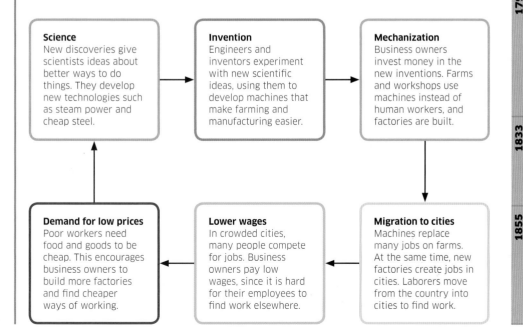

Science New discoveries give scientists ideas about better ways to do things. They develop new technologies such as steam power and cheap steel.

Invention Engineers and inventors experiment with new scientific ideas, using them to develop machines that make farming and manufacturing easier.

Mechanization Business owners invest money in the new inventions. Farms and workshops use machines instead of human workers, and factories are built.

Demand for low prices Poor workers need food and goods to be cheap. This encourages business owners to build more factories and find cheaper ways of working.

Lower wages In crowded cities, many people compete for jobs. Business owners pay low wages, since it is hard for their employees to find work elsewhere.

Migration to cities Machines replace many jobs on farms. At the same time, new factories create jobs in cities. Laborers move from the country into cities to find work.

An island of ideas

The many inventions of the 18th century were made possible by scientists and engineers, funded by rich entrepreneurs. Together they developed new machines, such as the steam engine, new ways of working, such as factory mass production, and new industrial processes, such as the Bessemer process for producing steel.

Farming with machines
1701-1831
A growing population called for more food and more efficient ways to grow it. In 1701, English inventor Jethro Tull created a seed drill that automatically sowed crops. Steam-powered plows appeared in the 1820s, and the American engineer Cyrus McCormick designed a mechanical harvester in 1831.

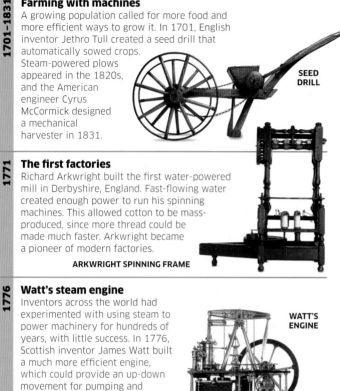

SEED DRILL

The first factories
1771
Richard Arkwright built the first water-powered mill in Derbyshire, England. Fast-flowing water created enough power to run his spinning machines. This allowed cotton to be mass-produced, since more thread could be made much faster. Arkwright became a pioneer of modern factories.

ARKWRIGHT SPINNING FRAME

Watt's steam engine
1776
Inventors across the world had experimented with using steam to power machinery for hundreds of years, with little success. In 1776, Scottish inventor James Watt built a much more efficient engine, which could provide an up-down movement for pumping and a circular movement for operating machines.

WATT'S ENGINE

Bridges of iron
1779
The era of modern bridge-building started in 1779 with the construction of the Ironbridge in Shropshire, England, the first bridge to be made entirely of solid cast iron. With stronger bridges and better-quality iron and steel, bridges could be built over longer distances, opening up new routes for roads and railways.

Gas lighting
1790
Gas from coal mines was burned in lamps to provide lighting in streets and homes. It was pumped through a network of pipes across major cities. The large-scale introduction of gas lighting in the 1790s was the work of William Murdoch, a Scottish engineer who also built steam engines. Gas lighting was brighter and more reliable than candles and oil lamps, allowing factories to remain open all night.

GAS STREET LIGHT

Brunel and the railways
1833
Isambard Kingdom Brunel was a bridge and railway engineer who oversaw the creation of much of Britain's rail network. At age 27 he became engineer to the Great Western Railway, where he constructed over 1,000 miiles (1,600 km) of track. He was famous for his innovative designs for bridges, viaducts, and tunnels.

The steel revolution
1855
In 1855, an Englishman named Henry Bessemer discovered a new, cheap way of making steel, using a machine called a "Bessemer converter" to burn impurities out of iron. Steel was essential for building railways, machinery, factories, and vehicles. By making it cheap and widely available, Bessemer's new process opened the way for a huge increase in the rate of industrialization.

How a steam engine works

The engine is powered by heat from coal burning in the firebox. Hot air from the fire passes along copper pipes through a water tank or boiler. This heats the water to boiling point, producing steam. The steam expands as it is heated, creating pressure inside the boiler.

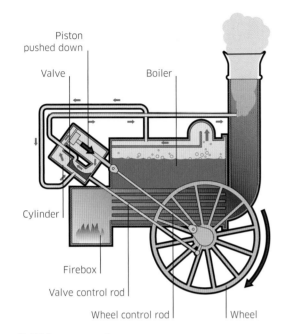

Piston pushed down
Valve
Boiler
Cylinder
Firebox
Valve control rod
Wheel control rod
Wheel

1 Piston moves down

An opening at the top of the boiler allows steam into sealed tubes called cylinders, one for each wheel. The pressure from the steam pushes down a piston inside the cylinder, which moves a control rod to turn the wheel. The turning of the wheel moves a valve inside the cylinder that controls the flow of steam.

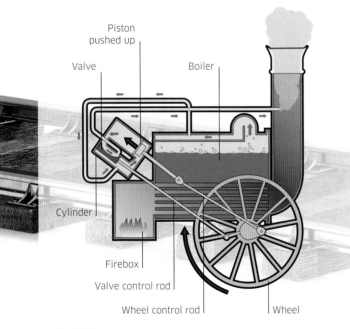

Piston pushed up
Valve
Boiler
Cylinder
Firebox
Valve control rod
Wheel control rod
Wheel

2 Piston moves up

When the piston reaches the bottom, the valve inside the cylinder switches the flow of steam from the top to the bottom of the cylinder. The steam now pushes the piston up, pulling on the wheel control rod to turn the wheel back to where it started. Steam and smoke from the firebox escape through the chimney.

The Age of Steam

For thousands of years, humans had relied on animal and people power to move heavy loads and drive machinery. This all changed in the late 18th century with the arrival of a bold new invention: the steam engine.

Steam engines operate by burning fuel to heat water until it boils. Hot steam from the boiling water is trapped to create pressure, which is used to drive machinery. This simple principle opened the way to powerful new engines. Steam engines were more flexible than windmills or waterwheels, which had to be built in specific places, and more powerful than humans or animals. They could drive factory and farm equipment, and pull plows across fields or trains along tracks. Larger models pumped vast amounts of water to drain mines and supply canal systems, and hauled blocks of stone and ore from quarries and mines. They were the driving force behind many of the innovations of the Industrial Revolution.

Water barrel
Water from this barrel kept the boiler topped off. The driver controlled the flow of water through pipes from the barrel to the boiler.

Tender (supply cart)
The engine required a constant supply of coal and water, kept on a cart pulled behind.

Train tracks

Stephenson's Rocket

The first steam locomotives were unreliable and very heavy. In 1829, a competition was held to design an engine to run on the newly built Liverpool to Manchester Railway. The winner was the Rocket, built by Robert Stephenson and his father, George.

27 mph (47 kph)—the Rocket's **top speed**.

75 miles (120 km)—the distance the Rocket traveled on its first day of trials.

4.7 tons—the **weight** of the **Rocket** steam locomotive.

311

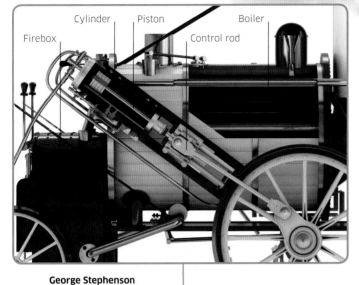

Firebox

Cylinder   Piston   Boiler

Control rod

Inside the engine
Early steam engines used a single large cylinder to power all the wheels at once. The Rocket had two angled cylinders, each connected directly to a single wheel with a control rod. This and other innovations, such as the blast pipe and a boiler with multiple tubes for hot air, made the Rocket faster and more efficient than any steam engine built before.

Smoke and steam

George Stephenson
Stephenson himself controlled the Rocket on its first demonstration.

Smokestack (chimney)
A blast pipe sucked air up through the chimney. The air was drawn in through the firebox, fanning the flames.

Stoker

Coal

Safety valve
This valve would allow steam to escape if the pressure rose too high, preventing explosions.

Control valves
These levers allowed the driver to control the flow of water and steam through the engine.

Cylinder
This sealed tube captured steam from the boiler and used it to push a piston, driving the wheels.

Steam dome
Steam from the boiler collected under this dome and was funneled into pipes leading to the cylinders.

Boiler
Water in this tank was heated by pipes, which ran through it carrying hot air from the furnace.

ROCKET.

Control rod
This rod transferred the in-out movement of the piston to the circular movement of the wheels.

Wooden wheels with steel rims

The course of the war

The war pitted 23 Union states of the North and West against 11 Confederate states of the South. The North had superior numbers, wealth, and weaponry, and despite some brilliant military successes, the South was eventually forced to surrender.

(1) April 12, 1861
Tensions between the North and South were running high. The war began when the Confederate army shot at Union soldiers stationed at Fort Sumter, South Carolina, and forced them to lower the American flag in surrender.

(2) July 21, 1861
The Confederates won their first battle near a small stream in Virginia called Bull Run. The Union answered by blockading the ports and borders of southern states, trying to wreck their economy.

(3) September 16–18, 1862
The Battle of Antietam, one of the bloodiest of the war, left 23,000 soldiers dead, wounded, or missing. The Confederates were beaten back in a turning point of the war.

(4) May 18–July 4, 1863
The city of Vicksburg beside the Mississippi River, held by the Confederates, was taken by Union troops. Control of the Mississippi was vital, since the South was using it to transport food and soldiers.

(5) July 1–3, 1863
In Gettysburg, Pennsylvania, the Union won the largest battle of the war after three days of fighting. Confederate leader General Lee lost 20,000 men, who were killed or wounded.

(6) April 9, 1865
With his troops surrounded, General Lee surrendered to General Ulysses S. Grant in a house in the village of Appomattox, Virginia.

SPRINGFIELD RIFLE MUSKET 1861

Abraham Lincoln

The 16th president of the United States, Abraham Lincoln was a brilliant orator. He was determined to keep the states of America together at all costs. After the war, he hoped to heal the divide between North and South, but was killed by a supporter of the South while at the theater in 1865.

"GOVERNMENT OF THE PEOPLE, BY THE PEOPLE, FOR THE PEOPLE SHALL NOT PERISH FROM THE EARTH."
ABRAHAM LINCOLN, SPEECH TO UNION FORCES AT GETTYSBURG, 1863

The Confederacy

Eleven Southern states broke away from the Union to form the Confederacy: North Carolina, South Carolina, Georgia, Alabama, Mississippi, Louisiana, Florida, Texas, Tennessee, Arkansas, and Virginia. They fought for states' rights and the right to own slaves. The Confederates had their own capital in Richmond, Virginia, and their own currency, flag (see left), and president–Jefferson Davis.

INDIANA

ILLINOIS

MISSOURI

KENTUCKY

TENNESSEE

ARKANSAS

Mississippi River

MISSISSIPPI

(4)

ALABAMA

FLORIDA

LOUISIANA

A nation divided

Battles were fought across America, but most of the fighting occurred in the states of Virginia and Tennessee, and along the border states– slave states that did not declare independence. Much of the conflict was near the Confederacy's capital, Richmond, Virginia, and the Union capital in Washington, DC.

2 The number of **Union** soldiers for every one **Confederate** soldier.

The number of **Americans killed** in the **Civil War** is nearly **equal** to the number who died in every other **foreign war** fought by the US since.

313

OHIO

③

⑤

②

Washington, DC,
Union capital

⑥

Union blockade
The Union set up a
naval blockade in the
Atlantic and Gulf of
Mexico to stop trade
to Southern ports.

VIRGINIA

Richmond,
Confederate capital

NORTH
CAROLINA

SOUTH
CAROLINA

①

GEORGIA

Artillery
Both sides in the war used
artillery fire to cause huge
numbers of casualties
among enemy troops.

The Union
The Union of the northern states,
led by President Abraham Lincoln,
had a larger army, including
200,000 freed slaves who joined
the fight. They also had greater
resources. Victory over the South
meant more than the ending of
slavery: the United States stayed
together as one nation with one
government. However, the
process of rebuilding the war-torn
country would be long and hard.

The Civil War

**The election of Abraham Lincoln as president in 1860 tore the US
in half, and the Civil War broke out between the North and South
over the rights of individual states and the issue of slavery.**

The US had been one country made up of many states, but in the mid-19th
century it became a divided nation. The northern states, made strong by
industry and immigrants from Europe, had little sympathy for the old-
fashioned farm culture of the South, which depended on slavery. The people
of the South suspected that the North was seeking to destroy their way of
life. When Abraham Lincoln became president, 11 Southern states feared
he would abolish slavery and left the Union. The war that followed divided
families and friends. More than 620,000 soldiers died, and even though
the country was finally reunited, bitterness remained for decades.

314 history ○ **THE MODERN WORLD**

80 The number of enemy **planes shot down** by the German **Red Baron** fighter pilot.

World War I

Half a century of power struggles, in which Germany and Austria-Hungary were set against France and Russia, ended with four years of bloody conflict that involved nearly every country in the world.

The war that followed was fought mainly in Europe, but fighting also spread to the Middle East, Africa, and Asia. Nations took part in bombing raids and chemical warfare, as well as experimenting with tanks, military aircraft, and submarines. However, most of the war was fought using ordinary artillery, machine guns, rifles, and horses. What was different about this war was the vast numbers of those involved: soldiers fought and died in the millions, and entire populations were expected to help make weapons and support the war.

Causes of the war

On June 28, 1914, the Archduke of Austria-Hungary was shot by a nationalist from Serbia in the Balkans. Austria-Hungary blamed Serbia for the killing and declared war. Russia offered to support Serbia. Germany declared war on Russia, then on France. Country after country rushed to defend their allies or declare war on their rivals until armies were on the move across the world. Most people believed the war would be over very quickly, but they were tragically mistaken.

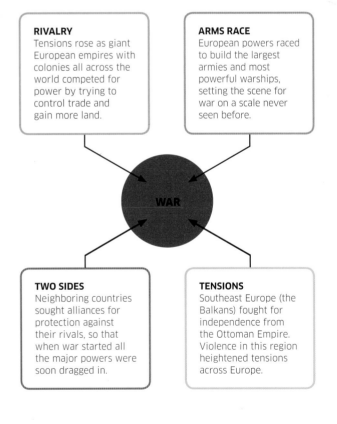

RIVALRY
Tensions rose as giant European empires with colonies all across the world competed for power by trying to control trade and gain more land.

ARMS RACE
European powers raced to build the largest armies and most powerful warships, setting the scene for war on a scale never seen before.

WAR

TWO SIDES
Neighboring countries sought alliances for protection against their rivals, so that when war started all the major powers were soon dragged in.

TENSIONS
Southeast Europe (the Balkans) fought for independence from the Ottoman Empire. Violence in this region heightened tensions across Europe.

Road to war
In the early 1900s, powerful European nations competed for trade and land, and built up large armies. Nations made agreements to support one another (alliances), but these were often fragile. Two groups of countries on opposite sides emerged: the Central Powers and the Triple Entente (Allies).

The fronts

The areas, or fronts, in which the war was fought went right across Europe. The two main zones, or theaters, of war were the Western Front and the Eastern Front. The Western Front stretched from the North Sea to the Swiss border and was made up of a continuous line of trenches. The Eastern Front, on the other side of Europe, saw the great armies of Germany and Austria-Hungary battle against Russia.

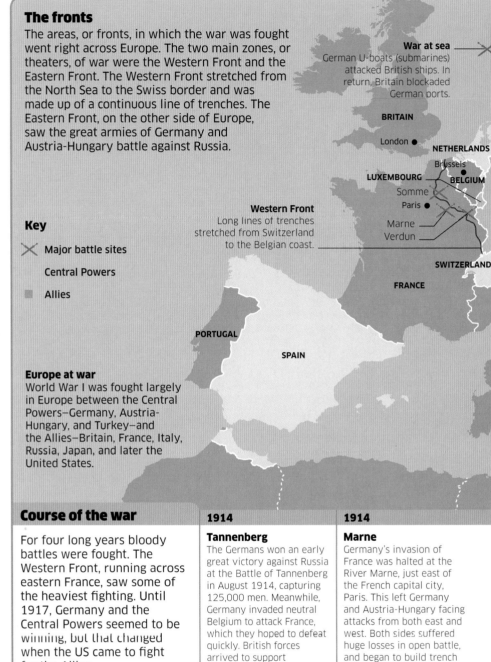

War at sea
German U-boats (submarines) attacked British ships. In return, Britain blockaded German ports.

BRITAIN

London ●

NETHERLANDS

Brussels
LUXEMBOURG   BELGIUM
Somme

Paris ●

Marne
Verdun

SWITZERLAND

FRANCE

Western Front
Long lines of trenches stretched from Switzerland to the Belgian coast.

PORTUGAL

SPAIN

Key

✕ Major battle sites

◼ Central Powers

◼ Allies

Europe at war
World War I was fought largely in Europe between the Central Powers—Germany, Austria-Hungary, and Turkey—and the Allies—Britain, France, Italy, Russia, Japan, and later the United States.

Course of the war

For four long years bloody battles were fought. The Western Front, running across eastern France, saw some of the heaviest fighting. Until 1917, Germany and the Central Powers seemed to be winning, but that changed when the US came to fight for the Allies.

1914

Tannenberg
The Germans won an early great victory against Russia at the Battle of Tannenberg in August 1914, capturing 125,000 men. Meanwhile, Germany invaded neutral Belgium to attack France, which they hoped to defeat quickly. British forces arrived to support Belgium and France.

1914

Marne
Germany's invasion of France was halted at the River Marne, just east of the French capital city, Paris. This left Germany and Austria-Hungary facing attacks from both east and west. Both sides suffered huge losses in open battle, and began to build trench systems for defense.

The war at home

World War I was the first "total" war, meaning not just soldiers but the whole civilian population were involved. The entire nation was expected to help keep the war effort going, by helping on the "Home Front." Civilians only received fixed rations of food to make sure enough could be sent out to the troops, and women took over many of the jobs of men sent to fight. Bombing raids on German, French, and some British cities brought the war into ordinary homes.

Everyone must play their part
This Russian poster reads: "All for the war." In wartime, women took men's places on farms, in factories, and in offices. Every man was expected to fight: military leader Lord Kitchener (far right) calls on British men to join the army.

RUSSIAN POSTER

On **Christmas Day** 1914, **British and German soldiers** on the Western Front stopped fighting to exchange gifts, sing carols, and even **play soccer**.

600 The **number of rounds** that a World War I machine gun could fire in **one minute**.

315

Russian revolution
A communist revolution swept across Russia in 1917, overthrowing the Tzar (emperor). Russian soldiers continued to fight until March 1918.

Eastern Front
Russia fought against Germany and Austria-Hungary all across Eastern Europe.

Italian Front
Fierce fighting took place in the mountains between Italy and Austria-Hungary.

Balkan front
Serbia fought against Germany, Austria-Hungary, and Bulgaria.

Arab revolt
The Arabs of North Africa and the Middle East rose up against the Ottoman Turks who ruled the region.

SWEDEN
EAST PRUSSIA
Tannenberg
Berlin
GERMANY
POLAND
RUSSIAN EMPIRE
Moscow
AUSTRIA-HUNGARY
ROMANIA
SERBIA
MONTENEGRO
BULGARIA
ITALY
ALBANIA
GREECE
Constantinople
Gallipoli
OTTOMAN EMPIRE

GERMAN GAS MASK AND CONTAINER

Mustard gas symbol

GERMAN GAS SHELL

A new kind of warfare

At the start of the war, armies on both sides were still using outdated tactics, such as cavalry and bayonet charges. However, with deadly weapons like machine guns widely available, these old tactics failed, resulting in huge numbers of deaths. By the end of the war, both sides had developed new strategies, as well as new weaponry, such as aircraft. Both sides used poison gas to kill off enemy soldiers. Horses, shown to be unsuited to the modern battlefield, were replaced by the first tanks.

Poison gas
At first there was no protection against poison gas, but by the middle of the war both sides carried gas masks. Around 30 types of gas were used, causing more than 1.2 million casualties.

230 The number of soldiers that perished each hour throughout the four-and-a-quarter years of the war.

1915–16	1916	1916	1918
Gallipoli British Empire forces, including many troops from Australia and New Zealand, launched an attack on the Ottoman Empire at Gallipoli, on the west coast of Turkey. They landed in April 1915, but suffered heavy casualties and were forced to withdraw.	**Verdun** Continuous fighting across the trenches produced a stalemate on the Western Front. Trying to break the deadlock, Germany launched an attack on the French fortifications at Verdun. After months of brutal fighting, the exhausted French army forced the Germans to retreat.	**Somme** The British and French, after little progress for two years, began the Big Push –a large-scale attack to break through German lines at the Somme in France. Thousands were mown down by German machine guns. More than 600,000 Allied troops were killed or wounded, for little gain.	**Hundred Days Offensive** Provoked by German submarine attacks on American ships, the US entered the war in 1917. In 1918, American, British, and French soldiers mounted a series of successful attacks, known as the Hundred Days Offensive, forcing the Central Powers to surrender.

BRITISH POSTER

'YOU ARE THE MAN I WANT'

The cost of the war

There had never before been a human conflict on this scale, and with it came huge cost to human life. More than half of the 65 million men who fought across the world were killed or wounded, and many died of disease. More than six million ordinary citizens died, from illness or starvation. Europe was left in ruins, and its systems of government, and the way people worked and lived, changed forever.

Military deaths
It is estimated that 15 million people died in World War I. Most of them were soldiers, especially in the armies of Russia and Germany.

Key
= 100,000 soldiers killed

RUSSIA
GERMANY
FRANCE
BRITISH EMPIRE
AUSTRIA-HUNGARY
ITALY
SERBIA
USA

1 MILLION
2 MILLION

316 history ∘ **THE MODERN WORLD**

6,000 miles (10,000 km)—the estimated **length** of the trenches across **France and Belgium**.

Trench warfare

Soldiers on both sides in World War I faced a lethal bombardment of bullets, shells, and poison gas. They lived and fought in deep trenches stretching great distances across the battlefields.

Both sides suffered horrific losses in the first few months of the war, as armies of massed infantry charged toward deadly machine guns. It became clear that neither side could break through the other's defenses. Instead they dug down into long lines of fortified trenches, which stretched all across Europe. The war became a stalemate that lasted for years, with soldiers camped in lines of trenches, facing each other across a strip of no man's land.

New weapons

World War I saw some of the highest rates of death and injury to frontline soldiers of any war in history. This was partly due to the development of powerful new weapons such as machine guns and high-explosive artillery shells, which could cause mass casualties in a very short space of time.

Artillery
The largest guns could bombard trench positions from miles away. A direct hit from an artillery shell would create a large crater, and could kill a dozen men in an instant.

Deadly enemies

Life in the trenches was extremely dangerous. Around 9.7 million soldiers were killed in combat, and many more were horribly wounded under a nearly constant barrage of bullets, shells, and poison gas.

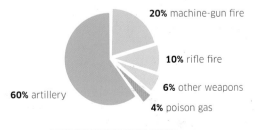

20% machine-gun fire
10% rifle fire
6% other weapons
60% artillery
4% poison gas

CAUSES OF DEATH OF SOLDIERS IN WORLD WAR I

Gas warfare
Both sides used poison gas as a weapon, and gas masks were essential.

Shell explosion
Artillery shells could be loaded with explosives, poison gas, or pieces of metal called shrapnel.

Life in the trenches

The trenches were a harsh place to live. In winter they filled with mud and ice, and they were infested with huge rats all year round. The soldiers were often cold and wet, hungry and exhausted, and to make matters worse, they knew an attack could come any moment.

No man's land
The land between the trenches was a sea of mud blasted by artillery shells. The bodies of dead soldiers often lay here for days because it was too dangerous to retrieve them.

Tunnel support

> **"What a bloodbath, what horrid images, what slaughter...**
> # Hell cannot be this dreadful."
> **Albert Joubaire, a French soldier at Verdun in 1916**

Underground war
As well as attacking above ground, both sides tried to tunnel into enemy trenches, to place explosives. Fierce battles were fought when enemy diggers met underground.

4,000 calories–daily ration of a British soldier in the trenches.

317

Firing bay
The bottom of the trench was dug to be deep enough that soldiers could walk along it without being exposed to enemy fire. Steps enabled soldiers to see out over no man's land, and snipers to fire on the enemy.

Periscope

Sandbags for protection

Field telephone

Sniper

Shell hole
Craters left by shell explosions filled with rainwater and mud, and could drown the unwary.

Barbed wire

Reconnaissance
During quiet times, small groups might be sent into no man's land to spy on enemy movement.

Pillbox
Concrete boxes were built to shelter machine guns and lookout posts.

Latrines
Under constant threat from enemy fire, even toilets and washrooms had to be built in trenches.

Soldiers' shelter

Firing bay
Soldiers standing here could look and fire out over no man's land. They had to beware of gunfire from enemy snipers.

Officers' dugout
Special rooms for officers were dug below ground.

318　history ○ THE MODERN WORLD

1.5 million **children died** during the **Holocaust**.

57 The number of **consecutive nights** **London** was bombed during **the Blitz**.

World War II

In September 1939, Germany, led by brutal dictator Adolf Hitler, stormed into Poland. This was the beginning of World War II. Lasting six long years, it was the deadliest conflict in history.

World War I was supposed to be "the war to end all wars," but defeated countries believed they had been treated badly by harsh peace terms. In the 1930s, a catastrophic global recession broke out, which left many people poor and destitute. Disillusioned, they began to turn to new, forceful leaders for solutions.

In Germany, the Nazi Party rose to power under Adolf Hitler. He launched mass invasions west into Europe and east into the USSR in search of more "living space" for the German people. At the same time, the Japanese fought to take control of Asia and the Pacific Ocean. The battle to defeat Germany, Japan, and their allies would spread across the globe, and cost the lives of millions.

Codes, spies, and propaganda

World War II was one of the first wars fought with modern technology and electronics. Both sides became very good at spying, and they used codes to pass on secret information. Spies and double agents did their best to outwit the enemy. In their own countries, they used posters, movies, and radio broadcasts to spread propaganda—powerful messages designed to stir national pride, loyalty, and hatred of the enemy.

Enigma
The Enigma machine was a German device used to send coded messages. It could only be read by another Enigma machine. The British cracked the codes in 1941 using an early form of computer.

Rotator cylinder
Letters are coded by a set of rotating wheels. They can only be decoded using the same settings.

Keyboard
When a letter is pressed, it sends an electrical signal to the rotator for coding.

Plugboard
The plugboard hugely increases the number of coding combinations.

Rise of Fascism
Fascism, a new form of nationalism, rose out of the ashes of World War I. As people struggled with mass unemployment and poverty, they were drawn to strong leaders such as Benito Mussolini (Italy) and Francisco Franco (Spain) who promised national unity and prosperity. In Germany, Adolf Hitler declared himself Führer (leader) and led the country to war.

Nazi symbol
This German army badge shows an eagle on top of a swastika—the symbol of the National Socialist German Workers Party (Nazis), led by Adolf Hitler.

Theaters of war
Battles raged on land, sea, and in the air across Western Europe, the Eastern Front, the Mediterranean, North Africa, and the Pacific and Atlantic oceans. Few nations remained neutral, supporting either the Allies (Britain, France, the US, and Russia) or the Axis (Germany, Italy, and Japan).

Battle of the Atlantic
The Allies needed to keep shipping lanes open, so essential supplies from the US could reach Britain and the USSR. German U-boats (submarines) sank many convoys, but the Allies eventually defeated the German navy.

United States of America
Neutral at the start of the war, the US helped the Allies with loans of money and materials. A surprise attack by Japan brought the US into the war in 1941.

NORTH AMERICA

ATLANTIC OCEAN

PACIFIC OCEAN

SOUTH AMERICA

Key
■ Allied nations

■ Axis nations

■ Countries conquered by the Axis

North Africa
The Axis and the Allies fought in North Africa from 1940 to 1943. British General Bernard Montgomery defeated German Field Marshal Erwin Rommel in tank battles across the desert.

16 million **American soldiers** served in **World War II**.

27 million **Soviet soldiers and civilians** died on the **Eastern Front**.

35,000 Allied **prisoners of war escaped** German and Italian **prisons** during **World War II**.

319

The Holocaust

Adolf Hitler was convinced that the German people were the "master race" and that other people, such as Jews, were inferior. Under German occupation, Jews were herded into ghettos where many starved to death. In 1942, Hitler instigated the Final Solution–the murder of all Jews. He set up concentration camps where "inferior" people such as Jews, homosexuals, gypsies, and Soviet prisoners of war were gassed to death in one of the most horrific campaigns in human history.

"I STILL BELIEVE, IN SPITE OF EVERYTHING, THAT PEOPLE ARE TRULY GOOD AT HEART."

ANNE FRANK, JEWISH VICTIM OF THE HOLOCAUST

The yellow star
Jews were forced to wear this yellow badge to identify them as Jewish. It became a symbol of Nazi persecution.

The course of the war

Hitler's forces quickly conquered large areas of Europe. He then attacked his former allies, the USSR, but was halted by fierce resistance. When the US joined the Allies in 1941, the tide began to turn. German forces were pushed back, and the Japanese were defeated in brutal fighting across Asia and the Pacific.

Sept 1, 1939

German invasion of Europe

Hitler's lightning invasion swiftly conquered Poland. The following year, German troops took Denmark, Norway, Belgium, the Netherlands, and most of France. The British were forced to evacuate 340,000 Allied troops at Dunkirk, France, in May 1940.

1940

Battle of Britain

During the Battle of Britain, German and British aircraft fought for control of the skies. Germany's defeat prevented a land invasion of Britain, but bombers began deadly air raids on British cities.

GAS MASK ISSUED TO CHILDREN IN BRITISH CITIES

June 1941

Operation Barbarossa

The Germans turned on their former allies, the USSR, reaching Moscow and Leningrad. But they were driven back by Soviet counterattacks and the harsh winter. Both sides suffered huge losses, and the Germans suffered their first defeat of the war.

Dec 7, 1941

Pearl Harbor

Japan, Germany's allies, mounted a surprise attack on American ships at Pearl Harbor, Hawaii, bringing the USA into the war. In June 1942, the US fleet defeated the Japanese Navy at the Battle of Midway in the Pacific Ocean, halting the Japanese advance.

Oct 1942

El Alamein

The Allies won a major victory when the British drove the Germans out of Egypt at the Battle of El Alamein.

DESERT RAT BANNER OF BRITISH FORCES IN NORTH AFRICA

Winter 1942

Stalingrad

The focus of the war on the Eastern Front, the brutal Battle of Stalingrad, USSR, involved unimaginable hardship as two armies fought for control of the city. The Soviet Red Army destroyed superior German forces, and soon began to march on Germany.

June 6, 1944

D-Day

After two years of planning, the Allies invaded Europe in Operation Overlord. To liberate France, 4,000 landing craft, 600 warships, and thousands of Allied aircraft hit five beaches in Normandy. Germany was forced to surrender just 11 months later.

Aug 6, 1945

Hiroshima

In the last act of the war, the Americans used a new weapon, the atomic bomb, to force the Japanese to surrender. They dropped bombs on the cities of Hiroshima and Nagasaki. The two explosions killed more than 300,000 people.

Europe

At the start of the war, most of mainland Europe fell to the Germans, whose *Blitzkrieg* (lightning war) tactics proved hugely successful. From 1942-43, the Allies began to fight back.

ASIA

EUROPE

AFRICA

The USSR

In 1941, the war widened when Hitler invaded the USSR. Early German successes were overturned by tenacious military and civilian resistance in one of the bloodiest campaigns of the war.

PACIFIC OCEAN

INDIAN OCEAN

AUSTRALIA

The Pacific

The Pacific theater of war included Japan, China, and Korea, and many small islands in Southeast Asia. The Japanese won early victories, but their advance was halted by the US Navy at the Battle of Midway in 1942.

30 mph (48 kph)—the **top speed** of the **Soviet T34 tank**.

200 miles (320 km)—the **range** of a **V-2 rocket**.

Modern warfare

World War II was the most destructive conflict in history, since modern technology created new and deadly weapons. The war saw the introduction of guided missiles, mass tank battles, jet engines, atomic weapons, and powerful bomber planes.

Hitler's armies planned to shock the Allies into surrender using surprise bomb attacks and rapid tank invasions—a strategy he called *Blitzkrieg* (lightning warfare). As the war went on, both sides built tanks, planes, and ships in huge numbers, and these weapons caused mass casualties and pulverized vast areas of land. Toward the end of the war, fleets of bombers numbering more than 1,000 pummeled cities for days and nights on end.

Bomber plane
During World War II, both sides used bombers to attack enemy cities: to destroy factories and damage enemy morale. German planes pounded British cities in 1940–41 in a series of attacks called the Blitz, while Allied aircraft leveled German cities such as Dresden in 1945.

Engines
Four powerful engines allowed the B-17 to reach a top speed of 290 mph (460 kph).

Bomb bay
The B-17 could carry up to 8,000 lb (3,600 kg) of bombs.

Oxygen tanks
These supplied breathable air to the crew at high altitudes.

Radio desk
A radio operator sat here to communicate with the bomber's home base.

Nose guns

Navigator
The navigator plotted the plane's course at this desk.

Bombardier
This officer controlled the release of bombs as close as possible to the target.

Cockpit
The pilot and copilot controlled the plane from here.

2.9 million tons—the total weight of bombs dropped by the Allies on Europe.

Propeller

90 The **number of airplanes** carried by a *Yorktown* class **aircraft carrier**.

1 million—the number of **houses in London** **destroyed** by **German air raids** during the **Blitz**.

321

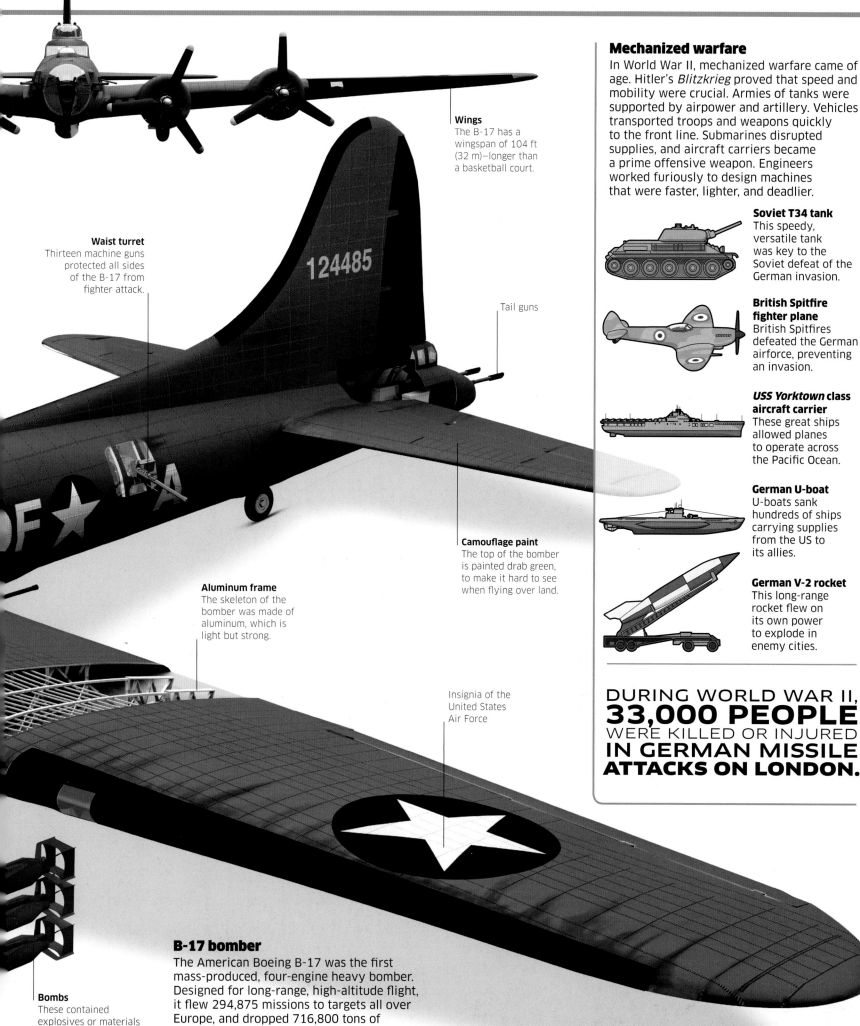

Wings
The B-17 has a wingspan of 104 ft (32 m)—longer than a basketball court.

Waist turret
Thirteen machine guns protected all sides of the B-17 from fighter attack.

124485

Tail guns

Camouflage paint
The top of the bomber is painted drab green, to make it hard to see when flying over land.

Aluminum frame
The skeleton of the bomber was made of aluminum, which is light but strong.

Insignia of the United States Air Force

Bombs
These contained explosives or materials for starting fires.

B-17 bomber
The American Boeing B-17 was the first mass-produced, four-engine heavy bomber. Designed for long-range, high-altitude flight, it flew 294,875 missions to targets all over Europe, and dropped 716,800 tons of bombs, mostly on German factories.

Mechanized warfare
In World War II, mechanized warfare came of age. Hitler's *Blitzkrieg* proved that speed and mobility were crucial. Armies of tanks were supported by airpower and artillery. Vehicles transported troops and weapons quickly to the front line. Submarines disrupted supplies, and aircraft carriers became a prime offensive weapon. Engineers worked furiously to design machines that were faster, lighter, and deadlier.

Soviet T34 tank
This speedy, versatile tank was key to the Soviet defeat of the German invasion.

British Spitfire fighter plane
British Spitfires defeated the German airforce, preventing an invasion.

USS Yorktown class aircraft carrier
These great ships allowed planes to operate across the Pacific Ocean.

German U-boat
U-boats sank hundreds of ships carrying supplies from the US to its allies.

German V-2 rocket
This long-range rocket flew on its own power to explode in enemy cities.

DURING WORLD WAR II, **33,000 PEOPLE** WERE KILLED OR INJURED **IN GERMAN MISSILE ATTACKS ON LONDON.**

322 history○ **THE MODERN WORLD**

18 of the **22 major cities in North Korea were flattened by air raids** in the Korean War.

A world divided

The Cold War saw two superpowers face off, backed by global alliances. The communist nations (marked in red), led by the USSR, were opposed by NATO (marked in blue), an alliance led by the US, and other allied countries around the world.

United States of America
The US was the most powerful NATO country. Its leaders worked to destabilize communist states across the world, but were not always successful.

United Kingdom
Allied with the US, the UK had an extensive spy network and its own arsenal of nuclear weapons.

The Space Race
Both sides raced to send people into space. The Soviets took the first victory when Russian pilot Yuri Gagarin orbited the Earth in 1961. But the Americans won the race when, in 1969, the crew of spacecraft *Apollo 11* became the first human beings to walk on the Moon.

The Cuban Missile Crisis
The island of Cuba was a communist state and an ally of the USSR. In 1962, the Soviets began to build missile launch sites in Cuba, within striking distance of major US cities. The Americans demanded the missiles be removed. Military conflict seemed inevitable, but at the last minute, the Soviets withdrew.

Nicaragua
Communist parties had the support of the people in countries across Central and South America. The US tried to undermine them, for example, by supporting a guerrilla rebellion in Nicaragua.

Communism in Africa
Communist parties formed in several African countries as they gained their independence from European empires. Backed by the USSR, they often battled with forces allied with NATO.

Global conflict

The battle between NATO and the USSR spread across the world. An "Iron Curtain" divided Europe between communist east and democratic west. Violent struggles broke out in Africa, Latin America, and Asia. In the end it was economic more than military force that brought the war to an end.

"FROM EACH ACCORDING TO **HIS ABILITY,** TO EACH ACCORDING TO **HIS NEEDS."**
COMMUNIST MOTTO

1945
As World War II came to an end, the Allied leaders arranged to divide Europe between them. The USSR forced Eastern European countries such as Poland and Hungary to turn to communism. By 1948, Europe was divided, with democracy in the west and communist rule in the east.

1948
The German capital, Berlin, in Soviet-controlled East Germany, was partly controlled by the US, Britain, and France. The Soviets tried to squeeze the Allies out by blocking roads and railways. The Americans and British got around the blockade by airlifting in more than a million tons of supplies.

1950
The US government feared that Soviet spies had found their way into key institutions such as the army and intelligence services. A Senator named Joe McCarthy began a campaign to hunt down enemy agents. His search became a witch hunt where innocent people were persecuted.

1956
Hungary, a Soviet ally in Eastern Europe, elected a new leader, Imre Nagy, who promised to reform the communist government. The USSR, determined to keep control of the country, sent tanks to restore Soviet control and remove Nagy from power. Many civilians were injured or killed.

1979
Soviet allies in Afghanistan were attacked by Islamic resistance fighters. The US supplied weapons and training to the rebels, while the USSR sent in an army to back up the communists. The war lasted for almost a decade, and millions of Afghan civilians were forced to flee their homes.

1987
The USSR was faced with economic collapse. A new leader, Mikhail Gorbachev, announced a policy of openness, reforming the communist government and seeking peace with NATO. In 1989, Gorbachev and US President George HW Bush announced the end of the Cold War.

6 million—the estimated **number of Afghan civilians forced to flee their homes** in the **Soviet-Afghan War**, 1979–88.

10 million **Polish people** joined the **Solidarity protest movement** in 1980, undermining communist rule.

323

The Iron Curtain
At the end of World War II, the USSR took control of much of Eastern Europe, by force where necessary. The dividing line between the two sides became known as the Iron Curtain.

USSR
The revolution of 1917 saw the Russian Empire become the USSR, the world's first communist state.

The Vietnam War
In 1954, Vietnam split into communist North and US-allied South. As tensions rose, the US sent troops to support South Vietnam. They were drawn into a brutal guerrilla war, and were forced to withdraw in 1973. South Vietnam was conquered by the North in 1975.

China
A brutal civil war saw China become a communist nation in 1949. Millions died in the decades of turbulence that followed.

Korea
Communist North Korea, aided by China and the USSR, battled the US and its allies for control of US-allied South Korea from 1950–53.

Sputnik
The USSR took a lead in the Space Race by launching the first man-made satellite, *Sputnik 1*, in 1957.

The Berlin Wall
Germany and its capital, Berlin, were split between the USSR, and the US, France, and Britain. The Soviets built a wall across Berlin to keep people from fleeing to the West. The wall was demolished in 1989 as the Cold War ended.

The Cold War

After World War II, the world was divided between two immensely powerful rivals: the communist USSR and the democratic US. Bitter enemies, these two superpowers faced off, backed by massive arsenals of nuclear weapons.

The people of the USSR (the Soviets) believed in communism, a system that shares all wealth equally. However, their government was often corrupt and oppressive. The US was a capitalist democracy, and its people enjoyed much greater freedom than those in communist countries. Both sides had vast stores of nuclear weaponry, enough to wipe each other out if they ever went to war. This threat of "mutually assured destruction" forced them to fight by other means, using spies and economic warfare to weaken the other's position. Most of their battles were fought in smaller countries such as Vietnam and Nicaragua, with the USSR trying to spread communism and the US fighting to prevent them from succeeding.

The great reformer
Mikhail Gorbachev reformed the USSR and sought peace with NATO. But he was ousted from power in 1991 and the USSR split apart.

324 history ○ THE MODERN WORLD

1968 The year **students and workers** all over Europe **marched in protest** against their governments.

The 1960s

Filled with political revolutions, struggles for independence, and teenage rebellion, the 1960s was a decade of change, in which old values and traditions were challenged by a new generation.

In Europe and the USA, the 1960s were a time of social change. A new generation, growing up after the horrors of World War II, looked forward with optimism and the belief they could change the world. They rejected their parents' values and challenged all forms of authority, embracing outrageous new styles of fashion, psychedelic art, and politically motivated music. At the same time, protest movements called for peace across the world, for the end to racial discrimination, and for equal rights for women.

The 1960s also saw wars in Vietnam, Nigeria, and Cyprus, and between Arabs and Israelis in the Middle East. Mao's Cultural Revolution turned Chinese society upside down. African countries achieved independence from their old colonial rulers, some becoming bright new democracies, while others slipped into civil war. Despite the turmoil, the decade ended with an astounding triumph for human science, technology, and bravery, when the first people set foot on the Moon.

Peace and love

Many people were shocked by the violence they saw on their new television screens, especially in news reports from the Vietnam War. Influenced by Eastern philosophies such as Hinduism and Buddhism, they formed protest movements calling for violence to be rejected in favor of peace and universal love. The Campaign for Nuclear Disarmament (CND) called for both sides in the Cold War to abandon nuclear weapons. The hippie movement, born in San Francisco, CA, called for a laid-back lifestyle promoting peace, love, and understanding.

War and peace

Despite numerous protests for peace, the 1960s became increasingly violent. Tensions grew between the US and the USSR, in a Cold War between East and West, and both sides built up massive arsenals of nuclear weapons. However, the 1960s also saw huge strides in the quest for equal rights. Discrimination against black people was outlawed in the US, and women gained greater control over their lives and choices.

Campaign for civil rights

At the beginning of the decade, many Southern states encouraged separation between white and black people (or segregation). In February 1960, four black students in South Carolina protested by sitting down at a "whites-only" lunch counter and refusing to leave. Their example sparked similar protests across segregated states.

The first man in space

On April 12 1961, the Russian Yuri Gagarin became the first person to journey to outer space. His spaceship, the *Vostok 1*, just large enough for one person, made a single orbit of the Earth. His flight lasted a total of 108 minutes from launch to landing.

Death of a president

President John F. Kennedy was shot and killed as he drove through the streets of Dallas, Texas. His murder shocked not just America, but the entire world, coming at a time of uncertainty and tension between Russia and the United States.

A NEWSPAPER REPORTS KENNEDY'S DEATH

CHICAGO DAILY NEWS

PRESIDENT IS KILLED

Texas Sniper Escapes; Johnson Sworn In

Story Begins on Next Page

1960	1961	1962	1963	1964

Independence across Africa

Up to World War II, much of Africa was ruled by European empires. These empires were greatly weakened by the war, and in 1960, 17 African countries gained independence, including Nigeria, Chad, Somalia, and Madagascar. The process of decolonization (giving power back to local people) would continue for many years.

Martin Luther King

The campaign for civil rights in the US was led by Dr. Martin Luther King, Jr. In August 1963, he gave a powerful speech to a crowd of campaigners in Washington, DC, calling for an end to racism. He was murdered five years later, but new laws in 1964 and 1965 banned racial discrimination.

The British invasion

Pop music became a powerful cultural force. British bands such as The Beatles and The Rolling Stones became world famous, storming the American charts in 1964.

KENYAN BANK NOTE SHOWING JOMO KENYATTA, THE COUNTRY'S FIRST PRESIDENT.

MARTIN LUTHER KING, JR., ADDRESSING CROWDS IN WASHINGTON, D.C.

"I HAVE A DREAM THAT MY FOUR **LITTLE CHILDREN WILL ONE DAY** LIVE IN A NATION WHERE **THEY WILL NOT BE JUDGED** BY THE COLOR OF THEIR SKIN BUT BY THE CONTENT **OF THEIR CHARACTER.**"

THE BEATLES ARRIVE IN THE USA

500,000 The **number of troops that entered Czechoslovakia** during the Prague Spring.

400,000 The number of **people who attended the Woodstock Festival.**

325

Volkswagen camper van

An icon of 1960s counterculture, these vans were perfect for people who wanted to drop out of mainstream society, travel the world, and try new things.

New art and fashion

Many parts of Europe and the US became very wealthy in the 1960s. Teenagers suddenly had buying power, and their shopping habits created new cultural trends. Artists such as Andy Warhol created Pop Art, using images from advertising, comic books, and movies. Young people didn't have to dress like their parents anymore, and fashion was transformed by designers such as Mary Quant. Carnaby Street in London became the center of this creative energy. In France, a New Wave of directors experimented with films focusing on realistic situations and the important social issues of the day.

"THE YOUNG TODAY ARE LESS MATERIALISTIC AND MORE INTELLIGENT THAN THEY'VE EVER BEEN."
MARY QUANT,
DESIGNER OF THE MINISKIRT, 1967

Fashion revolution

The miniskirt, by Mary Quant, is an icon of 1960s fashion. The older generation thought it was vulgar and indecent. The younger generation adored it. The new designs made models such as Twiggy (Lesley Hornby) overnight celebrities.

Vietnam War

In the bloodiest conflict of the Cold War, the US army supported South Vietnam against communist North Vietnam, who were allied with the USSR and China. The war was a disaster for the US, who were forced to withdraw after years of brutal fighting.

DOGTAGS USED TO IDENTIFY US SOLDIERS IN VIETNAM

China's Cultural Revolution

Communist China was led by Mao Zedong. He was loved by farmers and workers, but he suspected the educated middle class of trying to undermine him. In 1966, to strengthen his hold on power, he called for a Cultural Revolution to rebuild Chinese society. Schools and colleges were closed down. Millions of young people were taken out of education and sent to work on farms. Scientists, teachers, scholars, writers, and business managers were beaten and humiliated by mobs in the streets. The turbulence continued until Mao's death in 1976.

ABORIGINAL FLAG

Equality in Australia

The indigenous people of Australia –the Aborigines–campaigned for equality throughout the 1960s. Their lands had been taken by white settlers, they were denied access to education and healthcare, and many were not permitted to vote. In 1967, Australia finally granted citizenship to Aborigines, but the struggle for equality continued for many years.

Woodstock

The Woodstock Music and Art Fair was held In August 1969 on farmland near Bethel, NY. It summed up the youthful optimism of the decade as hundreds of thousands came to watch their heroes perform live. The festival featured performances by the decade's greatest musicians, such as Joan Baez, Janis Joplin, and Jimi Hendrix.

| 1965 | 1966 | 1967 | 1968 | 1969 |

The Six Day War

Israel had long been in dispute with its Arab neighbors. In 1967, fearing an attack led by Egypt, Israel struck first, capturing large areas of land in Egypt and Palestine in a war lasting just six days.

Prague Spring

Czechoslovakia had lived under communist rule since 1948, with the Czech government strongly influenced by the Soviet Union. In 1968, Czech leader Alexander Dubček tried to give the people new freedoms. The Soviets would not allow this and sent tanks into Prague, the Czech capital. Despite protests by the people of Prague, Dubček was removed from power and communist rule continued.

Moon landings

The decade ended with an extraordinary achievement. In July 1969, an American spacecraft carrying Neil Armstrong and Edwin "Buzz" Aldrin landed on the surface of the Moon. Around 600 million awestruck people watched the Moon landing live on their television screens.

Key

Israeli territory before the war

Land captured by Israel during the war

SATURN V

5 billion **mobile phones** were **in use globally** by 2011.

6.1 billion—**population of the world** at the **start of the 21st century.**

The 21st century

At the end of the 20th century, the world got ready to party. Huge celebrations took place across the globe to greet the year 2000, the start of the new millennium. The new century brought grave new challenges, but also amazing opportunities.

With the world's population expanding, humanity's demands on the planet are growing rapidly. As the 21st century goes on, scientists have become increasingly concerned that we may run out of some natural resources, and that human activity is causing dangerous changes to our environment. Many countries have also had to contend with devastating natural disasters. Terrorist attacks brought fear and conflict to many cities, and a global financial collapse increased the hardship for millions.

At the same time, the 21st century has seen astonishing new advances in technology. Smartphones and tablets have transformed the way we communicate, and the Internet has expanded hugely to give voices to users across the globe.

Digital revolution

The digital revolution began in the 1980s, when computers became cheap enough for people to buy and use at home. At first computers were big metal boxes, but today they are hidden in everyday objects, such as smartphones, tablets, MP3 players, and cameras. The Internet is rapidly evolving to play a central role in society, transforming cultural, economic, and political landscapes. There are thought to be more than 2 billion Internet users worldwide, all of whom can exchange information in an instant.

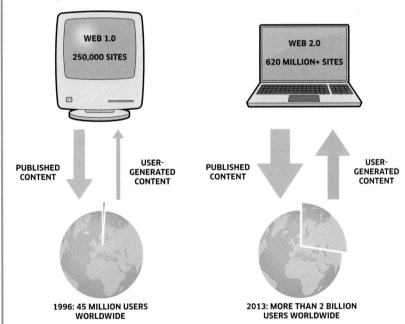

WEB 1.0
250,000 SITES

WEB 2.0
620 MILLION+ SITES

PUBLISHED CONTENT — USER-GENERATED CONTENT

PUBLISHED CONTENT — USER-GENERATED CONTENT

1996: 45 MILLION USERS WORLDWIDE

2013: MORE THAN 2 BILLION USERS WORLDWIDE

Web use
During the 1990s, most people only used the Internet to look up information. In the 21st century, the amount of user-generated content has hugely increased, with blogs and social networking sites allowing people to share their ideas and experiences.

IN 2001, GOOGLE INDEXED
250 MILLION IMAGES.
IN 2010, IT INDEXED
MORE THAN 10 BILLION.

The War on Terror

In 2001, a group of Islamist terrorists named al-Qaeda launched a series of attacks on targets in the US. A decade of conflict followed. The US and its allies launched a "War on Terror," invading Afghanistan to capture the terrorists and prevent further attacks. Meanwhile, al-Qaeda and their allies plotted to cause more deaths and destruction in other countries across the world.

Sept 2001

9/11
On September 11, 2001, the US suffered devastating terrorist attacks. Members of al-Qaeda, a global terrorist network of radical Muslims, hijacked four aircraft. They flew two into the World Trade Center in New York (pictured) and one into the Pentagon. The fourth crashed in Pennsylvania. Almost 3,000 people were killed in the attacks, which shocked the world.

The War in Iraq

In 1991, Saddam Hussein, leader of Iraq, ordered an invasion of neighboring Kuwait. His armies were driven out by an international force led by the US, but tensions remained high. In 2001, the international community suspected that Saddam Hussein possessed weapons of mass destruction capable of causing huge civilian casualties. As the War on Terror heightened tensions across the Middle East, the US and UK led an invasion of Iraq in 2003, toppling Saddam Hussein from power. Although the invasion lasted only a few weeks, violence would continue in Iraq for many years.

Saddam Hussein's statue is toppled
US tanks rolled into the Iraqi capital, Baghdad, in April 2003, signaling the end of the dictatorship of Saddam Hussein. Jubilant Iraqis toppled a massive statue of the former leader in a symbolic gesture of contempt.

Natural disasters

The first years of the 21st century were beset by natural disasters and extreme weather. In 2003, more than 40,000 people died in heat waves across Europe. In 2004, a huge tsunami caused devastation around the Indian Ocean, killing almost 230,000 people in 14 countries. The following year, a powerful storm, Hurricane Katrina, laid waste to the city of New Orleans, with wind speeds of 125 mph (200 kph). A massive earthquake devastated the island of Haiti in the Caribbean in 2010, killing more than 300,000 people and leaving millions homeless. In 2011, another earthquake triggered a tsunami in Japan, destroying homes and causing radioactive material to leak from the Fukushima nuclear power plant.

Global dangers
Countries all across the world experienced devastating natural disasters in the early years of the 21st century. Some were freak chance events, while others have been linked to changes in the world's climate.

Oct 2001

Invasion of Afghanistan
The US and its NATO allies launched Operation Enduring Freedom after the 9/11 attacks, in an effort to track down Osama bin Laden. The terrorist leader was thought to be in Afghanistan, where the Taliban government was allied with al-Qaeda. The invasion succeeded in overthrowing the Taliban, but violence continued in Afghanistan for years.

March 2004

Madrid bombings
On the eve of Spanish political elections, members of al-Qaeda exploded bombs on four trains in Madrid, killing 191 people and wounding 1,841. The Spanish government had supported the 2003 US-led invasion of Iraq. The Spanish public promptly voted that political party out of office and installed a party that withdrew Spanish troops from Iraq.

July 2005

London bombings
Britain experienced attacks on July 7, 2005, when terrorists carried out a series of suicide bombings on London's transport system. Three bombs exploded on underground trains, and one on a double-decker bus. An al-Qaeda website claimed that they had launched these attacks in retaliation for Britain's involvement in the wars in Iraq and Afghanistan.

May 2011

Death of Bin Laden
US President Barack Obama received intelligence that Osama bin Laden, the head of al-Qaeda, was hiding out in a compound in Abbottabad, Pakistan. In a daring night raid named Operation Neptune Spear, a US Navy Seal team shot dead bin Laden and four others. It was an important milestone in the War on Terror, but not an end to Islamist extremist terrorist attacks.

The Arab Spring
In 2010, a Tunisian man set fire to himself in protest to poor treatment by the Tunisian police. His rebellion sparked a wave of unrest that spread across the Arab world, in countries ruled by dictators or corrupt and oppressive governments. First, the Tunisian leader, Zine al-Abidine Ben Ali, was forced from power. Then dissent spread to Egypt, where President Hosni Mubarak resigned after massive popular protests. In 2011, there were uprisings in Yemen, Bahrain, Libya, and Syria. Libya's leader, Colonel Muammar Gaddafi, was overthrown by rebel fighters. Free elections took place in some Arab countries, but others such as Syria were thrown into civil war.

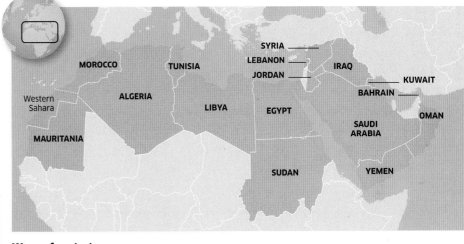

Wave of protest
Demonstrations in Tunisia spread to countries across the Middle East and North Africa.

Global financial crisis
In 2007, US banks realized that they had lent money for home mortgages to hundreds of thousands of customers who could not afford to pay them back. To make matters worse, the banks had bundled up the mortgages with other investments, worth billions of dollars. These suddenly lost value, threatening financial systems across the world. The value of investments plummeted, and huge banks collapsed in the US and Europe. The crisis brought poverty and unemployment to many countries across the globe.

Losses and bailouts
The crisis wiped 33 percent off the value of the world's companies. Governments were forced to pay out huge sums of money to keep their economies afloat.

2009 financial statistics

- Value of world's companies wiped out
- GDP (annual production) of US
- Money spent by European governments to prop up banks in debt

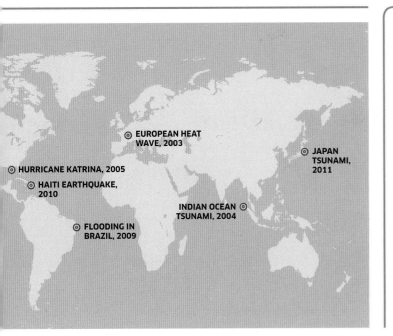

- EUROPEAN HEAT WAVE, 2003
- JAPAN TSUNAMI, 2011
- HURRICANE KATRINA, 2005
- HAITI EARTHQUAKE, 2010
- INDIAN OCEAN TSUNAMI, 2004
- FLOODING IN BRAZIL, 2009

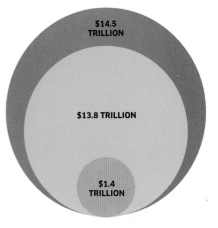

$14.5 TRILLION

$13.8 TRILLION

$1.4 TRILLION

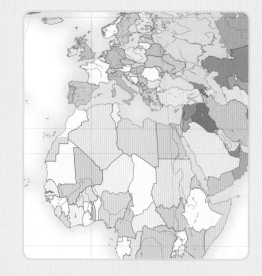

REFERENCE

Find out all about stars, wars, flags, empires, inventions, wonders of the world, record-breaking animals, and history's looniest leaders in the reference section. A useful glossary explains many of the terms used in this book.

Sky maps

These six maps fit together to form a map of the whole night sky. Together, the shape they create is known as the celestial sphere, and includes every star that can be seen from Earth. The stars can also be linked together into shapes called constellations—there are 88 constellations in total. Some have smaller shapes within them, which are called asterisms. The red lines on these maps divide the celestial sphere into different regions, each with a single constellation as its focus. The dots show stars—the bigger the dot, the brighter the star it represents.

The constellations

Andromeda	Canes Venatici
Antlia	Canis Major
Apus	Canis Minor
Aquarius	Capricornus
Aquila	Carina
Ara	Cassiopeia
Aries	Centaurus
Auriga	Cepheus
Boötes	Cetus
Caelum	Chamaeleon
Camelopardalis	Circinus
Cancer	Columba

THE NORTH POLAR SKY

The main feature of the north polar sky is Polaris, also known as the North Star or Pole Star. Although not a particularly bright star, it is important, because it lets navigators on land or sea find which way north is, and set their direction of travel accordingly. As the Earth's axis points to a spot very close to Polaris, the star appears to stay in virtually the same place, while the sky rotates around it.

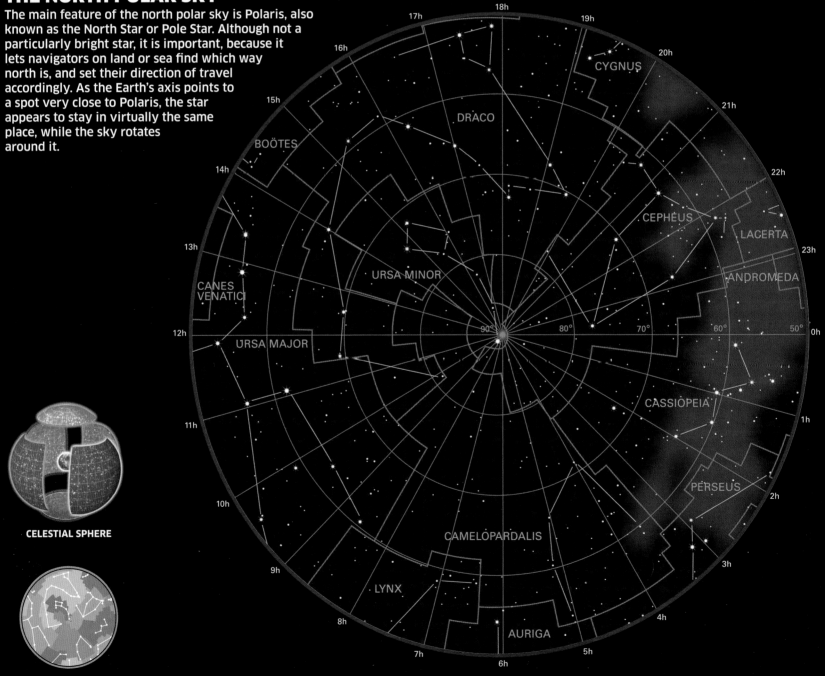

CELESTIAL SPHERE

CONSTELLATIONS

Coma Berenices	Fornax	Libra	Pavo	Scorpius	Ursa Minor
Corona Australis	Gemini	Lupus	Pegasus	Sculptor	Vela
Corona Borealis	Grus	Lynx	Perseus	Scutum	Virgo
Corvus	Hercules	Lyra	Phoenix	Serpens (Caput)	Volans
Crater	Horologium	Mensa	Pictor	Serpens (Cauda)	Vulpecula
Crux	Hydra	Microscopium	Pisces	Sextans	
Cygnus	Hydrus	Monoceros	Piscis Austrinus	Taurus	
Delphinus	Indus	Musca	Puppis	Telescopium	
Dorado	Lacerta	Norma	Pyxis	Triangulum	
Draco	Leo	Octans	Reticulum	Triangulum Australe	
Equuleus	Leo Minor	Ophiuchus	Sagitta	Tucana	
Eridanus	Lepus	Orion	Sagittarius	Ursa Major	

THE SOUTH POLAR SKY

While the northern hemisphere has Polaris to guide travelers, there is no equivalent south star. Here, observers must use a fairly complicated method to find the south celestial pole, since it lies in a faint and barren part of the night sky. However, the constellations nearby contain some wonderful stars, and there is a good view of our galaxy, the Milky Way.

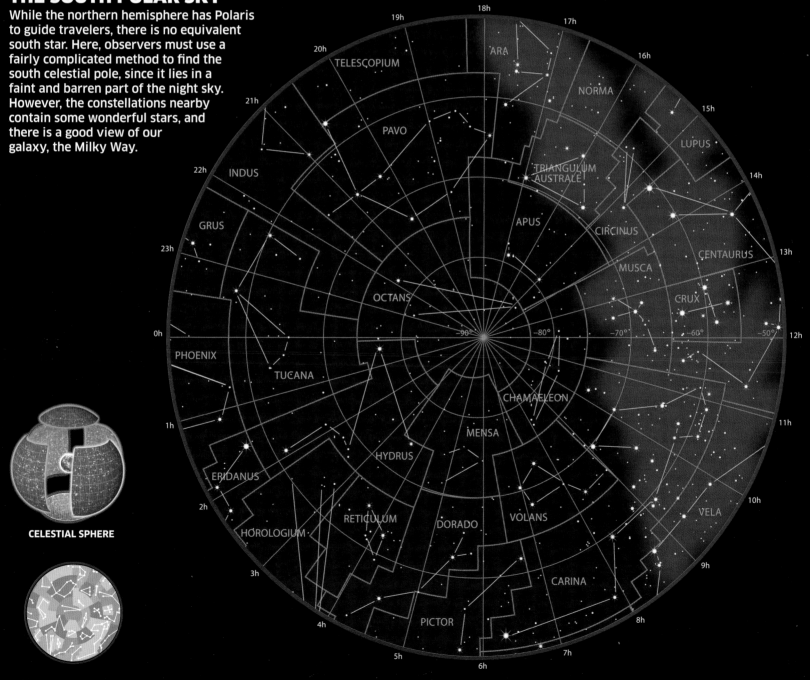

CELESTIAL SPHERE

CONSTELLATIONS

EQUATORIAL SKY CHART 1

This section of the night sky is best observed in the evenings of September, October, and November. It mainly consists of empty areas of space and faint stars, but there are some objects worth looking out for. In the Andromeda constellation you can see the Andromeda Galaxy, which is our largest neighboring galaxy. Just north of the celestial equator (shown as a yellow line here) is the Great Square of Pegasus, an asterism (part of a larger constellation). In Piscis Austrinus is Fomalhaut, the brightest star in this region.

CELESTIAL SPHERE

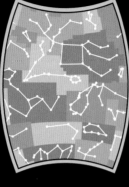

CONSTELLATIONS

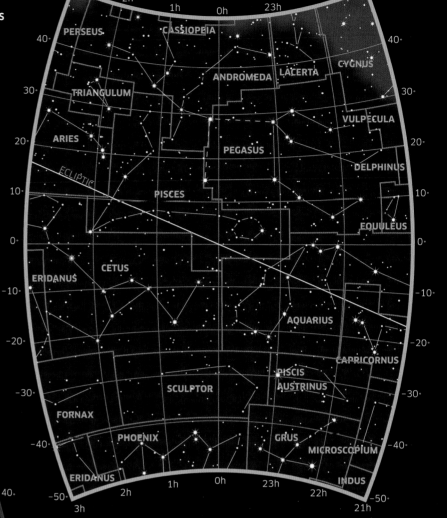

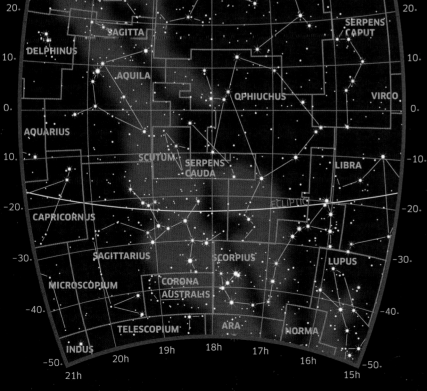

EQUATORIAL SKY CHART 2

This part of the night sky is filled with interesting star patterns and is best observed in the evenings of June, July, August, and September. The northern area is dominated by the Summer Triangle asterism, made up of three stars: Deneb, in the Cygnus constellation; Vega, in Lyra; and Altair, in Aquila. To the south is a curving arrangement of stars that forms the constellation Scorpius, and the constellation Sagittarius is also nearby.

CELESTIAL SPHERE   **CONSTELLATIONS**

EQUATORIAL SKY CHART 3

This part of the night sky is best observed in evenings in March, April, and May. It contains two of the brightest stars of the whole celestial sphere: reddish Arcturus, in Boötes, and bluish Spica, in Virgo. Virgo is the second-biggest constellation, and just to its south is the largest, Hydra, which weaves its way across—and beyond—the entire region. Just above the center and to the right are the stars that make up Leo, the Lion. One of the few constellations with an easily recognizable pattern, its head forms a distinctive backward question mark of six stars.

CELESTIAL SPHERE

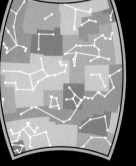

CONSTELLATIONS

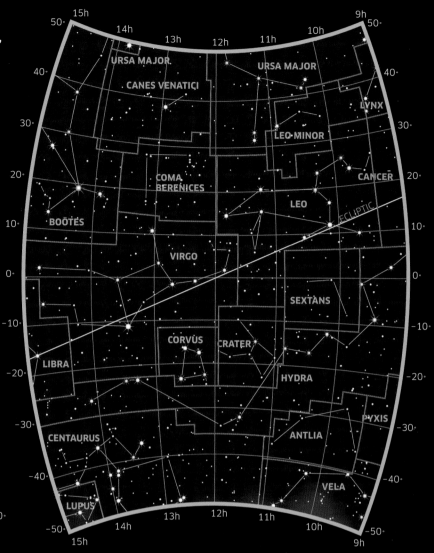

EQUATORIAL SKY CHART 4

This section of the night sky is best observed in the evenings of December, January, and February. It is one of the most stunning areas of the night sky as it contains more bright stars than any other. A good constellation to try to identify is Orion, which has an easily recognizable line of three bright stars across its center, known as Orion's Belt. Adjacent to Orion is Taurus, containing the star Aldebaran, as well as one of the celestial sphere's finest star clusters—the Pleiades or the Seven Sisters.

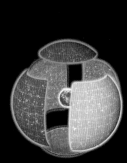

CELESTIAL SPHERE

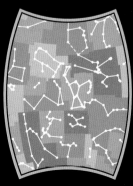

CONSTELLATIONS

The world

The Earth's surface is divided into seven large land masses called continents: Antarctica, North America, South America, Europe, Asia, Africa, and Australasia and Oceania. Most of this land is further divided into countries—194 in total. The only major exception is Antarctica, where there are no countries, although many nations claim ownership of parts of the land there.

Continental populations

There are now more than 7 billion people in the world. Asia is the most densely populated continent, with around 60 percent of the world's population, including the world's two most populous nations: China (1.3 billion people) and India (1.2 billion people). By contrast, there are never more than a few thousand people living the harsh climate of Antarctica at any one time—and these are mostly scientists doing research.

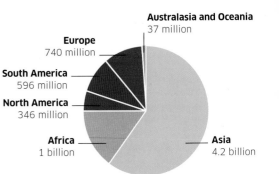

Australasia and Oceania
37 million

Europe
740 million

South America
596 million

North America
346 million

Africa
1 billion

Asia
4.2 billion

Dividing the world

This political map of the world, shows the continents and countries. An imaginary line known as the equator runs horizontally around the center of the Earth. The region either side of the equator—within the Tropic of Cancer to the north and the Tropic of Capricorn to the south—is known as the Tropics. This is the world's hottest region, where the Sun's rays strike the Earth directly.

Time zones

The Earth is also divided by imaginary vertical lines known as lines of longitude. For every 15° you head east or west, you either gain an hour or lose an hour. The world is divided into 24 of these time zones.

Continent size

The largest continent in the world is Asia. Australia and Oceania is the smallest continent, at only about a sixth of the size of Asia. The biggest country in the world is Russia, which crosses the border between Europe and Asia, at 6,601,668 miles² (17,098,242 km²). The second and third largest countries are Canada and the US, both in North America. Canada has a total area of 3,855,102 miles² (9,984,670 km²) and the US is 3,794,100 miles² (9,826,675 km²).

Australasia and Oceania
2,967,000 miles²
(7,687,000 km²)

Europe
3,998,000 miles²
(10,355,000 km²)

Asia
17,140,000 miles²
(44,391,000 km²)

Antarctica
5,500,000 miles²
(14,245,000 km²)

South America
6,880,000 miles²
(17,821,000 km²)

North America
9,362,000 miles²
(24,247,000 km²)

Africa
11,677,000 miles²
(30,244,000 km²)

With an area of 0.2 miles² (0.5 km²), Vatican City is the world's **smallest country.**

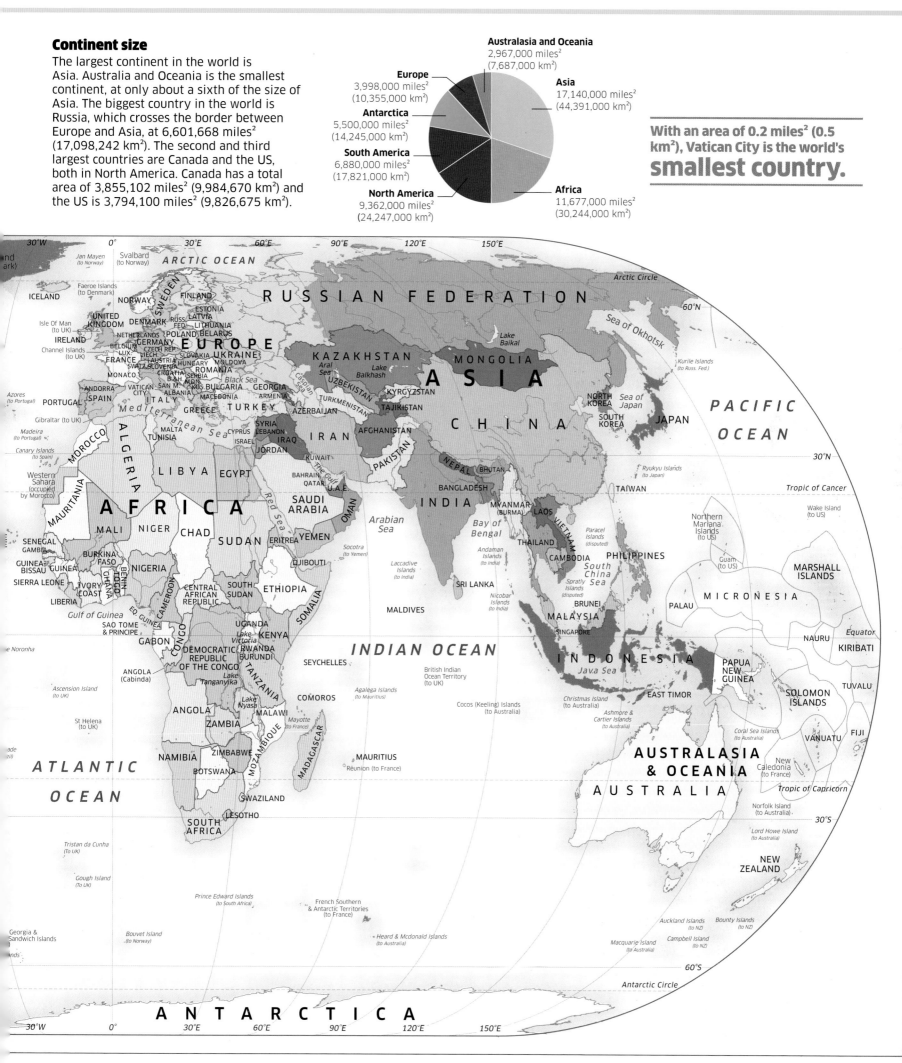

World flags

Every country has a national flag with a unique design that identifies it to other countries. There are no international rules for flag design—each country can choose any pattern, though they are usually based on the country's history or culture. Most flags are rectangular in shape, but the proportions of the rectangle are not always the same. This is not always the case, however—Nepal, for example, has a distinctive, nonrectangular flag, which looks like two triangles on top of each other. National flags first became widespread in the 19th century, but Denmark has the oldest national flag still in use, dating back as far as the 13th century.

AFRICA

ALGERIA	EGYPT	LIBYA	MOROCCO	TUNISIA
BENIN	BURKINA FASO	CAPE VERDE	GAMBIA	GHANA
GUINEA	GUINEA-BISSAU	IVORY COAST	LIBERIA	MALI
MAURITANIA	NIGER	NIGERIA	SENEGAL	SIERRA LEONE
TOGO	CAMEROON	CENTRAL AFRICAN REPUBLIC	CHAD	CONGO
DEM. REP. CONGO	EQUATORIAL GUINEA	GABON	SAO TOME & PRINCIPE	BURUNDI
DJIBOUTI	ERITREA	ETHIOPIA	KENYA	RWANDA
SOMALIA	SUDAN	SOUTH SUDAN	TANZANIA	UGANDA
ANGOLA	BOTSWANA	LESOTHO	MALAWI	MOZAMBIQUE
NAMIBIA	SOUTH AFRICA	SWAZILAND	ZAMBIA	ZIMBABWE
COMOROS	MADAGASCAR	MAURITIUS	SEYCHELLES	

NORTH AMERICA

CANADA	UNITED STATES OF AMERICA	MEXICO	BELIZE
COSTA RICA	EL SALVADOR	GUATEMALA	HONDURAS
NICARAGUA	PANAMA	ANTIGUA & BARBUDA	BAHAMAS
BARBADOS	CUBA	DOMINICA	DOMINICAN REPUBLIC
GRENADA	ST. VINCENT & THE GRENADINES	TRINIDAD & TOBAGO	ST. KITTS & NEVIS
ST. LUCIA	HAITI	JAMAICA	

SOUTH AMERICA

COLOMBIA	GUYANA	SURINAM	VENEZUELA	BOLIVIA	ECUADOR	PERU	BRAZIL	ARGENTINA
URUGUAY	CHILE	PARAGUAY						

EUROPE

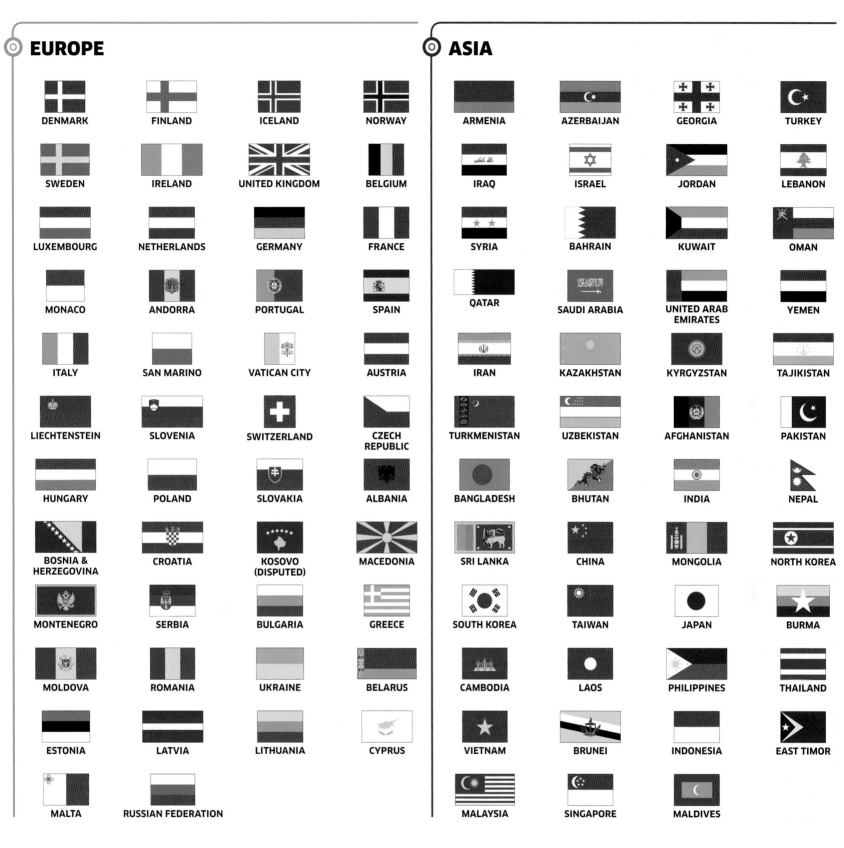

DENMARK · FINLAND · ICELAND · NORWAY

SWEDEN · IRELAND · UNITED KINGDOM · BELGIUM

LUXEMBOURG · NETHERLANDS · GERMANY · FRANCE

MONACO · ANDORRA · PORTUGAL · SPAIN

ITALY · SAN MARINO · VATICAN CITY · AUSTRIA

LIECHTENSTEIN · SLOVENIA · SWITZERLAND · CZECH REPUBLIC

HUNGARY · POLAND · SLOVAKIA · ALBANIA

BOSNIA & HERZEGOVINA · CROATIA · KOSOVO (DISPUTED) · MACEDONIA

MONTENEGRO · SERBIA · BULGARIA · GREECE

MOLDOVA · ROMANIA · UKRAINE · BELARUS

ESTONIA · LATVIA · LITHUANIA · CYPRUS

MALTA · RUSSIAN FEDERATION

ASIA

ARMENIA · AZERBAIJAN · GEORGIA · TURKEY

IRAQ · ISRAEL · JORDAN · LEBANON

SYRIA · BAHRAIN · KUWAIT · OMAN

QATAR · SAUDI ARABIA · UNITED ARAB EMIRATES · YEMEN

IRAN · KAZAKHSTAN · KYRGYZSTAN · TAJIKISTAN

TURKMENISTAN · UZBEKISTAN · AFGHANISTAN · PAKISTAN

BANGLADESH · BHUTAN · INDIA · NEPAL

SRI LANKA · CHINA · MONGOLIA · NORTH KOREA

SOUTH KOREA · TAIWAN · JAPAN · BURMA

CAMBODIA · LAOS · PHILIPPINES · THAILAND

VIETNAM · BRUNEI · INDONESIA · EAST TIMOR

MALAYSIA · SINGAPORE · MALDIVES

AUSTRALASIA AND OCEANIA

AUSTRALIA · NEW ZEALAND · PAPUA NEW GUINEA · FIJI · SOLOMON ISLANDS · VANUATU · MARSHALL ISLANDS · MICRONESIA · NAURU

PALAU · KIRIBATI · TUVALU · TONGA · SAMOA

Tree of life

Life has evolved into an amazing variety of forms, but they are all related to the first living things that appeared on Earth more than 3.8 billion years ago. This tree of life shows how the simplest single-celled organisms–prokaryotes such as bacteria–developed into the more complex single-celled eukaryotes and the multicelled plants, fungi, and animals.

The main groups of the diversity of life are shown in this diagram, including all the vertebrates or animals with backbones. Humans are part of the primate group of mammals, so we are also linked through billions of years of evolution to the simplest living organisms on the planet.

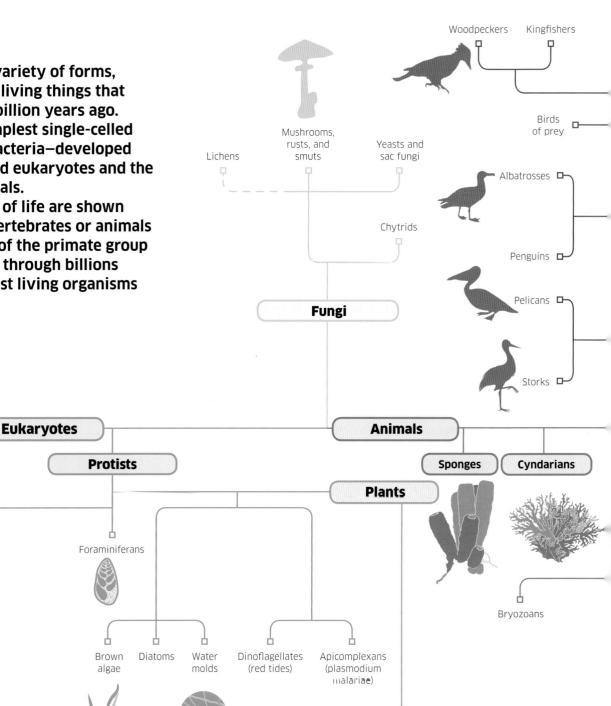

Woodpeckers   Kingfishers

Birds of prey

Mushrooms, rusts, and smuts

Lichens

Yeasts and sac fungi

Albatrosses

Chytrids

Penguins

Pelicans

Fungi

Storks

LIFE BEGINS

Archaea

Prokaryotes   **Eukaryotes**   **Animals**

Bacteria   **Protists**   **Sponges**   **Cyndarians**

Plants

Giardia   Foraminiferans

Bryozoans

Brown algae   Diatoms   Water molds   Dinoflagellates (red tides)   Apicomplexans (plasmodium malariae)

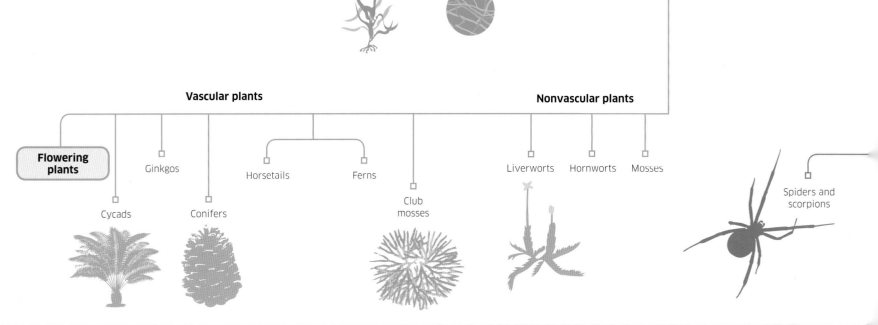

Vascular plants   **Nonvascular plants**

Flowering plants   Ginkgos   Horsetails   Ferns   Liverworts   Hornworts   Mosses

Cycads   Conifers   Club mosses   Spiders and scorpions

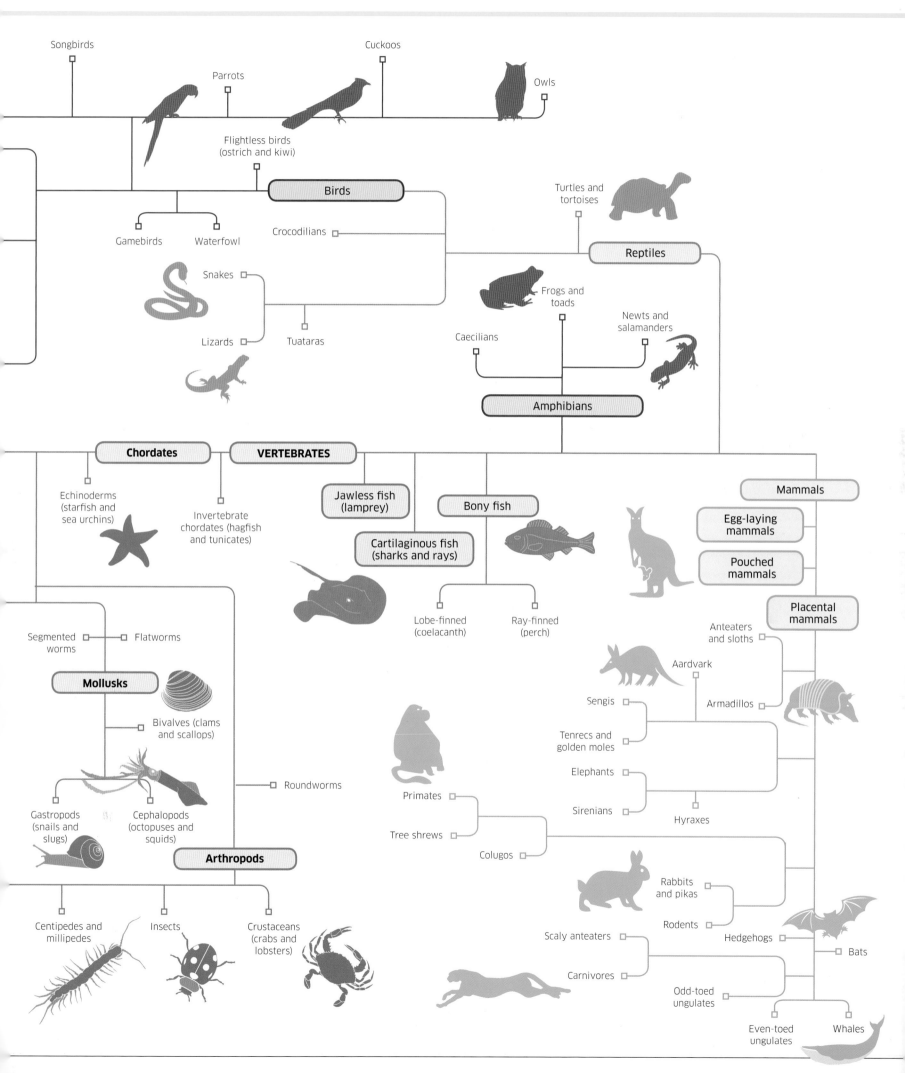

Songbirds

Cuckoos

Parrots

Owls

Flightless birds
(ostrich and kiwi)

Birds

Turtles and
tortoises

Gamebirds   Waterfowl   Crocodilians

Snakes

Reptiles

Frogs and
toads

Newts and
salamanders

Caecilians

Lizards   Tuataras

Amphibians

Chordates   **VERTEBRATES**

Echinoderms
(starfish and
sea urchins)

Invertebrate
chordates (hagfish
and tunicates)

Jawless fish
(lamprey)

Bony fish

Mammals

Egg-laying
mammals

Cartilaginous fish
(sharks and rays)

Pouched
mammals

Segmented
worms   Flatworms

Lobe-finned
(coelacanth)

Ray-finned
(perch)

Placental
mammals

Anteaters
and sloths

Mollusks

Aardvark

Sengis

Armadillos

Bivalves (clams
and scallops)

Tenrecs and
golden moles

Elephants

Primates

Gastropods
(snails and
slugs)

Cephalopods
(octopuses and
squids)

Roundworms

Sirenians

Hyraxes

Tree shrews

Arthropods

Colugos

Rabbits
and pikas

Centipedes and
millipedes

Insects

Crustaceans
(crabs and
lobsters)

Scaly anteaters

Rodents

Hedgehogs

Bats

Carnivores

Odd-toed
ungulates

Even-toed
ungulates   Whales

Nature's record breakers

Some animals are capable of the most amazing feats, moving at extraordinary speeds or producing incredibly loud noises. Others are remarkable for their size—either weighty giants or so small that it is difficult to imagine how their bodies function. Some live to advanced ages, while others survive for just a few days.

WEIGHTY WILDLIFE

Most of the heaviest animals, such as whales and giant sharks, live in the sea, where the ocean water supports their bodies.

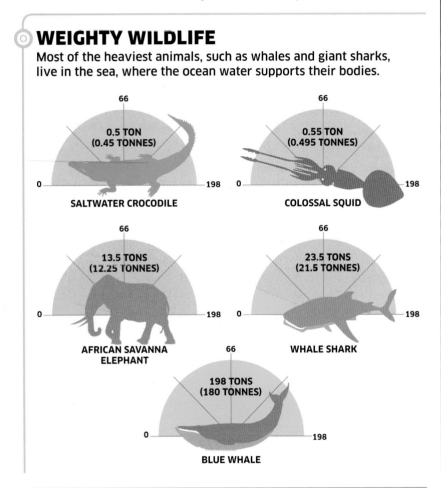

0.5 TON (0.45 TONNES)
SALTWATER CROCODILE

0.55 TON (0.495 TONNES)
COLOSSAL SQUID

13.5 TONS (12.25 TONNES)
AFRICAN SAVANNA ELEPHANT

23.5 TONS (21.5 TONNES)
WHALE SHARK

198 TONS (180 TONNES)
BLUE WHALE

GETTING AROUND

Some predators achieve astonishing speeds as they attack their prey. By contrast, the sloth seems to live its life in slow motion.

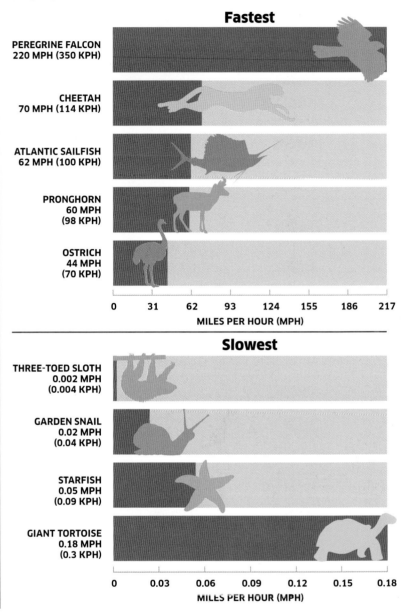

Fastest

PEREGRINE FALCON
220 MPH (350 KPH)

CHEETAH
70 MPH (114 KPH)

ATLANTIC SAILFISH
62 MPH (100 KPH)

PRONGHORN
60 MPH (98 KPH)

OSTRICH
44 MPH (70 KPH)

| 0 | 31 | 62 | 93 | 124 | 155 | 186 | 217 |

MILES PER HOUR (MPH)

Slowest

THREE-TOED SLOTH
0.002 MPH (0.004 KPH)

GARDEN SNAIL
0.02 MPH (0.04 KPH)

STARFISH
0.05 MPH (0.09 KPH)

GIANT TORTOISE
0.18 MPH (0.3 KPH)

| 0 | 0.03 | 0.06 | 0.09 | 0.12 | 0.15 | 0.18 |

MILES PER HOUR (MPH)

NOISIEST ANIMALS

The snapping shrimp stuns its prey with the loudest noise made by any animal, but luckily it only lasts for a split-second.

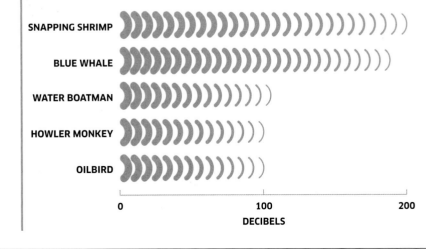

SNAPPING SHRIMP

BLUE WHALE

WATER BOATMAN

HOWLER MONKEY

OILBIRD

| 0 | 100 | 200 |

DECIBELS

JUMPING CREATURES

Craggy mountain terrain allows the snow leopard to leap huge distances to attack prey. Other animals jump to escape danger.

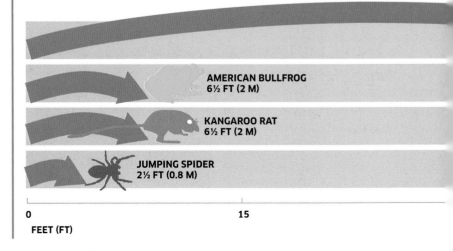

AMERICAN BULLFROG
6½ FT (2 M)

KANGAROO RAT
6½ FT (2 M)

JUMPING SPIDER
2½ FT (0.8 M)

| 0 | 15 |

FEET (FT)

ANIMAL LIFESPANS

Big animals tend to live longer than small ones, and some insects, such as mayflies, survive for just a few hours as flying adults.

Longest Lives (YEARS)

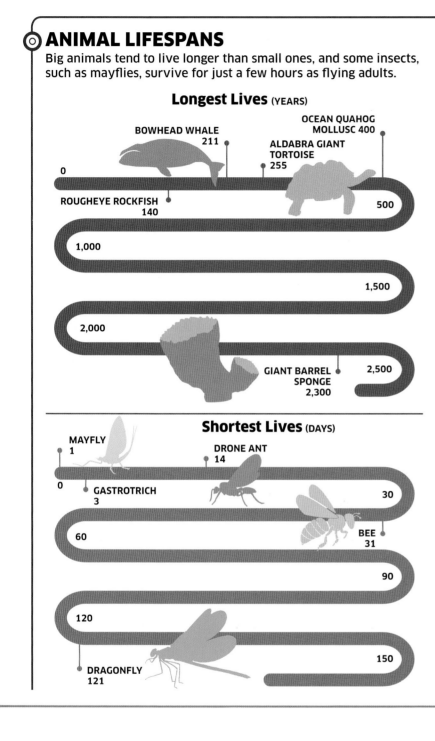

OCEAN QUAHOG
MOLLUSC 400

BOWHEAD WHALE
211

ALDABRA GIANT
TORTOISE
255

0

ROUGHEYE ROCKFISH
140

500

1,000

1,500

2,000

GIANT BARREL
SPONGE
2,300

2,500

Shortest Lives (DAYS)

MAYFLY
1

DRONE ANT
14

0

GASTROTRICH
3

30

60

BEE
31

90

120

150

DRAGONFLY
121

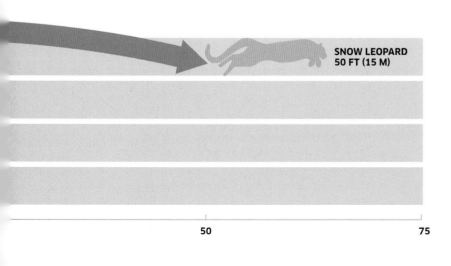

SNOW LEOPARD
50 FT (15 M)

50

75

TALL AND SMALL

The smallest animals are microscopic, such as the rotifers that live mainly in ponds and streams. Other creatures are giants that tower over all the other animals living alongside them.

Tallest

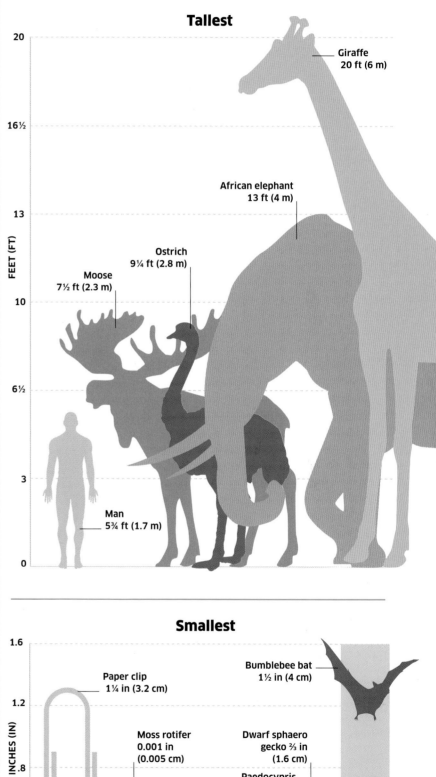

Giraffe
20 ft (6 m)

African elephant
13 ft (4 m)

Ostrich
9¼ ft (2.8 m)

Moose
7½ ft (2.3 m)

FEET (FT)

20

16½

13

10

6½

3

0

Man
5¾ ft (1.7 m)

Smallest

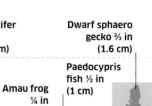

Bumblebee bat
1½ in (4 cm)

Paper clip
1¼ in (3.2 cm)

1.6

1.2

INCHES (IN)

.8

.4

0

Moss rotifer
0.001 in
(0.005 cm)

Dwarf sphaero
gecko ⅔ in
(1.6 cm)

Amau frog
¼ in
(0.8 cm)

Paedocypris
fish ½ in
(1 cm)

Conversion Tables

Measurements are important because they help people agree on things. Without accurate measurements, there would be no world records, cooking would be guesswork, and it would be hard to find clothes that fit. Ancient measurements were often based on body parts, which is why we still measure in units such as feet to this day. However, everyone's body is a different size, so now we use more standard measures.

MAKING CONVERSIONS

You can convert imperial measurements to metric ones or vice versa, by multiplying or dividing by a fixed number called a conversion factor. The only thing that cannot be converted in this way is temperature, which has its own unique method.

UNITS OF MEASUREMENT

There are two common systems for measuring most things. The traditional way is called imperial and it is still popular in the United States. The metric system is more suited to scientific work and is widely used in Europe. In metric, each measurement is linked to others by powers of 10.

AREA

METRIC	
100 square millimeters (mm²)	1 square centimeter (cm²)
10,000 square centimeters (cm²)	1 square meter (m²)
10,000 square meters (m²)	1 hectare (ha)
100 hectares (ha)	1 square kilometer (km²)
1 square kilometer (km²)	1,000,000 square meters (m²)
IMPERIAL	
144 square inches (sq in)	1 square foot (sq ft)
9 square feet (sq ft)	1 square yard (sq yd)
1,296 square inches (sq in)	1 square yard (sq yd)
43,560 square feet (sq ft)	1 acre
640 acres	1 square mile (sq mile)

LENGTH

METRIC	
10 millimeters (mm)	1 centimeter (cm)
100 centimeters (cm)	1 meter (m)
1,000 millimeters (mm)	1 meter (m)
1,000 meters (m)	1 kilometer (km)
IMPERIAL	
12 inches (in)	1 foot (ft)
3 feet (ft)	1 yard (yd)
1,760 yards (yd)	1 mile
5,280 feet (ft)	1 mile
8 furlongs	1 mile

LIQUID VOLUME

METRIC	
1,000 milliliters (ml)	1 liter (l)
100 liters (l)	1 hectoliter (hl)
10 hectoliters (hl)	1 kiloliter (kl)
1,000 liters (l)	1 kiloliter (kl)
IMPERIAL	
8 fluid ounces (fl oz)	1 cup
16 fluid ounces (fl oz)	1 pint (pt)
4 gills (gi)	1 pint (pt)
2 pints (pt)	1 quart (qt)
4 quarts (qt)	1 gallon (gal)
8 pints (pt)	1 gallon (gal)

MASS

METRIC	
1,000 milligrams (mg)	1 gram (g)
1,000 grams (g)	1 kilogram (kg)
1,000 kilograms (kg)	1 tonne (t)
IMPERIAL	
16 ounces (oz)	1 pound (lb)
14 pounds (lb)	1 stone
112 pounds (lb)	1 hundredweight
2,000 pounds (lb)	1 ton

TEMPERATURE

	FAHRENHEIT	CELSIUS
Boiling point of water	212°	100°
Freezing point of water	32°	0°
Absolute zero	−459°	−273°

TIME

METRIC AND IMPERIAL	
60 seconds	1 minute
60 minutes	1 hour
24 hours	1 day
7 days	1 week
52 weeks	1 year
1 year	12 months

TEMPERATURE

To convert from
Fahrenheit (°F) to Celsius (°C)
$C = (F − 32) \times 5 \div 9$

To convert from
Celsius (°C) to Fahrenheit (°F)
$F = (C \times 9 \div 5) + 32$

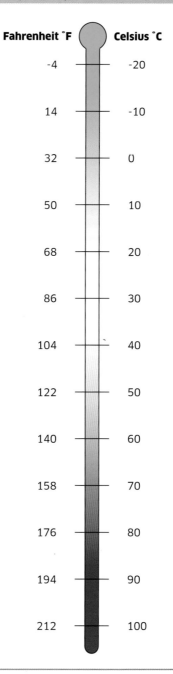

Fahrenheit °F	Celsius °C
−4	−20
14	−10
32	0
50	10
68	20
86	30
104	40
122	50
140	60
158	70
176	80
194	90
212	100

HOW TO CONVERT METRIC AND IMPERIAL MEASURES

TO CHANGE	TO	MULTIPLY BY	TO CHANGE	TO	DIVIDE BY
acres	hectares	0.40	hectares	acres	0.40
centimeters	feet	0.03	feet	centimeters	0.03
centimeters	inches	0.39	inches	centimeters	0.39
cubic centimeters	cubic inches	0.06	cubic inches	cubic centimeters	0.06
cubic feet	cubic meters	0.03	cubic meters	cubic feet	0.03
cubic inches	cubic centimeters	16.39	cubic centimeters	cubic inches	16.39
cubic meters	cubic feet	35.32	cubic feet	cubic meters	35.32
feet	centimeters	30.48	centimeters	feet	30.48
feet	meters	0.30	meters	feet	0.30
gallons	liters	3.79	liters	gallons	3.79
grams	ounces	0.04	ounces	grams	0.04
hectares	acres	2.47	acres	hectares	2.47
inches	centimeters	2.54	centimeters	inches	2.54
kilograms	pounds	2.20	pounds	kilograms	2.20
kilometers	miles	0.62	miles	kilometers	0.62
kilometers per hour	miles per hour	0.62	miles per hour	kilometers per hour	0.62
liters	gallons	0.26	gallons	liters	0.26
liters	pints	2.11	pints	liters	2.11
meters	feet	3.28	feet	meters	3.28
meters	yards	1.09	yards	meters	1.09
meters per minute	centimeters per second	1.67	centimeters per second	meters per minute	1.67
meters per minute	feet per second	0.05	feet per second	meters per minute	0.05
miles	kilometers	1.61	kilometers	miles	1.61
miles per hour	kilometers per hour	1.61	kilometers per hour	miles per hour	1.61
miles per hour	meters per second	0.45	meters per second	miles per hour	0.45
millimeters	inches	0.04	inches	millimeters	0.04
ounces	grams	28.35	grams	ounces	28.35
pints	liters	0.47	liters	pints	0.47
pounds	kilograms	0.45	kilograms	pounds	0.45
square centimeters	square inches	0.16	square inches	square centimeters	0.16
square inches	square centimeters	6.45	square centimeters	square inches	6.45
square feet	square meters	0.09	square meters	square feet	0.09
square kilometers	square miles	0.39	square miles	square kilometers	0.39
square meters	square feet	10.76	square feet	square meters	10.76
square meters	square yards	1.20	square yards	square meters	1.20
square miles	square kilometers	2.59	square kilometers	square miles	2.59
square yards	square meters	0.84	square meters	square yards	0.84
tonnes (metric)	tons (imperial)	1.10	tons (imperial)	tonnes (metric)	0.89
tons (imperial)	tonnes (metric)	0.89	tonnes (metric)	tons (imperial)	1.10
yards	meters	0.91	meters	yards	0.91

INCREDIBLE HISTORY

Throughout the ages, in every corner of the globe, history has been happening. From crazy rulers and child prodigies to huge empires and life-changing inventions, history is filled with people and events that often seem too incredible to be true. Here are some of the amazing events, inventions, and people that have gone down in history.

BIGGEST EMPIRES

The greatest empires in history ruled over large areas of land, often spanning many continents. Empires are ruled by a single monarch or an oligarchy (a small group of people, such as a powerful family). They rule over vast territories, and must maintain control of their lands as well as conquering new places if they want to expand. Here are the five biggest empires the world has ever seen.

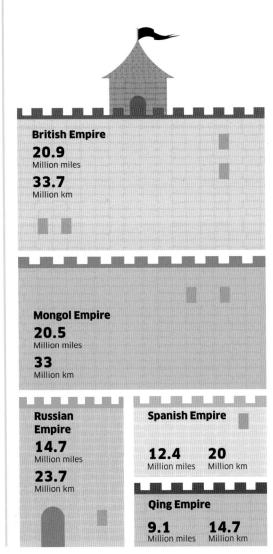

British Empire
20.9
Million miles
33.7
Million km

Mongol Empire
20.5
Million miles
33
Million km

Russian Empire
14.7
Million miles
23.7
Million km

Spanish Empire
12.4   **20**
Million miles   Million km

Qing Empire
9.1   **14.7**
Million miles   Million km

■ **British Empire**
At its peak in the late 19th century, the British empire covered about a quarter of Earth's land area. It was said that the "Sun never sets" on its lands.

■ **Mongol Empire**
Under the Genghis Khan, the empire of the Mongols (a group of eastern nomadic tribes) grew rapidly in the 13th and 14th centuries. It expanded across Asia, including China and Russia.

■ **Russian Empire**
The Russian Empire existed from 1721 until the Russian Revolution in 1917. At its peak in the middle of the 19th century, it stretched across Eastern Europe, Asia, and North America.

■ **Spanish Empire**
Under the rule of the Habsburg dynasty, the Spanish Empire became the major global power in the 16th and 17th centuries. Territories included North and South America and parts of Europe.

■ **Qing Empire**
Ruling for 267 years from the mid-17th century to the beginning of the 20th century, the Qing (Manchu) dynasty was the last imperial dynasty of China.

LONGEST WARS

Conflicts have been fought throughout history, all around the world. While some wars are resolved quickly, others continue for decades, or even a century, until the last battle is fought and won.

116 Years

The Hundred Years' War, 1337–1453
The longest in recorded history, this war was fought between the English and French. Despite the name, it lasted 116 years.

43 Years

The Punic Wars, 264–146 BCE
This was a series of three wars between Carthage (the major maritime power) and Rome (which controlled the Italian peninsula). Rome defeated Carthage, and destroyed the city in 146 BCE.

30 Years

The Thirty Years' War, 1618–1648
Although there were many reasons for this war, it was mainly a religious conflict between Catholics and Protestants. Mostly fought in Germany, it became a political war and changed Europe forever.

30 Years

The Wars of the Roses, 1455–1485
The fight for the crown of England lasted 30 years and was fought between the Houses of York and Lancaster. The Tudor king, Henry VII, led the House of Lancaster to victory over Richard III's House of York.

27 Years

The Peloponnesian War, 431–404 BCE
This war was fought between rival alliances of Greek city-states led by Athens and Sparta. Athens was strongest at sea, but Sparta was more powerful on land and eventually crushed the Athenian forces.

23 Years

Napoleonic Wars, 1796–1815
Napoleon Bonaparte was a skilled general who declared himself Emperor of France in 1804. He led France in a series of wars against other European powers, until his defeat at the Battle of Waterloo.

SHORTEST WARS

Not all conflicts are long and drawn out—some are over in just a few days. The shortest war ever began when the Zanzibar sultan's successor took control without gaining the permission of the British consul first. He fled from the palace almost immediately.

38 MINUTES

Anglo-Zanzibar, 1896
Between Britain and the Zanzibar Sultanate.

6 DAYS

Six Day War, 1967
Between Israel and neighboring states Egypt, Jordan, and Syria.

13 DAYS

Indo-Pakistan War, 1971
Between India and Pakistan.

14 DAYS

Serbo-Bulgarian War, 1885
Between Serbia and Bulgaria.

24 DAYS

Georgian-Armenian War, 1918
Between Georgia and Armenia.

AMAZING INVENTIONS

Our everyday lives would be very different if these inventions had never happened. From simple household objects to complex modern technology, these incredible discoveries have transformed the way we live and think, and changed the course of history.

1440: Printing press
Johannes Gutenberg's press let people make copies of writings quickly and cheaply.

1776: Steam engine
James Watt added a separate condensing chamber to the early steam engine, making it more efficient.

1876: Telephone
Alexander Graham Bell is famous for this invention, but many others claimed to have beaten him to it.

1879: Light bulb
This bright idea for electric light in the home was the invention of Thomas Edison and Joseph Swan.

1886: Car
German engineer Karl Benz took to the road in a three-wheeled car, powered by an internal combustion engine.

1903: Airplane
The Wright brothers invented a flying machine, which would revolutionize travel across the world.

1928: Penicillin
The accidental discovery of mold growing on bacteria led Alexander Fleming to discover the first antibiotic.

1941: Modern computer
The first electronic, programmable computer was invented by Konrad Zuse. It was called the Z3.

1969: Internet
The first network was set up by the Pentagon. Twenty years later, Tim Berners-Lee invented the World Wide Web.

LOONY LEADERS

Throughout history there have been many eccentric leaders. Some were just victims of bad publicity, while others were cruel oractually insane. Here is a selection of just a few of history's loony leaders.

Hatshepsut (1470s BCE)
This Egyptian ruler knew her people did not like the idea of a female pharaoh, so she put on a fake beard and called herself king instead of queen.

Ashurnasirpal II (ruled 884–859 BCE)
This Assyrian general enjoyed boasting about his conquests. An inscription at the entrance to his palace described the tortures inflicted on those who rebelled against him.

Nebuchadnezzar II (ruled 605–562 BCE)
A Babylonian king who believed that he was a cow, Nebuchadnezzar II spent seven years in a field, chewing his cud.

Peisistratus (560s BCE)
This Athenian citizen claimed he had been attacked, so the city let him have bodyguards. He then used his bodyguards to take over the city, becoming its ruler.

Nero (37–68)
This Roman emperor had his mother and adoptive brother killed. It is said that he captured Christians and had them burned in his garden at night, to provide light.

Caligula (12–41)
The Roman emperor Caligula was known for his cruelty and extravagance. He proclaimed himself a god, and expected people to worship him. He replaced the heads on many statues of gods so that they looked like him.

Irene of Athens (752–803)
Mother of Emperor Constantine VI, Irene of Athens had her son's eyes gouged out so that she could rule the Byzantine Empire on her own.

Basil II (958–1025)
After victory in battle with the Bulgarians in 1014, Emperor Basil of Byzantium ordered his troops to punish 15,000 Bulgarian prisoners by scooping out their eyes. A single man was allowed to keep one eye so that he could lead the others home.

Timur the Lame (1336–1404)
A nomadic warlord from modern-day Uzbekistan, this leader killed anyone who got in his way. On one occasion this meant all 30,000 inhabitants of a city.

Vlad III (1431–76)
Nicknamed Vlad the Impaler, this Transylvanian ruler marched into neighboring Bulgaria, where he captured 20,000 people and impaled them on stakes.

Farouk of Egypt (1920–65)
This Egyptian leader was a thief who enjoyed picking pockets while on state visits. He once stole an expensive pocket watch from Winston Churchill.

CHILD PRODIGIES

Some people are born brilliant, and achieve great things from a very young age. From musicians to mathematicians, these clever children made their mark on the world with their amazing achievements and impressive talents.

Avicenna (980–1037)
At 10, this Persian polymath (expert in many subjects) had memorized the Qur'an. He was a qualified physician at 18.

Blaise Pascal (1623–62)
This talented mathematician wrote a significant treatise on geometry at 16.

Maria Gaetana Agnesi (1718–99)
By 13, Agnesi could speak at least seven languages. She became a mathematician, linguist, and philosopher.

W. Amadeus Mozart (1756–91)
Mozart was playing keyboard and violin at the age of four, and composing music at five.

Jean F. Champollion (1790–1832)
This French linguist knew 12 languages by the age of 16. As an adult, he deciphered the Egyptian hieroglyphics.

Pablo Picasso (1881–1973)
Trained by his father, Picasso was painting incredible works of art from a very early age.

ANCIENT WONDERS

Admired and marveled by Ancient Greek travelers, the Seven Wonders of the Ancient World were amazing landmarks around the eastern Mediterranean rim. Only one, the Great Pyramids of Giza, still remains today.

Lighthouse of Alexandria
Built by the Nile River in the third century BCE, this was the world's first lighthouse. It used mirrors to reflect sunlight out to sea.

Great Pyramids of Giza
These three pyramids near Cairo are called Khufu, Khafra, and Menkaura. They were built as royal tombs for Egyptian pharaohs.

Statue of Zeus at Olympia
This statue of Zeus, the Greek god of thunder, was 40 ft (12 m) high. It was placed at Olympia, the site of the Ancient Olympic games.

Temple of Artemis at Ephesus
This large temple was built in honor of Artemis, the Greek goddess of the hunt and childbirth. It was made of marble, and had 127 columns.

Colossus of Rhodes
Made of bronze, this statue of Greek sun god Helios was 110 ft (33.5 m) tall. It stood for 60 years before falling during an earthquake.

Mausoleum at Halicarnassus
This enormous marble tomb was for Mausolus, the King of Carnia. It was built by his grieving wife Artemisia.

Hanging Gardens of Babylon
Built on a huge brick terrace, these gardens were said to be 75 ft (22 m) in the air. Many experts believe they may not have existed at all.

Glossary

ACCELERATION
In physics, a term meaning the rate of change in velocity.

ADAPTATION
The way in which a living species, such as an animal or a plant, has developed in appearance or behavior to fit in with its environment.

AGRICULTURE
Using the land to grow food crops or raise domestic animals.

ALGAE
Simple, often single-celled, organisms, some of which look like plants; algae are found in a variety of habitats but occur most commonly in water.

AMPHIBIAN
A cold-blooded animal, such as a frog or newt, that can live both in water and on land.

ANARCHY
Disorder in society, especially when there is no leader or government in control.

ANTENNA
A sensitive feeler on the head of an insect or a crustacean (for example, a lobster, crab, or housefly).

APARTHEID
An official policy of keeping people apart because of their racial origins. It was used to separate black Africans from white in South Africa.

ARCHAEA
A biological group of microscopic, single-celled organisms that look like bacteria but have different genes.

ARCHAEOLOGY
Study of the ancient past through looking at the remains of buildings and objects that people once used.

ARTHROPOD
An invertebrate (animal lacking a backbone) that has a jointed, outer body case. Arthropods include insects, spiders, crustaceans such as crabs and lobsters, and scorpions.

ASTEROID
A small object in space, made from a mixture of rock and metals, that orbits the Sun.

ATMOSPHERE
The layer of breathable gases, mainly oxygen and nitrogen, that surrounds Earth.

ATOM
The smallest particle of an element that has the same chemical makeup as the element.

AURORA
Bands of light in the sky caused by high-energy particles from space meeting atoms in the atmosphere.

BACTERIA
Microscopic, single-celled organisms, some of which are helpful—for example, by helping us to digest our food or keeping the soil healthy—while others are responsible for serious diseases.

BCE
Before Common Era: the years before 1 CE (start of the Common Era). This abbreviation has largely replaced BC (Before Christ).

BIOME
A large-scale biological community with a particular climate and certain types of plants—for example, a rainforest.

BLACK HOLE
A body of matter in space of such intense gravity that even light cannot escape from it.

BRONZE AGE
A period of ancient history, between about 2500–1200 BCE, when people mostly used bronze for making tools and weapons.

CAMOUFLAGE
The way animals blend in with their background or use disguises to escape notice by predators; this includes seasonal changes of coat color and mimicry of a more dangerous animal.

CANOPY
The topmost branches of the trees in a forest; canopy also means the part of a plant showing above ground.

CAPITALISM
A system for organizing society that is in favor of capitalists: people or private organizations that make a profit and accumulate wealth (capital) by producing goods and services.

CARNIVORE
A meat-eating animal with teeth especially shaped for tearing flesh.

CAVALRY
Historically, military troops mounted on horseback. The term now also means army units that move around in vehicles such as cars and tanks.

CE
Common Era: the years from 1 CE to the present day. This abbreviation has largely replaced AD (Anno Domini, Latin for "In the year of our Lord").

CELLULOSE
A substance found in plant cell walls that gives plants their structure.

CHLOROPHYLL
The green coloring in plants that enables them to absorb sunlight, which they use for photosynthesis (the process of converting water and carbon dioxide into their own food).

CHLOROPLASTS
Special structures in plant cells containing the green pigment chlorophyll.

CHROMOSOME
A threadlike structure, found in the nucleus of body cells, that is made up of coiled strands of DNA (an organism's genetic code).

CHRYSALIS
The hard, protective case, also called a pupa, which encloses the larva of an insect such as a moth or butterfly as it develops its adult form.

CITIZEN
A person who belongs to a city or a bigger community such as a state or country.

CITY-STATE
A city, together its surrounding territory, that has its own independent system of government. Athens, Sparta, and Corinth in ancient Greece were very powerful city-states.

CIVIL WAR
War between different political groups or regions within the same country.

CNIDARIA
A large group of marine animals, including jellyfish and many types of coral, which carry stinging cells in their tentacles.

COELACANTH
A deep-sea fish with a distinctive shape, long thought to be extinct. It has features very similar to those seen in fossil fish from the age of dinosaurs.

COLD-BLOODED
Describing an animal whose body heat depends on the temperature of its surroundings; reptiles, for example, are cold-blooded.

COLONY
A group of people who leave their native country to settle elsewhere but keep links with their homeland. Also: a group of animals, usually of one species, that live and work together.

COMBUSTION
A chemical reaction in which a substance, for example, a fuel oil, mixes and burns with oxygen.

COMET
Small astronomical body of ice and dust that orbits the Sun.

COMMUNISM
A political system based on the belief that property should not be owned by individual people but shared by all.

COMPOUND
A chemical substance in which two or more elements have bonded together.

COMPOUND EYE
The eyes of adult insects and some crustaceans consist of many sections. Each section has its own lens, and together they create a mosaic image.

CONSTELLATION
A group of stars that form a pattern in the sky; many constellations are named after animals or mythical characters.

CORE
The innermost and hottest part of Earth, consisting of a liquid outer layer around a solid center, both thought to be made of iron and nickel.

CRUST
Earth's hard, rocky, outermost layer.

CULTURE
The customs, beliefs, and behavior shared by a society.

DEMOCRACY
A political system in which people have power to control their government, usually by electing politicians to represent their views.

DETRITIVORE
An animal that feeds on dead plant or animal matter.

DNA
Abbreviation for deoxyribonucleic acid, the material packed inside chromosomes that holds all the instructions for making and maintaining a living body.

DYNASTY
A family or group that rules over a country for several generations.

ECHINODERM
A spiny-skinned marine animal with a radially symmetrical body: if it is divided through the middle in any direction the halves look exactly alike. This group includes starfish and sea urchins.

ECOSYSTEM
A community of animals and plants that share, and interact with, the same habitat.

ELECTRON
One of the tiny particles inside an atom; electrons have a negative electric charge.

ELEMENT
In chemistry, a simple substance made of atoms that are all of the same kind.

EMBRYO
The earliest stage in the development of an animal or plant. A human embryo forms when sex cells join.

EMPIRE
A group of countries or states united under one ruling power.

ENZYME
A substance in animals and plants that speeds up a chemical reaction.

EROSION
The process by which Earth's surface rocks and soil are worn away by the action of winds, water, and glaciers (moving ice).

ERUPTION
A violent discharge of lava, hot ashes, and gases from a volcano. Eruptions are the result of molten rock, or magma, working its way from the inside of Earth to the surface.

EXOPLANET
A planet that is outside our Solar System.

EXOSKELETON
A hard outer skeleton, such as that of insects and crustaceans, which supports and protects the body.

EXTINCTION
The disappearance from Earth of the last living representative of a species.

FAULT
A crack in Earth's surface where the rocks on either side have shifted in relation to each other, either upward downward, or sideways. The continuing movement of the rocks can cause earthquakes.

FETUS
The unborn young of an animal; in humans, what a baby is called from the ninth week of pregnancy onward.

FEUDALISM
A social system that developed in medieval times, when people of the serving classes (such as laborers and peasants) pledged support to their overlord in return for his protection.

FISSION
A splitting apart; nuclear fission is the splitting of the nucleus of an atom.

FOSSIL
The preserved remains of life from an earlier geological time.

FRICTION
The dragging force that occurs when one object moves over another.

FULCRUM
The fixed point on which a lever moves.

FUSION
A joining together; nuclear fusion is the joining of two atomic nuclei.

GALAXY
A gigantic group of stars, dust, and gas. Our own galaxy is the Milky Way.

GENE
One of the tiny units found inside cells that determine what a living thing looks like and how its body works. Genes are passed on from one generation to the next.

GESTATION
The period during which young develop in the womb.

GLACIER
A moving mass of ice, formed from accumulated snow. Some glaciers flow like rivers, while others are vast ice sheets such as those covering Antarctica and much of Greenland.

GRAVITY
The force that attracts one object to another and prevents things from floating off into space.

GUERRILLA
A member of a small, independent fighting force that operates by making surprise attacks on an enemy.

HABITAT
The area where an animal naturally makes its home.

HERBIVORE
An animal that feeds on plants.

HOMINID
A word meaning humanlike, which refers to humans and all our extinct ancestors. It can also include the great apes (chimpanzee, bonobo, gorilla, and orangutan).

HORMONES
Natural chemicals that are produced by glands and circulate in the bloodstream to have an effect on particular parts of the body.

HURRICANE
A violent tropical storm with torrential rain and high winds that reach more than 74 miles (119 kilometers) per hour.

IGNEOUS ROCK
Rock formed from magma—hot, liquid material inside Earth—that has come to the surface then cooled and hardened.

INDIGENOUS
Occurring naturally in a particular environment or country.

INERTIA
The tendency of an object to either stay still or to move in a straight line at an unchanging speed until a force acts upon it.

INFANTRY
The part of an army made up of soldiers who fight on foot.

INVERTEBRATE
An animal without a backbone: for example, an insect, a worm, or a crustacean.

ION
An atom that has lost or gained one or more electrons and as a result has either a positive or negative electrical charge.

IONOSPHERE
The area of Earth's atmosphere through which radio waves can be transmitted.

IRON AGE
The historical period characterized by the use of iron for making weapons and tools. The earliest known iron implements were found in the Middle East and southern Europe, and date to about 1200 BCE.

ISOTOPE
One of two or more atoms of a chemical element that have different numbers of neutrons (particles with no electric charge) compared to other atoms of the element.

KARST
A type of landscape formed from limestone rocks. Karst country includes steep cliffs and, below the surface, caves and tunnels where underground streams have slowly dissolved the soft limestone.

KERATIN
A tough protein found in the top layer of skin and also in hair, nails, horns, and hooves.

LAVA
Hot, liquid rock forced out of a volcano during an eruption.

LIGHT YEAR
A measurement used by astronomers, based on the distance that light travels in one year.

MAGMA
Hot, liquid rock that is found beneath Earth's surface.

MAMMAL
A warm-blooded animal that has a backbone, feeds its young on milk, and usually has a covering of fur.

MANTLE
The rocks that lie beneath Earth's crust (surface), extending almost to the innermost core, and making up most of our planet's weight.

MARSUPIAL
A mammal that carries its developing young in a pouch, usually on its stomach.

MASS
The amount of matter in an object.

MAUSOLEUM
A large tomb or, often, a splendidly impressive building for housing several tombs.

MEDIEVAL PERIOD
Also known as the Middle Ages, the period in European history that lasted from about the 5th to the 16th century.

MELANIN
Dark pigment that gives skin its color; it is also found in hair and the colored part of the eye (iris).

METAMORPHIC ROCK
Rock that has been changed from one type to another through immense heat or pressure underground.

METAMORPHOSIS
A change from one form to another, sometimes very different, form; metamorphosis is seen in animals such as insects and amphibians as they develop into adults.

METEORITE
A small body of rock or debris that falls to Earth from space.

MIGRATION
Seasonal mass movement of animals from one place to another in search of food and places to breed.

MINERAL
A solid, inorganic (nonliving) material occurring naturally in Earth; different minerals are classified according to their elements and crystal structure.

MITOCHONDRIA
Tiny organs inside a body cell that create energy to keep the cell alive.

MOLECULE
A group of atoms bonded together.

MONARCHY
A type of government in which a king or queen is recognized as the head of a country, even though he or she may have no real power.

MORAINE
Rocks and soil carried downhill by a glacier and deposited as heaps of debris.

NEBULA
A cloud of gas and dust in outer space; some nebulas are the debris from dead stars, others are where new stars form.

NEPHRON
One of millions of minute filtering units found in the kidneys.

NEUTRON
One of the tiny particles inside an atom; neutrons have no electric charge.

NOMADIC
Describing people who move from place to place, usually according to the seasons, but never establish a permanent settlement.

NUCLEUS
The control center of a body cell, where information about a living organism is held in the form of genes. Also: the central core of an atom.

NUTRIENTS
Food substances that are necessary for life and growth.

ORBIT
The path taken by an object—for example, a planet—that is circling around another.

ORGANISM
Any living thing, including an animal, a plant, or a microscopic lifeform such as a bacterium.

PERMAFROST
Ground that remains permanently frozen beneath the topsoil.

PHARAOH
Title given to a king in ancient Egypt. People believed that the pharaohs had sacred powers.

PHOTOSYNTHESIS
A chemical process by which plants use the energy from sunlight to make their own food.

PHYLUM
One of the major scientific divisions that group together living things according to what their ancestors were like and the way their bodies are made.

PLACENTA
In mammals, an organ that develops inside the womb during pregnancy. This acts as a supply line, providing the developing young with nourishing food and oxygen from the mother's bloodstream.

PLASMA
A gaslike cloud of electrically charged matter.

PLATE BOUNDARY
An area where the edges of the vast moving plates that make up Earth's crust come together.

POLYP
A form taken by some marine animals, such as jellyfish, sea anemones, and corals. Usually tube-shaped, polyps have a mouth at one end, and are attached firmly at the base to a rock or the seabed.

PREDATOR
An animal that hunts other animals for food.

PREHISTORY
The time before the development of civilizations, when people did not write things down.

PREY
An animal hunted by other animals for food.

PROPAGANDA
Information spread publicly to put forward ideas or political views; propaganda is sometimes used to cause deliberate harm to a person or group.

PROTISTS
Simple, single-celled life forms, most of which can be seen only under a microscope. Protists live in watery environments and include algae and mobile, animal-like protozoa.

PROTON
One of the tiny particles inside an atom; protons have a positive electric charge.

PUPA
The hard, protective case, also called a chrysalis, that encloses the larva of an insect as it develops into an adult.

QUARK
One of the particles that make up the other particles in the nucleus of an atom (neutrons and protons).

REACTANT
One of the ingredients that join together to cause a chemical reaction.

REPTILE
A cold-blooded, scaly-skinned vertebrate (animal with a backbone); reptiles include snakes and lizards.

REPUBLIC
A country without a royal family that is headed, usually, by a president who may or may not have been freely chosen by the people.

RETINA
A layer of light-sensitive cells lining the inside of the eyeball.

SCAVENGER
Meat-eating animal that feeds on the dead remains of other animals.

SEDIMENTARY ROCK
Rock formed from particles of older rocks that have settled in layers and hardened under compression.

SEISMIC ACTIVITY
The shock waves that can be felt after an earthquake.

SHALE
Rock formed from layers of clay deposited over millions of years.

SOLAR SYSTEM
The Sun together with its orbiting groups of planets, including Earth, and other smaller bodies such as asteroids.

SOLENOID
A wire coil that acts like a magnet when an electric current passes through it.

SONAR
A method that uses sound waves to detect objects and measure distances underwater.

STALACTITE
A natural structure, found hanging from the ceilings of caves and underground passages. Stalactites form slowly from deposits of lime carried in trickling water.

STALAGMITE
A natural structure found on the floors of caves and underground passages. Stalagmites slowly build up from deposits of lime carried in water dripping from stalactites in the ceiling.

STOMATA
Tiny openings on the undersides of leaves that control the amount of gas and moisture passing into and out of a plant.

STONE AGE
The period of prehistory, lasting more than two million years, when humans and their ancestors made most of their tools out of stone.

SUBDUCTION
A geological process in which one of the vast plates that make up Earth's crust is pushed beneath another.

SULTAN
In some Islamic countries, the traditional title given to the ruler.

SUNSPOT
A dark, cooler patch on the surface of the Sun.

SUPERNOVA
An exploding giant star.

TECTONIC PLATE
One of the large, slowly moving slabs into which Earth's crust is divided.

TENTACLES
Long, elastic structures, like arms, that some animals use for feeling, moving around, and picking up food.

TOXIN
A poisonous substance produced by a living organism such as an animal or a plant.

TRANSPIRATION
The evaporation of water from the leaves and stems of plants.

TSUNAMI
An enormous, rapidly rising ocean wave caused by an earthquake or volcanic activity under the sea. Tsunamis travel far and fast, causing widespread devastation inland.

TUNDRA
Cold, treeless region, snow-covered for many months of the year, where only low-growing, hardy plants and specially adapted animals can survive. Tundras occur in the Arctic and in high mountain areas.

VELOCITY
The speed at which something moves in a particular direction.

VERTEBRATE
An animal with a backbone.

VIRUS
Tiny lifeform that is a collection of genes inside a protective shell. Viruses can invade body cells, where they multiply, causing illnesses.

VISCOSITY
The measure of a liquid's ability to flow.

VIZIER
Title once given to a chief official in some Muslim countries.

VOLCANO
An opening in Earth's crust that provides an outlet for magma (hot, liquefied rock) when it rises to the surface.

WARM-BLOODED
Describing an animal that can keep its body heat at an almost constant level, regardless of whether the outside temperature is hot or cold.

Index

Acknowledgments

Smithsonian Project Coordinator:
Kealy Wilson

Smithsonian Enterprises:
Kealy Wilson, Product
Development Manager
Ellen Nanney, Licensing Manager
Brigid Ferraro, Director of Licensing
Carol LeBlanc, Senior Vice President

Reviewers for the Smithsonian:
National Museum of Natural History:
Dr. Don E. Wilson, Curator Emeritus,
Department of Vertebrate Zoology; Sally
Kuhn Sennert, USGS/Global Volcanism
Program, Department of Mineral Sciences;
Dr. Jeffrey E. Post, Geologist and Curator-
in-Charge, National Gem and Mineral
Collection; Dr. Nancy Knowlton, Sant Chair
of Marine Sciences; Dr. Michael Brett-
Surman, Museum Specialist for Fossil
Dinosaurs, Reptiles, Amphibians and Fish,
Department of Paleobiology; Thomas F.
Jorstad, Paleobiology Information Officer,
Department of Paleobiology; Dr. Gary
Krupnick, Head of the Plant Conservation
Unit, Department of Botany; Dr.
Christopher L. Mah, Research Collaborator,
Department of Invertebrate Zoology; Gary
F. Hevel, Research Collaborator,
Department of Entomology; Jeremy F.
Jacobs, Collections Manager, Division of
Amphibians and Reptiles; Christopher M.
Milensky, Museum Specialist, Division of
Birds, Department of Vertebrate Zoology;
Dr. M. G. (Jerry) Harasewych, Research
Zoologist and Curator of Marine Mollusks,
Department of Invertebrate Zoology; Jim
Harle, Map curator volunteer; Dr. Briana
Pobiner, Paleoanthropologist and Educator,
Human Origins Program; Salima Ikram,
Egyptology Unit Head, Department of
Anthropology; Dr. William W. Fitzhugh,
Curator of Archaeology and Director of
Arctic Studies Center, Department of
Anthropology; J. Daniel Rogers, Curator of
Archaeology, Department of Anthropology

National Portrait Gallery:
James G. Barber, Historian

National Air and Space Museum
Dr. F. Robert van der Linden, Chairman,
Aeronautics Division; Roger Connor,
Curator, Aeronautics Division; Andrew
Johnston, Geographer, Center for Earth
and Planetary Studies

*National Museum of African American
History and Culture*
Ester Washington, Director of Education

*Freer Gallery of Art and Arthur
M. Sackler Gallery*
Dr. Alexander Nagel, Assistant Curator of
Ancient Near East; James T. Ulak, Senior
Curator of Japanese Art; J. Keith Wilson,
Curator of Ancient Chinese Art; Debra
Diamond, Associate Curator of South and
Southeast Asian Art

*National Museum of American History,
Kenneth E. Behring Center*
David K. Allison, Associate Director for
Curatorial Affairs; Dwight Blocker Bowers,
Curator, Division of Culture and the Arts;
Roger E. Sherman, Associate Curator,
Division of Medicine and Science; Ann M.
Seeger, Deputy Chair and Curator, Division
of Medicine and Science; Dr. Paul F.
Johnston, Curator, Division of Work and
Industry; L. Susan Tolbert, Deputy Chair
and Curator, Division of Work and
Industry; Jennifer Locke Jones, Chair and
Curator, Division of Armed Forces History

The Smithsonian name and logo
are registered trademarks of the
Smithsonian Institution.

**The publisher would like to thank the
following people for their assistance in the
preparation of this book:** Sam Atkinson,
Ann Baggaley, Alexandra Beeden, Sreshtha
Bhattacharya, Jane Evans, Pakshalika
Jayaprakash, Suefa Lee, Vibha Malhotra,
Monica Saigal, Steve Setford, Sarah
Tomley, and Debra Wolter for editorial
assistance; Steve Crozier, Paul Drislane,
Mandy Earey, Gadi Farfour, Nidhi Mehra,
Anjana Nair, Priyabrata Roy Chowdhury,
Ankita Mukherjee, Ranjita Bhattacharji,
Niyati Gosain, Mark Lloyd, Payal Rosalind
Malik, Vaibhav Rastogi, Laura Roberts,
Mary Sandberg, and Sharon Spencer for
design assistance; Caroline Hunt for
proofreading; Elizabeth Wise for the index;
Aldebaran Robotics, Mark Burdett Rachel
Smart, Sarah Fowler, Professor Thomas
Hildebrandt, Richard Hook and Francoise
Delplancke-Stroebele of the European
Southern Observatory, and KwaZulu-Natal
Sharks Board for their expert advice; and
Kennis & Kennis Reconstructions for
models of early human ancestors.

**The publisher would like to thank the
following for their kind permission to
reproduce photographs:**

(Key: a-above; b-below/bottom; c-center;
f-far; l-left; r-right; t-top)

10 NASA: JPL (ftr); R. Williams (STScI) /
The Hubble Deep Field Team (cra). **11
Corbis**: NASA (tc/planet). **Dorling
Kindersley**: Julian Baum (tc/dwarf planet).
**NASA and The Hubble Heritage Team
(AURA/STScI)**: NASA / ESA / A. Nota (STScI
/ ESA) (ftr). **NASA**: (cr); JPL / University of
Arizona (tl); JPL / ESA / SOHO (tr). **Science
Photo Library**: (c); John Thomas (ftl); David
Parker (br); Mark Garlick (bl); Volker
Springel / Max Planck Institute For
Astrophysics (fbr). **13 NASA**: COBE / DMR
(cr). **14 ESO**: (fclb/crab nebula); S. Gillessen
et al (fcl/galactic centre). **NASA and The
Hubble Heritage Team (AURA/STScI)**:
NASA / ESA (fbl). **15 NASA**: ESA / Z. Levay
and R. van der Marel, STScI / T. Hallas / A.
Mellinger (br). **16 NASA and The Hubble
Heritage Team (AURA/STScI)**: NASA / ESA
/ M. Robberto (Space Telescope Science
Institute / ESA) (b). **17 SuperStock**: Science
Photo Library (b). **20 NASA**: K. Reardon
(Osservatorio Astrofisico di Arcetri, INAF)
IBIS, DST, NSO (cla). **22 NASA**: JPL (tc). **24
Science Photo Library**: Dr. Michael J.
Ledlow (clb). **25 NASA**: (br). **26 NASA**: (ftl);
JPL (crb). **28 NASA**: (c); JSC (br). **29 NASA**:
(tr). **33 NASA**: Chandra X-ray Observatory
/ ESA / JHU / R. Sankrit & W.Blair (r). **36
NASA**: (fcla/jupiter); SDO (fcla/sun); NASA
and The Hubble Heritage Team (STScI /
AURA)Acknowledgment: R.G. French
(Wellesley College), J. Cuzzi (NASA /
AMES), L. Dones (SwRI), and J. Lissauer
(NASA / AMES) (fcla/saturn). **Science Photo
Library**: NASA / JPL-Caltech (bl). **37
Science Photo Library**: David Ducros (cr).
42 Dorling Kindersley: Shutterstock (cla).
46 Dorling Kindersley: Tom Coulson (bl).
47 Alamy Images: G. Brad Lewis Agency /
Photo Resource Hawaii (cl, clb); Tom
Pfeiffer (bl). **50 Corbis**: Michael DeFreitas /
Robert Harding World Imagery (cra).
54 Dorling Kindersley: David Leffman /
Rough Guides (fcl). **55 Alamy Images**:
Photoshot Holdings Ltd (crb). **Dorling
Kindersley**: Greg Ward / Rough Guides (tr).
56 Dorling Kindersley: Natural History
Museum, London (fcl/copper). **58 Dorling
Kindersley**: NASA / Digitaleye / Jamie
Marshall (br). **59 Corbis**: (fbr). **64 Dorling
Kindersley**: Greg Ward / Rough Guides (bl).
65 Fotolia: Okea (tr). **66 Dorling
Kindersley**: Tim Draper / Rough Guides (cl).
71 NASA: Jacques Descloitres, MODIS Land
Science Team (bl). **76 Dorling Kindersley**:
Atlantic Digital (bl, tl). **Getty Images**: Flickr
/ www.MartyPhotography.com.au (cla).
Science Photo Library: Henning Dalhoff
(cl/l, cl/c, cl/r). **77 Corbis**: Annie Griffiths
Belt (tr). **78 Dorling Kindersley**: Jon
Hughes (cla); Andrew Kerr (c, crb, tr); Jon
Hughes and Russell Gooday (cra). **79
Dorling Kindersley**: Jon Hughes (crb, ca,
fcl); Jon Hughes and Russell Gooday (cra);
Andrew Kerr (c, bc, cla); Jon Hughes /
Bedrock Studios (cl); Richard Tibbets (clb).
80 Dorling Kindersley: Jon Hughes (cb);
Dennis Wilson - Staab Studios -
modelmaker (clb); Andrew Kerr (bl, br).
Science Photo Library: Roger Harris (bc).
81 Dorling Kindersley: Jon Hughes and
Russell Gooday (cla); Andrew Kerr (cra).
Science Photo Library: Mark Garlick (bc).
82 Dorling Kindersley: Natural History
Museum, London (cl). **84 Dorling
Kindersley**: Natural History Museum,
London (tr). **85 Dorling Kindersley**:
Dinosaur State Park, Connecticut (ftr);
Barrie Watts (ftl); Courtesy of the
Naturmuseum Senckenburg, Frankfurt (cr);
Natural History Museum, London (tr). **86
Dorling Kindersley**: Malcolm Coulson (c).
Dreamstime.com: Irochka (clb); Andrey
Sukhachev (cl). **89 Corbis**: Lilly /
Imagebroker (fbl). **Getty Images**: E+ /
KingWu (fclb). **92 Corbis**: Pulse (crb). **93
Alamy Images**: Martin Strmiska (fcr).
Corbis: Kai Schwabe / Westend61 (bc).
Dorling Kindersley: Tim Draper / Rough
Guides (cr). **94 Corbis**: Konrad Wothe /
Minden Pictures (bl). **Getty Images**: Flickr /
Nicolas Reusens (tr). **98 Corbis**: Tui De Roy
/ Minden Pictures (br). **Getty Images**:
Encyclopaedia Britannica / UIG (bl). **98-99
Dorling Kindersley**: Kenneth Lilly (b/
whale); John Temperton (b/diplodocus). **99
Corbis**: DLILLC (fbl); David Pattyn / Foto
Natura / Minden Pictures (fbr); Paul
Souders (bl). **Getty Images**: National
Geographic / Joel Sartore (br). **101 Corbis**:
Dave Fleetham / Design Pics (cr). **SeaPics.
com**: Doug Perrine (br). **103 SuperStock**:
Scubazoo / Science Faction (tr). **104
Dorling Kindersley**: Natural History
Museum, London (br, cra). **105 Corbis**:

Thomas Marent / Minden Pictures (br, bc); Wolfgang Thieme / DPA (bl). **naturepl.com**: Fabio Liverani (fbr). **108 Corbis**: Paul Marcellini (MYN) / Nature Picture Library (bc). **Dorling Kindersley**: David Peart (clb); Jerry Young (cb). **Getty Images**: Flickr Open / Peter Schoen (cra). **109 Dorling Kindersley**: Jerry Young (cr). **Science Photo Library**: Edward Kinsman (bc). 110 Science Photo Library: Dante Fenolio (tr); William H. Mullins (cl). **113 Corbis**: Mitsuaki Iwago / Minden Pictures (br). **SeaPics.com**: Doug Perrine (bl). **116 Corbis**: John Abbott / Visuals Unlimited (clb/bats); Denis Scott (bl); James Hager / Robert Harding World Imagery (cl); Thomas Marent / Minden Pictures (clb/lemur). **117 Dorling Kindersley**: Tim Shepard / Oxford Scientific Films (tr). **Fotolia**: Peter Kirillov (cla, clb). **119 Corbis**: DLILLC (br). **120 Corbis**: Flip Nicklin / Minden Pictures (cl). **Dorling Kindersley**: Jamie Marshall (clb); Kevin Jones (br). **121 Fotolia**: Vibe Images (br). **Getty Images**: The Image Bank / Gallo Images-Roger De La Harpe (crb); Minden Pictures / Ingo Arndt (cr); Oxford Scientific / Elliot Neep (bl, bc, fbl). **122 Dorling Kindersley**: Kanapaha Botanical Gardens (fbr); Alex Robinson / Rough Guides (bl). **Getty Images**: Visuals Unlimited, Inc. / Science VU (br). **123 Getty Images**: Stone / Lester Lefkowitz (br). **Science Photo Library**: Copyright Tom Van Sant / Geosphere Project, Santa Monica (bl). **125 Corbis**: Mark Moffett / Minden Pictures (br). **130 Photolibrary**: Moodboard (br). **131 Getty Images**: Oxford Scientific / Mark Conlin (tl); Oxford Scientific / Luis Javier Sandoval (crb). **132 Corbis**: Anthony Bannister / Gallo Images (cl). **135 Corbis**: Michael & Patricia Fogden (bl); Visuals Unlimited (fbl); Thomas Marent / Minden Pictures (fbr). **naturepl.com**: Edwin Giesbers (br); Mark Payne-Gill (cl, cr, fcr). **139 Corbis**: Zephyr / Science Photo Library (cl). **Dorling Kindersley**: Spike Walker (Microworld Services) (bl). **Dreamstime.com**: Irochka (bc). **Fotolia**: Dario Sabljak (ca). **Getty Images**: Stone / UHB Trust (c). **PunchStock**: Image Source (fcl). **SuperStock**: Science Picture Co. / Science Faction (fbl). **140 Science Photo Library**: Hybrid Medical Animation (cl). **144 Science Photo Library**: (br); Steve Gschmeissner (fbr); Prof. P. Motta / Dept. Of Anatomy / University "La Sapienza", Rome (bc). **145 Dorling Kindersley**: Zygote Media Group (br/unipennate, br/fusiform, br/multipennate, br/strap, br/triangular, br/circular). **151 Science Photo Library**: Susumu Nishinaga (bc). **153 Corbis**: Paul Anton (tr); Piet Mall / Stock4B (cr); Tetra

Images (cra). **155 Dorling Kindersley**: Halli Verrinder (br). **156 Science Photo Library**: Steve Gschmeissner (bl). **157 Science Photo Library**: (c). **158 Corbis**: Mike Watson / Moodboard (tc). **Dorling Kindersley**: Tony Graham (bc). **159 Corbis**: Photo Quest Ltd / Science Photo Library (tr). **161 Science Photo Library**: Thomas Deerinck / NCMIR (crb). **162 Dorling Kindersley**: Zygote Media Group (bl). **163 Science Photo Library**: Eye Of Science (cla). **164 Fotolia**: Aptyp_koK (bc). **Science Photo Library**: Sovereign, ISM (cl). **165 Alamy Images**: Image Source (cr). **Dorling Kindersley**: Zygote Media Group (l, tr, ftr). **166 Dorling Kindersley**: Medimation (cl). **167 Dorling Kindersley**: Zygote Media Group (c). **168 SuperStock**: Science Photo Library (tl). **168-169 Dorling Kindersley**: Zygote Media Group. **169 Dorling Kindersley**: Zygote Media Group (c, br). **The Natural History Museum, London**: (cr). **171 Science Photo Library**: Omikron (tc). **172 Science Photo Library**: Steve Gschmeissner (cb). **173 Science Photo Library**: Susumu Nishinaga (c). **174 Science Photo Library**: Steve Gschmeissner (cl, tl). **176 Dorling Kindersley**: Zygote Media Group (br, fbr). **177 Dorling Kindersley**: Zygote Media Group (tc, fclb, clb, cb, fbl, bl/l, bl/r, bc). **183 Getty Images**: Flickr / Gen Umekita (fbr). **Science Photo Library**: Dr. Najeeb Layyous (cr). **184-185 Getty Images**: Stone / Michel Tcherevkoff (b). **184 Science Photo Library**: (cra); AJ Photo (tr). **187 Corbis**: Ocean (fcrb); Visuals Unlimited (tc). **194 Getty Images**: Lionel Flusin / Gamma-Rapho Via Getty Images (cla). **Science Photo Library**: Claudia Marcelloni, CERN (br). **195 Science Photo Library**: CERN (cl). **202 Corbis**: John Nakata (c). **Science Photo Library**: Sandia National Laboratories (fbr); Sheila Terry (ca). **206 Dorling Kindersley**: The Science Museum, London (tr). **207 NASA**. **214 Dorling Kindersley**: National Maritime Museum, London (tr). **215 Corbis**: David Chapman / Design Pics (cr). **222 Getty Images**: E+ / Scott Hailstone (c); Jordrell Bank Observatory / AFP (bl). **223 Corbis**: Ocean (cr). **Dorling Kindersley**: Richard Trillo (br). **NASA**: SDO (bc). **Science Photo Library**: T-Service (cl). **225 Getty Images**: Photolibrary / Dennis Macdonald (bl). **228 ESO**: (bc, br); P. Barthel / Acknowledgments: Mark Neeser (Kapteyn Institute, Groningen) and Richard Hook (ST / ECF, Garching, Germany). (bl). **Science Photo Library**: European Southern Observatory / G. Hudepohl (tr). **241 Corbis**: Bohemian Nomad Picturemakers / Kevin R. Morris (cl). **Dorling Kindersley**: The Science

Museum, London (fcrb). **242 Dorling Kindersley**: The Science Museum, London (cra, cr). **243 NASA**: Dominic Hart / NASA / Ames (bl). **245 Corbis**: Boston Dynamics / DPA (fcr). **Courtesy of Warwick Mobile Robotics**: (tr). **250 Camera Press**: Marc Deville / Gamma (br). **Dorling Kindersley**: Natural History Museum, London (crb); Matthew Ward / The Trustees of the British Museum (tr). **Kennis & Kennis / Alfons and Adrie Kennis**: (tl, cra, bc). **The Natural History Museum, London**: (c). **251 Alamy Images**: Zev Radovan / BibleLandPictures (tr). **Kennis & Kennis / Alfons and Adrie Kennis**: (tl, cl, cra, crb, bc). **252 Dorling Kindersley**: The Museum of London (bl/bone shuttle); The Science Museum, London (clb/flint knife, clb/wood axe). **253 Corbis**: Nathan Benn / Ottochrome (br). **256 Dorling Kindersley**: David Peart (cl). **257 Dorling Kindersley**: John Hepver / The Trustees of the British Museum (t). **261 Dorling Kindersley**: Max Alexander / Tap Service Archaeological Receipts Fund, Hellenic Republic Ministry Of Culture (tr); Stephen Dodd / The Trustees of the British Museum (br); Nick Nicholls / The Trustees of the British Museum (cr, crb); Chris Christoforo / Rough Guides (cra). **265 Dorling Kindersley**: Ermine Street Guard (cr, cra). **266 Dorling Kindersley**: Christi Graham and Nick Nicholls / The Trustees of the British Museum (c). **268 Dorling Kindersley**: Peter Hayman / The Trustees of the British Museum (bl). **269 Dorling Kindersley**: National Maritime Museum, London (cla). **270 Dorling Kindersley**: Courtesy of Vikings of Middle England (fbl/axe, fbl/sax). **276 Dorling Kindersley**: Jewish Museum, London (bl). **277 Dorling Kindersley**: Karen Trist / Rough Guides (bc). **279 Corbis**: The Gallery Collection (br). **281 Dorling Kindersley**: Judith Miller / Sloan's (tr). **284 Dorling Kindersley**: The Science Museum, London (bl). **287 Dorling Kindersley**: The Science Museum, London (fbr); James Stevenson / National Maritime Museum, London (br). **National Maritime Museum, Greenwich, London**: (crb). **290 Corbis**: The Gallery Collection (b). **291 Dorling Kindersley**: Robbie Polley (cl). **Getty Images**: Karl Weatherly / Photodisc (bl). **295 Dorling Kindersley**: The Trustees of the British Museum (crb); David Gower / The Trustees of the British Museum (cr); Alan Hills / The Trustees of the British Museum (fcra, tr, br). **296 Dorling Kindersley**: Board of Trustees of the Royal Armouries (fcra, tr, cr). **298 Getty Images**: OFF / AFP (bl). **300 Dorling Kindersley**: Ray Moller / Wilberforth Collection, Hull

Museums (cl). **301 Dorling Kindersley**: Royal Geographical Society, London (bl); Wilberforce House Museum, Hull (cra). **302 Alamy Images**: The Art Archive (clb). **Corbis**: Stefano Bianchetti (br); Lebrecht Music & Arts (bc). **Dorling Kindersley**: National Maritime Museum, London (cr). **303 Corbis**: Lebrecht Music & Arts (bc); Michael Nicholson (fbl); Philadelphia Museum of Art (tr). **304 Getty Images**: Brendan Smialowski (cra). **305 Dorling Kindersley**: Chas Howson / The Trustees of the British Museum (br); Courtesy of Queens's Rangers (cra); National Constitution Center (c). **306 Getty Images**: De Agostini Picture Library (cb). **307 Dorling Kindersley**: Max Alexander (cb); Courtesy of David Edge (cr). **309 Alamy Images**: Streetlife (crb). **Dorling Kindersley**: B&O Railroad Museum, Baltimore, Maryland, USA (tl); Museum of English Rural Life, The University of Reading (tr); The Science Museum, London (cr, cra). **312 Dorling Kindersley**: Confederate Memorial Hall, New Orleans, LA (tc). **313 Dorling Kindersley**: Peter Keim (c). **314 Corbis**: (br). **315 Dorling Kindersley**: Imperial War Museum (fcr). **Getty Images**: Popperfoto (bl). **316 Dorling Kindersley**: Royal Artillery Museum / Royal Artillery Historical Trust (cl). **318 Dorling Kindersley**: Imperial War Museum, London (bl). **Getty Images**: Capt. Poston / IWM via Getty Images (br). **319 Dorling Kindersley**: By kind permission of The Trustees of the Imperial War Museum, London (tc); Eden Camp Museum, Yorkshire (cra). **Getty Images**: Hulton Archive (cl); Roger Viollet (c); Sgt. Lou Lowery / MCT / MCT via Getty Images (bc). **323 Alamy Images**: ITAR-TASS Photo Agency / Yuri Lizunov (bl). **324-325 Corbis**: Heide Benser (t); Hulton-Deutsch Collection (b). **324 Getty Images**: Central Press / Agence France Presse / Hulton Archive (bc). **325 Corbis**: Nathan Benn (cl). **Getty Images**: Popperfoto (tr). **326-327 Getty Images**: Gilles Bassignac / Gamma-Rapho Via Getty Images. **327 Corbis**: Masatomo Kuriya (tl).

All other images © Dorling Kindersley. For further information see: **www.dkimages.com**